Accounting Information Systems

Second Edition

Accounting Information Systems

Second Edition

Vernon J. Richardson
University of Arkansas
Xi'an Jiaotong Liverpool University

C. Janie Chang
San Diego State University

Rodney Smith
California State University, Long Beach

Mc Graw Hill Education

ACCOUNTING INFORMATION SYSTEMS, SECOND EDITION

This book is printed on acid-free paper.

1 2 3 4 5 6 7 8 9 LWI 21 20 19 18 17

ISBN 978-1-259-53887-2
MHID 1-259-53887-7

Chief Product Officer, SVP Products & Markets: *G. Scott Virkler*
Vice President, General Manager, Products & Markets: *Marty Lange*
Managing Director: *Tim Vertovec*
Marketing Director: *Natalie King*
Executive Brand Manager: *Steve Schuetz*
Director, Product Development: *Rose Koos*
Director of Digital Content: *Peggy Hussey*
Associate Director of Digital Content: *Kevin Moran*
Lead Product Developer: *Kris Tibbetts*
Marketing Manager: *Michelle Williams*
Market Development Manager: *Erin Chomat*
Digital Product Analyst: *Xin Lin*
Director, Content Design & Delivery: *Linda Avenarius*
Program Manager: *Daryl Horrocks*
Content Project Managers: *Heather Ervolino; Angela Norris*
Buyer: *Susan K. Culbertson*
Design: *Egzon Shaqiri*
Content Licensing Specialists: *Shawntel Schmitt (photo); Lori Slattery (text)*
Cover Image: *Shutterstock/Tatyana Vyc; Shutterstock/Rrrainbow*
Typeface: *10/12 STIXGeneral*
Compositor: *SPi Global*
Printer: *LSC Communications*

All credits appearing on page or at the end of the book are considered to be an extension of the copyright page.

Library of Congress Cataloging-in-Publication Data
Names: Richardson, Vernon J., author. | Chang, C. Janie, author. | Smith, Rodney (Business writer), author.
Title: Accounting information systems / Vernon J. Richardson, University of Arkansas, Fayetteville, C. Janie Chang, San Diego State University, Rodney Smith, California State University, Long Beach.
Description: Second edition. | New York, NY : McGraw-Hill Education, [2018]
Identifiers: LCCN 2016040033 | ISBN 9781259538872 (alk. paper)
Subjects: LCSH: Accounting—Data processing. | Information storage and retrieval systems—Accounting.
Classification: LCC HF5679 .R53 2018 | DDC 657.0285/53—dc23
LC record available at https://lccn.loc.gov/2016040033

mheducation.com/highered

About the Authors

Vernon J. Richardson *University of Arkansas; Xi'an Jiaotong Liverpool University*

Vernon J. Richardson is Professor of Accounting and the S. Robson Walton Distinguished Chair in the Sam M. Walton College of Business at the University of Arkansas. He also serves as Accounting Department chair. He is also a research fellow at the International Business School Suzhou, Xi'an Jiaotong Liverpool University. He received his BS, MAcc, and MBA from Brigham Young University and has a PhD in accounting from the University of Illinois at Urbana-Champaign. He has taught students at the University of Arkansas, University of Illinois, Brigham Young University, Aarhus University, University of Kansas, Xi'an Jiaotong Liverpool University, and the China Europe International Business School (Shanghai).

Dr. Richardson is a member of the American Accounting Association. He has served as president of the American Accounting Association Information Systems section. He was formerly editor at the *Accounting Review* and is currently an editor at *Accounting Horizons.* He also served as associate editor at *MIS Quarterly* and the *Journal of Information Systems.* He has published articles in the *Accounting Review, Journal of Information Systems, Journal of Accounting and Economics, Contemporary Accounting Research, MIS Quarterly, Journal of Management Information Systems, Journal of Operations Management,* and *Journal of Marketing.*

C. Janie Chang *San Diego State University*

C. Janie Chang is the Vern Odmark Professor of Accounting in the Charles W. Lamden School of Accountancy at San Diego State University (SDSU). She received her PhD from the University of California, Irvine. Before coming to SDSU, Dr. Chang served as Professor of Accounting Information Systems (AIS) at San Jose State University (SJSU). At SJSU, she established the undergraduate AIS program. She also taught students at University of California–Davis, University of California–Irvine, and California State University–San Marcos. Dr. Chang's teaching interests in AIS include information systems audit, data modeling, issues in e-business, and business networks and controls.

Dr. Chang is a member of the American Accounting Association and Information Systems Audit and Control Association (ISACA). She was formerly a co-editor at the *Review of Accounting and Finance.* Dr. Chang has studied issues in auditing, accounting, and information systems to investigate information processing of experts in addition to cross-cultural issues related to professional judgments and decisions. Her studies have been published in *Abacus, Auditing: A Journal of Practice and Theory, Behavioral Research in Accounting, Data Base, International Journal of Accounting, International Journal of Accounting Information Systems, Journal of Accounting Literature, Journal of Accounting and Public Policy,* and *Review of Accounting and Finance,* among others.

Rod Smith *California State University, Long Beach*

Rod Smith is Professor of Accountancy at California State University, Long Beach. He received his BS in Mathematics from the University of Oregon; MS in Financial Management from the Naval Postgraduate School, Monterey, California; and PhD in Management (Accounting) from University of California–Irvine. He previously taught at the University of Arkansas, University of California–Irvine, and University of Alaska.

Dr. Smith has published research in the *Accounting Review, Journal of Information Systems, Journal of Management Accounting Research, Journal of Accounting and Public Policy,* and *International Journal of Accounting Information Systems.* He is a certified public accountant (inactive), certified management accountant, and retired captain in the U.S. Coast Guard.

His research interests include use of financial and nonfinancial measures to assess organizational performance; accounting information systems, enterprise systems, business processes, and business value; design science; and systems dynamics and business process simulation.

Preface

Whether accountants work in public accounting or in industry, they use a variety of technology tools. The International Federation of Accountants (IFAC) describes four roles for accountants with respect to information technology: **(1) *users* of technology and information systems, (2) *managers* of users of technology and related information systems, (3) *designers* of information systems, and (4) *evaluators* of information systems.** As users, managers, designers, and evaluators of technology and technology-driven business processes, accountants must understand the organization and how organizational processes generate information important to management. To ensure that processes and systems are documented—and to participate in improvements to processes and systems—accountants must be business analysts.

This textbook aims to provide students with a variety of technology and business analysis concepts and skills. It is intended for use in the first Accounting Information Systems course at both the undergraduate and graduate levels. Ongoing changes in business technology—such as the move to Internet-based systems, Big Data and data analytics, software as a service, and mobile access to enterprise information, as well as increased security and control requirements—make technological skills more important than ever for accounting graduates. This textbook also aims to show how current changes in accounting and technology affect each of these roles. For example, the Sarbanes-Oxley Act affects financial reporting system controls, and XBRL changes system requirements and affects how companies develop and report financial information. We also consider the role of Big Data and data analytics and how they are used in financial accounting, managerial accounting, and auditing. Additionally, we consider both the COBIT and COSO frameworks to describe how organizations deal with risk management. In their roles as managers, designers, and evaluators, accountants must know how those frameworks affect their accounting and related information systems.

The core competencies of the American Institute of Certified Public Accountants (AICPA) emphasize accounting skills over content. This textbook emphasizes examples, problems, and projects through which students can develop the technological skills they need for their accounting careers. It uses real-world companies such as Starbucks, Walmart, Google, and Amazon that students can relate to. It takes a broad view of accounting information systems that emphasizes the accountants' roles in the use, management, design, and evaluation of the systems and the management information that they produce. To assist accounting students in experiencing the benefit of learning information technology/information services (IT/IS) concepts and using IT/IS skills in accounting, we focus on business processes, business requirements, how information technology supports those requirements, and how accountants contribute. In particular, this textbook helps students learn to:

- **Design business processes and represent them with standard documentation tools.** The role of the accounting function has evolved from stewardship and reporting to full partnership, supporting management decisions throughout the organization. As business analysts, accountants must be able to document business processes, identify potential improvements, and design and implement new business processes. Thus, this textbook helps develop business process modeling skills.
- **Design and implement well-structured databases to enable business processes.** Accountants must also understand how business processes generate data and how such data are structured, interrelated, and stored in a database system. To ensure that business processes and the database systems are documented and to participate

in improvements to processes and systems, accountants must understand and be able to model such systems. Thus, this textbook helps develop data modeling and database implementation skills.

- **Query databases to provide insights about the performance of business operations.** Most organizational information resides in databases. To support management decisions throughout the organization, accountants must understand how those data are structured and how to retrieve information to support business management decisions. Thus, this textbook develops skills on the use of Microsoft Access and databases in general. This textbook also develops data analytics tools through the use of Microsoft Excel and Tableau.
- **Evaluate internal control systems and apply business rules to implement controls and mitigate information systems risks.** Recent federal legislation—for example, the Sarbanes-Oxley Act of 2002 and COSO and COBIT guidance—emphasizes the importance of risk mitigation in modern organizations. Internal control systems must constantly evolve to meet a changing risk environment. Accountants are often the internal control experts and must, therefore, understand how internal controls should be implemented in business processes as part of the organization's overall risk mitigation and governance framework. Thus, this textbook presents specific material on internal control and accounting information systems, as well as general information about computer fraud and security. It also describes how to monitor and audit accounting information systems.

AIS 2e Content Updates

General Updates for the 2nd Edition

- Added additional End-of-Chapter Multiple Choice Questions and Problems throughout the text.
- Significantly revised many End-of-Chapter Problems for availability and auto-grading within Connect.
- Revised and added many new Discussion Questions in most chapters.

Chapter by Chapter Updates

Specific chapter changes for *Accounting Information Systems,* 2nd Edition, are as follows:

Chapter 1

- Updated the opening vignette, highlighting the use of **Starbucks** Clover coffee machines.
- Updated real-world references.
- Edited and updated the Progress Check questions.

Chapter 2

- Increased introductory coverage of BPMN.
- Added discussion of flow object types, including gateway and event types.
- Introduced repeating activities.
- Added introduction to data objects, data stores, and associations.

Chapter 3

- Updated discussion of how the multiplicities for associations indicate where foreign keys are posted in relational tables.
- Added discussion of business rules, decision requirements, and decision tables.

Chapter 4

- Updated the section on Using Microsoft Access to Implement a Relational Database. Figures 4.6 through 4.17 were updated using Microsoft Access 2013.
- Updated Appendix A. Figures 4.A1 through 4.A9 were updated using Microsoft Access 2013.

Chapter 5

- Added additional figures related to sales activity models.
- Updated the Chapter 5 Comprehensive Exercise.

Chapter 6

- Updated the Chapter 6 Comprehensive Exercise.

Chapter 7

- Updated BPMN diagrams to include revisions to Chapter 2.

Chapter 8

- Substantially modified the chapter to describe to students how to approach an integrated project.
- Created two new integrated projects with multiple versions to accommodate various class schedules and to allow instructors to rotate projects.
- The first of the two integrated projects is a more challenging project that includes issues related to managing inventory levels and internal inventory transfers. Other topics covered include multiple sales types, including Internet, wholesale, and retail sales, where customers can pay by cash, check, or credit card.
- The second of the two integrated projects is shorter and less challenging and focuses on wholesale sales from multiple distribution centers.

Chapter 9

- This is an all-new chapter emphasizing data analytics.
- Illustrated how data analytics is used to help **Starbucks** pick its store locations.
- Inserted an all-new explanation of how data analytics is used in business and accounting.
- Added an explanation and example of how Audit Data Standards provided by the AICPA are used to facilitate data analytics between a company's financial staff and the external auditors.
- Explained how the DATA Act recently passed by Congress gives firms specific responsibilities to protect privacy and the breach of individual identifying information.
- Illustrated data analytics and data analytics techniques in both Excel and Tableau.

Chapter 10

- Updated the opening vignette, highlighting Kevin Johnson, who has substantial technology leadership as **Starbucks**'s new president and chief operating officer.
- Added an all-new example and inserted an additional figure illustrating a digital marketing dashboard.
- Updated real-world references, particularly of examples of business intelligence.
- Edited and updated Progress Check questions.

Chapter 11

- Updated COSO Internal Control Framework to COSO 2013 by updating the five components and adding the 17 relevant principles of internal controls.
- Added Figure 11.2 to summarize COSO 2013 control components and principles.

Chapter 12

- Updated the opening vignette.
- Revised the contents of computer fraud and abuse as well as vulnerability assessment and management.
- Edited and updated the Progress Check questions.

Chapter 13

- Updated the opening vignette.

Chapter 14

- Added discussion of the IT Governance Institute Val IT Framework.

Chapter 15

- Added an all-new opening vignette, highlighting Gerri Martin-Flickinger as the **Starbucks** chief technology officer.
- Edited and updated Progress Check questions.

Chapter 16

- Updated the opening vignette highlighting technology used at **Walmart**.
- Updated Figure 16.2 with recent information technology project outcomes.

Main Features

Accounting Information Systems, 2nd Edition, focuses on the accountant's role as business analyst in solving business problems by database modeling, database design, and business process modeling.

Chapter Maps

Chapter Maps provide a handy guide at the start of every chapter. These remind students what they have learned in previous chapters, what they can expect to learn in the current chapter, and how the topics will build on each other in chapters to come. This allows them to stay more focused and organized along the way.

A look at this chapter

A look back

A look ahead

Chapter-Opening Vignettes

Do your students sometimes wonder how the course connects with their future? Each chapter opens with a vignette, which sets the stage for the rest of the chapter and encourages students to think of concepts in a business context.

Chapter **Two**

Accountants as Business Analysts

A look at this chapter

As users, managers, designers, and evaluators of technology and technology-driven business processes, accountants must understand the organization and how organizational processes generate information important to management. To ensure that processes and systems are documented—and to participate in improvements to processes and systems—accountants must also be business analysts. This chapter defines business process modeling and describes how it supports the roles of accountants. It explains the potential value of business process modeling. Finally, it describes the types of business process models and introduces basic modeling tools to guide the student's development of modeling skills.

A look back

Chapter 1 discussed the importance of accounting information systems and the role accountants play in those systems. It further described how investments in information technology might improve the ability to manage business processes and create value for the firm.

A look ahead

Chapter 3 introduces data modeling. It describes how data modeling supports the design, implementation, and operation of database systems. It introduces basic modeling tools that will be used throughout the rest of the text.

© AFP/Getty Images

One recent morning, I stopped at a very busy **Starbucks** in San Francisco. I looked at the line coming out of the door and immediately thought that it would take at least 20 minutes to get my morning coffee. Instead, I was pleasantly surprised at the efficiency of the employees who got me through that line in less than 2 minutes.

I watched closely as the Starbucks partners behind the counter executed the workflow of the process. One partner took my order and relayed my pastry order to another partner behind the pastry case. He also relayed my coffee order to the barista at the other end of the counter. As I moved through the line to the register, my order arrived just as I did, and a fourth partner

30

"I believe that the sequence of topics follows a logical pattern by moving from introducing the general concepts of AIS to students to internal controls and a need to automate them, to design of the DB—'backbone' of the IT system—and then to specific accounting cycles, and to general IT-related issues."

—Dmitriy Shaltayev, Christopher Newport University

"I like how it relates many of the concepts to real companies, like Starbucks."

—Linda Wallace, Virginia Tech

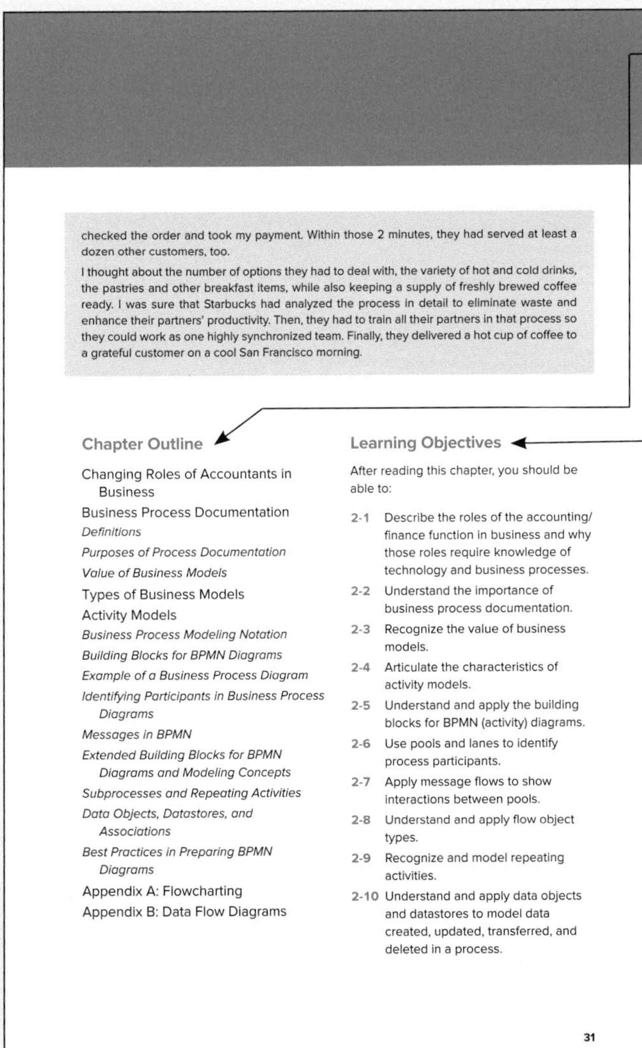

checked the order and took my payment. Within those 2 minutes, they had served at least a dozen other customers, too.

I thought about the number of options they had to deal with, the variety of hot and cold drinks, the pastries and other breakfast items, while also keeping a supply of freshly brewed coffee ready. I was sure that Starbucks had analyzed the process in detail to eliminate waste and enhance their partners' productivity. Then, they had to train all their partners in that process so they could work as one highly synchronized team. Finally, they delivered a hot cup of coffee to a grateful customer on a cool San Francisco morning.

Chapter Outline

Changing Roles of Accountants in Business
Business Process Documentation
Definitions
Purposes of Process Documentation
Value of Business Models
Types of Business Models
Activity Models
Business Process Modeling Notation
Building Blocks for BPMN Diagrams
Example of a Business Process Diagram
Identifying Participants in Business Process Diagrams
Messages in BPMN
Extended Building Blocks for BPMN Diagrams and Modeling Concepts
Subprocesses and Repeating Activities
Data Objects, Datastores, and Associations
Best Practices in Preparing BPMN Diagrams
Appendix A: Flowcharting
Appendix B: Data Flow Diagrams

Learning Objectives

After reading this chapter, you should be able to:

2-1 Describe the roles of the accounting/finance function in business and why those roles require knowledge of technology and business processes.
2-2 Understand the importance of business process documentation.
2-3 Recognize the value of business models.
2-4 Articulate the characteristics of activity models.
2-5 Understand and apply the building blocks for BPMN (activity) diagrams.
2-6 Use pools and lanes to identify process participants.
2-7 Apply message flows to show interactions between pools.
2-8 Understand and apply flow object types.
2-9 Recognize and model repeating activities.
2-10 Understand and apply data objects and datastores to model data created, updated, transferred, and deleted in a process.

31

Chapter Outline

Each chapter opens with an Outline that provides direction to the students about the topics they can expect to learn throughout the chapter.

Learning Objectives

Learning Objectives are featured at the beginning of each chapter. The objectives provide students with an overview of the concepts they should understand after reading the chapter. These Learning Objectives are repeated in the margin of the text where they apply.

"Well-written with great examples. Students should like reading this book."

—Marcia Watson, Mississippi State University

Integrated Project

Projects can generate classroom discussion, foster good teamwork, and prepare students for their accounting careers. Chapter 8 provides guidance to students on how to approach a systems project; related material provides information and data for the projects. There are now two different projects, so instructors can select the project level of difficulty to match the time available or the sophistication of their students. Both integrated projects require students to apply the different techniques they have learned in Chapters 5, 6, and 7 to a realistic situation. One project focuses on inventory management in a small business with multiple retail stores and a central warehouse. The second project also involves a small wholesale distribution business with multiple stores but without inventory management complications. Students use Microsoft Access to implement their data models and prepare financial reports in both projects.

LO 8-5
Employ the relational database to answer a variety of business performance questions

Prepare Queries

After importing all the data and setting the relationships to match the UML class diagram, you are ready to prepare queries for the financial statements and any other operational performance information. Each deliverable may require multiple queries. For example, to determine sales revenue for the quarter, you would first extend the SALES ITEMS table information to determine the amount for each item sold on each sale, as shown in Figure 8.11.

Then, using the query shown in Figure 8.11 and the SALES table, calculate the amount of each sale within the fiscal period, in this case the first calendar quarter, as shown in Figure 8.12. Set the criteria to constrain transactions to the first quarter. Sum the amount field, calculated as shown in Figure 8.11. Then, the summed amount from this query can be used to calculate overall sales revenue for the quarter in a subsequent query.

FIGURE 8.10
Setting Relationship between SALES and SALES ITEMS Tables

© Microsoft Excel

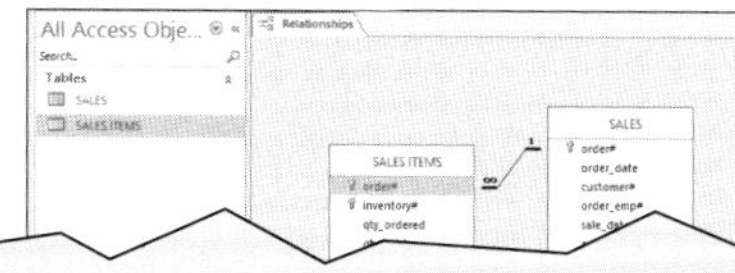

"I like comprehensive problems that extend across multiple chapters so students can see how different components of a problem fit together."

—Janice Benson, University of Wyoming

Data Analytics

Due to its importance and popularity, we have added an all-new chapter on data analytics (Chapter 9). That chapter introduces the importance and impact of data analytics in the business world and specifically on the accounting profession. Data analytics holds great value to these businesses, whether the data reveal certain patterns in their marketing or advertising, provide insight into seasonal trends, or offer anything else that could be relevant to the businesses' success. However, the value of data analytics is really only as valuable as the insight it provides. We highlight the importance of data analytics in accounting, especially in auditing. The chapter also introduces several data analytics techniques in Excel and Tableau.

LO 9-7
Use Excel spreadsheet tables for data analytics

DATA ANALYTICS TOOLS

Using Excel for Data Analytics

This section provides an introduction to the use of Excel to perform data analytics. Th example employs freely available U.S. Census data,[23] and it shows state and county popula tion and changes in population due to births and deaths over the period from 2010 to 201 This particular example uses only state population data as shown in Figure 9.2. Note that th data start in the first row of the worksheet, and any blank rows or blank columns are delete Thus, the data extend from cell A1 to cell AD52 with variable names in the first row. Th region numbers indicate areas of the country, such as Northeast or South. The division num bers represent further subdivisions of the regions, such as New England or South Atlanti We describe tab, section, and item selection as X > Y > Z, where X represents the Excel ta Y is the section of the ribbon bar, and Z is the specific icon on the ribbon bar.

The first step is to convert the raw data to a **table in Excel.** Click on any cell within th data. Select INSERT > Table > Table, as shown in Figure 9.3. A Create Table popup wi appear to specify where the data for the table are and whether the table has headers. If the are no blank rows or columns in the data, Excel will correctly identify the extent of the da for the table. Check the box to specify that the table has headers, as shown in Figure 9.

Progress Checks

These self-test questions and problems in the body of the chapter enable the student to determine whether he or she has understood the preceding material and to reinforce that understanding before reading further. Detailed solutions to these questions are found at the end of each chapter.

"I really like the Progress Check box. It is a great tool for students' self assessment."

—Chih-Chen Lee, Northern Illinois University

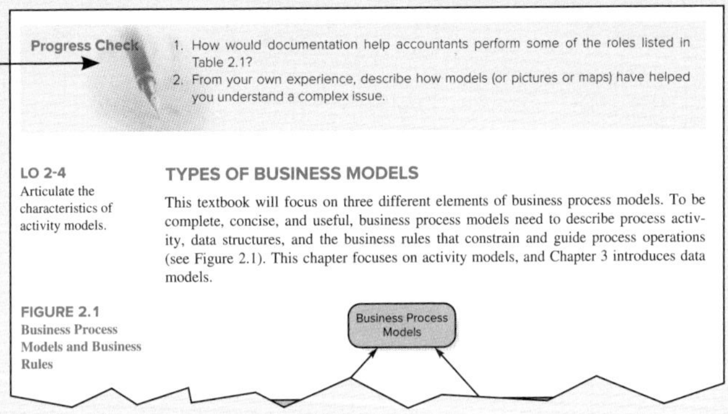

Progress Check

1. How would documentation help accountants perform some of the roles listed in Table 2.1?
2. From your own experience, describe how models (or pictures or maps) have helped you understand a complex issue.

LO 2-4
Articulate the characteristics of activity models.

TYPES OF BUSINESS MODELS

This textbook will focus on three different elements of business process models. To be complete, concise, and useful, business process models need to describe process activity, data structures, and the business rules that constrain and guide process operations (see Figure 2.1). This chapter focuses on activity models, and Chapter 3 introduces data models.

FIGURE 2.1
Business Process Models and Business Rules

Data Modeling and Microsoft Access

Chapter 3 describes how data modeling supports the design, implementation, and operation of database systems. Basic modeling tools are used throughout the rest of the text.

"This textbook would be good when using the database approach. It provides the information needed to develop and use a database without getting into the details of transaction processing (activities, documents, and internal control)."

—Janice Benson, University of Wyoming

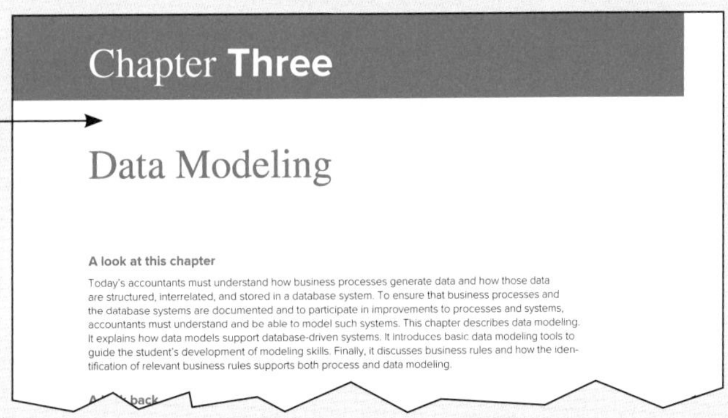

Chapter **Three**

Data Modeling

A look at this chapter

Today's accountants must understand how business processes generate data and how those data are structured, interrelated, and stored in a database system. To ensure that business processes and the database systems are documented and to participate in improvements to processes and systems, accountants must understand and be able to model such systems. This chapter describes data modeling. It explains how data models support database-driven systems. It introduces basic data modeling tools to guide the student's development of modeling skills. Finally, it discusses business rules and how the identification of relevant business rules supports both process and data modeling.

Connect Accounting for *Accounting Information Systems*

The 2nd Edition of *Accounting Information Systems* has a full Connect package, with the following features available for instructors and students.

- **SmartBook®** is the market-leading adaptive study resource that is proven to strengthen memory recall, increase retention, and boost grades. SmartBook, which is powered by LearnSmart, is the first and only adaptive reading experience designed to change the way students read and learn. It creates a personalized reading experience by highlighting the most impactful concepts a student needs to learn at that moment in time. As a student engages with SmartBook, the reading experience continuously adapts by highlighting content based on what the student has mastered or is ready to learn. This ensures that the focus is on the content he or she needs to learn, while simultaneously promoting long-term retention of material. Both students and instructors can use SmartBook's real-time reports to quickly identify the concepts that require more attention from individual students—or the entire class. The end result? Students are more engaged with course content, can better prioritize their time, and come to class ready to participate.
- **Online Assignments.** New to Connect for *Accounting Information Systems,* 2nd Edition, is the addition of all End-of-Chapter Multiple Choice questions as assignable. Additionally, applicable End-of-Chapter Problems from each chapter have been added to Connect in an auto-gradable format. Connect helps students learn more efficiently by providing feedback and practice material when and where they need it. Connect grades homework automatically, and students benefit from the immediate feedback that they receive, particularly on any questions they may have missed.

Example of End-of-Chapter Problem

Required:
Using the Cash table below, show the output for the following SQL query: **(Using the dropdowns, identify which rows and columns would included in the SQL query output shown below. Select "Not included" for rows and columns that would not be included in the output.)**

SELECT Account#, Balance
FROM Cash
WHERE Balance < 50000;

Cash	Included			
	Account #	Type	Bank	Balance
	BA-6	Checking	Boston 5	253
	BA-7	Checking	Shawmut	48,000
	BA-8	Draft	Shawmut	75,000
	BA-9	Checking	Boston5	950

- **Comprehensive Exercises and Integrated Project.** The setup information for the Comprehensive Exercises for Chapters 5 and 6 and the Integrated Project in Chapter 8 have been added to Connect, along with the ability for students to upload their submission files for their instructors to grade. Narrated videos explaining the background, setup, and goals of the Exercises and Project have also been provided.
- **Multiple Choice Quizzes.** The Multiple Choice Quizzes from the Online Learning Center have been revised and can now be assigned to students through Connect for grading.
- **Test Bank.** The Test Bank for each chapter has been updated and significantly expanded for the 2nd Edition to stay current with new and revised chapter material, with all questions available for assignment through Connect. Instructors can also create tests and quizzes from the Test Bank through our TestGen software.
- The Instructor and Student Resources have been updated for the 2nd edition and are available in the Connect Instructor Resources page. Available resources include Instructor Resource and Solutions Manuals, Comprehensive Exercise and Integrated Project setup and solutions files, PowerPoint presentations, Test Bank files, and other ancillary materials. All applicable Student Resources will be available in a convenient file that can be distributed to students for classes either directly, through Connect, or via courseware.

Example of Test Bank Question in Connect

Which of the following is <u>not</u> a best practice in preparing Unified Modeling Language (UML) Class diagrams?

- ○ Opt for simplicity.
- ○ Model each process separately.
- ○ Avoid crossing lines whenever possible.
- ○ Avoid confusing abbreviations.

McGraw Hill Education **connect®**

Required=Results

©Getty Images/iStockphoto

McGraw-Hill Connect®
Learn Without Limits

Connect is a teaching and learning platform that is proven to deliver better results for students and instructors.

Connect empowers students by continually adapting to deliver precisely what they need, when they need it, and how they need it, so your class time is more engaging and effective.

> 73% of instructors who use **Connect** require it; instructor satisfaction **increases** by 28% when **Connect** is required.

Connect's Impact on Retention Rates, Pass Rates, and Average Exam Scores

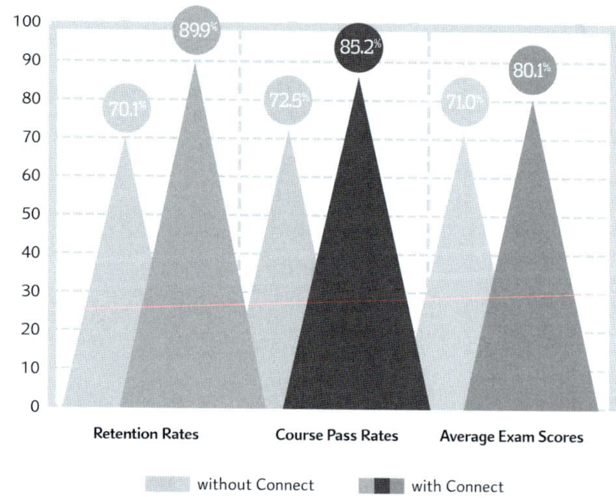

Using Connect improves retention rates by 19.8%, passing rates by 12.7%, and exam scores by 9.1%.

Analytics

Connect Insight®

Connect Insight is Connect's new one-of-a-kind visual analytics dashboard that provides at-a-glance information regarding student performance, which is immediately actionable. By presenting assignment, assessment, and topical performance results together with a time metric that is easily visible for aggregate or individual results, Connect Insight gives the user the ability to take a just-in-time approach to teaching and learning, which was never before available. Connect Insight presents data that helps instructors improve class performance in a way that is efficient and effective.

Impact on Final Course Grade Distribution

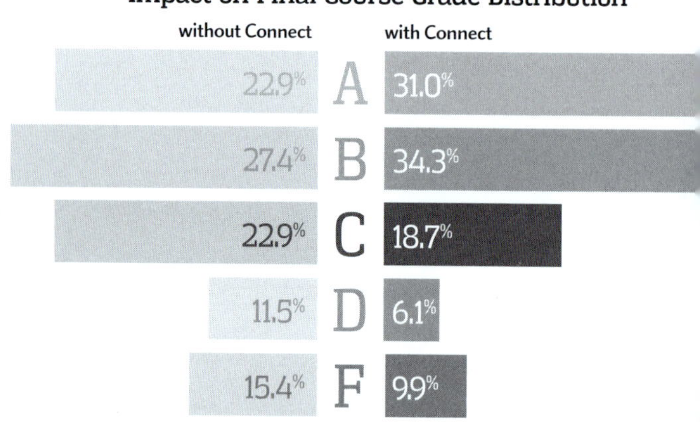

Acknowledgments

Throughout the development of this book, we were privileged to have the candid and valuable advice of our contributors, reviewers, and survey and focus group participants. These reviewers instructors provided us with priceless suggestions, feedback, and constructive criticism. The depth and sincerity of their reviews indicate that they are a devoted group of teacher-scholars. The content of the book over various versions and editions was greatly enhanced because of their efforts.

T. S. Amer
Northern Arizona University
Victoria Badura
Chadron State College
James Bay
University of Utah
Tanya Benford
Florida Gulf Coast University
Janice Benson
University of Wyoming
Jennifer Blaskovich
University of Nebraska, Omaha
A. Faye Borthick
Georgia State University
Kristine Brands
Regis University
Linda Bressler
University of Houston
Kimberly Brickler-Ulrich
Lindenwood University
Sandra Cereola
James Madison University
Siew Chan
Nova Southeastern University
Shifei Chung
Rowan University
Kim Church
Oklahoma State University
Ronald Clark
Auburn University
Curtis Clements
Abilene Christian University
Donna Free
Oakland University
Graham Gal
University of Massachusetts, Amherst
Andy Garcia
Bowling Green State University
David Gelb
Seton Hall University
Jan Gillespie
University of Texas

Terry Glandon
University of Texas, El Paso
Severin Grabski
Michigan State University
Gerry Grant
California State University, Fullerton
Rebekah Heath
St. Ambrose University
William Heninger
Brigham Young University
Kenneth Henry
Florida International University
Sarah Hill
Northcentral Technical College
Rani Hoitash
Bentley University
Diane Janvrin
Iowa State University
Nancy Jones
California State University, Chico
Grover Kearns
University of South Florida, St. Petersburg
Kevin Kobelsky
University of Michigan–Dearborn
Joseph Komar
University of St. Thomas
Don Kovacic
California State University, San Marcos
Brenda Lauer
Davenport University
Mark Lawrence
University of North Alabama
Yvette Lazdowski
Plymouth State University
Maria Leach
Auburn University
Chih-Chen Lee
Northern Illinois University
Picheng Lee
Pace University

Adena LeJeune
Louisiana College
Chan Li
University of Pittsburg
Tina Loraas
Auburn University
Lois Mahoney
Eastern Michigan University
James Mensching
California State University, Chico
Mike Metzcar
Indiana Wesleyan University
Bonnie Morris
West Virginia University
Johnna Murray
University of Missouri, St. Louis
Bruce Neumann
University of Colorado, Denver
Oluwakemi Onwuchekwa
University of Central Florida
Debra Petrizzo
Franklin University
Theresa Phinney
Texas A&M University
Ronald Premuroso
University of Montana
Helen Pruitt
University of Maryland
Jeffrey Pullen
University of Maryland
Austin Reitenga
University of Alabama
Mohd Rujob
Eastern Connecticut State University
Juan Manuel Sanchez
Texas Tech University
Paul San Miguel
Western Michigan University
Arline Savage
Cal Poly, San Luis Obispo
Lloyd Seaton
University of Northern Colorado
Dmitriy Shaltayev
Christopher Newport University
Lewis Shaw
Suffolk University
Robert Slater
University of North Florida
Kathleen Sobieralski
University of Maryland
Eileen Taylor
North Carolina State University
Ryan Teeter
University of Pittsburgh
Barbara Uliss
Metropolitan State University of Denver
Linda Wallace
Virginia Tech
Marcia Watson
Mississippi State University
Mitchell Wenger
The University of Mississippi
Veronda Willis
The University of Texas at Tyler
Darryl Woolley
University of Idaho
Al Chen Yuang-Sung
North Carolina State University

Dedications

To Joe and Mossi White, for being wonderful second parents.

—Vern Richardson

To my students and my family who have inspired and supported me.

—Janie Chang

To my wife, Gayla.

—Rod Smith

Brief Contents

Contents

Chapter **One**

Accounting Information Systems and Firm Value

A look at this chapter

Information plays a crucial role in today's information age. In this chapter, we discuss the importance of accounting information systems and the role accountants play in those systems. Firms invest in accounting information systems to create business value. In this chapter, we also describe investments in information systems to manage internal and external business processes and how they create value for the firm.

A look ahead

Chapter 2 examines the role of accountants as business analysts. The chapter defines business process modeling and describes how it supports the business analyst role of accountants. It explains the potential value of business process modeling and introduces basic modeling tools to guide the accountant's development of modeling skills.

© Kumar Sriskandan/Alamy

Walking in to **Starbucks** and ordering a latte, you notice the atmosphere and the quality and variety of its coffees and related offerings. What you may not immediately notice is the accounting information system that supports the recordkeeping, replenishment, financing, etc. To be sure, Starbucks has invested immense resources into planning, designing, and developing a number of accounting information systems to track information needed to run an effective business and to report to its shareholders and regulators (e.g., Internal Revenue Service and Securities and Exchange Commission) on its performance. This accounting information system tracks information as diverse as the number of hours worked each day by each of its 191,000 employees throughout the world to the amount of sales taxes to be paid and remitted to local and national tax authorities at its 22,000 stores in 66 countries.

In addition, through its Clover coffee machines (which track customer preferences through the cloud and also track the expiration dates of milk), Starbucks is always collecting information and making it accessible from headquarters. Many increasingly view Starbucks as a technology company. This chapter focuses on the role accounting information systems play in creating value for a firm such as Starbucks.

Source: *Forbes* Profile, 2015; *Computerworld*, 2014.

Chapter Outline

Introduction

Accountants as Business Analysts

Definition of Accounting Information Systems

A Simple Information System

Attributes of Useful Information

Data versus Information

Discretionary versus Mandatory Information

Role of Accountants in Accounting Information Systems

Specific Accounting Roles

Certifications in Accounting Information Systems

The Value Chain and Accounting Information Systems

AIS and Internal Business Processes

AIS and External Business Processes

The Supply Chain

Customer Relationship Management

AIS, Firm Profitability, and Stock Prices

AIS and Firm Profitability

AIS and Stock Prices

Learning Objectives

After reading this chapter, you should be able to:

1-1 Define an accounting information system, and explain characteristics of useful information.

1-2 Distinguish among data, information, and an information system.

1-3 Distinguish the roles of accountants in providing information, and explain certifications related to accounting information systems.

1-4 Describe how business processes affect the firm's value chain.

1-5 Explain how AIS affects firm value.

1-6 Describe how AIS assists the firm's internal business processes.

1-7 Assess how AIS facilitates the firm's external business processes.

1-8 Assess the impact of AIS on firm profitability and stock prices.

INTRODUCTION

Information on business facts, numbers, and other useful indicators for business purposes is all around us. Most firms consider information to be a strategic asset and will use it to develop a competitive advantage to run their business better than their competitors. **Starbucks**, for example, uses information about its customers, suppliers, and competitors to predict how much coffee it will sell and how much coffee it will need to purchase. If the company predicts more customers than it actually has, it will have excess coffee and may incur extra carrying costs of its inventory. If Starbucks underestimates the demand for its products, the store could potentially run out of coffee and miss out on profitable sales. Information is a strategic asset if the firm knows what information it needs, develops systems to collect that information, and uses that information to make critical decisions that will affect performance.

LO 1-1
Define an accounting information system, and explain characteristics of useful information.

ACCOUNTANTS AS BUSINESS ANALYSTS

Firms have access to a tremendous amount of data—for instance, transactional data produced from point-of-sale terminals or bank deposits, consumer behavior data, operational statistics generated throughout a supply chain, and more—that can contain valuable insights to enable decision making. With such data, firms can more easily benchmark activity and compare and contrast results. In that way, firms can determine the most effective way to allocate resources such as talent, capital, and expense dollars (e.g., marketing).[1]

At the same time, however, surveys suggest that 28 percent of senior financial executives say they have little or no information to predict the performance of their firms. Another 54 percent said they had only half the information needed to provide visibility into performance.[2]

Therefore, even with information all around us, it often lacks the needed relevance, clarity, and accuracy. To be sure, as you've learned in your classes to date, accountants keep financial records, prepare financial reports, and perform audits. Because the role of the accountant is to access and attest to the quality of information, accountants may increasingly be considered to be in the best position to serve as a business analyst in looking at the organization as a whole and discussing how best to optimize the overall performance.

Specific questions accountants might be able to address include such business opportunities as whether to outsource a business function to India, promote one electronics product over another based on which will sell best or be most profitable, or structure a warehouse lease in such a way as to minimize current or future taxes.

To address such critical, but diverse, business opportunities, accountants need to decide what information is required, then build an information system to access the necessary information, and finally analyze that information to offer helpful advice to management as input for their decisions.[3]

DEFINITION OF ACCOUNTING INFORMATION SYSTEMS

Of the many information systems that might be used in a firm, one type of information system is used in every firm: an **accounting information system (AIS)**. An AIS is defined as a system that records, processes, summarizes, and reports on business transactions to provide financial and nonfinancial information to facilitate decision making. In addition, an AIS is designed to ensure appropriate levels of internal controls (security measures to

[1] B. McCarthy, "A Manual for the Data-Driven Finance Chief," CFO.com (November 6, 2015).
[2] J. Hagel, "Why Accountants Should Own Big Data," *Journal of Accountancy* (November 2013.)
[3] F. Borthick, "Helping Accountants Learn to Get the Information Managers Want: The Role of the Accounting Information Systems Course," *Journal of Information Systems* 10, no. 2 (1996), pp. 75–85.

protect sensitive data) for those transactions. This is the focus of this book. Some might call an AIS just a financial reporting system. Others might include in their AIS a much broader set of data that includes nonfinancial information such as sales and marketing activities or the results of research and development expenditures. Viewed broadly, an AIS collects, processes, and reports information deemed useful in decision making.

The study of AISs lies at the nexus of two traditional disciplines: information systems and accounting. In this book, we will highlight knowledge from both of these disciplines to more fully understand an AIS. While an AIS could take the form of a paper-and-pencil manual bookkeeping system, we will view an AIS in this book as computerized systems.

A Simple Information System

An AIS, just like any system, can be explained using a general systems approach (as in Figure 1.1) with input, storage, processing, and output activities. We cover these activities in subsequent chapters, but the input may come in the form of sales recorded on a **Starbucks** cash register or point-of-sale terminal. Processing those data may take the form of getting the input into storage (such as a database or a data table). Processing might involve querying that database (e.g., using SQL queries) to produce the output in the form of a report for management use. As an example, Starbucks may query its sales database to report how much coffee it sells around Christmas to see if additional sales incentives need to be made to increase sales around Christmas in the future. Whether this report has information that is ultimately useful to management is covered in the next section.

FIGURE 1.1
A Simple Information System

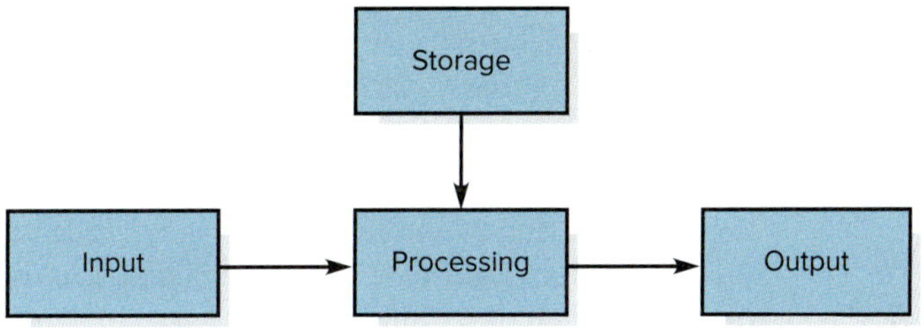

Attributes of Useful Information

To be most useful to decision makers, information from an AIS must be both relevant and reliable and have these attributes:

1. **Relevance**
   a. Predictive value (helps with forecasting the future).
   b. Feedback value (corrects or confirms what had been predicted in the past).
   c. Timeliness (available when needed or in time to have an impact on a decision).
2. **Reliability**
   a. Verifiable (can be confirmed by an independent party).
   b. Representational faithfulness (reports what actually happened).
   c. Neutrality (information is not biased).

Relevance

To be useful, information must be relevant to the decision maker. Information is relevant only if it would affect a business decision. In other words, information is relevant when it helps users predict what will happen in the future (predictive value) or evaluate how past decisions actually worked out (feedback value). It is also relevant if the information is received in time to affect their decisions (timeliness).

Reliability

Information is reliable if users can depend on it to be free from bias and error. Reliable information is verifiable by internal and external parties and faithfully represents the substance of the underlying economic transaction. If **Best Buy** sells a high-definition television for $3,200, it should be recorded and subsequently reported in its sales revenue account as $3,200. Accounting information should not be designed to lead users to accept or reject any specific decision alternative, but rather to offer reliable accounting information that is neutral, or free from bias, to let users make the best decisions.

Sometimes there are trade-offs between information that is relevant and information that is reliable. The best information may be information that only becomes reliable once an audit performed by external auditors is complete. But waiting for an audit to be completed may take so long that it is no longer relevant. The most relevant information may require an estimate of the value of a building, but that estimate might be subject to bias of the building appraiser, which will limit the information's reliability. Management often must make choices and trade off between relevance and reliability of the data.

For certain problems, the best information might include some information that tends to be more reliable (e.g., last period's sales, sales of competitors selling similar products) and other information that tends to be more relevant (estimates, appraisals, predictions gained by running regression models predicting year-ahead sales, etc.) that, in combination, complement each other and give management the necessary information.

AISs exist to provide useful information to decision makers. Considering the attributes of useful information helps AIS designers and users construct a system that delivers useful information.

LO 1-2
Distinguish among data, information, and an information system.

Data versus Information

Hal Varian, **Google**'s chief economist, explains that while data are widely available, "what is scarce is the ability to extract wisdom from them." In that short statement, we learn that data and the information actually needed to make decisions may well have different definitions. **Data** are simply raw facts that describe the characteristics of an event that, in isolation, have little meaning.

Useful Information or Just Data? On September 12, 2001, Walmart sold 88,000 U.S. flags, compared to only 6,400 that same day a year earlier.

Attributes of a simple sale of a U.S. flag at a **Walmart** store in Tempe, Arizona, may include the time and date of sale, bar code number, price, and quantity purchased. However, to be most useful to Walmart, these data must be processed in a meaningful way to provide information useful to Walmart management. Thus, Walmart management would like the information to potentially address such questions as:

- How many flags does Walmart need on hand to prepare for the July 4th holiday each year?
- What is the right price to charge for flags to maximize Walmart's profits?
- Which size of U.S. flag sells best in Tempe, Arizona; Stamford, Connecticut; or Champaign, Illinois? Does it depend on location?
- Do consumers replace flags, or do they last many years and not really need to be replaced?

Data are considered to be an input, whereas information is considered to be the output.

Information is defined as being data organized in a meaningful way to be useful to the user. Thus, data are often processed (e.g., aggregated, sorted, etc.) and then combined with the appropriate context. Decision makers typically require useful information to make decisions. As another example, while the sales prices of a particular toy might be just considered data, subtracting the cost of goods sold from the sales price to compute the net profit would be considered information if the data help a retailer decide whether to carry that particular toy in its inventory. To the extent that computers can process and organize data in a way that is helpful to the decision maker, it is possible that there may be so much information available to actually cause **information overload**, which we define as the difficulty a person faces in understanding a problem and making a decision as a consequence of too much information. Therefore, an AIS must be carefully designed to provide the information that is most useful without overwhelming the user.

The overall transformation from a business need and business event (like each individual sale of a U.S. flag) to the collection of data and information to an ultimate decision is called the **information value chain** and is reflected in Figure 1.2. If Walmart needs to know how many flags it should have at each location (i.e., business need), it will collect transactions involving flag sales (i.e., business event). Then it can take those data and turn them into useful information that might be used to make decisions on flag supply levels at each store. Certainly, the transformation from data to information is a key part of that value chain. Information that is useful (i.e., relevant or reliable) may get to the point of being knowledge and, ultimately, may be helpful in forming the basis for a decision.

FIGURE 1.2
Information Value Chain

Source: Statements on Management Accounting, Institute of Management Accountants, 2008.

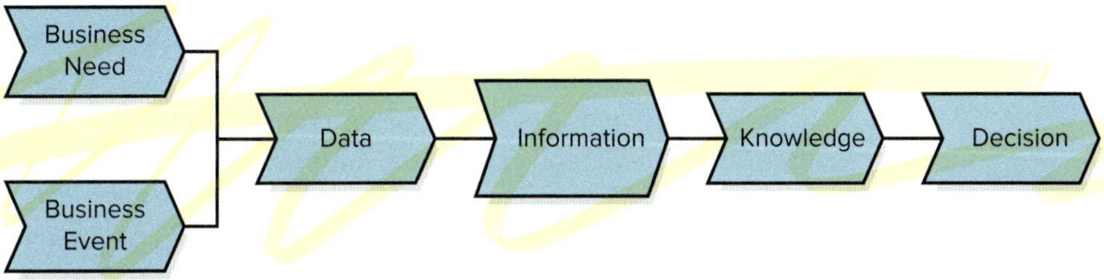

Discretionary versus Mandatory Information

Because you have already taken a few accounting classes, you understand the types of information that are recorded, processed, and subsequently reported for different purposes, including managerial, financial, or tax purposes. Managerial accounting information is generally produced for internal information purposes and would usually be considered to be **discretionary information** because there is no law requiring that it be provided to management. Management simply decides what information it needs to track and builds an information system to track it. For example, management may want an activity-based costing (ABC) system to figure out how overhead costs should be allocated at **Microsoft** to a set of products (like the Microsoft Surface Book as compared to a Microsoft XBox). The value of information equals the difference between the benefits realized from using that information and the costs of producing it. Because discretionary information is not required, management must determine if the benefits of receiving that information are greater than the costs of producing it.

In contrast, much of the financial and tax accounting information is produced for external information purposes such as for investors, banks, financial analysts, bondholders, and the Internal Revenue Service (IRS). This financial and tax accounting information would generally be considered to be **mandatory information**. As mentioned earlier, discretionary information should be produced if the value of the information it provides to management is worth more than the cost to produce it. However, mandatory information is usually produced at the lowest possible cost to comply with the laws of the regulators (e.g., Securities and Exchange Commission, IRS, state banking commission, state tax commission, etc.).

As early as 1989, **Starbucks** installed a costly computer network and hired a specialist in information technology from **McDonald's** Corporation to design a point-of-sale (cash register) system for store managers to use. Every night, stores passed their sales information to the Seattle headquarters, which allowed managers to highlight regional buying trends almost instantly.

An AIS is used to support the mandatory information required by tax returns.
© Digital Vision/Getty Images RF

Progress Check

1. Propose useful information that is relevant to a college basketball coach. Also propose useful information that is reliable to a college basketball coach.
2. Give an example of data versus information at a **Walmart** store.
3. Provide two types of discretionary information and two types of mandatory information that might come from an accounting information system.

LO 1-3
Distinguish the roles of accountants in providing information, and explain certifications related to accounting information systems.

ROLE OF ACCOUNTANTS IN ACCOUNTING INFORMATION SYSTEMS

In today's age, technology is a key tool in creating information systems for today's businesses. As a result, accounting and information technology are now more closely linked than ever. As information technology (IT) has gained operational and strategic importance in the business world, the role of accountants, understandably, must adjust as well. The International Federation of Accountants (IFAC) notes:

> IT has grown (and will continue to grow) in importance at such a rapid pace and with such far reaching effects that it can no longer be considered a discipline peripheral to accounting. Rather, professional accounting has merged and developed with IT to such an extent that one can hardly conceive of accounting independent from IT.[4]

Indeed, accountants have a role as business analysts and business partners; that is, they gather information to solve business problems or address business opportunities. They determine what information is relevant in solving business problems, create or extract that information, and then analyze the information to solve the problem. An AIS provides a systematic means for accountants to get needed information and solve a problem. Another illustration of the role of accountants in AIS comes from the Institute of Management Accounting. In this definition, note the role of the accountant in devising planning and performance information systems:

> Management accounting is a profession that involves partnering in management decision making, devising planning and performance management systems, and providing expertise in financial reporting and control to assist management in the formulation and implementation of a firm's strategy.[5]

Specific Accounting Roles

Understanding the design, use, and management of information technology is of vital importance to not only management accountants, but to all of those within the accounting profession. To recognize the needed competencies for accountants with respect to

[4]Source: "Information Technology Competencies in the Accounting Profession: AICPA Implementation Strategies for IFAC International Education Guideline No. 11," American Institute of Certified Public Accountants, 1996.
[5]Source: Institute of Management Accountants, *Statements on Management Accounting,* 2008.

information technology, it is important to recognize the potential role of accountants in accounting information systems, including the following:

1. The accountant as *user* of accounting information systems—whether it be inputting journal entries into an accounting system, using a financial spreadsheet to calculate the cost of a product, or using anti-virus software to protect the system, accountants use an AIS.
    - As an example, accountants serving in an audit role should be able to understand how to access their client's AIS and how to use at least one major computer-assisted auditing package (such as Audit Control Language, or ACL), an online or local database system, or a professional research tool.
2. The accountant as *manager* of accounting information systems (e.g., financial manager, controller, CFO).
    - Accountants serving as managers of AISs must be able to plan and coordinate accounting information systems and be able to organize and staff, direct and lead, and monitor and control those information systems.
3. The accountant as *designer* of accounting information systems (e.g., business system design team, producer of financial information, **systems analyst**).
    - Accountants serving in a design capacity must have significant practical exposure as they work to develop a system that will meet the needs of users. Specifically, they need to work with key phases of system analysis and design, such as the preparation of a feasibility analysis; information requirements elicitation and documentation techniques; data file design and documentation techniques; and document, screen, and report design techniques. In particular, accountants must understand business processes and the information requirements of other systems.
4. The accountant as *evaluator* of accounting information systems (e.g., IT auditor, assessor of internal controls, tax advisor, general auditor, consultant)
    - As will be discussed in Chapter 11, the **Sarbanes-Oxley Act of 2002 (SOX)** requires an evaluation of the internal controls in an AIS. As part of that act, and as part of a standard audit, accountants must be able to tailor standard evaluation approaches to an AIS and offer practical recommendations for improvement where appropriate. In addition, the accountant must be able to apply relevant IT tools and techniques to effectively evaluate the system.

In considering the information technology competencies in the accounting profession, the American Institute of Certified Public Accountants (AICPA) and International Federation of Accountants (IFAC) assume that, at a minimum, all accountants will be proficient in the AIS user role and at least one of the other listed roles (e.g., manager, designer, or evaluator). Accountants will be better users, managers, and evaluators of AISs if they understand the design of the system. Thus, throughout the text we touch on all of the roles that accountants have in the firms, but we particularly emphasize skills relevant to the designer role.

Certifications in Accounting Information Systems

In addition to the various roles that accountants play, accountants and related professionals may also seek various certifications to show they are proficient in specific areas of AISs. This will show their competence to specific employers or clients that need some specific services. There are three primary certifications that most directly apply to accounting and information systems (see Figure 1.3).

FIGURE 1.3
Certifications in Accounting Information Systems

Name	Certifying Body	Who They Are and What They Do	How to Qualify
Certified Information Systems Auditor (CISA)	Information Systems Audit and Control Association (ISACA) www.isaca.org	The CISA designation identifies those professionals possessing IT audit, control, and security skills. Generally, CISAs will perform IT audits to evaluate the accounting information system's internal control design and effectiveness.	To qualify as a CISA, a candidate must take an examination and obtain specialized work experience.
Certified Information Technology Professional (CITP)	American Institute of Certified Public Accountants (AICPA) www.aicpa.org	The CITP designation identifies accountants (CPAs) with a broad range of technology knowledge and experience. The CITP designation demonstrates the accountant's ability to leverage technology to effectively and efficiently manage information while ensuring the data's reliability, security, accessibility, and relevance. CITPs may help devise a more efficient financial reporting system, help the accounting function go paperless, or consult on how an IT function may transform the business.	A CPA can earn a CITP designation with a combination of business experience, lifelong learning, and an optional exam.
Certified Internal Auditor (CIA)	Institute of Internal Auditors (IIA) http://www.theiia.org/	The CIA designation is the only globally accepted certification for internal auditors and is the standard to demonstrate their competency and professionalism in the internal auditing field.	An individual can earn a CIA designation by having the required education, professional experience, and character references; the individual must also pass the CIA examination.

Progress Check

4. Would an IT auditor be considered to be a user, manager, evaluator, or designer of a client firm's accounting information system?
5. What would be the appropriate designation for someone who wants to be an IT auditor?
6. Let's suppose that **ConocoPhillips** is hiring accountants for an entry-level financial accounting position. Is it reasonable to expect accountants to be proficient in information technology?

LO 1-4
Describe how business processes affect the firm's value chain.

THE VALUE CHAIN AND ACCOUNTING INFORMATION SYSTEMS

Information technology (IT) is increasingly omnipresent! Worldwide spending on IT is expected to exceed $3.54 trillion in 2016.[6] Clearly, information technology is a huge investment that firms make, and they expect to create value through its use. How IT assists firms to carry out their internal and external business processes and, in turn, creates value is an important topic of this chapter.

A firm makes money by taking the inputs (e.g., raw materials, talented workers, buildings, equipment, etc.) and producing a more valuable output (e.g., iPhones available for

[6]"Worldwide IT Spending to Rise 0.6% to $3.54 Trillion in 2016: Gartner," *The Economic Times,* January 19, 2016.

sale, completed audit report, etc.). Take a university as an example. Universities admit students to the university (as inputs) and use their resources (curriculum, faculty, buildings, computers, etc.) to create a job-ready, educated graduate (the output). Arguably, the university creates value. If it is not creating value in one form or the other, it probably will not continue to survive.

Let's continue the discussion by defining **business value** as all those items, events, and interactions that determine the financial health and/or well-being of the firm. This value may come from suppliers, customers, or employees or even from information systems. Business value does not necessarily need to be determined by stock price or net income. A not-for-profit group like the **International Red Cross** may define business value as how many lives are saved, the amount of blood donated or the number of children that are immunized.

To consider how value is created, we begin by looking at the business processes. A business process is a coordinated, standardized set of activities conducted by both people and equipment to accomplish a specific task, such as invoicing a customer. To evaluate the effectiveness of each of its business processes, a firm can use Michael Porter's value chain analysis. A **value chain** is a chain of business processes for a firm. Products pass through all activities of the chain in order; at each activity, the product is expected to gain some value. It is important not to confuse the concept of the value chain with the actual cost of performing those activities. One way of looking at this is by considering a rough diamond. Although the cutting activity of a diamond may have a very low cost, this cutting activity adds much of the value to the end product because a cut diamond is much more valuable than a rough diamond. And a diamond cut well adds more value than a diamond cut poorly.

The value chain illustrated in Figure 1.4 shows both primary activities and support activities. Primary activities directly provide value to the customer and include the following five activities:

1. **Inbound logistics** are the activities associated with receiving and storing raw materials and other partially completed materials and distributing those materials to manufacturing when and where they are needed.
2. **Operations** are the activities that transform inputs into finished goods and services (e.g., turning wood into furniture for a furniture manufacturer; building a house for a home builder).
3. **Outbound logistics** are the activities that warehouse and distribute the finished goods to the customers.
4. **Marketing and sales activities** identify the needs and wants of customers to help attract them to the firm's products and, thus, buy them.
5. **Service activities** provide the support of customers after the products and services are sold to them (e.g., warranty repairs, parts, instruction manuals, etc.).

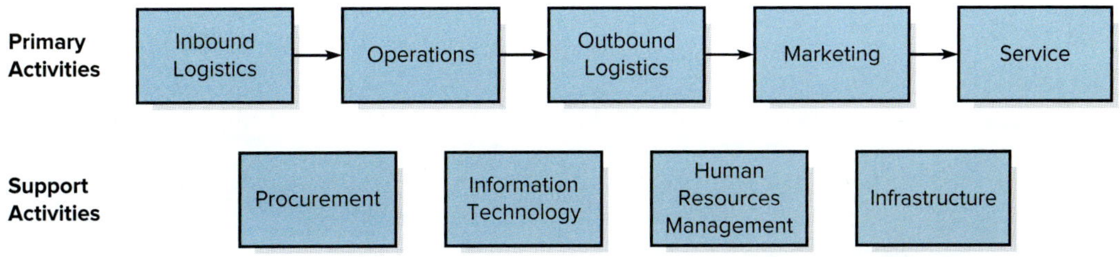

FIGURE 1.4
The Value Chain

These five primary activities are sustained by the following support activities:

1. **Firm infrastructure** activities are all of the activities needed to support the firm, including the CEO and the finance, accounting, and legal departments.
2. **Human resource management** activities include recruiting, hiring, training, and compensating employees.
3. **Technology** activities include all of the technologies necessary to support value-creating activities. These technologies also include research and development to develop new products or determine ways to produce products at a cheaper price.
4. **Procurement** activities involve purchasing inputs such as raw materials, supplies, and equipment.

LO 1-5
Explain how AIS affects firm value.

An AIS can add value to the firm by making each primary activity more effective and efficient. For example, AISs can assist with inbound and outbound logistics. This is done by finding efficiencies and cost savings in logistics (transportation and warehousing costs, etc.) in AISs and geographic information systems to help identify the lowest cost of getting items from one location to another. AISs can make marketing, sales, and service activities more valuable by summarizing data about key customers to help manage and nurture a firm's interactions with its clients.

As an example, **Amazon.com** is one of the best at fostering its interaction with its customers by keeping a record of their past purchases and product searches and using that information to recommend other similar products for its customers to consider (see highlighted circle in Figure 1.5 for an example). As another example, as the loan officers at a bank learn more about the financial products currently being used by its bank's customers through its AIS, they will be able to help identify additional bank products (e.g., insurance, CDs, mutual funds, etc.) to sell to their clients.

As detailed here, AIS can add value to the firm by making each support activity more effective and efficient. An AIS:

- Helps with the firm infrastructure by giving management information relevant to the decision makers.
- May also help provide the internal control structure needed to make sure the information is secure, reliable, and free from error (as discussed in Chapter 11).
- Helps produce external and internal financial reports efficiently and helps decision makers get timely access to the processed information. This may give the information to the decision maker in time to influence the decision.
- Supports the human resources function by assisting employees, who are arguably the most valuable asset of the firm. This assistance includes easy access to payroll information, compensation policies, benefits, tax benefits, and so on.
- Assists procurement by improving the effectiveness and efficiency of the supply chain. This helps ensure that the right product is at the right location at the right time, including receipts of raw material from suppliers to delivery of finished goods to the customers.

Progress Check

7. Consider the value chain for **Ford**. In your opinion, which primary activity is the most critical to creating value for the firm?
8. How does an AIS help **Wayfair** (a popular online furniture and furnishings store) find the right marketing strategy?
9. An AIS adds value to the supporting activities by making access to financial results available on a more timely basis. Why does this matter?

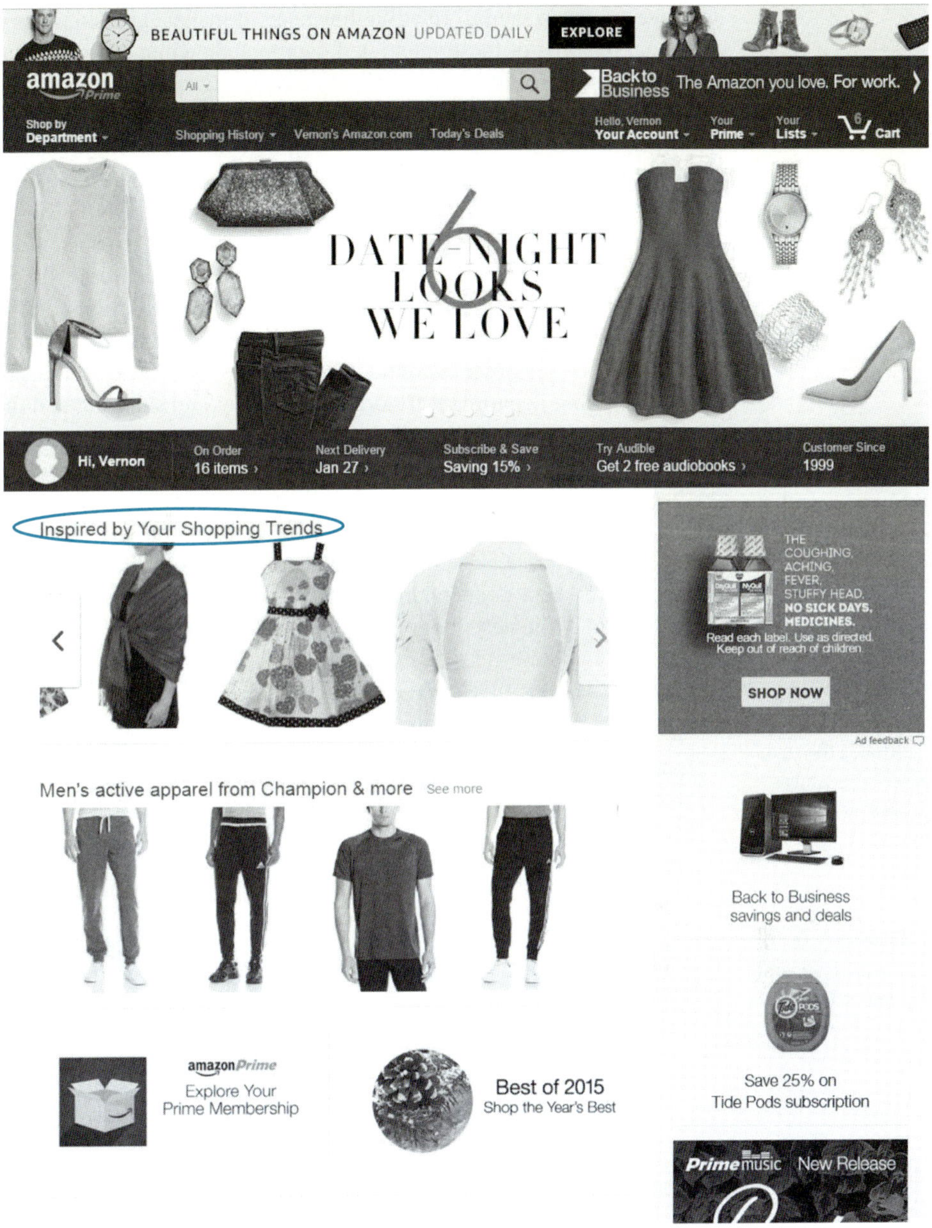

FIGURE 1.5
Amazon.com: "Inspired by Your Shopping Trends"

Source: Amazon.com

LO 1-6
Describe how AIS assists the firm's internal business processes.

AIS AND INTERNAL BUSINESS PROCESSES

Our discussion now turns to how an AIS can assist the firm with its internal business processes. An AIS within a firm is usually the foundation for an **enterprise system (ES)**—also called an enterprise resource planning (ERP) system. An enterprise system is a centralized database that collects data from throughout the firm. This includes data from orders, customers, sales, inventory, and employees. These data are then accumulated in the centralized database and made available to all enterprise system users, including accounting, manufacturing (or operations), marketing, and human resources. As the data are integrated into one single, centralized database to become useful information, authorized employees throughout the firm (from the CEO all the way to the lowest-paid line worker) have access to the information they need to make a decision. For most firms, the informational benefits of these integrated data include enhanced completeness, transparency, and timeliness of information needed to effectively manage a firm's business activities.

As an example, an enterprise system can automate a business process such as order fulfillment. The enterprise system can take an order from a customer, fill that order, ship it, and then create an invoice to bill the customer. As an example, when a customer service representative receives a customer order into an enterprise system, she has all the information needed to approve and complete the order (e.g., the customer's credit rating and order history from the finance module of the centralized database, the firm's inventory levels to see if the product is available from the warehouse module of the centralized database, and the shipping dock's trucking schedule from the logistics module of the centralized database). Once the order is complete, the enterprise system routes the order to the warehouse and shipping department for order fulfillment and shipping and then to the finance department to make sure the customer is invoiced. During the process, all workers in the various departments can see the same information and update it as needed. As problems arise (e.g., backordered products, returned products, trucker strike, etc.), the enterprise system gives all within the firm the most current information to address these issues.

The enterprise system serves as the backbone of the firm's internal business processes and serves as a connection to the external business processes with external partners as discussed in the next section.

LO 1-7
Assess how AIS facilitates the firm's external business processes.

AIS AND EXTERNAL BUSINESS PROCESSES

Firms do not work in isolation. They are always connected to both their suppliers and customers and their wants and needs. As shown in Figure 1.6, the AIS assists in business integration with external parties such as suppliers and customers. The firm's interaction with the suppliers is generally called *supply chain management,* and the interaction with its customers is generally called *customer relationship management.*

FIGURE 1.6
AIS and External Business Processes

The Supply Chain

Supply chain refers to the flow of materials, information, payments, and services from raw materials suppliers, through factories and warehouses, all the way to the final customers of the firm's products. A supply chain also includes the firms and processes that create and deliver products, information, and services to the final customers. The supply chain refers to a network of processes that delivers a finished good or service to the final customer. Figure 1.7 reflects the sourcing, manufacturing (making), and delivering to the customer for each member of the supply chain (assuming the **Unilever** product is made in China, sold to **Sam's Club** and convenience stores, and ultimately sold to an end customer). Handling the returns from the firm's customers and to the firm's suppliers also represents a significant process that requires substantial planning.

To make the supply chain function efficiently, supply chain tasks include processes such as purchasing, payment flow, materials handling, production planning and control, logistics and warehousing, inventory control, returns, and distribution and delivery.

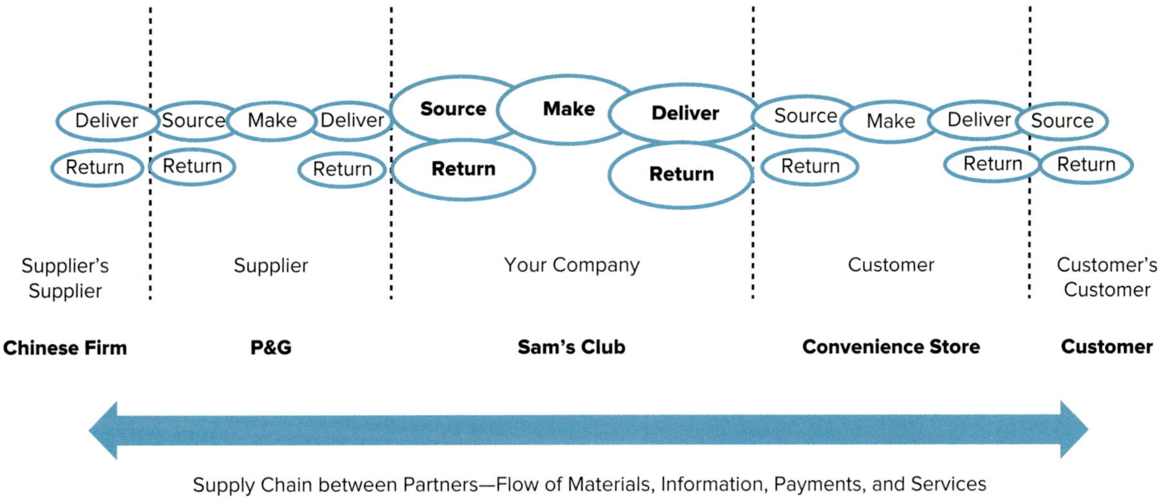

FIGURE 1.7
The Supply Chain

As an illustration, Michael Dell of **Dell Computer** explained one aspect of Dell's use of supply chain management software with suppliers as follows:

> We tell our suppliers exactly what our daily production requirements are so it is not, "Well, every two weeks deliver 5,000 to this warehouse, and we'll put them on the shelf, and then we'll take them off the shelf." It is, "Tomorrow morning we need 8,562, and deliver them to door number seven by 7 am."[7]

The software used to connect the focal firm with its suppliers is generally referred to as **supply chain management (SCM) software**. This software addresses specific segments of the supply chain, especially in manufacturing scheduling, inventory control, and transportation. This SCM software is designed to facilitate decision making and optimize the required levels of inventory to be ordered and held in stock. In the preceding example, Dell might produce expected demand for its products for the next year. As the dates get closer, the estimate is refined so the supplier has a better idea of what exactly will be needed. It is expected that this use of SCM software will optimize inventory and, in turn, will reduce the required amount of raw materials and finished goods inventory the firm will have to hold and thus lower product costs.

A recent study[8] found that firms implementing SCM software are able to reduce the amount of raw materials inventory on hand and reduce selling, general, and administrative expenses. They are also able to increase their gross margins and overall inventory turnover. This suggests that supply chain management systems allow inventory to be optimized to lower the amount of required inventory on hand while not decreasing sales.

Walmart has long been regarded as having one of the best supply chain systems in the world. One aspect of Walmart's supply chain management software is simply communicating the results of its retail sales to its top suppliers. Walmart's Retail Link database is

[7]Source: A. A. Thompson, A. J. Strickland and J. Thompson, *Strategic Management: Concepts and Cases,* 11th ed. (New York: McGraw-Hill, 2006).

[8]B. Dehning, V. J. Richardson, and R. W. Zmud, "The Financial Performance Effects of IT-Based Supply Chain Management Systems in Manufacturing Firms," *Journal of Operations Management* 25 (June 2007), pp. 806–24.

one of the world's largest databases and allows many of its suppliers to view real-time sales data of its products for each store. This allows suppliers to assess the demand for their products and to optimize their own level of inventory and related logistics costs. In turn, the cost savings generated from this process are passed on to Walmart itself and its customers.

Walmart uses its supply chain expertise to lower prices and fulfill its motto to "Save Money, Live Better."

© Justin Sullivan/Getty Images

Connection with Practice

One way of measuring the effectiveness of a supply chain is to calculate the fill rate. The fill rate is a calculation of the service level between two parties—generally, a supplier and a customer. The fill rate is a measure of shipping performance usually expressed as a percentage of the total order. The fill rate is often calculated as the value of order lines shipped on the initial order divided by the total value of the order. If the fill rate increases over time, this means the overall service level is improving. Supply chain management software would be expected to improve the fill rate and, in turn, the overall service levels.

Customer Relationship Management

The more a company can learn about its customers, the more likely it will be able to satisfy their needs. **Customer relationship management (CRM) software** is a term that describes the software used to manage and nurture a firm's interactions with its current and potential clients. CRM software often includes the use of database marketing tools to learn more about customers and to develop strong firm-to-customer relationships. CRM software also includes using IT to manage sales and marketing for current sales and customer service and technical support after the sale is done.

As mentioned in the opening vignette of this chapter, a good example of the need for CRM is **Starbucks**. After its quick expansion in the early 2000s, Starbucks felt like it had lost some of the original Starbucks customer coffeehouse experience. This caused a desire within Starbucks to make sure it understood its customers and their coffeehouse needs. Therefore, a recent initiative at Starbucks was implemented to learn more about its customers. The new chief information officer, Stephen Gillett, argues that his most crucial duty is to enhance Starbucks' ability to mine its customer data to help "reignite our passion with our customers." Starbucks uses loyalty cards (Starbucks' Reward cards) and surveys to track its customers' purchases and build profiles of its customers.[9]

As another example, **Royal Bank** (formerly Royal Bank of Canada) considers CRM software to be such an important part of its strategy that the stated objective of the bank is "to capture the full potential of our customer base through the use of customer information to deliver the right solutions in a consistent, professional manner at every point of contact."[10]

Connection with Practice

Salesforce.com is a popular vendor of CRM software. Note the explanation of CRM on the home page of its website:

> Build more meaningful and lasting relationships with your customers—better understand their wants and needs, identify new opportunities to help, and address any problems faster with an overview of every customer interaction.

Source: Accessed January 26, 2016, www.salesforce.com/what-is-salesforce/?d=70130000000mA5n&internal=true

Progress Check

10. Give an example of how supply chain management software might work for **General Motors**. What type of information does General Motors need to share with its suppliers?
11. Using CRM techniques, what information could universities gather about their current and prospective customers, the students? What information might be most useful to them in recruiting future students?

LO 1-8
Assess the impact of AIS on firm profitability and stock prices.

AIS, FIRM PROFITABILITY, AND STOCK PRICES

Throughout this chapter, we have tried to make the case that AIS facilitates value-creating activities. This section presents a direct test of whether an investment in AIS, in fact, creates value by considering whether an AIS investment led to more profits or higher market value.

AIS and Firm Profitability

One way to consider how AIS creates value is to look at an income statement. Accountants understand that to make more profits, a firm either needs to increase revenues or decrease expenses (or both!). Figure 1.8 illustrates how AIS affects the income statement, making the case for how an AIS may increase profitability.

In an academic study,[11] a positive association was found between the level of the firm's annual IT investment and its subsequent accounting earnings (as measured by return on

[9] T. Wallgum, "Starbucks' Next-Generation CIO: Young, Fast and in Control," *CIO Magazine,* January 2009, www.cio.com/article/474127/Starbucks_Next_Generation_CIO_Young_Fast_and_In_Control?page=3&taxonomyId=3123.

[10] "CRM Case Study: The Analytics That Power CRM at Royal Bank (of Canada)," www.mindbranch.com.

[11] K. Kobelsky, V. J. Richardson, R. Smith, and R. W. Zmud, "Determinants and Consequences of Firm Information Technology Budgets," *The Accounting Review* 83 (July 2008), pp. 957–96.

assets and return on sales), suggesting that IT investment does create value. In a completely different study,[12] researchers found both an improvement in profitability as well as stock returns around the implementation of supply chain information systems.

FIGURE 1.8
The Potential Effect of AIS on an Income Statement

Income Statement	Effect of AIS on Income Statement
Revenues	Customer relationship management (CRM) techniques could attract new customers, generating additional sales revenue.
Less: Cost of Goods Sold	Supply chain management (SCM) software allows firms to carry the right inventory and have it in the right place at the right time. This, in turn, will lower obsolescence as well as logistics and procurement costs.
Gross Margin	The gross margin will change as the result of changes in revenues or cost of goods sold due to the effects of AIS.
Less: Selling, General, and Administrative Expenses (SG&A)	An efficient enterprise system can significantly lower the cost of support processes included in sales, general, and administrative expenses.
Less: Interest Expense	SCM software allows the firm to carry less inventory. Less inventory leaves less assets to finance and may possibly reduce debt and its related interest.
Net Income	All combined, a well-designed and well-functioning AIS with investments in enterprise systems, SCM, and/or CRM may be expected to improve net income.

AIS and Stock Prices

Every time a firm makes an investment, it expects a return of its original investment as well as a return on that investment. This is the case for AIS investments as well. When an investment is announced by a public firm, stock market participants assess whether the investment will pay off or not, either by enhancing revenues or reducing expenses or some combination of both. If the stock market participants believe the future cash flows from the investment will increase for the firm, the stock price of that firm is expected to increase. If the stock market participants believe the future cash flows from the investment will decrease for that firm, the stock price is expected to fall.

An academic study[13] divided up announcements of 315 firms making new AIS investments. The study broke these announcements into three groups, depending on what strategic role the technology was expected to fill within the firm. If AIS investments simply replace human labor to automate business processes, they are defined as automate AIS investments. The automate process will typically digitize (i.e., put in a digital form) the business processes. Once digitized, this information can be automatically and easily summarized in a usable form (i.e., reports, etc.) for management use (defined as the IT strategic role of informate-up) or in a usable form to employees across the firm (defined as IT strategic role of informate-down). IT can also change the basis of competition and redefine business and industry processes (defined as the IT strategic role of transform). As an example, **FedEx**, which allows its customers to track their own packages on the web, changed the basis of competition for the express transportation industry by fundamentally redefining business processes and relationships.

[12]K. B. Hendricks, V. R. Singhal, and J. K. Stratman, "The Impact of Enterprise Systems on Corporate Performance: A Study of ERP, SCM and CRM System Implementations," *Journal of Operations Management* 25, no. 1 (January 2007), pp. 65–82.

[13]B. Dehning, V. J. Richardson, and R. W. Zmud, "The Value Relevance of Announcements of Transformational Information Technology Investments," *MIS Quarterly* 27, no. 4 (2003), pp. 637–56.

Using strategic role as a way to group the IT investments, the lowest strategic role for technology is to automate manual processes. The highest strategic role for technology is transform, with informate-up and informate-down having a medium strategic role. Here is a summary of these strategic roles:

- **Automate**—replace human labor in automating business processes.
- **Informate-up**—provide information about business activities to senior management.
- **Informate-down**—provide information about business activities to employees across the firm.
- **Transform**—fundamentally redefine business processes and relationships.

Figure 1.9 shows how the stock market responded (adjusted for level of risk and overall market returns) on the day the AIS investment was announced. This analysis assumes there were no other significant news events at the firm on the same day as the AIS investment announcement. On average, the 172 "automate" AIS investments increased firm market value by 0.05 percent and the 95 "informate" AIS investments increased firm market value by 0.40 percent. On average, the "transform" AIS investments increased firm market value by 1.51 percent. The authors found that those 48 AIS investments that transformed the business processes and changed the way business is done had the greatest impact on firm value. Automate and informate investments do have an impact, but they are substantially smaller than the value-enhancing impact of transform investments.

FIGURE 1.9
Stock Market Reaction to AIS Investments

Stock Market Increase around AIS Investment Announcements

AIS Investment Strategic Role

Automate	Informate*	Transform
0.05%	0.40%	1.51%

*Informate-up and Informate-down are consolidated in a single strategic role: Informate.

Progress Check

12. How does the use of supply chain management software reduce the cost of goods sold for a retailer like **Target**?
13. Many hospitals and doctor's offices are beginning to digitize the medical records of their patients. Would this be an example of an automate, informate, or transform IT strategic role?

Summary

Information plays a crucial role in the information age.

- Accountants play a critical role in recording, processing, and reporting financial information for decision making and control. An accounting information system (AIS) is defined as an information system that records, processes, and reports on transactions to provide financial information for decision making and control.
- The accounting profession (including the IFAC and the AICPA) recommends that accountants develop proficiency in at least two areas of information systems: as a user and as a manager, designer, or evaluator of information systems. Accountants often seek certification in information systems to show their level of proficiency to both prospective employers and clients.
- Firms invest in accounting information systems to create value. The value chain illustrates how, during each primary activity, the product should gain some value. An AIS serves an important role in providing value in each primary and supporting activity.

- An AIS creates value by managing internal and external business processes. Enterprise systems, sometimes called ERP or back-office systems, generally manage transactions within the firm. Supply chain management software is used to manage transactions and communications with suppliers. Customer relationship management software is used to manage and nurture the relationship with current and potential customers.
- An AIS generally helps make business processes more efficient and effective. A well-designed and well-functioning AIS can be expected to create value by increasing revenues and reducing expenses.

Key Words

accounting information system (AIS) (*4*) A system that records, processes, and reports on transactions to provide financial and nonfinancial information to make decisions and have appropriate levels of internal controls for those transactions.

automate (*19*) The use of technology to replace human labor in automating business processes.

business value (*11*) Items, events, and interactions that determine the financial health and well-being of the firm.

Certified Information Systems Auditor (CISA) (*10*) The CISA designation identifies those professionals possessing IT audit, control, and security skills. Generally, CISAs will perform IT audits to evaluate the accounting information system's internal control design and effectiveness.

Certified Information Technology Professional (CITP) (*10*) The CITP designation identifies accountants (CPAs) with a broad range of technology knowledge and experience.

Certified Internal Auditor (CIA) (*10*) The CIA designation is the certification for internal auditors and is the standard to demonstrate competency and professionalism in the internal auditing field.

customer relationship management (CRM) software (*16*) Software used to manage and nurture a firm's interactions with its current and potential clients. CRM software often includes the use of database marketing tools to learn more about the customers and to develop strong firm-to-customer relationships.

data (*6*) Raw facts or statistics that, absent a context, may have little meaning.

discretionary information (*7*) Information that is generated according to one's own judgment.

enterprise system (ES) (*13*) A centralized database that collects data from throughout the firm. Commercialized information system that integrates and automates business processes across a firm's value chain located within and across organizations.

firm infrastructure (*12*) Activities needed to support the firm, including the CEO and the finance, accounting, and legal departments.

human resource management (*12*) Activities include recruiting, hiring, training, and compensating employees.

inbound logistics (*11*) Activities associated with receiving and storing raw materials and other partially completed materials and distributing those materials to manufacturing when and where they are needed.

informate-down (*19*) The use of computer technology to provide information about business activities to employees across the firm.

informate-up (*19*) The use of computer technology to provide information about business activities to senior management.

information (*6*) Data organized in a meaningful way to the user.

information overload (*6*) The difficulty a person faces in understanding a problem and making a decision as a consequence of too much information.

information value chain (*7*) The overall transformation from a business need and business event to the collection of data and information to an ultimate decision.

mandatory information (*7*) Information that is required to be generated or provided by law or regulation.

marketing and sales activities (*11*) Activities that identify the needs and wants of their customers to help attract them to the firm's products and buy them.

operations (*11*) Activities that transform inputs into finished goods and services.

outbound logistics (*11*) Activities that warehouse and distribute the finished goods to the customers.

procurement (*12*) Activities that involve purchasing inputs such as raw materials, supplies, and equipment.

relevance (*5*) Information that is capable of making a difference in a decision.

reliability (*5*) Information that is free from bias and error.

Sarbanes-Oxley Act of 2002 (SOX) (*9*) A federal law in the United States that set new and enhanced standards for all U.S. public companies, management, and public accounting firms; a response to business scandals such as Enron, WorldCom, and Tyco International. It requires public companies registered with the SEC and their auditors to annually assess and report on the design and effectiveness of internal control over financial reporting.

service activities (*11*) Activities that provide the support of customers after the products and services are sold to them (e.g., warranty repairs, parts, instruction manuals, etc.).

supply chain (*14*) The flow of materials, information, payments, and services from raw materials suppliers, through factories and warehouses, all the way to the final customers of the firm's products.

supply chain management (SCM) software (*15*) Software that connects the focal firm with its suppliers. It generally addresses segments of the supply chain, including manufacturing, inventory control, and transportation.

systems analyst (*9*) Person responsible for both determining the information needs of the business and designing a system to meet those needs.

technology (*12*) Supports value-creating activities in the value chain. These technologies also include research and development to develop new products or determine ways to produce products at a cheaper price.

transform (*19*) The use of computer technology to fundamentally redefine business processes and relationships.

value chain (*11*) A chain of critical business processes at a company that creates value.

Answers to Progress Checks

1. Useful relevant information may include the number of times an opposing player goes to his left, makes a spin move, or shoots a three pointer instead of passing the ball. Receiving this relevant information in a timely manner may help the team prepare for its upcoming basketball games. An example of useful reliable information might include the information collected and verified by an independent official keeping the score and statistics of a basketball game. This information might include the score of the game, the shooting percentages, the numbers of blocks and steals by each team and player, the type of defense they used, whether players shoot with the left or right hand, the number of assists and turnovers, etc. Having an unbiased source of information allows the coach to use the information received without having to worry about whether the information is biased.
2. Data at **Walmart** might be any random factoid without context. An example might be that one store in the United States had sales of $1.2 million yesterday. It is only when put in context that the data become useful. If we know that the store is in Lawrence, Kansas, and that on the same date, a year earlier, the store had sales of $0.8 million, the data become information.
3. Two types of discretionary information include the cost of manufacturing each **Apple** iPad or the type of pastry that sells best with hot chocolate at **Starbucks**. Two types of mandatory information might be the amount of sales taxes collected and remitted to the state tax collector or the number of common shares of stock outstanding reported to the Securities and Exchange Commission.

4. Generally, an IT auditor would be considered to be an evaluator of a client firm's accounting information system. In general, an IT auditor will assess the accounting information system to ensure the audit risk (the risk of reaching an incorrect conclusion based on the audit findings) will be limited to an acceptable level.
5. The Certified Information Systems Auditor (CISA) designation would be the most appropriate credential for an IT auditor. In some cases, the Certified Information Technology Professional (CITP) designation would also be an appropriate credential.
6. Most, if not all, entry-level financial accounting positions would expect some reasonable level of proficiency as a user of accounting information systems, such as the ability to use a basic accounting/bookkeeping package (e.g., QuickBooks, Peachtree, Microsoft Excel, Microsoft Windows, etc.) However, the International Federation of Accountants suggests accountants have proficiency not only as a user but also as an evaluator, manager, or designer of an accounting information system. Some of that desirable proficiency will be gained in this textbook, so read carefully!
7. Clearly, all portions of the value chain have to be working well for **Ford** to be successful and create value for the firm and its shareholders. A case could be made for any and all of the primary activities. I will argue that marketing and sales are the most important because, to be successful, companies need to completely understand and then meet their customers' needs.
8. **Wayfair** is a popular online site for furniture and home furnishings. An AIS may help Wayfair find the right marketing strategy by figuring out where to advertise Wayfair's product offerings (e.g., banner ads, referral pages, Facebook ads, e-mails, etc.) to its customers. AIS may also help Wayfair figure out which products sell best and which products have the biggest profit margins to know which products to push.
9. An AIS can add value to the firm by providing financial results in time to make a difference to the decision maker. As an example, if the firm finds out quickly that one of its products is too expensive to manufacture, the firm may choose to discontinue the product or choose a cheaper way to manufacture it. If that financial information is not received until weeks or months later, then the firm will have lost profits.
10. Let's suppose that **General Motors** will decide how many Chevrolet Corvettes to produce at each plant. Once General Motors knows how many it will likely produce, the supply chain management software can immediately compute the specific parts needed and share this information with its suppliers. The suppliers can then plan and begin production of the parts they provide. For example, if General Motors plans to produce 50,000 Corvettes at its Kansas City assembly plant, the tire suppliers can plan on producing and delivering 200,000 tires to meet those needs.
11. Universities are increasingly using CRM techniques to catalog information about their students from overall trends about the new millennials (who prefer more choices, experiential learning, flexibility, etc.) to archiving individual inquiries (i.e., e-mail, Snapchat, Instagram, Facebook, Twitter, etc.) by each prospective student. Students generally don't like to be treated as one among the masses, so any information that might target a specific student need or interest would be particularly useful to recruiters.
12. Supply chain software can help reduce procurement, logistics, and inventory-carrying costs for **Target**. If the whole supply chain has a better idea of the final customer's demand of the product, it will reduce the need to carry more inventory than is needed or to miss customer sales by not having enough product on hand. This, in turn, will reduce procurement, logistics, and inventory-carrying costs.
13. Digitizing medical records is an example of the automate IT strategic role.

connect

Multiple Choice Questions

1. Accounting information systems: **LO 1-1**
    a. are always computerized.
    b. report only financial information.
    c. are an information system that records, processes, and reports on transactions to provide financial and nonfinancial information for decision making and control.
    d. require a CITP designation to understand.
2. Which of the following is *not* a characteristic of useful information? **LO 1-1**
    a. Predictive value
    b. Timeliness
    c. Verifiable
    d. Expensive to generate
3. Which of the following is considered to be mandatory information required by a regulatory body? **LO 1-2**
    a. U.S. tax return
    b. The cost to produce a textbook
    c. The number of U.S. flags that are sold on July 4
    d. The cost to build an all-new Starbucks restaurant in Shanghai, China
4. The correct order of effects in the value chain is: **LO 1-4**
    a. Inbound logistics → Operations → Service.
    b. Inbound logistics → Outbound logistics → Marketing and Sales.
    c. Inbound logistics → Operations → Outbound logistics.
    d. Inbound logistics → Operations → Marketing and Sales.
5. What designation would be most appropriate for those professionals possessing IT audit, control, and security skills? **LO 1-3**
    a. Certified Internal Auditor (CIA)
    b. Certified Public Accountant (CPA)
    c. Certified Information Technology Professional (CITP)
    d. Certified Information Systems Auditor (CISA)
6. A supply chain: **LO 1-7**
    a. supplies bicycle chains.
    b. refers to the flow of materials, information, payments, and services.
    c. is similar in function and purpose to the value chain.
    d. does not apply to a service firm like an accounting firm.
7. Customer relationship management software does *not* include information about: **LO 1-7**
    a. current customers.
    b. prospective customers.
    c. former customers.
    d. current suppliers.
8. IT strategic roles of AIS investments are classified as: **LO 1-8**
    a. automate, informate, transform.
    b. value creation, value destruction, value neutral.
    c. digitize, report, transform.
    d. automate, digitize, transport.

9. According to a recent study, the IT strategic role that has the greatest impact on shareholder value is: **LO 1-8**
   a. informate.
   b. digitize.
   c. automate.
   d. transform.
10. The income statement account most likely affected by an AIS investment in supply chain management software would be: **LO 1-8**
    a. revenues.
    b. cost of goods sold.
    c. selling, general, and administrative expenses.
    d. unearned revenue.
11. The balance sheet account most likely to be affected by supply chain management software would be: **LO 1-7**
    a. Owner's Equity.
    b. Inventory.
    c. Short-term Marketable Securities.
    d. Property, Plant, and Equipment.
12. Customer relationship management software would be most likely to affect which income statement account? **LO 1-7**
    a. Selling, General, and Administrative Expenses
    b. Interest Expense
    c. Revenues
    d. Cost of Goods Sold
13. Enterprise systems would generally be considered to be an: **LO 1-6, LO 1-7**
    a. internal business process.
    b. external business process.
    c. interior business process.
    d. exterior business process.
14. A systems analyst would generally be considered to fill which role with respect to accounting information systems? **LO 1-3**
    a. User
    b. Manager
    c. Designer
    d. Evaluator
15. Which of these represents the proper transformation from data to decision according to the information value chain? **LO 1-2**
    a. Data → Information → Knowledge → Decision
    b. Data → Knowledge → Information → Decision
    c. Data → Business Event → Information → Decision
    d. Data → Analysis → Information → Decision

Discussion Questions

1. Brainstorm a list of discretionary information that might be an output of an accounting information system and be needed by **Starbucks**. Prioritize which items might be most important, and provide support. **LO 1-2**
2. Explain the information value chain. How do business events turn into data, then into information, and then into knowledge? Give an example starting with the business event of the purchase of a CD at **Best Buy** all the way to useful information for the CEO and other decision makers. **LO 1-2**
3. Give three examples of types of discretionary information at your college or university, and explain how the benefits of receiving that information outweigh the costs. **LO 1-2**
4. After an NBA basketball game, a box score is produced detailing the number of points scored, assists made, and rebounds retrieved (among other statistics). Using the characteristics of useful information discussed at the beginning of the chapter, please explain how this box score meets (or does not meet) the characteristics of useful information. **LO 1-2**
5. Some would argue that the role of accounting is simply as an information provider. Will a computer ultimately completely take over the job of the accountant? As part of your explanation, explain how the role of accountants in information systems continues to evolve. **LO 1-3**
6. How do you become a Certified Information Technology Professional (CITP)? What do they do on a daily basis? **LO 1-3**
7. Explain the value chain for an appliance manufacturer, particularly the primary activities. Which activities are most crucial for value creation (in other words, which activities would you want to make sure are the most effective)? Rank the five value chain–enhancing activities in importance for an appliance manufacturer. **LO 1-4**
8. Which value chain–supporting activities would be most important to support a health insurance provider's primary activities? How about the most important primary activities for a university? **LO 1-4**
9. List and explain three ways that an AIS can add value to the firm. **LO 1-5**
10. Where does new-product development fit in the value chain for a pharmaceutical company? Where does new-product development for a car manufacturer fit in the value chain? **LO 1-4**
11. An enterprise system is a centralized database that collects and distributes information throughout the firm. What type of financial information would be useful for both the marketing and manufacturing operations? **LO 1-6**
12. Customer relationship management software is used to manage and nurture a firm's interactions with its current and potential clients. What information would **Boeing** want about its current and potential airplane customers? Why is this so critical? **LO 1-7**

Problems

connect

1. An article suggests:

> A monumental change is emerging in accounting: the movement away from the decades-old method of periodic financial statement reporting and its lengthy closing process, and toward issuing financial statements on a real-time, updated basis . . . real-time financial reporting provides financial information on a daily basis. Current technology allows for financial events to be identified, measured, recorded, and reported electronically, with no paper documentation.[14]

Indeed, many corporations are pressing their finance and accounting departments for more timely financial information and ad hoc analysis. Would a shift toward real-time financial statements make the financial information more useful or less useful? More or less relevant? More or less reliable? **LO 1-1**

[14] "Real-Time Accounting," *The CPA Journal*, April 2005.

2. Consider the following bar chart of how accounting professionals' activities have changed over time. Comment on how information technology affects the role of accountants. In what respect is this a positive trend or a negative trend? What will this bar chart look like in 2020? **LO 1-3**

Continuous Evolution in Accounting Professional Activities

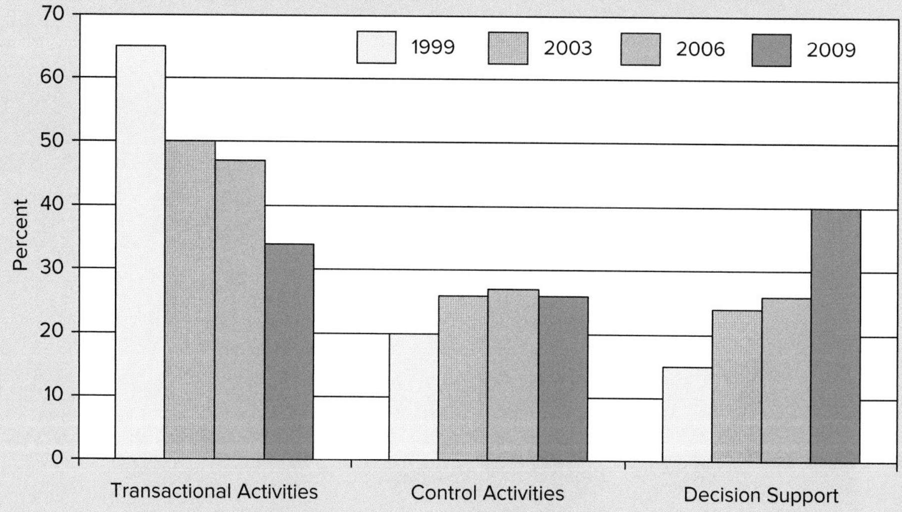

Source: *The Agile CFO: A Study of 900 CFOs Worldwide,* IBM, 2006.

connect 3. Match the value chain activity in the left column with the scenario in the right column: **LO 1-4**

1. Service activities	A. Surveys for prospective customers
2. Inbound logistics	B. Warranty work
3. Marketing and sales activities	C. Assembly line
4. Firm infrastructure	D. Delivery to the firm's customer
5. Human resource management	E. New-product development
6. Technology	F. Receiving dock for raw materials
7. Procurement	G. CEO and CFO
8. Outbound logistics	H. Buying (sourcing) raw materials
9. Operations	I. Worker recruitment

connect 4. Match the value chain activity in the left column with the scenario in the right column. **LO 1-4**

1. Customer call center	A. Operations
2. Supply schedules	B. Inbound logistics
3. Order taking	C. Procurement
4. Accounting department	D. Firm infrastructure
5. Staff training	E. Human resource management
6. Research and development	F. Technology
7. Verifying quality of raw materials	G. Service activities
8. Distribution center	H. Outbound logistics
9. Manufacturing	I. Marketing and sales activities

5. **John Deere**'s $4 billion commercial and consumer equipment division implemented supply chain management software and reduced its inventory by $500 million. As sales continued to grow, the company has been able to keep its inventory growth flat. How did the supply chain management software implementation allow John Deere to reduce inventory on hand? How did this allow the company to save money? Which income statement accounts (e.g., revenue, cost of goods sold, SG&A expenses, interest expense, etc.) would this affect? **LO 1-7**

6. **Dell Computer** used customer relationship management software called IdeaStorm to collect customer feedback. This customer feedback led the company to build select consumer notebooks and desktops pre-installed with the Linux platform. Dell also decided to continue offering Windows 10 as a pre-installed operating system option in response to customer requests. Where does this fit in the value chain? How will this help Dell create value? **LO 1-7**

connect

7. **Ingersoll Rand** operates as a manufacturer in four segments: Air Conditioning Systems and Services, Climate Control Technologies, Industrial Technologies, and Security Technologies. It installed an Oracle enterprise system, a supply chain system, and a customer relationship management system. The company boasts the following results.[15]

   - Decreased direct product costs by 11 percent.
   - Increased labor productivity by 16 percent.
   - Increased inventory turns by four times.
   - Decreased order processing time by 90 percent and decreased implementation time by 40 percent.
   - Ensured minimal business disruption.
   - Streamlined three customer centers to one.

   Take each of these results and explain how the three systems (enterprise system, supply chain system, and customer relationship management system) affected these financial results and created value for the firm. **LO 1-8**

connect

8. Using the accompanying explanations of each IT strategic role, suggest the appropriate IT strategic role (automate, informate, or transform) for the following types of IT investments. Depending on your interpretation, it is possible that some of the IT investments could include two IT strategic roles. **LO 1-8**

   a. Digital health records
   b. Google Maps that recommend hotels and restaurants along a trip path
   c. Customer relationship management software
   d. Supply chain management software
   e. Enterprise systems
   f. Airline flight reservations systems
   g. PayPal (www.paypal.com)
   h. Amazon.com product recommendation on your homepage
   i. eBay
   j. Course and teacher evaluations conducted online for the first time (instead of on paper)
   k. Payroll produced by computer

[15]Source: http://www.ediguys.net/pages/SCIS/ingersoll-rand-siebel-casestudy.pdf

IT Strategic Roles[16]

Automate IT Strategic Role

- Replace human labor by automating business processes.
- Virtually no IT-driven transformation efforts.
- IT providing enhancements to existing processes or practices.

Informate-Up/-Down IT Strategic Role

- Provide new data/information to empower management, employees, or customers.
- An intermediate level of IT-driven transformation efforts.
- Gain clearer picture of cause-and-effect relationships, greater understanding of operating environment.

Transform IT Strategic Role

- Fundamentally alter traditional ways of doing business by redefining business capabilities and/or (internal or external) business processes and relationships.
- Strategic acquisition to acquire new capabilities or to enter a new marketplace.
- Use of IT to dramatically change how tasks are carried out recognized as being important in enabling firm to operate in different markets, serve different customers, and gain considerable competitive advantage by doing things differently.

connect

9. Information systems have impact on financial results. Using Figure 1-8 as a guide, which system is most likely to impact the following line items on an income statement. The systems to consider are enterprise systems, supply chain systems, and customer relationship management systems. **LO 1-8**

Income Statement Item	System
Revenues	
Cost of goods sold	
Sales, general, and administrative expenses	
Interest expense	
Net Income	

connect

10. Accountants have four potential roles in accounting information systems: user, manager, designer, and evaluator. Match the specific accounting role to the activity performed. **LO 1-8**
    1. Controller meeting with the systems analyst to ensure accounting information system is able to accurately capture information to meet regulatory requirements
    2. Cost accountant gathering data for factory overhead allocations from the accounting information system
    3. IT auditor testing the system to assess the internal controls of the accounting information system
    4. CFO plans staffing to effectively direct and lead accounting information system

[16]B. Dehning, V. J. Richardson, and R. W. Zmud, "The Value Relevance of Announcements of Transformational Information Technology Investments," *MIS Quarterly* 27, no. 4 (2003), pp. 637–56.

connect 11. In 2013, Frey and Osborne[17] wrote a compelling article suggesting that up to 47 percent of total US employment is at risk due to computerization. The chart below suggests the probability that each occupation will lead to job losses in the next 20 years. **LO 1-8**

Selected Occupation	Probability of Job Loss
Tax preparers	0.99
Accountants and auditors	0.94
Retail salespersons	0.92
Sheet metal workers	0.82
Economists	0.43
Plumbers	0.35
Commercial drivers	0.18
Police	0.10
Chemical engineers	0.02
Preschool teachers	0.007
Physician and surgeon	0.004

1. Given these predictions, which jobs are most likely to be replaced by computerization? Those that primarily have tasks that automate, informate, or transform?
2. Noticing the high probability of predicted job loss in the accounting and auditing area, are those job losses expected to be due to automate, informate, or transform?
3. As accountants become business partners in giving critical information to management for decision making, are those tasks automate, informate, or transform?
4. Is the use of data analytics by accountants an example of automate, informate, or transform?

[17] C. B. Frey and M. A. Osborne, "The Future of Employment: How Susceptible Are Jobs to Computerisation?" (Oxford Martin School, University of Oxford, September 17, 2013), www.oxfordmartin.ox.ac.uk/downloads/academic/The_Future_of_Employment.pdf.

Chapter **Two**

Accountants as Business Analysts

A look at this chapter

As users, managers, designers, and evaluators of technology and technology-driven business processes, accountants must understand the organization and how organizational processes generate information important to management. To ensure that processes and systems are documented—and to participate in improvements to processes and systems—accountants must also be business analysts. This chapter defines business process modeling and describes how it supports the roles of accountants. It explains the potential value of business process modeling. Finally, it describes the types of business process models and introduces basic modeling tools to guide the student's development of modeling skills.

A look back

Chapter 1 discussed the importance of accounting information systems and the role accountants play in those systems. It further described how investments in information technology might improve the ability to manage business processes and create value for the firm.

A look ahead

Chapter 3 introduces data modeling. It describes how data modeling supports the design, implementation, and operation of database systems. It introduces basic modeling tools that will be used throughout the rest of the text.

© AFP/Getty Images

One recent morning, I stopped at a very busy **Starbucks** in San Francisco. I looked at the line coming out of the door and immediately thought that it would take at least 20 minutes to get my morning coffee. Instead, I was pleasantly surprised at the efficiency of the employees who got me through that line in less than 2 minutes.

I watched closely as the Starbucks partners behind the counter executed the workflow of the process. One partner took my order and relayed my pastry order to another partner behind the pastry case. He also relayed my coffee order to the barista at the other end of the counter. As I moved through the line to the register, my order arrived just as I did, and a fourth partner checked the order and took my payment. Within those 2 minutes, they had served at least a dozen other customers, too.

I thought about the number of options they had to deal with, the variety of hot and cold drinks, the pastries and other breakfast items, while also keeping a supply of freshly brewed coffee ready. I was sure that Starbucks had analyzed the process in detail to eliminate waste and enhance their partners' productivity. Then, they had to train all their partners in that process so they could work as one highly synchronized team. Finally, they delivered a hot cup of coffee to a grateful customer on a cool San Francisco morning.

Chapter Outline

Learning Objectives

After reading this chapter, you should be able to:

2-1 Describe the roles of the accounting/finance function in business and why those roles require knowledge of technology and business processes.

2-2 Understand the importance of business process documentation.

2-3 Recognize the value of business models.

2-4 Articulate the characteristics of activity models.

2-5 Understand and apply the building blocks for BPMN (activity) diagrams.

2-6 Use pools and lanes to identify process participants.

2-7 Apply message flows to show interactions between pools.

2-8 Understand and apply flow object types.

2-9 Recognize and model repeating activities.

2-10 Understand and apply data objects and datastores to model data created, updated, transferred, and deleted in a process.

LO 2-1
Describe the roles of the accounting/finance function in business and why those roles require knowledge of technology and business processes.

CHANGING ROLES OF ACCOUNTANTS IN BUSINESS

Over the past 15 years, a number of studies have highlighted the changing role of the accountant in business. Rapid changes in the global marketplace substantially affect the accounting profession. In the past, accountants typically focused on stewardship and reporting functions; they kept financial records, prepared financial reports, and performed audits. Now, they face the challenge of helping the enterprise to optimize its processes (financial, administrative, and operational) to achieve the competitive performance levels and maximize shareholder value.

Rapid changes in technology such as business intelligence (BI) and enterprise resource planning (ERP) systems have increased the availability of data throughout the organization. However, technology alone will not ensure good decision making. To be fully effective, the information produced by the technology must support the information requirements of the business's decision makers. Consequently, accountants are involved in supporting evidence-based decision making throughout the business. Although they continue to face the challenge of conducting their core transaction processing and reporting more efficiently, accountants must also act as business partners involved in a host of business management activities—including strategic planning, process improvement, and compliance management—to produce better management information for both internal and external stakeholders. Table 2.1 summarizes the traditional stewardship and reporting and accounting management roles, as well as the increasingly important business management support roles.

To perform all the roles described in Table 2.1 and be valuable business partners, accountants must first understand the business, as well as the various ways that the business

TABLE 2.1
Roles of the Accounting/Finance Function in Business

Stewardship and Reporting	Accounting/Finance Operations	Business Management Support
Regulatory compliance	Finance and accounting processes (procure to pay, order to cash, record to report, payroll and treasury)	Management information
Tax returns	Financial close—completing period-end accounts	Planning, budgeting, and forecasting
Stakeholder assurance	Financial consolidation, reporting, and analysis	Performance measurement, reporting, and analysis
Investor relations	Providing comprehensive management information	Performance management
Raising capital and loans	People management	Risk management—from strategic to operational, including fraud risk
Board reports	Using IT to make finance and accounting processes more efficient and effective	Investment appraisal
Statutory reporting		Cost management Supply chain management Value-based management Project management Change management Capital structure and dividend policy Strategic planning Professional expertise (e.g., merger and acquisition or tax)

Source: Based on *Improving Decision Making in Organisations: The Opportunity to Transform Finance* (London: CIMA, 2007), Figure 3.

collects data and summarizes and communicates business information. They must understand how the business delivers value to its customers, interacts with other businesses, and meets requirements for good corporate citizenship. They must also understand the risks that the business faces and the internal controls in place to mitigate those risks. Finally, they must understand how accounting information systems collect, summarize, and report business process information. This highlights the need for good documentation of business processes and business systems. To ensure that processes and systems are documented—and to participate in improvements to business processes and systems—accountants must also be business analysts.

BUSINESS PROCESS DOCUMENTATION

LO 2-2
Understand the importance of business process documentation.

Definitions

Before we describe how business analysis and business process modeling can support accountants' roles, we first present some definitions.

- **Business process**: A defined sequence of business activities that use resources to transform specific inputs into specific outputs to achieve a business goal. A business process is constrained by business rules.
- **Business analysis**: The process of defining business process requirements and evaluating potential improvements. Business analysis involves ascertaining, documenting, and communicating information about current and future business processes using business process modeling and related tools.
- **Business model**: A simple, abstract representation of one or more business processes.[1] A business model is typically a graphical depiction of the essential business process information.
- **Documentation**: Explains how business processes and business systems work. Documentation is "a tool for information transmission and communication. The type and extent of documentation will depend on the nature of the organization's products and processes."[2]

Purposes of Documentation

Documentation includes business process models, business rules, user manuals, training manuals, product specifications, software manuals, schedules, organization charts, strategic plans, and similar materials that describe the operation, constraints on, and objectives of business processes and systems. Although documentation has always been important for accounting information systems, the Sarbanes-Oxley Act of 2002 made documentation essential for businesses. That act requires managers to assess and attest to the business's internal control structure and procedures. The U.S. Securities and Exchange Commission (SEC) rules require "management to annually evaluate whether ICFR (internal control of financial reporting) is effective at providing reasonable assurance and to disclose its assessment to investors. Management is responsible for maintaining evidential matter, including documentation, to provide reasonable support for its assessment. This evidence will also allow a third party, such as the company's external auditor, to consider the work performed by management."[3] The act also requires external auditors to audit management's assessment of the effectiveness of internal controls and express an opinion on the

[1]In other contexts, the term "business model" is often used to describe the plan by which a company generates revenue.

[2]ISO 9001: 2008, International Standards Organization.

[3]SEC Interpretive Guidance 33-8810, issued June 27, 2007.

Documentation supports audits of business processes.

© Keith Brofsky/Getty Images

company's internal control over financial reporting.[4] Thus, documentation is necessary for internal audit to support management's assertions as well as external auditors to evaluate management's assertions on internal control over financial reporting.

In addition to Sarbanes-Oxley compliance requirements, documentation is important for the following reasons:

- *Training.* User guides, employee manuals, and operating instructions help employees learn how business processes and systems operate.
- *Describing current processes and systems.* Documentation provides an official description of how business processes and systems, including AIS, work. Thus, documentation supports internal and external audit requirements; establishes accountability; and standardizes communications within the business and between the business and its customers, suppliers, and other stakeholders.
- *Auditing.* Documentation provides audit trails, which can assist auditors in determining the effectiveness of internal controls.
- *Accountability.* Documentation includes checklists, delegations of authority, and similar assignments of responsibility. Thus, documentation would specify who is authorized to approve orders or sign checks, for example.
- *Standardized interactions.* Documentation clearly describes the inputs and outputs of business processes and systems and thus provides a common language for all parties that interact with the process or system.
- *Facilitating process improvement.* Because it describes the way processes currently work, documentation is also the basis for determining what should be changed. Well-managed businesses regularly review all processes with a view to continuous improvement in four major areas:

    1. Effectiveness: Are the outputs of the process obtained as expected?
    2. Efficiency: Can the same outputs be produced with fewer inputs and resources?
    3. Internal control: Are the internal controls working?
    4. Compliance to various statutes and policies: Does the process comply with constantly changing local, state, federal, and international laws and regulations?

LO 2-3

Recognize the value of business models.

Value of Business Models

Imagine a map of a city like Los Angeles, California, or even a small city like Fayetteville, Arkansas. How many words would it take to provide the same information as the map? Undoubtedly, the graphical representation (map) presents the information more concisely and perhaps more clearly than a written description. Business processes and systems can also be difficult to describe concisely using words alone. Thus, business models allow us to depict the important features of business processes and systems clearly and concisely.

Organizational change—including mergers, acquisitions, outsourcing, offshoring, product innovation, and continuous process improvement—and other business transformations are common. Change, however, can be expensive and risky. Careful planning is necessary to implement change in a way that minimizes those costs and risks. This is where business models create value. Business models provide communication, training,

[4]See Public Company Accounting Oversight Board (PCAOB) Auditing Standard No. 5, *An Audit of Internal Control over Financial Reporting That Is Integrated with an Audit of Financial Statements.*

analysis, and persuasion tools that are particularly suited for planning business transformations. Business models allow managers to assess what needs to be changed and plan how to make the change. In particular, business models create value in the following ways.

- *Managing complexity.* Models are simpler than the processes and systems they depict, but they incorporate the essential elements.
- *Eliciting requirements.* Models offer a communications tool that can be used to interview involved parties and discuss the impact of possible changes.
- *Reconciling viewpoints.* Models can combine various local views into one integrated view. Some models can be used to simulate potential outcomes from a change to better assess the impact of the change.
- *Specifying requirements.* Models can be the basis for documentation of the changed process or system. Additionally, some models can be used to generate working software directly.
- *Managing compliance.* Models can be used to identify legal and regulatory requirements and how those requirements affect business processes. When new laws are passed, the models quickly show where changes must be made to comply.
- *Supporting training.* Models can support training of employees on how to implement new business processes.
- *Managing and reusing knowledge.* Models support knowledge management, the practice of systematically capturing individuals' knowledge and making it available where needed throughout the organization. Business models can convert tacit knowledge, found only in people's heads, to explicit knowledge that can be taught to others.

Progress Check

1. How would documentation help accountants perform some of the roles listed in Table 2.1?
2. From your own experience, describe how models (or pictures or maps) have helped you understand a complex issue.

LO 2-4
Articulate the characteristics of activity models.

TYPES OF BUSINESS MODELS

This textbook will focus on three different elements of business process models. To be complete, concise, and useful, business process models need to describe process activity, data structures, and the business rules that constrain and guide process operations (see Figure 2.1). This chapter focuses on activity models, and Chapter 3 introduces data models.

FIGURE 2.1
Business Process Models and Business Rules

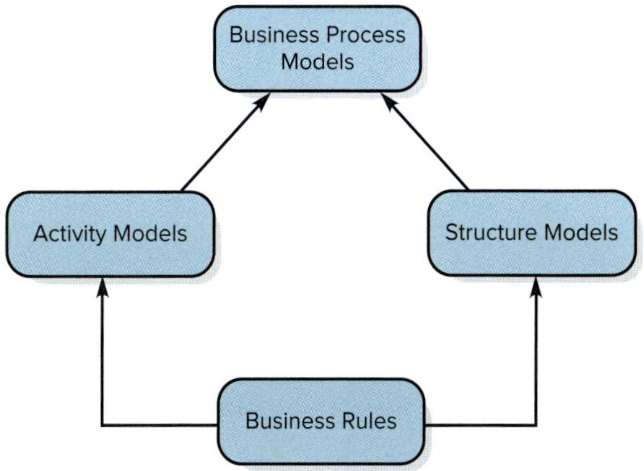

ACTIVITY MODELS

Activity models describe the sequence of workflow in a business process or processes. While the purpose of structure models is to create a blueprint for the development of a relational database to support the collection, aggregation, and communication of process information, the purpose of activity models is to represent the sequential flow and control logic of a set of related activities. They are tools for planning, documenting, discussing, and implementing systems; however, they also facilitate the use of those systems once implemented. Furthermore, they are important tools for analyzing and improving business processes.

Activity models, such as flowcharts, have been used to analyze business processes and design changes since well before 1920.[5] As technology changed, designers developed a variety of activity models, such as data flow diagrams, business process maps, and IDEF0 functional modeling method,[6] to document and analyze business process workflow.

Regardless of the specific modeling notation, workflow models must be able to describe:

1. Events that start, change, or stop flow in the process.
2. Activities and tasks within the process.
3. The sequence of flow between tasks.
4. Decision points that affect the flow.
5. Division of activity depending on organizational roles.

LO 2-5
Understand and apply the building blocks for BPMN (activity) diagrams.

Business Process Modeling Notation

For this textbook, we employ **business process modeling notation (BPMN)** for activity models, although the concepts discussed also apply to other modeling notation, such as UML activity diagrams and data flow diagrams.[7] The Object Management Group (OMG) also maintains the specifications for BPMN. The original specification for BPMN was issued in 2004. Since then, BPMN has been widely adopted because it was specifically designed for process modeling in a way that can be understood by businesspeople rather than software engineers (in contrast with UML activity diagrams). Additionally, there are free or inexpensive software products that support modeling and subsequent simulation of the process. The International Standards Organization (ISO) has adopted a specification for BPMN identical to OMG BPMN 2.0.1.

Good BPMN models have the following important characteristics:

1. They are correct. They do not violate BPMN standards.
2. They are clear. They describe the logic of a business process unambiguously, although they may not present the details of how individual tasks are performed.
3. They are complete. They show how the process starts, all the significant ends, and all important communications with relevant external parties.
4. They are consistent. Given the same facts about the process logic, all modelers should create similar models of the process.

Basic Building Blocks for BPMN Diagrams

Events include start, intermediate, and end events. Basic events are modeled as small circles, as shown in Figure 2.2. Start events have a single thin line circle. End events have

[5] D. J. Couger, "Evolution of Business System Analysis Techniques," *Computing Surveys* 5, no. 3 (1973), pp. 167–98. The article describes the use of flowcharts for industrial engineering by Frederick W. Taylor and others prior to 1920.

[6] See Federal Information Processing Standards Publication 183, www.idef.com.

[7] Data flow diagrams encompass elements of both activity and structure models, but they are primarily used to depict the sequence of data flows related to activities in a business process.

a single thick line circle. Intermediate events have a double thin line circle. Intermediate events affect the flow of a process, but do not start or end the process. Icons placed in events are used to further define event categories, such as message, timer, or error events.

Activities represent specific steps in the business process. Basic activities are modeled as rounded rectangles, as shown in Figure 2.2. Each activity is described with a short verb phrase placed within the rectangle (e.g., process credit card payment or bill customer). An activity can depict a single action or some logical combination of actions depending on the required level of detail to achieve the objectives of the business process analysis.

Sequence flows are represented by arrows to indicate the progression of activity within the process, as shown in Figure 2.2. The diagram should show the sequence of activity from left to right and top to bottom.

Gateways show process branching and merging as the result of decisions. Basic gateways are depicted as diamonds. Usually, gateways appear as pairs on the diagram. The first gateway shows the branching, and the second gateway shows merging of the process branches.

Annotations allow the modeler to add additional descriptive information to the model. Annotations are modeled with text inside a bracket connected to other model symbols with a dashed line.

FIGURE 2.2
Basic Elements of Business Process Diagrams

Element	Description	Symbol
Events	Events are things that happen; they affect the flow of the business process when they occur. For example, a start event begins a process, an intermediate event may change the flow, and an end event signals the end of the process.	start intermediate end
Activities	Activities are where the work takes place; they can represent processes, subprocesses, or tasks depending on the diagram's level of detail.	Activity
Sequence Flows	An arrow shows the normal sequence flow—i.e., the order of activities—in a business process diagram.	Sequence Flow →
Gateways	Gateways control the branching and merging of flow paths in the business process.	Gateway
Annotations	Text annotations allow the analyst to add descriptive information to the diagram.	text annotation

Example of a Business Process Diagram

Figure 2.3 illustrates a simple business process activity diagram showing the checkout process at a retail store. In this process, the customer presents items for checkout. The clerk scans items and identifies payment method. Then, the process branches depending on the nature of payment. The payment is accepted, and the process branches merge.

The clerk bags the items for the customer, and the process ends. Note that the start event can be labeled to explain the start event, and the gateway branches can be labeled to show the purpose of the branches (handling cash or credit payment in this case).

FIGURE 2.3
Sample Business Process Diagram

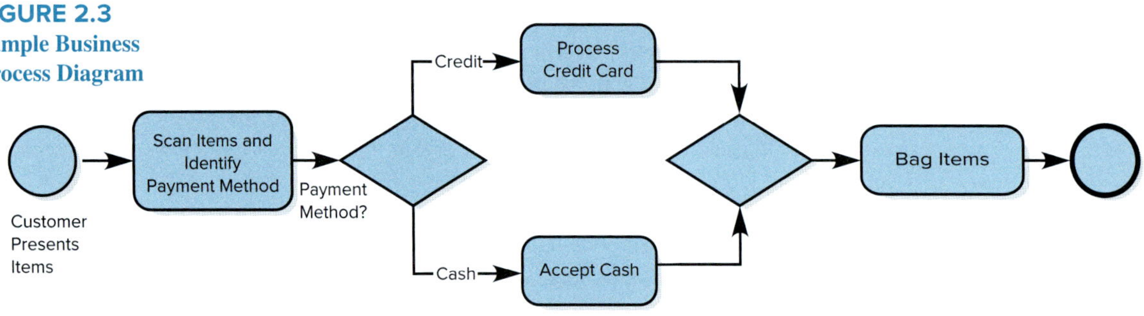

Figure 2.3 also demonstrates some other features of BPMN models. First, the models are usually presented left to right or top to bottom. All processes start with a start event and end with an end event, although there may be more than one end event. The flow of the process is shown by the sequence flow arrows. The sequence flows following the branching gateway are labeled to describe the circumstances under which the process would follow that specific flow. Each step in the process, each task, is named to describe the nature of the task. Tasks are named with a verb and an object, such as *bag items* and *accept cash.* The branching gateway represents an important question that affects the subsequent flow; in this case, the gateway questions the payment method. However, the gateway is not a decision. The information to answer the question is determined in the task labeled "Scan Items and Identify Payment Method." The second gateway shows that the two paths merge and the flow then continues. In this model, the second, merging, gateway is optional. Later, you will see models where the merging gateway is not optional.

Progress Check

3. Draw a business process model (using BPMN) of a drive-through window at a fast-food restaurant. What starts the process? What ends the process? What are the important steps? Are there any decision points that would require gateways?

LO 2-6
Use pools and lanes to identify process participants.

Identifying Participants in Business Process Diagrams

It is often important to identify who performs which activity in a business process. A participant is an actor or person that performs activities and interacts with other participants in a process. Participants include people, systems, organizations, and machines. Participants can also be identified by the role of the actor in the process. BPMN provides notation to identify both the organizations and the departments or individual actors participating in a process. The organization is identified by a **pool** and the department is identified by **lanes** within the pool, as shown in Figure 2.4. Every diagram contains at least one pool, but if there is only one pool, the pool may be presented without a boundary. Activities can be assigned to only one participant, and thus may appear in only one pool or lanes.

Let's examine Figure 2.4 more closely. You should note that regardless of the number of lanes in the pool, there is still one start event per pool and at least one end event.

FIGURE 2.4
Pools and lanes to Identify Participants

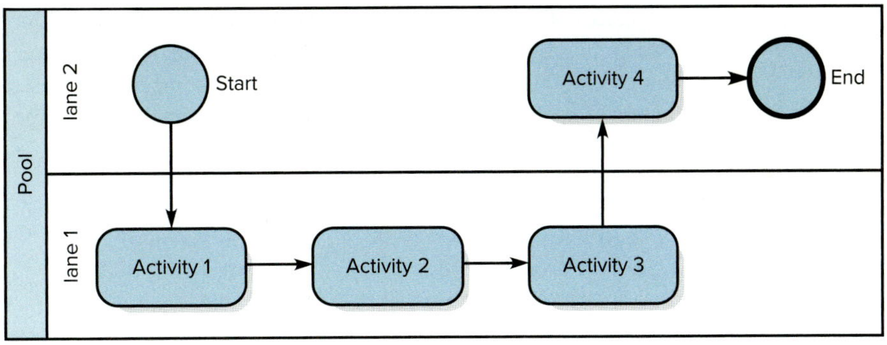

Each task is located in only one lane. Tasks may not span lanes. In other words, one task cannot be performed by two departments. The sequence must flow continuously from the start event to each end event, but the sequence flows can cross lane boundaries. Sequence flows, however, do not extend beyond one pool.

LO 2-7
Apply message flows to show interactions between pools.

Messages in BPMN

BPMN represents exchanges between two participants (pools) in the same process as message flows. For example, in a sales process with a customer pool and a store pool, the customer order would be represented as a message flow. The activities within a pool are organized by sequence flow, but the interactions between pools are represented as **message flows.** A message flow is shown as a dashed arrow with a small circle at the starting end, as shown in Figure 2.5.

FIGURE 2.5
Message Flow Symbol

Figure 2.6 provides a simple example of message flows between two pools. One pool represents a patient and the other pool represents the doctor's office. The patient becomes ill and calls the doctor's office for an appointment. The doctor's office receives the request and assigns the appointment. Each pool has a start event and in the case one event. The sequence flows are continuous from the start events to the end events and do not cross pool

FIGURE 2.6
Message Flow Example

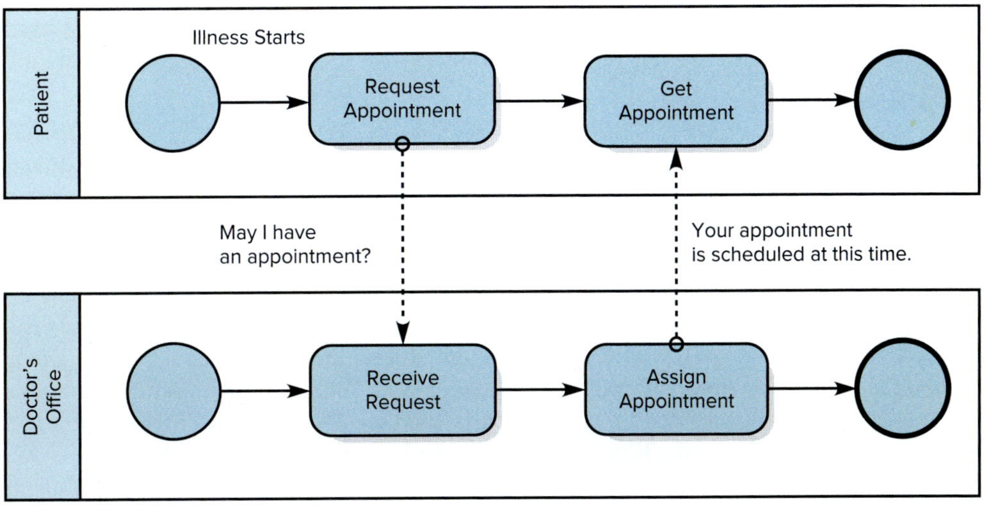

boundaries. The message flows are between pools and not within pools. While the nature of each message flow is pretty clear in this model, it is good practice to label the message flows. As models become more refined, it is sometimes necessary to define the specific content of each message flow to aid the implementation of the process.

Progress Check

4. Using Figure 2.6 as a guide, draw a simple model of a customer interacting with **Amazon.com**'s website to purchase an item. Assume the customer is an Amazon Prime™ member and can buy an item with 1-click (i.e., Amazon already has the credit card information). Use two pools and the associated message flows.

Usually, modelers are not very interested in activities in the external pool. So, if we are modeling the doctor's office process in Figure 2.6, we might not care about the activities in the patient's pool. Yet, we remain concerned about the message flows between the pools. So, we can make the patient's pool opaque, hiding the activities, but still showing the message flows. Figure 2.7 shows the opaque patient's pool. Note that the message flows now attach to the edge of the patient's pool.

FIGURE 2.7
Message Flow to Edge of Pool

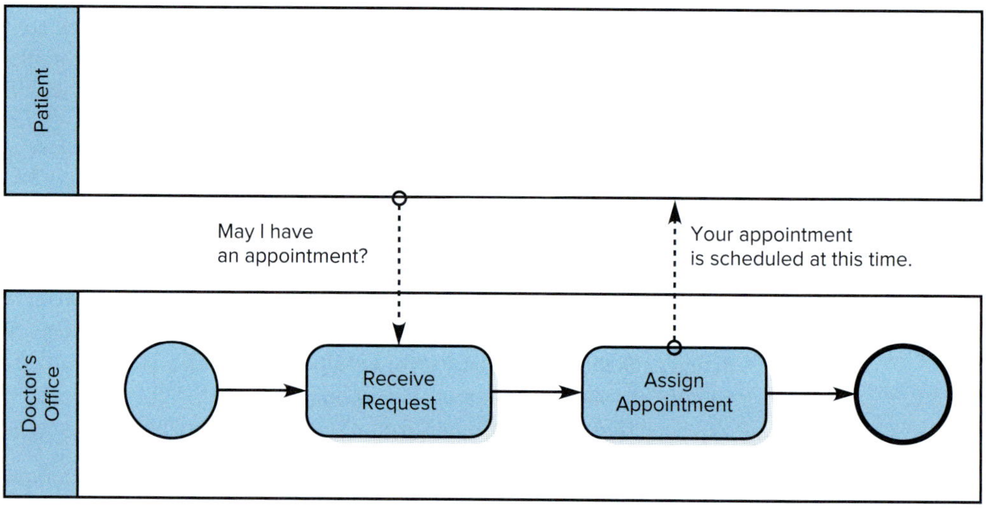

LO 2-8
Understand and apply flow object types.

Extended Building Blocks for BPMN Diagrams and Modeling Concepts

Token concept. BPMN uses the theoretical concept of a token flowing through the process to understand how various elements interact. A start event generates a token that must then be able to flow through the process until it reaches an end event, which consumes the token. In most cases, tokens only travel along sequence flows and pass through process flow objects. Process flow object behavior can be defined by how that element interacts with a token as it flows through the process. A token does not traverse message flows.

Flow object types. Flow objects include events, activities, and gateways. Sequence flows only connect to flow objects. Within BPMN, each flow object can be further characterized by type. To show the type of element, BPMN includes a type icon within the specific flow object. For example, a "timer" event would show the event with a clock face icon inside, and a "message" event would show the event with an envelope icon inside. Within this text, we will focus on the types that are widely used.

Gateway types. Figure 2.8 shows three common gateway types. Exclusive gateways pass the token along the path established by the gateway conditions. Inclusive gateways can create additional tokens depending on the number of paths taken after the branching gateway. Parallel gateways also create additional tokens for each path leaving the gateway. The merging gateways synchronize the process. For inclusive and parallel gateways, the merging gateways delay the flow until all tokens for that instance arrive, then one token proceeds along the exiting sequence flow.

FIGURE 2.8
Gateway Types

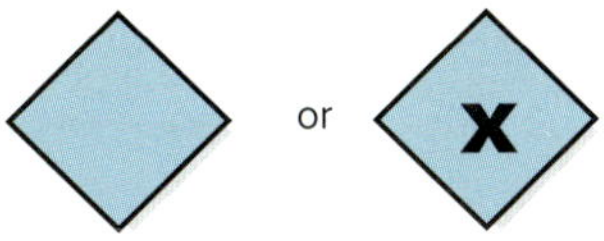	Exclusive gateway. For branching exclusive gateways, only one path can be taken out of the gateway for each instance of a process depending on the branching conditions.
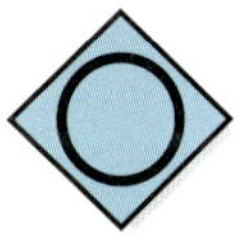	Inclusive gateway. For branching inclusive gateways, one or more paths can be taken out of the gateway for each instance of a process depending on the branching conditions. Merging inclusive gateways synchronize the flow.
	Parallel gateway. For branching parallel gateways, all paths are taken out of the gateway. Merging parallel gateways synchronize the parallel flows.

Consider the process of planning a trip. Figure 2.9 shows an example of an exclusive gateway where the trip will involve either traveling by air or traveling by car. In Figure 2.10 an inclusive gateway indicates that the planned trip could involve either traveling by air or traveling by car or both. In Figure 2.11 a parallel gateway indicates that the trip will involve air travel, car travel, and hotel stays.

FIGURE 2.9
Exclusive Gateway Example Where the Trip Involves Air Travel or Car Travel but Not Both

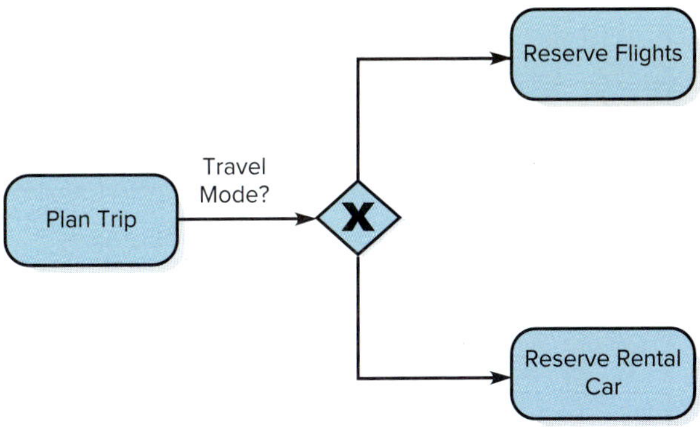

FIGURE 2.10
Inclusive Gateway Example Where the Trip May Involve Either Air Travel, Car Travel, or Both

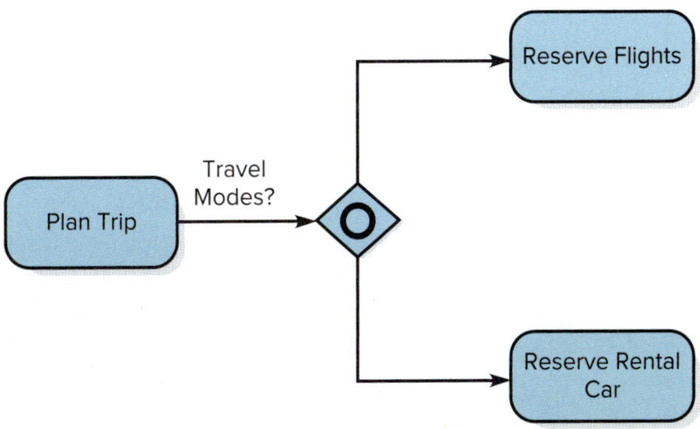

FIGURE 2.11
Parallel Gateway Example Where the Trip Involves Air Travel, Car Travel, and Hotel Stays

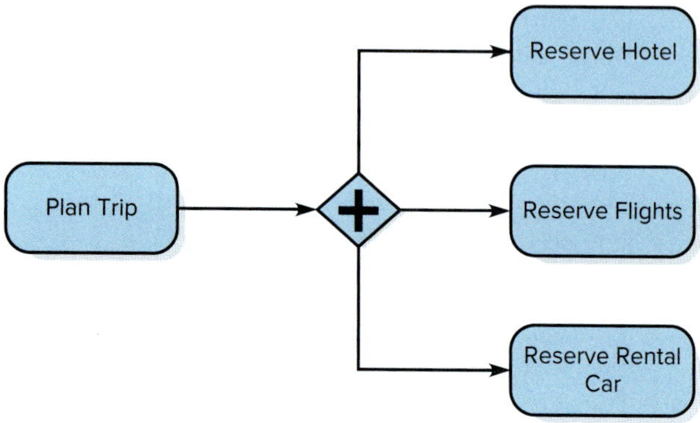

Event types. The basic flow objects include start events, intermediate events, and end events. Figure 2.12 shows common event types. First, message events either create (throw) or receive (catch) messages. Messages are communications from individual participants in a process. When modeled, the messages are shown as message flows. Second, timer events indicate a delay until a specific time and/or date or a specific cycle (such as 8 hours, 2 weeks). Third, error events indicate an interruption to the process. Intermediate error events are "boundary" events; they are attached to an activity and indicate an alternate process flow when an error occurs.

FIGURE 2.12
Event Types

	Start message (catching) event. This is used to begin a process based on an incoming message, such as a sales order. Start events can only receive (catch) messages and not send (throw) them.
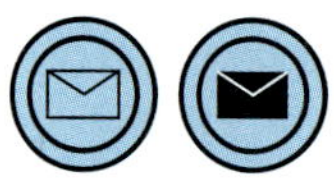	Intermediate message events. The white envelope is the catching event and the black envelope is the throwing event. These indicate that the process sends a message to or receives a message from an external participant.
	End message (throwing) event. This indicates that the process sends a message when it ends. End events can only send messages and not receive them.
	Start timer event. This is used to indicate a process that starts at a particular time or date, such as creating monthly budgets.
	Intermediate timer event. This indicates a delay in the process flow until a specific time or date or for a specified period.
	Intermediate error event. This is a boundary event, discussed in more detail below, to indicate the alternate process flow when an error occurs in an activity.

Figure 2.13 shows a generic example using message events. The process starts with a start message event that receives (catches) the "Request" message from the external participant. The process proceeds to the "Evaluate Request" task, and then the intermediate message event sends (throws) the "Evaluation" message flow to the external participant. The process flow continues to the next intermediate message event, where it waits (the token stops) until the external participant responds with the "Confirm" message flow. When the event catches the message, the sequence flow continues to the "Do Something" task and then the process ends. The end message event throws a message to the external participant that the process is done.

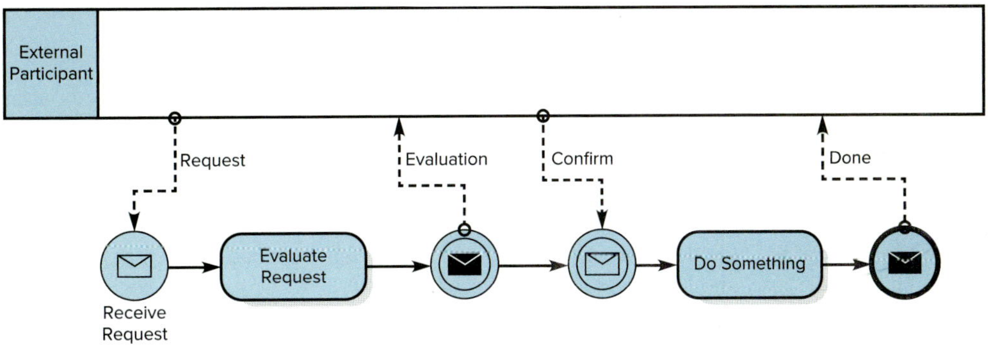

FIGURE 2.13
Message Events Example

Figure 2.14 shows an example using timer events and a boundary intermediate error event. The start timer begins the process two weeks before the birthday to be celebrated. The "Plan Party" task has an intermediate error event attached to its boundary (a boundary event). Specifically, this is an example of an interrupting boundary event that affects process flow when an error occurs in the Plan Party task. If an error occurs, then the process flows to the "Cancel Party" task and then ends. However, if the Plan Party task completes successfully, the process flows to the intermediate timer event and then waits two weeks (the token waits to proceed). After two weeks, the process continues to the "Hold Party" task and then ends.

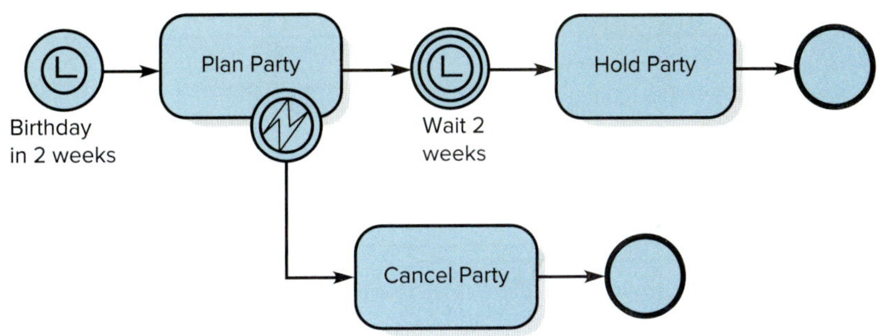

FIGURE 2.14
Timer and Error Events Example

In later chapters, we will discuss other types of boundary events, both interrupting and noninterrupting. Note that you could also model the process shown in Figure 2.14 using a task to test whether the plans are good and then using a gateway to branch to the Cancel Party task if the plans fail. The use of the error boundary event provides a clear and more concise way to show the error.

Task types. Finally, BPMN offers different task types, but task types are used less often than gateway and error types. There are tasks to send and receive messages. These would be modeled with envelope icons (white for receiving, black for sending) in the upper left corner of the task rectangle. These tasks correspond to catching and throwing message events, and in most cases, the message events are preferred. Normally, you would use the send and receive tasks when you need to attach boundary events to the task as you can't do that with events. Modelers are often tempted to use the send and receive tasks to forward work to the next task in the process. This is unnecessary because the sequence flow implies that the work is forwarded. So, send and receive tasks are only related to message flows. Next, there are business rules tasks. In a business rules task, one or more business rules are applied in order to produce a result or make a decision. There are several other task types, such as user, script, manual, service, etc., and users can define their own tasks. In most cases, there is little need to use other than the general abstract task type (without any type icon). In this textbook, we will not use task types.

LO 2-9
Recognize and model repeating activities.

Subprocesses and Repeating Activities

Activities are the place where work takes place in BPMN diagrams. An activity can represent a process, subprocess, or task. So far, we've focused on tasks, but sometimes it is helpful to show a higher level of abstraction. In other words, we might want to lump several related tasks together into a subprocess. Figure 2.15 shows how subprocesses are modeled. Subprocesses can be used to show processes that are reused in several other processes. They are a useful modeling tool when the modeler doesn't want to add unnecessary detail to a diagram, especially when that detail will be presented in another model.

Sometimes, we want to show that the same task is performed multiple times. In this case, we can show the task as looping. Looping tasks repeat until a condition is satisfied. This has the same effect as using a gateway that sends the process back to the task if the condition is not satisfied. When the number of times that a task will repeat is known in advance, we can use a multi-instance task. A parallel multi-instance task is performed several times by different actors at the same time. A sequential multi-instance task is performed several times by the same actor in sequence. Think about taking a test. Each student takes the test at the same time, so this would be an example of a parallel multi-instance task. Then, the instructor grades the tests sequentially, so this would be an example of a sequential multi-instance task.

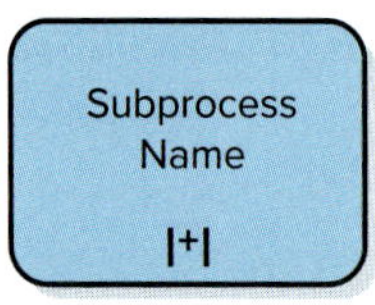	A collapsed subprocess contains other detailed processes that are hidden from view. It is modeled with the activity rectangle with a plus sign in a box at the bottom center. The details of the subprocess are normally shown in another diagram.
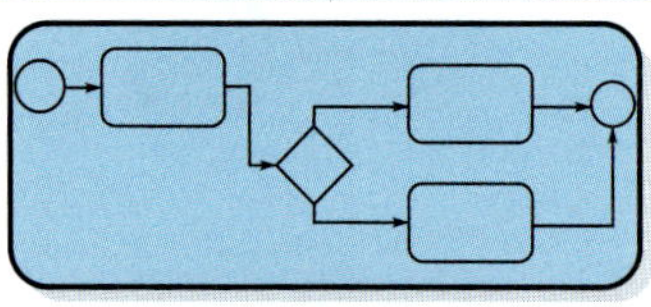	An expanded subprocess embeds the subprocess in the current process. The subprocess is contained within the activity rectangle and includes start and end events.
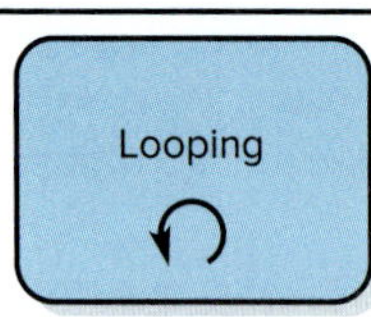	A looping task repeats until a condition is satisfied, such as until all e-mail in the inbox is checked.
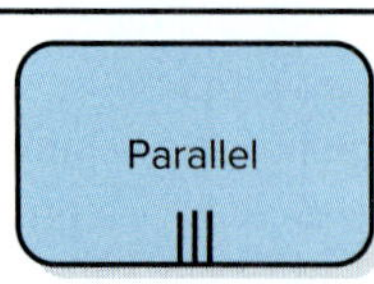	A parallel multi-instance task is performed several times at the same time, such as when several different people perform the same task at the same time in the process.
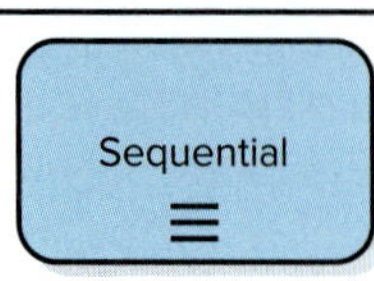	A sequential multi-instance task is performed several times in sequence, such as when an instructor grades tests for several students.

FIGURE 2.15
Subprocesses and Repeating Activities

LO 2-10
Understand and apply data objects and datastores to model data created, updated, transferred, and deleted in a process.

Data Objects, Datastores, and Associations

Processes create, update, transfer, and delete data in various forms. Sometimes the data management is implicit. At other times, it is important to explicitly model where data are created or used. The two main BPMN elements used to model data are the data object and the datastore, as shown in Figure 2.16. Data objects are modeled with document icons. Datastores are modeled with a disk icon. Associations are dotted lines that show the movement of data between the data objects and datastores and activities. Associations may use arrowheads to show the direction of data flow.

FIGURE 2.16
Data Objects, Datastores, and Associations

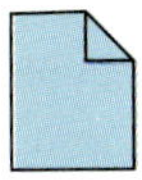	A data object. This element represents data that are only available for the duration of a process.
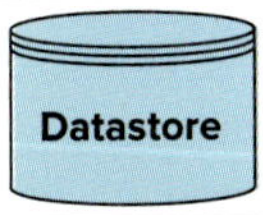	A datastore. This element represents data that are available across processes.
	An association connecting a data object/store to an activity. The arrowhead shows the direction of data flow when necessary.

Figure 2.17 shows alternative examples of one simple process with a data object. The process starts and the actor buys concert tickets. Time passes until the date of the concert and then the actor attends the concert using the tickets. The same data object, tickets, can be repeated in the process as necessary to avoid confusion. In our simple example, the first alternative seems to make more sense, since it is clear that one ticket data object is created and then used. If it is necessary for other processes to access the stored ticket information, then tickets should be modeled as a datastore.

FIGURE 2.17
Examples of Process Using Data Objects

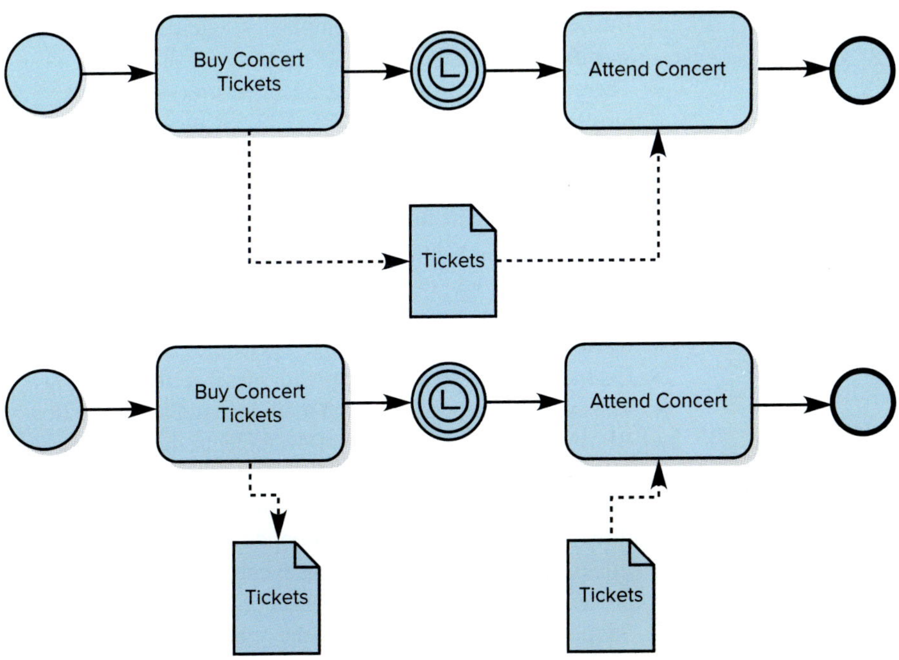

Best Practices in Preparing BPMN Diagrams

The primary objective of process activity modeling is to describe the important steps in a business process clearly, concisely, and accurately. Diagrams are tools to aid in planning, documenting, discussing, implementing, and using systems. Here are some modeling best practices that can enhance the use of models for these purposes.

1. Focus on one business process at a time.
2. Clearly identify the events that start and end the process.
3. Include essential elements, but avoid distracting detail.
4. Think about a token flowing from the start event through the process to the end event; the flow of the token should be clear for all paths through the process.
5. Label activities clearly with a verb and an object (e.g., pay invoice).
6. Model iteratively, getting feedback to improve accuracy and clarity.
7. Use message flows to show interactions between process participants. Remember that tokens do not flow across message flows.
8. Each pool must have a start and at least one end.
9. Make the external participant's pool opaque, hiding the elements in that pool, when the external participants activities are not important for the model. When the pool is opaque, attach the message flow arrows to the edge of the pool.
10. Use sequence flows within pools and not between pools.

Summary

Information plays a crucial role in the information age.

- Accountants' roles in business are evolving rapidly.
- Accountants are increasingly involved in business management support.
- Business process documentation is essential for training, describing current processes and systems to support internal and external audits, establishing accountability, and communicating among employees and various stakeholders.
- Business process documentation provides a starting point for business process improvement.
- Business models manage complexity, elicit requirements, reconcile viewpoints, and specify operating requirements for business processes.
- There are two major types of business process models: activity models and structure models.
- Activity models show the flow of work in a business process.
- BPMN provides a notation for specifying workflow.
- BPMN notation includes flow objects: events, activities, sequence flows, and gateways that allow process branching.
- BPMN allows the identification of participants in a process through the use of pools and swimlanes.
- BPMN message flows document exchanges between pools.
- External pools may be opaque with message flows attached to the edge of the pool.
- The token concept is a method to understand sequence flow within a process.
- BPMN establishes types for flow objects, i.e., events, gateways, and tasks, to help describe specific uses.
- Intermediate error events are an example of boundary events that interrupt the normal flow of a process when an error condition occurs.
- Timer events are used to indicate events that occur at a specific time or date or cause the process to wait for a specific period of time.
- Subprocesses represent collections of tasks.
- Data objects and datastores allow modeling of process information processing requirements.

Key Words

activities (37) In business process modeling, activities represent specific steps in a business process.

activity models (36) Models that describe the sequence of workflow in a business process or processes.

annotations (37) Model elements that allow the modeler to add additional descriptive information to the model. Annotations are modeled with text inside a bracket connected to other model symbols with a dashed line.

business analysis (33) The process of defining business process requirements and evaluating potential improvements. Business analysis involves ascertaining, documenting, and communicating information about current and future business processes using business process modeling and related tools.

business model (33) A simple, abstract representation of one or more business processes. A business model is typically a graphical depiction of the essential business process information.

business process (33) A defined sequence of business activities that use resources to transform specific inputs into specific outputs to achieve a business goal.

business process modeling notation (BPMN) (36) A standard for the description of activity models.

data flow diagram (DFD) (52) Another type of activity model that graphically shows the flow of data through a system and also incorporates elements of structure models.

documentation (33) An information transmission and communication tool that explains how business processes and business systems work.

events (36) Important occurrences that affect the flow of activities in a business process. BPMN includes symbols to define start, intermediate, and end events.

flowcharts (47) Visualizations of a process activity; they are activity models much like models using BPMN.

gateways (37) Show process branching and merging as the result of decisions. Basic gateways are depicted as diamonds. Usually, gateways appear as pairs on the diagram. The first gateway shows the branching, and the second gateway shows merging of the process branches.

lanes (or swimlanes) (38) BPMN symbols that provide subdivisions of pools to show, for example, functional responsibilities within an organization.

message flows (39) BPMN represents exchanges between two participants (pools) in the same process as message flows, which are modeled as dashed arrows.

pools (38) BPMN symbols used to identify participants, actors, or persons that perform activities and interact with other participants in a process.

process maps (48) Simplified flowcharts that use a basic set of symbols to represent a business process activity.

sequence flows (37) BPMN symbols that show the normal sequence of activities in a business process. Sequence flows are modeled as solid arrows, with the arrowhead showing the direction of process flow.

Appendix A

Flowcharting

WHAT IS A FLOWCHART?

Like business process models, **flowcharts** are visualizations of a process activity. Flowcharts have been widely used since they were first introduced in the 1920s. Modern techniques such as UML activity diagrams and BPMN are extensions of flowcharts. Flowcharts are useful tools for systems development, process documentation, and understanding internal controls. Three types of flowcharts are often used by accountants. These three types typically differ in the level of detail modeled.

1. *Systems flowcharts* provide an overall view of a system, including the inputs, activities, and outputs of the process.
2. *Process maps* use the basic set of flowchart symbols to provide a representation of the steps within a business process. **Process maps** are conceptually similar to business process diagrams created with BPMN.
3. *Document flowcharts* present the flow of documents through an entity, often describing the areas within the entity with responsibility for particular tasks.

BASIC BUILDING BLOCKS FOR FLOWCHARTS

The basic flowchart symbols shown in Figure 2.A1 are similar to, and serve the same basic functions as, the BPMN symbols for activity models.

- *Start/End.* Each flowchart should show the flow of process activities from one start to one or more logical ends. The start and end steps are drawn as ovals.
- *Tasks/Activities.* Tasks or activities represent specific steps in the business process. Basic activities are modeled as rectangles. Each activity is described with a short verb phrase placed within the rectangle (e.g., process credit card payment or bill customer). An activity can depict a single action or some logical combination of actions depending on the required level of detail to achieve the objectives of the business process analysis.
- *Sequence Flows.* Sequence flows are represented by arrows to indicate the progression of activity within the process. The diagram should show the sequence of activity from left to right and top to bottom.
- *Decisions.* Decisions are modeled as diamonds with multiple exits (sequence flows) based on the result of decisions.

FIGURE 2.A1
Basic Elements of Flowcharts

Element	Description	Symbol
Start/End	The Start/End steps indicate the beginning and ending of the process flow.	Start
Tasks/Activities	Tasks/Activities are the steps that describe the work; they can represent individual tasks or collections of tasks depending on the diagram's level of detail.	Task/Activity
Sequence Flows	An arrow shows the normal direction of flow—i.e., the order of activities—in a diagram.	Sequence Flow
Decisions	Decision diamonds portray the nature of the decision and the exit options.	Decision

EXAMPLE OF BUSINESS PROCESS FLOWCHART

Figure 2.A2 shows a simple business process activity diagram depicting the checkout process at a retail store. In this process, the customer presents items for checkout. The clerk scans items and identifies payment method. Then the process branches depending on the nature of payment. The payment is accepted, and the process branches merge. The clerk

FIGURE 2.A2
Sample Business Process Flowchart

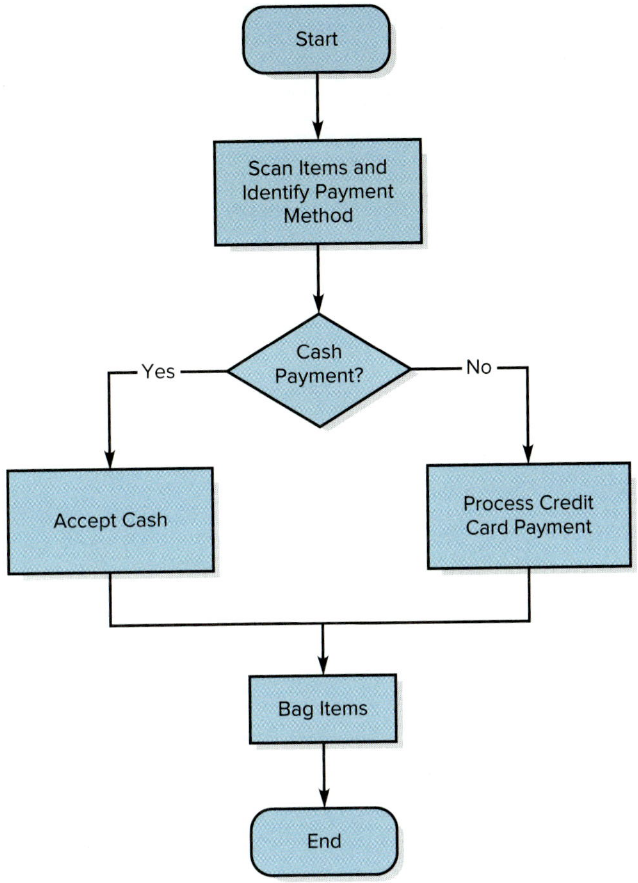

bags the items for the customer, and the process ends. Note that the start event can be labeled to explain the start event, and the gateway branches can be labeled to show the purpose of the branches (handling cash or credit payment in this case).

ADDITIONAL FLOWCHART SYMBOLS

The additional symbols shown in Figure 2.A3 are also widely used to depict specific operations within flowcharts. While none of these symbols are necessary for system flowcharts, they are often used in document flowcharts to differentiate manual and system operations and the media used in the process.

Element	Description	Symbol
Input/Output; Journal/ Ledger	The parallelogram is a generalized symbol for input or output when the medium is not specified.	In/Out
Input/Output of Document(s) or Report(s)	The document symbol indicates hard-copy documents or reports coming into or going out of the process.	One Document Multiple

(continued)

FIGURE 2.A3
Additional Flowchart Symbols

Element	Description	Symbol
Online Keying	This symbol indicates data entry using online devices such as a computer or a handheld device.	
Storage Offline	This symbol indicates storage, typically of documents, not accessible by computer. File-ordering sequence is indicated as follows: N = numerically, A = alphabetically, D = by date.	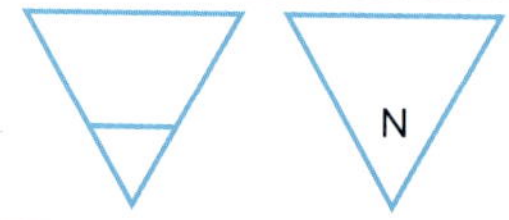
Magnetic Disc Storage	This symbol includes database (online) storage accessible by computer.	
Manual Task/Activity	This symbol indicates a manual task. If the flowchart differentiates between manual and computer operations, the basic task/activity symbol shown in Figure 2.A1 then shows a computer operation.	
On/Off Page Connectors	This symbol indicates data entry using online devices such as a computer or a handheld device.	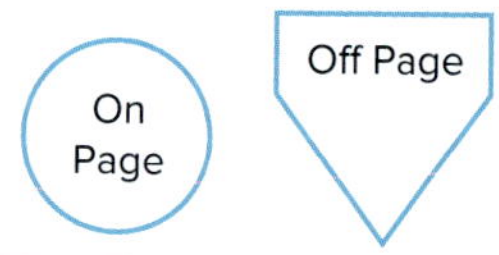
Annotation	This symbol is to add descriptive comments or explanatory notes to clarify the process.	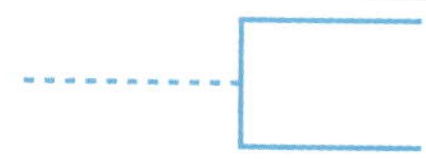

FIGURE 2.A3
(continued)

SHOWING RESPONSIBILITY

Deployment flowcharts show both the sequence of steps in a process as well as the organizational responsibility for each step. Like business process models (BPMN), deployment flowcharts use swimlanes to represent different organizational units or functions. These flowcharts are particularly useful in identifying the multiple handoffs between organization units in a process. These handoffs can be sources of problems, and making these steps clear can help identify those problems. Additionally, deployment flowcharts are useful in documenting processes for activities such as employee training. The flowchart in Figure 2.A4 illustrates swimlanes and responsibilities.

SHOWING OPPORTUNITY

Opportunity flowcharts highlight opportunities for improvement by, for example, separating value-added from cost-added activities within a process. Opportunity flowcharts use swimlanes to separate the activities that add value from those that add to the costs of the process, such as the costs of redoing work, waiting for information, waiting for parts, or correcting problems in general. Value-added activities are those that are essential to producing the process's product or service given the current state of technology, even if the process runs perfectly every time. Cost-added-only activities are those related to checking for defects, reworking, or supplying missing information.

For example, Figure 2.A5 shows the simple process of printing out and turning in an assignment document. If the process went as expected, we would select the printer, print the document, and turn in the assignment. The example assumes that, in some cases, the printer can be out of paper, which requires adding more paper before proceeding, or that the print cartridges could be out of ink, which requires replacing the cartridges and reprinting the document.

FIGURE 2.A4
Flowchart with Swimlanes Showing Responsibility

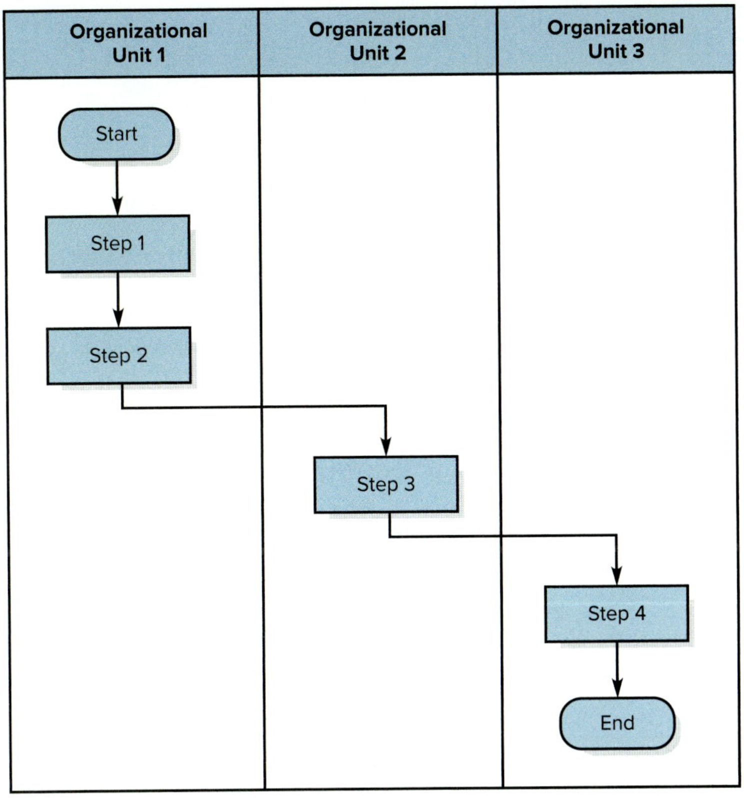

FIGURE 2.A5
Opportunity Flowchart Example of a Document Printing Process

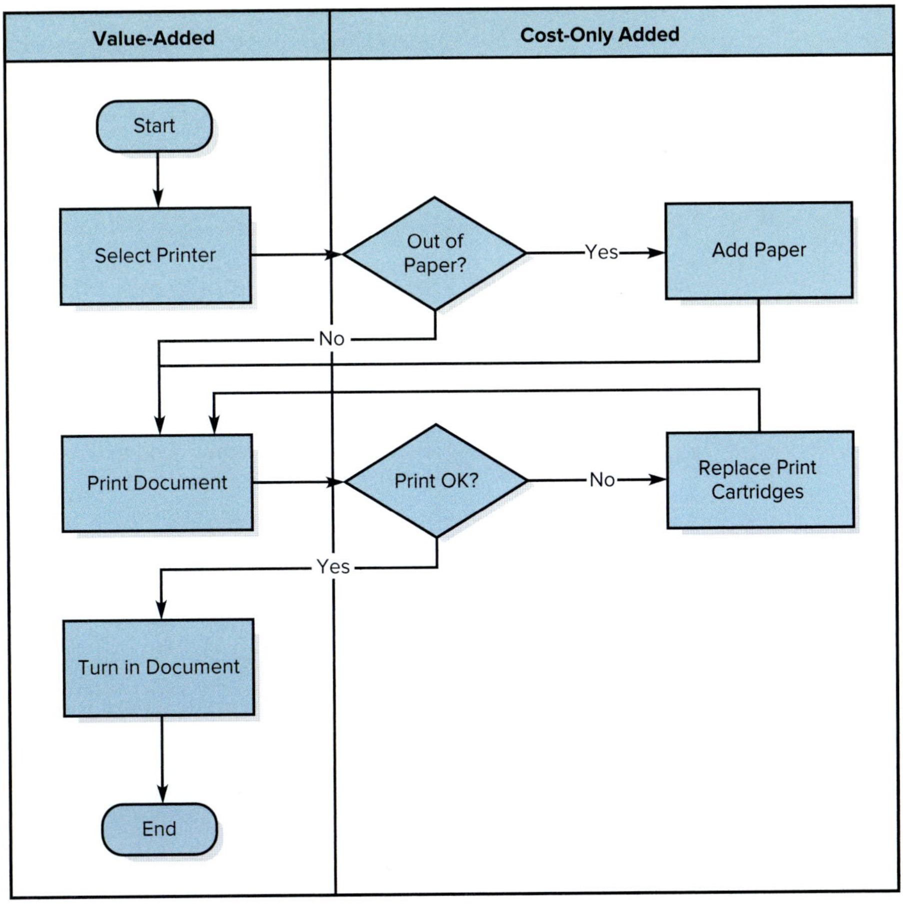

Appendix B

Data Flow Diagrams

WHAT IS A DATA FLOW DIAGRAM (DFD)?

A **data flow diagram (DFD)** represents graphically the flow of data through a system, such as one or more business processes. Data flow diagrams are often used to perform structured systems analysis and design, whereby a system is described at increasing levels of detail to facilitate new systems design. DFDs use a limited set of symbols (see Figure 2.B1) and are easily read and understood. Unlike most flowcharts, DFDs specifically represent the datastores—that is, the system files affected by or supporting the process—as well as the data that flow to and from the datastores. DFDs have no start and end symbols, which is also unlike flowcharts and BPMN business process diagrams. Instead, data flow diagrams present the external sources of—or destinations for—the data.

FIGURE 2.B1
Basic Elements of Data Flow Diagrams

Element	Description	Symbol
Process	The activities within a system that use or generate data (e.g., Receive customer order).	Process
Data Source or Destination	The entities that interact with the system (e.g., customers, employees, or bank).	Source/ Destination
Datastores	This symbol describes the physical or electronic data storage.	Datastore
Data Flows	This symbol shows the flow of data (e.g., an order coming from a customer); data flows are named to indicate the data content.	data flow 1

BASIC BUILDING BLOCKS FOR DATA FLOW DIAGRAMS

The following describes basic building blocks for data flow diagrams. The structure of these diagrams is substantially different from the structure of BPMN activity models.

- *Processes* are activities that use or generate data. Depending on the software tools used to draw DFDs, processes may be represented with circles or rectangles with rounded corners. As with BPMN diagrams and flowcharts, processes are given names using short verb phrases (e.g., receive customer order). A process must have at least one or more data flows coming in and going out.
- *Terminators* are external entities that are either sources or destinations for data. Terminators are typically represented with rectangles. Examples of terminators are customers, suppliers, or other entities external to the particular system being represented.
- *Datastores* represent the physical or electronic repositories of data within the system. Datastores are typically represented as rectangles with one or both ends open.
- *Data flows* represent the flow of physical or electronic data through the system. These are represented by arrows that show the direction of data flow.

EXAMPLE OF A DFD

Figure 2.B2 shows a simple example of a DFD showing the checkout process at a retail store. In this process, the customer (external source) presents items for checkout. The system includes scanning and bagging the items and accepting payment while updating sales and inventory records.

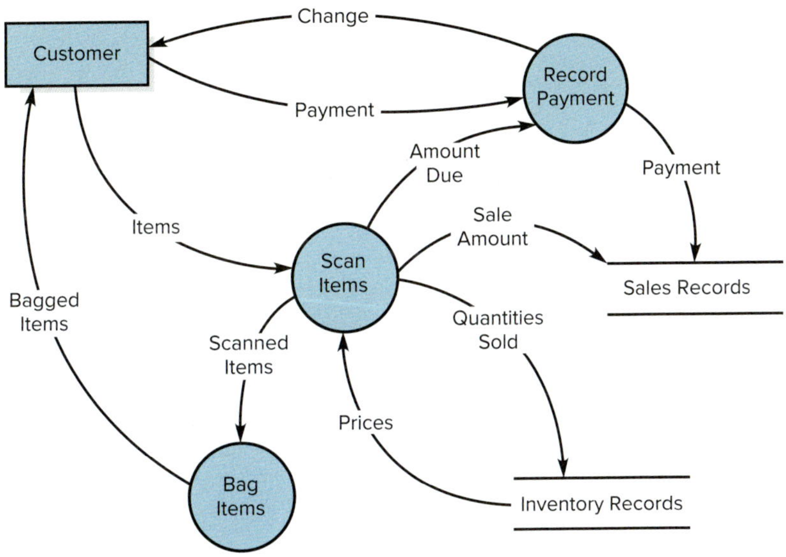

FIGURE 2.B2 Sample Level 0 DFD of Customer Checkout System

NESTING OR EXPLODING DFDs

DFDs describe a system at increasing levels of detail to facilitate new systems design. The context diagram shows the entire system as one process and identifies all relevant external sources and destinations for data, as well as the type of data coming from or going to those external entities. Then, subsequent models showing increasing detail would be identified as level 0, level 1, and level 2. Each process in a DFD is designated by the level and the number of the process. In Figure 2.B2, for example, assuming that is the level 0 diagram, then *Scan Items* could be designated process 1.0. If any subprocesses of *Scan Items* are subsequently modeled, those would be designated 1.1, 1.2, and so on.

BEST PRACTICES FOR DFDs

There are several best practices to ensure that DFDs provide useful descriptions of systems. Similar to flowcharts and BPMN diagrams, DFDs are a communications tool. Thus, the names given to processes, datastores, data flows, and external entities are important. The names should be clear to the system users. With regard to modeling specific elements of the diagram, modelers should remember that processes do not spontaneously generate or absorb data. Processes only modify data; therefore, all processes should have at least one data flow coming in and going out, and the data flow out of a process should be different than the data flow in. Datastores support the system's processing requirements, so every datastore should be connected to at least one process in the system. Finally, systems are developed to respond to inputs from external entities or to deliver information to external entities, so every external entity must be connected to at least one data flow.

USING DFDs FOR SYSTEM DOCUMENTATION

To form complete documentation for a system, the business analyst would augment the DFDs with additional information. For example, the analyst would define each datastore completely, specifying the fields, data types, data limits, and formats. The analyst would also define each element of a data flow in terms of the specific fields that it contains. Plus, the analyst would describe the business rules or logic for each process and confirm those with the process owners.

Answers to Progress Checks

1. Documentation is important to almost all accounting/finance functions listed.
2. The answer depends on the student, but all of us have used maps. Many of us have assembled a product from **IKEA**. Most of us have installed software on our computers.
3. Here's a simple business process model (without pools and swimlanes) for a fast-food drive-through:

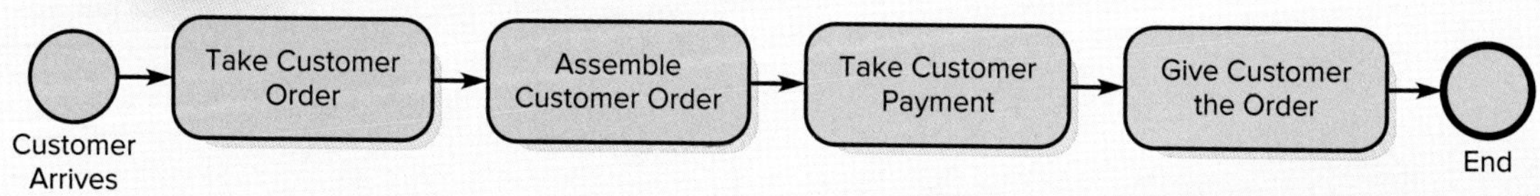

4. Here is one possible example of a process model using pools and message flows to show a customer interacting with **Amazon.com**'s website to purchase an item.

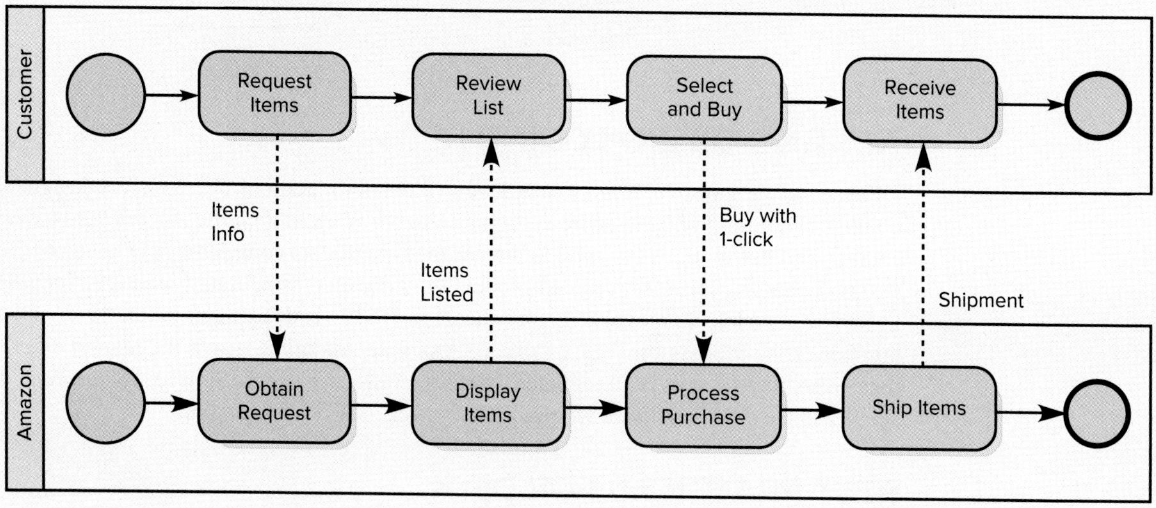

connect

Multiple Choice Questions

1. Which of the following is not a role of the accounting function in business? LO 2-1
   a. Financial close
   b. Regulatory compliance
   c. Project management
   d. Using IT to make finance and accounting processes more efficient
   e. All of the above are roles of the accounting function.

2. Which of the following is not an example of business process documentation? **LO 2-2**
    a. Business process models
    b. Training manuals
    c. Organization charts
    d. Internal audit
    e. All of the above are examples of business process documentation.
3. Which of the following is not a purpose of business process documentation? **LO 2-2**
    a. Facilitating process improvement
    b. Specifying accountability
    c. Training
    d. Supporting internal audit
    e. All of the above are purposes of business process documentation.
4. Which of the following best describes the value of business models? **LO 2-3**
    a. A communication tool
    b. A planning tool
    c. A process improvement tool
    d. A tool for managing complexity
    e. All of the above
5. Which of the following describes how participants in a process are identified in BPMN? **LO 2-6**
    a. Message flows
    b. Swimlanes
    c. Pools
    d. Gateways
    e. Both b and c
    f. Both a and d
6. Which of the following symbols is used to represent a gateway in BPMN? **LO 2-5**

a. 

b. 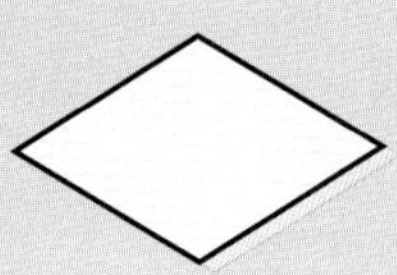

c. 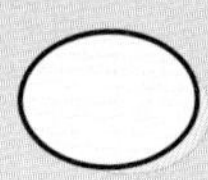

d. 

7. Which of the following symbols is used to represent sequence flow in BPMN? **LO 2-5**

a. 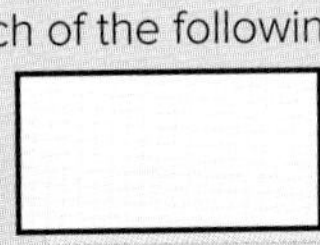

b. 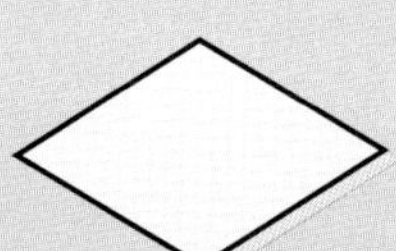

c. 

d. 

8. Which of the following statements about BPMN is not true? **LO 2-5**
    a. Arrows represent sequence flows.
    b. The BPMN specification is maintained by the Object Management Group (OMG).
    c. Events are modeled with a circle symbol.
    d. Annotations allow the modeler to add descriptive text.
    e. All of the above are true.
9. Which of the following describe characteristics of good BPMN models? **LO 2-5**
    a. They are clear.
    b. They are complete.
    c. They are consistent.
    d. They are correct.
    e. All of the above

10. Which of the following statements about sequence flows is not true? **LO 2-5**
   a. Sequence flows are continuous from the start event through activities and gateways, if any, to an end event in a pool.
   b. Sequence flows may not cross pool boundaries.
   c. Sequence flows may not cross lane boundaries.
   d. Tokens move along sequence flows.
   e. None of the above
11. Which of the following best describes message flows? **LO 2-7**
   a. Message flows are continuous within each pool.
   b. Message flows are modeled with solid arrows.
   c. Message flows represent exchanges between pools.
   d. Message flows may not cross pool boundaries.
   e. Message flows may not cross lane boundaries.
12. Which of the following is not true about the token concept? **LO 2-8**
   a. The token concept is a theoretical concept that describes process flow.
   b. The start event generates a token.
   c. The end event consumes the token.
   d. Tokens do not traverse message flows.
   e. All of the above are true
13. Which of the following is not a flow object? **LO 2-8**
   a. Gateways
   b. Message events
   c. Activities
   d. Message flows
   e. Timer events
14. Which of the following best describes an exclusive gateway? **LO 2-8**
   a. The only gateway in a BPMN diagram
   b. A gateway that does not connect to message flows
   c. A gateway with only one exit path per instance of a process
   d. A gateway where all exit paths are taken for each instance of a process
   e. None of the above
15. Which of the following best describes an inclusive gateway? **LO 2-8**
   a. The gateway that is shared among two pools
   b. A gateway with one or more exit paths per instance of a process
   c. A gateway with only one exit path per instance of a process
   d. A gateway where all exit paths are taken for each instance of a process
   e. None of the above
16. Which of the following is true about start events? **LO 2-8**
   a. A start event can catch a message.
   b. A start event cannot be a timer event.
   c. A start event can throw a message.
   d. A start event cannot be a message event.
   e. None of the above is true.
17. Which of the following is true about end events? **LO 2-8**
   a. An end event can catch a message.
   b. An end event can throw a message.

c. An end event can be a timer event.
d. An end event can be shared among pools.
e. None of the above is true.

18. Which is the following is true about intermediate timer events? **LO 2-8**
    a. The process delays until a specific date or time.
    b. The process delays for a specific period of time, e.g., 1 day.
    c. The process delays for an unspecified amount of time.
    d. The process delays until a message is received.
    e. Both a and b are true.
19. Which of the following best describes an intermediate error event? **LO 2-8**
    a. It is a boundary event attached to the boundary of an activity.
    b. It indicates alternate sequence flow begins when an error occurs.
    c. It is modeled with a leaning Z or flash sign.
    d. All of the above describe intermediate error events.
    e. None of the above describes intermediate error events.
20. Which of the following best describes a looping task? **LO 2-9**
    a. The task repeats until a condition is satisfied.
    b. A looping task only repeats twice.
    c. A looping task is modeled as a subprocess.
    d. A looping task happens multiple times in parallel.
    e. None of the above
21. Which of the following best describes a data object? **LO 2-10**
    a. It is modeled with a document icon.
    b. It represents data that are only available for the duration of the process.
    c. It is linked to tasks with data associations.
    d. It is different from a datastore.
    e. All of the above describe data objects.
22. Which of the following are true with respect to data associations? **LO 2-10**
    a. It is modeled as a dotted arrow.
    b. The association arrowhead shows the direction of data flow.
    c. Tokens flow across data associations.
    d. Gateways can be used to show optional data updates.
    e. Both a and b are true.

Discussion Questions

1. Do you think that your accounting education has prepared you for all roles of an accountant in business (see Table 2.1)? Which roles do you feel best prepared for? Which roles do you feel least prepared for? Why? **LO 2-1**
2. Choose one of the Accounting/Finance Operations roles in Table 2.1. How could a BPMN activity model help an accountant better understand that role? **LO 2-1**
3. Compare BPMN activity diagrams with flowcharts and DFDs. What is different? What is the same? When would one notation be better or worse than another? **LO 2-1, LO 2-4**
4. Consider the Stewardship and Reporting role of accountants shown in Table 2.1. What information would you need to collect and use to manage the regulatory compliance function? **LO 2-3, LO 2-4**
5. Assume that your company has BPMN diagrams of all their main processes. How could they use this information? **LO 2-5**

6. Describe some situations that might lead you to conclude that a BPMN diagram is not complete. **LO 2-6**
7. Each activity/task can only be assigned to one pool or lane. Why is that an important rule? **LO 2-5, LO 2-8**
8. Describe situations where you would use exclusive, inclusive, and parallel gateways? **LO 2-8**
9. Your process waits until you receive a response from your customer. What kind of flow object would you use to show this? **LO 2-8**
10. Give some examples of processes that would start with a timer event based on your experience. **LO 2-4**

Problems

connect

1. Consider the following narrative describing the process of filling a customer's order at a **Starbucks** branch:

   A Starbucks customer entered the drive-through lane and stopped to review the menu. He then ordered a Venti coffee of the day and a blueberry muffin from the barista. The barista recorded the order in the cash register. While the customer drove to the window, the barista filled a Venti cup with coffee, put a lid on it, and retrieved the muffin from the pastry case and placed it in a bag. The barista handed the bag with the muffin and the hot coffee to the customer. The customer has an option to pay with cash, credit card, or Starbucks gift card. The customer paid with a gift card. The barista recorded the payment and returned the card along with the receipt to the customer.

   Use BPMN to model Starbucks' process of taking a customer order using the following independent assumptions:

   a. No additional assumptions. Identify the start and end events and the tasks that the barista performs. Include any gateways whenever there are alternative tasks. **LO 2-5**

   b. The barista prepares each item in the order before delivering the order to the customer. Model the process to include a looping task. **LO 2-5, LO 2-9**

   c. The coffee needs time to brew and isn't immediately available. The barista asks the customer if he wants to wait. If the customer waits, 5 minutes will pass, and then the coffee can be prepared. Model the process to include an intermediate error event and a intermediate timer event. **LO 2-5, LO 2-8**

   d. The manager wants to see the interaction between the barista and the customer. Model the process with two pools, message flows, and intermediate message events to show that interaction. **LO 2-5, LO 2-6, LO 2-7**

connect

2. Consider the following narrative describing the process of going to class:

   Larry awoke to his alarm clock buzz. He got up and dressed for the day. Then, he ate a hearty breakfast of oatmeal, toast, orange juice, and coffee. He grabbed his books and prepared to leave for school. Before he left home, he checked the weather. If it looked like rain, he put on a jacket and took his umbrella, and he drove to school. If it looked sunny, he left his jacket and umbrella at home and walked to school. If he drove to school, he parked his car and walked to class. If he walked to school, he went straight to class.

   Use BPMN to model Larry's process of going to class using the following independent assumptions:

   a. No additional assumptions. Identify the start and end events and the tasks Larry performs, including any gateways whenever there is a decision to be made. **LO 2-5**

   b. Larry arrives at school early. Use an intermediate timer event to show the delay between arriving at school and going to class. **LO 2-5, LO 2-8**

   c. Larry doesn't own a car. If it is raining, he texts his friend Jazmin for a ride. She texts back whether she's available or not, and Larry either rides with her or walks to school in the rain. **LO 2-5** connect 3. Consider the following narrative describing the process of planning a vacation:

> Yannis is planning a trip to Hawaii with a friend. They first decide when they want to go and how much they can afford to spend. Then, they make their flight and hotel reservations. They wait until the scheduled departure. They travel to Hawaii and stay in the hotel. They enjoy a number of tourist activities. When their time in Hawaii is done, they fly home.

Use BPMN to model the process using the following independent assumptions:

a. When in Hawaii, they enjoy a number of tourist activities. Include a looping task to show this. LO 2-5, LO 2-9

b. There is a possibility that the hotel room and/or flights aren't within their budget. If reservations are too expensive, they will try different dates. If reservations are still too expensive, they will cancel their trip. Use a collapsed subprocess and an intermediate error event to model these assumptions. LO 2-5, LO 2-8

connect 4. Consider the following narrative describing the process of preparing an income tax return:

> Each year before April 15, you file your income taxes. You collect multiple W-2 and 1099 documents. You prepare your tax return and double-check it for accuracy. You file your forms.

Use BPMN to model the process using the following independent assumptions. Use inclusive gateways to model simultaneous events.

a. When you prepare your tax return, you download multiple forms from the IRS website. You fill out the forms, double-check your work, and then print them out. If you owe money, you write a check. You mail your tax return along with the check if you owe money. If you are getting a refund, you wait to receive your refund by check and deposit your refund in your bank account. LO 2-8

b. When you prepare your tax return, you use cloud-based tax software. You answer the questions and the tax software prepares the tax return for you. Once you've double-checked your work, you enter your checking account details and file your return electronically. If you owe money, the IRS will automatically deduct the amount from your checking account in 7 days. If you are getting a refund, the IRS will deposit the refund directly into your checking account. LO 2-8

connect 5. Consider the following narrative describing the process of registering a car with the DMV:

> Heide lives in California and it is time to renew her automobile registration. The California DMV sends her a renewal form and indicates that she needs a smog check for her automobile. She takes her car to the smog check station. She completes the smog check. If the smog check is successful, she can then go to the DMV website and renew her registration, paying with a credit card. Two weeks later she receives a new registration form and tags for her license plates. She puts the registration in the glove box of her car and places the tags on her license plates.

Use BPMN to model this process using the following independent assumptions:

a. No additional assumptions. Use a messaging start event to begin the process. LO 2-8

b. If the car fails the smog check, Heide must schedule maintenance service with her dealer. She completes the service and returns for a new smog check. If the car passes, she can complete the renewal process. LO 2-8

c. Heide uses the renewal form information at the smog check station. The smog check station provides a smog check certificate that Heide submits along with the renewal form to update her registration on the DMV website. She places the new registration document in her car. Use data objects to represent these documents. LO 2-8, LO 2-10

Additional problems are available in connect only.

Chapter Three

Data Modeling

A look at this chapter

Today's accountants must understand how business processes generate data and how those data are structured, interrelated, and stored in a database system. To ensure that business processes and the database systems are documented and to participate in improvements to processes and systems, accountants must understand and be able to model such systems. This chapter describes data modeling. It explains how data models support database-driven systems. It introduces basic data modeling tools to guide the student's development of modeling skills. Finally, it discusses business rules and how the identification of relevant business rules supports both process and data modeling.

A look back

Chapter 2 described the roles of accountants as users, managers, designers, and evaluators of technology and technology-driven business processes. To perform in those roles, accountants need to ensure that processes and systems are documented—and to participate in improvements to processes and systems. Thus, accountants must be business analysts. The chapter continued to introduce types of business process models as well as the potential value of business process modeling.

A look ahead

In the next several chapters, we use business process and data models to examine sales, acquisition, conversion, and related management processes.

© Purestock/SuperStock

Recently, **Starbucks** replaced a variety of systems with **Oracle**'s application suite. According to Karen Metro, vice president of global business system solutions for Starbucks, "Many of our systems had grown up in silos and were loosely connected, and we were having a hard time keeping them upgraded or getting the functionality we needed out of those systems. **Accenture** came in to help us review the state of the environment and put together a global program to deploy standardized business processes and systems around the world." About 200 people from both Accenture and Starbucks worked full time for 3 years on the project. The software was first implemented in Europe, then North America, and finally China. Starbucks expects a variety of performance benefits, including improved margins. In particular, the software will help Starbucks understand where its money is spent and "leverage that with our suppliers around the world."

Source: Information provided by Accenture case study posted on its website, www.accenture.com, 2009.

Chapter Outline

Learning Objectives

After reading this chapter, you should be able to:

3-1 Understand the purpose of structure models.

3-2 Understand and apply the building blocks for UML class (structure) diagrams.

3-3 Describe multiplicities for a UML class diagram.

3-4 Understand how to implement a relational database from a UML class diagram.

3-5 Understand process decision requirements and how business rules support process decisions.

3-6 Describe business rules and the various forms of rules.

LO 3-1
Understand the purpose of structure models.

STRUCTURE MODELS

Structure models describe the data and information structures inherent in a business process or processes. The primary purpose of these models is to create a blueprint for the development of a relational database to support the collection, aggregation, and communication of process information. They are tools for planning, documenting, discussing, and implementing databases; however, they also facilitate the use of databases after they are implemented.

For more than 50 years, **data models** have been used to represent the conceptual contents of databases to communicate with the users of those databases. For example, Charles Bachman developed data structure diagrams, also known as Bachman diagrams, in the 1960s. Using similar notation, Peter Chen developed entity-relationship modeling in 1976 to describe the entities (e.g., people, things, and events) and the relationships among entities in databases. Since then, a number of others have offered a variety of notations to describe the elements of databases, but the concepts in all variations are similar.

A model of logical database structures must be able to describe:

1. The entities or things in the domain of interest.
2. The relationships among those things.
3. The cardinalities that describe how many instances of one entity can be related to another.
4. The attributes or characteristics of the entities and relationships.

Unified Modeling Language Class Diagrams

This textbook employs the Unified Modeling Language (UML) class diagram notation for structure models, although the concepts also apply to other notation standards, such as entity-relationship modeling. The Object Management Group is a not-for-profit consortium of computer industry members that maintains and publishes the specification for the UML. **Class diagrams** are one type of diagram within UML and are similar in many ways to entity-relationship diagrams. They describe the logical structure of a database system.

LO 3-2
Understand and apply the building blocks for UML class (structure) diagrams.

Building Blocks for UML Class Diagrams

Classes

A **class** is any separately identifiable collection of things (objects) about which the organization wants to collect and store information. Classes can represent organization resources (e.g., trucks, machines, buildings, cash, investments), persons (e.g., customers, employees), events (e.g., sales, purchases, cash disbursements, cash receipts), and conceptual structures (e.g., accounts, product categories, budgets). Classes are typically implemented as tables in a relational database, where individual instances of objects are represented as rows in the table.

Cash disbursements represent events in a class. The class symbol would be name only such as bank account.
© Image Source/Getty Images

Each class is represented by a rectangle with three compartments, as shown in Figure 3.1. The top compartment shows the name of the class. The middle compartment shows the attributes (data elements) shared by all instances in the class. The bottom compartment describes operations that each instance in the class can perform. The attribute and operation compartments are optional. In this text, we will typically omit the attribute and operations compartments and use the class symbol with only the name of class when depicting classes.

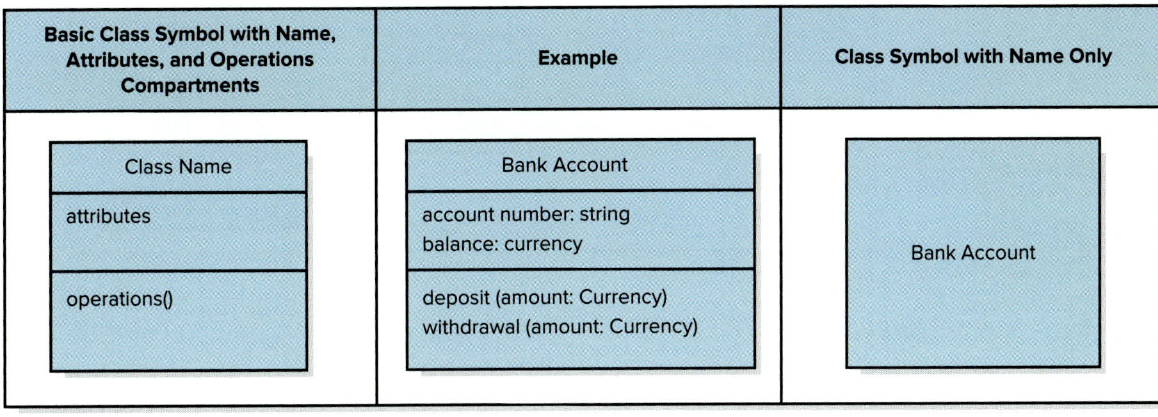

FIGURE 3.1
Class Notation

Associations

An **association** depicts the relationship between two classes. For example, customers (class) *participate* in sales (class); professors (class) *teach* courses (class); employees (class) *work for* organizations (class). It allows navigation between instances in one class and instances of another class, such as linking customer information to a particular sale. A generic association is drawn as a line connecting two classes. When the business purpose of the association is not clear, the association can be named by placing the text name on the line, as shown in Figure 3.2. Association names are verbs or verb phrases that indicate why instances of one class relate to instances of another class.

FIGURE 3.2
Classes with Associations

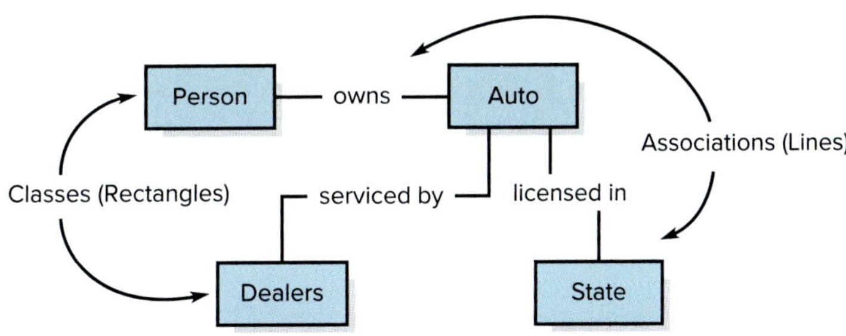

LO 3-3
Describe multiplicities for a UML class diagram.

Multiplicities

Multiplicities describe the minimum and maximum number of times instances in one class can be associated with instances in another class. Multiplicities for a class are represented by a pair of numbers placed on the opposite side of the association. In a binary association, there would then be two sets of multiplicities. Minimum values can be 0 or 1. The minimum values of multiplicities indicate whether participation in the relationship is optional (0) or mandatory (1). The maximum values can be 1 or many (*). In Figure 3.3, for example, it is optional for a person to own an automobile, but it is mandatory that each auto be owned by a person (assuming the auto class represents registered automobiles). The maximum values for a pair of multiplicities for a single association describe the nature of the relationship between classes: one-to-one, one-to-many, or many-to-many. In Figure 3.3, for example, a person could own many autos, so this is a one-to-many relationship.

FIGURE 3.3
Multiplicities
Each Person owns a minimum of 0 and a maximum of many Autos. Each Auto is owned by a minimum of 1 and a maximum of 1 Person.

Example of Association with Multiplicities

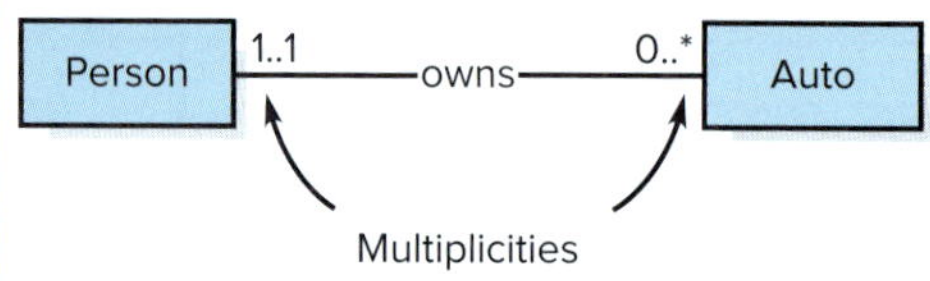

Options for Multiplicities

Indicator	Meaning
0..1	Zero or one
1..1	One only
0..*	0 or more
1..*	1 or more

Attributes

Attributes are data elements that describe the instances in a class. Figure 3.4 lists the attribute names for the classes in a domain of interest (related to taking orders from customers) and identifies primary and foreign keys. The full specification of attributes would also include data type, default value (if any), **constraints** on the value (such as minimum and maximum possible values), and other descriptive information.

Primary Keys. A **primary key (PK)** is an attribute or combination of attributes that uniquely identifies each instance in a class or row in a table. Primary keys can be modeled as part of the attribute list for each class on the UML class diagram; often, however, they are defined in the supporting documentation, such as the table listing shown in Figure 3.4, especially when using class symbols that only show the class name, as shown earlier in Figure 3.2. The primary key is a unique identifier for each instance in the class. For example, the "State" class in Figure 3.2 collectively defines all the states. Each state is an instance in that class, and each state would be identified by a unique primary key, such as the abbreviations AR, CA, WA, and so on.

FIGURE 3.4
List of Tables with Attribute Names

Customers	[Customer_Number (PK), Customer_Name, Customer_City, Customer_State, Customer_Zip, Customer_Phone]
Orders	[Order_Number (PK), Order_Date, Delivery_Date, Order_Amount, Shipping_Cost, Customer_Number (FK)]
Order_Items	[Order_Number + Product_Number (PK), Quantity_Ordered, Price]
Inventory	[Product_Number (PK), Product_Description, Quantity_on_Hand (QOH), Unit_of_Issue, Current_List_Price, Standard_Cost]

There are often several candidates for the primary key of a class or database table. There are several important criteria that guide the selection of appropriate primary keys:

- The primary key must uniquely identify each instance of the class (or row of the table). Consequently, the designer should avoid anything that could be duplicated, such as names.
- The primary key cannot be null (blank) under any circumstances. For this reason, the designer should avoid using attributes for the primary key that are potentially unavailable for any instance of the class; for example, not everyone has a Social Security number.
- The primary key cannot change over time.
- The primary key should be controlled by the organization that assigns it. When the assigning organization does not control the primary key values, it becomes difficult to ensure uniqueness. For example, names are not good primary keys.
- A primary key with sequential values makes it easier to recognize gaps in the data.
- All else equal, shorter primary key values are better than longer ones because shorter keys ease data entry, indexing, and retrieval.

Foreign Keys. A **foreign key (FK)** is an attribute or combination of attributes that allows tables to be linked together. A foreign key is linked *to the primary key of another table* to support a defined association. In Figure 3.3, for example, the Auto class would include a foreign key to match the primary key for the Person class to support the Owns association. In the table attribute listing shown in Figure 3.4, the primary key of the Customers Table is Customer_Number. The foreign key Customer_Number in the Orders Table allows rows in the Orders Table to be linked to corresponding rows in the Customers Table.

Progress Check

1. Consider students enrolled in courses taught by professors. Draw a simple class diagram with associations that describes the registration process. *Hint:* Include courses, students, and professors.
2. Add multiplicities to your diagram. Can a student be enrolled in many courses? Can a course have many students enrolled?
3. Create a listing of the tables with attributes. What are the primary keys? What attributes do you think go with each table definition?

Other Relationships

The generic relationship between two classes is modeled as an *association*, as described earlier. However, UML includes modeling notation for other types of relationships: **generalization** (or inheritance), **aggregation,** and **composition,** as shown in Figure 3.5. These special-purpose relationship notations should be used when they clarify relationships in a particular model, but they can also be modeled using associations.

Other Useful UML Class Model Notation

UML is semantically rich; it provides notation that accommodates a wide variety of modeling situations. We have outlined the basic notation that should allow you to build most

Relationship Notation	Explanation
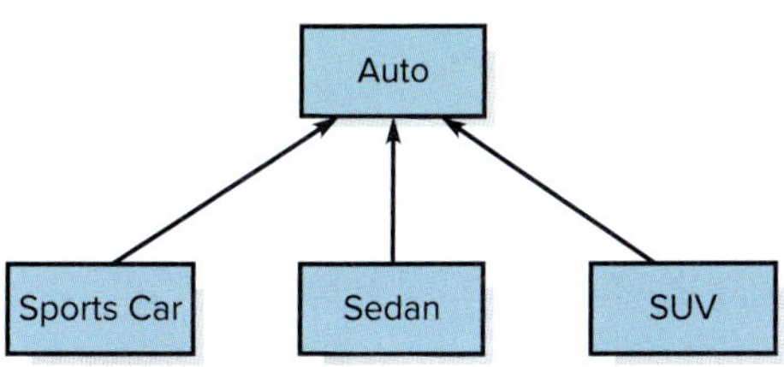	Generalization relationships allows grouping of things that share common characteristics. They reduce redundancy because the shared characteristics only need to be modeled once. For example, sports cars, sedans, and SUVs are all autos. They have many common elements, such as vehicle identification numbers (VINs), horsepower, gas mileage, etc. The subtypes (sports car, sedan, and SUV) also have unique characteristics that separately identify them.
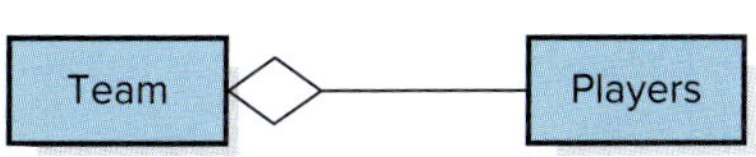	Aggregation relationships describe classes that are often considered together. Although players could exist separately from a team, they are part of a team. Aggregation relationships could be nested, for example, when the team is part of a league.
	Composition relationships are a form of aggregation. In this case, however, chapters do not exist separately from the books.

FIGURE 3.5
UML Notation for Other Relationships

Other Notation	Explanation
	Notes allow the modeler to add explanations. Notes can also be used to describe constraints. A note could be attached to a particular class rectangle with a dashed line.
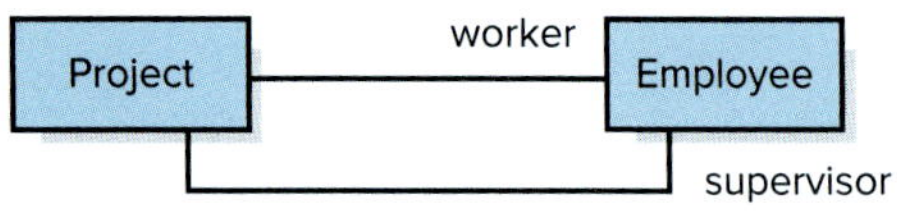	Role designation is helpful when the association between two classes depends on the specific role that objects in one class take on. In this example, employees work on a project, but one employee supervises the project. Different roles often result in different multiplicities.
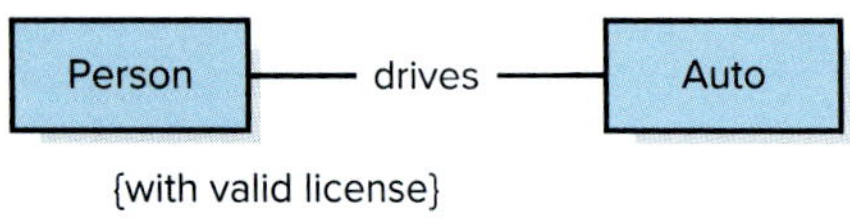	Constraints can be modeled with notes or a constraint can be placed near the constrained end of an association. In this example, only persons with valid drivers licenses should participate in the drive association.

FIGURE 3.6
Other Useful Class Diagram Notations

business process structural models. However, there are three other UML class model notations that can be particularly useful for modeling business processes from an accounting viewpoint. These three notations are described in Figure 3.6.

Best Practices in Preparing Class Diagrams

The primary objective of a class diagram is to describe the important elements of a domain of interest clearly, concisely, and accurately. As noted previously, class diagrams are tools to aid in planning, documenting, discussing, implementing, and using database systems. Here are some modeling best practices that can enhance the use of models for these purposes.

1. Use common terminology in the organization for class names (e.g., sales, orders, clients), and avoid confusing abbreviations.
2. Link classes on the diagram only when there is a clear business purpose for the relationship.
3. Avoid crossing lines where possible because that increases the potential for misreading the diagram.
4. Use consistently sized class rectangles to avoid an unwanted emphasis on a larger symbol.
5. Avoid running association lines close together because they may be hard to follow.
6. Opt for simplicity; show only what you need to show.
7. Focus first on the accuracy of the content, then address appearance.
8. Use notes to explain more complex situations.

UML CLASS MODELS FOR RELATIONAL DATABASE DESIGN

LO 3-4
Understand how to implement a relational database from a UML class diagram.

As we noted at the beginning of this chapter, the primary purpose of structure models is to create a blueprint for the development of a relational database to support the collection, aggregation, and communication of process information. They are tools for planning, documenting, discussing, and implementing databases. This section describes basic processes

FIGURE 3.7
Mapping Classes to Tables

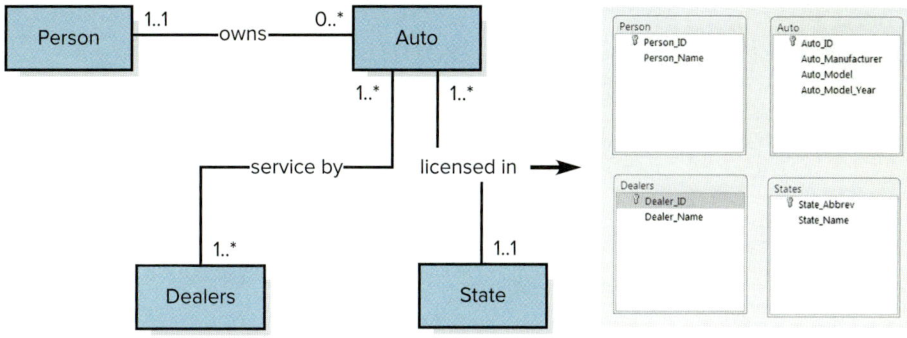

for mapping a UML class diagram to a relational database schema, which defines the tables, fields, relationships, keys, etc., in the database.[1]

1. *Map classes to tables.* The first step is to map the classes to tables. In Figure 3.7, for example, the UML class diagram (shown earlier in Figure 3.2 without multiplicities) would map to four tables in the relational database. Each instance of the class maps to a row in the corresponding table.
2. *Map class attributes to table fields and assign primary keys.* Map the attributes for each class to fields in the corresponding relational table. If the primary keys have not been designated, determine an appropriate primary key for each relational table. In the example shown in Figure 3.7, the primary keys for the tables are indicated by **Microsoft** Access's primary key symbol, a gold key icon.
3. *Map associations to foreign keys.* Each association in Figure 3.7, except the "serviced by" association between Dealers and Auto, will be implemented by adding foreign keys. The maximum multiplicities on each side of an association determine the foreign key placement. The figure indicates that one person owns a maximum of many autos. This is an example of a one-to-many relationship that will be implemented with a foreign key. A one-to-one relationship occurs when the maximum multiplicity on each side of the association is 1, and, in general, one-to-one relationships will also be implemented with a foreign key.
   a. There is a rule of thumb that can help identify where the foreign key is placed. Remember that each association is implemented in your database with a foreign key or a linking table, as described later. Assume a one-to-many relationship—that is, a relationship where the maximum multiplicity on one side of the association is 1 and the maximum multiplicity on the other side of the association is many. The foreign key is posted toward the "many" side of the association. In other words, the primary key for the class on the 1 side of the association is posted as a foreign key for the class on the "*" side of the association. Thus, in Figure 3.7 the primary key for Person is posted in Auto as a foreign key, and the primary key of State is also posted in Auto as a foreign key. Table 3.1 provides general rules for posting foreign keys based on the type of association between two classes.
   b. The minimum multiplicities are often determined by the timing of entries to both tables involved in one association. If an entry in one table must match an entry in the other table, then the minimum is 1. If an entry in one table can occur without an entry in the other table, then the minimum is 0. In Figure 3.7, we've assumed that each auto is owned by one person, and you can't have any auto listed in the Auto table without a corresponding owner in the Person table. Thus, the minimum

[1] Schemas can also define other database requirements, such as levels of access, but this section focuses on designing the basic elements.

TABLE 3.1
Posting Foreign Keys[a]

[a] The foreign key is the primary key of the related table; however, foreign keys may be assigned different names if it improves understanding.

[b] Foreign keys can be posted in either table, but the minimum multiplicity of 0 indicates an optional association for that table and a general rule provides the most efficient option for posting the foreign key.

Multiplicity for A	Multiplicity for B	Relationship Type	General Rules for Posting Foreign Keys
0..1	0..1	One-to-one[b]	Post foreign key in either A or B but not both
0..1	1..1	One-to-one	Post foreign key in A
0..1	0..*	One-to-many	Post foreign key in B
0..1	1..*	One-to-many	Post foreign key in B
1..1	0..1	One-to-one	Post foreign key in B
1..1	1..1	One-to-one	Post foreign key in either A or B but not both
1..1	0..*	One-to-many	Post foreign key in B
1..1	1..*	One-to-many	Post foreign key in B
0..*	0..1	One-to-many	Post foreign key in A
0..*	1..1	One-to-many	Post foreign key in A
0..*	0..*	Many-to-many	Create linking table
0..*	1..*	Many-to-many	Create linking table
1..*	0..1	One-to-many	Post foreign key in A
1..*	1..1	One-to-many	Post foreign key in A
1..*	0..*	Many-to-many	Create linking table
1..*	1..*	Many-to-many	Create linking table

multiplicity next to Person is 1. Conversely, an individual in the Person table may or may not own an auto. If the individual did not own an auto, there would be no matching auto in the Auto table. In this case, the matching entry is optional and the minimum multiplicity next to Auto is 0. Note that the minimum is 0 even if some individuals own autos. As long as our requirements indicate that some individual may not own an auto, the minimum is 0.

4. *Create new tables to implement many-to-many relationships.* A many-to-many relationship is when the maximum multiplicity is * on both ends of the association, regardless of the minimum multiplicities. In this situation, the database designer creates a new table to implement the association. The default primary key for the new table is the combination of the two primary keys for the associated tables. In Figure 3.7, for example, each Auto can be serviced by many Dealers, and each Dealer can service many Autos. Thus, the "serviced by" association is implemented by creating a new table with a primary key that includes both Auto_ID and the Dealer_ID (called a concatenated or composite key), as shown in Figure 3.8.

FIGURE 3.8
Implementing a Many-to-Many Relationship
In theory, every relationship type can be implemented with a linking table as shown in this figure.

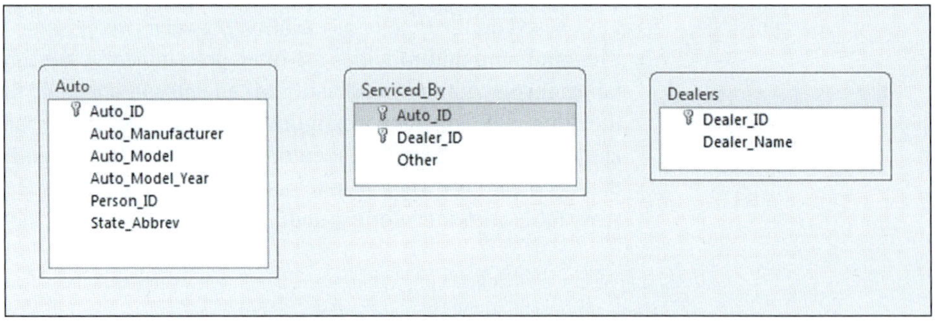

FIGURE 3.9
Mapping Class Diagram Associations to Relationships

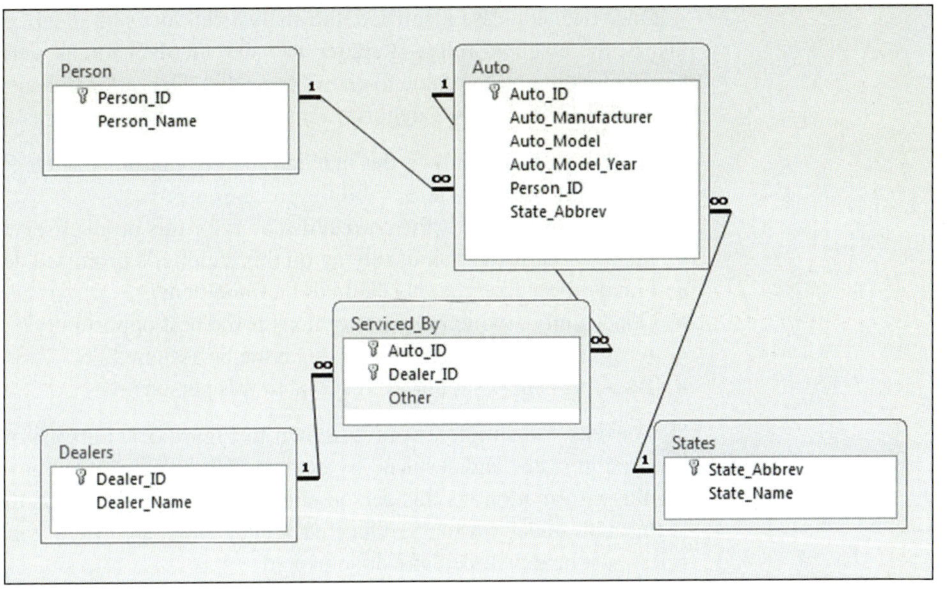

5. *Implement relationships among tables.* Create relationships among the relational tables to match the associations shown on the class diagram. After the foreign keys are posted and the linking tables created for the many-to-many relationships, the database designer can implement the relationships, as shown in Figure 3.9. Note that each half of the composite primary key for the Serviced_By table acts as a foreign key: Auto_ID in the Serviced_By table links to Auto_ID in the Auto table and Dealer_ID in Serviced_By table links to Dealer_ID in the Dealers table.

The set of relational tables shown in Figure 3.9 then implements the class diagram shown in Figure 3.4. In other words, the class diagram is the blueprint from which the database is built. Just as inadequate plans result in substandard buildings, an incomplete or erroneous class diagram will result in an ineffective database. It is easier to change the blueprint than change the building, and it is easier to change the class diagram (and ensure that it is correct) than to change the database.

LO 3-5
Understand process decision requirements and how business rules support process decisions.

DECISION REQUIREMENTS AND BUSINESS RULES

In addition to the process activities described in Chapter 2 and the information structures introduced in this chapter, analysts also need to focus on the process decision-making requirements. Then, business rules can be developed to support those decision-making requirements. Recognizing the importance of decision making in business processes, the Object Management Group recently issued version 1.0 of its standard for Decision Model and Notation (DMN).

Decision modeling involves four basic steps that are performed iteratively:

1. Identify decisions required in the process.
2. Describe and document these decisions and how they impact the business objectives for the process.
3. Specify decision requirements in terms of the information and knowledge required to make the decision.
4. Decompose and refine the requirements, determining where existing business rules apply and where new business rules need to be developed.

Once decisions are identified, the analyst can focus on identifying the decision logic—that is, the business rules—required to make the decision as well as the contextual input data that would be available to decision makers. Operational decisions depend on the business process but can be categorized into several general types as follows:

- Eligibility or approval—is this individual or organization eligible for this product or service?
- Validation—is this claim valid for processing?
- Calculation—what is the correct discount for this product/service for this customer?
- Risk—what is the risk of relying on this supplier's promised delivery date?
- Fraud—how likely is this claim to be fraudulent?
- Opportunity—which of these options is the best opportunity?
- Assignment—to whom should this issue be assigned?
- Targeting—how should we respond to this person?

Consider the simple example shown in Figure 3.7. Persons own automobiles that are licensed in states and serviced by dealers. What decisions might be involved in processing this information? Is this person eligible to own this auto? Is this license request valid? Is this auto under warranty? Once each decision is identified, the corresponding business rules must be developed and documented.

LO 3-6
Describe business rules and the various forms of rules.

Business Rules and Decision Tables

Business rules support decision making in business processes. They standardize and constrain process action. A **business rule** is a succinct statement of a constraint on a business process. It is the logic that guides the behavior of the business in specific situations. Business rules are typically written in text, not modeled; however, they influence the structure and flow of models. Business rules establish multiplicities in class models, and they set criteria for branching in activity models.

Rule: Credit card payments are allowed if the card is MasterCard.
© Thomas Trutschel/Photothek via Getty Images

There are several forms for business rules. To put these in context, let's consider a simple example of customer payments at a restaurant. Suppose the restaurant accepts cash or credit card payments as long as the credit card is American Express. Additionally, the restaurant only accepts payments in U.S. dollars, not foreign currency, and it does not accept checks. These payment constraints involve the following rule forms:

- *Obligatory.* This rule form states what should occur: Payment should be made in U.S. dollars.
- *Prohibited.* This rule form states what should not occur: No payments by check.
- *Allowed.* This rule form states what is allowed under what conditions: Credit card payments are allowed if the card is American Express.

Rules are stated in short sentences, as described earlier. In an attempt to formalize the statement of rules, the Object Management Group published a standard, titled "Semantics of Business Vocabulary and Business Rules" (SBVR), in 2008.[2] SBVR sets standards for stating business rules using natural language. The standard describes operative business rules, such as the three forms just described: obligatory, prohibited, and allowed. It also describes similar structural rules that describe fundamental characteristics—such as, "It is

[2]For further information on SBVR, see www.omg.org/spec/SBVR/1.0/.

necessary that each sale be made to a customer"—rather than operating policy rules that are stated in terms of preferred outcomes.

Rules must be enforceable. So, there must be related enforcement-level information that describes how to deal with potential violations. Enforcement levels include strict enforcement, pre-override, and post-override. If a rule is strictly enforced, violations are not authorized. If a rule is subject to pre-override, violations are allowed if authorized in advance. If a rule is subject to post-override, violations are allowed if authorized after the violation. When rules are subject to override, there should also be a statement of who can authorize a violation. Additionally, certain rules can be considered guidelines, which are generally followed but not enforced. The enforcement level can vary for different parts of the organization.

Rules are valuable because they make modeling business processes easier. They limit the number of options to those allowed by business policy. The rules for a business process establish systems requirements when acquiring new technology. However, rules can also inhibit process improvements because they can be tied to outdated technology. Thus, a close examination of business rules—and the business reasons for them—can reveal unnecessary constraints. In most situations, however, business rules are not stated formally; they are implicit. The process analysis should, therefore, elicit important business rules.

Decision tables combine multiple business rules to support likely circumstances requiring a decision. A decision table consists of a name, a set of inputs, a set of outputs, and a set of rules. The rules associate the inputs to the decision outputs at that point in the process. Figure 3.10 presents a sample decision table where three rules are shown as rows in the table. The table name is *Discounts.* The columns *Customer Type* and *Size of Order* are the inputs to the decision. The *Discount to Offer* is the output of the decision. The number column could be indexed to identify the process, decision, and rule, but in this case it simply numbers the three rule options.

FIGURE 3.10
Sample Decision Table

Discounts			
Number	**Customer Type**	**Size of Order**	**Discount to Offer**
1	Business	<10	10%
2	Business	>=10	15%
3	Individual	All	5%

Summary

- Structure models, such as UML class models, describe the information structures of one or more business processes.
- Structure models allow communication about database design.
- Structure models support the design, implementation, and use of databases.
- The building blocks for UML class diagrams include classes, associations, multiplicities, and attributes.
- Attributes for each class include the primary key, foreign keys, and other attributes describing characteristics of the class.
- Primary keys uniquely define each instance of a class (and each row in a relational database table).
- Foreign keys allow tables to be linked together.
- Foreign keys are primary keys of other tables posted in the current table to allow linking.
- Other class diagram relationships include generalizations, aggregations, and compositions.
- Associations model the business purpose of a relationship between two classes, such as the role that members of one class have with respect to the other class.

- UML class models can be used to create tables by mapping classes to tables, mapping class attributes to table fields, mapping associations to foreign keys depending on the multiplicities of the association, and creating new tables to implement many-to-many relationships.
- Analysts must understand process decision requirements to truly understand how the process should perform.
- Business rules and decision tables establish business policies and constrain business processes.

Key Words

aggregation relationship (65) A special-purpose UML notation representing the relationship between two classes that are often considered together, such as when a sports league is made up of a collection of teams.

association (63) UML symbol that depicts the relationship between two classes; it is modeled as a solid line that connects two classes in a model.

attributes (64, 73) Data elements that describe instances in a class, very much like fields in a database table; characteristics, properties, or adjectives that describe each class.

business rule (70) Succinct statements of constraints on business processes; they provide the logic that guides the behavior of the business in specific situations.

cardinalities (74) *See* multiplicities.

class (62) Any separately identifiable collection of things (objects) about which the organization wants to collect and store information. Classes can represent organization resources (e.g., trucks, machines, buildings, cash, investments), persons (e.g., customers, employees), events (e.g., sales, purchases, cash disbursements, cash receipts), and conceptual structures (e.g., accounts, product categories, budgets). Classes are typically implemented as tables in a relational database, where individual instances of the class are represented as rows in the table.

class diagrams (62) Structure models prepared using UML notation.

composition relationship (65) A special-purpose UML notation representing the relationship between two classes that are often considered together, similar to aggregation relationships, except in composition relationships, one class cannot exist without the other, such as a book and the chapters that compose the book.

constraints (64) Optional or mandatory guidance about how a process should perform in certain situations.

data models (62) A graphic representation of the conceptual contents of databases; data models support communication about database contents between users and designers of the database.

entities (73) The people, things, and events in the domain of interest; in UML notation, entities are modeled as classes.

foreign key (FK) (65) Attribute that allows database tables to be linked together; foreign keys are the primary keys of other tables placed in the current table to support the link between the two tables.

generalization relationship (65) A special-purpose UML symbol that supports grouping of things that share common characteristics; it reduces redundancy because the shared characteristics need only be modeled once.

multiplicities (63) UML symbols that describe the minimum and maximum number of times an instance of one class can be associated with instances of another class for a specific association between those two classes; they indicate whether the two classes are part of one-to-one, one-to-many, or many-to-many relationships.

primary key (PK) (64) An attribute or a combination of attributes that uniquely identifies an instance of a class in a data model or a specific row in a table.

relationship (73) The business purpose for the association between two classes or two database tables; *see* association.

structure model (62) A conceptual depiction of a database, such as a UML class model or an entity-relationship model.

Entity-Relationship Diagrams

WHAT IS AN ENTITY-RELATIONSHIP DIAGRAM?

An entity-relationship diagram (ERD) represents graphically the logical data structure of a system, such as a database supporting one or more business processes. ERDs were originally proposed in a 1976 paper[3] by Peter Chen as a tool to capture the conceptual design (schema) of a relational database system, and ERD modeling techniques have evolved over time. Fundamentally, ERDs and UML class models are equivalent tools for modeling data structures.

BASIC BUILDING BLOCKS OF ERDS

Not surprisingly, the basic building blocks of ERDs include entities and relationships. Each entity has attributes that describe its characteristics. Entities correspond to tables in a relational database where the attributes are the fields in the table. Each relationship indicates a business purpose for connecting two or more entities. Relationships correspond to the links between tables. Cardinalities (i.e., multiplicities) define how one entity links to another. See Figure 3.A1.

FIGURE 3A.1
Basic Elements of Entity-Relationship Diagrams

Element	Description	Symbol
Entity	Separately and uniquely identifiable things of interest in a system.	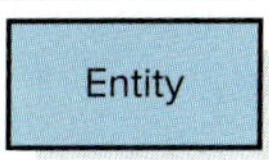
Relationship	Associations between two entities reflecting a business purpose (Chen's notation).	
Relationship with Cardinalities	Associations between two entities reflecting a business purpose (information engineering style), where the ends indicate the cardinalities.	

Entities represent separately and uniquely identifiable things of interest in a system, for example, customers, employees, sales, inventory, and cash receipts. Entities are modeled as rectangles. Entities correspond to classes in UML class models.

Relationships represent associations between entities, for example, customers (entity) *participate in* (relationship) sales (entity). Relationships are modeled as diamonds. Relationships correspond to associations in UML class models.

Attributes are characteristics of entities; for example, customer attributes could include name, address, city, state, zip code, and credit limit. Attributes correspond to fields in a relational table, so the selection of attributes for an entity should reflect efficient table design, as discussed within Chapter 3.

[3] P. P. Chen, "The Entity-Relationship Model: Toward a Unified View of Data," *ACM Transactions on Database Systems* 1 (1976), pp. 9–36.

Cardinalities describe the nature of the relationship between two entities; they describe how many instances of an entity relate to one instance of another entity—for example, each *customer* may *participate in* many *sales*. Cardinalities correspond to multiplicities in UML class diagrams.

ERD EXAMPLE USING CHEN'S NOTATION

Figure 3.A2 shows a simple ERD using min-max cardinality notation. The two entities are Singers and Songs. The relationship between the two entities shows that we are modeling the singers that recorded the songs. This example uses min-max notation to describe the cardinalities. The cardinalities next to the Singers entity indicate the minimum (0) and maximum (N) number of songs that each singer recorded. The cardinalities next to the Songs entity indicate the minimum (1) and maximum (1) number of singers that recorded each song.

FIGURE 3.A2
ERD Example Using Chen's Notation

ERD EXAMPLE USING INFORMATION ENGINEERING NOTATION

Figure 3.A3 shows the same example as Figure 3.A2 using information engineering notation. Again, the two entities are Singers and Songs. In this case, however, the purpose of the relationship between the two entities is not as clearly identified. The "crow's feet" markings on the relationship line indicate the cardinalities. The cardinality notation next to the Singers entity indicates there is one singer for each song. Note that a double line symbol (—||—) is sometimes used to indicate one and only one (mandatory). The cardinality notation next to the Songs entity indicates a singer can record many songs (optional). Thus, there may be singers in the database who did not record any songs, but each song must be recorded by one singer.

FIGURE 3.A3
ERD Example Using Information Engineering Notation

CARDINALITY OPTIONS

In general, there are four options for each cardinality. The minimum can be zero (the relationship is optional) and the maximum can be either one or many, or the minimum can be one (the relationship is mandatory) and the maximum can again be either one or many. Considering the cardinalities at each end of the relationship between two entities (entity A and entity B), there are three basic types of relationships (see Figure 3.A4):

- *One-to-one (1:1).* One instance of entity A is related only to one instance of entity B. For example, each sale earns one cash receipt.
- *One-to-many (1:N).* One instance of entity A is related to many instances of entity B (or vice versa). For example, a customer participates in many sales.
- *Many-to-many (M:N).* Many instances of entity A are related to each instance of entity B and many instances of entity B are related to entity A. For example, a sale can include many inventory items, and each inventory item could be sold on many sales.

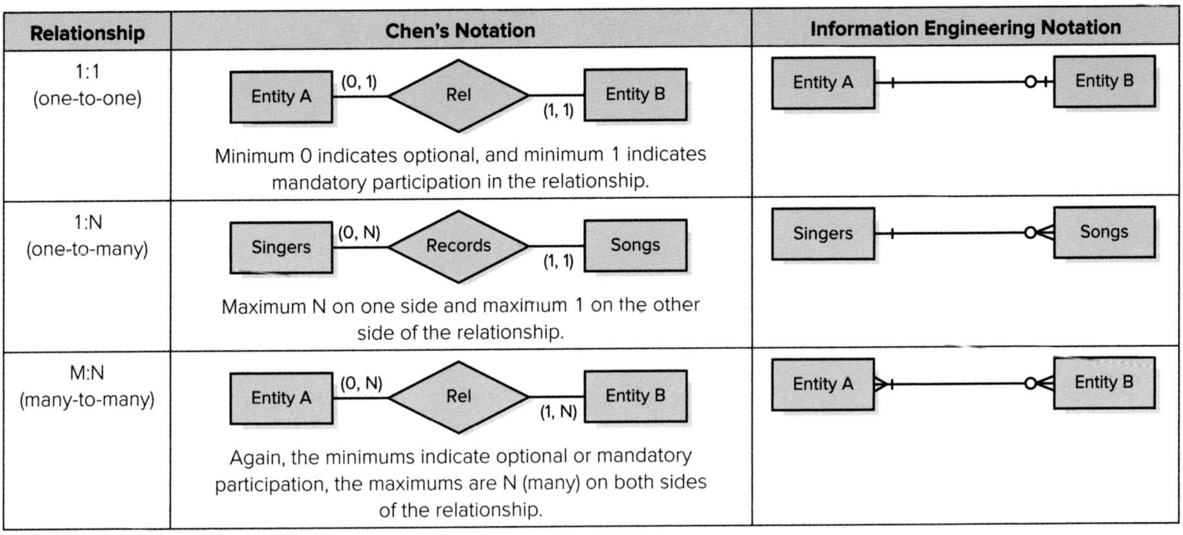

FIGURE 3.A4
Examples of Cardinality Options Using Both Chen's Notation and Information Engineering Notation

Answers to Progress Checks

1. The class diagram would look something like this:

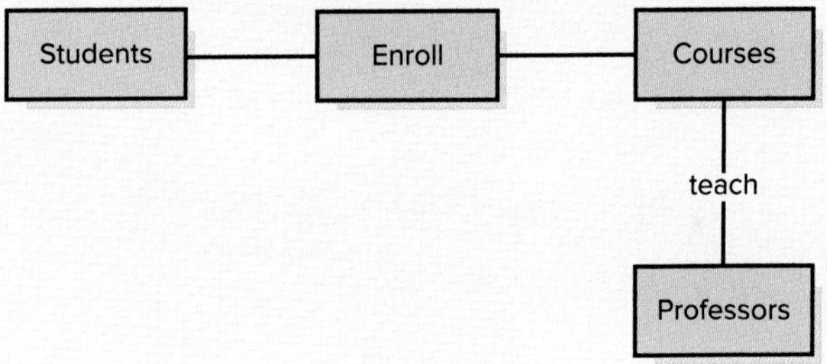

2. With multiplicities:

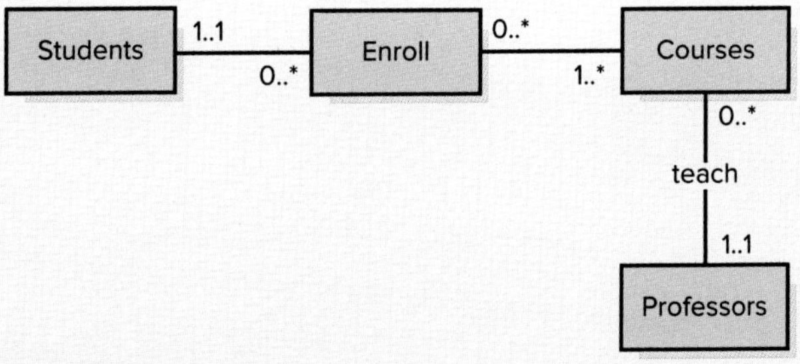

Note that this assumes that each course only has one professor teaching it and students have not yet enrolled in some courses.

3. The table structure would look something like this:

Students	[Student ID (PK), Student Name, Student Address, Student e-mail, . . .]
Enroll	[Enrollment transaction number (PK), Enrollment date, Student ID (FK), . . .]
Courses	[Course number (PK), Course Name, Course Description, Professor ID (FK), . . .]
Professors	[Professor ID (PK), Professor Name, Professor Department, . . .]

Mc Graw Hill Education connect

Multiple Choice Questions

1. Which of the following is not an objective of a structure model? **LO 3-1**
    a. Designate things of interest in the business domain.
    b. Describe characteristics of things of interest in the business domain.
    c. Support relational database design.
    d. Describe the sequence of activities.
    e. All of the above are objectives of structure models.

2. Which of the following symbols is used to represent a class in a UML class diagram? **LO 3-2**

    a. 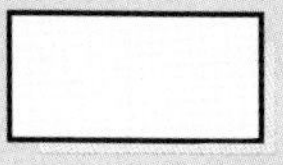

    c. 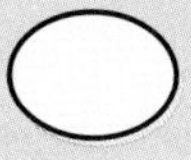

    b. 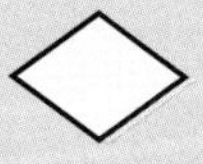

    d. 

3. Which of the following statements concerning this class diagram with multiplicities is not true? **LO 3-2, LO 3-3**

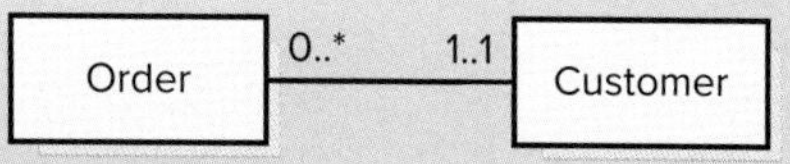

    a. An order can involve only one customer.
    b. A customer can place only one order.
    c. A customer can place many orders.
    d. A customer may not have ordered yet.
    e. All of the above are true.

4. Which of the following statements is true about the following class diagram? **LO 3-2, LO 3-3**

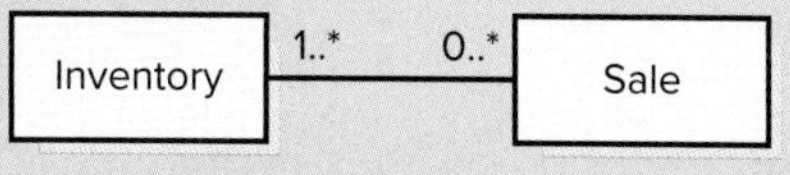

    a. A sale can involve zero inventory items.
    b. A sale can involve one inventory item.
    c. A sale can involve many inventory items.
    d. A and C are true.
    e. B and C are true.

5. Which of the following is an example of an *obligatory* business rule? **LO 3-6**
    a. Customers must provide a valid credit card number.
    b. Customers must enter a shipping address.
    c. Customers may not enter a post office box as a shipping address.
    d. Customers may use Visa or MasterCard.
    e. Both a and b are obligatory business rules.

6. Which of the following is not an enforcement level for a business rule? **LO 3-6**
    a. Strict enforcement
    b. Optional enforcement
    c. Pre-override enforcement
    d. Post-override enforcement
    e. Guideline

7. Contrast the UML class diagrams with the entity-relationship diagrams shown in Appendix A. Which of the following pairs are not equivalent? **LO 3-1, LO 3-2, LO 3-3**
   a. Class and Entity
   b. Class and Relationship
   c. Association and Relationship
   d. Multiplicity and Cardinality
   e. All of these are equivalent.
8. Which of the following best describes the meaning of this diagram? **LO 3-2, LO 3-3**

   a. Each sale can result in many subsequent cash receipts.
   b. Each cash receipt can apply to many sales.
   c. All sales must have cash receipts.
   d. Each sale can result in only one cash receipt.
   e. None of the above
9. Which of the following best describes the meaning of this entity-relationship diagram? **LO 3-2, LO 3-3**

   a. Every student is enrolled in many classes.
   b. Every class must have at least one student enrolled.
   c. Every student must be enrolled in at least one class.
   d. No students are enrolled in any classes.
   e. None of the above
10. Which of the following best describes the meaning of this UML class diagram? **LO 3-2, LO 3-3**

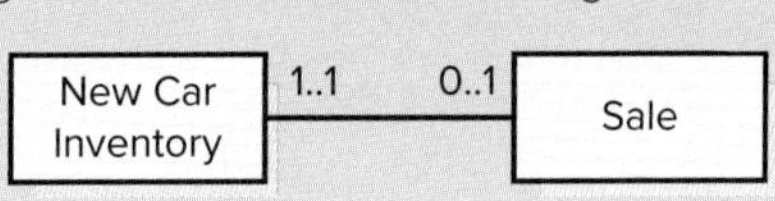

   a. Each new car can be sold once.
   b. A sale can involve multiple new cars.
   c. Each new car can be sold multiple times.
   d. No new cars are in inventory.
   e. None of the above

Refer to this diagram to answer questions 11 through 20.

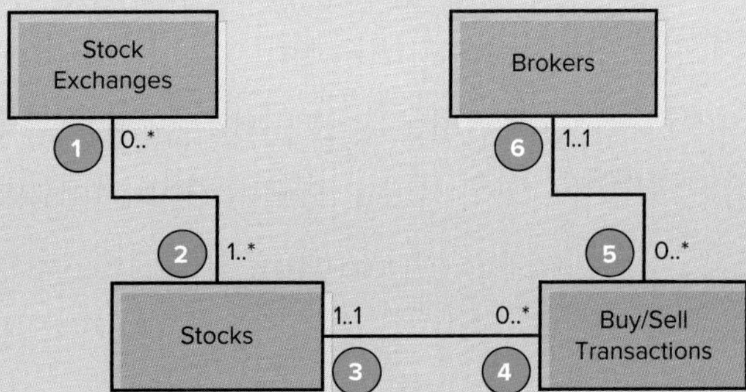

11. Which of the following best describes the meaning of the multiplicities next to the number 1 in the preceding diagram? LO 3-2, LO 3-3
    a. Stocks are traded in only one exchange.
    b. Stocks are traded in at least one exchange.
    c. Stocks are traded in a minimum of zero exchanges.
    d. Stocks are traded in a maximum of many exchanges.
    e. Both c and d are correct.
12. Which of the following best describes the meaning of the multiplicities next to the number 2 in the preceding diagram? LO 3-2, LO 3-3
    a. Each exchange trades at least one stock.
    b. Each exchange trades only one stock.
    c. Each exchange trades a minimum of zero stocks.
    d. Each exchange trades a maximum of many stocks.
    e. Both a and d are correct.
13. Which of the following is true to implement the Stock Exchanges and Stocks classes and the association between them in the preceding UML class diagram in a database? LO 3-2, LO 3-3, LO 3-4
    a. The primary key of Stocks is a foreign key in Stock Exchanges.
    b. The primary key of Stock Exchanges is a foreign key in Stocks.
    c. The association between Stocks and Stock Exchanges is implemented as a linking table.
    d. Both a and b are true.
    e. None of these is true.
14. Which of the following best describes the meaning of the multiplicities next to the number 3 in the preceding diagram? LO 3-2, LO 3-3
    a. Each transaction involves at least one stock.
    b. Each transaction involves only one stock.
    c. Each transaction involves a minimum of zero stocks.
    d. Each transaction involves a maximum of many stocks.
    e. Both a and b are correct.
15. Which of the following best describes the meaning of the multiplicities next to the number 4 in the preceding diagram? LO 3-2, LO 3-3
    a. Each stock is bought/sold at least once.
    b. Each stock is bought/sold only once.
    c. Each stock is bought/sold a maximum of many times.
    d. Each stock is bought/sold a minimum of many times.
    e. Both a and c are correct.
16. Which of the following is true to implement the Buy/Sell Transactions and Stocks classes and the association between them in the preceding UML class diagram in a database? LO 3-2, LO 3-3, LO 3-4
    a. The primary key of Stocks is a foreign key in Buy/Sell Transactions.
    b. The primary key of Buy/Sell Transactions is a foreign key in Stocks.
    c. The association between Stocks and Buy/Sell Transactions is implemented as a linking table.
    d. Both a and b are true.
    e. None of these is true.

17. Which of the following best describes the meaning of the multiplicities next to the number 5 in the preceding diagram? LO 3-2, LO 3-3
    a. Each Broker is involved in one Buy/Sell Transaction.
    b. Each Broker is involved in many Buy/Sell Transactions.
    c. Each Broker is involved in a minimum of one Buy/Sell Transaction.
    d. Each Broker is involved in a minimum of zero Buy/Sell Transactions.
    e. Both b and d are correct.
18. Which of the following best describes the meaning of the multiplicities next to the number 6 in the preceding diagram? LO 3-2, LO 3-3
    a. Each Buy/Sell Transaction involves one Broker.
    b. Each Buy/Sell Transaction involves many Brokers.
    c. Each Buy/Sell Transaction involves a minimum of zero Brokers.
    d. Each Buy/Sell Transaction involves a maximum of many Brokers.
    e. Both a and d are correct.
19. Which of the following is true to implement the Buy/Sell Transactions and Brokers classes and the association between them in the preceding UML class diagram in a database? LO 3-2, LO 3-3, LO 3-4
    a. The primary key of Brokers is a foreign key in Buy/Sell Transactions.
    b. The primary key of Buy/Sell Transactions is a foreign key in Brokers.
    c. The association between Brokers and Buy/Sell Transactions is implemented as a linking table.
    d. Both a and b are true.
    e. None of these is true.
20. Which of the following is true to implement the Stock Exchanges and Brokers classes in the preceding UML class diagram in a database? LO 3-2, LO 3-3, LO 3-4
    a. The primary key of Brokers is a foreign key in Stock Exchanges.
    b. The primary key of Stock Exchanges is a foreign key in Brokers.
    c. The association between Brokers and Stock Exchanges is implemented as a linking table.
    d. Both a and b are true.
    e. None of these is true.
21. Which of the following is not a general category of operational decision? LO 3-5
    a. Eligibility
    b. Accumulation
    c. Validation
    d. Risk
    e. Opportunity
22. Which of the following is not a basic step in modeling process decision requirements? LO 3-5
    a. Identify process steps.
    b. Document decisions and how they impact business objectives.
    c. Decompose and refine requirements.
    d. Specify decision information and knowledge requirements.
    e. Identify required decisions.

Discussion Questions

1. Consider the following one-to-one association between classes. You are mapping the diagram to a set of relational tables. Where would you post the foreign key? Why would you post it there? **LO 3-1, LO 3-2, LO 3-3, LO 3-4**

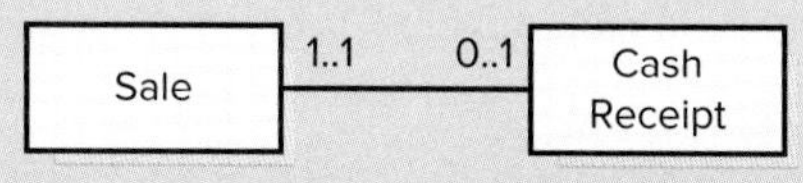

2. Consider the sale and cash receipt classes shown in Discussion Question 1. What kind of business is this (in terms of its payment requirements from customers)? How would the multiplicities change if the business (e.g., a used car dealer) accepted multiple payments over time? **LO 3-1, LO 3-3**
3. Consider the following model and corresponding relational tables. Describe the meaning of the diagram in words. Assume that Students are identified by Student ID Number and Courses are identified by Course Number. List the relational tables that would implement the diagram (you may make assumptions about the nonidentifying fields in the tables). **LO 3-1, LO 3-2, LO 3-3, LO 3-4**

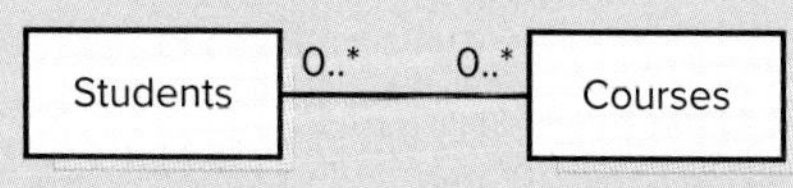

4. How would the following model look if you used a composition relationship? Which is more descriptive? *Hint:* Consider a composition relationship. **LO 3-1, LO 3-2**

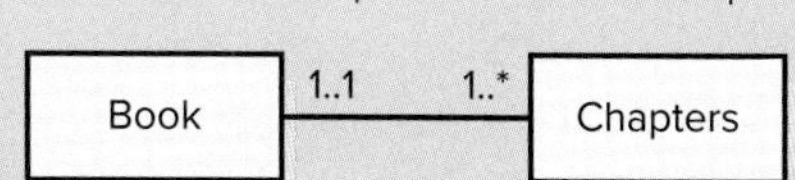

5. Consider the diagram in Discussion Question 4. Identify some examples of classes that would be modeled with a compostion model. Identify some examples of classes that would be modeled with an aggregation relationship model. **LO 3-1, LO 3-2**
6. Think about the process you went through to enroll in this class. What business rules do you think applied to the enrollment process? Are all of these rules written? Why or why not? **LO 3-5, LO 3-6**
7. Think about the last time that you purchased something over the Internet. What did the checkout page look like? What categories of operational decisions do you think were made by the website operator. What business rules applied? **LO 3-5, LO 3-6**
8. Compare the UML class diagram shown in Figure 3.3 with the entity-relationship diagram shown in Figure 3.A2. Describe the differences and the similarities. **LO 3-1, LO 3-2**
9. In your college career, you may have attended several universities. Draw a simple UML class diagram or an entity-relationship diagram showing your relationship with those universities. Now add the multiplicities or cardinalities. Would the multiplicities/cardinalities be different if the diagram was drawn from the university's perspective rather than your perspective? Why or why not? **LO 3-1, LO 3-2, LO 3-3**
10. Describe some real-world examples of (a) one-to-one relationships, (b) one-to-many relationships, and (c) many-to-many relationships. Which do you think is most common? Which does a relational database handle most easily? **LO 3-3, LO 3-4**

Problems

connect

1. Identify the classes and associations in the following narrative, and draw a class diagram with multiplicities: **LO 3-2, LO 3-3**

   Dr. Franklin runs a small medical clinic specializing in family practice. She has many patients. When the patients visit the clinic, she may perform several tests to diagnose their conditions. She bills the patient one amount for the visit plus additional amounts for each test.

connect 2. Identify the classes and associations in the following narrative, and draw a class diagram with multiplicities: **LO 3-2, LO 3-3**

> Paige runs a small frozen yogurt shop. She buys several flavors of frozen yogurt mix from her yogurt supplier. She buys plastic cups in several sizes from another supplier. She buys cones from a third supplier. She counts yogurt and cones as inventory, but she treats the cups as an operating expense and doesn't track any cup inventory.

connect 3. Write out a set of relational tables that correspond to the class diagram that you prepared for Problem 1. Identify primary and foreign keys. **LO 3-4**

connect 4. Write out a set of relational tables that correspond to the class diagram that you prepared for Problem 2. Identify primary and foreign keys. **LO 3-4**

connect 5. Develop a UML class diagram with classes, associations, and multiplicities based on the following narrative: **LO 3-2, LO 3-3**

> The Multnomah County Library provides a variety of services to citizens of the county. First, the library offers a number of traditional books and movies that may be checked out by patrons. Each patron may check out up to 5 books and 2 movies at one time. The library also offers several computers for patron use. The library tracks computer use sessions. Each patron may use the computer for up to 30 minutes per session. The library also maintains a number of small meeting rooms that patrons may reserve for classes or events during normal operating hours. Although library services are offered to all county citizens, each patron must obtain a library card to check out books, use the computers, or reserve a room.

connect 6. Use the UML class diagram you created for Problem 5 to create an Access database for the library. Make up at least three fields for each table, including one field that will be the primary key. **LO 3-4**

Additional problems are available in connect only.

Chapter **Four**

Relational Databases and Enterprise Systems

A look at this chapter

Databases serve as a means of organizing information. We focus on relational databases that store information in tables. We explore relational database principles, including primary and foreign keys, basic requirements of database design, and data retrieval using Structured Query Language (SQL). We also explain enterprise systems (or ERP systems) using a relational database system and their relevance to the organization.

A look back

Chapter 3 described data modeling, explaining how data models support database-driven systems. It introduced basic data modeling tools to guide the student's development of modeling skills. The chapter also provided a discussion of business rules and how identifying relevant business rules supports both process and data modeling.

A look ahead

Chapters 5 through 8 use data models to describe business processes such as sales to cash collection, procurement to pay, and product conversion.

© Tim Boyle/Getty Images

As **Starbucks'** main competitor in the northeast United States, **Dunkin' Donuts** looks to use relational database technology to help determine who ends up on the corner of your block first!

To help it win this race, Dunkin' Donuts is using a new system that helps it more quickly close deals with its new franchisees. Franchisees apply to run a Dunkin' Donuts franchise, pay the franchise fee after the approval process, and then pay royalties on each dollar of sales thereafter. Dunkin' Donuts' management uses the system to manage information about these potential franchisees, including the status of each potential deal and the status of the franchisee financing. This is particularly important in the competition against Starbucks, which doesn't franchise its stores, so its growth isn't delayed by issues with finding suitable franchise operators and getting them signed up to sell coffee in a timely fashion.

Dunkin' Donuts' managers use this dashboard-type system to get a geographic view of regions where deals are stalling; it then has the ability to drill down to see which specific item is slowing down the process. It can identify potential deals in locations that are too close in proximity. Key metrics the company is tracking and monitoring include the average cycle time to complete a franchise deal and the expected size of those deals.

Source: *Informationweek*, 2007, www.informationweek.com/news/global-cio/showArticle.jhtml?articleID=199001001; www.betheboss.ca/franchise_news_april_2007%5Cdunkin-donuts-crm161.cfm.

Chapter Outline

Learning Objectives

After reading this chapter, you should be able to:

4-1 Describe the advantages of relational databases.

4-2 Explain basic relational database principles.

4-3 Describe how to query using Structured Query Language (SQL).

4-4 Understand the purpose and basic framework for an enterprise system.

4-5 Assess how cloud computing facilitates enterprise systems.

INTRODUCTION

A **database** is a collection of related data for various uses. Databases used in a business setting often maintain information about various types of objects (e.g., raw materials inventory), events (e.g., sales transactions), people (e.g., customers), and places (e.g., retail store). In databases today, three types of data models are used: the hierarchical model, the network model, and the relational model.

Hierarchical data models were widely used in mainframe database management systems. Hierarchical data models organize data into a tree-like structure that allows repeating information using defined parent/child relationships. One example of a tree-like structure is financial statements, where a financial statement element (parent) can be decomposed into finer elements (child). More specifically, assets (parent) can be decomposed into current assets (child 1) and noncurrent assets (child 2). Current assets (parent) could be further decomposed into cash and cash equivalents (child 3), accounts receivable (child 4), and inventory (child 5). You can see how the hierarchical relationships define the relationships among the data elements associated with a balance sheet in a tree-like structure. In a hierarchical data model, data elements are related to each other using a notation known as 1:N mapping (one parent: more than one child), also known as one-to-many relationships.

A **network data model** is a flexible model representing objects and their relationships. The network model allows each record to have multiple parent and child records or M:N mapping, also known as many-to-many relationships. These form a lattice structure (often looking like a big net) connecting parent and child records together.

LO 4-1
Describe the advantages of relational databases.

The **relational data model** is a data model that stores information in the form of related two-dimensional tables. It allows designers and users to identify relationships at the time the database is created or much later whenever new informational requirements from the data model are desired. While hierarchical and network data models require relationships to be formed at the database creation, relational data models can be made up as needed.

Relational data models are the dominant data model form in use today, likely because they offer many advantages over other data models, including:

1. ***Flexibility and scalability.*** As business and informational requirements change, relational data models are able to handle these changes quickly and easily. For this flexibility, the relational data model for databases is the most popular data model today.
2. ***Simplicity.*** A relational data model is a relatively simple model that is easy to communicate to both database users and database developers.
3. ***Reduced information redundancy.*** A relational data model requires each piece of data to be recorded only in one place, eliminating the need for information to be stored in multiple places in the organization. This also helps keep the information updated because the information only has to be updated once in one database, which can help avoid data inconsistency.

For the remainder of the chapter, we focus on the use of relational databases.

Definitions for Databases

Before we get into the details of how relational databases are created and used in an organization, it is useful to define a few terms related to databases.

- **Database management system (DBMS)**—The DBMS is defined as a computer program that creates, modifies, and queries the database. Specifically, the DBMS is designed to manage a database's storage and retrieval of information.

- **Data dictionary**—The data dictionary describes the data fields in each database record such as field description, field length, field type (e.g., alphanumeric, numeric), and so on.
- **Database administrator**—The database administrator is responsible for the design, implementation, repair, and security of a firm's database.

Progress Check

1. A database is an organized collection of data for various uses. Name three uses for a sales database at **Bed Bath & Beyond.**
2. Relational data models allow changes to the data model as information needs change. **General Motors** has recently expanded into China and been very successful. How does the use of a relational data model help General Motors' database designers and database users?

FUNDAMENTALS OF RELATIONAL DATABASES

LO 4-2
Explain basic relational database principles.

Entities and Attributes

First, it is important to describe entities and attributes of a relational database. As introduced in Chapter 3, a class (also called an entity) in the relational database model could be a person, place, thing, transaction, or event about which information is stored. Customers, sales, products, and employees are all examples of classes. Classes could be grouped into resources (R), events (E), and agents (A) in data modeling.[1] *Resources* are those things that have economic value to a firm, such as cash and products. *Events* are the various business activities conducted in a firm's daily operations, such as sales and purchases. *Agents* are the people who participate in business events, such as customers and salespeople.

Attributes are characteristics, properties, or adjectives that describe each class. Attributes for customer may include the Customer ID, Customer Last Name, Customer First Name, and Customer Address. Attributes for sales could be Invoice Number, Customer ID, Date, and Product Number. Attributes for products may include Product Number, Product Name, and Product Price.

There are three main constructs in a relational database: tables, attributes, and records. The primary construct is called a table or relation for data storage, with rows and columns much like a spreadsheet. Each table in a database represents either a class or a relationship among classes. Tables need to be properly linked to make a relational database. The columns in a table are called fields and represent the attributes or characteristics of the class or relationship. The rows in a table are called records or tuples. A record represents all the specific data values that are associated with one instance.

Keys and Relationships

Logical relationships within a relational database model are created by using primary keys and foreign keys. A simplistic illustration of a relational database for Gizmos and Gadgets (a reseller of smartphones) appears in Figure 4.1. As defined in Chapter 3, a **primary key (PK)** is an attribute or combination of attributes that uniquely identifies a specific row in a table. Notice the Customer ID in the Customer table is the primary key that uniquely

[1]The REA model was first conceptualized by William E. McCarthy in 1982. See W. E. McCarthy, "The REA Accounting Model: A Generalized Framework for Accounting Systems in a Shared Data Environment," *The Accounting Review,* July 1982, pp. 554–78.

Products of Gizmos and Gadgets.

The McGraw-Hill Companies/Ashley Zellmer, photographer

identifies the customer. In this case, the telephone number of the customer serves as the Customer ID. In Figure 4.1, the primary key that uniquely identifies a sale in the Sales table is the invoice number, and the primary key that uniquely identifies each product in the product table is the product number.

A **foreign key (FK)** in the relational database model serves as an attribute in one table that is a primary key in another table. A foreign key provides a logical

FIGURE 4.1
Illustration of a Relational Database Using Primary Keys and Foreign Keys for Gizmos and Gadgets, a Phone Reseller

Gizmos and Gadgets June 12, 2017 Invoice #13131

To: Mark Wagstaff
168 Apple Rd., Rockville, MD 20852
602-966-1238

Product No.	Description	Price	Amount
1233	Apple iPhone 5g	399.00	399.00
		Order Total	399.00

Customer Table

Customer ID	Customer Last Name	Customer First Name	Customer Address
602-966-1238	Wagstaff	Mark	168 Apple Rd., Rockville, MD 20852
602-251-7513	Waite	Seth	2500 Campanile Dr., NY, NY 10001

Primary Key

Foreign Key

Sales Table

Invoice No.	Customer ID	Date	Product No.
13131	602-966-1238	6/12/17	1233
13945	602-966-1238	8/28/17	1334
14995	602-251-7513	11/21/17	1233
15123	602-251-7513	12/11/17	5151
15127	602-251-7513	12/12/17	3135

Primary Key

Foreign Key

Primary Key

Product Table

Product No.	Product Name	Product Price
1233	Apple iPhone 5g	399.00
1334	Motorola Droid	299.00
1233	Apple iPhone 5g	399.00
5151	iPhone cover	32.00
3135	Apple Charger	23.00

relationship, or a link, between two tables. For example, notice the link between the Customer table and the Sales table by use of the foreign key, Customer ID, in Figure 4.1. Also, notice the link between the Sales table and the Product table by use of the foreign key Product No. in the Sales table.

Basic Requirements of Tables

The approach of relational database imposes requirements on the structure of tables. If these basic requirements are not fulfilled or if data redundancy exists in a database, anomalies may occur. The requirements include the following:

- The **entity integrity rule**—the primary key of a table must have data values (cannot be null).
- The **referential integrity rule**—the data value for a foreign key must either be null or match one of the data values that already exist in the corresponding table.
- Each attribute in a table must have a unique name.
- Values of a specific attribute must be of the same type (example: alpha or numeric).
- Each attribute (column) of a record (row) must be single-valued. This requirement forces us to create a relationship table for each many-to-many relationship.
- All other nonkey attributes in a table must describe a characteristic of the class (table) identified by the primary key.

Progress Check

3. Describe how primary keys and foreign keys link tables in a relational database. *(Hint: Use Figure 4.1 to help describe how they work.)*

USING MICROSOFT ACCESS TO IMPLEMENT A RELATIONAL DATABASE

Introduction to Microsoft Access

Microsoft Access is a program in the Microsoft Office Suite. Access is a simple database management system that can be used to run databases for individuals and small firms. In practice, many larger firms choose more complicated database systems like MySQL server or Microsoft SQL Server. The Access system is composed of seven objects that are used to implement relational databases.

The basic building block of a database is the *table*. A table is used to store data, which consist of a series of rows (records) and columns (attributes) connected by relationships (links between tables). All data stored in the database will be stored in tables. Tables are linked by the use of foreign keys, forming an interconnected network of records that taken together are the relational database.

When users want to find answers to questions in the database, such as "how many customers do I have?" they use **queries**. Queries are a tool used to retrieve and display data derived from records stored within the database. This can range from listing all customers who live in Oregon, which is a subset (dynaset) of records in the customer table, to the balance in Accounts Payable, which must draw data from multiple tables. Calculations and data sorting are often performed with queries.

Forms are utilized by users to enter data into tables and view existing records. In viewing existing records, forms are powered by queries that allow data from multiple tables to be displayed on each form. Often, a firm that uses a fully electronic accounting information system will allow end users to directly update the database through the use of forms.

Reports are used to integrate data from one or more queries and tables to provide useful information to decision makers. Unlike a form, the report does not allow users to edit database information. In an accounting database, reports might consist of a sales invoice to be mailed to customers or the year-end balance sheet to show stakeholders the financial position of the firm. The applications of reports are limited only by data that have been stored in the database.

Access also allows for web-based forms, called **pages**, which allow data to be entered into the database in real time from outside of the database system. This type of application might be used to allow customers to place orders through the firm's website.

For more advanced users, Access offers **macros**. Macros are defined by users to automate processes such as opening a specific form.

Finally, Access's code can be altered by the use of **modules**. Some Microsoft applications come with modules built in that will be automatically added onto Access, like the **PayPal** module that facilitates integration with the organization's PayPal account. Other modules can be coded using Visual Basic script to alter the fundamental processes at the heart of Access.

Steve's Stylin' Sunglasses

Steve's Stylin' Sunglasses (SSS) is a retail store that designs and manufactures custom sunglasses. Every pair of sunglasses Steve, the owner, creates is unique and is therefore fairly expensive to buy. The excellent reputation for quality products and the stellar customer service provided by SSS have attracted new and returning customers.

To promote sales, Steve allows payments to be made periodically over time based on a zero-interest installment plan. However, a down payment is required. Though most customers pay for their sunglasses in full with either cash or credit card, some choose to take advantage of the payment plan option. Steve has noticed that the installment plan is utilized most frequently by customers buying multiple pairs of sunglasses at one time. Steve's policy on installment sales is that each payment from a customer must be clearly marked for one specific sale.

Because Steve is directly supervising two salespeople, who are paid on commission, he prefers to keep all sales separate to facilitate oversight of the revenue cycle. Steve does not collect any data on his customers until they make their first purchase at the store. However, he insists on storing data on every customer because each customer is entitled to free cleanings and adjustments.

Steve handles the bulk of the behind-the-scenes work at the store, including designing the sunglasses. As a result, he employs two salespeople—Frank and Sandra—who deal with the customers. When a customer walks through the door, the first available salesperson greets and assists that customer from the beginning to the end of the transaction, including helping select the best pair of sunglasses and ringing up the sale on the cash register. To that point, Frank and Sandra also act as the company's cashiers, and in that capacity, they take turns making weekly trips to **Bank of America** to deposit the cash receipts. The company has a few bank accounts with Bank of America.

A Data Model and Attributes for Steve's Stylin' Sunglasses' Sales Process

In Figure 4.2, we use a UML class diagram to draft a data model for the sales process of SSS. Notice that an REA data model presents classes in the UML diagram in three general categories: resources, events, and agents.

The central column in Figure 4.2 includes two events (i.e., business activities)—Sales and Cash Receipt. The Sales event conducted by SSS involves one resource (Inventory)

FIGURE 4.2
The Data Model for Sales Process of Steve's Stylin' Sunglasses

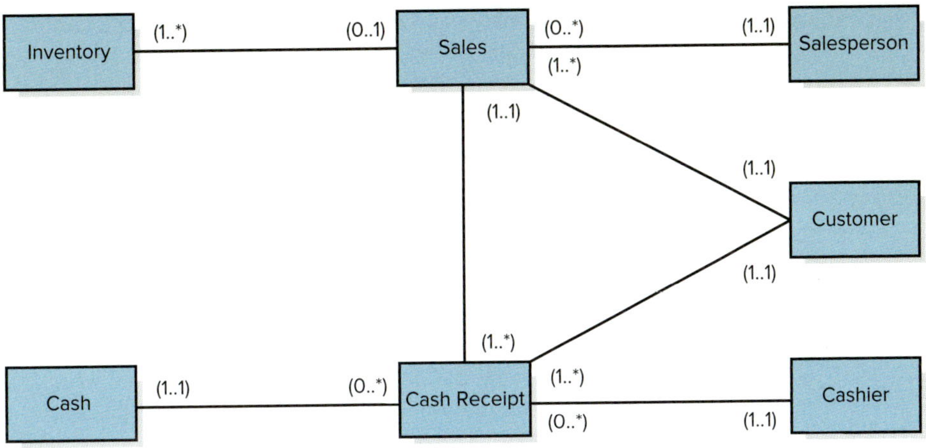

and two agents (Salesperson and Customer). The Cash Receipt event involves one resource (Cash) and two agents (Cashier and Customer). The two events are related. One would decrease the resource of SSS (selling inventories), which leads to the other that would increase the recourse of SSS (collecting cash). They are economic events involving exchanging resources with external agents (i.e., customers).

Please notice that the class Cash contains information of the bank accounts that SSS has. You can consider Cash as Bank Accounts in the diagram. To simplify, you may also consider each record in the Cash Receipt event as a check from a customer.

Multiplicities in Steve's Stylin' Sunglasses' Data Model

Figures 4.3, 4.4, and 4.5 explain the multiplicities regarding the sales event of Steve's Stylin' Sunglasses.

FIGURE 4.3
Explanations on Multiplicities Related to the Sales Event

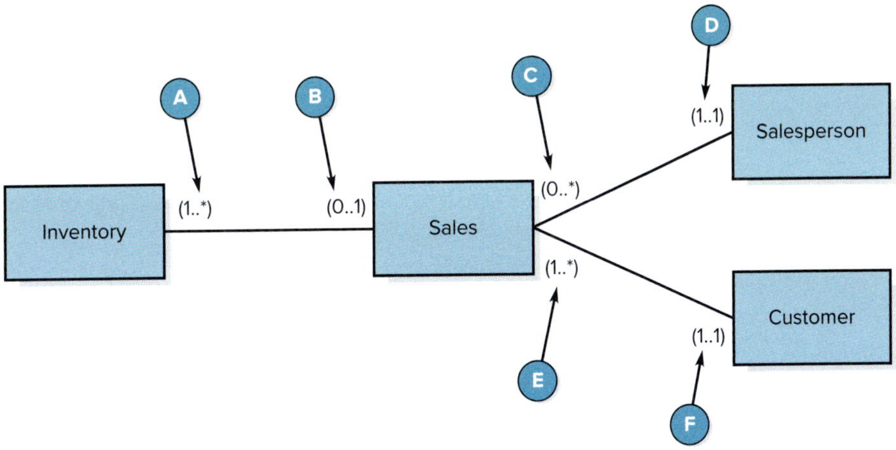

(A) SSS may sell more than one pair of sunglasses to a customer at one time.

(B) Every pair of sunglasses SSS creates is unique and could be sold once only. Zero means a pair of sunglasses could be designed but not yet sold.

(C) The shop employs two employees who can act as salespersons. At a minimum, a salesperson (new) may not handle any sale transaction yet, and at most, each salesperson could handle many sale transactions.

(D) One and only one salesperson greets and assists a customer from the beginning to the end of a sale transaction.

(E) SSS has repeat customers. Customer data are recorded after the first purchase.

(F) Each sale involves one and only one customer.

FIGURE 4.4
Explanations on Multiplicities Related to the Cash Receipt Event

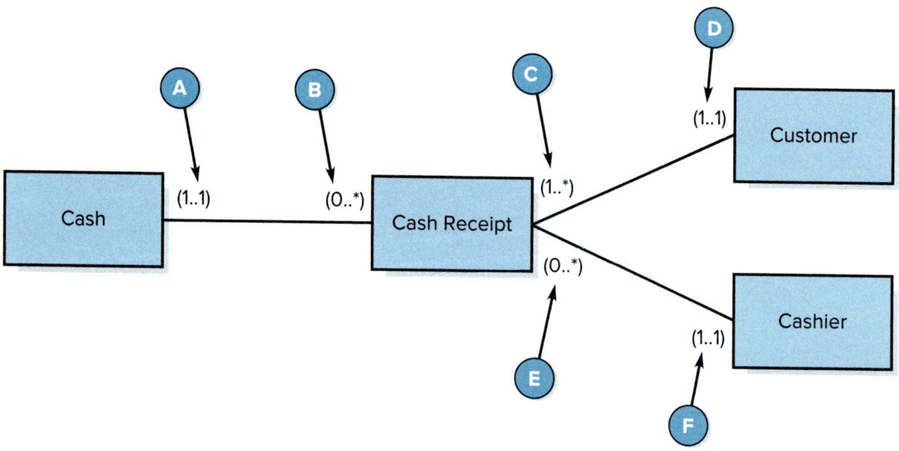

(A) Each cash receipt is deposited in one and only one bank account.

(B) Each bank account could have no deposit or many deposits from the cash receipt event.

(C) Each customer has the option for an installment plan (i.e., SSS will have many cash receipts from one customer). The "1" means a down payment is required.

(D) Each cash receipt is from one and only one customer.

(E) The shop employs two employees who can act as cashier. A cashier (new) may not handle any cash receipt yet, or a cashier could take charge of many cash receipts.

(F) Each cash receipt (e.g., a check from a customer) is handled by one and only one cashier.

FIGURE 4.5
Explanations on Multiplicities between the Sales and Cash Receipt Events

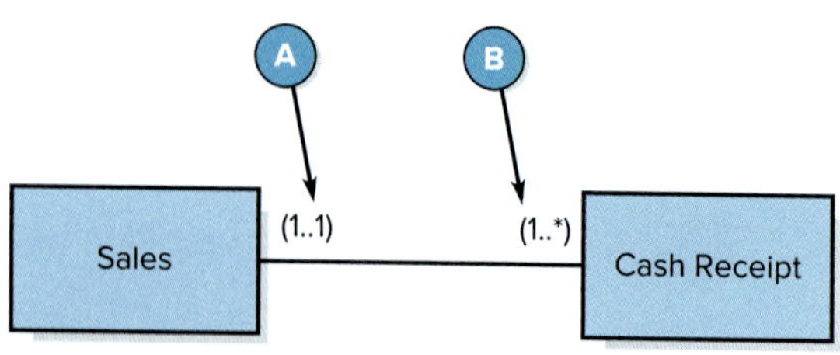

(A) Each cash receipt is for one and only one sale transaction.

(B) Each sale transaction may have at least one cash receipt (i.e., a down payment is required), and at most many cash receipts from customers (i.e., installment sales).

Given the data model in Figure 4.2, we assume the following attributes for each table.

Customer	[Customer_Number (PK), Customer_First_Name, Customer_Last_Name, Customer _Address, Customer_City, Customer_State, Customer_Zip, Customer_Email]
Salesperson	[Salesperson_Number (PK), Salesperson_First_Name, Salesperson_Last_Name, Salesperson_SSN]
Cashier	[Cashier_Number (PK), Cashier_First_Name, Cashier_Last_Name, Cashier_SSN]
Sales	[Sale_Number (PK), Sale_Date, Sale_Amount, Payment_Type, Customer_Number (FK), Salesperson_Number (FK)]
Cash_Receipt	[Receipt_Number (PK), Receipt_Date, Receipt_Amount, Customer_Number (FK), Cashier_Number (FK), Sale_Number (FK), Account_Number (FK)]
Cash	[Account_Number (PK), Bank_Name, Bank_Address, Bank_Contact_Person, Balance]
Inventory	[InventoryID_Number (PK), Description, Completion_Date, Cost, Price, Sale_Number (FK)]

Using Access to Implement a Simple Database for Steve's Stylin' Sunglasses

Getting Started in Access

Step 1. Open Access.

Step 2. Access will ask you to choose from available templates. Select "Blank database" (see Figure 4.6).

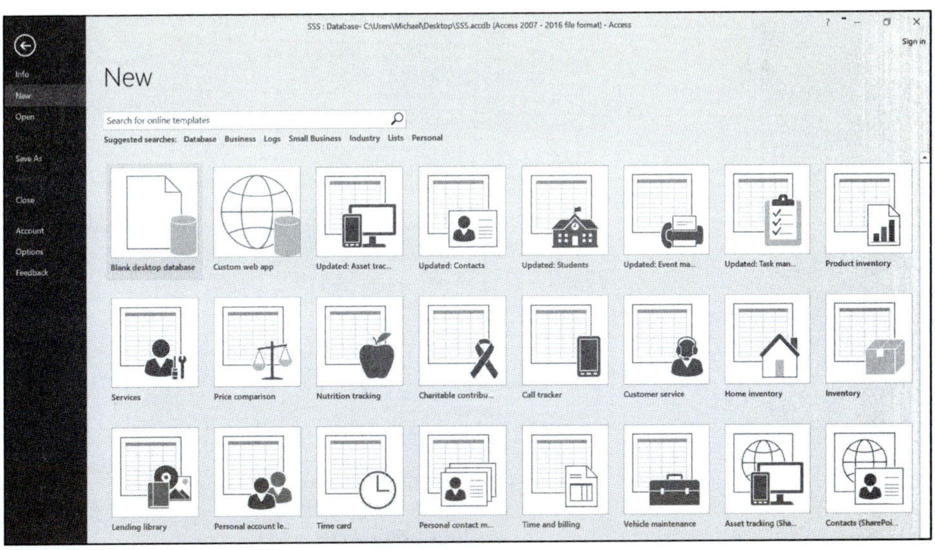

FIGURE 4.6
Starting Access

© Microsoft Access

Step 3. To change the name of the database, click File → Save Database As; then save the database as "SSS." You will likely get a message saying "All objects must be closed before you save the database" (see Figure 4.7). Click "Yes."

Step 4. Ensure that the ribbon marked "Enable content" is enabled.

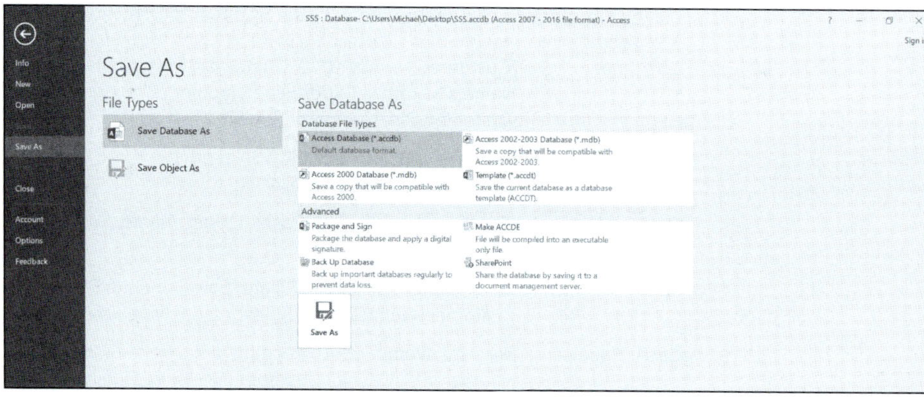

FIGURE 4.7
Save a Database in Access

Creating New Tables in Access

Refer to the tables and attributes designed based on the data model (Figure 4.2). This is the database we will be constructing. The first table is the Customer table.

Step 1. Click the tab Create → Table (see Figure 4.8). (Note: The Table Design button will create a table and open it in Design View. See Figure 4.9.)

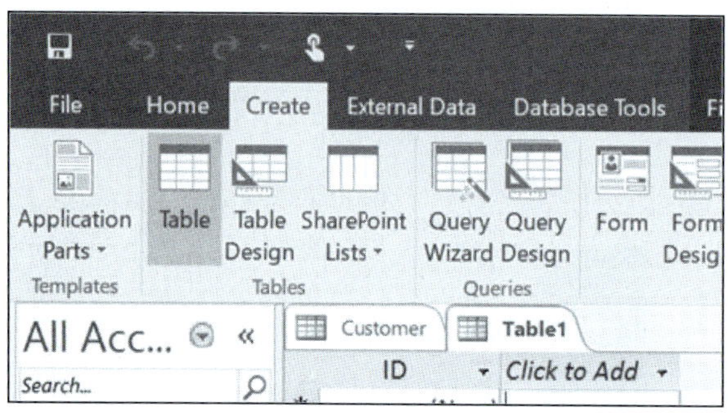

FIGURE 4.8
Create a Table in Access

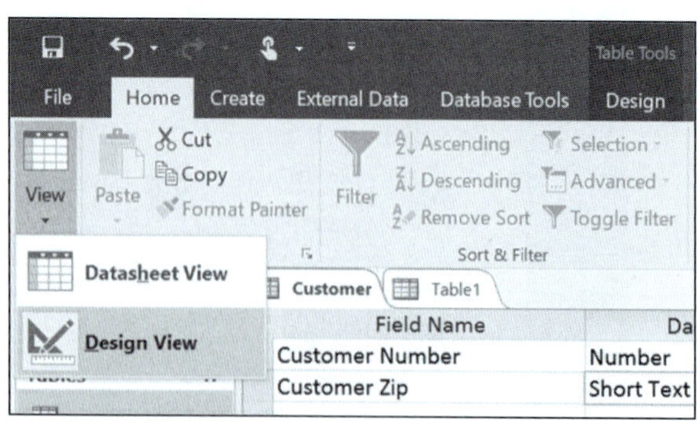

FIGURE 4.9
Create a Table in Design View

Step 2. Click the tab Home → View (dropdown menu) → Design View (see Figure 4.9).

Step 3. You will be prompted to Save As, so save the table as "Customer." This table will contain the records of Steve's Stylin' Sunglasses' customers. Note the Field Name, Data type, and Description columns. You will use these to configure the Customer table (see Figure 4.10).

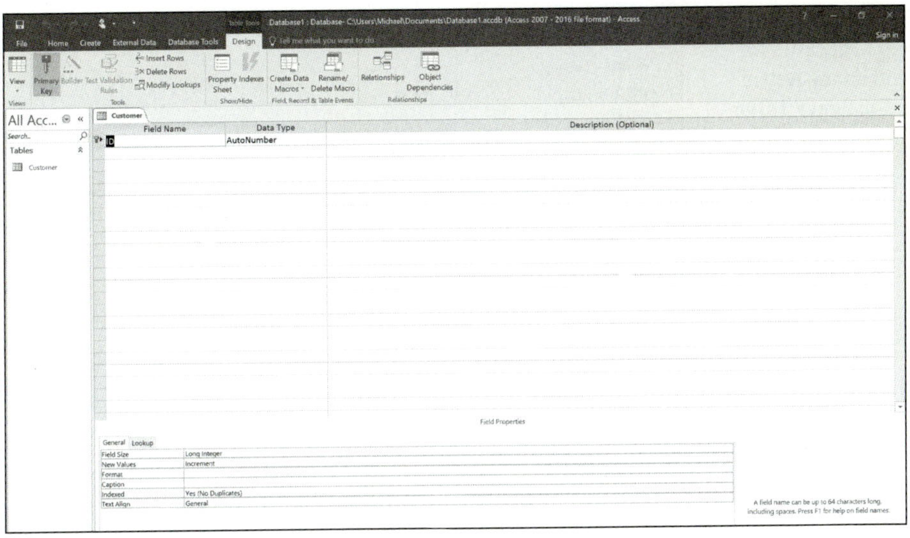

FIGURE 4.10
The Design View of the Customer Table

Step 4. The first attribute of the Customer table will be its primary key. Currently, the primary key is named ID. Highlight ID in the Field Name column and change it to "Customer Number." A field name names an attribute in a table. It may contain 64 characters and may not contain periods, exclamation points, or brackets because they are used in Visual Basic scripts. You should see a key icon next to the Customer Number (see Figure 4.11). If it is not there, right click and select "Primary Key" or look for the primary key button on the design tab of the ribbon.

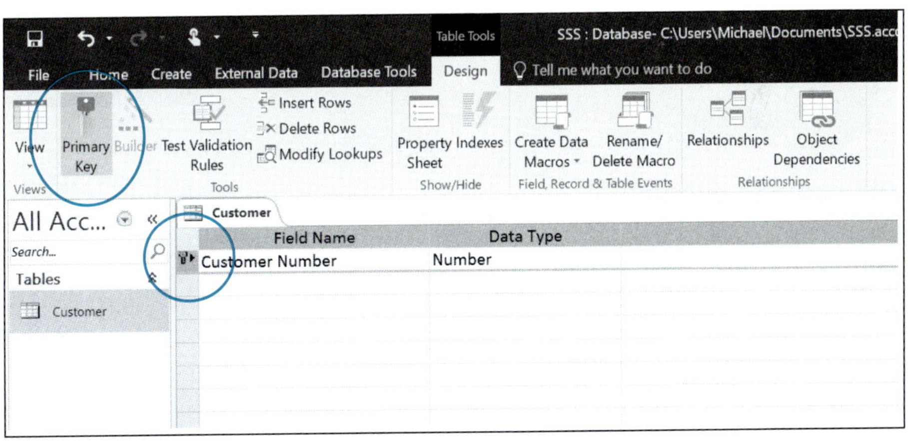

FIGURE 4.11
Create the Primary Key of the Customer Table

Step 5. Click on the dropdown button for the Data Type and select Number. This will force any data entered into this field to be in the form of a number. Take some time to familiarize yourself with the options on this menu. Description field (Figure 4.10), when used, allows useful information about the attribute to be provided to users.

Step 6. It is a good practice to set Field Properties for each attribute. For example, for Customer Number, we would set the Field Size to Long Integer and the Validation Rule to Like "######". By doing so, we will ensure that all Customer Numbers are six digits long (i.e., six pound signs). The Validation Text of "Customer # should be 6 numbers" provides an error message to tell users what they did wrong. Because this is a primary key, choose the Required field as "Yes" and the Indexed field as "Yes (No Duplicates)" (see Figure 4.12).

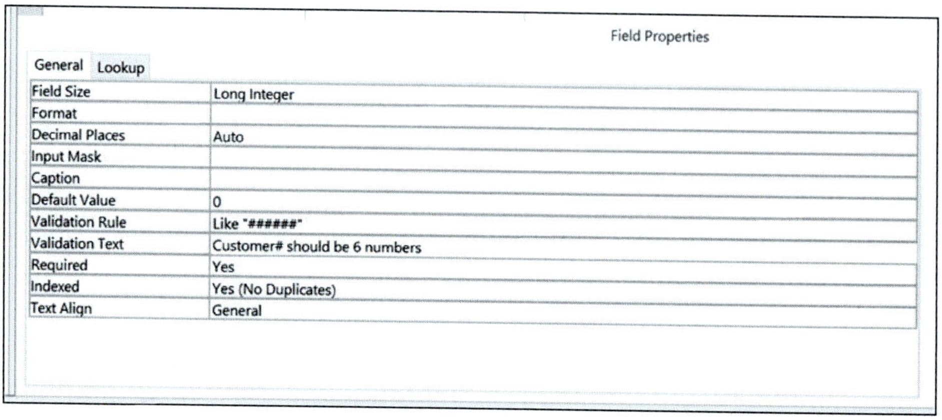

FIGURE 4.12
Field Properties for the Primary Key of the Customer Table

© Microsoft Access

Step 7. For some fields, it is appropriate to use an Input Mask. For example, Customer Zip should have an Input Mask. To do this, select the attribute Customer Zip and click in the Input Mask area in the Field Properties box. You will see to the right a button with ". . ." on it. Click this button to bring up the Input Mask Wizard window as shown in Figure 4.13. Select Zip Code from the menu and click Next and Finish.

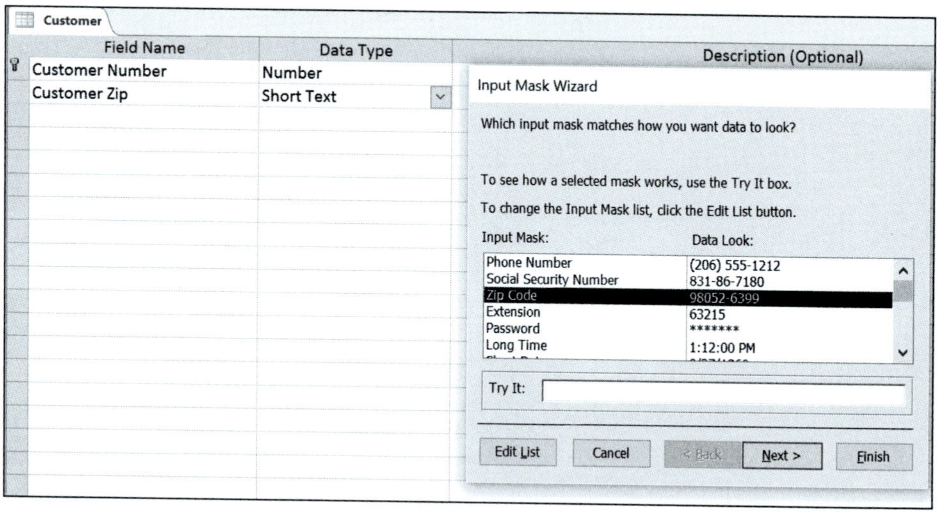

FIGURE 4.13
Input Mask for Customer Zip Field

© Microsoft Access

Step 8. Create the rest of the tables and attributes given before, using appropriate data types and properties. Generally, validation rules are used for primary keys. The attributes of the Sales table are shown in Figure 4.14. For other fields such as Sale Date in the Sales table, you will also use Input Masks.

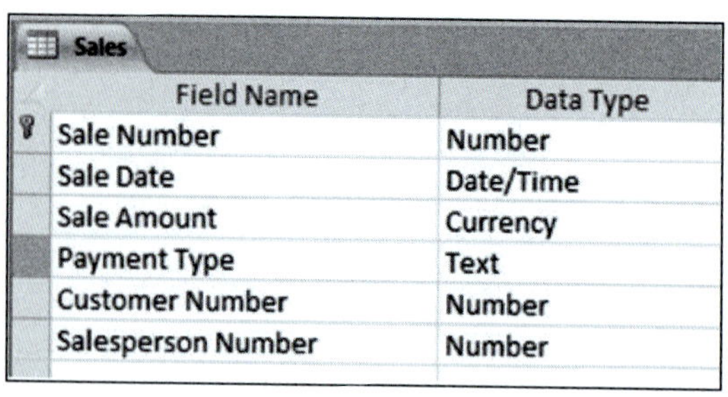

FIGURE 4.14
Attributes of the Sales Table

© Microsoft Access

Creating Relationships in Access

In order to implement a relationship in Access, you must use a foreign key. Note that the names of the two fields (the primary key in one table and the foreign key in the other table) do not have to be the same. You will create links between these similar fields in Access' Relationship window.

Step 1. To pull up the Relationship window, click Database Tools → Relationships (see Figure 4.15).

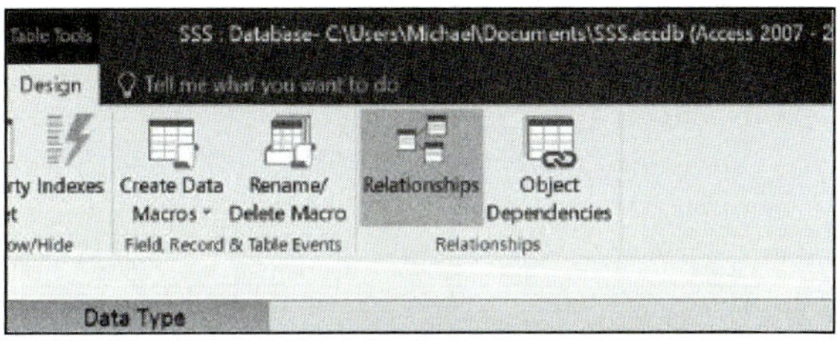

FIGURE 4.15 **Open the Relationship Window in Access**

© Microsoft Access

Step 2. Click the Show Table button in the Design tab to pull up a list of all your tables. Select all your tables and press the Add button. Arrange the tables in the form similar to the data model.

Step 3. Click each primary key that you want to link and drag it to its respective foreign key in another table. Be sure to check the "Enforce Referential Integrity" box for each relationship (see Figure 4.16).

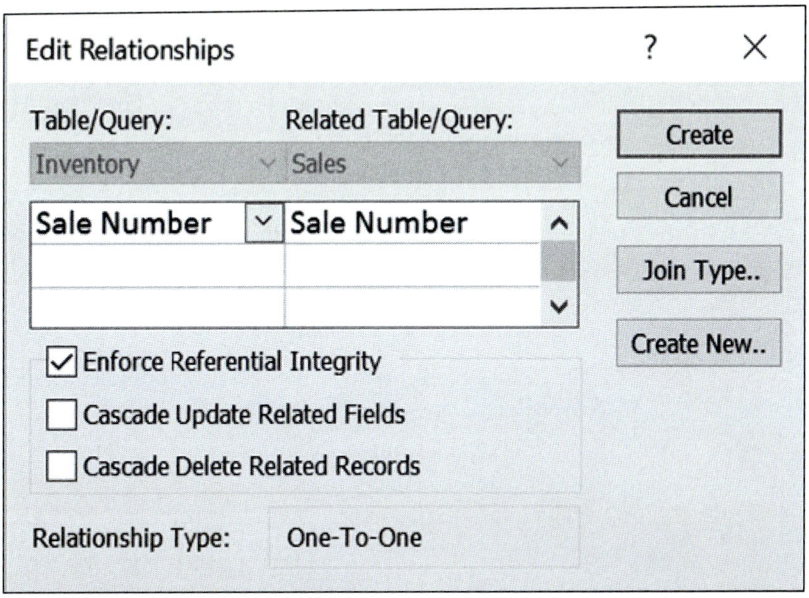

FIGURE 4.16 **Enforce Referential Integrity in Linking Tables**

© Microsoft Access

Step 4. Upon completion of this process for all relationship among the tables, the Relationship window should look like Figure 4.17. A referential database has been created in Access for Steve's Stylin' Sunglasses.

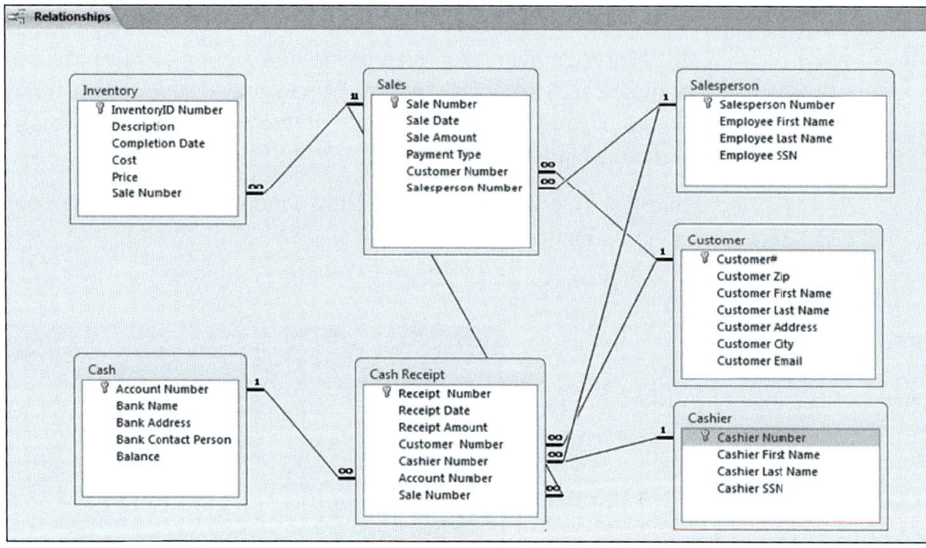

FIGURE 4.17 A Database for Steve's Stylin' Sunglasses

STRUCTURED QUERY LANGUAGE (SQL)

LO 4-3 Describe how to query using Structured Query Language (SQL).

SQL (usually pronounced "Sequel") stands for **Structured Query Language** and is a computer language designed to query data in a relational database. SQL is based on relational algebra and allows a user to query and update the database. In a database, while queries allow the user to access, read, and report on desired data, the responsibility of actually making physical changes to the relational database belongs to the database management system (DBMS). The four most basic operations—Create, Read, Update, and Delete (CRUD)—must be supported in a DBMS. SQL provides the "INSERT" operator (i.e., a command) to create new records, the "SELECT" operator to read or retrieve data, the "UPDATE" operator to update records, and the "DELETE" operator to delete existing records from the database.

The SELECT operator is used to begin a query. The SELECT operator tells the query which columns (or attributes) of a table should be included in the query result. A query includes a list of columns in the final result immediately following the SELECT operator. An asterisk (*) can also be used to specify that the query should return all columns of the queried tables. SELECT is the most useful operator in SQL, with optional keywords and clauses that include the following:

1. The FROM clause to the SELECT operator indicates the name of table(s) from which to retrieve data.

SQL Example 1: Given the attributes in the Customer table in Figure 4.18, how is a query used to find the salesperson for each customer?

FIGURE 4.18 Customer

Customer#	Name	A/R Amt	SP#
C-1	Bill	345	E-12
C-2	Mick	225	E-10
C-3	Keith	718	E-10
C-4	Charlie	828	E-99
C-5	Ron	3,200	E-10

If we use the following SQL commands, we are asking SQL to select the Customer#, Name, and SP# attributes from the Customer Table:

SELECT Customer#, Name, SP#

FROM Customer;

We will get the following query result (Figure 4.19):

FIGURE 4.19

Customer#	Name	SP#
C-1	Bill	E-12
C-2	Mick	E-10
C-3	Keith	E-10
C-4	Charlie	E-99
C-5	Ron	E-10

2. The WHERE clause states the criteria that must be met to be shown in the query result. There are many search criteria that you can specify for the final result. Search criteria using relational operators, the BETWEEN operator, and the LIKE operator are very common in SQL commands (Figure 4.20).

FIGURE 4.20
Cash Receipt

Remittance Advice#	Amount	Bank Account#	Date	Customer Number	Cashier Number
RA-1	1,666	BA-6	25-JUL-2017	C-2	E-39
RA-2	10,000	BA-7	26-JUL-2017	C-2	E-39
RA-3	72,000	BA-7	15-AUG-2017	C-1	E-39
RA-4	32,600	BA-7	15-AUG-2017	C-5	E-39
RA-5	1,669	BA-6	25-AUG-2017	C-2	E-39

SQL Example 2:

If we use the following SQL command, we are asking SQL to retrieve all cash receipt information for customer C-2 from the table called "Cash Receipt."

SELECT *

FROM [Cash Receipt]

WHERE [Customer Number] = 'C-2';

Please note that the asterisk (*) following the SELECT SQL statement is a wild card indicating all columns should be selected. The brackets are needed following the FROM and WHERE clauses because there are spaces in the table and attribute names. In addition, if any table name or attribute name contains one or more spaces, we have to use brackets such as [Cash Receipt] to make sure it is considered as one table or one attribute in SQL.

We will get the following query result (Figure 4.21):

FIGURE 4.21

Remittance Advice#	Amount	Bank Account#	Date	Customer Number	Cashier Number
RA-1	1,666	BA-6	25-JUL-2017	C-2	E-39
RA-2	10,000	BA-7	26-JUL-2017	C-2	E-39
RA-5	1,669	BA-6	25-AUG-2017	C-2	E-39

Notice the WHERE command eliminated those rows that did not have Customer Number equal to C-2.

SQL Example 3: Assume you would like to use a query to find the salesperson for each customer, and you would like to show the name of each salesperson as part of the result. Data are presented in Figures 4.22 and 4.23.

Customer#	Name	A/R Amt	SP#
C-1	Bill	345	E-12
C-2	Mick	225	E-10
C-3	Keith	718	E-10
C-4	Charlie	828	E-99
C-5	Ron	3,200	E-10

FIGURE 4.22
Customer

SP#	SP_Name
E-10	Howard
E-12	Pattie
E-34	Stephanie
E-99	David

FIGURE 4.23
Salesperson

If we use the following SQL commands, we are asking SQL to select the Customer#, Name, SP#, and SP_Name attributes from the Customer table and Salesperson table:

```
SELECT Customer#, Name, SP#, SP_Name
FROM Customer, Salesperson
WHERE Customer.SP#=Salesperon.SP#;
```

It is critical that we include WHERE here to link two tables. SP# is a foreign key in the Customer table. We use it to link the Salesperson table with the Customer table.

We will get the following query result (Figure 4.24):

FIGURE 4.24

Customer#	Name	SP#	SP_Name
C-1	Bill	E-12	Pattie
C-2	Mick	E-10	Howard
C-3	Keith	E-10	Howard
C-4	Charlie	E-99	David
C-5	Ron	E-10	Howard

The above example shows a "one to many" relationship. That is, each customer is served by a salesperson and each salesperson can serve many customers.

3. The GROUP BY operator is used with aggregate functions on the query results based on one or more columns.

SQL Example 4: Refer to the Cash Receipt table in SQL Example 2 (Figure 4.20). Assume you would like to know the total cash receipt amount from each customer. If you use the following SQL commands, you can get the result.

```
SELECT [Customer Number], SUM(Amount)
FROM [Cash Receipt]
GROUP BY [Customer Number];
```

The query results will be (Figure 4.25):

FIGURE 4.25

Customer Number	Amount
C-2	13,335
C-1	72,000
C-5	32,600

4. The ORDER BY clause identifies which columns are used to sort the resulting data. If there is no ORDER BY clause, the order of rows returned by a SQL query will not be defined.

   SQL Example 5: Refer to the Cash Receipt table in SQL Example 2 (Figure 4.20). If we use the following SQL commands instead, the amount of cash receipt would be ordered in ascending amount (ASC) or descending amount (DESC). The result (Figure 4.26) is different from that of Example 2.

   SELECT *

   FROM [Cash Receipt]

   WHERE [Customer Number] = 'C-2'

   ORDER BY Amount ASC;

FIGURE 4.26

Remittance Advice#	Amount	Bank Account#	Date	Customer Number	Cashier Number
RA-1	1,666	BA-6	25-JUL-2017	C-2	E-39
RA-5	1,669	BA-6	25-AUG-2017	C-2	E-39
RA-2	10,000	BA-7	26-JUL-2017	C-2	E-39

5. The INSERT INTO operator inserts data into a SQL table. For example, you can insert a row into the Cash Receipt table with the following SQL commands:

   INSERT INTO [Cash Receipt]

   VALUES ('RA-6', 5000, 'BA-7', '28-AUG-2017', 'C-2', 'E-39');

   After insertion, the Cash Receipt table will have one more row and the result of the execution is as follows (Figure 4.27):

FIGURE 4.27
Cash Receipt

Remittance Advice#	Amount	Bank Account#	Date	Customer Number	Cashier Number
RA-1	1,666	BA-6	25-JUL-2017	C-2	E-39
RA-2	10,000	BA-7	26-JUL-2017	C-2	E-39
RA-3	72,000	BA-7	15-AUG-2017	C-1	E-39
RA-4	32,600	BA-7	15-AUG-2017	C-5	E-39
RA-5	1,669	BA-6	25-AUG-2017	C-2	E-39
RA-6	5,000	BA-7	28-AUG-2017	C-2	E-39

6. The UPDATE operator is for updating data in a SQL table. For example, you can use the following SQL UPDATE command to change the Amount value from 5000 to 6000 for the inserted entry of RA-6. You often need to use the command SET for the updated data value.

   UPDATE [Cash Receipt]

   SET Amount = 6000

   WHERE [Remittance Advice#] = 'RA-6';

7. The DELETE FROM operator deletes data from a SQL table. For example, to delete the entry previously inserted, you can use the following SQL commands:

   DELETE FROM [Cash Receipt]

   WHERE [Remittance Advice#] = 'RA-6';

   After executing the DELETE command, the record of Remittance Advice# 'RA-6' will be deleted from the Cash Receipt table, and the table will look the same as the original one.

8. The SELECT DISTINCT clause selects a column without showing repetitive values.

   SQL Example 6: Refer to the Cash Receipt table in SQL Example 2(Figure 4.20). You can retrieve each customer number once from the Cash Receipt table with the following command:

   SELECT DISTINCT [Customer Number]

   FROM [Cash Receipt];

   You will get the following query result (Figure 4.28):

FIGURE 4.28

Customer Number
C-2
C-1
C-5

9. The BETWEEN operator can be used to specify the end points of a range. Possible criteria can be "WHERE Amount BETWEEN 1000 AND 2000" or "WHERE Date BETWEEN '01-JAN-2017' AND '31-DEC-2017'." Assuming that you are interested in finding out cash receipt entries made in July, then you can issue the following SQL command to retrieve those entries.

   SELECT *

   FROM [Cash Receipt]

   WHERE Date BETWEEN '01-JUL-2017' AND '31-JUL-2017'

   The query result will be (Figure 4.29):

FIGURE 4.29

Remittance Advice#	Amount	Bank Account#	Date	Customer Number	Cashier Number
RA-1	1,666	BA-6	25-JUL-2017	C-2	E-39
RA-2	10,000	BA-7	26-JUL-2017	C-2	E-39

10. Membership Operator (IN) allows you to test whether a data value matches the specified target values.

    SQL Example 7: Refer to the Cash Receipt table in SQL Example 2 (Figure 4.20). Assume you would like to know the total cash receipt amount from customers C-1 and C-2. If you use the following SQL commands, you can get the result shown in Figure 4.30, which is different from that of Example 4.

    SELECT [Customer Number], SUM(Amount)

    FROM [Cash Receipt]

    WHERE [Customer Number] IN ('C-1', 'C-2')

    GROUP BY [Customer Number];

    The query results will be:

FIGURE 4.30

Customer Number	Amount
C-1	72,000
C-2	13,335

In addition, there are six relational operators in SQL. Their definitions are listed here:

Relational Operators	Meaning
=	equal
! = or < >	not equal
<	less than
< =	less than or equal to
>	greater than
> =	greater than or equal to

Given the data in Figure 4.20, if you are interested in those entries with an amount ≥10000, you can use the following SQL commands.

```
SELECT *
FROM [Cash Receipt]
WHERE Amount > = 10000;
```

You will get the following query result back (Figure 4.31):

FIGURE 4.31

Remittance Advice#	Amount	Bank Account#	Date	Customer Number	Cashier Number
RA-2	10,000	BA-7	26-JUL-2017	C-2	E-39
RA-3	72,000	BA-7	15-AUG-2017	C-1	E-39
RA-4	32,600	BA-7	25-AUG-2017	C-5	E-39

SQL language provides several convenient aggregate functions to be used in SQL commands. These aggregate functions include AVG, SUM, MAX, MIN, and COUNT. Their definitions are as follows:

- AVG(X): gives the average of column X.
- SUM(X): gives the summation of all rows that satisfy the selection criteria for column X.
- MAX(X): gives the maximum value of column X.
- MIN(X): gives the minimum value of column X.
- COUNT(X): gives the number of rows that satisfy the given condition.

To query the total amount and average amount from the Cash Receipt table, use

```
SELECT SUM(Amount), AVG(Amount)
FROM [Cash Receipt];
```

To query the largest amount entry from the Cash Receipt table, use

```
SELECT MAX(Amount)
FROM [Cash Receipt];
```

To query the total amount that occurred in July from the Cash Receipt table, use

```
SELECT SUM(Amount)
FROM [Cash Receipt]
WHERE Date BETWEEN '01-JUL-2017' AND '31-JUL-2017';
```

SQL create commands, update commands, and many other SQL query commands as well as SQL functions are beyond the scope of this textbook. See, for example, www.w3schools.com/sql/ for a list of popular SQL query commands.

Progress Check

4. What does the SQL command SELECT * do?
5. What SQL command would you use to order an amount in descending order?
6. What SQL commands would you use if you wanted to query transactions made in July from the Cash Receipt table?

LO 4-4
Understand the purpose and basic framework for an enterprise system.

ENTERPRISE SYSTEMS

Before enterprise systems were developed, each function within the organization (finance, accounting, human resources, procurement, manufacturing, etc.) had its own information system that met its own needs. However, imagine the challenge for a company like **General Motors** to predict, budget, and manage its costs for producing a new Corvette! The company would have to get production information from the manufacturing database, costs from the accounting database, and labor information and costs from the human resources database and attempt to integrate them. Because of these types of problems and the power of integrated information, enterprise systems were developed, including major, commercial enterprise systems such as SAP/ERP, Oracle ERP, and Microsoft Dynamics.

In fact, for a popular ERP product (SAP/ERP) installation, there are more than 10,000 tables that are all linked to each other!

Enterprise systems (ESs), also known as enterprise resource planning (ERP) systems, are commercialized information systems that integrate and automate business processes across a firm's value chain located within and across organizations. Typically, an enterprise system uses a relational data model as a basis for the information system. The use of primary and foreign keys links the hundreds of tables that form the basis for the enterprise system.

As mentioned in Chapter 1, ESs accommodate the integration and support of the various business processes and information needs of a company by integrating multiple modules to help a manufacturer or other business manage the important parts of its business, including product planning, parts purchasing, inventory maintenance, supplier interaction, customer service, and order tracking. ESs can also include application modules for the accounting, finance, and human resources aspects of a business. ESs are applicable to all types of businesses. In fact, most universities now use enterprise systems to manage course registration and student accounts (including the payment of library fines and parking tickets!).

Figure 4.32 offers a list of potential modules available from SAP. You can quickly see the breadth of the offering that would come from a typical enterprise systems vendor.

Managers (and auditors) can trace the creation of information throughout business processes and also identify the participants in each process. Therefore, ES has a higher level of internal transparency compared to the typically isolated legacy systems. For example, once one user from the sales department enters a customer order, users from the inventory department can see this information immediately and begin to process the customer order. At the same time, users from the accounting department can use this information to prepare the customer invoice and recognize revenue once it has been earned. Database transactions in ES are often designed to track specific details of any given business transaction, including who entered the data into the system, who modified it, and who actually used it.

FIGURE 4.32
List of Modules Available from SAP

List of SAP Modules Available for Implementation	
Financial Applications	
FI	Financial Accounting
CO	Controlling
EC	Enterprise Controlling
IM	Investment Management
PS	Project System
Human Resources	
PA	Personnel Administration
PT	Personnel Time Management
PY	Payroll
Logistics Applications	
SD	Sales and Distribution
MM	Materials Management
PP	Production Planning and Control
LE	Logistics Execution
QM	Quality Management
CS	Customer Service

The purported informational benefits of an enterprise system include enhanced completeness, transparency, and timeliness of information needed to manage effectively an organization's business activities.[2]

The enterprise system serves as the backbone of the company's internal business processes and serves as a connection with the external business processes for supply chain and customer relationship management systems.

Challenges of Enterprise System Implementation

Although the standard enterprise system software is packaged and technically sound, all types of challenges emerge from both a technical and organizational perspective when it comes time to custom-fit the software to a particular organization's needs. More specifically, organizations face many challenges in implementing enterprise systems, including the following:

1. Integrating various modules within the enterprise system.
2. Integrating with external systems such as the information system of a supplier and/or customer.
3. Integrating with the firm's own existing legacy systems.
4. Converting data from existing legacy systems to the enterprise system.
5. Getting any big project implemented at a firm. This might include scope creep (i.e., increasing the number of changes to the software initially planned), cost overruns, time delays, and so on. In addition, this means getting adequate training for employees and getting them to actually adopt the new software when they might feel their old system seemed to meet their needs just fine.

These challenges can be overwhelming and some are specifically addressed in Chapter 16. Here, we provide an illustration of a few of the high-profile examples of firms that had failed or challenged enterprise system implementations, as well as the resulting damage inflicted on the firm:

[2]H. Klaus, M. Rosemann, and G. G. Gable, "What Is ERP?," *Information Systems Frontiers* 2, no. 2 (2000), p. 141.

Hershey was not able to deliver Hershey Kisses for Halloween in 1999 right after the first attempt to implement its enterprise system.
© JILL JARSULIC/KRT/Newscom

1. **Hershey**

   Hershey spent $115 million on a failed enterprise system implementation attempt of SAP R/3, Siebel CRM, and Manugistics supply chain applications during the Halloween season, which caused huge candy disruptions in 1999. This failed attempt prevented Hershey from delivering $100 million worth of Hershey Kisses for Halloween that year, causing a third-quarter sales drop of 12.4 percent. Earnings that year were off by 18.6 percent (compared with the previous year), and that caused the stock price to fall by 8 percent.

2. **Nike**

   In 2000, a $400 million i2 upgrade to **Nike**'s supply chain and enterprise systems gave the shoe and athletic company $100 million in lost sales, a 20 percent stock dip, and a collection of class-action lawsuits.

3. **Hewlett-Packard (HP)**

   In 2004, **HP**'s enterprise system implementation went awry. Gilles Bouchard, then-CIO of HP's global operations, said, "We had a series of small problems, none of which individually would have been too much to handle. But together they created the perfect storm." The project eventually cost HP $160 million in order backlogs and lost revenue—more than five times the project's estimated cost.

4. **Enterprise System Failure at a University**

   During fall semester 2004, more than 27,000 students at the University of Massachusetts, Stanford University, and Indiana University were unable to find their classes and unable to collect their financial aid checks due to a flawed ERP system. However, after a couple frustrating days and weeks, everyone eventually got their checks and class schedules![3]

5. **Fox Meyer**

   Fox Meyer, once the nation's fourth-largest distributor of pharmaceuticals, blamed its enterprise system fiasco as the reason for its bankruptcy in 1996.

6. **Shane Co.**

   Shane Co., the family-owned jewelry retailer that sought bankruptcy in 2009, told a U.S. judge that the company's decline was triggered partly by delays and cost overruns for a $36 million SAP AG enterprise system.

Enterprise Systems Computing in the Cloud

LO 4-5
Assess how cloud computing facilitates enterprise systems.

Providing sufficient computing power in an organization to run an enterprise system can be challenging. In recent years, **cloud computing** has emerged as a potential alternative to host enterprise systems and other firm computing needs. Cloud computing is Internet-based computing, where shared resources, software, and information are provided to firms on demand. Just like an electrical grid can handle electricity needs on the fly, cloud

[3] www.cio.com/article/486284/10_Famous_ERP_Disasters_Dustups_and_Disappointments.

computing can handle computing needs on the fly. Cloud computing is simply a set of pooled computing resources that are delivered over the Internet.

Cloud computing can easily host enterprise system applications. Enterprise system applications can quickly scale to the requirements of the computing task by making hundreds of servers and related resources available when they are required. When using cloud computing, firms do not need to worry about buying more computers to meet increasing computing traffic demands or about huge computing traffic spikes. They will simply pay for the computing power they use, much like you pay for the amount of electricity you use in your home or work.

Cloud computing, of course, has disadvantages as well. Ensuring that any sensitive data are secure and backed up frequently by the host is often a concern of cloud computing clients. Making sure the host has minimal down time and adequate processing speed at all times are also concerns. But perhaps the biggest concern is that cloud computing requires the client to have a constant Internet connection. If, for some reason, the Internet connection goes down, the system will not function. This represents an obvious downside on a firm's business that uses cloud computing for its interfaces with their enterprise system.

Progress Check

7. Why are enterprise systems so much better than legacy systems that firms are willing to invest the time, money, and effort to risk implementing such systems?
8. From Figure 4.32, which SAP modules would an accounting firm implement to track its billable hours for the audit staff?

Summary

- Relational databases offer efficient, effective databases for a firm. Their flexibility and scalability along with their simplicity offer powerful advantages for a firm and its information systems.
- Relational databases rely on primary and foreign keys to link tables.
- Structured Query Language (SQL) is used with relational databases to query the database.
- Enterprise systems are based on relational databases and link many different modules and functions of the firm to give integrated information to the firm's management and workers throughout the firm.
- Cloud computing is a recent innovation that could host a firm's enterprise systems such as SAP's cloud-based ERP software Business ByDesign.

Key Words

attributes (*85*) Data elements that describe instances in a class, very much like fields in a database table; characteristics, properties, or adjectives that describe each class.

cloud computing (*104*) Internet-based computing, where shared resources, software, and information are provided to firms on demand; using redundant servers in multiple locations to host virtual machines.

data dictionary (*85*) Describes the data fields in each database record such as field description, field length, field type (e.g., alphanumeric, numeric), etc.

database (*84*) A shared collection of logically related data for various uses.

database administrator (*85*) The person responsible for the design, implementation, repair, and security of a firm's database.

database management system (DBMS) (*84*) A computer program that creates, modifies, and queries the database. Specifically, the DBMS is designed to manage a database's storage and retrieval of information.

enterprise system (ES) (*102*) A centralized database that collects data from throughout the firm. Commercialized information system that integrates and automates business processes across a firm's value chain located within and across organizations.

entity integrity rule (*87*) The primary key of a table must have data values (cannot be null).

foreign key (FK) (*86*) Attribute that allows database tables to be linked together; foreign keys are the primary keys of other tables placed in the current table to support the link between the two tables.

form (*87*) Forms are utilized by users to enter data into tables and view existing records.

hierarchical data model (*84*) Organizes data into a tree-like structure that allows repeating information using defined parent/child relationships.

macro (*88*) Macros are defined by Access users to automate processes such as opening a specific form.

module (*88*) Some Microsoft applications come with modules built in that will be automatically added onto Access.

network data model (*84*) A flexible model representing objects and their relationships; allows each record to have multiple parent and child records or M:N mapping, also known as many-to-many relationships.

pages (*88*) Access pages allow data to be entered into the database in real time from outside of the database system.

primary key (PK) (*85*) An attribute or a combination of attributes that uniquely identifies an instance of a class in a data model or a specific row in a table.

query (*87*) Query in Access is a tool used to retrieve and display data derived from records stored within the database.

referential integrity rule (*87*) The data value for a foreign key must either be null or match one of the data values that already exist in the corresponding table.

relational data model (*84*) Stores information in the form of related two-dimensional tables.

report (*88*) Reports in Access are used to integrate data from one or more queries and tables to provide useful information to decision makers.

Structured Query Language (SQL) (*96*) A computer language designed to retrieve data from a relational database.

Answers to Progress Checks

1. There could be different answers for this question. Three possible answers are as follows:
   a. Which **Bed Bath & Beyond** products are selling the best.
   b. Which products the company needs to advertise or which need a price reduction.
   c. How many of which product to order for tomorrow, next week, and next month from its suppliers.
2. If relational data models are not used, database designers and database users have to predict information uses in the future, even when their business model (the way they make money) changes. This is one of the key reasons relational data models (and relational databases) are used.
3. The primary key of one table serves as a foreign key in another table. When they are matched together, they are able to link two distinct tables in preparation for querying, updating, or modifying.
4. The SQL statement "SELECT *" requests that all columns in a table be selected for use in the query.

5. The SQL clause "ORDER BY Amount DESC" would be used.
6. The following SQL commands should be used.

```
SELECT *
FROM [Cash Receipt]
WHERE Date BETWEEN '01-JUL-2014' AND '31-JUL-2014';
```

7. The power of integration of the various modules and functions (e.g., accounting, marketing, procurement, manufacturing, etc.) across the organization makes an enterprise system particularly valuable to not only management, but also to workers throughout the enterprise.
8. The SAP module PT Personnel Time Management appears to be the most applicable module for tracking billable hours for the audit staff.

Appendix A

Creating a Form for Data Entry and Display

Forms are utilized to enter data into tables and view existing records. This appendix provides a tutorial to create a simple form for Steve's Stylin' Sunglasses (SSS) to enter customer information into the Customer table and display the customer records one by one.

Step 1. Open the SSS database in Microsoft Access.

Step 2. Display all the tables on the left-hand side of the database window, and highlight the Customer table. Click on the Form Wizard icon in the form section of the Create tab (Figure 4.A1).

FIGURE 4.A1
Create a Form in Access

© Microsoft Access

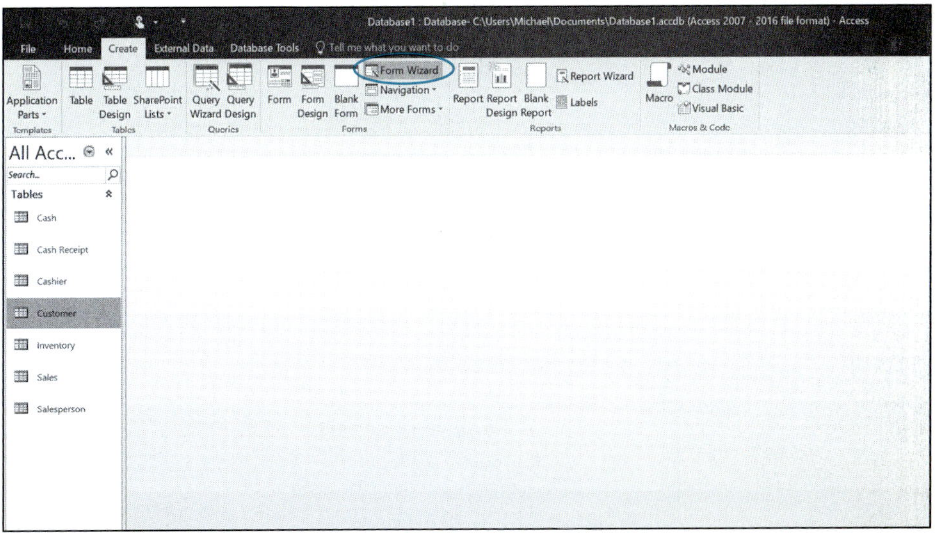

Step 3. In the pop-up Form Wizard window, select Customer table from the Table/Queries pull-down menu, and select all seven fields for inclusion in the form (Figure 4.A2).

FIGURE 4.A2
Select Fields Using Form Wizard

© Microsoft Access

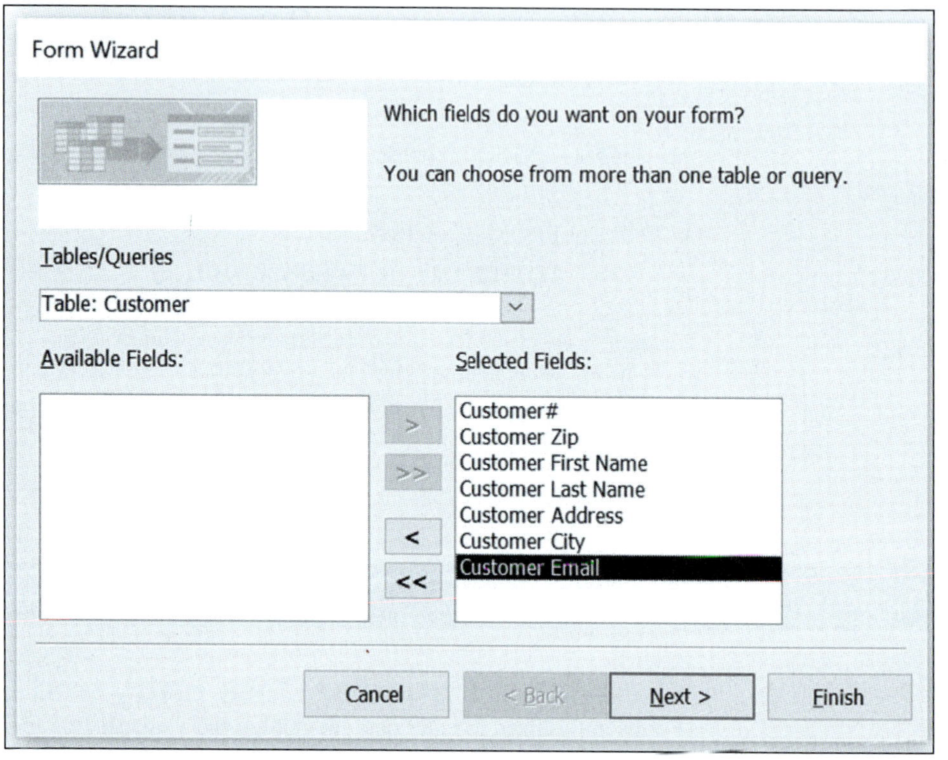

Step 4. Click the Next button. You will see four types of form layouts. Choose "Columnar" as the form layout (Figure 4.A3).

FIGURE 4.A3
Select a Layout Using Form Wizard

© Microsoft Access

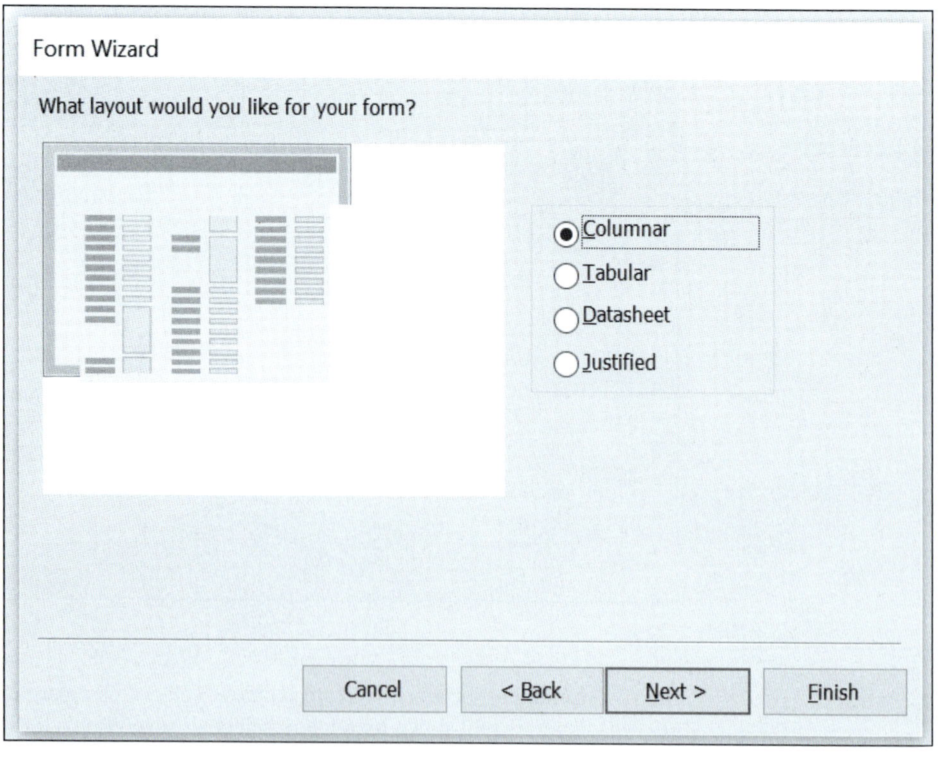

Step 5. Click the Next button. Name the title of the form "Customer Form" and select "Modify the form's design" as indicated in Figure 4.A4. Click Finish and a screen resembling Figure 4.A5 will appear.

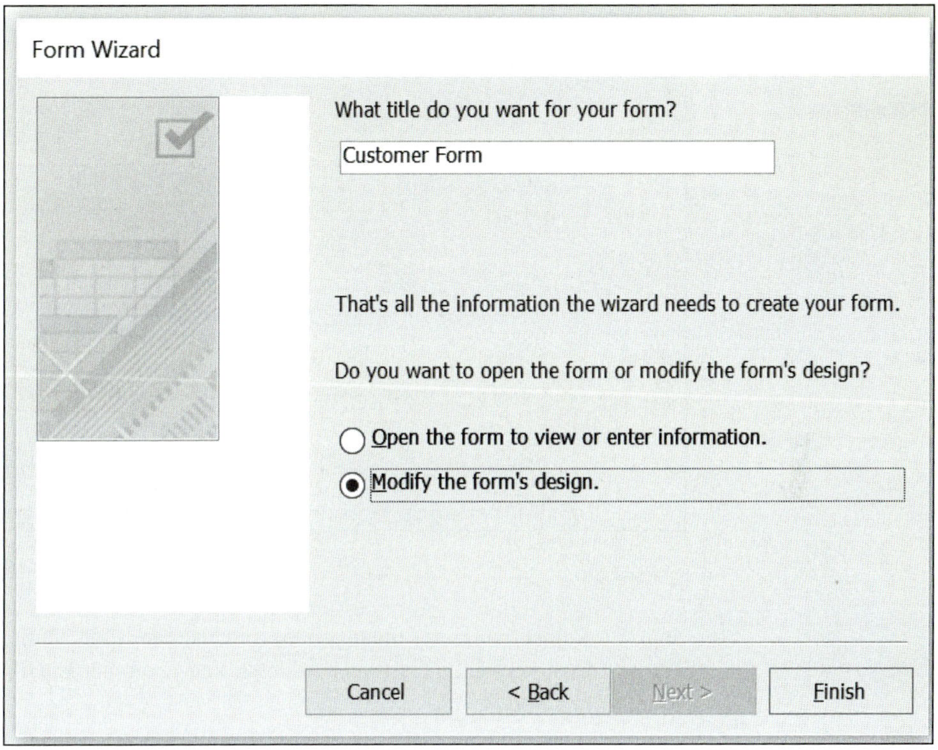

FIGURE 4.A4
Give a Title to the Form

© Microsoft Access

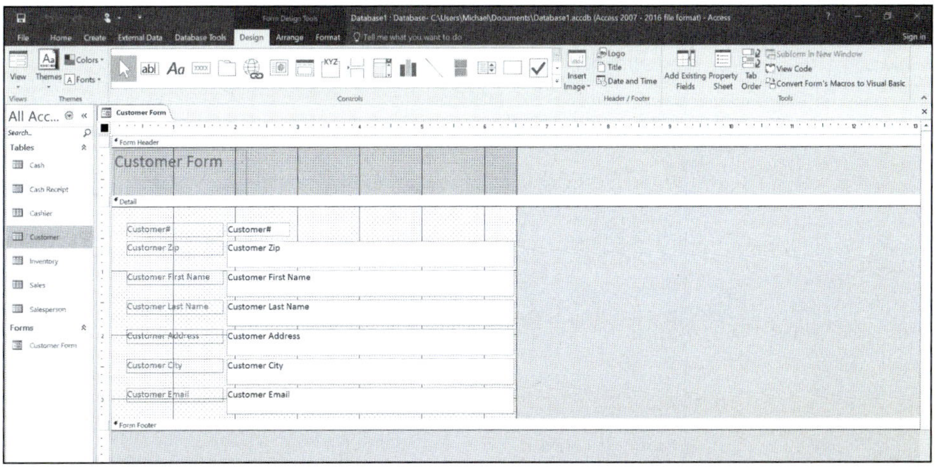

FIGURE 4.A5
Draft a Customer Form

© Microsoft Access

Step 6. Figure 4.A5 is the design view of the Customer Form in which you can format the form. The Customer Zip text field looks too wide. Select the Customer Zip field and resize it (Figure 4.A6).

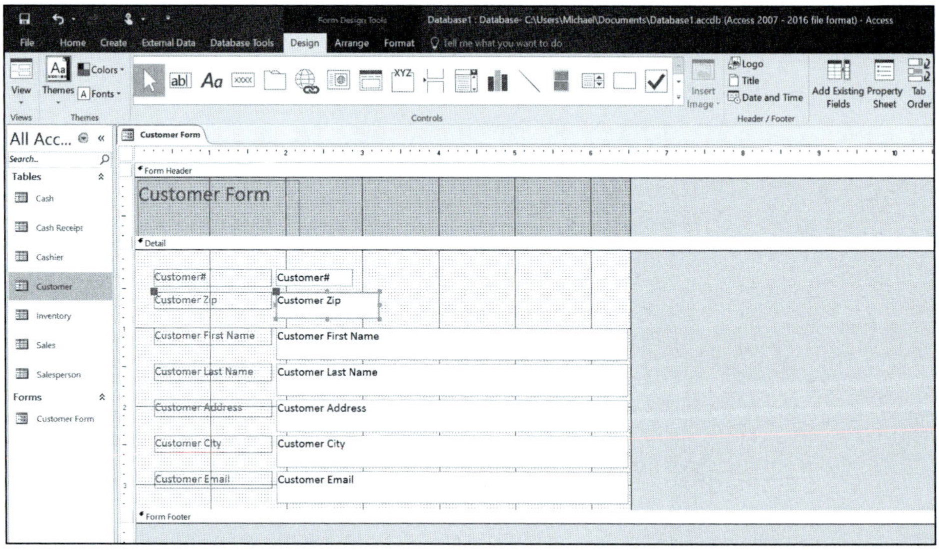

FIGURE 4.A6
Modify the Customer Form

© Microsoft Access

Step 7. Adjust the size of the text field for Customer First Name, Customer Last Name, Customer City, Customer Address, and Customer Email. Make the form look like Figure 4.A7.

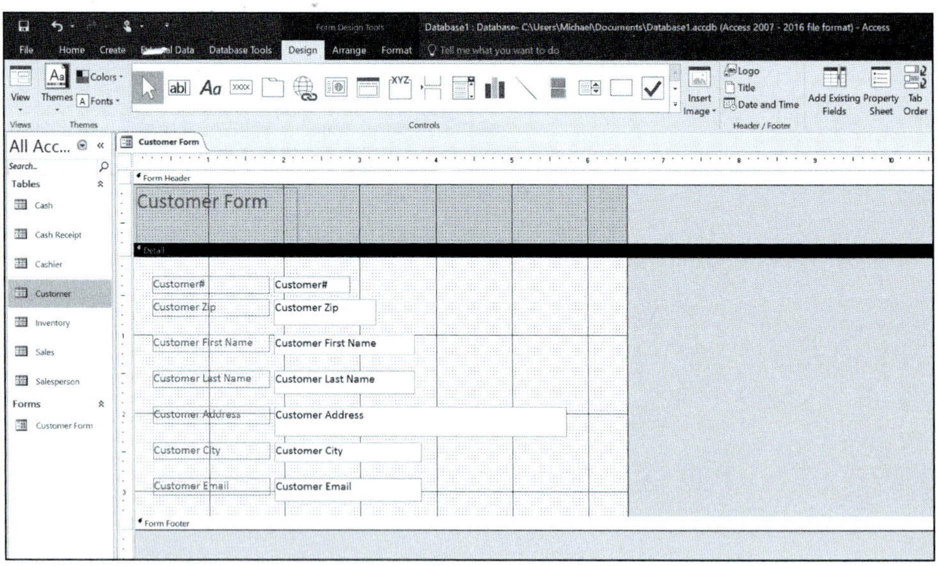

FIGURE 4.A7
Continue Modifying the Customer Form

© Microsoft Access

Step 8. In order to enter data using the form, we need to switch to Form View. Click on the Form View icon in the View section of the File tab (Figure 4.A8).

FIGURE 4.A8
Switch from the Design View to the Form View

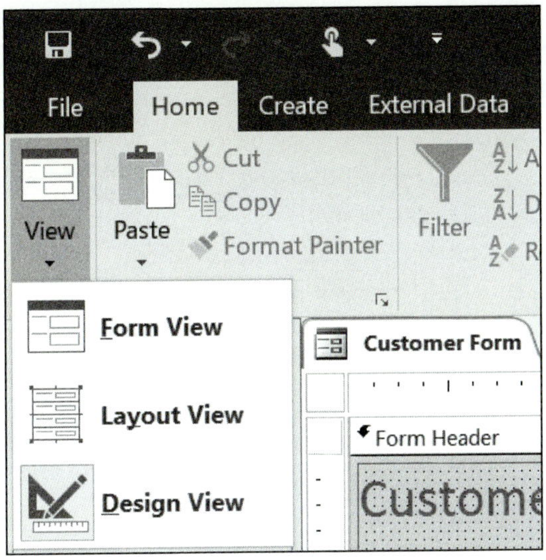

Step 9. In Form View, enter a new customer record as follows—Customer Number: 100001, Customer First Name: John, Customer Last Name: Smith, Customer Address: 2105 East Main Street, Customer Zip: 80202-4781, Customer City: Denver, Customer Email: Joh_S@gmail.com. If you would like to add the second record using this form, click on the triangle symbol icon on the record line at the bottom of the Customer Form. It will display another blank page for data entry.

Step 10. Close and save the Customer Form. Double-click on the Customer table on the left-hand side of the database window to open the table. You will see the new record has already been entered into the Customer table (Figure 4.A9).

FIGURE 4.A9
Form View of the Customer Form

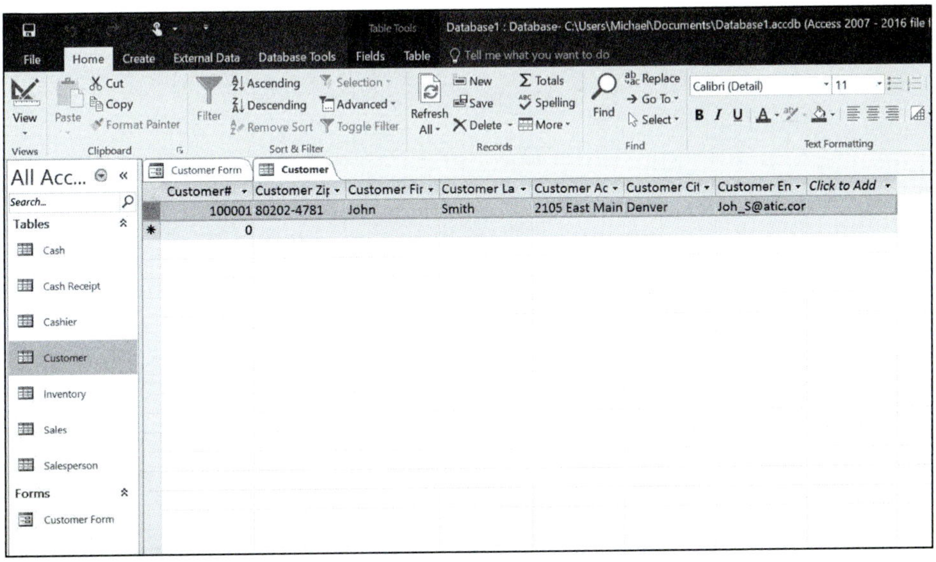

Step 11. Save and close the SSS file.

In this exercise, you learned how to create a form to enter customer information into the Customer table (steps 2 to 7) and how to review customer information one by one using the form (step 9).

connect

Multiple Choice Questions

1. In the hierarchical data model, the mapping from parent to child is: **LO 4-2**
   a. 1:1 (one-to-one).
   b. 1:N (one-to-many).
   c. N:N (many-to-many).
   d. N:1 (many-to-one).
2. Advantages of relational data models generally include: **LO 4-1**
   a. reduced information redundancy.
   b. low cost.
   c. ease of implementation.
   d. efficiency.
3. A class in a relational database model is defined as: **LO 4-2**
   a. the sum of a whole.
   b. characteristics or properties of a table.
   c. person, place, thing, transaction, or event about which information is stored.
   d. being or existence, especially when considered as distinct, independent, or self-contained.
4. Which statement about enterprise systems is correct? **LO 4-4**
   a. Most enterprise systems are designed mainly for accounting and finance functions.
   b. **SAP, Oracle**, and **Microsoft** all offer products for enterprise systems.
   c. Most enterprise systems are designed for the service industry.
   d. Small companies do not use enterprise systems at all.
5. Refer to Figure 4.2; if Steve's Stylin' Sunglasses accepts installments without requiring a down payment, the multiplicities between Sales and Cash Receipts should be changed to: **LO 4-2**
   a. Sales (0..1) - (1..*) Cash Receipts.
   b. Sales (1..1) - (0..*) Cash Receipts.
   c. Sales (1..1) - (1..1) Cash Receipts.
   d. Sales (0..*) - (1..1) Cash Receipts.
   e. None of the above is correct.
6. The FROM clause to the SELECT statement used in SQL indicates: **LO 4-3**
   a. the name of the table(s) from which to retrieve data.
   b. the name of the column(s) from which to retrieve data.
   c. the name of the database(s) from which to retrieve data.
   d. the name of the query from which to retrieve data.
7. The WHERE clause to the SELECT statement used in SQL states the criteria that must be met: **LO 4-3**
   a. to run a query.
   b. to be included as an attribute in the table.
   c. to be included in the database.
   d. to be shown in the query result.

8. The "ORDER BY Amount ASC" clause to the SELECT statement used in SQL suggests that: **LO 4-3**
   a. the amount of the query result will be listed in ascending order.
   b. the amount of the query result will be listed in descending order.
   c. the data attribute ASC be shown in order.
   d. none of the above.
9. SAP modules available for implementation include: **LO 4-4**
   a. Payroll, Personnel Time Management, and Enterprise Management.
   b. Payroll, Financial Accounting, and Enterprise Management.
   c. Financial Accounting, Payroll, and Sales and Distribution.
   d. Sales and Distribution, Financial Accounting, and Procurement.
10. Cloud computing: **LO 4-5**
   a. takes energy from the sun and clouds.
   b. is Internet-based computing, where shared resources, software, and information are provided to firms on demand.
   c. requires a firm to make an extensive investment in hardware and software to meet firm needs.
   d. can meet computing needs today but is not expected to meet tomorrow's computing needs.
11. What kind of relationship does a network data model represent? **LO 4-1**
   a. One-to-one relationship
   b. One-to-many relationship
   c. Many-to-one relationship
   d. Many-to-many relationship
12. Which of the following is a valid primary key for a cash receipt table? **LO 4-2**
   a. Purchase order number
   b. Check number
   c. Cash receipt number
   d. Receipt amount
13. Which of the following is used in SQL to begin a query? **LO 4-3**
   a. BEGIN
   b. SELECT
   c. INPUT
   d. INSERT
14. The GROUP BY operator in SQL is used to: **LO 4-3**
   a. aggregate functions on the query results based on one or more columns.
   b. identify which columns are used to sort the resulting data.
   c. state the criteria that must be met to be shown in the query result.
   d. indicate the name of the table from which to retrieve data.
15. When using Microsoft Access, the main function of "Table" is to: **LO 4-2**
   a. store data.
   b. report data.
   c. retrieve data.
   d. analyze data.

Discussion Questions

1. Explain the differences among hierarchical, network, and relational data models. What makes the relational data model the most popular data model in use today? LO 4-1
2. What are the basic requirements of a relational database? LO 4-2
3. Structured Query Language (SQL) is used to retrieve data from a database. Why would an accountant need to learn SQL? LO 4-3
4. Figure 4.32 lists the modules available from SAP. List and explain which modules would be most appropriate for either Maytag or a manufacturing company you are familiar with. LO 4-4
5. Given the description of Hershey's failed enterprise system implementation from the chapter, which of the four challenges of the enterprise system described in the chapter seem to best explain what happened? Use Google or Yahoo! to get more details on this case to help answer this question. LO 4-4

Problems

Cash

Account#	Type	Bank	Balance
BA-6	Checking	Boston5	253
BA-7	Checking	Shawmut	48,000
BA-8	Draft	Shawmut	75,000
BA-9	Checking	Boston5	950

connect 1. Use the Cash table above to show the output for the following SQL query:

```
SELECT Account#, Balance
FROM Cash
WHERE Balance < 50000;
```

connect 2. Use the Cash table above to show the output for the following SQL query:

```
SELECT Account#, Balance
FROM Cash
WHERE Bank = 'Boston5'
ORDER BY Amount DESC;
```

connect 3. Use the Cash table above to write a SQL query to show a list of checking accounts. Hint: Filter the results on the Type field.

connect 4. Use the Cash table above to write a SQL query to show the total of all of the balances. Hint: Use the SUM function.

5. Consider the UML diagram used to model Steve's Stylin' Sunglasses' (SSS) sales data. Draw a new UML diagram assuming that SSS sells mass-produced brand-name sunglasses instead of custom sunglasses.

connect 6. Think about data collected and used by Netflix. LO 4-1, LO 4-2
   a. Identify three tables that would contain customer or subscription data.
   b. For each table identified in a, list five attributes (you may include primary and foreign keys as well as non-key attributes).
   c. Describe each attribute using elements from a data dictionary (e.g., description, field length, field type, etc.).
   d. Why would Netflix be interested in storing and tracking these attributes (e.g., to enhance customer service or future customer sales, to sell more affiliated products to customers, etc.)?

7. Cloud computing has plenty of appeal for many firms, especially those that have immense computing needs. Why do you think some might be reluctant to have their data and computing power originating from the cloud? LO 4-5

8. Use the **Access_Practice.accdb** database to complete the following tasks in Access. LO 4-2
   a. The database contains three tables containing information about this company's sales process: Inventory, Sales, and SalesItems. Use the Relationships window to link the tables together.
   b. The SalesItems table records the quantity and price of each item sold on each sale (sales may include more than one item). Calculate the extended amount of sale (call it Amt) for each item (Quantity * UnitPrice). Include InvoiceID, InventoryID, Quantity, and UnitPrice in the query. Name the query Item_Extension_Calculation.
   c. Calculate the total dollar amount of *each sale*. Include InvoiceID, InvoiceDate, CustomerID, and EmployeeID from the Sales table and the Amt from the Item_Extension_Calculation query. Name the query Sale_Amount_Calculation.
   d. Calculate total sales for *each inventory item*.
   e. Calculate *total sales*.
   f. Calculate the month in which each sale occurred. Include InvoiceID and InvoiceDate from the Sales table. Name the query Sales_Months. *(Hint:* Look for the Month function in the expression builder.)
   g. Calculate the sum of sales for each month.
9. This problem continues Problem 8. Use the **Access_Practice.accdb** database that you have been working on to complete the following tasks. LO 4-2
   a. Go to the Relationships screen and connect the five tables, enforcing referential integrity.
   b. Calculate the total sales for each customer. Include CustomerID and CompanyName from the Customer table and the calculated sale amount from the Sale_Amount_Calculation query. Name the query Total_Customer_Sales.
   c. Generate an e-mail user name for each employee using the first letter of the employee's first name and the first five letters of the employee's last name, e.g., Rod Smith = > rsmith. Include EmployeeID, EmployeeFirstName, and EmployeeLastName in the query. Name the query Employee_Email_Generator.
   d. Calculate the total sales for each month.
   e. Determine which customer had the highest average sales amount. *(Hint:* Sort in descending order.)
   f. Assume the employees earn a 5 percent commission on sales. Calculate the total commission due to each employee. Use two queries to do these calculations.

Background for Problems 10 to 14

Ellen Novotny started an online bookstore in 2017. You are Ellen's best friend and promised to help her. Ellen asked you to create a small database to track the information on books and authors. You created the following tables: Author, Book, and Author_Book. The table Author_Book is a relationship table to link the Author table and Book table because of the many-to-many relationship between the two tables. That is, each author may write many books and each book may have multiple authors. In general, each customer can purchase many books in a single transaction. Also, copies of the same book can be sold to different customers. Once an order is processed, the books are shipped right away. Based on these tables you have (see below), help Ellen to extract the information she needs from the database.

Author

Author ID	Last Name	First Name	Email	Phone number
AU-1	Adams	Eric	Eric168@yahoo.com	(714) 833-2419
AU-2	Brown	Jennifer	jenifferb@gmail.com	(619) 596-0012
AU-3	Davis	Keith	keithd@gmail.com	(212) 342-5680
AU-4	Newport	Kevin	kevinn@hotmail.com	(301) 947-7741
AU-5	Pham	John	johnpham@gmail.com	(617) 645-3647
AU-6	Sviokla	Julia	jsviokla@yahoo.com	(805) 498-1688

Book

Book ID	Title	Area	Year	Edition	Publisher
B-1	Accounting Principles	Financial Accounting	2016	8	Wiley
B-2	Cost Management	Management Accounting	2017	3	McGraw-Hill
B-3	Accounting Information Systems	Information Systems	2017	2	McGraw-Hill
B-4	Individual Taxation 2017	Taxation	2018	6	Pearson
B-5	Intermediate Accounting	Financial Accounting	2016	1	Wiley
B-6	Advanced Accounting	Financial Accounting	2017	1	McGraw-Hill

Author_Book

Author ID	Book ID
AU-1	B-2
AU-1	B-5
AU-2	B-6
AU-3	B-2
AU-3	B-3
AU-4	B-2
AU-5	B-4
AU-6	B-1
AU-6	B-6

Customer

Customer ID	Last Name	First Name	Email
C-1	Black	Emily	Ewb2003@yahoo.com
C-2	Brown	Jack	jackjack@gmail.com
C-3	Easton	Anderson	anderson.easton@gmail.com
C-4	Jennix	May	jennixm@hotmail.com
C-5	Venable	Judy	Judy.Venable@gmail.com
C-6	White	Ashley	Ashley2015@yahoo.com
C-7	Williams	Eric	Williams_e@yahoo.com

Sales_Line_Item

Sales Date	Customer ID	Book ID	Quantity	Unit price
9/1/2017	C-7	B-3	1	$205
9/1/2017	C-7	B-1	1	$221
9/1/2017	C-1	B-6	30	$195
9/2/2017	C-5	B-2	60	$199
9/2/2017	C-5	B-5	25	$210
9/2/2017	C-3	B-2	1	$245
9/2/2017	C-3	B-6	1	$215
9/2/2017	C-3	B-4	1	$160
9/3/2017	C-2	B-1	1	$221

10. Ellen asks you to give her a list of the books that each author wrote. Write a complete SQL statement to provide the information to Ellen, including author names, book titles, publishers, and the years of publication.
11. Ellen wants to know how many books each author wrote. Write a SQL statement to provide such information to Ellen.
12. You are going to send e-mails to inform the customers that the books ordered have been shipped. Write a SQL statement to obtain the complete information on the book title(s), unit price(s), and the number of each book purchased to be sent to the customers.
13. Ellen wants to know how many copies of each book were sold. Write a SQL statement to obtain the necessary information you think Ellen wants. **LO 4-3**
14. Ellen wants to know the dollar amount of total sales made on September 1, 2017. Write a SQL statement to obtain the necessary information you think Ellen wants. **LO 4-3**

connect

15. The Cash Receipt table below contains seven attributes. Which of those could possibly be foreign keys? **LO 4-2**

Cash Receipt

Remittance Advice #	Date	Amount	Customer #	Check #	Invoice #	Cashier #
RA-220	11/02/2016	2549.90	C-12	201	S-101	E-13345
RA-278	11/10/2016	699.90	C-5	1457	S-108	E-13347
RA-276	11/30/2016	1209.70	C-9	392	S-107	E-13345
RA-289	11/30/2016	949.95	C-28	2558	S-105	E-13346

connect

16. A sales invoice typically includes the date of sale, salesperson, customer data, items included in the sale, and amount. Which foreign keys should be added to the following table to link all of these data elements? **LO 4-2**

Sales

Invoice #	Date	Amount
S-101	10/05/2016	2549.90
S-105	11/01/2016	949.95
S-107	11/02/2016	1209.70
S-108	11/06/2016	699.90

Additional problems are available in connect only.

Chapter Five

Sales and Collections Business Process

A look at this chapter

This chapter examines the sales and cash collection process. We use a comprehensive example to develop activity and structure models of the process. We show how the activity model in conjunction with business rules can be used to develop, implement, and monitor control activities. We show how the structure model can be used to develop a relational database to support information processing requirements. The chapter includes a comprehensive exercise in which students prepare UML class models and then develop the corresponding Microsoft Access database to prepare specific financial information.

A look back

Chapters 2 and 3 described types of business process models and introduced basic modeling tools to guide the student's development of modeling skills. Chapter 4 introduced relational databases and Microsoft Access. We use those skills to examine activity and structure models for the sales and collection process.

A look ahead

In the next chapter, we examine the purchasing and cash disbursement process. We again use the basic modeling tools from Chapters 2, 3, and 4 to examine activity and structure models and corresponding database structures for the process.

© James Leynse/Getty Images

In April 2008, **Starbucks** started offering additional benefits to registered Starbucks Card holders when they use their cards at Starbucks stores in the United States and Canada:

1. Complimentary customization on select syrups and milk alternatives (e.g., soy milk).
2. Complimentary Tall beverage of choice with the purchase of one pound of whole bean coffee.
3. Free refills on brewed coffee during the same visit.
4. Two hours daily of free, in-store Wi-Fi.
5. The opportunity to join Starbucks in supporting charitable causes.

Speaking about this sales initiative, Starbucks CEO Howard Schultz said, "Already, one in seven customers uses the Starbucks

Card, and now we are taking the first steps toward recognizing these customers by providing them value beyond any other coffeehouse. It is the personal relationship our customers have with our brand, our stores, and our baristas that is the foundation of our success. Through this initiative, we are making it even easier to make the Starbucks Experience your own."

At the same time, Starbucks introduced its Pike Place Roast, aimed at providing its customers a "unique, consistent, and fresh brewed coffee experience." It also began making coffee in smaller batches to ensure that its coffee is always fresh.

Starbucks' senior management clearly recognizes the importance of its sales process, and the continuing improvement of its customers' experiences, to its success and long-term growth. What kinds of information do you think Starbucks needs to manage and improve its sales process?

Chapter Outline

Learning Objectives

After reading this chapter, you should be able to:

5-1 Describe the business activities that comprise the sales and collection process.

5-2 Develop an activity model of the sales and collection process using BPMN.

5-3 Understand and apply different activity modeling options.

5-4 Develop business rules to implement controls for the sales and collection process.

5-5 Develop a structure model for the sales and collection process using UML class diagrams.

5-6 Use multiplicities to implement foreign keys in relational tables.

5-7 Implement a relational database from the UML class diagram of the sales and collection process.

LO 5-1
Describe the business activities that comprise the sales and collection process.

SALES AND COLLECTION PROCESS

The sales and collection process includes business activities related to selling products and services, maintaining customer records, billing customers, and recording payments from customers. It also includes activities necessary to manage accounts receivable, such as aging accounts and authorizing credit. Certainly, the sales and collection processes generate accounting transactions to record revenue, accounts receivable, and cash receipts. They also affect cost of goods sold and inventory for companies that sell merchandise.

Figure 5.1 describes typical accounting transactions resulting from the sales and collection process. **Sales** are typically made in exchange for **cash** or credit. The transaction may also require collection of sales tax. A cash sale increases cash. A credit sale results in an account receivable. **Accounts receivable** are monies owed to the firm from the sale of **products** or services. A sale of goods also results in a corresponding recognition of cost of goods sold expense and reduction of inventory. When the customer subsequently pays for the goods or services sold on credit, cash is increased and accounts receivable are reduced.

We apply the tools introduced in Chapters 2, 3, and 4 to a comprehensive example of the sales and collection process. For this example, we take on the role of business analysts helping a small business, Sunset Graphics Inc., document its business processes. In this chapter, we first describe the sales and collection activities using BPMN, and then we define the typical information structure using UML class diagrams. Finally, we use the UML class diagrams to build a database to collect and report sales and collection information. Throughout, we describe business rules that establish potential process controls.

FIGURE 5.1
Accounting Transactions for the Sales and Collection Process

Oct 1	**Accounts Receivable**	1,350.54	
	Sales Tax Payable		100.04
	Sales		1,250.50
	Sold products on credit to Smith, Inc. Invoice No. 459		
Oct 1	**Cash**	1,452.87	
	Sales Tax Payable		107.62
	Sales		1,345.25
	Sold products for cash		
Oct 1	**Cost of goods sold**	750.30	
	Inventory		750.30
	Recording cost of sales		
Oct 31	**Cash**	1,350.54	
	Accounts Receivable		1,350.54
	Received payment from Smith, Inc. for Invoice No. 459		

SUNSET GRAPHICS EXAMPLE

Company Overview

Virgil and Linda B (their family name is Bartolomucci, but everyone calls them Mr. and Mrs. B) started their company more than 20 years ago and have grown it into a successful graphic design and printing business. They design and sell signs and banners, lettering and vinyl graphics for vehicles and boats, corporate promotional items, and silk-screened T-shirts and embroidered gear, among other products. Recently, Virgil and Linda decided that they wanted to try and step back from the day-to-day operations. Before they did that, they decided that it was time to review their business processes to develop better documentation, improve processes, and establish consistency in customer service. They also wanted to be sure that effective internal controls were in place because they wouldn't be on site as often.

Designing for customer specifications.
© Ingram Publishing/SuperStock

Sunset Graphics' Sales and Collection Process Description

Because most of its products are designed to customer specifications, Sunset usually prepares a **quote** for the **customer** that carefully describes the products and services it will provide. If the customer likes the quote, he or she will place the **sales order** for all or part of the quoted products and services. At that point, Sunset may order any products not in inventory from its suppliers. When it receives the products, Sunset then applies the graphics. When the entire order is complete, Sunset delivers the products to the customer. In some cases, Sunset applies the graphics or installs the products at the customer's site. When the job is complete, it bills the customer and either collects payment immediately or allows the customer to pay within 30 days, depending on the customer's credit.

LO 5-2
Develop an activity model of the sales and collection process using BPMN.

SUNSET GRAPHICS' ACTIVITY MODELS

Basic Sales Activity Model

After talking with Virgil and Linda B about their sales and collection process, our first task was to draw a simple activity model using BPMN. As shown in Figure 5.2, the start of the process occurs when the customer requests a quote. Then, a series of tasks takes place in sequence until the customer pays for the products and services and the process ends. Sunset records sales when the products and services are delivered to the customer. Although some customers do not place orders after getting a quote, Virgil allowed that most do.

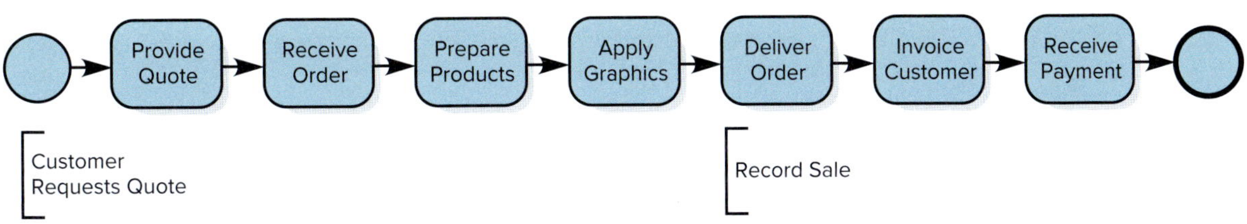

FIGURE 5.2
Basic Sales Activity Model

LO 5-3
Understand and apply different activity modeling options.

Refining the Model to Show Collaboration

Business process analysis is an iterative process. After thinking about the basic model, Linda remarked that much of their business involved interaction with customers, and the basic model doesn't really show that interaction. We agreed, but said that BPMN also allows *pools* that show different participants in a process. *Message flows* (shown by dashed arrows) between pools describe the interaction between participants.

To illustrate, we prepared Figure 5.3 that shows the customer's activities in one pool and Sunset Graphics' activities in the other pool. We explained that each pool needs a start and end event, and the *sequence flow* (shown by the solid arrows) within a pool continues from the start event to the end event without a break. This type of activity model is called a **collaboration** model in BPMN, and the interaction between participants is called **choreography.**

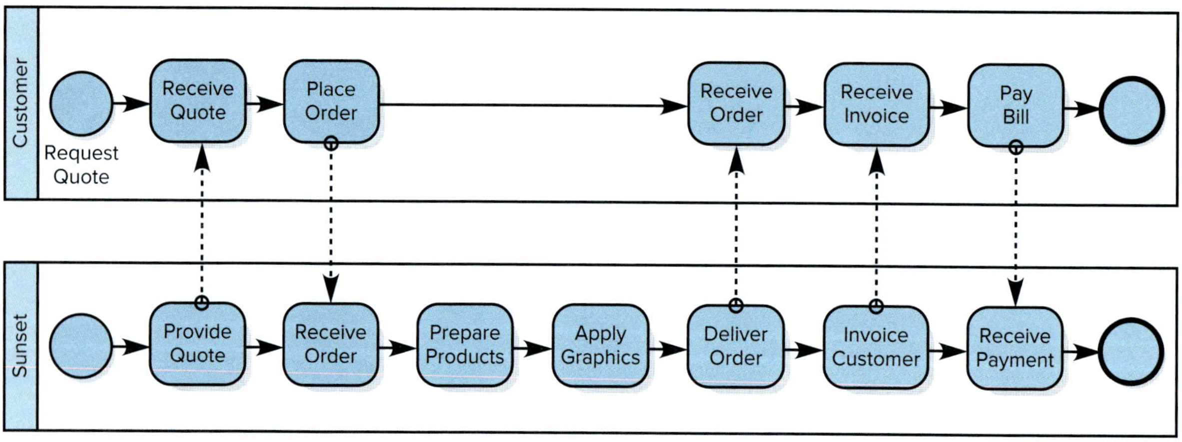

FIGURE 5.3
Collaboration Sales Activity Model

Linda said that this model more clearly shows the interactions, but she really did not care about customers' activities. She was just concerned about the choreography of interactions between the pools and the orchestration of Sunset's activities (the sequence of activities within one pool is called an **orchestration**). We understood and changed the model. Figure 5.4 now hides the customer's activities, but it shows the important message flows between participants. We told Linda that we could also hide Sunset's activities and just show the choreography between participants, but she liked this model.

Progress Check

1. What information does the collaboration model in Figure 5.4 tell you that is different from the basic model shown in Figure 5.2?
2. From your own experience, describe how you would change Figure 5.4 to reflect another sales and collection process.

Refining the Model to Consider Exceptions

Virgil then asked how we would model potential exceptions to the typical process flow. For example, he said that sometimes Sunset's suppliers don't have the products that Sunset needs to complete the job, and it has to notify the customer and cancel the job. We weren't ready to model details of the purchasing process yet, but we could model it generally as a *collapsed* **subprocess** and also allow for the exception. A collapsed subprocess contains a series of steps that are hidden from view. Because this was getting more complicated, we temporarily dropped the pools and revised the basic sales model.

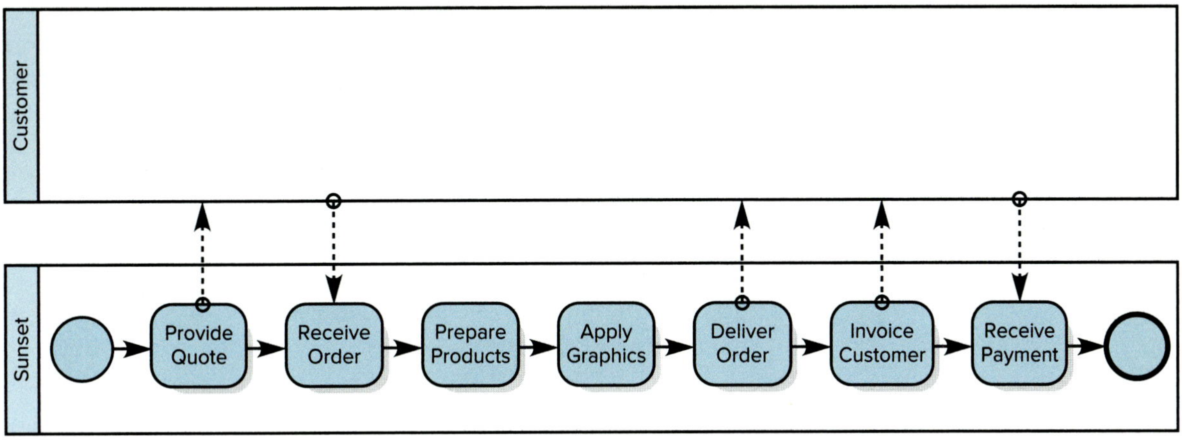

FIGURE 5.4
Collaboration Sales Activity Model

Figure 5.5 now models the purchasing exception when products are not available. We show the exception that occurs when the product is not available as an *intermediate* **error event** attached to the subprocess. When the exception occurs, the customer is notified and the process ends. Under normal conditions, the process continues as before.

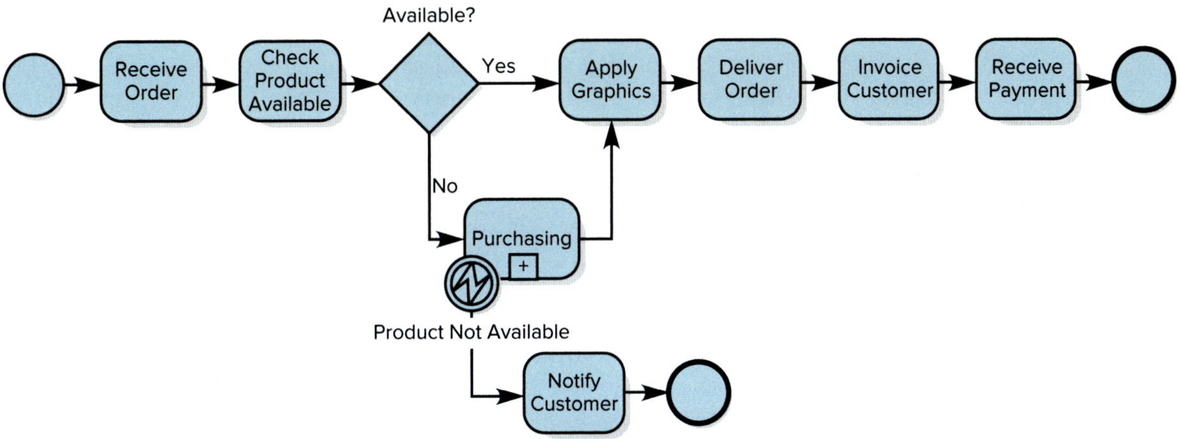

FIGURE 5.5
Sales Activity Model with Exception

Virgil loved it. He said that is exactly what happens at times. Then, he asked about the invoice customer and review payment tasks. He said they don't always get paid immediately and sometimes have to send another invoice. Because he was starting to understand BPMN, he asked if we could also use a boundary event to show that the payment was not received on time. We applauded him for how well he understood the tools. Yes, we can use an *intermediate timer boundary event* to show the exception. Virgil says that he waits 2 weeks after the payment due date to send a new invoice. Figure 5.6 adds the intermediate timer boundary event to the process. The timer event would be triggered when the payment is not received within 2 weeks.

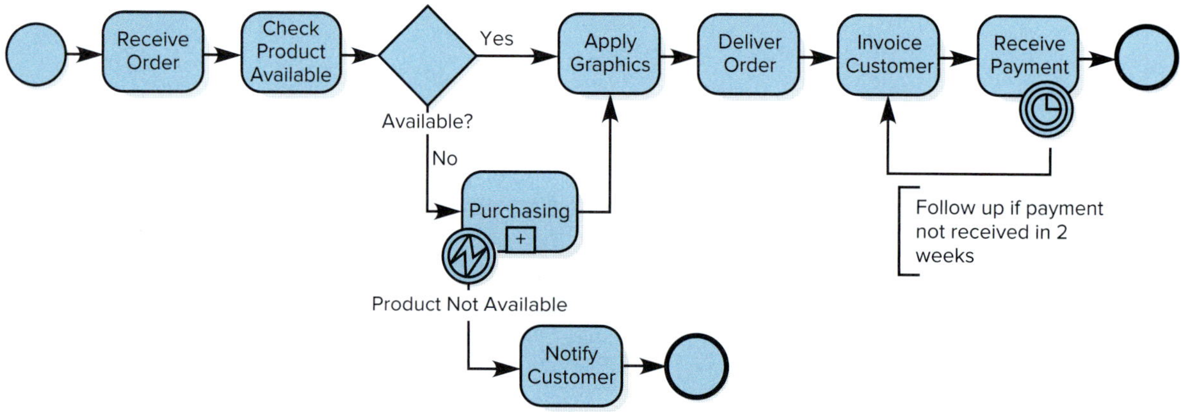

FIGURE 5.6
Sales Activity Model with Intermediate Boundary Events

LO 5-4
Develop business rules to implement controls for the sales and collection process.

BUSINESS RULES AND SUNSET GRAPHICS' SALES AND COLLECTION PROCESS CONTROLS

Next, we wanted to talk about controls over the sales and collection process because Virgil and Linda planned to step back from the day-to-day operations. We said that we would like to implement controls by developing business rules for the process. We explained to Virgil and Linda that a business rule is a compact statement that constrains some aspect of business activity. Business rules help ensure that information systems operate in a consistent and effective manner to achieve organizational objectives.

Virgil remarked that business rules seemed similar to internal controls. He quickly pulled out his laptop and went to the COSO website, www.coso.org.[1] He paraphrased its definition, "Internal control is broadly defined as a process designed to provide reasonable assurance regarding the effectiveness and efficiency of operations, reliability of financial reporting, and compliance with applicable laws and regulations." We answered that business rules are not processes; they are constraints on the process. However, you could think of business rules as control activities. COSO describes control activities as including approvals, authorizations, verifications, reconciliations, reviews of operating performance, security of assets, segregation of duties, and other activities designed to address risks to achievement of the entity's objectives. After thinking about it, Virgil agreed. He understood that business rules implement specific control activities for a particular business process. He just wasn't sure how to do it.

We explained that business rules are developed by identifying three elements: event, condition, and action. The first step is to identify important business events. Then, we need to know your conditions that would affect your intention or objective for each event. Finally, we determine the appropriate actions to take based on the conditions. For example, we've already listed important business events in the activity models, so let's examine Sunset's sales and collection process in Figure 5.4 and develop some possible business rules.

Both Virgil and Linda were now involved, so we started with the first step in the process: provide quote. We asked what their intention was for this step. They replied that they wanted to provide quotes accurately and promptly because the quote was extremely important in winning the customer's business. We then asked about the constraints that should be applied to the activity because a Sunset partner would prepare the quotes in the future. Virgil responded that the partner should provide the quote to the customer within 1 day of the customer's request. Linda added that they wanted to control approvals so that

[1]See Chapter 11 for more complete explanation of COSO (Committee of Sponsoring Organizations of the Treadway Commission) and internal control elements.

a manager approved large value quotes. That way, they could be sure that Sunset would not be overextended by taking on a large job that it could not accomplish on time.

Next, we asked about the accounting information system controls over the process. We explained that **access controls** limit who can use and change records in the system. This helps implement appropriate segregation of duties. Virgil said that the partners who provide quotes should not also manage the inventory and set prices, so they should not have access that would allow them to modify product and price information. Finally, we said we need **application controls** to ensure data integrity and an audit trail. For example, we need to control the assignment of quote numbers to make sure all of them are accounted for. Plus, we need to establish appropriate ranges or limits for each value that Sunset's partners can add or change in the system.

With Virgil and Linda's direction, we were able to develop an initial set of business rules for the sales and collection process. They articulated their intentions for every step in the process, and then we set business rules to segregate duties and limit partner authority appropriately. Table 5.1 shows the initial set of business rules for Sunset's sales and collection process.

Process Steps	Intention	Partner Authority/Action	Access Controls	Application Controls
Provide Quote	Provide quotes promptly and accurately.	Partner must provide quote within 1 business day of request; manager must approve quotes > $5,000.	Partners preparing quotes cannot modify established product and service prices.	System must provide quote number control, default values, range and limit checks, and create audit trail.
Receive Order	Record order promptly and accurately; ensure customer credit is authorized.	Partner must record order within 1 hour of receipt; manager must approve orders > $5,000; credit manager must approve credit order > $1,000.	Partners accepting orders cannot modify established product and service prices; partners accepting orders cannot approve request for customer credit > $1,000.	System must provide order number control, default values, range and limit checks, and create audit trail; system links quote to order.
Prepare Products and Apply Graphics	Prepare products promptly; ensure products match order; ensure quality products.	Partner must check all products for defects and show defective products/graphics to manager; partner must prepare products and apply graphics to meet required delivery schedule.	Partners preparing products cannot modify order.	System must allow the partner to modify only the status information; system must assign current date by default.
Deliver Order	Deliver order on date requested; ensure customer accepts delivery.	Partner delivering order must verify that delivery matches order.	Partners delivering products cannot modify order.	System must supply delivery information and not allow modification.
Invoice Customer	Invoice customer promptly; monitor until paid.	Partner must invoice customer no later than 3 business days after delivery.	Partner preparing invoice cannot modify order; before preparing the invoice, make sure the product has been delivered.	System must supply invoice number; invoice information must be filled in automatically from order.
Receive Payment	Record and deposit receipt promptly.	Partner receiving payment must record receipt immediately and deposit intact on same day.	Partner receiving payment cannot modify order or invoice.	System must supply receipt number, default to current date, default payment value to order amount.

TABLE 5.1
Using Business Rules to Implement Internal Controls

LO 5-5
Develop a structure model for the sales and collection process using UML class diagrams.

SUNSET GRAPHICS' STRUCTURE MODELS

We proceeded to examine Sunset Graphics' information requirements by preparing UML class diagrams that describe their sales and collection process. As described in Chapter 3, the primary purpose of a UML model of the sales and collection process is to create a blueprint for the development of a relational database to support the collection, aggregation, and communication of process information. To develop UML class diagrams, we follow the **REA** framework (resources, events, and agents) as a proven approach to describing business processes in a way that meets both accounting and broad management information requirements.

UML Class Model for Quotes

Virgil and Linda B outlined Sunset's process for preparing quotes for customers. They call their employees partners. In this case, a Sunset partner works with the customer to document how Sunset will meet the customer's requirements. The Sunset partner will prepare the quote, and the customer will confirm the quote. The quote specifies the prices and quantities of Sunset's products and services to be delivered. So, our preliminary model shows Sunset's **resources** (Products), the Quote **event**, and the two **agents** (Sunset Partner and Customer) that participate in the event.

In Figure 5.7, we've numbered the three relevant associations: (1) the Sunset Partner to Quote event association, (2) the Customer to Quote event association, and (3) the Quote events to Products resource association. The multiplicities for association number 1 indicates that each Sunset Partner may participate in a minimum of zero Quotes and a maximum of many Quotes, but each Quote involves only one Sunset Partner.[2] Similarly, for association number 2, each Customer may participate in zero to many Quotes and each Quote is prepared for only one Customer. For association number 3 each Quote specifies prices and quantities for at least one product (minimum of one and maximum of many). Each product may be listed on many quotes (but some products may not yet be listed on quotes). Associations 1 and 2 represent **one-to-many relationships** between classes. Association number 3 represents a **many-to-many relationship**. As we discuss later, the nature of these relationships determines how the associations are implemented in the relational database.

FIGURE 5.7
UML Class Diagram for Quotes

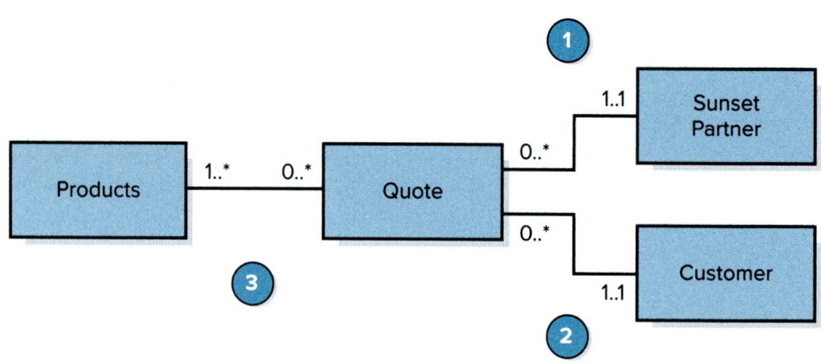

UML Class Model for Adding Orders

Next, Virgil and Linda B described how Sunset's quotes typically result in one or more orders from the customer. Of course, the same customer is involved in both the quote and the order, but a different Sunset partner could take the order. Sunset does not always prepare quotes prior to taking an order because some of its products are ready for delivery

[2] When describing multiplicities, we refer to the instances of the class—for example, Quotes refers to the individual quotes that are instances of the Quote class (or rows in the Quote table).

and do not need to be customized. When the customer places the order, Sunset has a formal commitment from the customer that will result in a sale when Sunset completes the delivery. Sunset does not deliver products and services until the order is complete, so there is a one-to-one relationship between orders and subsequent sales.

Figure 5.8 adds the Order event. We highlight association 4 because it links the Customer's order to the previous quote. Other associations with Order are similar to associations with Quote. The multiplicities for association 4 indicate that each Quote is related to a minimum of zero Orders, which may happen if the Customer does not place an order but also indicates that orders follow quotes in time (i.e., there can be delay between the quote and the customer order). Each Quote may be related to more than one Order if the Customer places partial orders, such as when the customer needs certain products and services immediately but others can wait. Orders are related to a minimum of zero Quotes and a maximum of one Quote.

FIGURE 5.8
UML Class Diagram for Orders and Quotes

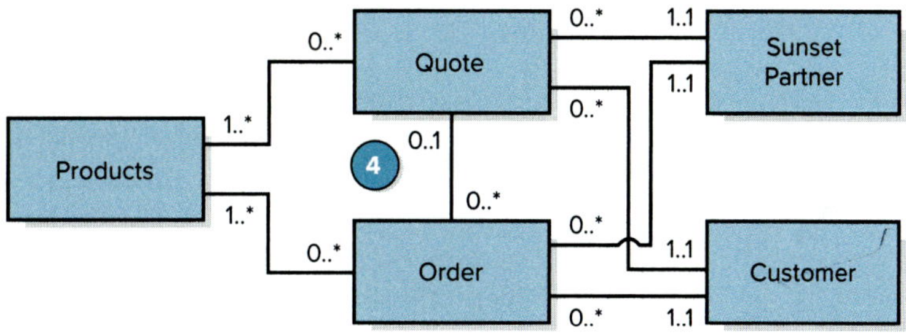

UML Class Model for Adding Cash Receipts

Linda B then remarked that some customers pay Sunset as soon as it delivers the products and services. However, Virgil said that Sunset's business and government customers are usually offered credit terms. In some situations, the customers may send one check for several orders. In any case, a Sunset partner records the **cash receipt** from the customer. All cash receipts are deposited in their primary bank account daily.

Figure 5.9 adds the Cash Receipt event and the Cash resource (e.g., bank accounts) to the UML class diagram. As with Orders and Quotes, a Sunset Partner and Customer both participate in the Cash Receipt event, and the multiplicities for these associations are similar to the earlier associations between agents and events. We've highlighted the association between Orders and Cash Receipts *events* (number 5) and the association between the Cash Receipts event and the Cash resource (number 6). For association number 5, the multiplicities indicate that each Cash Receipt is linked with a minimum of one Order and a maximum of many Orders (one customer payment for multiple orders), and each Order is linked to a minimum of zero (not paid yet) and a maximum of one (paid in full) Cash Receipt. Thus, the delivered Orders for which there are no Cash Receipts define Sunset's accounts receivable. For association number 6, the multiplicities indicate that each Cash Receipt is deposited into one account (Cash resource), and each account could have many Cash Receipts.

Progress Check

3. Describe when a Sales/Order might be preceded by the Quote activity.
4. Could the order event be divided into two events: Orders and Sales? If so, when does this make sense?

FIGURE 5.9
UML Class Diagram for Orders and Cash Receipts

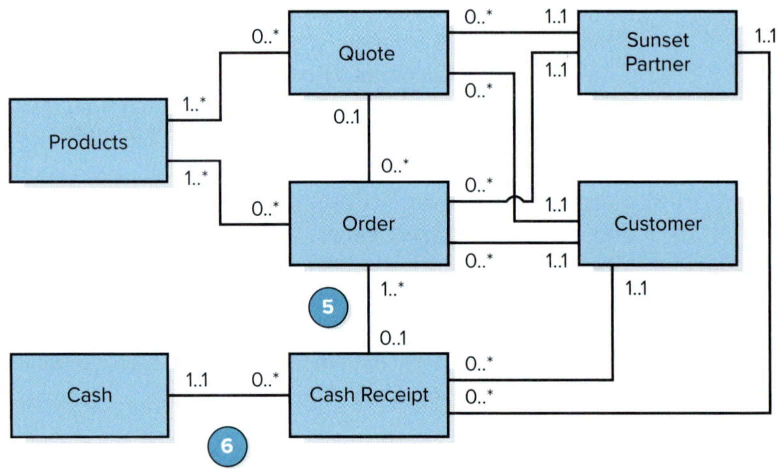

UML Class Model for Adding Categorical Information

Both Virgil and Linda now agree that the model generally represents their sales and collection process, but they wondered how to include product categories and order status information that they use for management. For example, they categorize their products into t-shirts and gear for silk screening and embroidery, lettering material for vehicles and boats, sign and banner material, customer artwork, and printing materials (card stock and stationery items). Additionally, they have a number of different categories for their promotional products. They also track the status of their orders (e.g., waiting for supply, pending graphic application, ready for delivery, and delivered).

We replied that companies often apply guidelines, constraints, and descriptive information to their resources, events, and agents to help manage the business process. Additionally, companies need to summarize the economic activity to support management's information requirements. Generically, these other classes can be called **type images**.[3] For Sunset, we can model product category and order status information by adding two classes to the basic model, as shown in Figure 5.10.

In Figure 5.10, the Product Category and Order Status classes allow Sunset to establish appropriate categories for the related classes (i.e., Products for Product Categories and Orders for Order Status). Association number 7 highlights the two associations between the underlying class and its type image. The multiplicities for both associations reflect that each category/status can apply to many instances of the underlying class. For example, each Product Category comprises many Products. Once implemented in a relational database, these type images allow process information to be summarized by category.

Type images could also support control activities by designating responsibilities. For example, a Sunset Partner could be assigned inventory management responsibility for one or more Product Categories, as shown by association number 5. The multiplicities for association number 8 indicate that one Sunset Partner is assigned to each Product Category, but some Sunset Partners could be assigned to manage multiple Product Categories.

LO 5-6
Use multiplicities to implement foreign keys in relational tables.

UML Class Model for Supporting Relational Database Planning

Virgil B had no more questions about the UML class diagrams of Sunset's sales and collection process, but he did wonder how the model would be implemented in the relational

[3]See, e.g., G. Geerts and W. McCarthy, "Policy Level Specifications in REA Enterprise Information Systems," *Journal of Information Systems* 20, no.2 (2006), pp. 37–63.

FIGURE 5.10
UML Class Diagram for Orders and Cash Receipts with Type Images

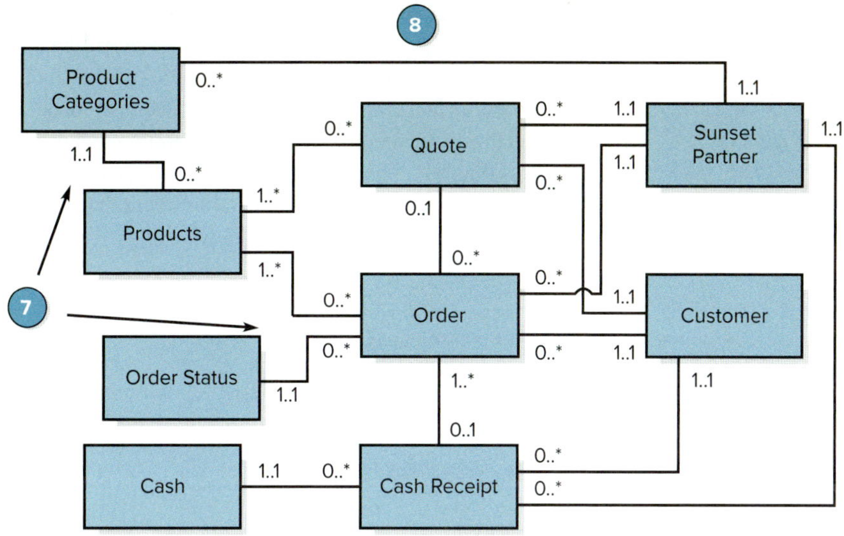

database. He knew that relational databases implement links between tables through foreign keys.[4] "How do you know where to put the foreign keys," he asked.

We said that once you understand the multiplicities, it is pretty easy to determine where to put the foreign keys. Let's use some of the associations that we've already discussed as examples. Figure 5.11 shows the one-to-many relationship between Customers and Orders. We've included some sample attributes for the classes. The «pk» notation indicates the primary keys; the «fk» notation indicates the foreign keys. Thus, *Cust_num* (customer number) is the primary key for the Customer table, and *Order_num* (order number) is the primary key for the Order table. The multiplicities indicate that each Customer can be linked with multiple Orders, but each Order only involves one Customer. Foreign keys are primary keys of linked tables, so either the *Cust_num* is a foreign key in the Orders table or the *Order_num* is the foreign key in the Customer table. Remember that properly designed relational tables cannot have multivalued fields. Thus, the *Order_num* cannot be a foreign key in the Customer table because each Customer can participate in multiple Orders. Instead, the *Cust_num* must be placed in the Orders table as the foreign key, as shown in Figure 5.11.

FIGURE 5.11
Using Multiplicities to Determine Foreign Key Implementation for One-to-Many Relationships

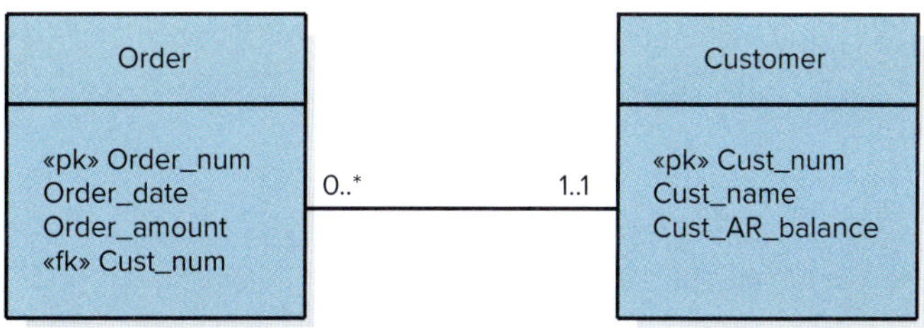

Next, we have to determine what to do with the many-to-many relationships, as shown between Order and Products in Figure 5.12. In this case, we need to turn the many-to-many relationship into two one-to-many relationships that can be easily implemented in a relational database. To do that, we define the Order Items class and model a *composition* association between Orders and Order Items as shown in Chapters 3 and 4. Note that the

[4]See Chapter 4 for a complete discussion of foreign keys and referential integrity.

primary key of Order Items is the combination of *Order_num* and *Prod_num* (called concatenated key or composite key): *Order_num* in Order Items links to *Order_num* in Orders and *Prod_num* in Order Items links to *Prod_num* in Products. The Order Items table will include *quantity ordered* and *price* attributes because those attributes depend on both the Order and the Product ordered.[5] Although we could have modeled Order Items on the original UML class diagram, identifying the many-to-many relationship serves the same purpose because, in either case, the Order Items table would have to be defined when the model is implemented.[6]

FIGURE 5.12
Implementing Many-to-Many Relationships

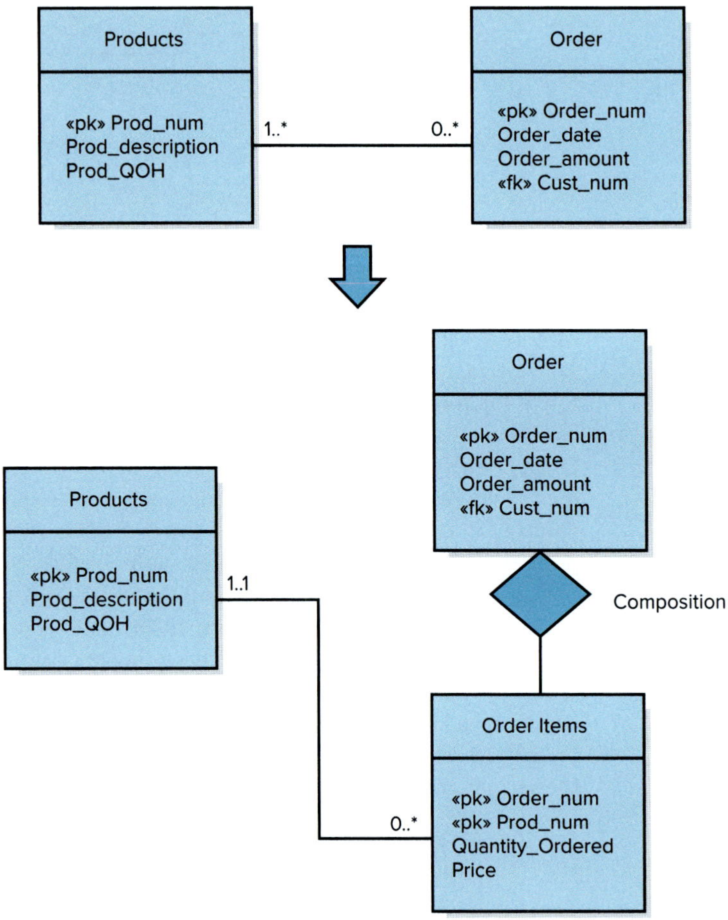

Progress Check

5. Refer to Figure 5.10. Where does the foreign key go for the Customer to Cash Receipt association?
6. Where would the foreign keys go in the Order to Cash Receipt association?

[5] Think about your cash register receipt at the grocery store—one sale includes many items.

[6] Additionally, the Order Items class cannot exist without the Order class, and because it can be derived from other classes, some argue that it should not be modeled.

LO 5-7
Implement a relational database from the UML class diagram of the sales and collection process.

SUNSET GRAPHICS' RELATIONAL DATABASE

Virgil and Linda B were now interested in seeing how the structure model would be implemented in a relational database for Sunset. For this example, we use Microsoft Access, but the process would be similar for any database-driven system. We encourage students to use the following description to implement a relational database to support information requirements for the sales and collection process.

Relational Database Planning for Attributes

During the model development process, we reviewed Sunset's existing documents to determine specific data requirements for each class/table. We then followed the guidance in the previous section to determine allocation of foreign keys. This resulted in a list of tables, attributes, data types, field sizes and primary and foreign keys, as shown in Table 5.2.

PK/FK	Attribute Name	Type	Size
	Table: tblBankAccounts		
PK	Account_number	Text	10
	Bank_routing_number	Text	10
	Bank_balance	Currency	8
	Bank_name	Text	15
	Bank_branch	Text	15
	Bank_phone_number	Text	15
	Table: tblCashReceipts		
PK	Receipt_number	Text	10
	Receipt_date	Date/Time	8
	Receipt_amount	Currency	8
FK	Customer_number	Text	10
	Customer_check_number	Text	10
FK	Received_by	Text	10
FK	Bank_account_number	Text	10
	Receipt_deposit_date	Date/Time	8
	Table: tblCustomers		
PK	Customer_number	Text	15
	Customer_name	Text	30
	Customer_address	Text	30
	Customer_address_2	Text	30
	Customer_city	Text	20
	Customer_state	Text	2
	Customer_zip	Text	5
	Customer_contact	Text	30
	Customer_phone	Text	15
	Customer_established_date	Date/Time	8
	Customer_last_activity	Date/Time	8
	Customer_balance	Currency	8
	Table: tblOrderItems		
PK	Order_number	Text	10
PK	Product_number	Text	10
	Order_quantity	Integer	2
	Order_price	Currency	8
	Table: tblOrders		
PK	Order_number	Text	10
	Order_date	Date/Time	8
FK	Customer_number	Text	10
FK	Quote_number	Text	10
FK	Order_taken_by	Text	10
	Order_required_by	Date/Time	8
	Order_delivered	Date/Time	8
	Order_total_amount	Currency	8
	Order_instructions	Memo	—
FK	Receipt_number	Text	10
FK	Order_status	Text	10
	Table: tblOrderStatus		
PK	Order_status_code	Text	10
	Order_status_description	Text	255
	Table: tblPartners		
PK	Partner_number	Text	10
	Partner_first_name	Text	15
	Partner_last_name	Text	15
	Partner_hire_date	Date/Time	8
	Partner_SocSecNo	Text	11
	Partner_Address	Text	50

TABLE 5.2
Sunset Database Table and Attribute Definitions

(continued)

PK/FK	Attribute Name	Type	Size
	Partner_Address2	Text	50
	Partner_City	Text	20
	Partner_State	Text	2
	Partner_Zip	Text	10
	Partner_phone	Text	14
	Partner_cellphone	Text	14
	Table: tblProductCategory		
PK	Product_category_number	Text	10
	Product_category_description	Text	255
	Product_category_manager	Text	10
	Product_category_notes	Memo	—
	Table: tblProducts		
PK	Product_number	Text	10
	Product_description	Text	255
	Product_price	Currency	8
	Product_unit_of_sale	Text	10
	Product_category	Text	10
	Product_quantity_on_hand	Integer	2
	Product_notes	Memo	—
	Table: tblQuoteItems		
PK	Quote_number	Text	10
FK	Product_number	Text	10
	Quote_quantity	Integer	2
	Quote_price	Currency	8
	Quote_notes	Text	255
	Table: tblQuotes		
PK	Quote_number	Text	10
	Quote_date	Date/Time	8
FK	Customer_number	Text	10
FK	Quote_by	Text	10
	Quote_amount	Currency	8

TABLE 5.2
(continued)

Create Database and Define Tables

The next step is to create a new, blank Microsoft Access database and create the tables described in Table 5.2 with the following steps:

1. Create the Table Design as shown in Figure 5.13 by selecting the CREATE tab; then select the Table Design icon on the ribbon bar.
2. Define each attribute listed for the table in Table 5.2 by typing the field name, selecting the data type, and setting the field size, as shown in Figure 5.14.
3. Set the primary key by selecting the appropriate field and clicking the Primary Key icon on the ribbon bar, as shown in Figure 5.15.
4. Save the table.
5. Repeat until all the tables are defined.

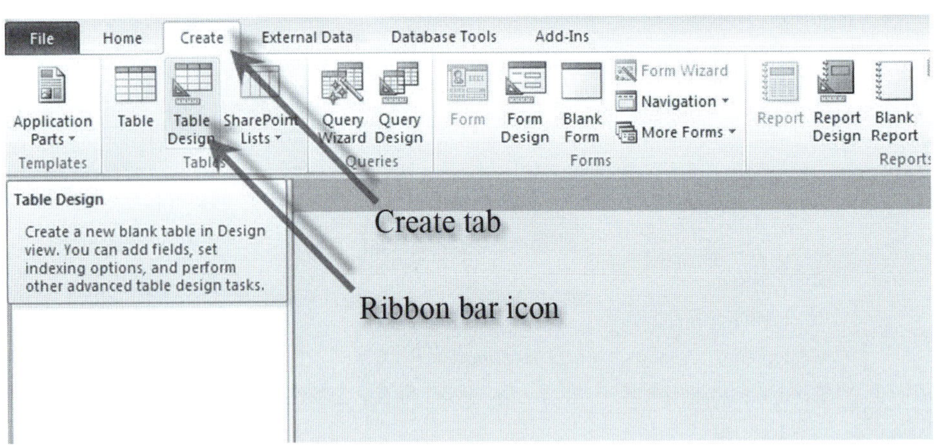

FIGURE 5.13
Create the Table Design

© Microsoft Access

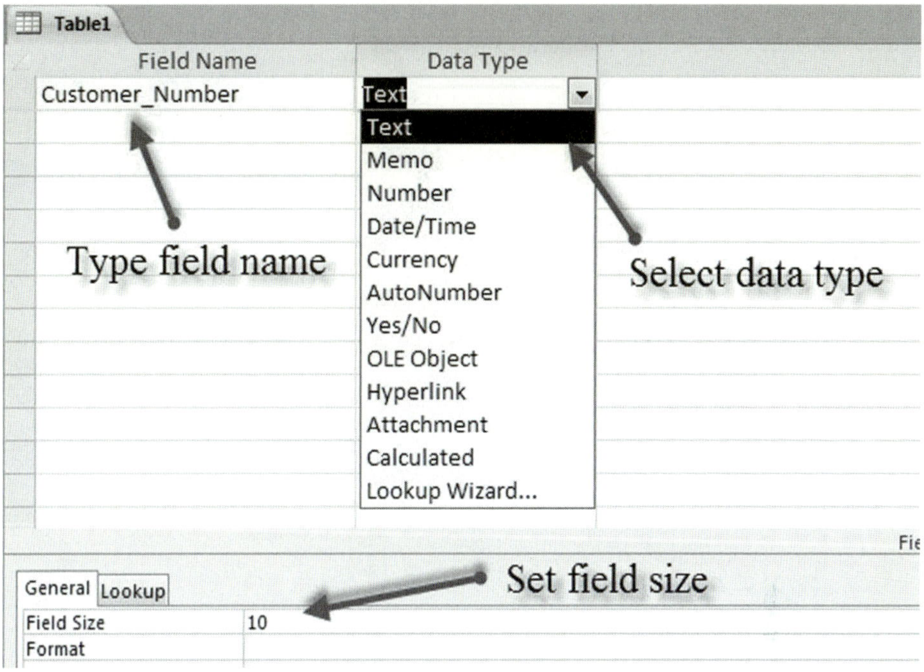

FIGURE 5.14
Define the Fields in the Table

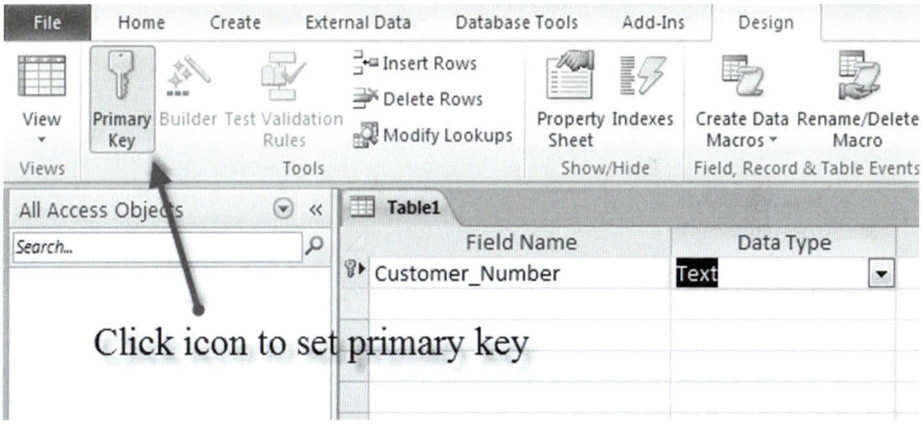

FIGURE 5.15
Set the Primary Key for the Table

Set Relationships

After the tables are defined, the next step is to establish the links between tables. Click on the DATABASE TOOLS tab and select the Relationships icon on the ribbon bar as shown in Figure 5.16. Then, as shown in Figure 5.17, add all the tables to the relationships screen and connect foreign keys to primary keys so that the relationships mimic the UML class diagram shown in Figure 5.9.

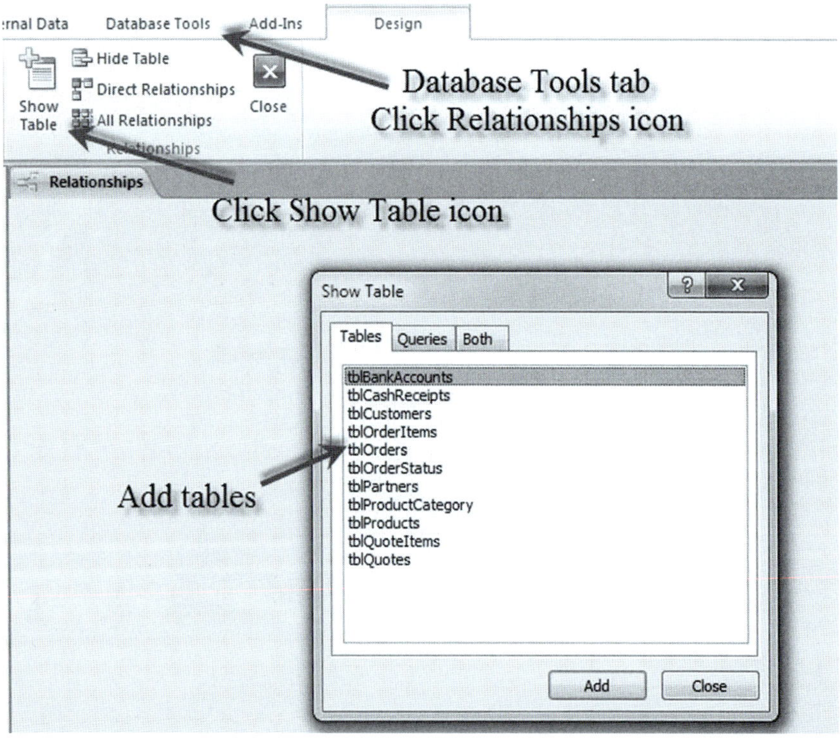

FIGURE 5.16
Set Relationships

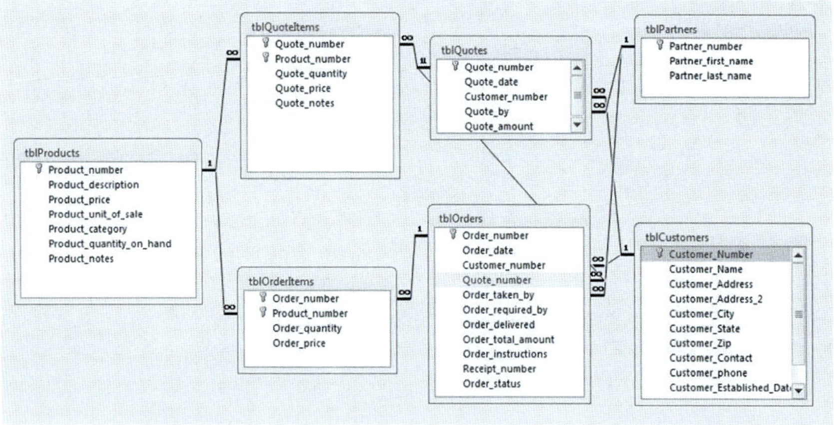

FIGURE 5.17
Partially Linked Tables with Referential Integrity Enforced

COMPREHENSIVE EXERCISE: BAER BELLY BIKINIS' SALES TO RETAILERS

Baer Belly Bikinis Inc. (BBB) is a small business located in Santa Monica, California. It sells swimwear and related products to specialty stores throughout the United States. It also sells its products to individuals over a company website. Paige Baer founded BBB almost 10 years ago after she graduated from the Fashion Institute of Design and Merchandising. She recognized the need for swimsuits sold as separates. Her business has grown rapidly, and now BBB has a large following of customers who want to be able to mix and match to find their ideal swimsuit. Currently, BBB products are carried in more than 1,000 specialty swimwear boutiques and online retailers.

During an initial interview with Paige Baer, she outlined BBB's business processes. She acknowledged that she doesn't know much about accounting and information technology.

As the business grew, her accounting suffered and information systems were added piecemeal. So, she is looking forward to an assessment of her requirements and recommendations that would position BBB for substantial further growth.

First, Paige described BBB sales to independent boutique retailers. BBB uses a group of independent sales representatives to sell its products to boutique retailers around the country. These sales representatives are not BBB employees. They are paid commissions based on the dollar volume of sales. After working with the sales representatives, individual retailers call BBB to place their order for the upcoming season. BBB will then ship the products when they become available. The retailers are expected to pay for shipments within 30 days. BBB offers a prompt payment discount for payment within 10 days.

The following material summarizes BBB's activities to prepare for and conduct the sales process:

- Summer
  - BBB finalizes designs for next year's products and prepares catalog materials with information on its future products.
- Fall to Spring
  - BBB sales representatives (independent agents working on commissions) visit retailers to develop sales. (BBB's payment of commissions to sales representatives is outside the scope of this case, although you should include the Sales Reps in your model and database.)
  - BBB's retailer customers place orders for one of two deliveries in season: (1) early spring (April) and (2) early summer (May/June). BBB records information on its retailers before they place any orders.
- Upon receipt of finished goods from their manufacturer in April and May, BBB ships products to retailers.
- Retailers' payments are due 30 days after shipment and include shipping costs. Some retailers pay late. Some take advantage of the prompt payment discounts.

BBB Finished Goods Inventory

BBB tracks its inventory by catalog number (catalog#). Each product is identified by color code, use (e.g., tops or bottoms), and type (e.g., the specific design of the piece). The color codes reflect the color and fabric design options, and they can change each year. At the beginning of the season, the quantity on hand of each item is zero. The quantity on hand increases when BBB gets deliveries from its manufacturer (outside the scope of this case) and decreases as it ships the products to the retailers to fill orders.

BBB Shipments

BBB makes one shipment for each retailer order and records revenue when the products are shipped. Warehouse employees prepare the shipments. All shipments are made under BBB's contract with a shipping company. BBB charges customers for the cost of the shipment, so the amount due from the retailers depends on the wholesale price of each item, the quantity shipped, and the shipping cost for the shipment. Payments to the shipping company are outside the scope of this case.

BBB Cash Receipts

Retailer customers send payment by check according to the payment terms (BBB standard payment terms are 2% 10 days net 30, meaning they receive a 2% discount on any amount they pay within 10 days with the net balance due within 30 days). The payment from the retailer customer always applies to only one order, but sometimes the retailers send multiple checks for that order. A BBB employee (accounts receivable) logs cash receipts from retailers. At the end of the day, the cash receipts are deposited intact into one bank account (BBB's main account). Each cash receipt is tracked by unique sequential cash receipt number.

Exercise Requirements

1. Based on the preceding information and the following attributes list, prepare a UML class model and corresponding table listing describing BBB's sales to retailers. List the tables in the following order: resources, events, agents, type images, and linking tables. Identify the primary keys and foreign keys in each table.
2. [optional] Based on the preceding information, prepare a BPMN activity model that describes BBB's Sales to Retailers process. The model should begin with retailers placing orders and end when BBB collects payments for the sales to the retailers.
3. Your instructor will provide an Excel spreadsheet with the BBB information. Create a new Access database, and import each worksheet in the spreadsheet into the database. Set appropriate primary keys.
4. After importing all the data, create relationships among tables to implement your data model.
5. Prepare queries to answer the following questions:
   a. What was BBB's total revenue?
   b. What is BBB's account receivable balance for each retailer customer as of the end of June?
   c. Which BBB product generated the largest sales volume? (List all products in descending order of sales dollars).

Attribute Listing for BBB

Bank Name
Cash Account Balance April 1
Cash Account Description
Cash Account#
Cash Receipt#
Customer Address
Customer City State Zip
Customer Name
Customer Phone
Customer#
Delivery Date
Employee Address
Employee City
Employee Department
Employee First Name
Employee Hire Date
Employee Last Name
Employee Pay Amount
Employee Phone
Employee Salary/Wage
Employee Zip
Employee#
Fabric Color Code
Fabric Color Name
Fabric Cost per Yard
Finished Inventory Catalog#
Finished Inventory Description
Finished Inventory Quantity on Hand
Flat Rate Ship Charge
Inventory Type Use
Order Date
Order Employee#
Order#
Quantity Ordered
Receipt Amount
Receipt Date
Requested Date
Retail Price
Sales Rep Area
Sales Rep Email Address
Sales Rep Name
Sales Rep Phone
Sales Rep#
Ship Date
Shipping Employee#
Shipping Cost
Size of Inventory Item
Standard Cost of Inventory Item
Supervisory Employee#
Type Code
Wholesale Price
Yards Fabric Required for This Inventory Type

Summary

- From an accounting standpoint, we must account for sales, accounts receivable, and cash collection in the sales and collection process.
- Sunset Graphics Inc. provides an ongoing example of how to model the sales and collection process.
- Activity models can show the basic steps in the process and the collaborations between the company and its customers, as well as exceptions to the process.
- Business rules implement internal control activities.
- There is a standard structure model pattern for the sales and collection process that shows the economic reality of the process.
- The standard pattern is tailored to a specific organization by adding type images to collect management information.
- The structure model provides a blueprint for a relational database that will collect, store, and report sales and collection information.
- The comprehensive exercise reinforces the concepts presented in the chapter.

Key Words

access controls (*125*) Limit who can use and change records in the system; for example, passwords control who can use an application.

accounts receivable (*120*) Monies owed by customers for prior sales of goods or services. In a data modeling context, accounts receivable are calculated as each customer's sales less corresponding cash receipts.

agents (*126*) The people or organizations who participate in business events, such as customers and salespeople.

application controls (*125*) Ensure data integrity and an audit trail; for example, new invoices are assigned sequential numbers; specific to a subsystem or an application to ensure the validity, completeness, and accuracy of the transaction.

cash (*120*) The organization's monies in bank or related accounts. The instances of the class are individual accounts. This is considered a resource.

cash receipts (*127*) Record receipts of cash from external agents (e.g., customers) and the corresponding deposit of those receipts into cash accounts. This is considered an event.

choreography (*122*) The interaction (message flows) between two participants (modeled as pools) in a process modeled using BPMN.

collaboration (*122*) A BPMN model showing two participant pools and the interactions between them within a process.

customer (*121*) The external agent in the sales and collection process.

error event (*123*) An intermediate event in a BPMN model showing processing for exceptions to the normal process flow.

events (*126*) Classes that model the organization's transactions, usually affecting the organization's resources, such as sales and cash receipts; Important occurrences that affect the flow of activities in a business process. BPMN includes symbols to define start, intermediate, and end events.

many-to-many relationship (*126*) Exists when instances of one class (e.g., sales) are related to many instances of another class (e.g., inventory) and vice versa. These relationships are implemented in Access and relational databases by adding a linking table to convert the many-to-many relationship into two one-to-many relationships.

one-to-many relationship (*126*) Exists when instances of one class are related to multiple instances of another class. For example, a customer can participate in many sales, but each sale involves only one customer.

orchestration (*122*) In BPMN, the sequence of activities within one pool.

product (*120*) Class representing the organization's goods held for sale, that is, the organization's inventory. This is considered a resource.

quote (*121*) Description of the products and/or services to be provided to a customer if ordered.

REA (*126*) Resource-event-agent framework for modeling business processes, originally developed by William McCarthy.

resources (*126*) Those things that have economic value to a firm, such as cash and products.

sales (*120*) Events documenting the transfer of goods or services to customer and the corresponding recognition of revenue for the organization.

sales order (*121*) Event documenting commitments by customers to purchase products. The sales order event precedes the economic event (sale).

subprocess (*122*) Represent a series of process steps that are hidden from view in BPMN. The use of subprocesses in modeling helps reduce complexity.

type image (*128*) Class that represents management information (such as categorizations, policies, and guidelines) to help manage a business process. Type image often allows process information to be summarized by category.

Appendix A

Generic REA Model with Multiplicities for the Sales and Collection Process

GENERIC PATTERN WITH MULTIPLICITIES

Figure 5.A1 shows a generic sales and collection process UML diagram. There are two resources, *inventory* and *cash;* there are two events, *sales* and *cash receipts;* and there are two agents, *employees* (internal agent) and *customers* (external agent). In this example, let's assume that the inventory is something tracked by universal product code (UPC). UPC are those bar codes you see on literally millions of products, such as soap, breakfast cereal, and packages of cookies. The cash resource represents the various bank accounts that would make up this enterprise's cash balance on its balance sheet. The sales event records information about individual sales transactions (e.g., transaction number, date, total dollar amount). The cash receipt event records information about payments received from customers and deposited into one of the bank accounts (e.g., receipt number, receipt date, receipt dollar amount, customer check number). The employees agent records information about the enterprise's employees, including those employees who handle sales transactions. The customers agent records information about actual and potential customers (let's assume that customer information is recorded in some cases when customers ask for product information and before they participate in their first sale, and let's also assume that the company only receives cash from customers).

FIGURE 5.A1
Generic Sales and Collection UML Diagram

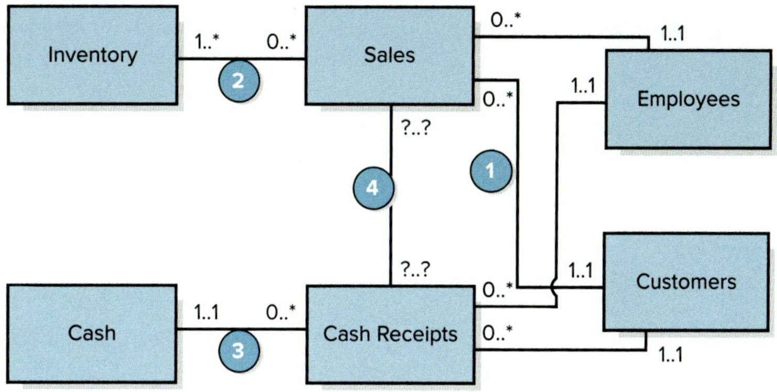

Consider association 1 between *customers* and *sales*. The multiplicities indicate that each customer participates in a minimum of zero and a maximum of many sales. Does this seem reasonable? The minimum of zero means that we can record information about customers before they participate in any sale. On the other side of the association, the multiplicities indicate that each sale involves one and only one customer. Again, does this seem reasonable? Notice that the multiplicities for the other associations between agents and events are the same. In fact, these are the typical multiplicities for those associations. There are circumstances where they might be different, but those circumstances occur infrequently.

Next, consider association 2 between the *sales* event and *inventory* resource. The multiplicities indicate that each sale involves a minimum of one and a maximum of many inventory items. For example, you visit your local **Starbucks** and buy one coffee, a tea for your friend, plus two scones. The multiplicities also indicate that each inventory item can be sold zero times or many times. Starbucks has to put an item on its menu before it can be sold, so it could have inventory items that have not yet been sold. But the same inventory item can be sold many times—as long as the quantity on hand is greater than zero. The multiplicities on this association are typical when the inventory is carried at a type of product level, such as when the inventory is identified by UPC. If the company sells high-value items, the multiplicities would differ. (How?)

Now, consider association 3 between the *cash receipt* event and the *cash* resource. These multiplicities indicate that each cash receipt (e.g., one check from a customer) is deposited into one and only one account, and each account is associated with a minimum of zero cash receipts and a maximum of many cash receipts. These multiplicities reflect typical business practices. Cash receipts are deposited into one account (when you deposit money via an ATM, you are putting it in one account, right?).

Finally, consider the duality association 4 between the *sales* and *cash receipt* events. The question marks indicate that these multiplicities depend on the nature of the business. Some businesses require payment at the time of the sale. Some allow payment terms. Some provide revolving accounts for their customers. Some collect payments in advance of the sale (e.g., magazine subscriptions). So, there are no typical multiplicities for this association.

Although we discourage memorization of data modeling elements, students often find that multiplicities are easier to understand once they see the typical sets for particular associations. We therefore recommend that students recognize and use the standard patterns for multiplicities as shown in Figure 5.A1, remembering that those standard multiplicities could change depending on the particular circumstances of the business.

Answers to Progress Checks

1. The collaboration model shown in Figure 5.4 highlights the interactions between Sunset Graphics and its customers. Figure 5.2 shows the sequence of activities for the sales process without identifying information coming into or out of each activity.
2. The answer depends on the choice of firm. Take **Amazon.com,** for example. Amazon collects payments at the time of the order and does not invoice customers.
3. Companies that provide quotes typically build or tailor their products to the specific customer requirements compared to companies that simply sell available products.
4. The order event could be separated into orders and sales when one order could result in multiple sales or one sale could involve multiple orders.
5. The foreign key for the Customer to Cash Receipt association in Figure 5.9 would be posted in the Cash Receipt table.
6. The foreign key for the Order to Cash Receipt association in Figure 5.9 would be posted in the Order table.

connect

Multiple Choice Questions

1. Which of the following is not an activity within the sales and collection process? **LO 5-1**
   a. Selling products and services
   b. Billing customers
   c. Managing inventory
   d. Recording payments from customers
   e. All of the above are sales and collection activities.
2. The sales and collection process is the point of contact between the firm and which set of external business partners? **LO 5-1**
   a. Investors
   b. Customers
   c. Employees
   d. Vendors
   e. All of the above
3. Which of the following sales and collection process activities can result in the creation of an account receivable? **LO 5-1**
   a. Receiving a sales order from a customer
   b. Shipping ordered products to the customer
   c. Billing the customer
   d. Recording payment from the customer
   e. None of the above

4. Which of the following describes message flows between pools? **LO 5-2**
   a. Orchestrations
   b. Sequence flows
   c. Choreography
   d. Intermediate events
   e. None of the above
5. Which of the following statements is true? **LO 5-2, LO 5-3**
   a. Each pool must have a start event.
   b. Sequence flows are shown by arrows with a solid line.
   c. Message flows are shown by arrows with a solid line.
   d. Each pool must have more than one swimlane.
   e. Both a and b are true.
6. Which of the following is not a purpose of a subprocess in BPMN? **LO 5-3**
   a. Reducing complexity
   b. Presenting higher-level process descriptions
   c. Creating alternative activities
   d. Developing a reusable model
   e. All of the above are purposes of subprocesses in BPMN.
7. What is the purpose of an intermediate error event? **LO 5-3**
   a. Indicates a change in flow due to a process exception
   b. Indicates the end of a process
   c. Indicates the start of a collapsed subprocess
   d. Describes the activities that will occur when there is not an error
   e. None of the above
8. Which of the following is an example of a business rule implementing access controls? **LO 5-4**
   a. The warehouse containing inventory must be locked when the inventory manager is not present.
   b. User's recording collections cannot modify sales records.
   c. The computer system shall generate an audit trail.
   d. Internal auditors shall be used.
   e. Both a and b are business rules implementing access controls.
9. Which of the following is not part of the REA framework? **LO 5-5**
   a. Agents
   b. Type images
   c. Resources
   d. Events
   e. All of the above are part of the REA framework.
10. How do you implement a one-to-many relationship in a relational database? **LO 5-6**
    a. Post a foreign key.
    b. Create a new table.
    c. Combine two fields to create a primary key.
    d. Create an association.
    e. None of the above

Use this diagram to answer multiple choice questions 11 through 32.

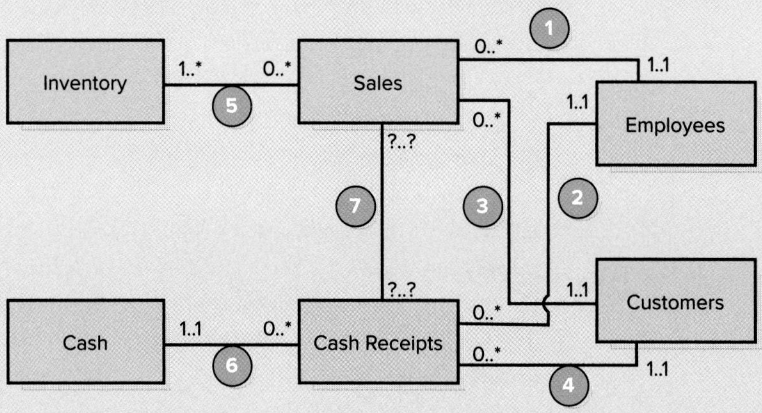

11. Refer to the association marked with the number 1 in the preceding diagram. Which of the following is the best description of the association? **LO 5-5, LO 5-6**
    a. Each employee participates in at least one sale.
    b. Each employee participates in a minimum of zero sales.
    c. Each employee participates in a maximum of one sale.
    d. Each employee participates in at least two sales.
    e. None of these are a description of the association.
12. Refer to the association marked with the number 1 in the preceding diagram. Which of the following is the best description of the association? **LO 5-5, LO 5-6**
    a. Each sale may involve multiple employees.
    b. Each sale may involve no employees.
    c. Each sale is associated with a minimum of one employee.
    d. Each sale is associated with a maximum of many employees.
    e. None of these are a description of the association.
13. Refer to the association marked with the number 2 in the preceding diagram. Which of the following is the best description of the association? **LO 5-5, LO 5-6**
    a. Only cashiers handle cash receipts.
    b. Each employee is associated with many cash receipts.
    c. One employee may be associated with many cash receipts.
    d. Each employee is associated with a minimum of one cash receipt.
    e. None of these are a description of the association.
14. Refer to the association marked with the number 2 in the preceding diagram. Which of the following is the best description of the association? **LO 5-5, LO 5-6**
    a. Each cash receipt may involve multiple employees.
    b. Each cash receipt may involve no employees.
    c. Each cash receipt is associated with only one employee.
    d. Each cash receipt is associated with a maximum of many employees.
    e. None of these are a description of the association.
15. Refer to the association marked with the number 3 in the preceding diagram. Which of the following is the best description of the association? **LO 5-5, LO 5-6**
    a. Each customer participates in a maximum of one sale.
    b. Each customer participates in at least one sale.
    c. Each customer participates in a minimum of zero sales.

d. Each customer eventually participates in at least two sales.

e. None of these are a description of the association.

16. Refer to the association marked with the number 3 in the preceding diagram. Which of the following is the best description of the association? **LO 5-5, LO 5-6**

a. Each sale is associated with a minimum of one customer.

b. Each sale may involve multiple customers.

c. Each sale is associated with a maximum of many customers.

d. Each sale may involve no customers.

e. None of these are a description of the association.

17. Refer to the association marked with the number 3 in the preceding diagram. What is the best interpretation if the minimum multiplicity next to Customers is 0 instead of 1? **LO 5-5, LO 5-6**

a. Some customers don't pay.

b. Some customers place orders but don't pick up their items.

c. Some sales are made in cash and customer information is not recorded.

d. Some customers never buy anything.

e. None of these interpret this situation appropriately.

18. Refer to the association marked with the number 4 in the preceding diagram. Which of the following is the best description of the association? **LO 5-5, LO 5-6**

a. Each customer pays in cash at the time of the sale.

b. Each customer is associated with a maximum of many cash receipts.

c. Each customer is associated with more than one cash receipt.

d. Each customer is associated with a minimum of one cash receipt.

e. None of these are a description of the association.

19. Refer to the association marked with the number 4 in the preceding diagram. Which of the following is the best description of the association? **LO 5-5, LO 5-6**

a. Each cash receipt may involve no customers.

b. Each cash receipt is associated with only one customer.

c. Each cash receipt may involve multiple customers.

d. Each cash receipt is associated with a maximum of many customers.

e. None of these are a description of the association.

20. Refer to the association marked with the number 5 in the preceding diagram. Which of the following is the best description of the association? **LO 5-5, LO 5-6**

a. Each sale may involve a maximum of many inventory items.

b. Each sale may involve a minimum of zero inventory items.

c. Each sale involves one inventory item.

d. Each sale may involve two inventory items.

e. None of these are a description of the association.

21. Refer to the association marked with the number 5 in the preceding diagram. Which of the following is the best example of a business rule that constrains the association? **LO 5-4, LO 5-5**

a. Sales are allowed if they include at least one inventory item.

b. Sales are prohibited if they include more than one inventory item.

c. Sales must include at least one inventory item.

d. Sales are allowed with the manager's approval in advance.

e. None of these are the best example of a business rule.

22. Refer to the association marked with the number 5 in the preceding diagram. Which of the following is the best description of the association? **LO 5-5, LO 5-6**
    a. Each inventory item must be sold at least once.
    b. Each inventory item may be sold many times.
    c. Each inventory item is associated with a minimum of one sale.
    d. Each inventory item is associated with a maximum of one sale.
    e. None of these are a description of the association.
23. Refer to the association marked with the number 6 in the preceding diagram. Which of the following is the best description of the association? **LO 5-5, LO 5-6**
    a. Each cash receipt is deposited into multiple cash accounts.
    b. Each cash receipt is associated with a minimum of zero cash accounts.
    c. Each cash receipt is associated with a maximum of many cash accounts.
    d. Each cash receipt is deposited into one cash account.
    e. None of these are a description of the association.
24. Refer to the association marked with the number 6 in the preceding diagram. Which of the following is the best description of the association? **LO 5-5, LO 5-6**
    a. Each cash account may be associated with many cash receipts.
    b. Each cash account is associated with one cash receipt.
    c. Each cash account is associated with a minimum of one cash receipt.
    d. Each cash account is associated with a maximum of one cash receipt.
    e. None of these are a description of the association.
25. Refer to the association marked with the number 7 in the preceding diagram. Assume that customers pay for all sales in full at the end of the month. Which of the following is the multiplicity that should be found next to the cash receipts class? **LO 5-5, LO 5-6**
    a. 0..*
    b. *..*
    c. 0..1
    d. 1..1
    e. 1..*
26. Refer to the association marked with the number 7 in the preceding diagram. Assume that customers pay for all sales during the month in full at the end of the month. Which of the following is the multiplicity that should be found next to the sales class? **LO 5-5, LO 5-6**
    a. 0..*
    b. *..*
    c. 0..1
    d. 1..1
    e. 1..*
27. Refer to the association marked with the number 7 in the preceding diagram. Assume that customers pay for all sales during the month in full at the end of the month. Which of the following is the best example of a business rule that constrains the association? **LO 5-4, LO 5-5**
    a. Customers are allowed to pay for sales on credit.
    b. Customers must pay for sales at the time of the sale.
    c. Customers are prohibited from paying for sales on credit.
    d. Customers may delay payment for a sale upon approval by the manager.
    e. None of these are an example of an appropriate business rule for the association.

28. Refer to the association marked with the number 5 in the preceding diagram. What is the best description of the type of inventory that this company sells? **LO 5-5, LO 5-6**
    a. High-value items such as automobiles
    b. Customized products
    c. Items identified by UPC (bar codes)
    d. Tickets to concerts
    e. None of these correctly describes the type of inventory.
29. Assume you are implementing a database from the preceding diagram. How many tables would the database include? **LO 5-5, LO 5-6, LO 5-7**
    a. 6
    b. 7
    c. 5
    d. 4
    e. You can't tell from the information provided.
30. Assume you are implementing a database from the preceding diagram. Which of these is the best way to implement the relationship identified by the number 3? **LO 5-5, LO 5-6, LO 5-7**
    a. Post the primary key of customers in sales as a foreign key.
    b. Post the primary key of sales in customers as a foreign key.
    c. Create a linking table between sales and customers.
    d. All of these are acceptable.
    e. None of these are acceptable.
31. Assume you are implementing a database from the preceding diagram. Which of these is the best way to implement the relationship identified by the number 6? **LO 5-5, LO 5-6, LO 5-7**
    a. Post the primary key of cash in cash receipts as a foreign key.
    b. Post the primary key of cash receipts in cash as a foreign key.
    c. Create a linking table between cash and cash receipts.
    d. All of these are acceptable.
    e. None of these are acceptable.
32. Assume you are implementing a database from the preceding diagram. Which of these is the best way to implement the relationship identified by the number 5? **LO 5-5, LO 5-6, LO 5-7**
    a. Post the primary key of sales in inventory as a foreign key.
    b. Post the primary key of inventory in sales as a foreign key.
    c. Create a linking table between sales and inventory.
    d. All of these are acceptable.
    e. None of these are acceptable.

Discussion Questions

1. The sales and collection process generates revenue, accounts receivable, and cash flow information for a firm's financial statements. What other information do you think managers would like to collect? **LO 5-1**
2. What kinds of businesses collect cash before recording the corresponding sales? How would that different sequence affect internal control requirements? **LO 5-1**
3. Draw a basic sales activity model using BPMN for a fast-food restaurant. Draw a second basic sales activity model using BPMN for a traditional restaurant. Discuss similarities and differences. How would you add taking reservations to the second model? **LO 5-2**
4. Draw a collaboration diagram that shows two pools and the message flows between a fast-food restaurant and its customers. How would you change that diagram for a traditional restaurant? **LO 5-2, LO 5-3**

5. Draw UML class diagrams for fast-food and traditional restaurants. Discuss similarities and differences. How would you add taking reservations to the second model? LO 5-2, LO 5-3
6. Using Amazon.com as an example, prepare a collaboration sales activity model. What is the difference between an online process and a traditional brick-and-mortar store process? LO 5-3
7. From your experience, think about the sales process for an online or brick-and-mortar store. Describe some business rules that help provide internal controls over that process. LO 5-4
8. What classes and associations would be included in a model that describes the information needed for a query that calculates the accounts receivable balance for each customer? Describe differences in the information for the *open-invoice method,* where customers pay according to specific invoices, versus the *balance-forward method,* where customers pay balances on monthly statements. LO 5-5

Problems

connect

1. The Beach Dude (BD) employs a legion of current and former surfers as salespeople who push its surfing-oriented products to various customers (usually retail outlets). This case describes BD's sales and collection process.

   Each BD salesperson works with a specific group of customers throughout the year. In fact, they often surf with their customers to try out the latest surf gear. The BD salespeople act laid-back, but they work hard for their sales. Each sale often involves hours of surfing with their customers while the customers sample all the latest surf wear. Because BD makes the best surfing products, the customers look forward to the visits from the BD salespeople. And they often buy a lot of gear. Each sale is identified by a unique invoice number and usually involves many different products. Customers pay for each sale in full within 30 days, but they can combine payments for multiple sales.

   BD manages its clothing inventory by item (e.g., XL BD surfer logo T-shirts), identified by product number, but it also classifies the items by clothing line (the lines are differentiated by price points as well as the intended use of the clothing, e.g., surfing products, casual wear, etc.). LO 5-5, LO 5-6, LO 5-7

   a. Draw a UML class diagram that describes the Beach Dude's sales and collection process.
   b. Using Microsoft Access, implement a relational database from your UML class diagram. Identify at least three fields per table.
   c. Describe how you would create queries in the relational database to determine the Beach Dude's accounts receivable.

connect

2. The Bob White Karate Studio has been a local fixture for almost 40 years. The studio offers training in American Kenpo Karate to students from 3 years old to 80 years old. Students select one of several programs: (a) monthly payments, (b) semi-annual payments, or (c) the black belt program. Each of these programs allows them to take group classes as well as one or more private lessons with a qualified black belt instructor, depending on the program selected. For example, the monthly program includes one private lesson, the semi-annual program includes three private lessons, and the black belt program includes one lesson per week until the student attains black belt rank. Additionally, students may purchase additional private lessons, as well as uniforms, sparring gear, and various studio insignia and clothing items. The additional half-hour private lessons are priced as packages, which include 5, 10, 20, 40, or 60 lessons, and the price also varies depending on whether the lessons are provided by senior or junior instructors. When students purchase a package, they are assigned to a particular instructor for the duration of the package. Students typically pay for anything they buy at the time of their purchase, but established students are sometimes allowed to purchase on credit. In that case, they generally must pay within 2 weeks. While all studio employees are also instructors, only a few employees handle sales transactions and accept payments. LO 5-2, LO 5-3, LO 5-5, LO 5-6, LO 5-7

   a. Draw a BPMN activity diagram that describes the Bob White Karate Studio's sales and collection process.
   b. Prepare a UML class diagram with classes, associations, and multiplicities.

c. Using the preceding information and the following attributes list, prepare a listing of the relational tables necessary to support this sales and collection process. List the tables in the following order: resources, events, agents, type images, and linking tables.

Attributes:

Cash account#
Cash account balance
Credit card number for this sale
Date sale paid
Employee/instructor#
Employee name
Employee rank
Instructor type
Inventory item#
Inventory item description
Inventory item price
Inventory item quantity on hand (QOH)
Private lesson package#
Private lesson package description
Private lesson package price
Program#
Program description
Program price
Quantity of instructors of this type
Quantity of this inventory item purchased on this sale
Sale#
Sale amount
Sale date
Sale paid (Y/N)
Student#
Student current rank
Student name
Student original enrollment date

3. Beach Rentals (BR) maintains an inventory of rental houses near universities and leases those houses to student renters. This case describes their rental business process. BR agents—former marketing majors renowned for their fast-talking and flamboyant lifestyles—work with potential renters and sign the rental contracts for BR.

   BR tracks its houses by city, neighborhood, and distance from campus. BR assigns one specific BR agent to each neighborhood to manage rentals for all houses in that neighborhood, but each BR agent may be assigned to multiple neighborhoods. BR cashiers collect the rent and are bonded for security purposes. Because cashiers never become agents (or vice versa), BR tracks BR cashiers separately from BR agents, although both are identified by employee numbers.

   BR sets rental rates to its student customers by considering such matters as number of bedrooms and age of the house. Additionally, BR applies a monthly rental surcharge to each house that depends solely upon its neighborhood designation; for example, upscale neighborhoods have higher surcharges and less desirable neighborhoods have lower surcharges. The same surcharge applies for the life of the lease. Every house has a rental surcharge, and all houses in a particular neighborhood have the same surcharge.

   Prospective renters, usually students, contact BR to inquire about renting a house. When a potential renter contacts BR, a BR agent is assigned to assist him or her. That BR agent remains the person's point of contact for as long as he or she continues to deal with Beach Rentals. BR records information on each potential renter as soon as he or she contacts BR to inquire about a house.

   BR agents negotiate the rental contracts with the students. Each rental contract must last at least 6 months, and 12-month contracts get a 5 percent discount. BR also charges a damage fee that is due along with the first month's rent when the rental contract is signed. The BR agent earns a 10 percent commission on each rental contract, and BR tracks the year-to-date (YTD) commission earned for each of the BR agents. Of course, the BR agents compete with one another to see who earns the highest commissions, and BR fosters the competition by giving an annual award to its "best" agent.

   When multiple students want to rent one house, BR requires that they designate the primary renter—the one who will be responsible for paying the rent. BR also gathers information about all the other occupants of the house and designates them as secondary renters. All the student renters, however, sign the rental contract, and BR assigns a unique renter number to each occupant. The students may not change primary renter for the term of a contract. BR cashiers collect the rental payments monthly from the primary renters. BR records information concerning employees, house owners, bank accounts, and neighborhoods in the database before the renters are involved in any events. **LO 5-5, LO 5-6, LO 5-7**

a. Prepare a UML class diagram with classes, associations, and multiplicities.
b. Using the preceding information and the following attributes list, prepare a listing of the relational tables necessary to support this sales and collection process. List the tables in the following order: resources, events, agents, type images, and linking tables.
c. Using the list of relational tables and Microsoft Access, define the relational tables and establish the relationships among tables necessary to implement Beach Rentals' sales and collection process in Access.

Attributes:

Agent employee#
Agent name
Agent real estate license status
Bank account#
Bank account balance
Bank name and address
Cash receipt $ amount
Cash receipt#
Cashier employee#
Cashier name
City name
Damage fee
House street address
House zip code
Monthly rent
Neighborhood name
Number of bedrooms
Number of houses in this city
Rent discount for 12-month contract
Rental contract#
Rental contract begin date
Rental contract duration in months
Rental surcharge amount
Renter bank and routing numbers
Renter name
Renter number#
YTD rental commissions

Additional problems are available in connect only.

Chapter Six

Purchases and Payments Business Process

A look at this chapter

This chapter examines the purchases and payments process. We continue the comprehensive example to develop activity and structure models of the process. We show how the activity model in conjunction with business rules can be used to develop, implement, and monitor control activities. We show how the structure model can be used to develop a relational database to support information processing requirements.

A look back

Chapter 5 examined the sales and collection processes. It began the comprehensive example that we use to examine typical process activities and data structures.

A look ahead

In the next chapter, we examine the conversion process, whereby companies transform raw material into finished goods. We again use the basic modeling tools from Chapters 2 and 3 and database design methods presented in Chapter 4 to examine activity and structure models for the process.

© MachineHeadz/Getty Images.

In a 2002 interview,[1] David Norton, **Starbucks**' vice president of logistics, talked about its global supply chain: "Rapid global growth requires comprehensive, integrated strategies focused on the needs of our retail stores, license and joint venture partners. We have a formal process for developing both strategic and operating plans which ensures we link manufacturing, procurement, and logistics to the needs of the business."

Norton went on to describe the role of technology: "Technology has become increasingly a staple of the supply chain rather than a driver. There have been few significant advances on the physical distribution side of the supply chain in years. In the information arena, the pattern seems to be over-commit and under-deliver. Systems are generally harder, more costly, and take longer to implement than has been the promise. The evolution of systems over the past 15 years might be even characterized as a journey from homegrown proprietary systems through best-of-breed/homegrown combinations, and finally to monolithic ERP environments. And

[1] Reported January 1, 2002, www.SupplyChainBrain.com.

my experience is that the integrated, monolithic ERP environments simply lack the flexibility to meet unique business requirements. We believe the best place to be today is combining the best of different applications. And our IT professionals here at Starbucks are comfortable with this because of advances in business integration systems/tools that enable this approach."

Finally, describing what it takes to design and operate integrated supply chain management tools, Norton noted, "A lot of folks come into the business and don't understand that you need a solid item master, a solid price master, a solid customer master, a solid order management system, a solid inventory system—all tied in nicely with AP [accounts payable] and AR [accounts receivable]—and if you don't have any of that stuff right, you can just about forget everything else."

Clearly, technology is important to Starbucks for the management of its supply chain. What kinds of information do you think Starbucks needs to manage and improve its supply chain?

Chapter Outline

Learning Objectives

After reading this chapter, you should be able to:

6-1 Describe the business activities that comprise the purchase and payment process.

6-2 Develop an activity model of the purchase and payment process using BPMN.

6-3 Understand and apply different activity modeling options.

6-4 Develop business rules to implement controls for the purchase and payment process.

6-5 Develop structure models for the purchase and payment process using UML class diagrams.

6-6 Implement a relational database from the UML class diagram of the purchase and payment process.

LO 6-1
Describe the business activities that comprise the purchase and payment process.

PURCHASES AND PAYMENTS PROCESS

The purchases and payments process includes business activities related to buying inventory from **suppliers** maintaining supplier records, and making payments to suppliers for trade accounts payable while taking appropriate **purchase discounts**. The purchases and payments process generates accounting transactions to record **purchases, accounts payable,** and **cash disbursements.** The process also affects inventory values as purchases are added to inventory. Figure 6.1 describes typical transactions resulting from the purchases and payments process.

We will apply the tools introduced in Chapters 2, 3, 4, and 5 to a comprehensive example of the purchases and payments process. We first describe the process activities using BPMN, and then we define the typical information structure using UML class diagrams. Finally, we use the UML class diagrams to build a database to collect and report relevant process information. We also describe business rules that establish potential process controls.

FIGURE 6.1
Accounting Transactions for Purchases and Payments Process

Oct 1	Purchases (or Inventory)*	1,495.50	
	Accounts Payable		1,495.50
	Purchased inventory on credit from Richardson & Sons, Inc.		
	Invoice 1125 dated Oct 1, terms 2/10, net 30		
Oct 11	Accounts Payable	1,495.50	
	Purchase Discounts		29.91
	Cash		1,465.59
	Paid Richardson & Sons, Inc. for Invoice 1125 dated Oct 1		
	less 2% discount		
* Debit to Purchases or Inventory account depends on whether the			
company uses a periodic or perpetual inventory system.			

SUNSET GRAPHICS EXAMPLE

Company Overview

As described in Chapter 5, Virgil and Linda B own and operate Sunset Graphics. They design and sell signs and banners, lettering and vinyl graphics for vehicles and boats, corporate promotional items, and silk-screened T-shirts and embroidered gear, among other products. Recently, they decided that it was time to review their business processes to develop better documentation, improve processes, and establish consistency in customer service. They also wanted to be sure that effective internal controls were in place. This comprehensive example assumes that we are business analysts who are helping Virgil and Linda accomplish these goals.

Sunset Graphics' Purchases and Payments Process Description

Linda B does most of the buying and also pays most of the bills for Sunset, so she explained the process. When Sunset needs to purchase items, it usually follows a straightforward process:

1. Research prices and product availability.
2. Select the best price and availability combination, and send a **purchase order** to the supplier.

3. Receive the items from the supplier (and record the purchase and accounts payable).
4. Pay the supplier according to the credit terms.

LO 6-2
Develop an activity model of the purchase and payment process using BPMN.

SUNSET GRAPHICS' ACTIVITY MODELS

Basic Purchases Activity Model

After talking with Linda B about their purchases and payments process, our first task was to draw a simple business process model using BPMN. As shown in Figure 6.2, the start of the process occurs when Sunset needs to purchase items to fulfill a customer order or to replenish inventory. Then, a series of tasks takes place in sequence until Sunset pays for the items and the process ends. Sunset records purchases and updates inventory when it receives the items.

FIGURE 6.2
Basic Purchases Activity Model

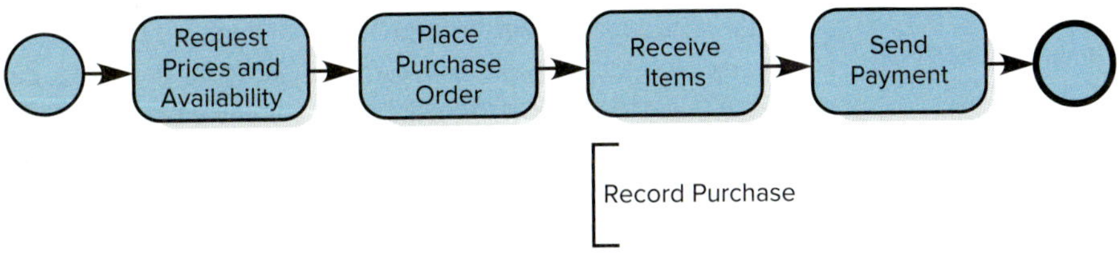

LO 6-3
Understand and apply different activity modeling options.

Refining the Model to Show Collaboration

After reviewing models for the sales and collection process in Chapter 5, Linda was starting to understand these models. She remarked that she liked the **collaboration** model better because it shows the interactions with the external parties that Sunset relies on. So, she asked if we could prepare a collaboration model of the purchases and payments process. Of course, we said we could. In this case, the *pools* would show suppliers and Sunset, with *message flows* (shown by dashed arrows) between pools describing the interaction between participants. In fact, if you are primarily interested in the interactions, you don't need to model the **orchestration** within either pool. To illustrate, we prepared Figure 6.3, which shows the two pools for the suppliers and Sunset Graphics and the **choreography** between them.

FIGURE 6.3
Collaboration Purchases Activity Model

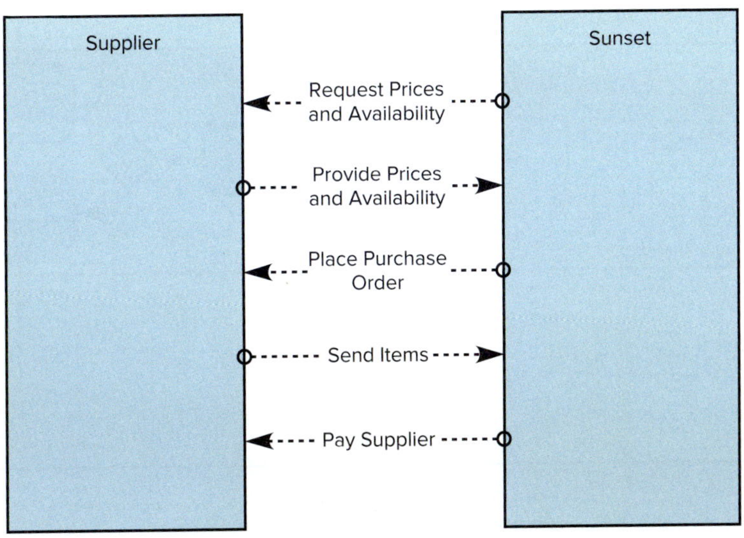

Linda thought that this model offered a good overview of their typical purchase and payment process. It showed the choreography of interactions between the pools. However, she reminded us that she would not be doing most of Sunset's buying and bill paying in the future. Because she was delegating those jobs, she thought that she should separate the buying duties from the payment duties for better internal control. She wondered if we could prepare a model that shows the process while highlighting different jobs within Sunset. We said that we could, and we reminded her about lanes in BPMN that allow us to model those different jobs.

Linda thought that showing the different jobs would provide better process documentation. However, she also noted that sometimes they do not get acceptable items from the supplier and have to send them back. She asked if we could also allow for that in the model. We prepared Figure 6.4 to show her a model with lanes that also allows for the return of deficient items.

In Figure 6.4, we included lanes for the buyer, receiving, and accounts payable (A/P) jobs that will exist at Sunset after Linda delegates her duties. We combined the Request Prices and Availability and Place Purchase Order activities in the original model shown in Figure 6.2 with a **subprocess** because we want to expand on those activities later. We also added another step to assess the items after receiving them from the supplier. Then, we included a **gateway** to branch into two possible courses of action. If the items are not acceptable, Sunset returns them to the supplier and the process ends. If the items are

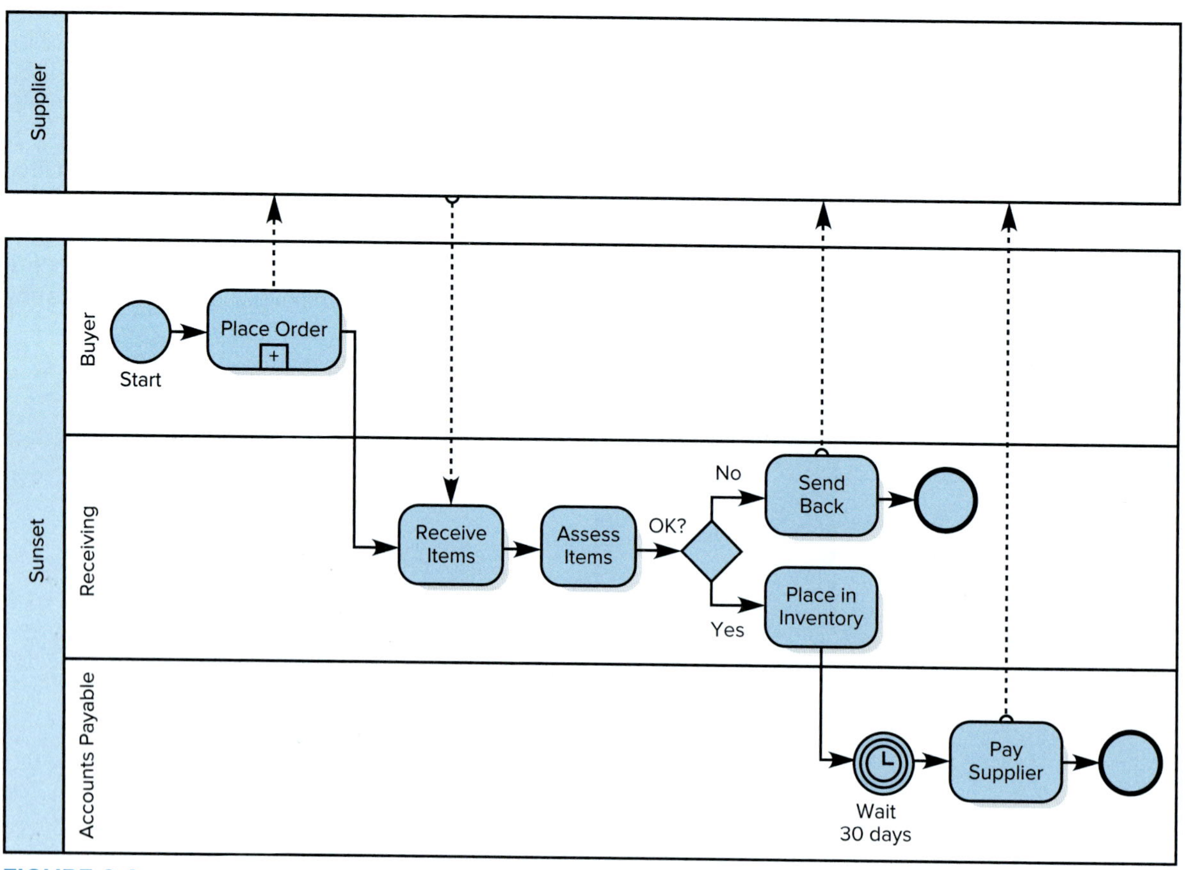

FIGURE 6.4
Expanded Collaboration Purchases Activity Model with Lanes

acceptable, they are placed in inventory; 30 days later (depending on credit terms), Sunset sends a payment to the supplier. Because there are two possible paths that do not reconnect, we include two end events.

Because we added some new notation, we explained what the new symbols mean. The gateway is modeled with the diamond. In this case, the gateway branches into two exclusive paths. We noted that with BPMN 2.0, gateways don't represent activities, so we needed to include the assessment activity, Assess Items, before the gateway. We also included an **intermediate timer event** (the **intermediate event** symbol with clock hands) to represent the time delay, Wait 30 days, before payment. **Timer events** represent a delay in the flow of a process. They can indicate a delay to (1) a specific date, such as December 31; (2) a relative time, such as 30 days; or (3) a relative repetitive date, such as next Friday at 5:00 p.m.

Progress Check

1. In Figure 6.4, at what point would Sunset record the purchase?
2. From your own experience, describe how you would change Figure 6.4 to reflect another purchases and payments process. What if the customer purchased over the Internet and paid by credit card?

LO 6-4
Develop business rules to implement controls for the purchase and payment process.

BUSINESS RULES AND SUNSET GRAPHICS' PURCHASES AND PAYMENTS PROCESS CONTROLS

Next, we wanted to talk about planning controls over the purchases and payments process to give Virgil and Linda more confidence in the integrity of the process when they stepped back from the day-to-day operations. As with the sales and collection process, we want to define controls by developing business rules for the process. First, we need to identify important business events and define Sunset's intention or objective for each event. Then, we determine the appropriate actions to take based on the conditions. For example, we've already listed important business events in the business process models, so let's examine Sunset's purchases and payments process in Figure 6.4 and develop some possible business rules.

Again, Virgil and Linda summarized their objectives for the steps in the process. Of course, their overall goal was to purchase needed items from reliable suppliers at the best possible prices to meet required delivery schedules. They also wanted to be sure that these suppliers were paid on time, taking prompt payment discounts where appropriate, so they could maintain positive, long-term relationships. Because they were not going to directly supervise the process anymore, they wanted to be sure that effective controls were applied.

Adding new purchases to inventory.
© Digital Vision/Getty Images

We outlined some standard controls over the purchases and payments process, suggesting segregation of ordering, receiving, and payment duties.

Process Steps	Intention	Partner Authority/ Action	Access Controls	Application Controls
Place Order	Order products from reliable suppliers at the best available prices to meet required delivery time.	Manager approval required for orders >$5,000; partner ordering products must not manage inventory.	Partner preparing purchase orders cannot modify product inventory records, receive items, or pay suppliers.	System must provide purchase order number control, default values, and range and limit checks and must create an audit trail.
Receive Items	Record receipt of items promptly and accurately.	Partner receiving items must not be same partner who ordered the items.	Partner receiving items cannot modify purchase orders or inventory records; they cannot view purchase order quantity ordered information.	System must only allow partner to enter the number of items received, subject to range and limit checks on quantities received; date of receipt defaults to current date.
Assess Items	Reject defective items; record acceptance promptly and accurately.	Partner assessing items must not be same partner who ordered the items.	Partner assessing items cannot modify purchase orders or inventory records.	System must only allow partner to record the assessment; date of assessment defaults to current date.
Place in Inventory	Place accepted items in proper inventory locations promptly.	Partner placing the items in inventory must not be same partner who ordered the items.	Partner placing items in inventory cannot modify purchase orders.	System must specify where items are to be placed.
Send Items Back	Return defective items to suppliers promptly.	Manager approval required for defective items return.	Partner returning items cannot modify supplier information.	System must supply supplier return address.
Pay Supplier	Pay suppliers accurately, taking cost-effective discount terms.	Partner making payment must not be partner who ordered items or received/ accepted items.	Partner making payments cannot modify purchase orders and receipt/ acceptance records.	System must supply supplier payment information and amount of payment; payment date defaults to current date.

TABLE 6.1
Using Business Rules to Implement Internal Controls

We reiterated that *access controls* limit which of their partners can view and change records in the system and help implement appropriate segregation of duties. We also need *application controls* to ensure data integrity and an audit trail. For example, we need to control the assignment of purchase order and receiving report numbers to make sure all of them are accounted for. Plus, we need to establish appropriate ranges or limits for each value that Sunset's partners can add or change in the system.

With Virgil and Linda's direction, we developed an initial set of business rules for the purchases and payments process. They articulated their intentions for every step in the process, and then we set business rules to segregate duties and limit partner authority appropriately. Table 6.1 shows the initial set of business rules for Sunset's purchases and payments process. We noted that we would need to set application controls for almost every attribute updated during data entry.

LO 6-5
Develop structure models for the purchase and payment process using UML class diagrams.

SUNSET GRAPHICS' STRUCTURE MODELS

Linda B seemed pleased with the business process models so far. However, Virgil B was more interested in planning Sunset's new database. He'd already set up the sales and collection tables in Access, and he was waiting for the purchases and payments model so he could set up these tables, too. So, we proceeded to examine Sunset Graphics' purchases and payments information requirements. As described in Chapter 3, the primary purpose of our UML class diagram of the purchases and payments process is to create a blueprint for the development of a relational database to support the collection, aggregation, and communication of process information. As in Chapter 5, we follow the **REA** framework (**resources, events,** and **agents**) as a proven approach to describing business processes in a way that meets both accounting and broad management information requirements.

Basic UML Class Diagram for Purchases and Payments

We quickly reviewed Sunset's requirements for the purchases and payments process with Virgil B. In this case, a Sunset Partner (agent) selects the Supplier (agent) and issues a Purchase Order (event) as indicated by the number 1 on Figure 6.5. The Purchase Order specifies the prices and quantities of Products (resource) ordered. The Supplier (agent) sends, and a Sunset Partner (agent) receives (Receipts event), the products (resource) as indicated by the number 2 on Figure 6.5. The **receipt** triggers the recognition of the purchase and the corresponding account payable in the accounting records. Then, when the payment is due, a Sunset Partner (agent) pays (cash disbursement event) the Supplier (agent) from a Cash account (resource) as indicated by the number 3 on Figure 6.5.[2] The payment reduces accounts payable.

We showed Virgil the basic model, and he noticed that this model looked very similar to the sales and collection process model. Although the events were different, the resources and the Sunset Partner agent were the same. We said that this was a typical purchases and payments process. We always start with this basic diagram when we model the purchases and payments process, and then we modify it to reflect the unique information structure of a particular company. The Purchase Orders event represents Sunset's commitment to purchase **products** and pay the supplier, although commitments do not affect the financial statements. The Receipts event does affect the financial statements because it records the purchase for those items received and accepted and records the increases to accounts payable. The Cash Disbursement event also affects financial statements because it records decreases to **cash** and decreases to accounts payable.

FIGURE 6.5
Basic UML Class Diagram for Purchases and Payments

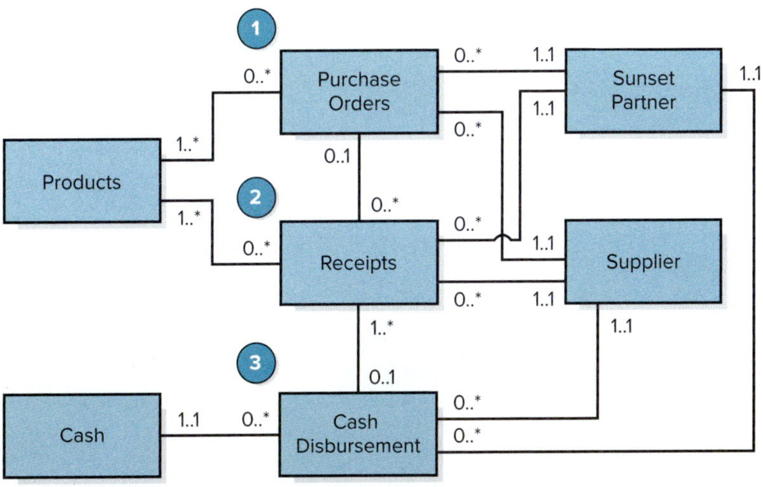

[2]Note that UML class diagrams reflect data structure and do not necessarily reflect the sequence of events.

Virgil said that he thought he understood multiplicities pretty well from our sales and collection process models, but he wanted to review a couple of them to make sure. For example, the multiplicities for the association between Purchase Orders and Products specify a **many-to-many relationship.** Each purchase order requests a minimum of one and a maximum of many products, and each product might not yet have been ordered and could be ordered many times.[3] We said that was correct but asked Virgil to explain the multiplicities for the Purchase Orders to Receipts association. He thought about it for a minute because he was not sure why a Purchase Order could be associated with multiple Receipts or why a Receipt could be related to a minimum of 0 Purchase Orders. We answered that we thought some Receipts were purchased over-the-counter from suppliers without first issuing a Purchase Order. Additionally, we thought that some Purchase Orders could result in partial shipments from the Supplier. Virgil responded that he could see how the model reflected those assumptions, but our assumptions were not correct. He said that Sunset always records a Purchase Order, even for over-the-counter purchases, and does not accept partial shipments.

Refining the UML Class Diagram for Purchases and Payments

Because Virgil said that Sunset always records Purchase Orders for a purchase and never accepts partial shipments, we revised the diagram. Because there is always a **one-to-one relationship** between Purchase Orders and Receipts, we can collapse the two classes into one and simplify the diagram (even though receipts happen after the orders). The new Purchases (event) class in Figure 6.6 would record purchase orders and include an attribute to indicate that the products were received. This is similar to the way we modeled Orders in the sales and collection process.

Each Purchase is associated with a minimum of 0 and a maximum of 1 Cash Disbursement because Sunset usually pays for purchases 30 days after receipt and pays in full. Each Cash Disbursement is associated with a minimum of 0 and a maximum of many Purchases because Sunset writes checks for other purposes and combines payments for multiple purchases from the same supplier when possible.

FIGURE 6.6 Revised UML Class Diagram for Purchases and Payments

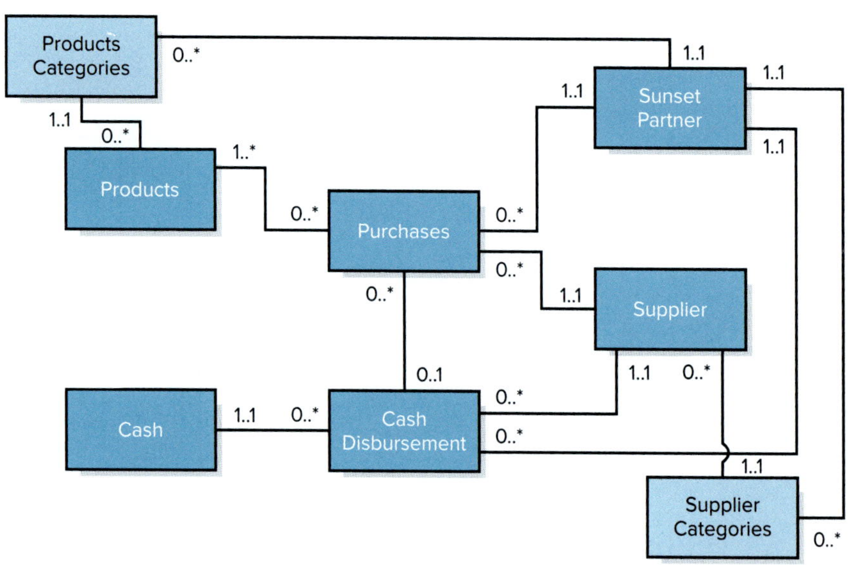

[3]We assume that products are identified before they are ordered.

Because we were refining the diagram, we added the **type image** for Product Categories that we also identified in the sales and collection process. Virgil then said that they also categorize their suppliers, so he suggested that we add a type image for Supplier Categories. He was really starting to understand UML class diagrams. We also added the association between Sunset Partners and Product Categories to reflect the assignment association that we identified in the sales and collection process.

Virgil agreed that Figure 6.6 accurately reflected their purchases and payments process. He was anxious to get started on defining the database. He recognized the composition association between Purchases and Purchase Items reflected by the many-to-many relationship between Purchases and Products. He said he understood how to post the foreign keys (see Chapters 3 and 4).

Progress Check

3. Describe when you would define two events—purchase orders and purchases—instead of combining them.
4. Review Figure 6.6 and explain when you might consider an association between Product Categories and Supplier Categories.

LO 6-6

Implement a relational database from the UML class diagram of the purchases and payments process.

SUNSET GRAPHICS' RELATIONAL DATABASE

Virgil and Linda B were both interested in implementing the purchases and payments UML class diagram in a relational database for Sunset. Again, we use Microsoft Access, but the process would be similar for any database-driven system. We encourage students to use the following description to implement a relational database to support information requirements for the purchases and payments process.

Relational Database Planning for Attributes

During the model development process, we reviewed Sunset's existing documents to determine specific data requirements for each class/table. We then followed the guidance in Chapter 3 to determine allocation of foreign keys. This resulted in a list of tables, attributes, data types, field sizes, and primary and foreign keys as shown in Table 6.2.

PK/FK	Attribute Name	Type	Size
	Table: tblBankAccounts		
PK	Account_number	Text	10
	Bank_routing_number	Text	10
	Bank_balance	Currency	8
	Bank_name	Text	15
	Bank_branch	Text	15
	Bank_phone_number	Text	15
	Table: tblCashDisbursements		
PK	Check_Number	Text	10
	Check_Amount	Currency	8
	Check_Date	Date/Time	8
FK	Supplier_Number	Text	10
FK	Account_Number	Text	10
FK	Partner_Number	Text	10
	Table: tblPartners		
PK	Partner_number	Text	10
	Partner_first_name	Text	15
	Partner_last_name	Text	15
	Partner_hire_date	Date/Time	8
	Partner_SocSecNo	Text	11
	Partner_Address	Text	50
	Partner_Address2	Text	50
	Partner_City	Text	20
	Partner_State	Text	2

TABLE 6.2
Sunset Database Table and Attribute Definitions

(continued)

PK/FK	Attribute Name	Type	Size
	Partner_Zip	Text	10
	Partner_phone	Text	14
	Partner_cellphone	Text	14
	Table: tblProductCategory		
PK	Product_category_number	Text	10
	Product_category_description	Text	255
	Product_category_manager	Text	10
	Product_category_notes	Memo	—
	Table: tblProducts		
PK	Product_number	Text	10
	Product_description	Text	255
	Product_price	Currency	8
	Product_unit_of_sale	Text	10
FK	Product_category	Text	10
	Product_quantity_on_hand	Integer	2
	Product_notes	Memo	—
	Table: tblPurchaseItems		
PK	Purchase_Order_number	Text	10
PK	Product_number	Text	10
	Purchase_Order_quantity	Integer	2
	Purchase_Order_price	Currency	8
	Received_quantity	Integer	2
	Accepted_quantity	Integer	2
	Table: tblPurchases		
PK	Purchase_Order_Number	Text	10
	Purchase_Order_Date	Date/Time	8
FK	Prepared_by	Text	10
FK	Supplier_Number	Text	10
	Received_Date	Date/Time	8
	Purchase_Order_Amount	Currency	8
	Required_by	Date/Time	8
FK	Check_Number	Text	10
	Memo	Memo	—
	Table: tblSupplierCategory		
PK	Supplier_category_number	Text	10
	Supplier_category_description	Text	255
	Supplier_category_purchases_YTD*	Currency	8
	Supplier_category_notes	Memo	—
	Table: tblSuppliers		
PK	Supplier_Number	Text	15
	Supplier_Name	Text	25
	Supplier_Contact_Name	Text	20
	Suppllier_Address	Text	30
	Supplier_Address_2	Text	30
	Supplier_City	Text	20
	Supplier_State	Text	2
	Supplier_Zip	Text	5
	Supplier_phone	Text	15
	Supplier_web_site	Hyperlink	—
FK	Supplier_Category	Text	10

* Year to date

TABLE 6.2
(continued)

Creating the Database and Defining the Tables

The next step is to create a new, blank Microsoft Access database and create the tables described in Table 6.2. Then, establish *relationships* between the tables as shown in Figure 6.7 and as described in Chapter 5. At that point, Sunset's purchases and payments process database is set up.

FIGURE 6.7
Linked Tables with Referential Integrity Enforced

© Microsoft Access

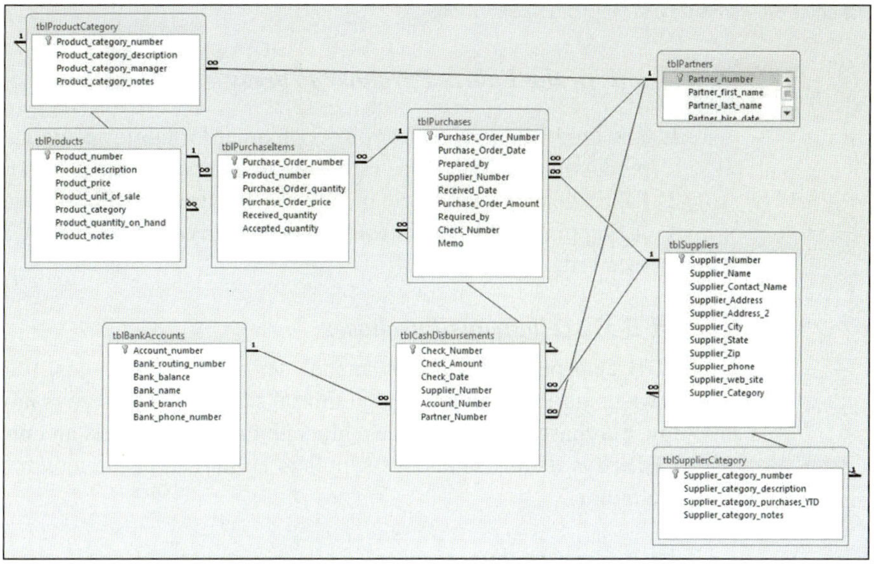

COMPREHENSIVE EXERCISE: BAER BELLY BIKINIS' PURCHASES OF FABRIC

As outlined in Chapter 5, Baer Belly Bikinis Inc. (BBB) is a small business located in Santa Monica, California. It sells swimwear and related products to specialty stores throughout the United States. It also sells its products to individuals over a company website. Paige Baer founded BBB almost 10 years ago after she graduated from the Fashion Institute of Design and Merchandising. She recognized the need for swimsuits sold as separates. Her business has grown rapidly, and now BBB has a large following of customers who want to be able to mix and match to find their ideal swimsuit. Currently, BBB products are carried in more than 1,000 specialty swimwear boutiques and online retailers.

During an initial interview with Paige Baer, she outlined BBB's business processes. She acknowledged that she doesn't know much about accounting and information technology. As the business grew, her accounting suffered and information systems were added piecemeal. So, she is looking forward to an assessment of her requirements and recommendations that would position BBB for substantial further growth.

This case examines BBB purchases of fabric. BBB's production staff selects the fabric and materials for the swimsuits. This case also examines BBB purchases of and miscellaneous supplies and services.

BBB Purchases of Fabric

BBB works closely with local fabric vendors to determine the color themes for each season's products. When BBB has received enough orders from the retailer customers to estimate the quantity of swimsuits and products to manufacture, BBB then orders the required quantities of fabric and related materials from the fabric vendors. BBB pays each fabric vendor at the end of the month for all purchases during the month. For each fabric order, there is one receipt. For each receipt of fabric, there is one order. Consequently, the order and purchases (receipts) can be modeled as one event.

Assessing fabric purchase requirements.
© Todd Wright/Blend Images/Getty Images

Details of the Fabric Purchase Process

1. The Production supervisor places an order for fabric according to internal estimates of production quantities (the estimates are not part of the project).
2. Fabric vendors ship fabric in bulk to BBB usually within 2 weeks of the order.
3. A Shipping and Warehouse employee receives the bulk fabric and verifies quantities received.

BBB Miscellaneous Purchases

BBB also purchases miscellaneous services and supplies, such as electricity, water, sewage, garbage, phone, and janitorial services. It also pays monthly rent on the building, purchases office supplies, hires photo shoot models and photographers, and so on. BBB pays its miscellaneous suppliers at the end of the month for all purchases during the month.

BBB Cash Disbursements

BBB assigns sequential numbers to each check issued. All checks for purchases (both fabric and miscellaneous) are written on its main bank account.

Exercise Requirements

1. Based on the preceding information and the following attributes list, prepare a UML class model and corresponding table listing describing BBB's purchases and payments process. List the tables in the following order: resources, events, agents, type images, and linking tables. Identify the primary keys and foreign keys in each table. [optional] Prepare a second UML model that combines the fabric and miscellaneous purchases events and the fabric and miscellaneous vendor agents. Show how you might model a way to differentiate among the types of vendors.
2. [optional] Based on the preceding information, prepare a BPMN activity model that describes BBB's purchases and payments process. The model should begin with BBB placing orders with its vendors and end when BBB makes payments for the purchases to the vendors.
3. Your instructor will provide an Excel spreadsheet with the BBB information. Create a new Access database, and import each worksheet in the spreadsheet into the database. Set appropriate primary keys.
4. After importing all the data, create relationships among tables to implement your data model.
5. Prepare queries to answer the following questions:

   a. What were BBB's total purchases of fabric in the second quarter (April to June)?
   b. What is BBB's accounts payable balance for each fabric as of April 15?
   c. Based on the information available, what is the quantity on hand in yards for each fabric color code as of April 15?

Attribute Listing for BBB

Bank Name	Employee#
Cash Account#	Employee Address
Cash Account Balance Beginning (April 1)	Employee City
Cash Account Description	Employee Department
Check#	Employee First Name
Check Amount	Employee Hire Date
Check Pay Date	Employee Last Name

Employee Pay Amount
Employee Phone
Employee Salary/Wage
Employee Zip
Fabric Color Code
Fabric Color Name
Fabric Cost per Yard
Fabric Inventory Quantity on Hand
Fabric Purchase Date Received
Fabric Purchase Order#
Fabric Purchase Order Date
Fabric Purchase Quantity in Yards
Fabric Purchase Received By
Fabric Purchase Total Amount
Fabric Vendor#
Fabric Vendor Address1
Fabric Vendor Address2
Fabric Vendor Company
Fabric Vendor Item Number
Fabric Vendor State
Fabric Vendor Type
Fabric Vendor Zip
Miscellaneous Purchase#
Miscellaneous Purchase Amount
Miscellaneous Purchase Date
Miscellaneous Purchasing Employee#
Miscellaneous Vendor#
Miscellaneous Vendor Address1
Miscellaneous Vendor Address2
Miscellaneous Vendor Company
Miscellaneous Vendor Item Number
Miscellaneous Vendor State
Miscellaneous Vendor Zip
Order Employee#
Pay Employee#
Vendor Type

Summary

- From an accounting standpoint, we must account for purchase orders, the receipt of goods and services (purchases), accounts payable, and cash disbursements (payments) in the purchases and payments process.
- Sunset Graphics Inc. provides a continuing example of how the purchases and payments process is modeled.
- BPMN activity diagrams can provide the basic sequence of tasks or can be extended to describe specific organizational responsibilities for tasks.
- Business rules implement controls over the purchases and payments process.
- UML class diagrams for the purchases and payments process are built on the standard REA pattern and look very similar to sales and collection process structure diagrams.
- Type images categorize information about agents and resources and show assignments.
- The structure models are the blueprint from which relational databases are designed and implemented.
- A comprehensive example reinforces the concepts presented in the chapter.

Key Words

accounts payable (*152*) Amounts owed to suppliers for goods and services received. In a data modeling context, accounts payable are calculated based on receipts (purchases) from each supplier less the corresponding payments (cash disbursements) to those suppliers.

agents (*157*) The people or organizations who participate in business events, such as customers and salespeople.

cash (*157*) The organization's monies in bank or related accounts. The instances of the class are individual accounts. This is considered a resource.

cash disbursements (*152*) Record payments of cash to external agents (e.g., suppliers) and the corresponding reduction in cash accounts. This is considered an event.

choreography (*153*) The interaction (message flows) between two participants (modeled as pools) in a process modeled using BPMN.

collaboration (*153*) A BPMN model showing two participant pools and the interactions between them within a process.

events (*157*) Classes that model the organization's transactions, usually affecting the organization's resources, such as sales and cash receipts; Important occurrences that affect the flow of activities in a business process. BPMN includes symbols to define start, intermediate, and end events.

gateway (*154*) Shows process branching and merging as the result of decisions. Basic gateways are depicted as diamonds. Usually, gateways appear as pairs on the diagram. The first gateway shows the branching, and the second gateway shows merging of the process branches.

intermediate event (*155*) Occurs between start and end events and affects the flow of the process.

intermediate timer event (*155*) Intermediate events that indicate a delay in the normal process flow until a fixed amount of time has elapsed.

many-to-many relationship (*158*) Exists when instances of one class (e.g., sales) are related to many instances of another class (e.g., inventory) and vice versa. These relationships are implemented in Access and relational databases by adding a linking table to convert the many-to-many relationship into two one-to-many relationships.

one-to-one relationship (*158*) Exists when instances of one class (e.g., sales) are related to only one instance of another class (e.g., cash receipts) and each instance of the other class is related to only one instance of the original class.

orchestration (*153*) In BPMN, the sequence of activities within one pool.

product (*157*) Class representing the organization's goods held for sale, that is, the organization's inventory. This is considered a resource.

purchase discount (*152*) An offer from the supplier to reduce the cost of a purchase if payment is made according to specified terms, usually within a specified time.

purchase order (*152*) A commitment event that precedes the economic purchase event. It records formal offers to suppliers to pay them if the supplier complies with the terms of the purchase order.

purchases (*152*) Records the receipt of goods or services from a supplier and the corresponding obligation to pay the supplier. These are considered events.

REA (*157*) Resource-event-agent framework for modeling business processes, originally developed by William McCarthy.

receipt (*157*) Same as the purchases event.

resources (*157*) Those things that have economic value to a firm, such as cash and products.

subprocess (*154*) Represents a series of process steps that are hidden from view in BPMN. The use of subprocesses in modeling helps reduce complexity.

suppliers (*152*) In the UML diagram of the purchases and payments process, the external agents from whom goods and services are purchased and to whom payments are made.

timer events (*155*) Indication of a delay in the flow of a process to a specific date, an elapsed time (for example, 30 days), or a relative repetitive date, such as every Friday.

type image (*159*) Class that represents management information (such as categorizations, policies, and guidelines) to help manage a business process. Type image often allows process information to be summarized by category.

Generic REA Model with Multiplicities for the Purchases and Payments Process

GENERIC PATTERN WITH MULTIPLICITIES

Figure 6.A1 shows a generic purchases and payments process UML diagram. There are two resources, *inventory* and *cash;* there are two events, *purchases* and *cash disbursements;* and there are two agents, *employees* (internal agent) and *suppliers* (external agent).

FIGURE 6.A1
Generic Purchases and Payments UML Diagram

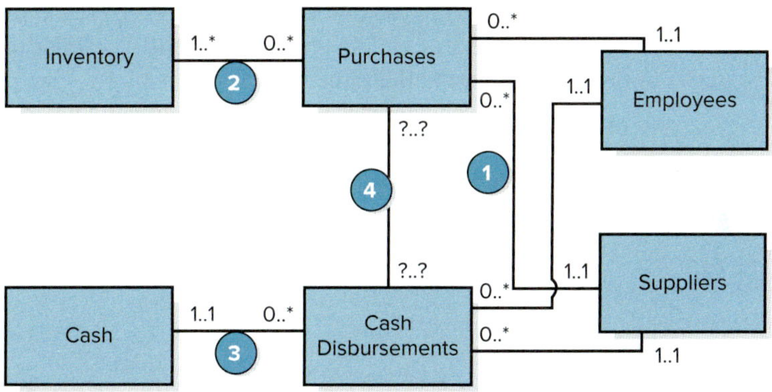

In this example, let's assume that the inventory is something tracked by universal product code (UPC). UPC are those bar codes you see on literally millions of products, such as soap, breakfast cereal, and packages of cookies. The cash resource represents the various bank accounts that would make up this enterprise's cash balance on its balance sheet. The purchases event records information about individual purchase transactions (e.g., transaction number, date, total dollar amount). The cash disbursement event records information about payments made to suppliers from one of the bank accounts (e.g., check number, check date, check dollar amount). The employees' agent records information about the enterprise's employees, including those employees who handle purchases transactions. The suppliers agent records information about actual and potential suppliers (let's assume that supplier information is recorded in some cases before the firm orders anything from them, and let's also assume that the company only writes checks to suppliers).

Figure 6.A1 shows the generic REA model. You should immediately notice the similarity with the sales and collection process diagram shown in Appendix A of Chapter 5. Consider association 1 between *suppliers* and *purchases.* The multiplicities indicate that each supplier participates in a minimum of zero and a maximum of many sales. Does this seem reasonable? The minimum of zero means that we can record information about suppliers before they participate in any sale. On the other side of the association, the multiplicities indicate that each purchase involves one and only one supplier. Again, does this seem reasonable? Notice that the multiplicities for the other associations between agents and events are the same. In fact, these are the typical multiplicities for those associations. There are circumstances where they might be different, but those circumstances occur infrequently.

Next, consider association 2 between the *purchases* event and *inventory* resource. The multiplicities indicate that each purchase involves a minimum of one and a maximum of many inventory items. The multiplicities also indicate that each inventory item can be purchased zero times or many times. The multiplicities on this association are typical when the inventory is carried at a type of product level, such as when the inventory is identified by UPC code.

Now, consider association 3 between the *cash disbursement* event and the *cash* resource. These multiplicities indicate that each cash disbursement (e.g., one check) is paid from one and only one account, and each account is associated with a minimum of zero cash disbursements and a maximum of many cash disbursements. These multiplicities reflect typical business practices. Think about paying bills using your bank's online banking feature. You log on, select the account, and then pay the bill. The amount of the payment is subtracted from that one account.

Finally, consider the duality association 4 between the *purchases* and *cash disbursement* events. The question marks indicate that these multiplicities depend on the nature of the business as well as the terms of the particular purchase. Payments could be made before, after, or at the same time as the purchase. One payment could be made for several purchases, or one purchase could involve several payments. So, there are no typical multiplicities for this association.

We recommend that students recognize and use the standard patterns for multiplicities as shown in Figure 6.A1, remembering that those standard multiplicities could change depending on the particular circumstances of the business.

Answers to Progress Checks

1. Sunset would record the purchase when the items are received and accepted, so the purchase is recognized with the Place in Inventory activity.
2. If they purchased over the Internet, they would pay when they placed the order. The Pay Supplier activity would then occur during the Place Order process.
3. You would define two events when there is not a one-to-one relationship between purchase orders and purchases.
4. You would link Product Categories and Supplier Categories if summary information depended on both the product and supplier categories, for example, year-to-date sales for this product category and this supplier category.

Multiple Choice Questions

1. Which of the following is not an activity in the purchases and payments process? **LO 6-1**
   a. Request prices
   b. Receive items
   c. Pay for items
   d. Bill customers
   e. All of the above are activities in the purchases and payments process.

2. Which activity results in an increase to accounts payable? LO 6-1
   a. Request prices
   b. Place purchase order
   c. Receive items
   d. Return rejected items
   e. Send payment
3. *Choreography* describes which of the following? LO 6-2, LO 6-3
   a. Sequence of activities in a process
   b. Message flows between pools
   c. Process gateways
   d. Both a and c
   e. Both b and c
4. Which of the following is not an example of an application control? LO 6-4
   a. Range checks ensure that purchases are limited to valid amounts.
   b. Employee making disbursements cannot modify purchase orders.
   c. System supplies supplier address for the payment.
   d. System creates audit trail documenting all changes.
   e. All of the above are examples of application controls.
5. Which of the following describes the purpose of an intermediate timer event? LO 6-3
   a. Indicates receipt of a message
   b. Indicates branching
   c. Indicates delay
   d. Both a and c
   e. Both b and c
6. Which of the following is a resource in a purchases and payments structure model? LO 6-5
   a. Employee labor
   b. Receipt of goods
   c. Paying by check
   d. Inventory
   e. Supplier
7. Which of the following is an agent in a purchases and payments structure model? LO 6-5
   a. Employee labor
   b. Receipt of goods
   c. Cash disbursement
   d. Inventory
   e. Supplier
8. Which of the following is an event in a purchases and payments structure model? LO 6-5
   a. Cash
   b. Inventory
   c. Employee
   d. Cash disbursement
   e. None of the above

9. Which of the following events would indicate recording of a purchase in the AIS? **LO 6-5**
   a. Issue Purchase Order
   b. Receive Goods
   c. Make Payment
   d. Transfer Inventory
   e. None of the above
10. In a typical relational database supporting the purchase and payment process, which of the following tables is likely to have the most foreign keys? **LO 6-5**
   a. Employee table
   b. Supplier table
   c. Inventory table
   d. Cash disbursement table
   e. Cash table

Use the following diagram to answer Questions 11 through 27.

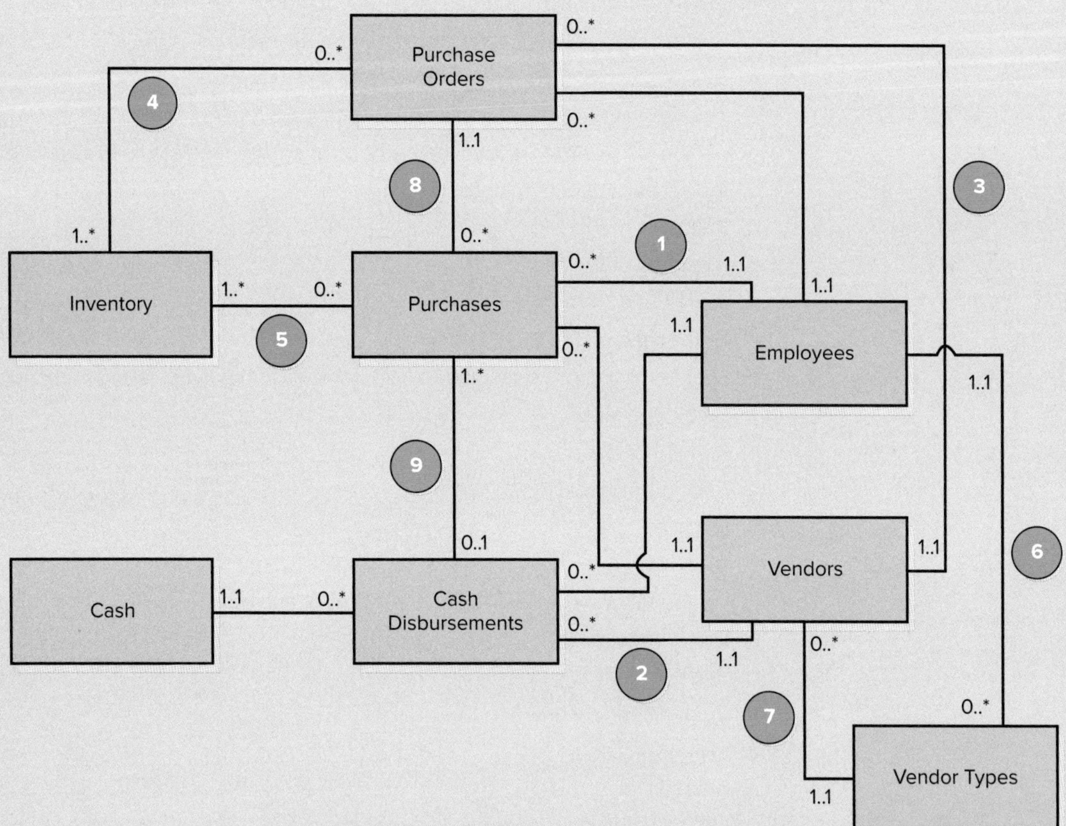

11. Refer to the association marked with the number 1 in the preceding diagram. Which of the following is the best description of the association? **LO 6-5**
   a. Each employee participates in a minimum of zero purchases.
   b. Each employee participates in at least one purchase.
   c. Each employee participates in a maximum of one purchase.
   d. Only employees in the shipping and receiving department receive purchases.
   e. None of these are a description of the association.

12. Refer to the association marked with the number 1 in the preceding diagram. Which of the following is the best description of the association? **LO 6-5**
    a. Each purchase is received by multiple employees.
    b. Each purchase is received by one employee.
    c. Each purchase can be received by a maximum of many employees.
    d. Each purchase can be received by a minimum of zero employees.
    e. None of these are a description of the association.
13. Refer to the association marked with the number 2 in the preceding diagram. Which of the following is the best description of the association? **LO 6-5**
    a. Each vendor always receives multiple cash disbursements.
    b. Each vendor receives a minimum of zero cash disbursements.
    c. Each vendor receives a maximum of one cash disbursement.
    d. Each vendor is paid by check.
    e. None of these are a description of the association.
14. Refer to the association marked with the number 2 in the preceding diagram. Which of the following is the best description of the association? **LO 6-5**
    a. Each cash disbursement is made to many vendors.
    b. A cash disbursement can be made to zero vendors
    c. Each cash disbursement is made to a maximum of one vendor.
    d. Each cash disbursement is made to a minimum of zero vendors.
    e. None of these are a description of the association.
15. Refer to the association marked with the number 3 in the preceding diagram. Which of the following is the best description of the association? **LO 6-5**
    a. Vendors may receive many purchase orders.
    b. Vendors must receive at least one purchase order.
    c. Vendors receive a minimum of one purchase order.
    d. Vendors receive a maximum of one purchase order.
    e. None of these are a description of the association.
16. Refer to the association marked with the number 3 in the preceding diagram. Which of the following is the best description of the association? **LO 6-5**
    a. Each purchase order is issued to many vendors.
    b. Each purchase order is issued to zero vendors.
    c. Each purchase order is issued to a maximum of many vendors.
    d. Each purchase order is issued to a minimum of one vendor.
    e. None of these are a description of the association.
17. Refer to the association marked with the number 4 in the preceding diagram. Which of the following is the best description of the association? **LO 6-5**
    a. Each purchase order specifies a type of inventory.
    b. Each purchase order is associated with a maximum of many inventory items.
    c. Each purchase order is associated with a minimum of zero inventory items.
    d. Some purchase orders do not list inventory items.
    e. None of these are a description of the association.

18. Refer to the association marked with the number 4 in the preceding diagram. Which of the following is the best description of the association? **LO 6-5**
    a. Each inventory item is ordered one time.
    b. Each inventory item is ordered zero times.
    c. Each inventory item is ordered on a minimum of zero purchase orders.
    d. Each inventory item is ordered on a minimum of one purchase order.
    e. None of these are a description of the association.
19. Refer to the association marked with the number 4 in the preceding diagram. Which of the following is the best way to implement the association in a relational database? **LO 6-5, LO 6-6**
    a. Post the primary key of purchase orders as a foreign key in inventory.
    b. Post the primary key of inventory in purchase orders as a foreign key.
    c. Create a linking table with a concatenated primary key.
    d. Record the date of the purchase order in the inventory table.
    e. None of these are a description of the correct implementation.
20. Refer to the association marked with the number 5 in the preceding diagram. Which of the following is the best description of the association? **LO 6-5**
    a. Each inventory item is associated with a minimum of one purchase.
    b. Each inventory item is purchased one time.
    c. Each inventory item is purchased zero times.
    d. Each inventory item is associated with a minimum of zero purchases.
    e. None of these are a description of the association.
21. Refer to the association marked with the number 5 in the preceding diagram. Which of the following is the best description of the association? **LO 6-5, LO 6-6**
    a. Purchases increase the quantity-on-hand of inventory items.
    b. Each purchase includes a minimum of zero inventory items.
    c. Each purchase includes a minimum of two inventory items.
    d. A purchase may be associated with a maximum of one inventory item.
    e. None of these are a description of the association.
22. Refer to the association marked with the number 5 in the preceding diagram. Which of the following is the best way to implement the association in a relational database? **LO 6-5**
    a. Create a linking table with a concatenated primary key.
    b. Post the primary key of purchases as a foreign key in inventory.
    c. Post the primary key of inventory in purchases as a foreign key.
    d. Post the purchases primary key in inventory and the inventory primary key in purchases.
    e. None of these are a description of the correct implementation.
23. Refer to the association marked with the number 6 in the preceding diagram. Which of the following is the best description of the association? **LO 6-5**
    a. Some employees are also vendor types.
    b. Employees only deal with authorized vendor types.
    c. Some employees are assigned to work with specific vendor types.
    d. Some vendor types are not issued purchase orders.
    e. None of these are a description of the association.

24. Refer to the association marked with the number 6 in the preceding diagram. Which of the following is the best way to implement the association in a relational database? LO 6-5
    a. Post the primary key of vendor types in employees as a foreign key.
    b. Post the primary key of employees as a foreign key in vendor types.
    c. Create a linking table with a concatenated primary key.
    d. The association does not require foreign keys.
    e. None of these are a description of the correct implementation.
25. Refer to the association marked with the number 7 in the preceding diagram. Which of the following is the best description of the association? LO 6-5
    a. Some vendors are not in a vendor type.
    b. Employees do not deal with vendors that are not in a vendor type.
    c. Vendors are classified by type.
    d. Each vendor type must contain at least one vendor.
    e. None of these are a description of the association.
26. Assume that you are drawing an activity (BPMN) diagram of the process. Which of the following is not true about your diagram? LO 6-5
    a. The issue purchase order task occurs before the receive purchases task.
    b. The purchases task could be modeled as a looping task to show multiple purchases following one purchase order.
    c. The process starts when a customer places a sales order.
    d. The process ends when the vendor is paid.
    e. All of these are true about the diagram.
27. Assume that you are drawing a collaboration activity (BPMN) diagram of the process. Which of the following would not be message flows on your diagram? LO 6-5
    a. Purchase order
    b. Delivery (of the purchase)
    c. Check/cash disbursement
    d. Inventory update
    e. All of these are message flows for the diagram.

Discussion Questions

1. Business rules implement internal controls. Review Table 6.1 and describe which business rules implement segregation of duties. Classify each of those business rules as obligatory, prohibited, or allowed as described in Chapter 3. LO 6-4
2. Walmart uses a vendor-managed inventory system, where the inventory is owned and managed by the vendor until it is delivered from Walmart's distribution center to the stores. What implications does this system have for Walmart's purchases and payments process? LO 6-1
3. Draw an activity model using BPMN for the process that you followed when you purchased your textbooks for the current semester. LO 6-2, LO 6-3
4. Refer to Figure 6.5. Describe the types of businesses that would employ a similar diagram for their purchases and payments processes. What other alternative approaches are there? Describe some businesses that would use these alternatives for the purchases and payments process structure. LO 6-2

5. Recall that type images apply guidelines, constraints, and descriptive information, as well as categorizing the economic resources, events, and agents for a business process. Figure 6.6 shows two examples of type images for Sunset Graphics. Are there other possible type images that could be added to the diagram to help Sunset's managers manage the purchases and payments process? **LO 6-5**
6. Some larger companies and government entities issue contracts for major purchases and then issue specific purchase orders to their contractors according to the terms of the contract. The contract can specify prices and payment terms as well as other administrative procedures. How would the use of contracts affect the standard process flow as shown in Figure 6.2? How would it affect the UML class diagram for the purchases and payments process? **LO 6-5**
7. Sunset Graphics often buys inventory after receiving a sales order from the customer. Suppose you are asked to prepare one UML class diagram that combines both the sales and collection process and the purchases and payments process. What would be shared among those processes? What would be unique to each process? Why? **LO 6-5**
8. What classes and associations would be included in a model that describes the information needed for a query that calculates the accounts payable balance for each supplier? Describe the logic of that query. (In other words, what steps would you follow to compute that balance?) **LO 6-5, LO 6-6**

Problems

connect

1. The following narrative describes the purchase and payment process for The Tablet Store. Use the narrative to answer the questions below. The Tablet Store recently opened to sell iPads and other tablet computing devices. It purchases its tablets directly from the manufacturers (e.g., **Apple**, **Samsung**, and **Dell**). To order tablets, a Tablet Store employee submits a purchase order to the manufacturer electronically. Each purchase order could stipulate several different models of tablets from one manufacturer. The manufacturers typically deliver the tablets to the store within two weeks after they receive the purchase order. The Tablet Store pays for each shipment within 30 days after receipt. If there are multiple orders to the same manufacturer, the Tablet Store occasionally combines payments, issuing one check for multiple receipts. All of the Tablet Store checks are drawn on one bank account. **LO 6-5, LO 6-6**
   a. Draw a UML class diagram that describes the Tablet Store's purchases and payments process.
   b. Using Microsoft Access, implement a relational database from your UML class diagram. Identify at least three fields per table.
   c. Describe how you would use the relational database to determine the Tablet Store's accounts payable.

connect

2. The following narrative describes the purchase and payment process for Quick Jet Inc. Use the narrative to answer the questions below. Quick Jet Inc. provides air taxi service to the wealthy, including celebrities, sports stars, and business executives. Quick Jet employees negotiate long-term leases with airplane leasing companies. Each lease involves one plane. Quick Jet categorizes its planes according to passenger capacity and normal flying range. Quick Jet makes monthly lease payments for its planes. If it leases multiple planes from the same lease company, it combines payments. **LO 6-2, LO 6-3, LO 6-5**

   Maintenance
   The company has no maintenance staff of its own, so it also contracts with a number of airplane maintenance companies to perform the routine maintenance required to keep its fleet airworthy. It issues orders against the contracts for specific maintenance required for the planes. To comply with FAA regulations, it tracks the details of the specific maintenance performed on each plane. To facilitate the tracking, each maintenance order specifies the maintenance services for one plane. Quick Jet pays for all the maintenance performed by each maintenance contractor within 15 days, according to the terms of the contracts, and may combine payments.

Miscellaneous Purchases

Quick Jet also provides each of its pilots with credit cards so they can purchase fuel and miscellaneous supplies at the various airports they use. The pilots turn in detailed lists of their purchases that identify the supplier, the date, the amount purchased, and the prices, as well as the plane for which the items were purchased. Each list is assigned a miscellaneous purchase number. Quick Jet pays the credit card bills in full each month upon receipt from the credit card company.

Other Information

Quick Jet keeps information about the plane leasing companies, the plane maintenance contractors, miscellaneous suppliers, and the credit card companies in one vendor file. However, it tracks plane leases, maintenance contracts, maintenance orders, and miscellaneous purchases separately (separate events). Quick Jet categorizes its employees according to their job assignments (e.g., pilots, purchasing employees, A/P clerks). It also categorizes vendors according to the services/goods they provide. It puts information about its agents, resources, and type images in the database before linking to other classes.

a. Draw a BPMN activity diagram that describes Quick Jet's purchases and payments process.

b. Prepare a UML class diagram with classes, associations, and multiplicities.

c. Using the preceding information and the following attributes list, prepare a listing of the relational tables necessary to support this sales and collection process. List the tables in the following order: resources, events, agents, type images, and linking tables.

Attributes:

Cash account#
Cash account balance
Check#
Check amount
Check date
Date this misc. purchase billed by credit card company
Employee#
Employee hire date
Employee name
Employee type
Employee type description
Lease#
Lease date
Lease monthly payment amount
Misc. supply purchase#
Misc. supply purchase date
Number of vendors of this type
Plane#
Plane maintenance contract#
Plane maintenance contract date
Plane maintenance contract duration
Plane maintenance item performed on this order for this plane
Plane maintenance order#
Plane maintenance order date
Plane miles since last maintenance
Plane type
Plane type passenger capacity
Plane type range in miles
Vendor#
Vendor Name
Vendor type
Vendor type description
Year-to-date (YTD) purchases from this vendor type

3. The following narrative describes a purchase and payment process and a sales and collection process for BR Management Company. Use the narrative to answer the questions below. BR Management Company (BRMC) operates apartment complexes and earns revenues by renting out the apartments in those complexes. BRMC assigns an agent/manager to each complex (one manager can manage several complexes) to handle day-to-day operations, such as maintaining the property and signing rental contracts. This case describes the maintenance and rental processes. LO 6-5

Complexes and Apartments

BRMC has acquired 15 and built several more apartment complexes over the past 2 years. It identifies complexes by address and apartments by the combination of address and apartment number. BRMC categorizes each apartment according to a number of factors, including the quality of its furnishings, number of rooms, and size. There are 27 apartment categories at present, each identified by unique category number. Because each complex presents a unique set of luxury appointments and amenities, BRMC determines the standard monthly rental fee by considering both the apartment category and complex; for example, 2 bedroom 1 bath apartments (category 21) rent for $850 per month in the Broadway complex, but the same category apartments rent for $1,450 per month in the Naples complex.

Maintenance

BRMC keeps its apartments and complexes in top condition. The BRMC agents monitor the condition of the facilities. Whenever the condition falls below BRMC standards, the agents hire contractors to bring the apartment back up to specifications. BRMC classifies each maintenance job by job type, and it matches the job type to the contractor type that can best perform the job. The BRMC agent then selects one specific contractor for the job from that contractor type. Each contractor may belong to several contractor types. Each maintenance job involves either one apartment or the common areas of the complex. BRMC tracks the maintenance performed on apartments and complex common areas.

Rentals

BRMC agents negotiate rental contracts with tenants. Each rental contract governs one year-long lease of an apartment. Although there is a standard monthly rental fee for each apartment in each building, agents may negotiate higher or lower rents if they see the need to do so. It is important to have a full record of the actual rent for all apartments. When there is more than one tenant per apartment, every tenant must sign the rental contract. BRMC assigns a unique tenant ID number to each tenant and issues them ID cards to control access.

Cash Receipts and Disbursements and Other Information

To simplify the case, the cash resource, the cashier agent, and the cash receipt and disbursement events (although they would certainly exist) are eliminated. You should *not* model those in your solution. All agents, resources, and types are put into the database before they are linked to other classes.

a. Prepare an integrated UML class diagram with classes, associations, and multiplicities.
b. Using the preceding information and the following attributes list, prepare a listing of the relational tables necessary to support BRMC's processes. List the tables in the following order: resources, events, agents, type images, and linking tables.

Attributes:

Actual completion date of job	Apartment square footage
Actual cost of this job	Apartment#
Actual monthly rent	Category
Agent monthly salary	Contractor name
Agent name	Contractor phone number
Apartment category#	Contractor quality rating
Apartment complex address	Contractor type

Contractor#
Count of rooms in apartment
Count of this type of contractor
Date complex was constructed
Employee#
Job type
Maintenance job#
Number of available apartments in this category
Projected completion date of job
Rental contract date
Rental contract#
Standard cost for this job type
Standard monthly rent
Tenant credit rating
Tenant ID#
Tenant name
Total complex square footage
Vendor#
Year to date (YTD) advertising $ for this
YTD $ spent on this job type
YTD $ spent on this job type in this complex

Additional problems are available in connect only.

Chapter **Seven**

Conversion Business Process

A look at this chapter

This chapter examines the conversion process whereby manufacturing companies convert raw material into finished goods. We continue our comprehensive example to develop activity and structure models of the process. We show how the activity model in conjunction with business rules can be used to develop, implement, and monitor control activities. We show how the structure model can be used to develop a relational database to support information processing requirements.

A look back

Chapter 6 examined the purchases and payments processes. It continued the comprehensive example that we are using to examine typical process activities and data structures.

A look ahead

Chapter 8 provides a hands-on project to review Chapters 5, 6, and 7.

© Ingram Publishing/SuperStock

Starbucks roasts its coffee in roasting plants distributed around the United States. One plant is a nondescript, 320,000-square-foot warehouse building located in Kent, Washington. Other roasting plants are located in Carson Valley, Nevada; York, Pennsylvania; and Amsterdam, Netherlands. The coffee beans are stacked in 150-pound burlap bags, and each bag is marked to identify the country of origin.

The bags of green coffee beans are stacked over a large metal grate in the floor. A worker cuts open the bag and the beans pour through the grate. They are pulled into a washer that separates foreign material. After washing, the beans are weighed, sorted, and stored for roasting. They are transferred into large roasters that can hold up to 600 pounds of beans. The roasting process is carefully controlled by computer. As the beans roast, they slowly turn brown. When the beans pop, the flavor is released.

The beans are transferred to cooling vats that turn and toss them to stop further roasting. Workers test the roasted beans. Soon, they are bagged and boxed for shipment. On average, the roasted beans will be in stores within 3 days.

To keep a constant flow of quality product to their worldwide network of stores, Starbucks needs to monitor its conversion process closely. In addition to the cost information that affects its financial statements, what other information is necessary for Starbucks' management of this process?

Chapter Outline

Learning Objectives

After reading this chapter, you should be able to:

7-1 Describe the business activities that comprise the conversion process.

7-2 Develop an activity model of the conversion process using BPMN.

7-3 Understand and apply different activity modeling options.

7-4 Develop business rules to implement controls for the conversion process.

7-5 Develop a structure model for the conversion process using UML class diagrams.

7-6 Implement a relational database from the UML class diagram of the conversion process.

LO 7-1
Describe the business activities that comprise the conversion process.

CONVERSION PROCESS

The conversion process is inherently more complicated than the sales and collections and purchases and payments processes described in the previous two chapters, primarily because of increased recordkeeping requirements and variations in the sophistication of the process itself among companies. Many types of businesses employ conversion processes, including bakeries, wineries, breweries, restaurants, car repair shops, construction companies, equipment manufacturers, automobile manufacturers, and so on.[1] The conversion process includes business activities related to maintaining inventories of raw material and finished goods, producing finished goods from raw material, tracking direct labor and direct equipment costs, and applying overhead.

The conversion process generates accounting transactions to record the transfer of raw material to work-in-process and work-in-process inventory to finished goods. In addition to the cost of raw materials, the conversion process must also account for direct labor and other direct costs incurred in determining the cost of goods manufactured. The allocation of overhead and indirect costs to work-in-process is typically based on direct labor-hours, although overhead could be allocated based on a number of cost drivers in an activity-based costing system. More specifically, conversion costs are typically accounted for at standard, where the standard is based on management estimates, and then the costs are updated to reflect actual costs incurred. Figure 7.1 describes typical transactions resulting from the conversion process. In addition to the accounting transactions, the specific details of the conversion process are often tracked to the individual job.

In this chapter, we continue to apply the tools introduced in Chapters 2 through 6 to a comprehensive example of the conversion process. We first describe the process activities using BPMN, and then we define the typical information structure using UML class diagrams. Finally, we use the UML class diagrams to build a database to collect and report relevant process information. We also describe business rules that establish potential process controls.

SUNSET GRAPHICS EXAMPLE

Company Overview

As described in Chapters 5 and 6, Virgil and Linda B own and operate Sunset Graphics. They design and sell signs and banners, lettering and vinyl graphics for vehicles and boats, corporate promotional items, and silk-screened T-shirts and embroidered gear, among other products. Recently, Virgil and Linda decided that it was time to step back from the day-to-day operations. Before they did, they wanted to review their business processes to develop better documentation, improve processes, and establish consistency in customer service. They also wanted to be sure that effective internal controls were in place because they wouldn't be on site as often.

Sunset Graphics' Conversion Process Description

Until recently, Sunset didn't track its conversion costs. If labor was involved in preparing products for a customer's order, Sunset simply billed the customer a flat rate for the service. The company didn't assign any labor or overhead costs to its products. However, that changed when it signed a major contract to provide a variety of signs and banners to state agencies. The terms of the contract required that Sunset include direct labor, direct

[1]We focus on companies that use job cost accounting methods, although the models could apply generally to companies that also use process costing methods.

FIGURE 7.1
Typical Conversion Process Accounting Transactions

Sep 1	**Work-in-Process Inventory**	**2,875,50**	
	Raw Material Inventory		**2,875.50**
	Record transfer of raw material to Work-in-process		
Sep 2	**Manufacturing Wages**	**4,650.00**	
	Cash		**4,650.00**
	To record manufacturing payroll		
Sep 2	**Work-in-Process Inventory**	**3,250.00**	
	Manufacturing Wages		**3,250.00**
	To record direct labor		
Sep 2	**Manufacturing Overhead**	**1,400.00**	
	Manufacturing Wages		**1,400.00**
	To record indirect labor		
Sep 2	**Manufacturing Overhead**	**1,945.25**	
	Utilities Payable		**1,945.25**
	To record manufacturing overhead costs		
Sep 2	**Work-in-Process Inventory**	**4,062.50**	
	Manufacturing Overhead		**4,062.50**
	To allocate manufacturing overhead to		
	work-in-process at 125% of direct labor		
Sep 3	**Finished Goods**	**10,188.00**	
	Work-in-Process Inventory		**10,188.00**
	Record transfer of work-in-process to finished goods		

equipment costs, and overhead in the cost of its products. Although Sunset used job costing for this contract, Virgil and Linda B began to wonder if job costing could be used to provide better information about the real costs of their products.

Virgil and Linda B explained their conversion process. Demand for products under the state contract fluctuated but often required short delivery times, so they decided to keep a safety stock of those products (**finished goods inventory**) on hand. When inventory levels dropped below certain levels, they then authorized production to replenish the inventory. To reduce delays, they also decided to maintain a **raw materials inventory,** although they wanted to keep those inventory levels as low as possible. It required some planning, but they created bills of material that identified the raw material required for each product and estimated the required inventory levels to keep production smooth and meet demand.

They summarized Sunset's conversion process as follows:

1. When the quantity on hand of a product drops below the minimum level, the item manager authorizes production to increase the quantity on hand.
2. Based on the bill of material for that item, they issue material into work-in-process.
3. Sunset partners then construct the items.
4. Upon completion, the products are placed in inventory.

LO 7-2
Develop an activity model of the conversion process using BPMN.

SUNSET GRAPHICS' ACTIVITY MODELS

Basic Conversion Activity Model

After talking with Virgil and Linda B about their conversion process, our first task was to draw a simple activity model using BPMN. As shown in Figure 7.2, the start of the process occurs when Sunset needs to replenish finished goods inventory. Then, the production authorization starts production activities, including the issue of raw material (R/M) and the use of direct labor. Work continues until the required quantity of the finished good item is prepared. At that point, production is complete, and the finished goods inventory is updated.

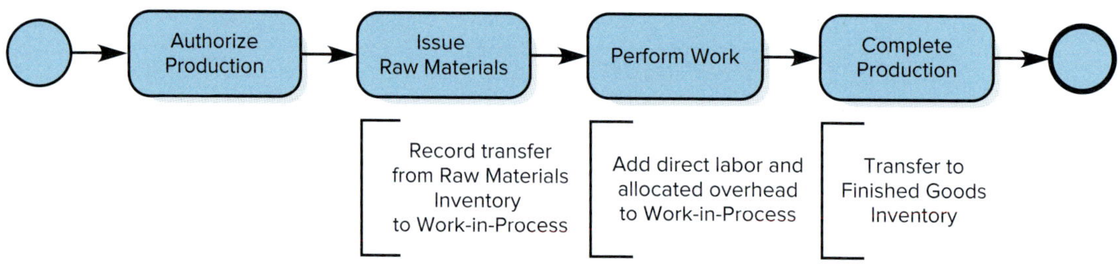

FIGURE 7.2
Basic Conversion Activity Model

LO 7-3
Understand and apply different activity modeling options.

Refining the Model

Virgil remarked that a collaboration model would not make much sense here. All the work is within Sunset. We agreed, but we said that swimlanes could show the different functions within Sunset to help clarify responsibilities. Both Virgil and Linda thought that, yes, it would clarify responsibilities. Virgil then added that sometimes they performed the work in a series of batches to make the process more manageable. Plus, they didn't necessarily issue all the raw materials at once. Sometimes, they started a batch, issued some raw materials, worked on those, and then issued more raw materials. They repeated these steps until they finished production.

We said that it would be pretty easy to add those refinements to the model, but we wondered if there was anything else to consider. Linda then added that they always inspect the work before it is added to the finished goods inventory, and if it doesn't meet quality standards, they discard the bad items and replace them. Finally, while partners place the finished items in inventory, the inventory manager updates the records.

Virgil was confident that he understood BPMN now. He suggested that the model could use multiple lanes and show the looping to reflect Sunset's conversion process. He then sketched the model shown in Figure 7.3. This model showed two lanes: (1) for the inventory manager and (2) for the Sunset employees who perform the work. This model shows the inventory manager authorizing production. Then, the conversion partners set up the batch, issue raw materials, and perform work making the finished good item. At that point, a partner inspects the work and if the work does not meet quality standards, the **intermediate error event** directs the process flow to the "discard items" activity. The sequence then loops back to issue more raw materials. If the batch is not finished, the **gateway** also directs the sequence flow back to issue more raw materials, and the steps are repeated until the batch is done. Then, a second gateway branches, depending on whether all batches are complete. If not, the sequence flow is directed back to the "set up batch" activity and the steps repeat until all batches are done. The conversion partners complete production by placing the finished items in inventory, and the inventory manager updates the inventory records.

We congratulated Virgil on his understanding of activity modeling. We said that his model would work, but we might be able to simplify it a little. We could use a looping

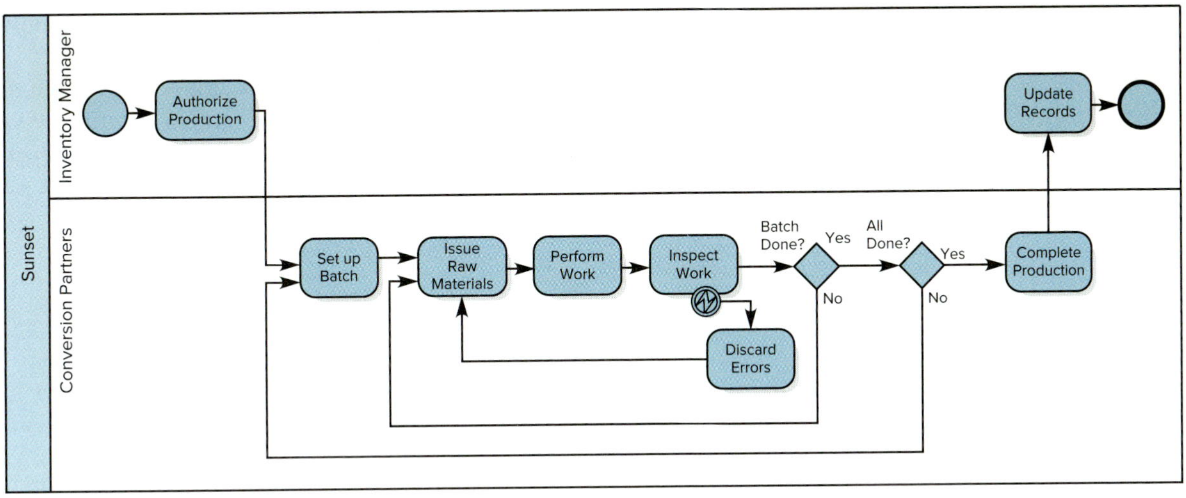

FIGURE 7.3
Conversion Process with Swimlanes and Loops

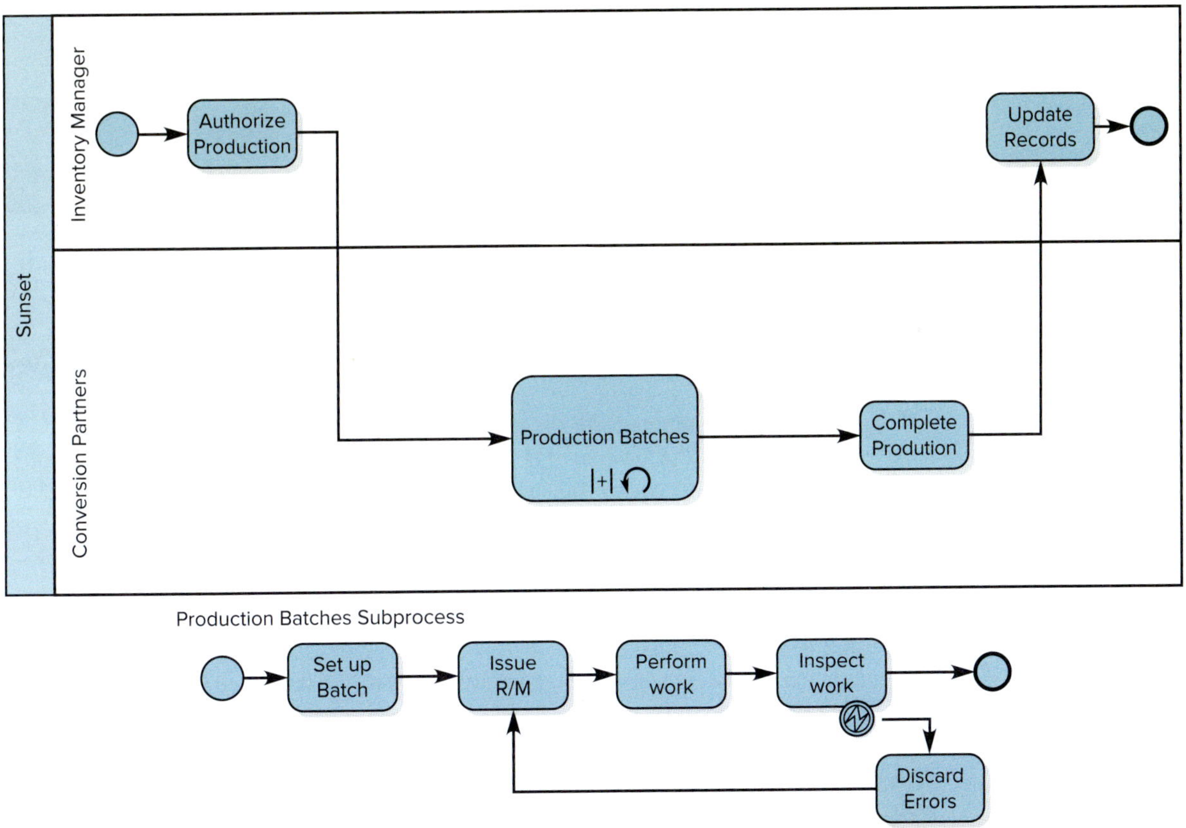

FIGURE 7.4
Conversion Process with Looping Collapsed Subprocess and Separate Production Batches Subprocess

collapsed subprocess (see Chapter 2) to represent the batch activities. The subprocess loops until all batches are done. The steps in the subprocess are then shown separately as in Figure 7.4. In this case, the original model was not that complicated, so either diagram is understandable. When certain parts of any process are complex, it can often improve understanding of the overall process if the complex parts are modeled separately. Then, one diagram shows the overall flow at a higher level, and the separate subprocess can show the more complex part of the process at a lower level of detail.

Both Virgil and Linda agreed that this model accurately describes their process. We noted that for internal control, we probably should have identified a third lane to show the separate "inspect work" function. The same partners who perform the work should not inspect the work. Virgil acknowledged that we were probably right, but we could leave that change for another day.

Progress Check

1. How would you change Figure 7.3 to show a separate organization unit performing the inspect work function?
2. Could you model the intermediate error event with a gateway instead? What would that look like?

LO 7-4
Develop business rules to implement controls for the conversion process.

BUSINESS RULES AND SUNSET GRAPHICS' CONVERSION PROCESS CONTROLS

Again, we asked Virgil and Linda B about controls over the conversion process. As with the other processes, we intended to define controls by developing business rules for the process. First, we needed to identify important business events and define Sunset's intention or objective for each event. Then, we determined the appropriate actions to take based on the conditions. For example, we've already listed important business events in the activity models, so let's examine Sunset's conversion process in Figures 7.2 and 7.3 to develop some possible business rules.

Inspecting work and discarding defects.
© Tetra Images/Getty Images

Virgil and Linda summarized their objectives for the steps in the process. Of course, their overall goal was to ensure finished products were available to meet expected demand. Because they were not going to directly supervise the process anymore, they wanted to be sure that effective controls were applied.

We outlined some standard controls over the conversion process, suggesting segregation of authorizing, issuing, and conversion work duties. We reiterated that *access controls* limit which of their partners can view and change records in the system and help implement appropriate segregation of duties. We also need *application controls* to ensure data integrity and an audit trail. For example, we need to control the assignment of production authorization and material issue numbers to make sure they are all accounted for. Plus, we need to establish appropriate ranges or limits for each value that partners can add or change in the system.

With Virgil and Linda's direction, we developed an initial set of business rules for the conversion process. They articulated their intentions for every step in the process, and then we set business rules to segregate duties and limit partner authority appropriately. Table 7.1 shows the initial set of business rules for Sunset's conversion process. We noted that we would need to set application controls for almost every attribute updated during data entry.

TABLE 7.1
Using Business Rules to Implement Internal Controls

Process Steps	Intention	Partner Authority/Action	Access Controls	Application Controls
Authorize Production	Partner with proper authority authorizes production to ensure finished goods are available to meet expected demand.	Supervisor must authorize production >$5,000.	Partner authorizing production cannot modify inventory records.	System must provide authorization order number control, default values, and range and limit checks; must also create audit trail.
Issue Raw Material	Issues from raw material according to bill of material recorded accurately.	Partner issuing material must not be same partner who authorized production.	Partner recording issue of material cannot modify bill of material.	System must only allow partner to enter the number of items issued based on bill of material, subject to range and limit checks on quantities; date defaults to current date.
Perform Work	Direct labor costs recorded promptly and accurately.	Partner performing direct labor must not be same partner authorizing production.	Partner recording labor costs cannot modify production authorization.	System must provide control numbers, hours, costs range, and limit checks; date defaults to current date.
Inspect Work and Discard Defects	Inspection ensures that only products meeting quality standards are allowed.	Partner inspecting work must not be a partner performing work.	Partner recording inspection cannot modify inventory records.	System must provide limit checks; date defaults to current date.
Complete Production	Finished product inventory must be updated promptly and accurately.	Partner placing products in finished inventory must not be same partner authorizing production.	Partner recording update of inventory records cannot modify production authorization.	System must default date to current date; inventory update limit is based on authorization.

LO 7-5
Develop a structure model for the conversion process using UML class diagrams.

SUNSET GRAPHICS' STRUCTURE MODELS

Now, both Virgil and Linda B looked forward to adding the conversion process features to Sunset's new database. This would mean that their database could handle their entire supply chain encompassing purchasing, making, and selling their products. We proceeded to examine Sunset Graphics' conversion information requirements. As described in Chapter 3, the primary purpose of our UML class diagram of the conversion process is to create a blueprint for the development of a relational database to support the collection, aggregation, and communication of process information. As in Chapters 5 and 6, we follow the **REA** framework (resources, events, and agents) as a proven approach to describing business processes in a way that meets both accounting and broad management information requirements.

Basic UML Class Diagram for Conversion

Based on what Virgil and Linda told us about their conversion process, we thought it was very close to a generic conversion process model shown in Figure 7.5. As indicated by numbers 1 and 2, an employee **(agent)** with supervisory responsibility authorizes

FIGURE 7.5
Generic UML Class Diagram for the Conversion Process

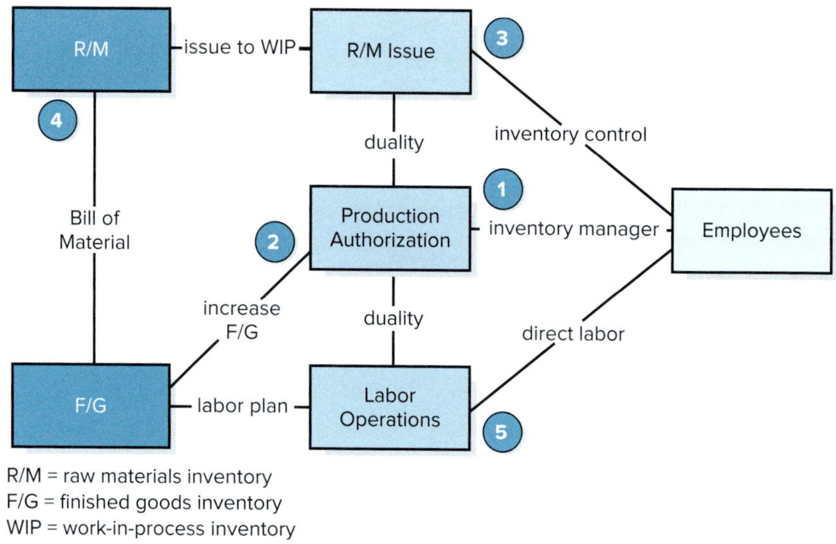

production **(event)** of one or more finished goods items **(resources).** Next, numbers 3 and 4 denote that an employee (agent) issues (event) the raw material (resource) into **work-in-process inventory** based on the bills of material for the finished goods items. Finally, number 5 shows that production employees perform work to make sure the finished goods are items and their direct labor are recorded **(labor operations event).**

We explained that the association between finished goods and labor operations indicates the planned labor. The bill of materials association between finished goods and raw material indicates the planned material content of each finished goods item. The two duality associations link the raw material issue and labor operations events to the production authorization. Thus, the data structure captures information about both planned and actual conversion activity.

Virgil said that he understood most of the diagram, but where is the work-in-process inventory resource? We explained that we don't need to model a separate work-in-process inventory because we can calculate that value at any time. For example, the **raw material issue event** records the value of items issued into work-in-process. The labor operations event records the value of direct labor added to work-in-process. The labor plan association establishes standard overhead allocation rates. Until the job is complete, the accumulated material, labor, and overhead costs increase work-in-process inventory. When the job is complete, which would be recorded in the initial **production authorization event,** the cost of goods manufactured increase the finished goods inventory value.

Refining the UML Class Diagram for Sunset's Conversion Process

Virgil thought Sunset's bill of materials should be more than an association, although he agreed that the company's conversion process resembled the generic model. For Sunset, the bill of materials contains more than a simple link between Sunset's material (raw materials) and its final products (finished goods). He also believed that they really had no defined labor plan. Sunset just recorded direct labor incurred and used a simple overhead allocation scheme.

We replied that it was easy to modify the generic process diagram to reflect Sunset's information requirements for the conversion process. We could "promote" the bill of materials association to a **type image** class because there was more detail involved. Also, the

Updating finished goods inventory.
© Steve Cole/Getty Images

bill of materials association is typically a **many-to-many relationship** between raw materials and finished goods because each raw material item could be used for multiple finished goods items and vice versa. We would likely create a table to implement that association anyway. We could also remove the labor plan association between the finished goods resource and the labor operations event. We developed the class diagram shown in Figure 7.6 reflecting those modifications, including multiplicities, and also keeping the association between Sunset Partners and Product Categories from the sales and collection process.

Virgil and Linda both thought that the revised class diagram accurately reflected their information requirements. However, they had some hypothetical questions about modeling the conversion process to make sure they understood it perfectly. For example, they asked how we would modify the model if Sunset used equipment in the conversion process and wanted to record direct equipment costs. We replied that we would simply add an equipment resource to capture information about the equipment, and then we would add an equipment operations event to record the costs of the use of the equipment. They said that made sense; an event records costs applied to work-in-process and a resource captures permanent information about the things available for use in the process. We added that type images can specify the plan for resource use, and then the plan could be compared to the actual usage recorded in the events.

FIGURE 7.6
Revised UML Class Diagram for Sunset's Conversion Process

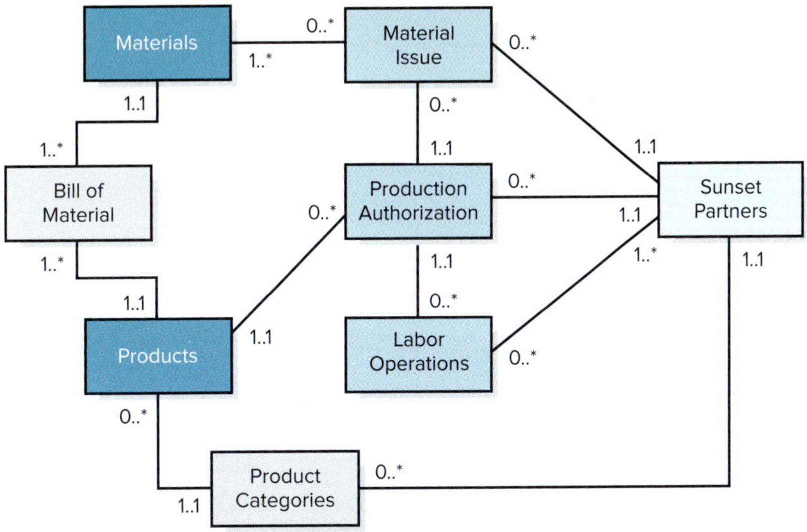

Progress Check

3. Figure 7.6 dropped the labor plan association. Could Sunset instead have "promoted" the labor plan association to a type image? How would that affect the diagram?
4. Add the equipment resource and equipment operations event to the diagram, and define the multiplicities.

LO 7-6
Implement a relational database from the UML class diagram of the conversion process.

SUNSET GRAPHICS' RELATIONAL DATABASE

Virgil and Linda B were both interested in implementing the conversion UML class diagram in a relational database for Sunset. Again, we use Microsoft Access, but the process would be similar for any database-driven system. We encourage students to use the following description to implement a relational database to support information requirements for the conversion process.

Relational Database Planning for Attributes

During the model development process, we again reviewed Sunset's existing documents to determine specific data requirements for each class/table. We then followed the guidance in Chapters 3 and 4 to determine allocation of foreign keys. This resulted in a list of tables, attributes, data types, field sizes, and primary and foreign keys as shown in Table 7.2.

Creating the Database and Defining the Tables

The next step is to create a new, blank Microsoft Access database and create the tables described in Table 7.2. Then, establish relationships between the tables as shown in Figure 7.7 following the process outlined in Chapter 5. At that point, Sunset's conversion process database is set up.

PK/FK	Attribute Name	Type	Size
	Table: tblBill_of_Material		
PK	BOM_number	Text	10
	Issue_sequence	Integer	8
	Standard_quantity	Double	8
FK	Product_number	Text	10
FK	Material_number	Text	255
	Special_handling	Memo	—
	Table: tblLabor_Operations		
PK	Labor_ops_Number	Text	10
FK	Prod_auth_number	Text	10
	Labor_ops_description	Memo	—
	Table: tblLabor_Operations_Partners		
PK	Labor_ops_number	Text	10
PK	Partner_number	Text	10
	Actual_direct_labor_hours	Long Integer	4
	Actual_direct_labor_wage	Currency	8
	Table: tblMaterial_Issue		
PK	Material_Issue_number	Text	10
	Issue_date	Date/Time	8
FK	Issued_by	Text	10
FK	Prod_auth_number	Text	255

PK/FK	Attribute Name	Type	Size
	Table: tblMaterial_Issue_Materials		
PK	Material_issue_number	Text	10
PK	Material_number	Text	10
	Qty_issued	Long Integer	4
	Table: tblMaterials		
PK	Material_number	Text	10
	Material_description	Text	255
	Material_price	Currency	8
	Material_quantity_on_hand	Integer	2
	Material_notes	Memo	—
	Table: tblPartners		
PK	Partner_number	Text	10
	Partner_first_name	Text	15
	Partner_last_name	Text	15
	Partner_hire_date	Date/Time	8
	Partner_SocSecNo	Text	11
	Partner_Address	Text	50
	Partner_Address2	Text	50
	Partner_City	Text	20
	Partner_State	Text	2
	Partner_Zip	Text	10

TABLE 7.2
Sunset Database Tables and Attribute Definitions for the Conversion Process

PK/FK	Attribute Name	Type	Size
	Partner_phone	Text	14
	Partner_cellphone	Text	14
	Table: tblProduct_Category		
PK	Product_category_number	Text	10
	Product_category_description	Text	255
FK	Product_category_manager	Text	10
	Product_category_notes	Memo	—
	Table: tblProduction_ Authorizations		
PK	Prod_auth_number	Text	255
	Prod_auth_date	Date/Time	8
FK	Partner_number	Text	10
FK	Product_Number	Text	10
	Scheduled_qty_to_produce	Long Integer	4
	Actual_qty_produced	Long Integer	4
	Scheduled_completion_date	Date/Time	8
	Actual_completion_date	Date/Time	8
	Overhead_rate	Single	4
	Total_material_cost	Currency	8
	Total_direct_labor	Currency	8
	Total_overhead	Currency	8
	Total_COGM*	Currency	8
	Table: tblProducts		
PK	Product_number	Text	10
	Product_description	Text	255
	Product_price	Currency	8
	Product_unit_of_sale	Text	10
FK	Product_category_number	Text	10
	Product_quantity_on_hand	Integer	2
	Product_notes	Memo	—

*Cost of goods manufactured.

TABLE 7.2 *(continued)*

FIGURE 7.7
Linked Conversion Process Tables with Referential Integrity Enforced

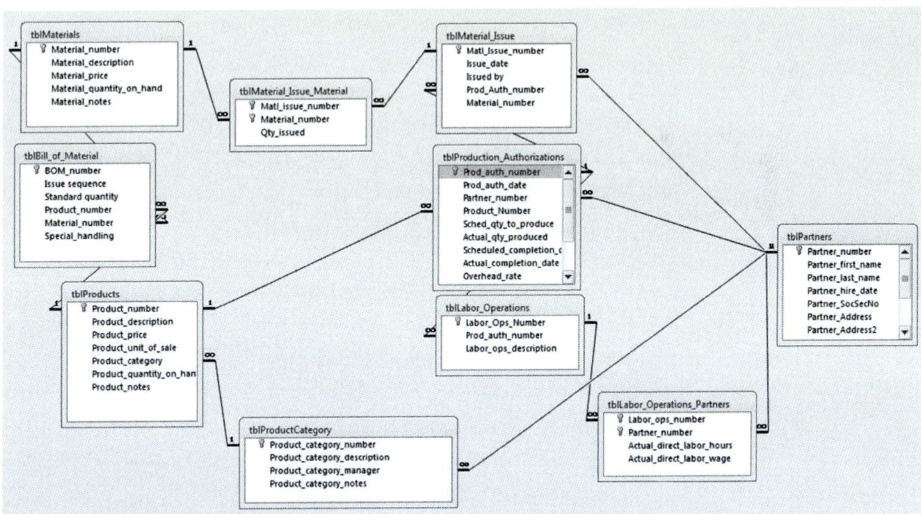

Summary

- From an accounting standpoint, we must account for transfers of raw materials into work-in-process, direct labor, allocated overhead, and the cost of goods manufactured in the conversion process.
- Sunset Graphics provides an ongoing example of how to model the conversion process.

- Activity models can show the basic steps in the process and the collaborations between the company and its customers, as well as exceptions to the process.
- Business rules implement internal control activities.
- There is a standard structure model pattern that allows for collection of accounting information for the conversion process—including issues of raw material into work-in-process and recording direct labor and allocated overhead—such that cost of goods manufactured includes material, labor, and overhead costs.
- The standard pattern is tailored to a specific organization by adding type images to collect management information.
- The structure model provides a blueprint for a relational database that will collect, store, and report sales and collection information.

Key Words

agents (*183*) The people or organizations who participate in business events, such as customers and salespeople.

events (*184*) Classes that model the organization's transactions, usually affecting the organization's resources, such as sales and cash receipts; Important occurrences that affect the flow of activities in a business process. BPMN includes symbols to define start, intermediate, and end events.

finished goods inventory (*179*) For a manufacturing company, the inventory (REA resource) that has completed the manufacturing process and is held for sale to customers.

gateway (*180*) Shows process branching and merging as the result of decisions. Basic gateways are depicted as diamonds. Usually, gateways appear as pairs on the diagram. The first gateway shows the branching, and the second gateway shows merging of the process branches.

intermediate error event (*180*) Occurs between start and end events and affects the flow of the process. Intermediate error events represent interruptions to the normal flow of the process and start the exception flow.

labor operations event (*184*) In the conversion process, an event that represents the recording of labor (and any associated overhead) costs applied to work-in-process.

many-to-many relationship (*185*) Exists when instances of one class (e.g., sales) are related to many instances of another class (e.g., inventory) and vice versa. These relationships are implemented in Access and relational databases by adding a linking table to convert the many-to-many relationship into two one-to-many relationships.

production authorization event (*184*) In a UML class model of the conversion process, an event that records the authorization to produce one or more finished good inventory items.

raw material issue event (*184*) In a UML class diagram of the conversion process, an event that records the transfer of raw materials into work-in-process.

raw materials inventory (*179*) For a manufacturing company, the inventory (REA resource) acquired for use (conversion) in the manufacturing process.

REA (*183*) Resource-event-agent framework for modeling business processes, originally developed by William McCarthy.

resources (*184*) Those things that have economic value to a firm, such as cash and products.

type image (*184*) Class that represents management information (such as categorizations, policies, and guidelines) to help manage a business process. Type image often allows process information to be summarized by category.

work-in-process inventory (*184*) For a manufacturing company, the value of raw materials, direct labor, and manufacturing overhead in production but not yet finished.

Answers to Progress Checks

1. You could modify Figure 7.3 by creating an additional swimlane within the Sunset pool for the inspection organizational unit.
2. You could modify Figure 7.3 by adding an additional gateway following the Inspect Work activity with two branches: (a) linking to the Discard Items activity and (b) linking to the Batch Done gateway.
3. An association can be promoted to a type image if it needs to contain more information or link to other classes. Apparently, Sunset's labor operations do not vary according to the specific product. If they did, it could promote the labor plan association shown in Figure 7.6 to a labor plan class as in Figure 7.7. That type image class would link to the products class and the labor operations class.
4. An equipment class would be an additional resource. It would be linked to the products class if the equipment varied according to the specific product. The equipment operations class, like the labor operations class, would record the use of the equipment to add that cost to the costs of production.

Mc Graw Hill Education connect

Multiple Choice Questions

1. Which of the following is an activity in the conversion process? **LO 7-1**
   a. Authorize production
   b. Issue raw material
   c. Perform work
   d. Transfer completed work to finished goods
   d. All of the above are activities in the conversion process.
2. Which of the following activities results in work-in-process moving to finished goods inventory? **LO 7-1**
   a. Authorize production
   b. Inspect work
   c. Complete production
   d. Issue raw material
   e. None of the above
3. Which of the following describes the purpose of a lane within a pool in BPMN? **LO 7-2, LO 7-3**
   a. Indicates the start of the process
   b. Indicates the end of the process
   c. Identifies different activity flow options
   d. Distinguishes specific responsibilities for performing different tasks
   e. None of the above

4. Which of the following is not a purpose of using lanes to describe the conversion process? **LO 7-2, LO 7-3**
   a. Document the sequence of activities in the process
   b. Expose potential problems in the handoff between organizational units
   c. Show important decision points, and identify responsibility for those decisions
   d. Establish internal control activities, such as segregation of duties
   e. All of the above
5. Which of the following is a business rule implementing access control for the conversion process? **LO 7-4**
   a. Employee authorizing production cannot modify inventory records.
   b. System must provide control numbers.
   c. Employees preparing quotes cannot modify established prices.
   d. System must create audit trail whenever records are changed.
   e. None of the above
6. Consider a UML class diagram of the conversion process that uses the REA framework. Which of the following events begins a typical conversion process? **LO 7-5**
   a. Assign employees to departments
   b. Authorize production
   c. Issue raw material into work-in-process
   d. Sell finished goods
   e. None of the above
7. Review Figure 7.6. Which of the following describes the purpose of the Labor Operations event? **LO 7-5**
   a. Add the cost of direct labor to work-in-process inventory
   b. Control the specific labor activities
   c. Ensure that labor is performed
   d. Identify production employees
   e. None of the above
8. Review Figure 7.7. Which of the following is a correct posting of a foreign key to implement the model in a relational database? **LO 7-5**
   a. Labor Operations primary key becomes a foreign key in Production Authorization.
   b. Products primary key becomes a foreign key in Bill of Material.
   c. Product Categories primary key becomes a foreign key in Sunset Partners.
   d. Products primary key becomes a foreign key in Product Categories.
   e. All of the above are correct.
9. Review Figure 7.7. Which of the following describes the purpose of the Bill of Material class? **LO 7-1, LO 7-5**
   a. Record the invoices from suppliers for materials purchased
   b. Record the planned raw material contents of each finished good
   c. Record the authorization of production
   d. Describe the labor required for each finished good
   e. None of the above.
10. Compare Figure 7.6 with Figure 7.7. Which of the following describes the differences between those two figures? **LO 7-5**
   a. Figure 7.7 includes *tblLabor_Operations_Partners* to implement the many-to-many relationship between *tblPartners* and *tblLabor_Operations*.
   b. Figure 7.7 includes *tblMaterial_Issue_Material* to implement the many-to-many relationship between *tblMaterial_Issue* and *tblMaterials.*

c. Figure 7.6 includes the minimum multiplicities to specify data integrity requirements.

d. Figure 7.7 only shows maximum cardinalities between linked tables.

e. All of the above are differences between the two figures.

Refer to the following integrated diagram, showing part of the purchases and sales processes linked to the conversion process, for Questions 11 through 25.

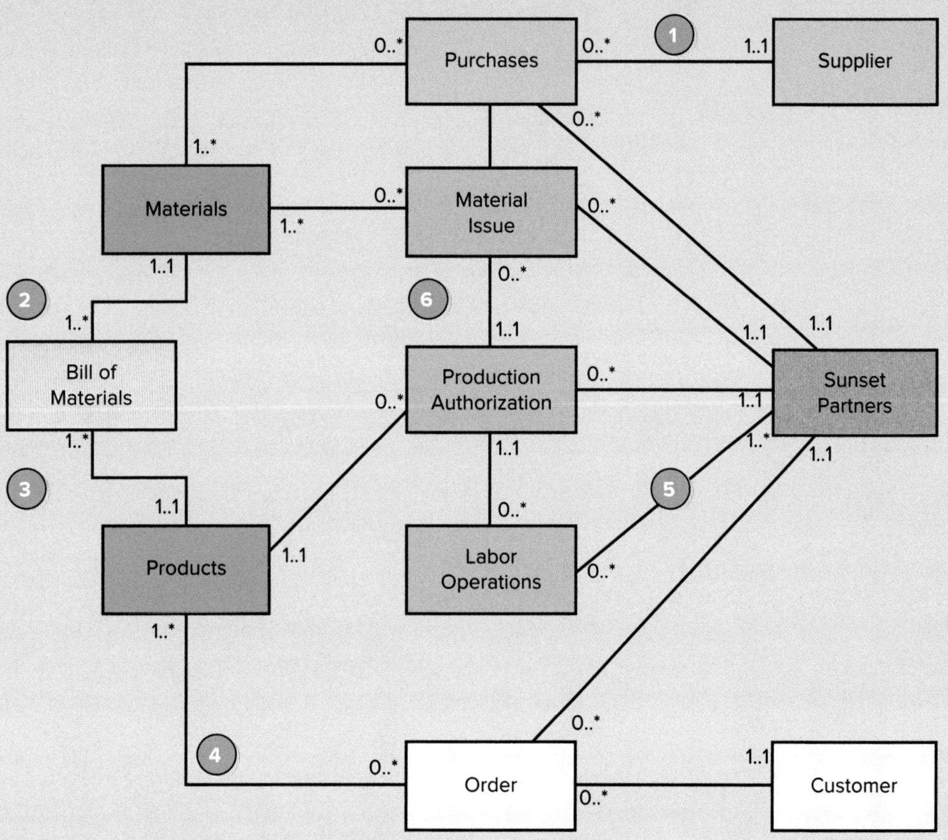

11. Refer to the association marked with the number 1 in the preceding diagram. Which of the following is the best description of the association? LO 7-5
    a. Each supplier participates in a minimum of zero purchases.
    b. Each supplier participates in at least one purchase.
    c. Each supplier participates in a maximum of one purchase.
    d. Supplier is the internal agent in the purchase process.
    e. None of these is a description of the association.
12. Refer to the association marked with the number 1 in the preceding diagram. Which of the following is the best description of the association? LO 7-5
    a. Each purchase involves one supplier.
    b. Each purchase involves multiple suppliers.
    c. Each purchase involves a minimum of zero suppliers.
    d. Some purchases are made after a production authorization.
    e. None of these is a description of the association.

13. Refer to the association marked with the number 2 in the preceding diagram. Which of the following is the best description of the purpose of the association? **LO 7-5**
    a. The association links finished goods to the corresponding bill of materials.
    b. The association links purchases to raw materials.
    c. The association identifies the raw materials in a bill of materials.
    d. All of these descriptions are purposes of the association.
    e. None of these are a description of the purpose of the association.
14. Refer to the association marked with the number 2 in the preceding diagram. Which of the following is the best description of the association? **LO 7-5**
    a. Each bill of materials entry specifies one raw material.
    b. Each bill of materials entry specifies multiple raw materials.
    c. Each bill of materials is related to a minimum of zero raw materials.
    d. Each bill of materials is related to a maximum of many raw materials.
    e. None of these is a description of the association.
15. Refer to the association marked with the number 2 in the preceding diagram. Which of the following is the best description of the association? **LO 7-5**
    a. Each raw material is related to a minimum of zero bills of materials.
    b. Each raw material is related to a maximum of one bill of materials.
    c. A raw material item could be related to multiple bills of materials.
    d. A raw material item could be related to no bill of materials.
    e. None of these is a description of the association.
16. Refer to the association marked with the number 2 in the preceding diagram. Which of the following is the best way to implement the association in a relational database? **LO 7-5**
    a. Post the primary key of bill of materials as a foreign key in raw materials.
    b. Post the primary key of raw materials as a foreign key in bill of materials.
    c. Create a linking table between raw materials and bill of materials.
    d. The location of the foreign key is optional.
    e. None of these is the best way to implement the relationship.
17. Refer to the association marked with the number 3 in the preceding diagram. Which of the following is the best description of the purpose the association? **LO 7-5**
    a. Links actual material costs to each finished goods item produced.
    b. Links actual labor costs to each finished goods item produced.
    c. Specifies planned material costs for each finished goods item.
    d. Specifies planned labor costs for each finished goods item.
    e. None of these is a description of the purpose of the association.
18. Refer to the association marked with the number 3 in the preceding diagram. Which of the following is the best description of the association? **LO 7-5**
    a. Each bill of materials is related to a minimum of zero finished goods.
    b. Each bill of materials is related to a minimum of one finished good.
    c. Each bill of materials is related to a maximum of many finished goods.
    d. Each bill of materials is not necessarily related to a finished good.
    e. None of these is a description of the association.
19. Refer to the association marked with the number 3 in the preceding diagram. Which of the following is the best way to implement the association in a relational database? **LO 7-5**
    a. Post the primary key of bill of materials as a foreign key in finished goods.
    b. Post the primary key of finished goods as a foreign key in bill of materials.

c. Create a linking table between finished goods and bill of materials.
d. The location of the foreign key is optional.
e. None of these is the best way to implement the relationship.

20. Refer to the association marked with the number 4 in the preceding diagram. Which of the following is the best description of the purpose of the association? **LO 7-5**
    a. Shows that the conversion and sales process are integrated via finished goods.
    b. Shows that the conversion process is triggered by an order for a finished good.
    c. Links finished goods produced by the conversion process to orders (by customers).
    d. Links finished goods to subsequent cash receipts in the sales process.
    e. None of these is a description of the purpose of the association.
21. Refer to the association marked with the number 4 in the preceding diagram. Which of the following is the best description of the association? **LO 7-5**
    a. Each finished good is related to one order.
    b. Each finished good is related to many orders.
    c. Each finished good is related to a minimum of one order.
    d. Each finished good is related to a maximum of one order.
    e. None of these is a description of the association.
22. Refer to the association marked with the number 5 in the preceding diagram. Which of the following is the best way to implement the association in a relational database? **LO 7-5**
    a. Post the primary key of Sunset partners as a foreign key in labor operations.
    b. Post the primary key of labor operations as a foreign key in Sunset partners.
    c. Create a linking table between Sunset partners and labor operations.
    d. The location of the foreign key is optional.
    e. None of these is the best way to implement the relationship.
23. Refer to the association marked with the number 5 in the preceding diagram. Which of the following is the best description of the association? **LO 7-5**
    a. Each labor operation is related to one Sunset partner.
    b. Each labor operation is related to many Sunset partners.
    c. Labor operations are related to a minimum of zero Sunset partners.
    d. Labor operations are related to a maximum of one Sunset partner.
    e. None of these is a description of the association.
24. Refer to the association marked with the number 6 in the preceding diagram. Which of the following is the best description of the purpose of the association? **LO 7-5**
    a. Authorizes the issue of raw materials.
    b. Controls the transfer of raw materials to work-in-process.
    c. Relates specific raw material issues to the controlling authorization.
    d. All of these describe the purpose of the association.
    e. None of these describes the purpose of the association.
25. Refer to the association marked with the number 6 in the preceding diagram. Which of the following is the best description of the association? **LO 7-5**
    a. Each production authorization is related to a minimum of zero material issues.
    b. Each production authorization is related to a minimum of one material issue.
    c. Each production authorization is related to a maximum of one material issue.
    d. Each production authorization is related to a maximum of zero material issues.
    e. None of these is a description of the association.

Discussion Questions

1. Think about the roles of accountants presented in Table 2.1 from Chapter 2. Why should accountants be involved in developing and reviewing the bills of materials? LO 7-1
2. Describe some businesses that use conversion processes. Do they all use the same sequence of activities? Do they all share the same information structure? Discuss some of the differences in those conversion processes. LO 7-1
3. Think about the UML class diagrams for the sales and collection process described in Chapter 5 and the purchases and payments process described in Chapter 6. If you were asked to prepare an integrated model that shows those two processes as well as the conversion process, where would the models intersect/integrate? Why? What elements are unique to each process? LO 7-5
4. In Figure 7.6, the Labor Operations event tracks direct labor incurred in the conversion process. What event tracks indirect labor? LO 7-1, LO 7-5
5. Describe how you would change Figure 7.6 to implement an activity-based costing system with three different cost drivers. LO 7-1, LO 7-5
6. Put Figure 7.6 in the context of the overall supply chain that starts with the purchases and payments process (Chapter 6) and ends with the sales and cash receipts process (Chapter 5). How would you expand Figure 7.6 to describe Sunset's entire supply chain? LO 7-1, LO 7-5
7. Business rules implement internal controls. Review Table 7.1 and classify each of those business rules listed as access controls as obligatory, prohibited, or allowed, as described in Chapter 2. Select two of those business rules and rephrase them, so an obligatory rule is now a prohibited rule, a prohibited rule is now an allowed rule, and so on. LO 7-4
8. Compare the generic UML class diagram for the conversion process shown in Figure 7.5 with a generic sales and collection diagram, similar to Figure 5.9. Identify the similarities and differences and then explain why they exist. LO 7-5

Problems

connect

1. The Rubber Duck Brewing Company is a new microbrewery. Rubber Duck's brewing process converts beer raw ingredients—malt extract, malted grain, adjuncts (rice or corn), hops, yeast, and water—into brewed beer. Over time, Rubber Duck has developed a unique recipe for each of its brewed beers. The recipe describes the specific ingredients, the sequence of brewing steps, the specific equipment, and the type of employees required for each step in the brewing process for each beer. Each step in the recipe may involve multiple ingredients (e.g., barley, hops, malts, and yeast) and multiple pieces of equipment, but it only requires one type of employee.

   Rubber Duck assigns a unique ingredient number to each ingredient so it can track the quantity on hand. It tracks its brewed beer by the beer name: pale ale, amber ale, porter, stout, lager, pilsner, and so forth. When Rubber Duck decides to brew one of its beers, a supervisor issues a "Brew Order" for that beer, specifying the quantity in gallons to be brewed. Then, the brewing process begins. Several Rubber Duck employees perform each brewing step. Rubber Duck tracks the amount of each raw ingredient actually used in each step as well the time spent by each employee on each step.

   Rubber Duck tracks its brewing equipment (e.g., mash tuns, whirlpools, fermenters, and conditioning tanks) by equipment item number, and it also tracks which equipment is used and how long it is used in each brewing step. Each brewing step often requires more than one piece of equipment, and some pieces of equipment are used on multiple brewing steps, although many are used in only one step. For safety, Rubber Duck only allows employees to operate equipment that they are qualified to use.

   When the brewing process is complete, the brewed beer is stored in large copper tanks for aging. Ales require relatively little aging (less than 3 weeks), while lagers may require longer aging (up to 5 weeks). The copper tanks are tracked separately from other brewing equipment. Aging of the beer is not part of the brewing process; it takes place after the brewing process.

a. Prepare a UML class diagram that captures Rubber Duck's brewing process.
b. Using the preceding information and the following attributes list, prepare a listing of the relational tables, indicating the primary key (PK) and foreign keys (FK) for each table. **LO 7-5**
c. (Optional) Use the UML class diagram and the listing of relational tables to prepare a relational database in Access. **LO 7-6**

Attributes:

Actual aging time to date for the brewed beer in this copper tank
Actual quantity of this ingredient used in this brew step
Actual time for this equipment used in this brew step
Brew order date
Brew order number (brew#)
Brew quantity in gallons
Brew step description
Brew step number (brew step#)
Brewed beer description
Brewed beer name
Brewed beer quantity on hand (QOH)
Brewing recipe step description
Brewing recipe step number (recipe step#)
Copper tank capacity in gallons
Copper tank number (tank#)
Date this employee qualified to operate this equipment
Employee name
Employee number (emp#)
Employee type
Employee type description
Equipment item description
Equipment item number (equip#)
Ingredient description
Ingredient number (ingred#)
Ingredient quantity-on-hand (QOH)
Number of employees of this type
Planned aging time for this brewed beer
Planned time for this equipment in this step
Quantity of beer in this tank (in gallons)
Standard quantity of this ingredient used in this recipe step
Time spent by this employee on this brew step

connect

2. Penny loves pastries. She wanted everyone else to love pastries, too, so she started Penny's Pastries in Orange County about 3 years ago. After a shaky start, she scored a big contract with **Starbucks** to provide pastries to all stores in southern California. This case describes Penny's daily baking process. Penny's bakery starts preparing fresh pastries every morning about 1:00 a.m. for delivery to local stores by 5:30 a.m. The selection and quantity of pastries vary according to the day of the week as well as the time of the year. **LO 7-2, LO 7-3, LO 7-5**

Inventories

Although Penny has a number of her own specialties, she makes many of her baked products according to Starbucks' requirements. So, every day she makes some of her own pastries for sale in her bakeries as well as all the pastries for the various Starbucks locations. Currently, her finished goods inventory can include more than 50 different kinds of pastries and baked products. Because of the volume that Penny produces, she maintains an extensive inventory of the ingredients that she uses in her baked goods, such as flour, butter, milk, chocolate, and cinnamon.

Baking Plans

Penny carefully plans the contents and preparation of each finished product (pastry and baked good). There are two parts to her formal plans—an ingredient list and a recipe—for each baked product. The ingredient list specifies the quantity of each ingredient required for each finished product. The recipe defines the sequence of steps that her bakers follow to prepare each finished product. The recipe steps also set the standard number of labor-hours, as well as the specific equipment used, to prepare a standard batch of each finished product.

Daily Baking Process

Early each morning, the supervisor prepares a daily baking order that specifies the quantities of all the different finished products to be prepared that day. As soon as the various products and quantities are known, an inventory clerk uses the ingredient list to issue all the ingredients necessary for the day, moving them from the storeroom to the baking area. In some cases, the clerk may issue ingredients several different times for each daily baking order so that none of the refrigerated items are left out longer than necessary. Penny assigns sequential issue numbers to each issue during the day, and the clerk carefully records the quantity of each ingredient issued.

Penny's bakers prepare the finished products in batches. Each batch produces one finished baked good product. A supervisor (who could be different from the supervisor who issued the baking order) issues a batch order to start the baking process for that batch. The bakers then prepare the ingredients in a series of baking steps according to the recipe for that product using the equipment and ovens specified in the recipe. Penny's bakery has an array of ovens and baking equipment, tracked by equipment number, to keep up with the daily baking production volumes. Because each oven has different characteristics, the baking time for each product can depend on the particular oven used. The baking steps usually involve mixing ingredients, preparing the pastries, placing the prepared items in an oven for baking, and then removing the products and placing them on cooling racks, ready for packing. Each actual baking step may involve the use of multiple pieces of baking equipment and multiple bakers. Penny carefully tracks actual hours of labor and equipment use for each baking step.

General Information

Penny does not separately identify employees as supervisors, inventory clerks, or bakers. There is one employee entity. Information on ingredient lists, recipes, finished products, ingredients, and employees is put into the database before those entities are linked to events or type images.

a. Draw a BPMN activity diagram that describes Penny's baking process.

b. Prepare a UML class diagram with classes, associations, and multiplicities.

c. Using the preceding case information and the following attributes list, prepare a listing of the relational tables necessary to support this conversion process. List the tables in the following order: resources, events, agents, type images, and linking tables.

Attributes:

Actual baking time for this baking step and this oven
Baking order#
Baking order date
Baking step#
Batch#
Batch finish time
Batch start time
Employee#
Employee hours worked on this baking step
Employee name
Employee pay rate
Equipment#
Equipment description
Equipment manufacturer
Finished product#
Finished product description
Finished product number of calories
Finished product price
Finished product QOH

- Ingredient#
- Ingredient cost
- Ingredient description
- Ingredient list#
- Ingredient list description
- Ingredient QOH
- Ingredient unit of issue
- Issue#
- Issue date/time
- Qty of this baked product ordered by this daily baking order
- Qty of this baked product prepared in this batch
- Qty of this ingredient issued on this issue#
- Qty of this ingredient required for this finished product
- Recipe step#
- Recipe step description
- Standard baking time for this recipe step with this oven
- Standard labor hours for this recipe step
- Total labor hours for this baking step

Additional problems are available in connect only.

Chapter **Eight**

Integrated Project

A look at this chapter

This chapter builds on the business process modeling and database design material in earlier chapters. It describes how to approach a business analysis and integrated systems development project involving multiple business processes. The project itself, designed as a group assignment, is available separately. To complete the project successfully, each group must plan and execute a realistic systems design and development project. The finished product will include activity and structure models of a company's business processes, which can support enhanced internal controls, more effective use of an AIS and related information technology to improve the company's performance, and the development relational database system and appropriate queries necessary to prepare financial and managerial accounting reports.

A look back

Chapter 7 completed the comprehensive example describing Sunset Graphics' business processes. It presented basic activity and structure models for the company's conversion process, as well as a description of the database to support that process.

A look ahead

Chapter 9 introduces business intelligence, data analytics, and data visualization concepts and tools.

Howard Schultz, Founder, President, and Chief Executive Officer of Starbucks.

After **Starbucks** implemented the **Oracle** E-business Suite, it had the IT backbone necessary to leverage a variety of other applications to support its business processes. As part of the Oracle implementation, **Accenture** worked with Starbucks to standardize business processes around the world. The Oracle ERP system resides on top of Oracle's database system, and that allows reuse and redistribution of the information collected. Starbucks' enterprise data warehouse (EDW) leverages that data to support Starbucks' internal business users.

By 2008, thousands of stores could directly access the EDW through web-based dashboards. Using a business intelligence reporting tool from **MicroStrategy Inc.**, individual users could develop customized operational performance reports. MicroStrategy's reports can even be delivered by e-mail on preset schedules.

Although Starbucks closed a number of retail stores in response to the economic downturn, its overall revenues increased from 2008 to 2010. More importantly, its revenue per store is back above $1 million in the United States. Its operating income has almost doubled since 2008, and its operating margin increased from 8.1% to 13.8% in 2010. Clearly, Starbucks has been successful at reducing costs and increasing margins. Without standardized processes and integrated systems providing reliable and timely information for decisions, it is unlikely that it could have achieved this success.

Chapter Outline

Project Planning

Define Business Requirements

Prepare Activity Diagrams Using BPMN

Prepare Structure Diagram

Import Data into Access, Create Efficient Tables, and Set Relationships

Prepare Queries

Learning Objectives

After completing the project outlined in this chapter, you should be able to:

8-1 Plan and manage a business analysis project

8-2 Develop activity models of multiple business processes, and use those models to assess potential risks and opportunities for process improvements

8-3 Develop an integrated UML class diagram for a business

8-4 Use the UML class diagram to design and implement a relational database system in Microsoft Access™

8-5 Employ the relational database to answer a variety of business performance questions

LO 8-1
Plan and manage a business analysis project

PROJECT PLANNING

Figure 8.1 describes a suggested sequence of activities to complete an integrated business analysis project. Such projects represent "ill-structured" problems that require careful planning and attention to detail. Thus, the first step is to prepare a project plan in as much detail as possible. Develop a problem statement and the timeline to accomplish the project on time. Identify the major steps you will undertake to complete the project, when they need to be completed, and who will perform them. There are additional project planning tools, such as Gantt charts, that can help define the elements of the plan. Refer to Chapter 16 of this text for a description of project planning/management elements. Regardless of the planning tool used, the plan should identify the specific tasks necessary to complete the project, when each task must be completed, and who will complete each task. The project plan then serves as the management tool to keep progress on track to successful and on-time completion.

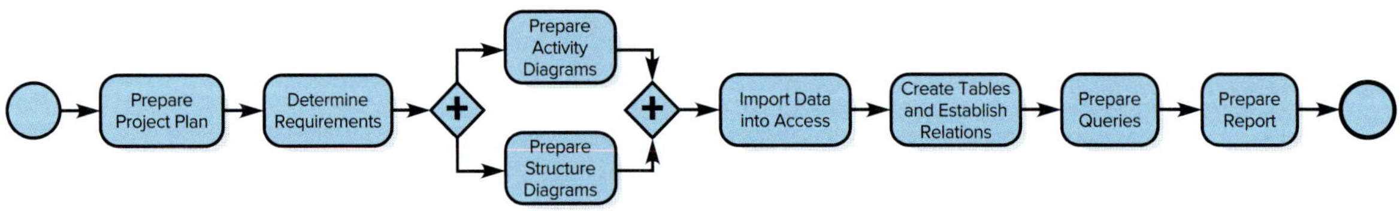

FIGURE 8.1
Suggested Project Steps

Define Business Requirements

Step 2 is to define the business requirements. The requirements discovery process involves fact-finding to determine who, what, when, where, why, and how business activities are performed. The process typically requires review of business documents as well as interviews with managers and employees. As the project team gathers requirements, they set the context of the project as shown in Figure 8.2. The focal organization is placed at the center of the diagram as an opaque pool. The external organizations that interact with "Your Company" are also shown as opaque pools. The goal is to identify all the message flows between the focal organization and the external organizations. The processes and systems within the focal organization must be able to respond to incoming message flows and efficiently deliver controlled outgoing message flows.

After establishing the context, the project team defines the activities, actors, data objects and artifacts (such as forms and documents), events, systems, and goals for the focal organization. For each activity, specify the goals of the activity and the inputs and outputs and define the actors that perform the activity, the documents created and used in the activity, and the events that affect the flow of activities. These elements will support the preparation of both your activity and structure diagrams.

LO 8-2
Develop activity models of multiple business processes, and use those models to assess potential risks and opportunities for process improvements

Prepare Activity Models Using BPMN

After gaining an understanding of the organization's business processes, document each current process with a business process activity diagram using business process modeling notation (BPMN). This is often an iterative process. First, prepare simple diagrams that show the basic steps performed in each process identified from your context diagram. Figure 8.3 shows a basic example of the sales process.

After you establish that your basic diagram is correct, then define who performs each activity and the artifacts that are created, updated, or used in the process. For example,

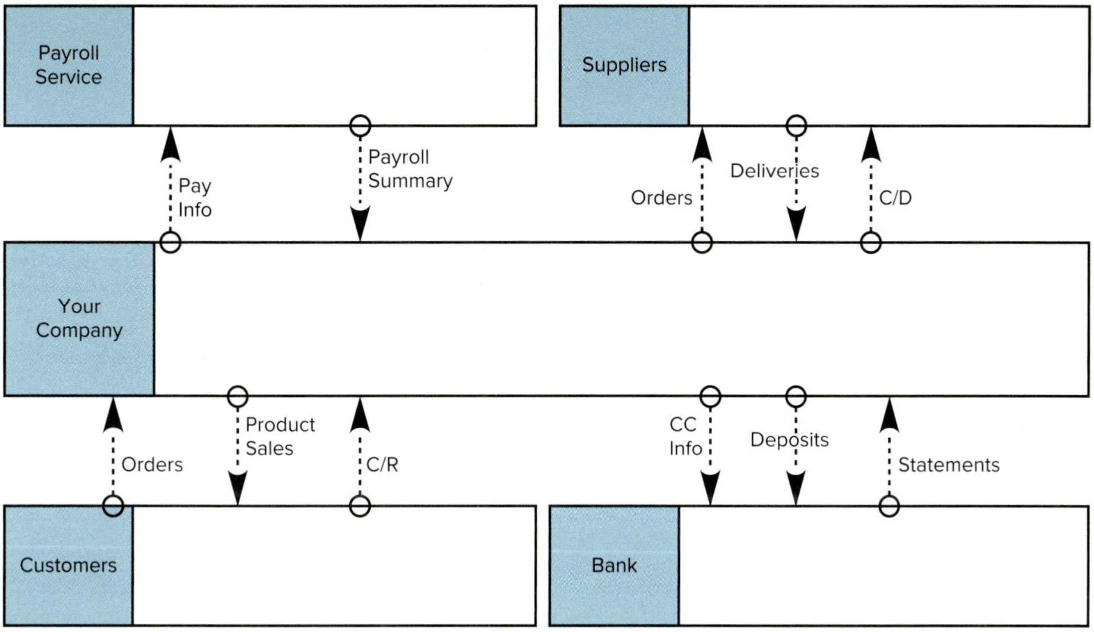

FIGURE 8.2
Project Context Diagram
C/D = cash disbursement; C/R = cash receipt; CC = credit card.

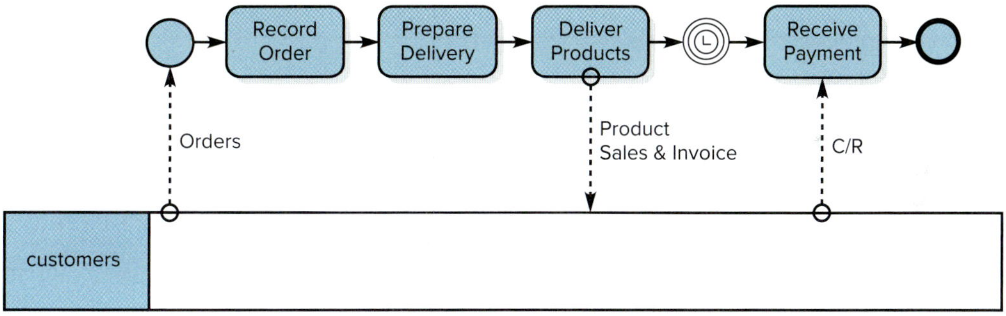

FIGURE 8.3
Basic Sales Process

Figure 8.4 expands the sales process to show that the shipping and receiving department receives the order, prepares the delivery, and delivers the products to the customer. The accounting department then receives the payment at the end of the month. Figure 8.4 also shows that the *Record Order* activity creates the Order form, which is used in the *Prepare Delivery* activity. The *Prepare Delivery* activity creates the Invoice (Inv), which is used in the *Receive Payment* process to confirm that the cash receipt matches the amount that the customer was billed.

Figure 8.4 shows the steps in the process if everything works as designed. However, it does not allow for errors or exceptions. So, the next step in the process is to include events and activities that allow for those exceptions, as shown in Figure 8.5. Figure 8.5 adds an intermediate error event to the *Prepare Delivery* activity to model circumstances where products are not available. When the error event is triggered, the process flow changes to include the *Cancel Order* activity, which then updates the Order form to record the

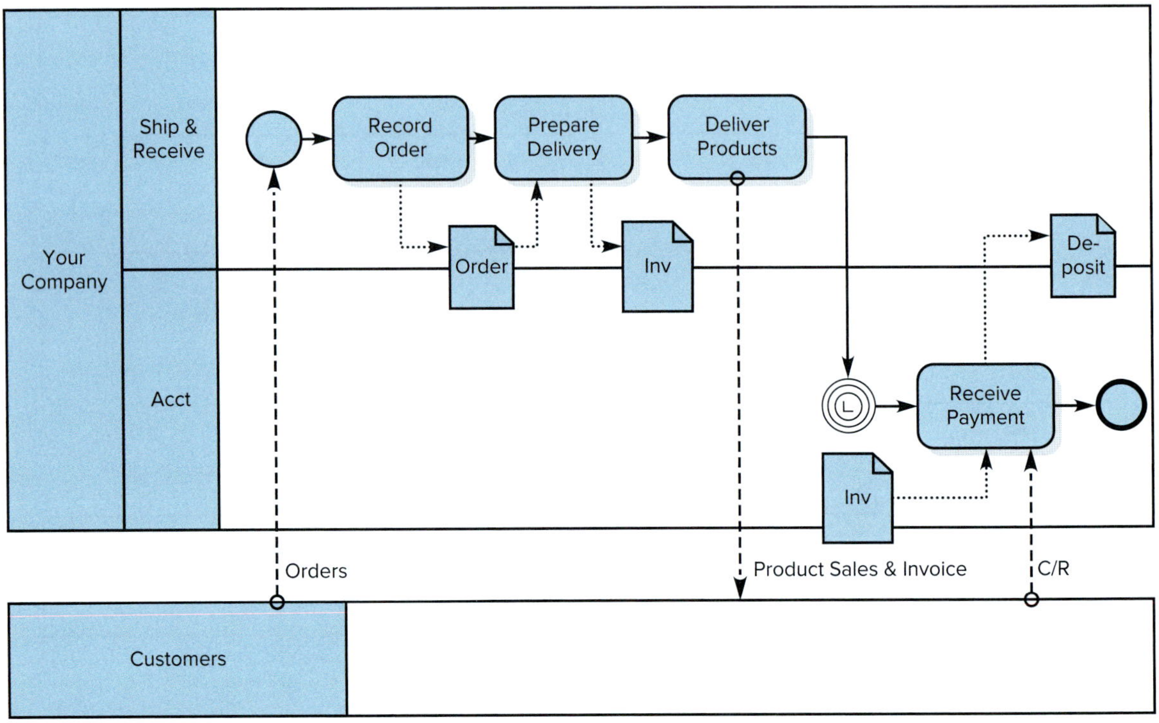

FIGURE 8.4
Expanded Sales Process

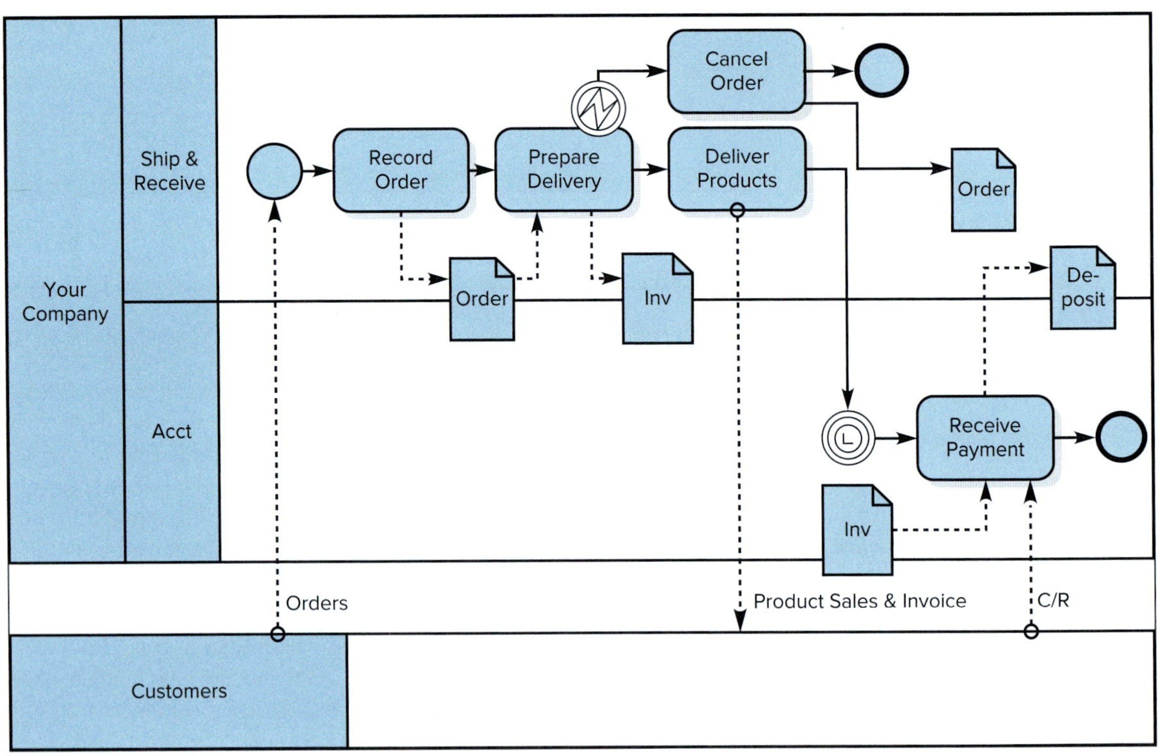

FIGURE 8.5
Expanded Sales Process with Exceptions

cancellation. Note that the Cancel Order process could also include notifying the Customer of the cancellation, although that is not modeled in this example. The project team should document the business rules that guide decisions within each activity.

Once the project team confirms the accuracy of the models, the next step is to examine the models for potential changes to increase control or improve efficiency. At this point, the team should consider material in Chapters 11 and 12 of this text to ensure effective internal controls. To improve efficiency, each activity should be examined to determine whether it adds value to the process. Value-added activities are those that are essential for production regardless of the technology used. Activities that only add cost and not value should be eliminated where possible. Cost-added activities include those that involve non-essential movements, waiting, approvals, corrections, or revisions.

LO 8-3
Develop an integrated UML class diagram for a business

Prepare Structure Diagram

Using the information gained from discovering the business requirements, the project team then prepares an integrated UML class diagram that shows the data requirements for the organization. The class diagram should articulate with the BPMN activity diagrams. The class diagram must capture information about each data object in the activity diagrams. Material in Chapters 5, 6, and 7 of this text provides standard patterns that can be the basis for the integrated diagram. Figure 8.6 shows a sample integrated UML class diagram using the REA framework. It includes four separate processes: sales, purchases of inventory, purchases of administrative expense items, and payroll. Clearly, the number of classes and associations would be very difficult to implement directly in Access without the diagram to guide the construction of the database. The diagram also helps plan the queries that will be used to prepare the financial statements. The events—sales, purchases of inventory, purchases admin, and timecards—will affect the income statement. The duality relationships between events, such as between purchases of inventory and C/D, can be used to determine items, such as payables and receivables, on the balance sheet. The inventory and cash resources will result in assets on the balance sheet. The cash disbursement (C/D) and cash receipt (C/R) events represent transactions affecting the statement of cash flows.

LO 8-4
Use the UML class diagram to design and implement a relational database system in Microsoft Access™

Import Data into Access, Create Efficient Tables, and Set Relationships

At this point, the project team is ready to create the Access database or more generally the AIS. For the purpose of the integrated project, your instructor will provide data in an Excel spreadsheet. In other projects, you might have to move data from existing systems into a new AIS. In either case, the UML class diagram will be the blueprint that you will follow. It is likely that the data will include redundancies and occasional typographical errors. You will need to correct those. After importing the data, you will need to set appropriate primary keys, check data types, and modify tables as necessary to be sure that they are efficient. Then, create the relationships among tables, enforcing referential integrity. Failing to enforce referential integrity will affect the reliability of your queries.

One common issue is dealing with information that must be split into multiple tables. For example, sales information may contain data about sales events mixed with data about the items sold on each sale. Such data would need to be split into the sales table and a sales items linking table. For example, Figure 8.7 shows sales data in a flat file before importing into Access. Although it appears that order# should be the primary key, the highlighted section shows redundant data for order #O9007. So, this table should be split so that order# is unique and the information about the inventory sold for each order is in a separate table. The table can be split in Excel or in Access. First, however, you have to determine which fields go in which table. Note that *order_date*, *customer#*, *order_emp#*, *sale_date*, and *cash_receipt#* are the same regardless of how many inventory items are included. Those

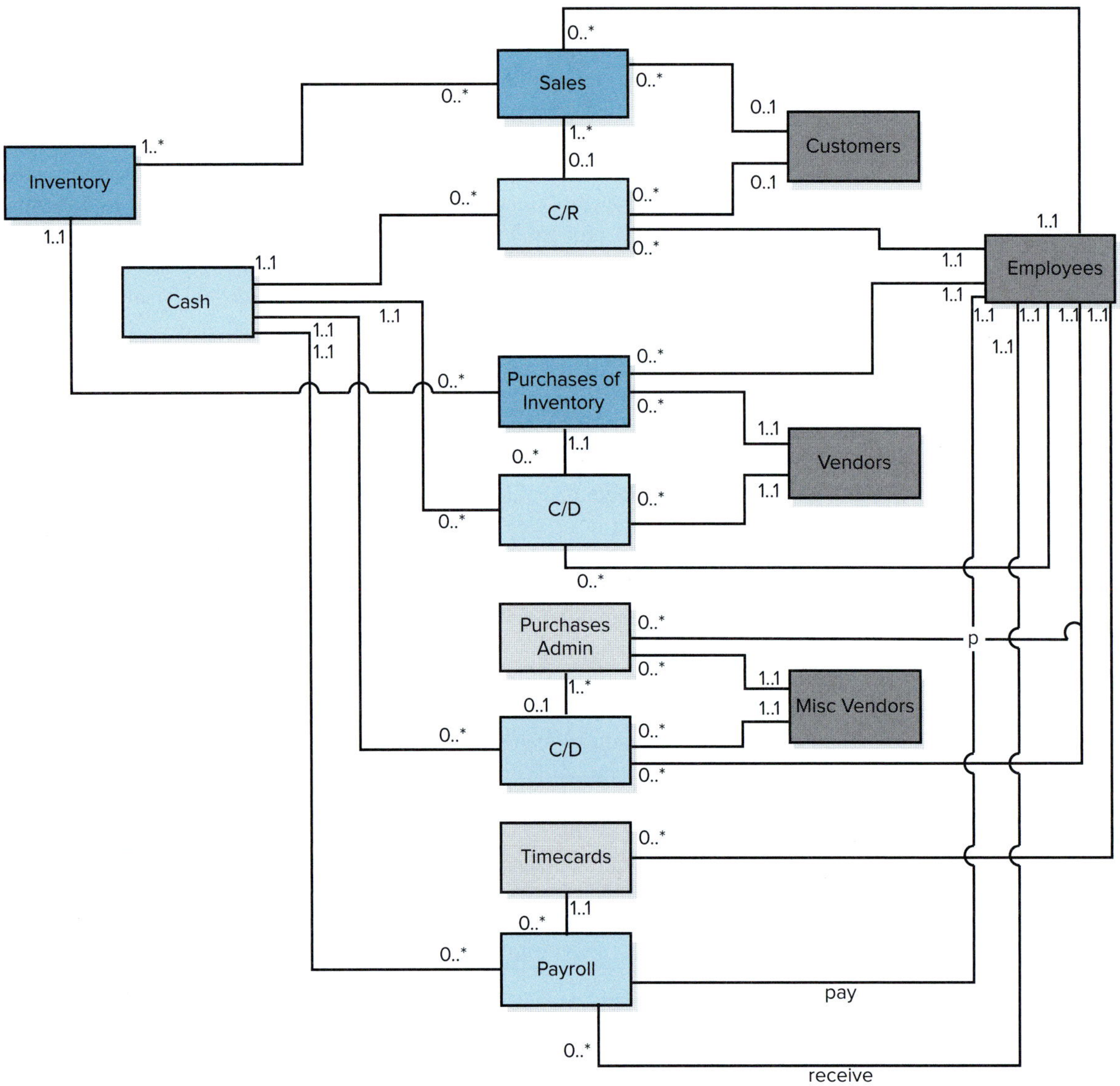

FIGURE 8.6

Sample Integrated UML Class Diagram

C/R = cash receipts; C/D = cash disbursements.

fields will go with the sales table. On the other hand, *qty_ordered*, *qty_sold*, and *sale_price* depend on both the order and the inventory item. Those fields will go in the sales items table. The primary key of the sales items table will be *order#* plus *inventory#*.

To set up the tables in Excel, select the first six columns and copy them to a new worksheet. Rename that worksheet as SALES. Then select order#, inventory#, qty_ordered, qty_sold, and sale_price to copy to a different worksheet, and rename that worksheet as SALES ITEMS. Next, to remove the duplicates in the SALES worksheet, select all six columns. Click on the DATA tab and select the Remove Duplicates icon on the ribbon bar. The Remove Duplicates box appears as shown in Figure 8.8. With all the boxes next to the column headings checked, click on the OK button. This will remove the duplicates and the data in the SALES table will look like Figure 8.9.

order#	order_date	customer#	order_emp#	sale_date	cash_receipt#	inventory#	qty_ordered	qty_sold	sale_price
O90001	12/29/2017	Atla_013	E2154	1/1/2018	CR_91117	P17008	50	52	$13.56
O90002	12/30/2017	Atla_015	E9481	1/4/2018	CR_91122	P17006	90	88	$14.44
O90003	12/31/2017	Atla_011	E8519	1/7/2018	CR_91080	P17001	90	84	$10.78
O90004	1/1/2018	Atla_010	E8519	1/8/2018	CR_91110	P17005	50	47	$13.89
O90005	1/2/2018	Atla_003	E3477	1/4/2018	CR_91091	P17013	30	27	$15.00
O90006	1/3/2018	Atla_001	E2154	1/4/2018	CR_91001	P17013	20	18	$15.00
O90007	1/4/2018	Atla_010	E9481	1/8/2018	CR_91110	P17010	100	93	$ 7.67
O90007	1/4/2018	Atla_010	E9481	1/8/2018	CR_91110	P17013	30	27	$15.00
O90007	1/4/2018	Atla_010	E9481	1/8/2018	CR_91110	P17015	80	75	$16.67
O90008	1/5/2018	Atla_008	E2154	1/10/2018	CR_91121	P17007	40	39	$10.89
O90009	1/5/2018	Atla_001	E9481	1/8/2018	CR_91001	P17007	130	129	$10.89
O90010	1/6/2018	Atla_010	E2154	1/15/2018	CR_91110	P17002	130	120	$11.11

FIGURE 8.7
Sample Mixed Sales Data

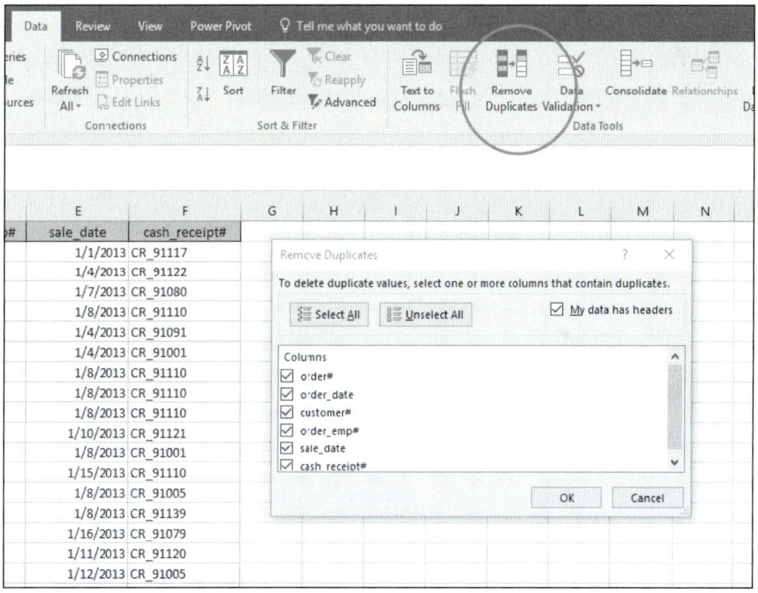

FIGURE 8.8
Removing Duplicates in the SALES Table

FIGURE 8.9
SALES Table with Duplicates Removed

order#	order_date	customer#	order_emp#	sale_date	cash_receipt#
O90001	12/29/2017	Atla_013	E2154	1/1/2018	CR_91117
O90002	12/30/2017	Atla_015	E9481	1/4/2018	CR_91122
O90003	12/31/2017	Atla_011	E8519	1/7/2018	CR_91080
O90004	1/1/2018	Atla_010	E8519	1/8/2018	CR_91110
O90005	1/2/2018	Atla_003	E3477	1/4/2018	CR_91091
O90006	1/3/2018	Atla_001	E2154	1/4/2018	CR_91001
O90007	1/4/2018	Atla_010	E9481	1/8/2018	CR_91110
O90008	1/5/2018	Atla_008	E2154	1/10/2018	CR_91121
O90009	1/5/2018	Atla_001	E9481	1/8/2018	CR_91001
O90010	1/6/2018	Atla_010	E2154	1/15/2018	CR_91110

Import the data in the SALES and SALES ITEMS worksheets into Access. During the import, select order# as the primary key for the SALES table but no primary key for the SALES ITEMS table. After the import, open the SALES ITEMS table in design view and select both order# and inventory# as the primary key. Then, set the relationship between SALES and SALES ITEMS as shown in Figure 8.10.

LO 8-5
Employ the relational database to answer a variety of business performance questions

Prepare Queries

After importing all the data and setting the relationships to match the UML class diagram, you are ready to prepare queries for the financial statements and any other operational performance information. Each deliverable may require multiple queries. For example, to determine sales revenue for the quarter, you would first extend the SALES ITEMS table information to determine the amount for each item sold on each sale, as shown in Figure 8.11.

Then, using the query shown in Figure 8.11 and the SALES table, calculate the amount of each sale within the fiscal period, in this case the first calendar quarter, as shown in Figure 8.12. Set the criteria to constrain transactions to the first quarter. Sum the amount field, calculated as shown in Figure 8.11. Then, the summed amount from this query can be used to calculate overall sales revenue for the quarter in a subsequent query.

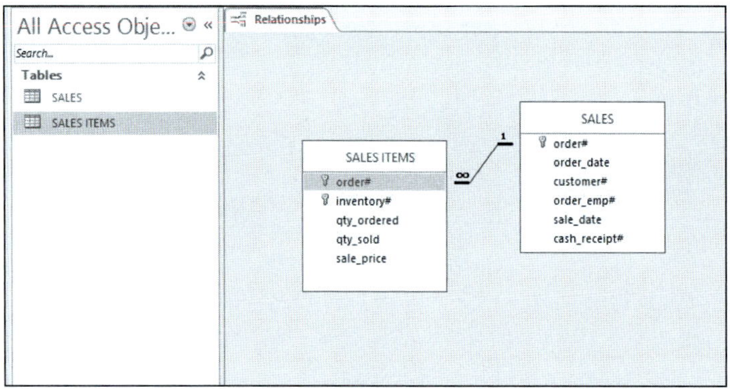

FIGURE 8.10
Setting Relationship between SALES and SALES ITEMS Tables

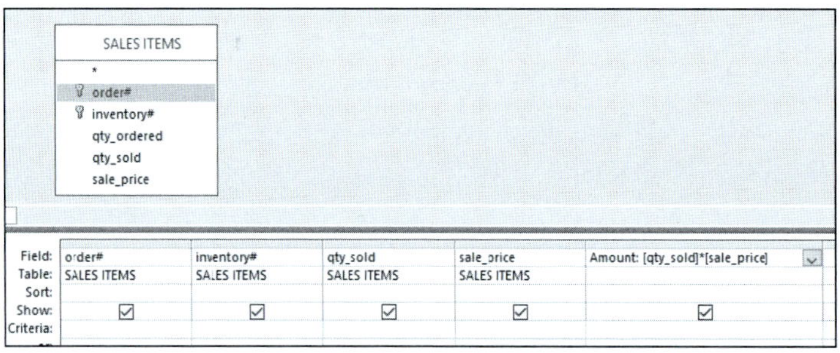

FIGURE 8.11
Calculating Amounts from the SALES ITEMS Table

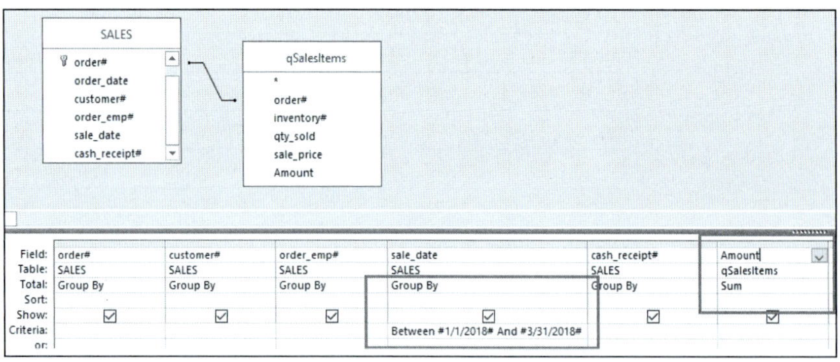

FIGURE 8.12
Summing Amounts for Each SALE

Summary

- This chapter outlines the approach to an integrated business analysis project.
- The project involves
  - Using project planning and management tools
  - Defining business requirements
  - Preparing an integrated UML class diagram
  - Preparing activity diagrams using BPMN
  - Importing data into Access from Excel
  - Cleaning and correcting data and data structures
  - Preparing queries to provide financial information

Chapter 9

Data Analytics in Accounting

A look at this chapter

This chapter introduces the importance and impact of data analytics on the business world and, specifically, on the accounting profession. Due to the increasing power and capabilities of certain technologies, the amount of data collected for various business purposes is increasing dramatically. These large datasets, or Big Data, hold great value to these businesses, whether the data reveal certain patterns in their marketing or advertising, provide insight into seasonal trends, or offer anything else that could be relevant to the businesses' success. However, the value of Big Data is really only as valuable as the insight it provides. If there is no way to properly slice and dice the data into an understandable form, then the value of the data is greatly diminished. This is where data analytics comes in—data analytics involves using tools to process these large amounts of data into a form that is easily accessible and understandable by business decision makers.

A look back

In Chapter 8, we provided the comprehensive project in which we integrated data models and prepared a database that could be queried to develop important reports necessary for decision making.

A look ahead

Chapter 10 provides a description of how AIS facilitates management reporting, including using data warehouses, business intelligence, and dashboards. In addition, it also explains the development and emerging use of eXtensible Business Reporting Language (XBRL).

© GIANLUIGI GUERCIA/AFP/Getty Images

Store openings at **Starbucks** in 2011 and 2012 represented some of the best store opening revenues in their history. How did Starbucks do it? It combined demography, data, and science in data analytics tools to pick its store locations. It embarked on these tools because Starbucks wanted to open 1,500 more stores in the United States without cannibalizing sales of existing stores. Such data analytics were used to pinpoint stores —including drive-through and smaller stores—in locations that were more convenient for customers. The result was clearly more traffic and improved sales.

Talking about the use of data analytics tools, CFO Troy Alstead notes that Starbucks has ". . . more discipline and rigor around new store development and the monitoring of new store performance and returns, today, than we ever have before." Alstead continued, "The most recent class of [newly opened] stores, particularly in the Americas, have consistently produced great returns, exceeding our hurdle rates." In fact, it is clear that Starbucks' president of the Americas and United States was pleased with these results and will continue to use them in the future, noting, ". . . we strongly believe that as a result of the demography, the data, the science and the experience we have, that these locations in the returns will mirror what we've been able to accomplish in 2011 and 2012." Data analytics seems to be pervasive in every type of business decision at Starbucks and will continue well into the future.

Source: http://data-informed.com/data-driven-location-choices-drive-latest-starbucks-surge/#sthash.y1pCr6V9.dpuf.

Chapter Outline

Learning Objectives

After reading this chapter you should be able to:

9-1 Define *Big Data* and *data analytics*

9-2 Describe the benefits and costs of using data analytics

9-3 Understand the impact of data analytics on business

9-4 Understand the impact of data analytics on accounting

9-5 Describe how audit data standards are useful in sharing data between a company and its auditors in preparation for data analysis

9-6 Explain the responsibilities of firms and auditors on privacy and data protection

9-7 Use Excel spreadsheet tables for data analytics

9-8 Use Excel pivot tables for data analytics and visualization

9-9 Use Excel Power Pivot for data analytics and visualization

9-10 Use Tableau for data analytics and visualization

LO 9-1
Define *Big Data* and *data analytics*

BIG DATA AND DATA ANALYTICS

As technology advances at an alarming rate, there are much more data that could be captured than ever before. In addition, storage of such large amounts of data becomes more feasible as the cost of data storage decreases. This trend is projected to continue exponentially into the future. Business leaders increasingly understand the power of this technology and recognize the value that data can have in an increasingly competitive global marketplace. During this technological era, Big Data and data analytics are having transformational effects on businesses. At a high level, **Big Data** is defined as datasets that are too large and complex for businesses' existing systems to handle utilizing their traditional capabilities to capture, store, manage, and analyze these datasets. The three Vs—volume, velocity, and variety—are often used to represent the defining features of Big Data.[1] *Volume* refers to the massive amount of data involved. *Velocity* refers to the fact that the data come in at quick speeds or in real time, such as streaming videos and news feeds. *Variety* refers to unstructured and unprocessed data, such as comments in social media, e-mails, global positioning system (GPS) measurements, etc.

One of the main challenges in the Big Data realm is acquiring relevant information that can be extracted or computed from the dataset. We define **data analytics** as the science of examining raw data (now often described as Big Data), removing excess noise from the dataset, and organizing the data with the purpose of drawing conclusions for decision making. Data analytics is useful for a business to examine patterns and trends in large datasets. That is, the process of data analytics aims at transforming raw data into valuable information. Data analytics plays a vital role in today's business world by examining the data to generate models for predictions of patterns and trends. If the data couldn't be analyzed to provide meaningful insight, the Big Data would not be nearly as valuable. Effective data analytics provides a way to search through large and unstructured data to identify unknown patterns or relationships.[2] Then, these data are organized in a meaningful structure to be extracted in order to provide useful information. Data analytics often involves the technologies, systems, practices, methodologies, databases, and applications used to analyze diverse business data to help organizations make sound and timely business decisions.[3]

Progress Check

1. How would considering weather patterns to predict corn production qualify as data analytics?
2. Using their definitions and the textbook discussion, compare and contrast the terms *Big Data* and *data analytics.*

LO 9-2
Describe the benefits and costs of using data analytics

THE BENEFITS AND COSTS OF THE USE OF DATA ANALYTICS

What differentiates Big Data from other types of data is determined "by whether these data push the limit of capabilities of information systems that work with these data."[4] Companies generally face two important limiting factors in their business systems when

[1]Kyunghee Yoon, Lucas Hoogduin, and Li Zhang, "Big Data as Complementary Audit Evidence," *Accounting Horizons* 29, no. 2 (June 2015), pp. 431–438.

[2]Roger S. Debreceny and Glen L. Gray, "IT Governance and Process Maturity: A Multinational Field Study," *Journal of Information Systems* 27, no. 1 (Spring 2013), pp. 157–188.

[3]H. Chen, R. H. L. Chiang, and V. C. Storey, "Business Intelligence Research," *MIS Quarterly* 34, no. 1 (2010), pp. 201–203.

[4]Miklos A. Vasarhelyi, Alexander Kogan, and Brad M. Tuttle, "Big Data in Accounting: An Overview," *Accounting Horizons* 29, no. 2 (June 2015), pp. 381–396.

dealing with Big Data: storage and processing. Depending on the size and resources of the company, the amount of data the company can feasibly store varies greatly. Many companies choose to use a cloud platform to lower the cost of data storage. In terms of processing Big Data, the processing power required to obtain information valuable to the company could be enormous or even impossible.

The data itself might have a cost to acquire (such as the cost to acquire weather pattern data, Twitter data, or economic data, etc). Another cost is that raw data must be scrubbed from extraneous data and noise to become useful. This is generally referred to as the **extract, transform, and load (ETL)** process. Reformatting, cleansing, and consolidating large volumes of data from multiple sources and platforms can be especially time-consuming. In fact, data analytics professionals estimate that they spend between 50 percent and 90 percent of their time cleaning data for analysis.[5] This, too, has an explicit cost that includes the salaries of the data analytics scientists and the cost of the technology to prepare and analyze the data. As with other information, there is a cost to produce these data. Of course, the organization will want to ensure that the cost to extract, process, analyze, and store such information is exceeded by the benefits of receiving such information.

Progress Check

3. What are some examples of the cost involved in performing data analytics?

LO 9-3
Understand the impact of data analytics on business

THE IMPACT OF DATA ANALYTICS ON BUSINESS

Many companies address the likely possibility that the data their organizations hold are, in fact, influencing their market value. A study from McKinsey Global Institute estimates that Big Data could generate up to $3 trillion in value per year in just a subset of industries impacted.[6] Big Data and data analytics could very much transform the manner in which companies run their businesses in the near future. According to a study produced by CapGemini and EMC, it is clear that Big Data is a disruptive force and must be addressed.[7] That is, the real value of data comes from data analytics. With a wealth of data on their hands, companies are empowered by using data analytics to discover various patterns, investigate anomalies, forecast future behavior, and so forth. For example, with insight provided through data analytics, companies could do more directed marketing campaigns based on patterns observed in their data, giving them a competitive advantage over companies that do not use this information to improve their marketing strategies. Patterns discovered from historical data enable businesses to identify future opportunities and risks. In addition to producing more value externally,

[5] "One-Third of BI Pros Spend Up to 90% of Time Cleaning Data," http://www.eweek.com/database/one-third-of-bi-pros-spend-up-to-90-of-time-cleaning-data.html," June 2015 (accessed March 15, 2016).

[6] "Open Data: Unlocking Innovation and Performance with Liquid Information," McKinsey Global Institute, http://www.mckinsey.com/insights/business_technology/open_data_unlocking_innovation_and_performance_with_liquid_information, October 2013 (accessed September 7, 2015).

[7] Louis Columbus, "56% of Enterprises Will Increase Their Investment in Big Data over the Next Three Years," *Forbes,* http://www.forbes.com/sites/louiscolumbus/2015/03/22/56-of-enterprises-will-increase-their-investment-in-big-data-over-the-next-three-years/, March 22, 2015 (accessed January 9, 2016).

studies show that data analytics affects internal processes, improving productivity, utilization, and growth.[8]

Data analytics often also involves data management and business intelligence with domain knowledge of business functional areas. Given the impact of Big Data, there will be an increasing amount of investments in data analytics. Therefore, there is an increasing demand for data analytics–related tasks. Data analytics skill sets are often composed of acquiring/cleansing data, creating data structures/models, and mining/analyzing data. The skills associated with data analytics are relevant across industries, including scientific, medical, manufacturing, technical services, information technologies, retail trade, government, and more.[9]

According to the results of 18th Annual Global CEO Survey conducted by PricewaterhouseCoopers (PwC), many CEOs express that they put a high value on data analytics, and 80% of them place data mining and analysis as the second-most important strategic technology for CEOs. In fact, per PwC's 6th Annual Digital IQ survey of more than 1,400 leaders from digital businesses, the area of investment that tops CEOs' list of priorities is business analytics.[10]

Progress Check

4. Let's assume a brand manager at Procter & Gamble identifies that an older demographic might be concerned with the use of its Olay™ products and its impact on their skin. How might Procter & Gamble use data analytics to assess if this is a problem?
5. Most uses of data analytics seem to be associated with external applications, like how data analytics might help a company market its products to other demographics. But data analytics also can have an impact on internal processes. Given the higher cost of paying employees to work overtime, consider an example of how data analytics might be helpful to reduce its overtime direct labor costs in a manufacturing setting.

LO 9-4
Understand the impact of data analytics on accounting

THE IMPACT OF DATA ANALYTICS ON ACCOUNTING

Financial Reporting

We refer to financial reporting as the responsibility internal to the firm of issuing financial statements and financial reports, an effort generally led by the CFO and controller. Financial reporting includes a number of estimates and valuations that might be better evaluated through use of data analytics. Both internal and external data could be used to address many of the questions that face financial reporting. Many financial statement accounts are just estimates, so accountants often ask themselves questions like this to evaluate those estimates:

1. How much of the accounts receivable balance will be collected?
2. Is any of our inventory obsolete? Are customers still interested in it? Should our inventory be valued at market or cost (applying the lower-of-cost-or-market rule)?
3. Is our goodwill correctly valued, or has it been impaired? Due to conservatism, do we need to write it down or write it off?
4. Is our property, plant, and equipment overvalued in the current real estate market?

[8]Joseph Kennedy, "Big Data's Economic Impact," https://www.ced.org/blog/entry/big-datas-economic-impact, December 3, 2014 (accessed January 9, 2016).

[9]Louis Columbus, "Where Big Data Jobs Will Be in 2015," *Forbes,* http://www.forbes.com/sites/louiscolumbus/2014/12/29/where-big-data-jobs-will-be-in-2015/, December 29, 2014 (accessed January 9, 2016).

[10]"Data Driven: What Students Need to Succeed in a Rapidly Changing Business World," PwC, http://www.pwc.com/us/en/faculty-resource/assets/PwC-Data-driven-paper-Feb2015.pdf, February 2015 (accessed January 9, 2016).

One way that data analytics may be used is to scan the environment—that is, by scanning social media to identify potential risks and opportunities to the firm. For example, in a business intelligence sense, it may allow a firm to monitor its competitors and its customers to better understand opportunities and threats around them. Are their competitors, customers, or suppliers facing financial difficulty that might affect their interactions with them? Data analytics may also allow an accountant or auditor to assess the probability of a goodwill write-down, warranty claims, or the collectability of bad debts based on what customers, investors, and other stakeholders are saying about the company in blogs and in social media. This information might help the firm determine both its optimal response to the situation and appropriate adjustment to its financial reporting.

Auditing

Data analytics plays a very critical role in the future of an audit. "As the business landscape for most organizations becomes increasingly complex and fast-paced, there is a movement toward leveraging advanced business analytic techniques to refine the focus on risk and derive deeper insights into an organization."[11] In fact, in PwC's 18th Annual Global CEO Survey, 86% of CEOs say they find it important to champion digital technologies and emphasize a clear vision of using technology for a competitive advantage, while 85% say they put a high value on data analytics. This sentiment has been reverberating through industry circles for several years now and has triggered many public accounting firms to invest in technology and personnel to capture, organize, and analyze these data to provide expanded services and added value to their clients. As a result, data analytics is expected to be the next innovation in the evolution of the audit and professional accounting industry.

Given the fact that operational data abound and are easier to collect and manage, combined with CEOs' desires to utilize such data, the accounting firms will be approaching their engagements with a different mindset. No longer will they be simply checking for material misstatements, fraud, and risk in financial statements or merely reporting their findings at the end of the engagement. Now, audit professionals will be collecting and analyzing the company's data similar to how an internal cost accountant or business analyst would in order to help management make better business decisions. This means that external auditors will stay engaged with clients beyond the audit. This is a significant paradigm shift. The audit process will be changed from a traditional process toward a more automated one, which will allow audit professionals to focus more on the logic and rationale behind data queries and less on the gathering of the actual data.[12] As a result, audits will not only yield important findings from a financial perspective, but also information that can help companies refine processes, improve efficiency, and anticipate future problems.

"It's a massive leap to go from traditional audit approaches to one that fully integrates big data and analytics in a seamless manner."[13]

Data analytics also expands auditors' capabilities in services such as testing for fraudulent transactions and automating compliance-monitoring activities (e.g., filing financial reports with the SEC or IRS). This increase in automation will also result in both higher quality and consistency of the audit and will help auditors identify issues earlier, thereby reducing surprises.[14] Greater insight into the client's operations would result in a more thorough audit and a better client experience. The ability to accurately identify risks would

[11] "Adding Insight to Audit: Transforming Internal Audit through Data Analytics," Deloitte, http://www2.deloitte.com/content/dam/Deloitte/ca/Documents/audit/ca-en-audit-adding-insight-to-audit.pdf (accessed January 10, 2016).

[12] "Data Driven," PwC.

[13] "How Big Data and Analytics Are Transforming the Audit," EY, https://eyo-iis-pd.ey.com/ARC/documents/EY-reporting-issue-9.pdf, April 2015 (accessed January 27, 2016).

[14] "Simplifying the Audit through Innovation," PwC, http://www.pwc.com/us/en/audit-assurance-services/financial-statement-audit.html (accessed January 10, 2016).

become more transparent whether it consists of security breaches or flawed processes. Additionally, corporate compliance with changing regulations could be more accurately monitored. The benefits of competent data analytics services are not limited to the audit services. IT advisory/consulting and tax services would also benefit from the greater insight provided by data analytics from the audit team because the analyses could provide a seamless big picture among functional areas. Financial and operational projection models could be developed to allow for quick and accurate "what-if" business forecasting.

It is clear that data analytics will transform the audit profession in several ways. Both internal and external auditors can benefit significantly through its use. By using data analytics, auditors are able to spend less time looking for evidence, which will allow more time for presenting their findings and making judgments. This will help eliminate some of the mundane tasks involved with audit and will lead to a more interesting and challenging experience for auditors. Data analytics will also allow auditors to vastly expand sampling beyond current traditional sample sizes and, in many cases, may be able test the full population of transactions.[15] With data analytics, auditors will also be able to work from anywhere at any time, given the data will be at the ready, and there will no longer be a need to pull data at the client site.

Another aspect of the audit profession that will change as a result of data analytics is the clients' expectations. Clients will begin to expect deeper and broader insights and faster and more efficient delivery, as well as innovative thinking from their auditors.[16] Overall, the use of data analytics brings forth significant and exciting changes to the audit profession. Auditors who adapt early to these changes will have a significant advantage over slow movers, as the harnessing of data analytics will provide notable benefits in the upcoming years.

Managerial and Tax Accounting

Data analytics also will increasingly play an important role in both managerial and tax accounting.

Accountants reporting to the CEO have lots of data (e.g., data warehouses, data marts, dashboards, etc.) that may be useful in providing support for managerial decision making. Likewise, planning tax-minimization strategies also may use data analytics to see what and how transactions can be optimized to reduce taxes.

Progress Check

6. How will data analytics change the external audit?
7. How can data analytics allow an accountant or auditor to assess the probability of a goodwill write-down, warranty claims, or the collectability of bad debts?

LO 9-5
Describe how audit data standards are useful in sharing data between a company and its auditors in preparation for data analysis

AUDIT DATA STANDARDS

In the preceding sections, we mentioned the substantial cost and effort involved in cleaning and scrubbing data to make the information ready for analysis. In fact, up to 90% of data analytics professionals' time is spent cleaning the data. However, if both the provider and the user (e.g., a company and its external auditor) of the data had the same data standards for their data, this cost of cleaning and formatting the data could be alleviated. For this

[15]"Big Data and Analytics in the Audit Process: Mitigating Risk and Unlocking Value," EY, http://www.alumnievents.ey.com/pdfs/ey-big-data-and-analytics-in-the-audit-process.pdf (accessed January 10, 2016).

[16]Joe Ucuzoglu, "How and Why the Audit Has to Evolve Rapidly," *Financial Reporting* (Financial Executives International), http://daily.financialexecutives.org/how-and-why-the-audit-has-to-evolve-rapidly/, March 26, 2015 (accessed January 10, 2016).

reason, the American Institute of Certified Public Accountants (AICPA) worked to develop **audit data standards (ADS).** ADS is a set of standards for data files and fields typically needed to support an external audit in a given financial business process area. These standards also include questionnaires that may need to be considered to ensure that the data to be accessed are a complete and valid population. While the AICPA's most immediate goal is to support the financial statement audit process, in practice, there may be very similar data requirements for external audit, internal audit, and compliance testing.[17]

Because there is wide variability in the file and field names and data types in underlying accounting and enterprise systems, the objective of the ADS is to produce data in a standard structure that can then be used consistently across financial audits of most organizations. The potential benefits include the following:

- Reduces the time and effort involved in accessing data by
  - Providing a precise request of what data are required and the format in which the data should be provided.
  - Reducing the risk that incorrect or incomplete data will be provided by IT.
  - Reducing the need for an IT specialist to clean or scrub the data.
  - Potentially having financial reporting systems (such as SAP or Oracle) output this information directly.
- Works well with standard audit and risk analytic tests often run against datasets in specific accounts or groups of accounts (such as inventory or accounts receivable or sales revenue transactions).
- Allows software vendors (such as **ACL Inc.**) to produce data extraction programs for given enterprise systems to help facilitate fraud detection and prevention and risk management.
- Facilitates testing of the full population of transactions, rather than just a small sample.
- Connects/interacts well with XBRL GL Standards (to be introduced in Chapter 10).

In Figure 9.1, we present the general ledger standards suggested under the ADS. Please note the fields, field names, data types, and lengths, as well as a description of what is included in the general ledger. Note, for example, field 12, which specifies whether this is a debit or credit, as well as field 17, which is the User ID of the individual who approved the journal entry. While the actual financial reporting system may vary (e.g., Oracle, Peoplesoft, SAP, etc.), the idea is that they all have the ability to output a file with these characteristics, which would then be easily imported into an external auditor's software.

FIGURE 9.1 **Standards for the General Ledger under Audit Data Standards**[18]

Field #	Field Name	Data Type	Length	Description
1	Journal_ID	TEXT	100	Identifier that is unique for each journal entry. May require concatenation of multiple fields.
2	Journal_ID_Line_Number	TEXT	100	Identifier that is unique for each line within a journal entry.
3	JE_Header_Description	TEXT	256	Description of the entire journal entry as described by the journal entry header.
4	JE_Line_Description	TEXT	256	Description of the individual line within the journal entry.

(continued)

[17]Audit Standard Library (as of July 2015), http://www.aicpa.org/interestareas/frc/assuranceadvisoryservices/pages/auditdatastandardworkinggroup.aspx (accessed March 16. 2016).

[18]Source: http://www.aicpa.org/InterestAreas/FRC/AssuranceAdvisoryServices/DownloadableDocuments/AuditDataStandards/AuditDataStandards.GL.July2015.pdf (accessed on March 16, 2016). Used by permission of AICPA.

FIGURE 9.1
(continued)

Field #	Field Name	Data Type	Length	Description
5	Source	TEXT	25	Posting source (code for source form which the journal entry originated, such as sales journal, cash receipts, journal, general journal, payroll journal, accountant manual entry, spreadsheet, and so on).
6	Business_Unit_Code	TEXT	25	Used to identify the business unit, region, branch, etc., at the level that financial statements are being audited and for which the trial balance is generated.
7	Effective_Data	DATE		The date of the journal entry, no matter what date the entry is received or entered.
8	Fiscal_Year	TEXT	4	Fiscal year in which Effective_Date occurs: YYYY for delimited, CCYY-MM-DD fiscal year end (ISO 8601).
9	Period	TEXT	10	Fiscal period in which the Effective_Date occurs. Examples include W1–W53 for weekly periods, M1–M12 for monthly periods, and Q1–Q4 for quarterly periods.
10	GL_Account_Number	TEXT	100	Identifier for the GL financial account. The GL_Account_Number in this file must match the GL_Account_Number used in the Trial_Balance and Chart_Of_Accounts files.
11	Amount	NUMERIC		Transaction monetary amount recorded in the functional or group currency for the entity under audit.
12	Amount_Credit_Debit_Indicator	TEXT	1	Indicates whether the amount is a credit or debit. "C" = credit; "D" = debit.
13	Amount_Currency	TEXT	3	The functional or group currency related to the amount.
14	Entered_By	TEXT	25	User_ID (from User_Listing file) for person who created the record.
15	Entered_Date	DATE		Date the journal entry was entered into the system. This is sometimes referred to as the creation date.
16	Entered_Time	TIME		The time this transaction was entered into the system. ISO 8601 represents time in 24-hour time (hhmm) (e.g., 1:00 p.m. = 1300)
17	Approved_By	TEXT	25	User ID (from User_Listing file) for person who approved the entry.
18	Approved_Date	DATE		The date the entry was approved.
19	Last_Modified_By	TEXT	25	User_ID (from User_Listing file) for the last person modifying this entry.
20	Last_Modified_Date	DATE		The date the entry was last modified before posting.
21	Reporting_Amount	NUMERIC		The amount recorded in the currency in which a reporting entity prepares its financial statements.

Field #	Field Name	Data Type	Length	Description
22	Reporting_Amount_Currency	TEXT	3	The currency in which a reporting entity prepares its financial statements (for example, USD, EUR)
23	Local_Amount	NUMERIC		Amount in the local country currency where the transaction originated.
24	Local_Amount_Currency	TEXT	3	The currency used for local country reporting requirements (e.g., USD, EUR; see ISO 4217 coding).
25	Reversal_Indicator	TEXT	1	Indicates whether this entry is a reversal or to be reversed. "1" = entry is a reversal, "2" = entry is to be reversed, and empty ("") = none of the above or system generated indicators.
26	Reversal_Journal_ID	TEXT	100	When the Reversal_Indicator=1, this identifies the Journal_ID of the entry being reversed.

Progress Check

8. Why is the use of ADS helpful for the external auditor?
9. Why is the use of ADS helpful for the company being audited?

LO 9-6
Explain the responsibilities of firms and auditors on privacy and data protection

RESPONSIBILITIES OF FIRMS AND AUDITORS REGARDING PRIVACY AND DATA PROTECTION

Just as firms have great opportunity to use Data Analytics to their benefit, firms and auditors also bear an important responsibility to protect personally identifying information from being compromised and exposed to unauthorized parties. This section discusses the DATA Act as a way to address privacy and data protection. DATA defines personally identifying information and describes procedures that can be used to prevent the compromise of such information.

National Standard for Privacy and Data Protection

The U.S. House of Representatives passed the **Data Accountability and Trust Act of 2009 (DATA)**[19] in hopes of creating a national standard for privacy and data protection. DATA would supersede a wide variety of state laws requiring organizations entrusted with personally identifying information to notify individuals when their information has been exposed to unauthorized parties. DATA also provides a universal definition of personally identifying information and requires organizations to implement and maintain formal security programs to prevent unauthorized access to personally identifying information.

DATA also sets steep penalties for violations, which fall into two categories:

- Failure to comply with security program requirements.
- Failure to follow the breach notification rules.

[19]H.R. 2221—Data Accountability and Trust Act, 111th Congress (2009–2010), https://www.congress.gov/bill/114th-congress/house-bill/580 (accessed February 24, 2016).

The two types of penalties are calculated differently. The amount for security program penalties is based on the number of days the organization is found to be noncompliant multiplied by a maximum of $11,000 per day. Notification penalties are calculated by multiplying the number of violations (or individuals they failed to notify) by up to $11,000. DATA sets the maximum penalty for violations to be $5 million for each type of violation, making it possible for a single organization to pay up to $10 million for both violations.[20]

Personally identifying information

A central component of any data protection law is the definition of **personally identifying information.** The definition is critical because it not only spells out what types of information need to be protected, but also helps organizations strip out elements of datasets to avoid having to protect them.

DATA defines personally identifying information as any of these items:

1. Individual's first name or initial and last name
2. Address
3. Phone number

in combination with any one or more of the following data elements for that person:

1. Social Security number.
2. Driver's license number, passport number, military identification number, or other similar number issued on a government document used to verify identity.
3. Financial account number, or credit or debit card number, and any required security code, access code, or password that is necessary to permit access to an individual's financial account.

Similarly, the Office of Management and Budget defines personally identifying information in a potentially more concise way:

> (1) any information that can be used to distinguish or trace an individual's identity, such as name, social security number, date and place of birth, mother's maiden name, or biometric records; and (2) any other information that is linked or linkable to an individual, such as medical, educational, financial, and employment information.[21]

However, on their own, the following do not constitute personal identifiable information because more than one person could potentially also have these data characteristics:

- Date of birth.
- Place of birth.
- Business telephone number.
- Business mailing or e-mail address (as opposed to personal e-mail address).
- Education information (like university attended).
- Race.
- Religion.
- Financial information.
- Geographical indicators.
- Employment information.
- Medical information.

[20]Richard Mackey, "Understanding the Data Accountability and Trust Act," http://searchsecurity.techtarget.com/magazineContent/Understanding-the-Data-Accountability-and-Trust-Act (accessed February 24, 2016).

[21]OMB Memorandum M-07-16, "Safeguarding Against and Responding to the Breach of Personally Identifiable Information."

A **breach of security** is the unauthorized access to or acquisition of data in electronic form that contain personal information. However, DATA may allow the data owner to avoid the process of notification if the data owner determines that there is no reasonable risk of identity theft, fraud, or unlawful activity. As an example, encrypted information exposed to unauthorized parties would not be considered a breach of data.

In the event of a breach, DATA would require data owners to notify the Federal Trade Commission and directly notify each individual whose data have been exposed within 60 days of the discovery of the breach.

The data owner may notify affected individuals in written or electronic form. However, electronic notification is only acceptable if the individual has consented to receiving official communications in that manner. For the cases in which the business does not have complete contact information for the affected individuals, the data owner may do these three things to notify them:

1. E-mail to the fullest extent possible.
2. Publish a notice on its website.
3. Provide notification in print and broadcast media for areas in which the victims reside.

Preventing the Compromise of Information

DATA benefits citizens because businesses are required to notify affected people when breaches occur. The overall approach of ensuring that companies and auditing firms formally protect information is to implement sound technical controls that include risk assessment and treatment and follow a uniform set of notification and support procedures. This promises to reduce the incidences of identity compromise and create incentives to improve overall security.

DATA also requires organizations to implement a security program designed to prevent compromise of the information. Companies and accounting firms are required to do the following:

- Establish a contact person to be responsible for overseeing the program.
- Develop, document, and maintain a security policy for the collection, use, sale, dissemination, and maintenance of personally identifying information.
- Maintain contracts with third parties with access to the information to establish controls that meet the requirements of the act.
- Formalize a process to identify risks and vulnerabilities of potential breaches, and implement appropriate administrative and technical controls to mitigate the risk of compromise of the personally identifying information.
- Implement and define a process for securely disposing of both digital and paper records that might include personally identifying information.[22]

Progress Check

10. When would a mobile phone number for a customer be considered "personally identifying information"?

[22]PwC Presentation on Data Centric Security Management, https://chapters.theiia.org/san-francisco/ChapterDocuments/PwC%20Presentation%20-%20Data%20Centric%20Security%20Management.pdf (accessed February 24, 2016).

LO 9-7
Use Excel spreadsheet tables for data analytics

DATA ANALYTICS TOOLS

Using Excel for Data Analytics

This section provides an introduction to the use of Excel to perform data analytics. The example employs freely available U.S. Census data,[23] and it shows state and county population and changes in population due to births and deaths over the period from 2010 to 2015. This particular example uses only state population data as shown in Figure 9.2. Note that the data start in the first row of the worksheet, and any blank rows or blank columns are deleted. Thus, the data extend from cell A1 to cell AD52 with variable names in the first row. The region numbers indicate areas of the country, such as Northeast or South. The division numbers represent further subdivisions of the regions, such as New England or South Atlantic. We describe tab, section, and item selection as X > Y > Z, where X represents the Excel tab, Y is the section of the ribbon bar, and Z is the specific icon on the ribbon bar.

The first step is to convert the raw data to a **table in Excel.** Click on any cell within the data. Select INSERT > Table > Table, as shown in Figure 9.3. A Create Table popup will appear to specify where the data for the table are and whether the table has headers. If there are no blank rows or columns in the data, Excel will correctly identify the extent of the data for the table. Check the box to specify that the table has headers, as shown in Figure 9.4.

	A	B	C	D	E	F	G	H	I	J	K	L	M	N
1	SUMLEV	REGION	DIVISION	STATE	COUNTY	STNAME	POP2010	POP2011	POP2012	POP2013	POP2014	POP2015	BIRTHS2010	BIRTHS201
2	40	3	6	1	0	Alabama	4,785,161	4,801,108	4,816,089	4,830,533	4,846,411	4,858,979	14,226	59,68
3	40	4	9	2	0	Alaska	714,021	722,720	731,228	737,442	737,046	738,432	2,892	11,71
4	40	4	8	4	0	Arizona	6,408,208	6,468,732	6,553,262	6,630,799	6,728,783	6,828,065	20,937	86,10
5	40	3	7	5	0	Arkansas	2,922,394	2,938,538	2,949,499	2,957,957	2,966,835	2,978,204	9,439	38,44
6	40	4	9	6	0	California	37,334,079	37,700,034	38,056,055	38,414,128	38,792,291	39,144,818	123,324	509,767
7	40	4	8	8	0	Colorado	5,048,254	5,119,480	5,191,731	5,271,132	5,355,588	5,456,574	16,791	65,91
8	40	1	1	9	0	Connecticut	3,579,717	3,589,759	3,593,541	3,597,168	3,594,762	3,590,886	9,489	37,6
9	40	3	5	10	0	Delaware	899,791	907,916	917,099	925,353	935,968	945,934	2,847	11,2
10	40	3	5	11	0	District of Columbia	605,126	620,472	635,342	649,540	659,836	672,228	2,243	9,
11	40	3	5	12	0	Florida	18,849,890	19,105,533	19,352,021	19,594,467	19,905,569	20,271,272	50,872	213,21
12	40	3	5	13	0	Georgia	9,713,454	9,812,280	9,917,639	9,991,562	10,097,132	10,214,860	32,489	132,6
13	40	4	9	15	0	Hawaii	1,363,980	1,378,227	1,392,641	1,408,765	1,420,257	1,431,603	4,646	19,15
14	40	4	8	16	0	Idaho	1,570,986	1,584,134	1,596,097	1,612,785	1,634,806	1,654,930	5,971	22,95
15	40	2	3	17	0	Illinois	12,841,249	12,861,882	12,875,167	12,889,580	12,882,189	12,859,995	41,836	162,42
16	40	2	3	18	0	Indiana	6,490,590	6,516,845	6,538,283	6,570,518	6,597,880	6,619,680	20,961	83,45
17	40	2	4	19	0	Iowa	3,050,694	3,065,389	3,076,636	3,092,224	3,109,481	3,123,899	9,967	37,85
18	40	2	4	20	0	Kansas	2,858,824	2,869,917	2,886,281	2,894,630	2,902,507	2,911,641	9,992	40,11
19	40	3	6	21	0	Kentucky	4,347,937	4,367,882	4,382,667	4,398,500	4,412,617	4,425,092	13,691	55,3
20	40	3	7	22	0	Louisiana	4,544,951	4,575,381	4,603,676	4,627,491	4,648,990	4,670,724	14,573	62,31
21	40	1	1	23	0	Maine	1,327,695	1,328,257	1,328,888	1,328,778	1,330,256	1,329,328	3,443	12,6
22	40	3	5	24	0	Maryland	5,788,409	5,844,171	5,890,740	5,936,040	5,975,346	6,006,401	18,461	73,5
23	40	1	1	25	0	Massachusetts	6,565,036	6,611,797	6,657,780	6,708,810	6,755,124	6,794,422	18,647	73,1
24	40	2	3	26	0	Michigan	9,877,369	9,876,589	9,886,879	9,900,506	9,916,306	9,922,576	29,102	113,98
25	40	2	4	27	0	Minnesota	5,310,903	5,348,119	5,380,443	5,420,541	5,457,125	5,489,594	17,500	68,3
26	40	3	6	28	0	Mississippi	2,970,316	2,977,999	2,985,660	2,990,976	2,993,443	2,992,333	9,421	39,7
27	40	2	4	29	0	Missouri	5,996,052	6,010,587	6,025,468	6,043,708	6,063,827	6,083,672	19,012	76,2
28	40	4	8	30	0	Montana	990,643	997,746	1,005,157	1,014,402	1,023,252	1,032,949	3,068	11,9
29	40	2	4	31	0	Nebraska	1,830,025	1,842,383	1,855,973	1,869,300	1,882,980	1,896,190	6,515	25,73
30	40	4	8	32	0	Nevada	2,703,440	2,718,819	2,754,874	2,790,366	2,838,281	2,890,845	8,892	35,8
31	40	1	1	33	0	New Hampshire	1,316,708	1,318,344	1,321,393	1,322,660	1,327,996	1,330,608	3,269	12,9
32	40	1	2	34	0	New Jersey	8,803,881	8,842,934	8,874,893	8,907,384	8,938,844	8,958,013	26,529	106,
33	40	4	8	35	0	New Mexico	2,064,741	2,078,226	2,084,792	2,086,890	2,085,567	2,085,109	6,649	27,80
34	40	1	2	36	0	New York	19,402,920	19,523,202	19,606,981	19,691,032	19,748,858	19,795,791	61,414	243,1
35	40	3	5	37	0	North Carolina	9,558,979	9,651,025	9,747,021	9,845,432	9,940,387	10,042,802	29,914	121,04
36	40	2	4	38	0	North Dakota	674,530	685,326	702,265	723,626	740,040	756,927	2,341	9,19
37	40	2	3	39	0	Ohio	11,540,766	11,545,442	11,551,783	11,572,232	11,596,998	11,613,423	34,809	137,

FIGURE 9.2
State Population Data in Excel

[23]There are many federal government datasets freely available at http://www.data.gov. The example dataset is from one showing U.S. county populations and changes in population for the period 2010 to 2015.

FIGURE 9.3
Creating a Table in Excel

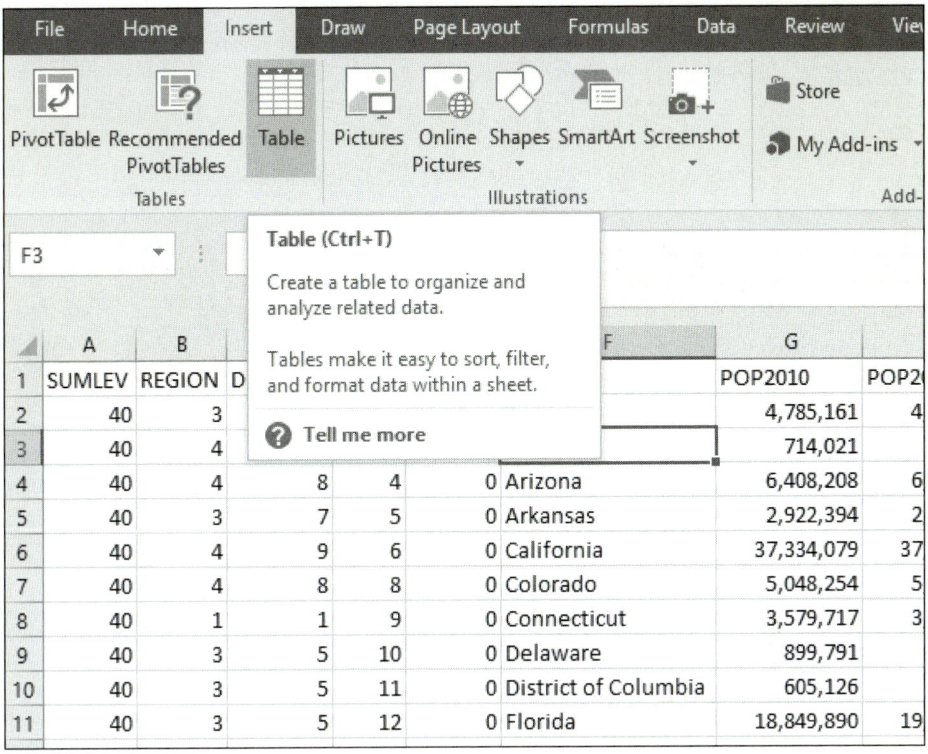

FIGURE 9.4
Create Table Popup

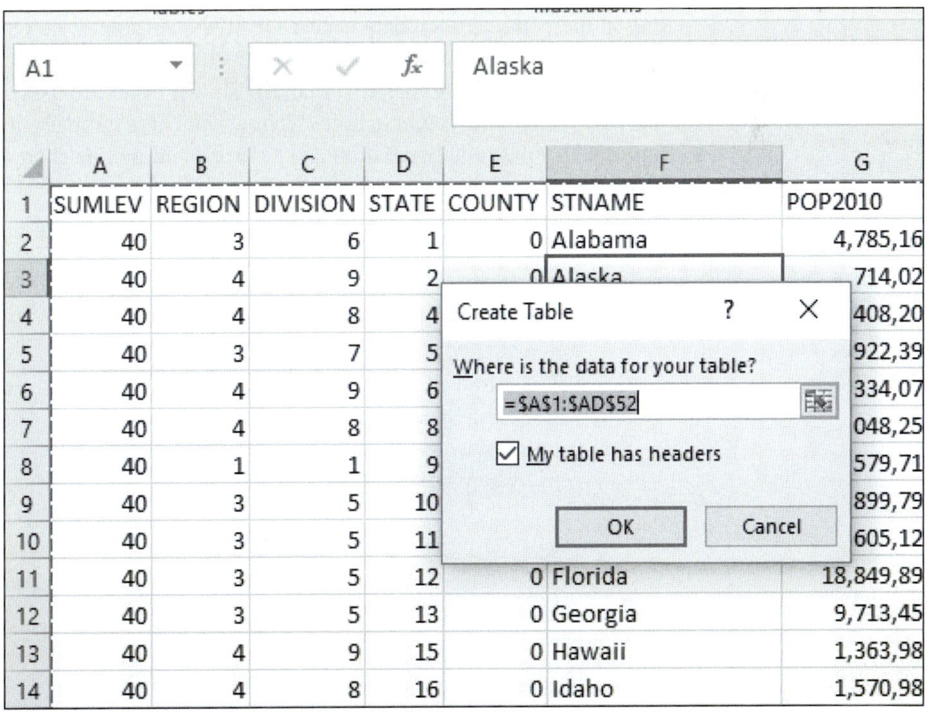

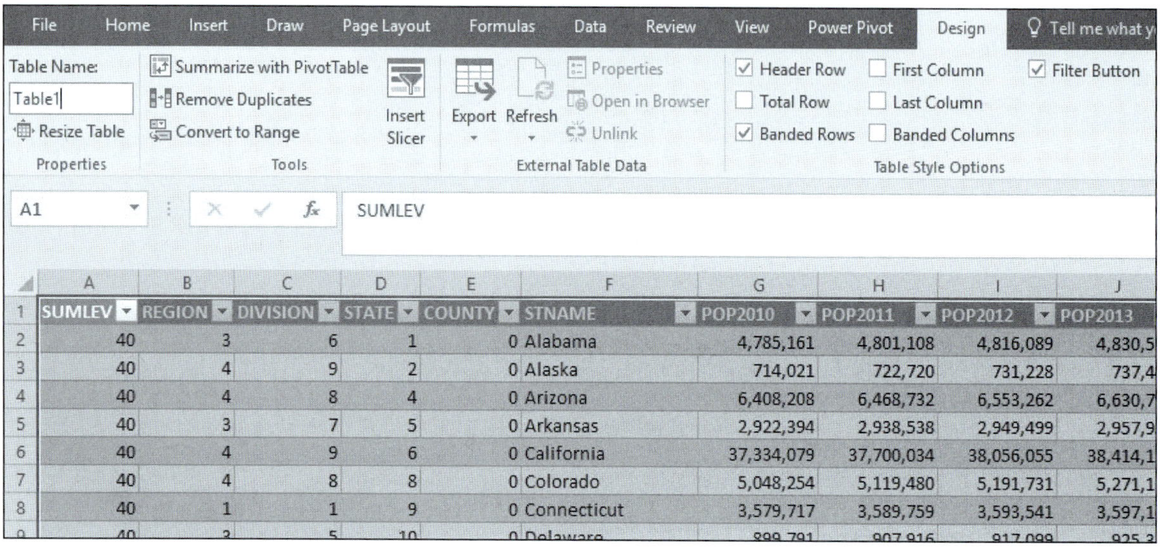

FIGURE 9.5
Table with Default Design

Select OK to create the table. Excel will apply a default design that creates a style for the header row, adds filter buttons to each column, and bands the rows with alternating colors, as shown in Figure 9.5. To apply a different style, select DESIGN > Table Styles and choose a new style from the available options.

Excel tables directly support some basic data analytics. For example, to add a Total Row at the bottom of the data, select DESIGN > Table Style Options and check the box next to Total Row. Then, navigate to the new totals row at the bottom of your table. Use the pull-down menus to add desired totals, as shown in Figure 9.6. Use the totals in conjunction with the column filters to quickly view and chart summary information. For example, Figure 9.7 shows total population and a corresponding line chart for each year for states in the Northeast region.

FIGURE 9.6
Adding Totals to the Table

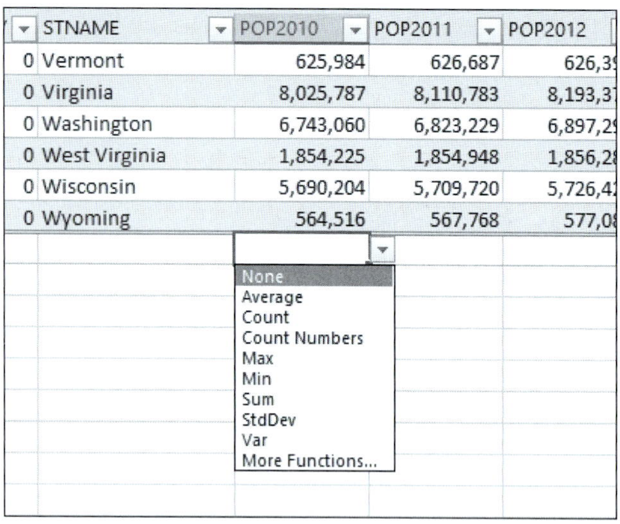

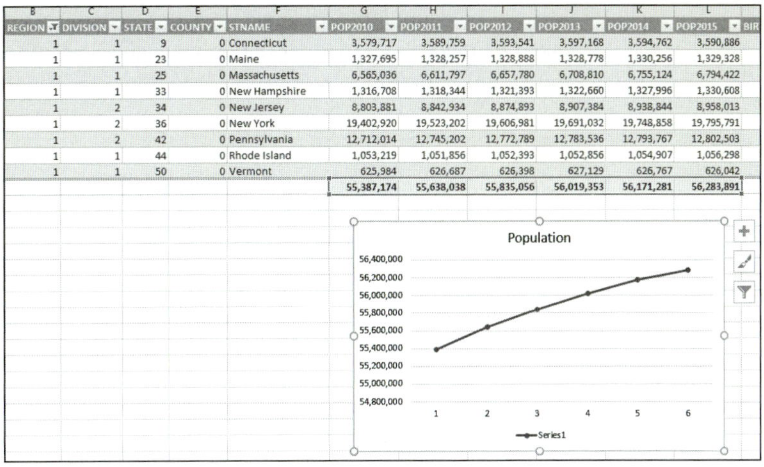

FIGURE 9.7
Using Filters and Totals for Analysis

Progress Check

11. Could you create a table in Excel and add a totals row? Use data from the integrated project in Chapter 8 and try it.

LO 9-8
Use Excel pivot tables for data analytics and visualization

Creating and Using Excel Pivot Tables

This section introduces **Excel pivot tables** for more flexible data analytics. Although pivot tables can be created from any Excel data, it is helpful to first create a table with your data as described earlier. Select any cell in your table; then select DESIGN > Tools > Summarize with PivotTable as shown in Figure 9.8. The Create PivotTable popup will appear, using the table name (we replaced the default table name, Table1, with *StatePop* in

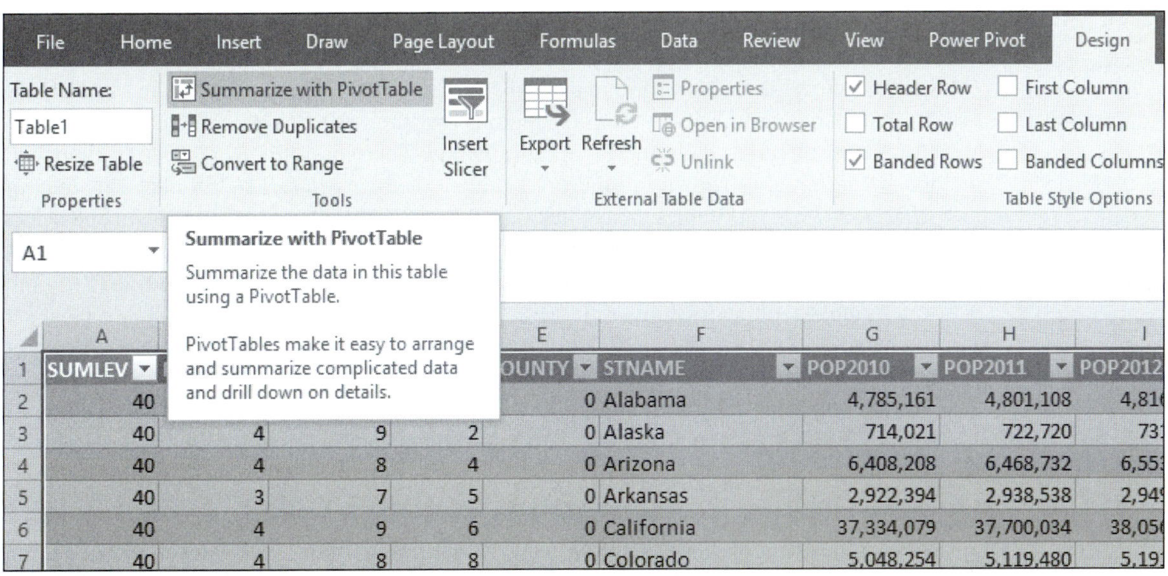

FIGURE 9.8
Summarizing with a Pivot Table in Excel

the example) as the table or range of data.[24] Then, select where you want the PivotTable report to be placed. The default option is placing the PivotTable report in a new worksheet, as shown in Figure 9.9.

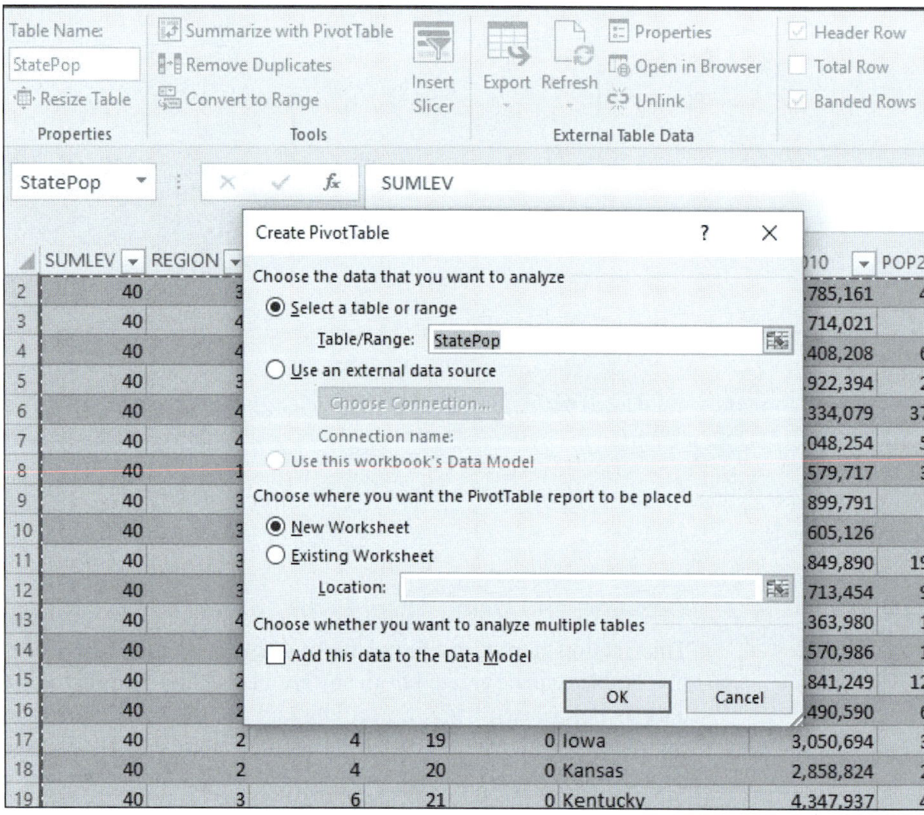

FIGURE 9.9
The Create PivotTable Popup

Excel creates a blank pivot table and shows a list of the fields—the names in the header row in the table—to use in defining the PivotTable report, as shown in Figure 9.10. To summarize the births in 2015 by region, first drag the *REGION* field down into the Rows area directly below the PivotTable Fields. Then, drag the *BIRTHS2015* field into the Values area, as shown in Figure 9.11. Note that the *BIRTHS2015* field reads *Sum of BIRTHS2015* in the Values area. Click on *Sum of BIRTHS2015* to view a menu and select the Value Field Settings, as shown in Figure 9.12. When the Value Field Settings box appears, select the Number Format button and change the format of the *BIRTHS2015* field to a number with zero decimal places and comma separators. At this point, we changed the name of *Sum of BIRTHS2015* to *Total Births 2015* to be more descriptive. The pivot table now shows the four regions and the total births in each region in 2015, as well as the overall total of births in a Grand Total row. To change the design of the PivotTable report, select DESIGN > Layout > Grand Totals or Subtotals to turn totals on or off.

Using Slicers to Filter Results in an Excel Pivot Table

Pivot tables become more flexible when you combine them with slicers. To illustrate, first drag the REGION field out of the Rows area and drag STNAME (state name) into

[24]You can change the table name on the Design tab ribbon bar in the Properties section.

FIGURE 9.10
The PivotTable Fields List

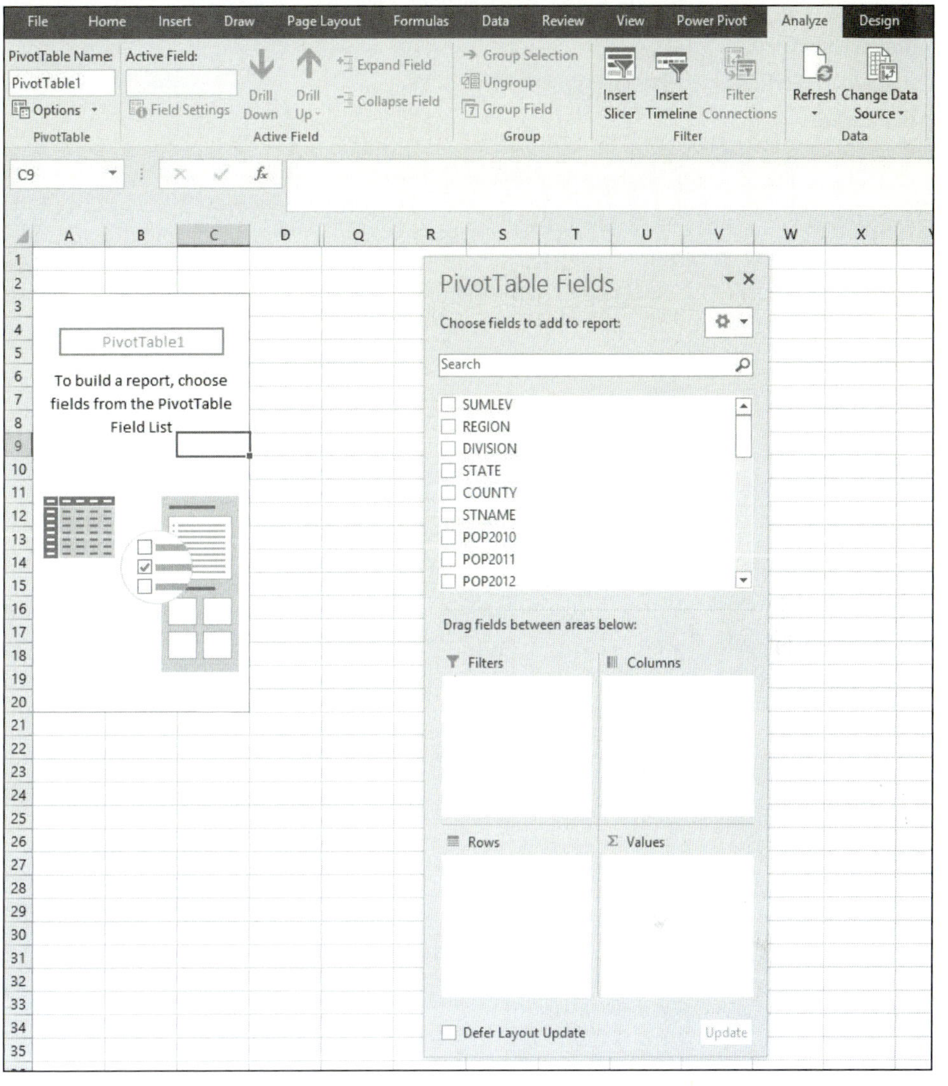

the Rows area. Now, the pivot table shows the total births in 2015 in each state. Assume you want to know how the number of births have changed since 2010, and you want to compare the changes among states in each region. There are several ways to accomplish this, but one easy and flexible way is to use calculated fields and slicers. First, calculate a new field to show the percentage change in births. Select ANALYZE > Calculations > Fields, Items & Sets. Choose Calculated Field from the menu that appears. On the Insert Calculated Field box, name the calculated field "Pct Change in Births" and create the formula *(BIRTHS2015-BIRTHS2010)/BIRTHS2010* in the Formula line. Click OK, and the new field will appear at the bottom of the PivotTable Fields list. Drag it into the Values area. Follow the steps outlined earlier to go to the Value Field Settings and change the number format to percentage. We then changed the name of the Values field from "Sum of Pct Change in Births" to "State Pct Change in Births" to create the pivot table in Figure 9.13.

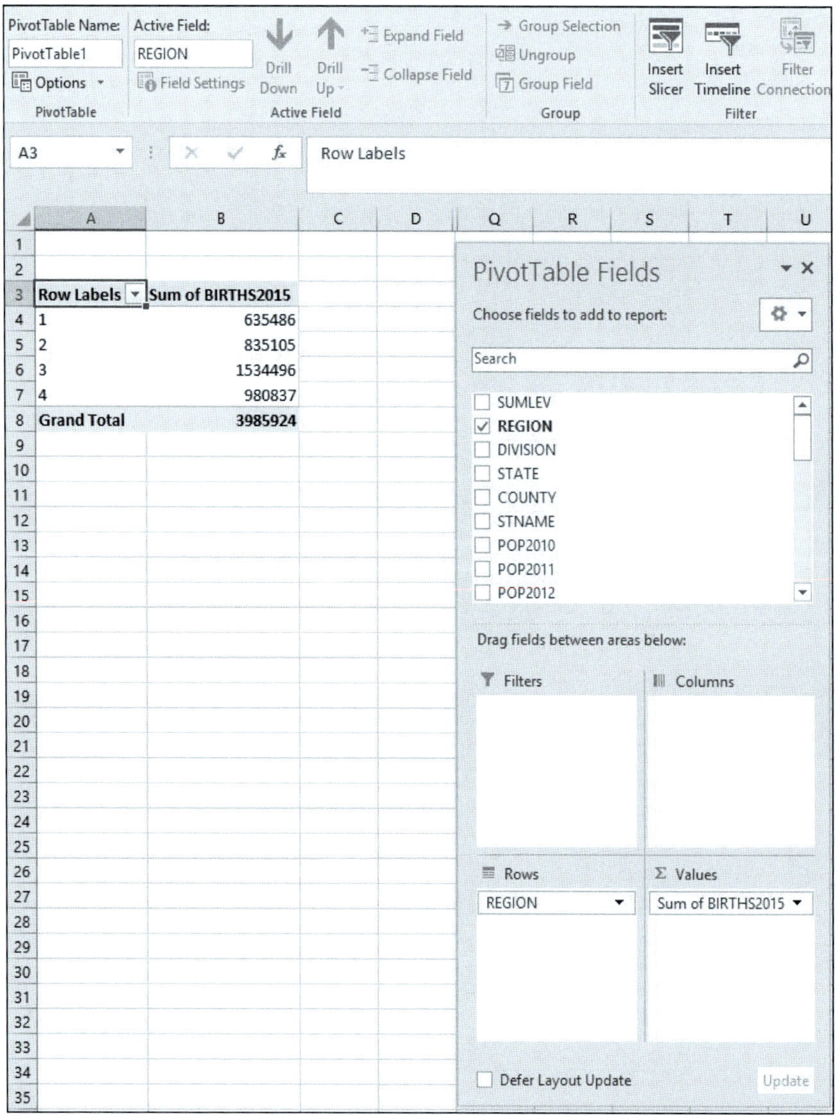

FIGURE 9.11
Summarizing Births in 2015 by Region

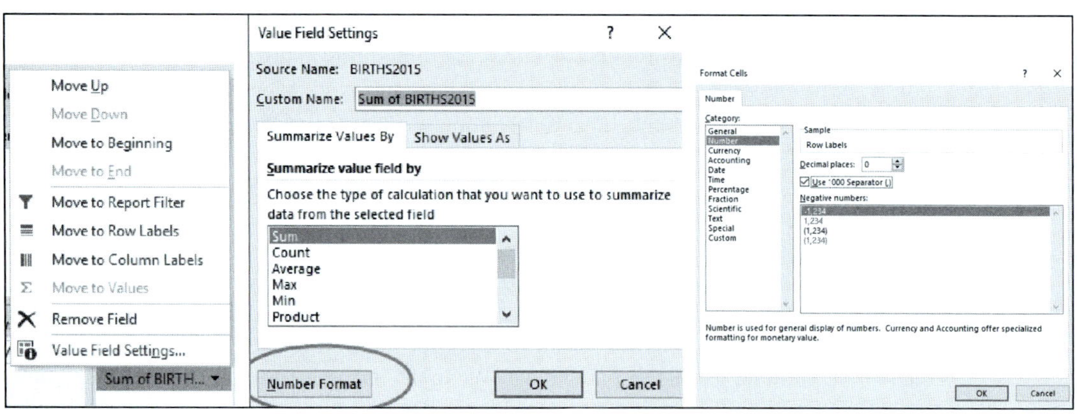

FIGURE 9.12
Value Field Settings and Formatting

FIGURE 9.13
Pivot Table Showing Percentage Change in Births by State

Row Labels	State Pct Change in Births
Alabama	310%
Alaska	298%
Arizona	317%
Arkansas	301%
California	309%
Colorado	299%
Connecticut	282%
Delaware	288%
District of Columbia	328%
Florida	334%
Georgia	302%
Hawaii	315%
Idaho	281%

To add a slicer, select ANALYZE > Filter > Insert Slicer. Be sure to click in your pivot table area to see the Analyze tab. When the Insert Slicer box appears, check the REGION field and click OK. The REGION slicer appears, as shown in Figure 9.14. Select Options > Slicer Styles to change the design of the slicer. Select the slicer, then click Options > Buttons > Columns or Options > Buttons > Height or Width to change the number of columns and size of the buttons. Click on a slicer button to select a specific region; hold the Ctrl key and select another button to show multiple regions. Click the small red x on the filter symbol at the top right of the slicer to clear the selections. Figure 9.15 shows the use of the slicer to select region number 4 (West region) in the pivot table and the corresponding pivot chart. This simple example hints at the possibilities for data analytics using pivot tables, pivot charts, and slicers. Creative users can build on this example to create interactive dashboards that present multiple organizational performance measures with relatively little effort.

Row Labels	State Pct Change in Births
Alabama	310%
Alaska	298%
Arizona	317%
Arkansas	301%
California	309%
Colorado	299%
Connecticut	282%
Delaware	288%
District of Columbia	328%
Florida	334%
Georgia	302%

REGION
1
2
3
4

Region Number	Region Name
1	Northeast
2	Midwest
3	South
4	West

FIGURE 9.14
Pivot Table with Slicer to Select REGION

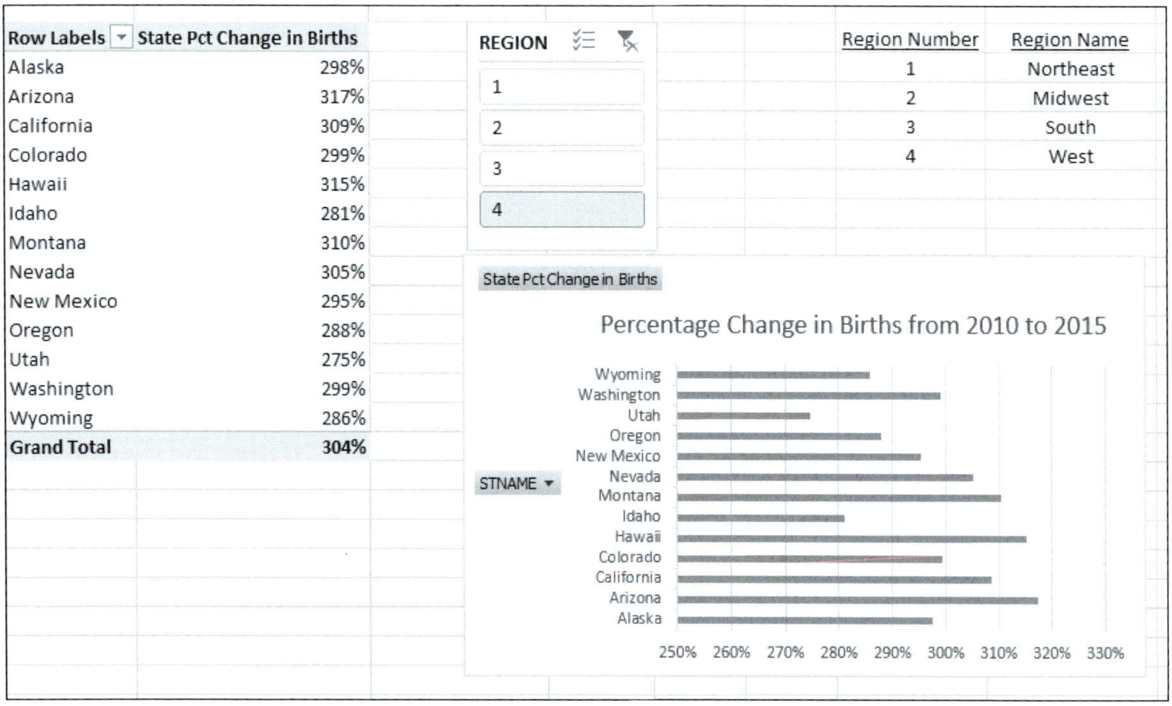

FIGURE 9.15
Pivot Table and Pivot Chart Controlled with Slicer

Progress Check

12. Could you create a pivot table with a slicer in Excel? Use data from the integrated project in Chapter 8 and try it.

LO 9-9
Use Excel Power Pivot for data analytics and visualization

Using Excel Power Pivot as a Data Manager

This section introduces the use of **Power Pivot,** an Excel add-in available for Excel 2010 and later. Power Pivot allows you to combine data from multiple sources, such as Excel and Access tables, and establish relationships to create an integrated database. In some ways, Power Pivot provides the functionality found in Microsoft Access. For this simple example, we continue working with the dataset from the U.S. Census showing population by state. First, create three Excel tables: one for the population by state data, another for the region numbers and names, and the last for division numbers and names. These will be the three tables linked using Power Pivot.

As stated, Power Pivot is an Excel add-in. To add it to Excel, select FILE > Options. When the Excel Options screen appears, select Add-ins. Then, select COM Add-ins, as shown in Figure 9.16. Then, check the box for Power Pivot on the list of COM add-ins. The Power Pivot tab is now added to the tabs on your Excel worksheet, as shown in Figure 9.17.

The next step is to add each table to the data model. For each worksheet, select POWER PIVOT > Add to Data Model. The Power Pivot for Excel screen will appear. Use the Excel icon on the Power Pivot quick access toolbar to switch back to the Excel workbook to add other tables. After adding the three tables to Power Pivot, go to Diagram View in Power

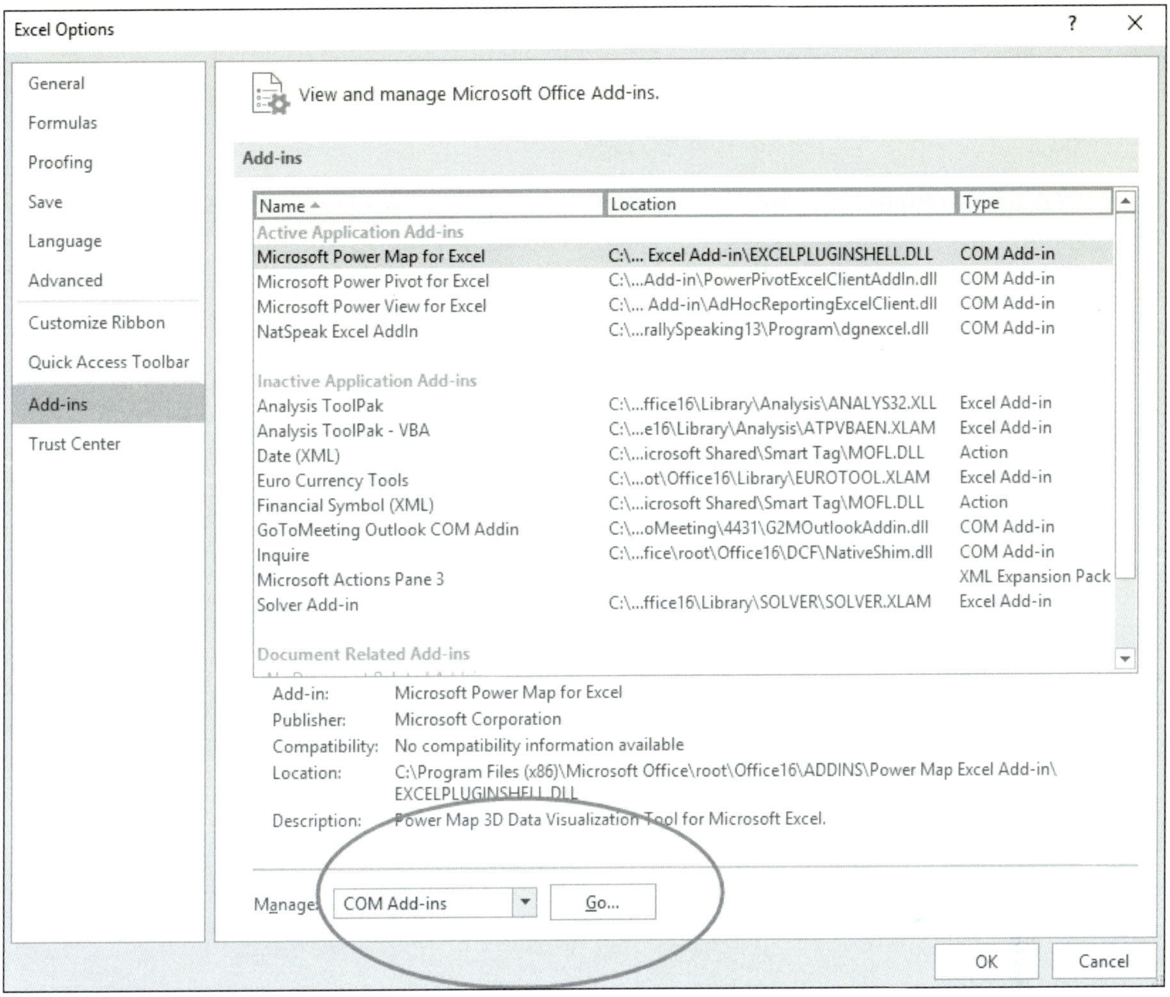

FIGURE 9.16
Adding Power Pivot to Excel

FIGURE 9.17
Excel Tabs after Successfully Adding Power Pivot

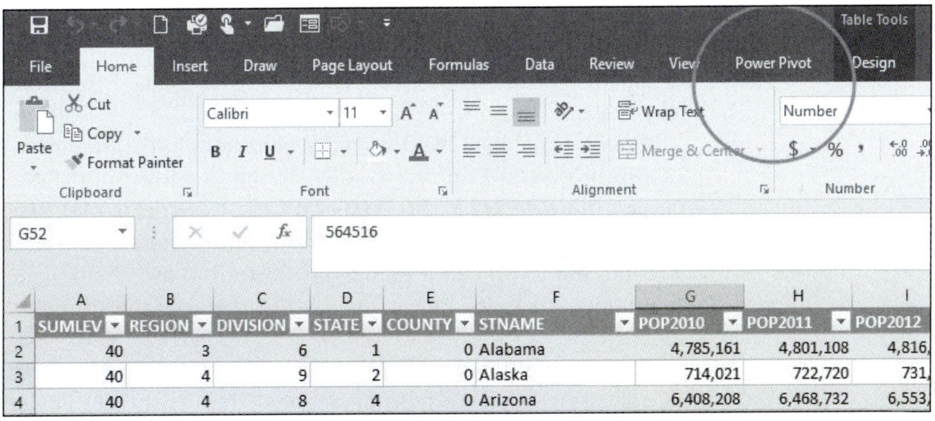

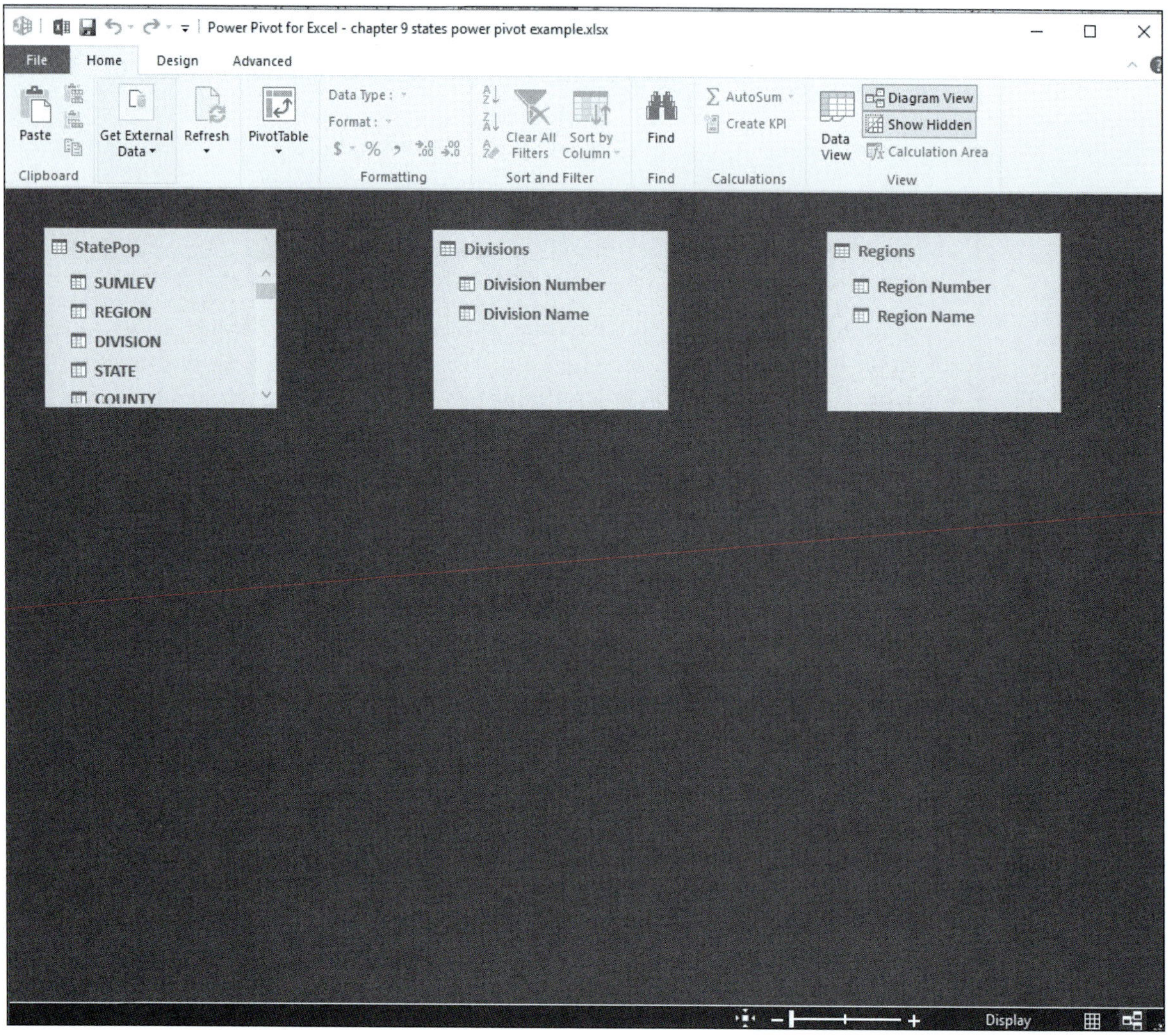

FIGURE 9.18
Power Pivot Diagram View

Pivot, as shown in Figure 9.18. Drag and drop the connections REGION to Region Number and DIVISION to Division Number to create relationships between tables, as shown in Figure 9.19. Select DESIGN > Relationships > Manage Relationships to edit or delete the relationships.

Now, we calculate the percentage change in births. Return to Data View by selecting HOME > View > Data View. Move to the first row in the first blank column. Enter the formula =*([BIRTHS2015]-[BIRTHS2010])/[BIRTHS2010]*, starting with the equal sign and then pointing to the cells in the table to complete the formula. Note that Power Pivot does not use Excel cell designations; instead, it uses field names for the formula. After entering the formula, Power Pivot will fill all the rows in your data table, as shown in Figure 9.20.

To complete this simple Power Pivot example, we will create a pivot table using the calculated field and the links among the tables created in Power Pivot. Select HOME > PivotTable, and then choose the option to create both a pivot table and chart, as shown in Figure 9.21. Note that the PivotTable fields section shows all three Power Pivot tables

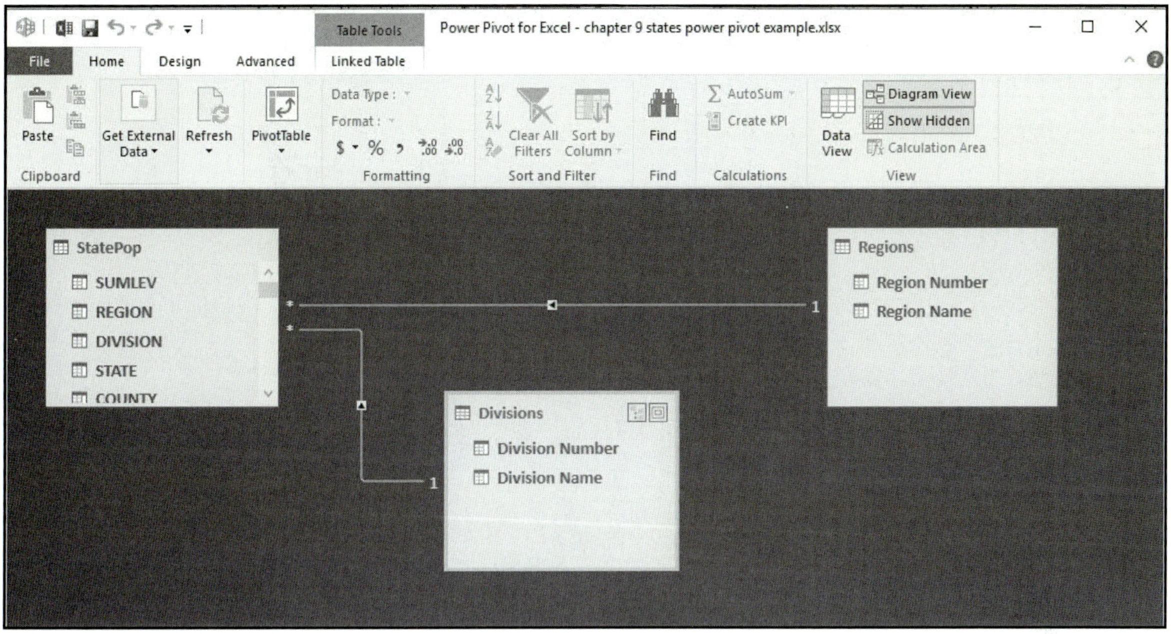

FIGURE 9.19
Setting Relationships in Power Pivot Diagram View

© Microsoft Excel

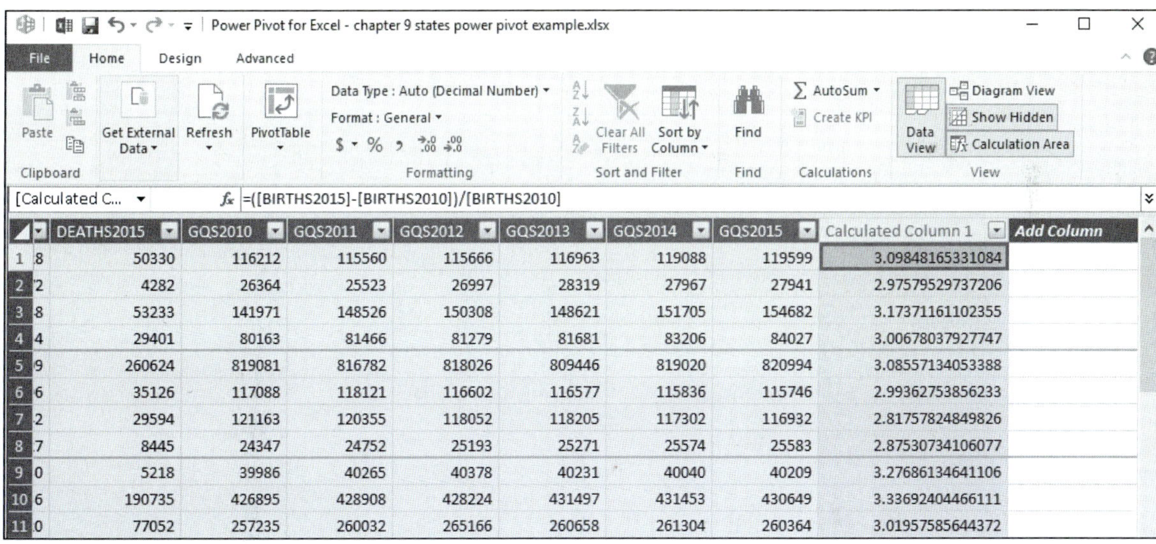

FIGURE 9.20
Calculating a New Field in Power Pivot

© Microsoft Excel

rather than listing the fields in one table. For this example, we select the Division Name field for the rows and the new calculated field showing percentage changes in births as our value field. After some formatting, the results look like Figure 9.22. Our pivot chart clearly shows that West South Central had the largest percentage increase and New England had the smallest percentage increase in births from 2010 to 2015. Finally, we can complete the example by adding a slicer by selecting ANALYZE > Filter > Insert Slicer to allow users to select one or more regions for analysis, as shown in Figure 9.23.

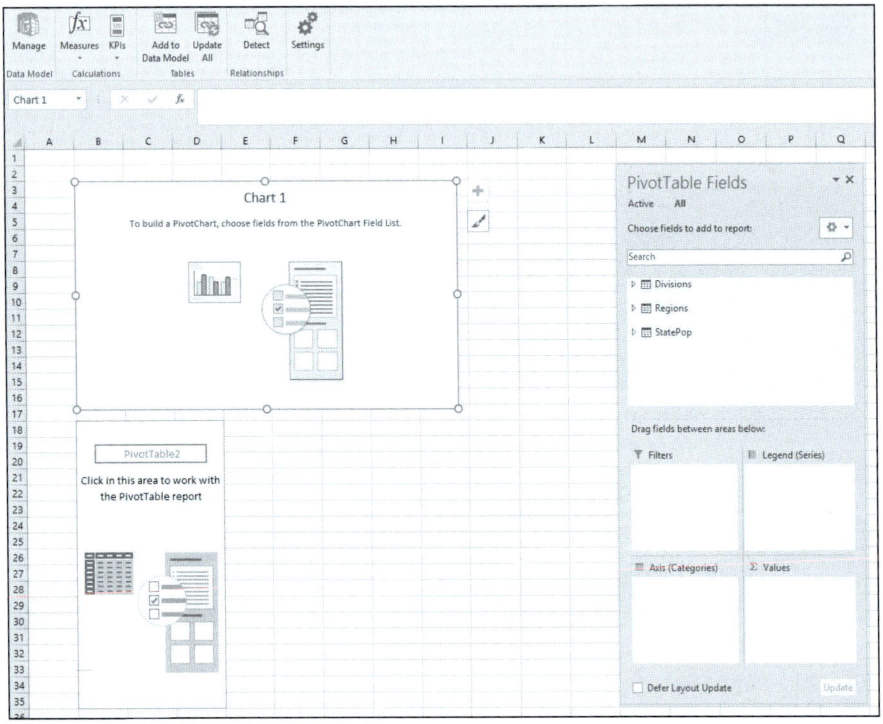

FIGURE 9.21
Ready to Define the Pivot Table and Chart

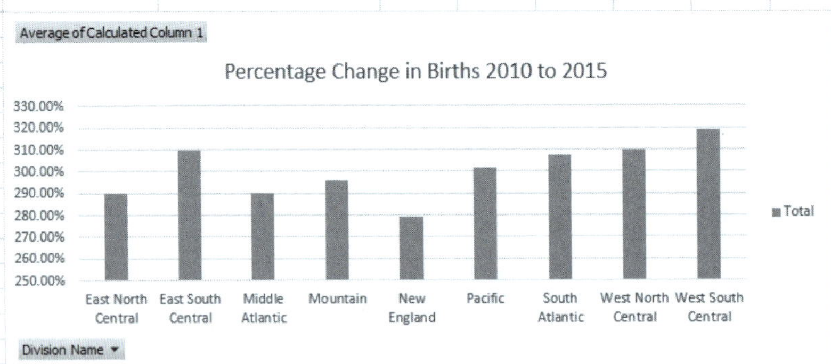

Row Labels	Percentage Change in Births
East North Central	289.97%
East South Central	309.76%
Middle Atlantic	290.13%
Mountain	296.14%
New England	279.10%
Pacific	301.74%
South Atlantic	307.27%
West North Central	309.96%
West South Central	319.06%
Grand Total	**300.45%**

FIGURE 9.22
Populated Pivot Table and Chart

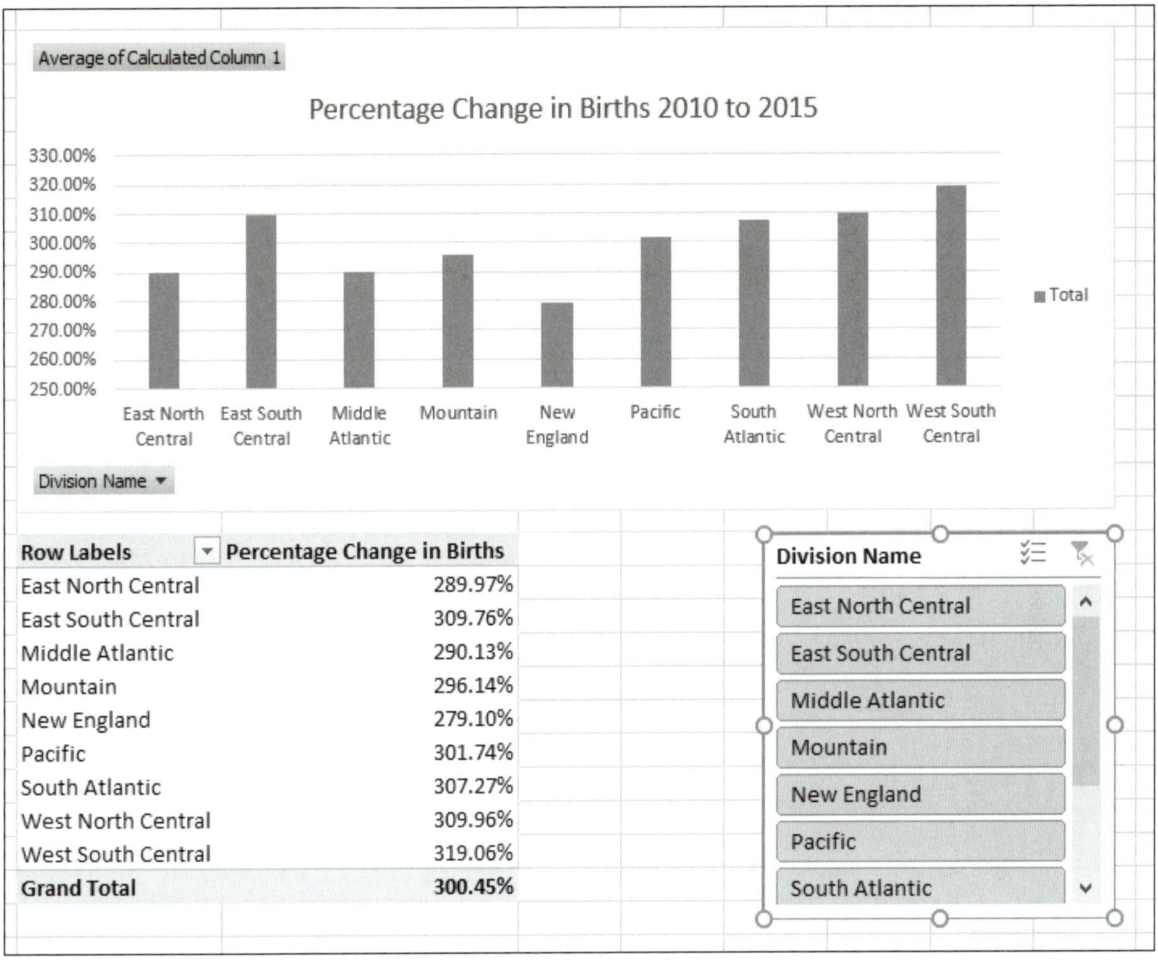

FIGURE 9.23
Adding a Division Name Slicer to the Populated Pivot Table and Chart

Progress Check

13. Could you set up Power Pivot in Excel and add a pivot table and chart? Use data from the integrated project in Chapter 8 and try it.

LO 9-10
Use Tableau for data analytics and visualization

Using Tableau for Data Visualization and Analysis

Tableau Desktop[25] is a relatively new tool for data analysis and visualization. In Excel, many of the data analysis functions have been added to extend its functionality. Yet, it remains primarily a tool to analyze and manipulate data in worksheets, and the extensions to perform analysis are sometimes cumbersome. Conversely, Tableau is designed specifically for data analysis and visualization. It is a powerful tool, and this section only briefly introduces some of its capabilities. The following descriptions assume that Tableau Desktop is downloaded and installed on your local computer. We recommend that users take advantage of the free tutorials available at http://www.tableau.com/learn/training.

[25]Tableau Desktop is available for free trial from http://www.tableau.com. Additionally, it has an academic program that provides fully licensed versions of its product for academic use.

Tableau will connect to various data sources, including Excel, text, and Access. For this example, we use the same Census data showing populations by state used in the earlier examples. After starting Tableau, the first step is to connect to the data, as shown in Figure 9.24. On the initial screen, select Connect > Excel and navigate to the Excel file location. After opening the Excel workbook, Tableau asks you to select the worksheets to use and then establish the relationships between the worksheets. Drag the worksheet names to the area designated, as shown in Figure 9.25, and then set the relationships between tables, as

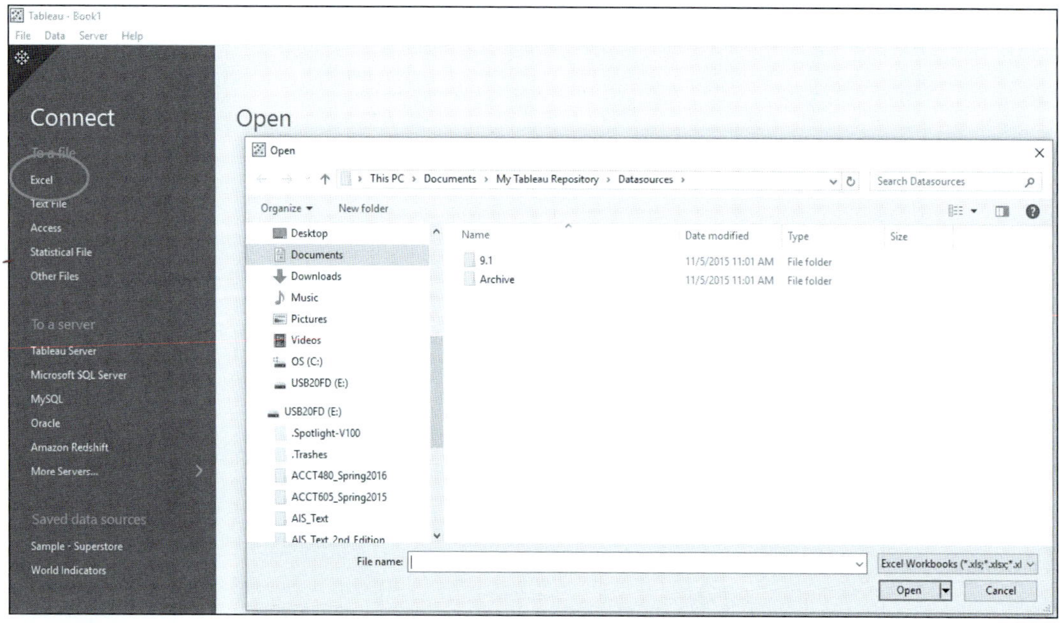

FIGURE 9.24
Connecting to an Excel File in Tableau

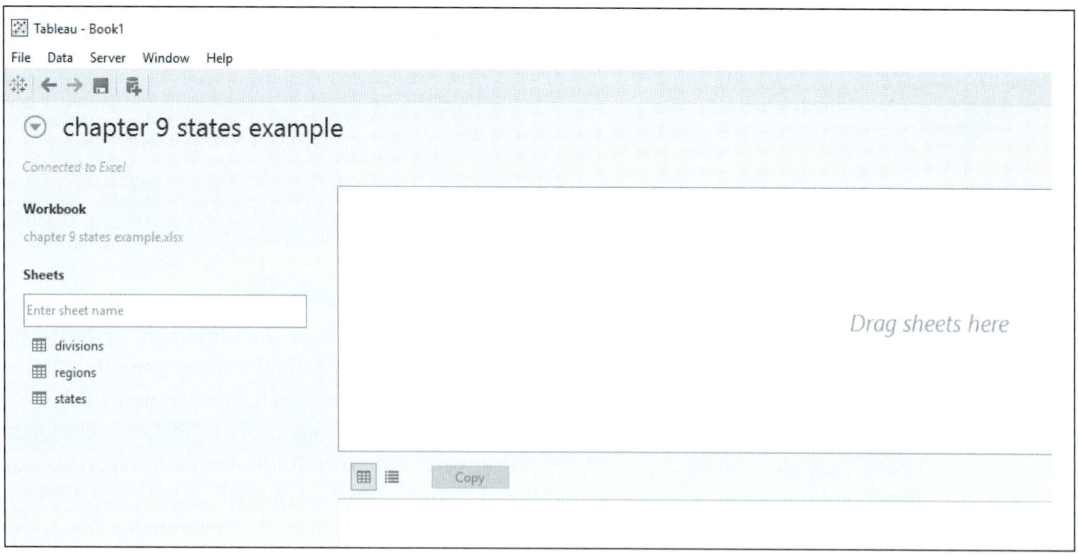

FIGURE 9.25
Selecting Worksheets to Use

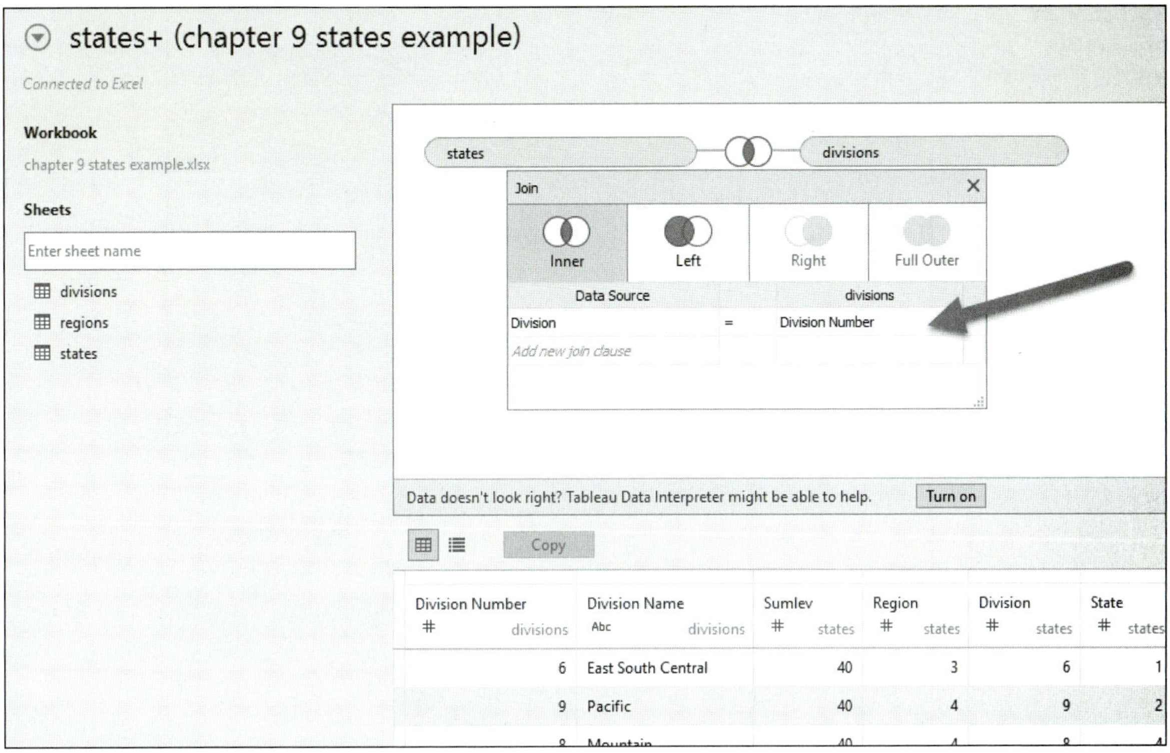

FIGURE 9.26
Setting Relationships between Worksheets

shown in Figure 9.26. Thus, the States worksheet is linked to the Division worksheet by connecting the Division field in States to the Division Number in Divisions.

After linking the worksheets in the Data Source screen, move to Sheet 1 to start the analysis, as shown in Figure 9.27. The data are shown in the data pane on the left, where text fields are listed at the top as Dimensions and numeric fields are listed below as Measures. The areas in the workspace with names like Pages, Filters, Marks, etc., are called Shelves and Cards. Drag and drop fields from the data pane to the Shelves and Cards to set up the analysis. First, drag the Division Name from the data pane to the Rows area, as shown in Figure 9.28. Next, calculate the percentage change in births in much the same way as the earlier examples. Use the pull-down menu at the top of the data pane and select the option Create Calculated Field, as shown in Figure 9.29. A dialog box opens. Enter the name of the new field in the text box at the top. Then, drag and drop fields to calculate the percentage change in births, as shown in Figure 9.30. Click OK to finish.

Next, drag the new calculated field to the analysis area, as shown in Figure 9.31. The default is to sum the calculated field, *Pct Change in Births,* for each division. We changed the default to, instead, calculate the average *Pct Change in Births* for each division as shown in the Marks area. Now to chart the data, select the chart type from the Show Me pane. In this case, we chose horizontal bars, as shown in Figure 9.32. To improve the display, we adjusted the axis to start at 2 instead of 0. That completes the analysis for this simple example, but Tableau has many more features. For example, it has a Dashboard feature that allows users to add various data visualizations to a Dashboard screen for quick review. Tableau also has an extensive set of charting and display options. It is a powerful tool to support data analytics and visualization.

FIGURE 9.27
Tableau Data Analysis Worksheet Setup

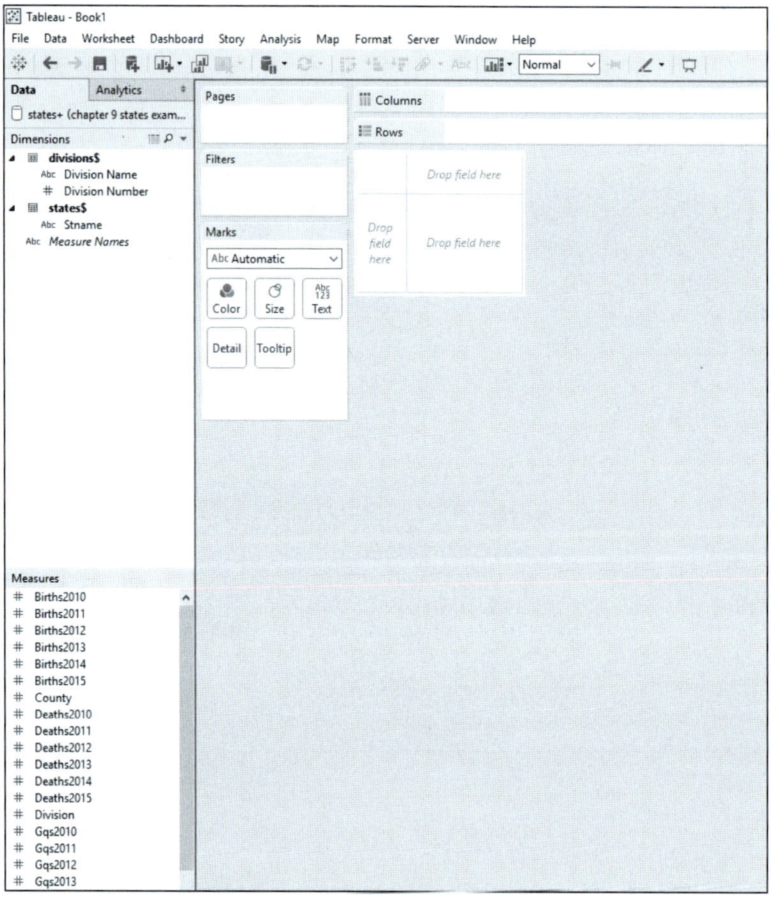

FIGURE 9.28
Selecting Rows for Tableau Data Analysis

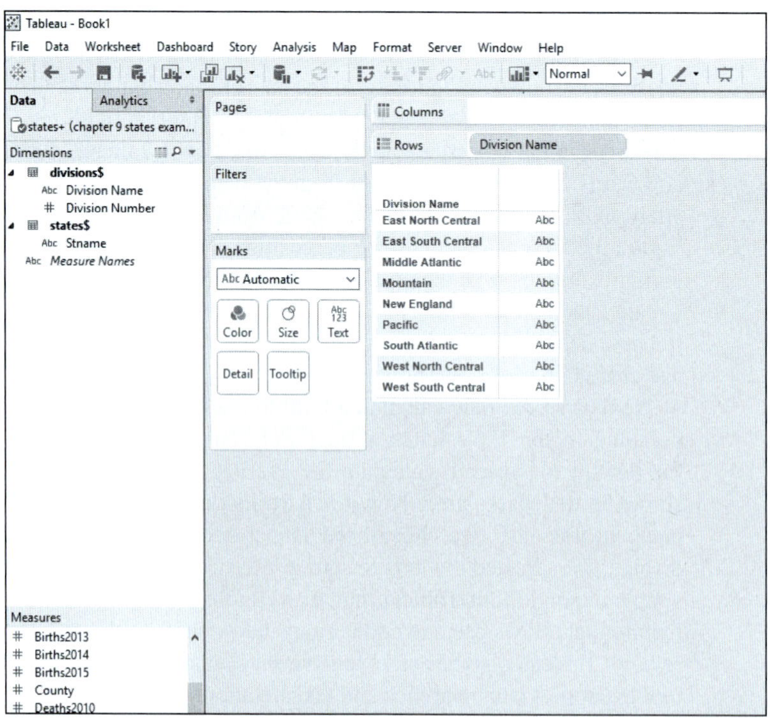

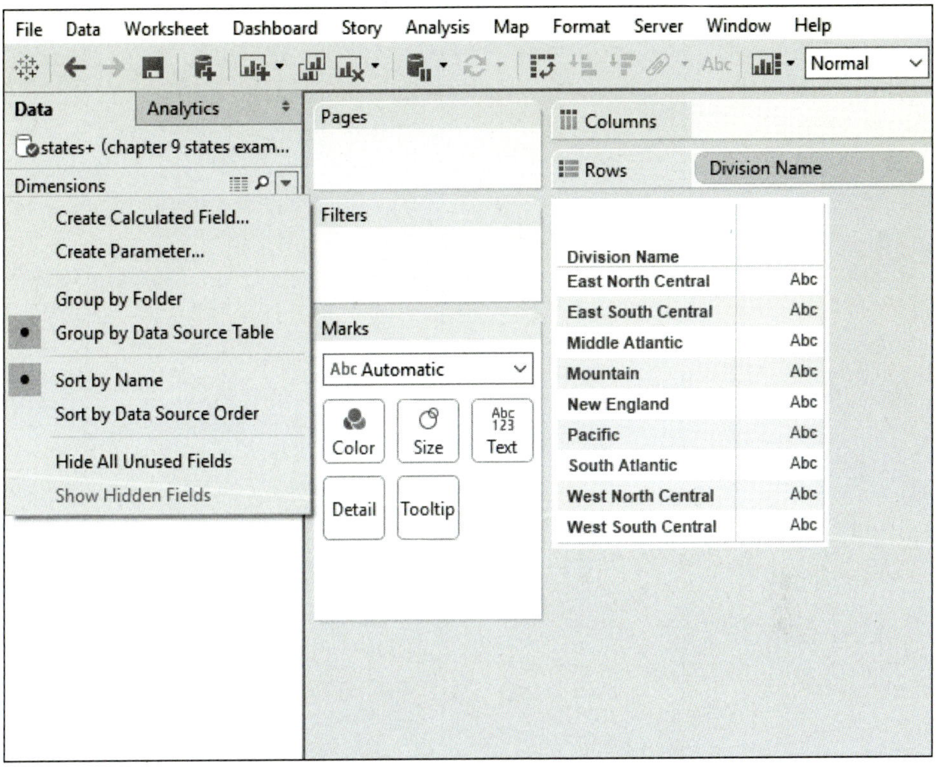

FIGURE 9.29 Menu Option for Creating Calculated Field

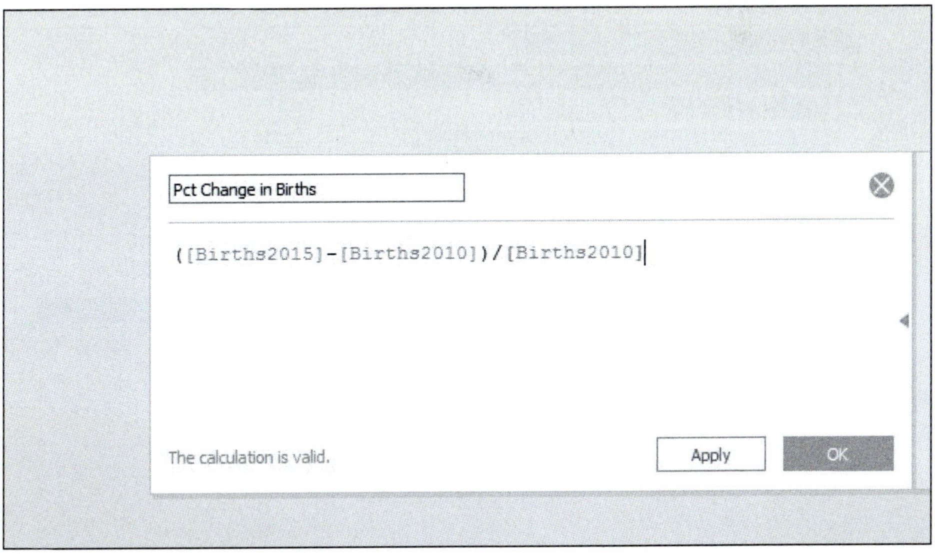

FIGURE 9.30 Creating Calculated Field

FIGURE 9.31
Using the Calculated Field in the Analysis

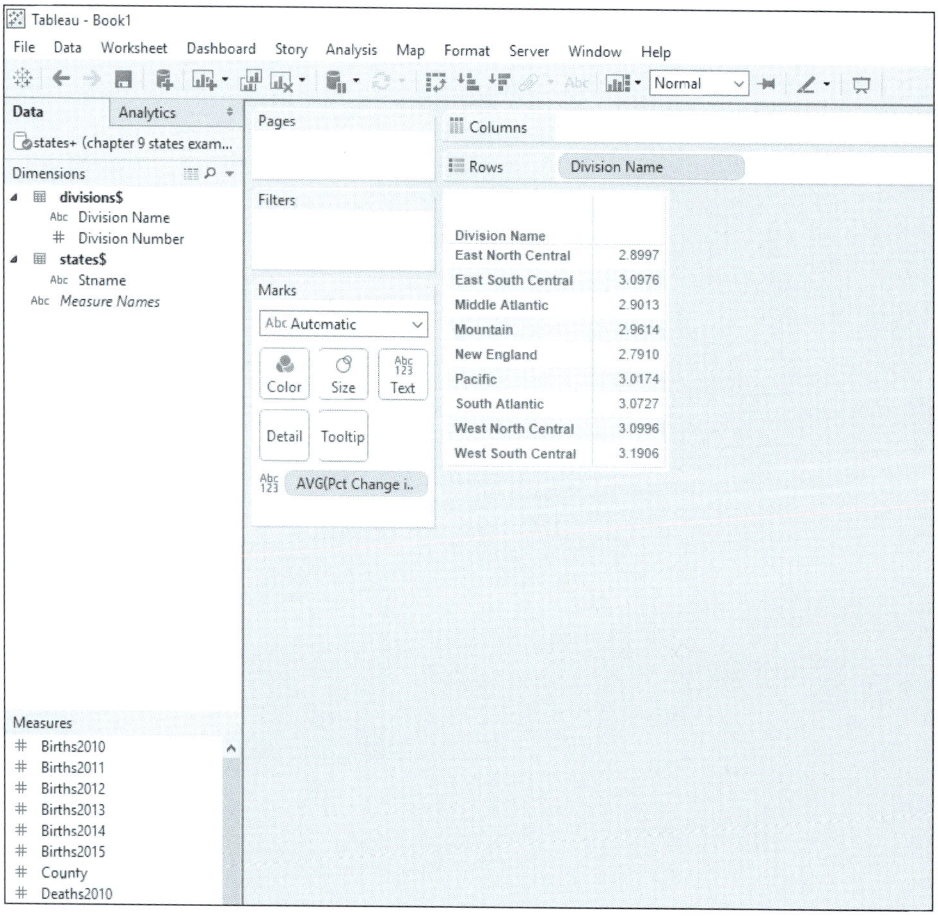

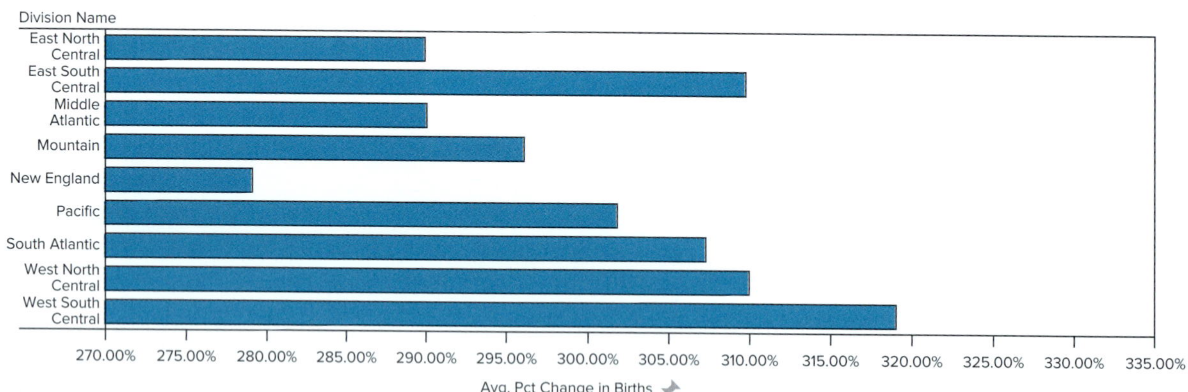

FIGURE 9.32
Charting the Data

Progress Check

14. Could you use Tableau for data visualization? Download the free trial and use data from the integrated project in Chapter 8 and try it.

Summary

- Big Data is datasets that are too large and complex for businesses' existing systems to handle utilizing their traditional capabilities to capture, store, manage, and analyze these datasets, whereas data analytics is the science of examining raw data (now often described as Big Data), removing excess noise from the dataset, and organizing the data with the purpose of drawing conclusions for decision making.
- There are often significant costs associated with getting data ready for analysis, including the cost to acquire the data as well as the cost to extract and reformat them to get them ready for analysis.
- Data analytics may help businesses unlock value in their firms by improving marketing strategies; identifying future opportunities and risks; and improving productivity, utilization, and growth.
- Data analytics may affect the financial reporting and internal and external auditing areas. In financial reporting, for example, scanning social media might be helpful in identifying potential risks and opportunities to the firm. In auditing, data analytics might be useful in helping both internal and external auditors perform audit tests on the population of transactions rather than just a sample.
- The American Institute of Certified Public Accountants (AICPA) worked to develop audit data standards (ADS) to set standards on the data files and fields typically needed to support an external audit in a given financial business process area.
- The Data Accountability and Trust Act of 2009 (DATA) proposes a national standard for privacy and data protection by requiring organizations entrusted with personally identifying information to carefully work to safeguard the data they maintain and to notify individuals when their information has been exposed to unauthorized parties.
- Microsoft Excel provides a number of tools to support data analytics and visualization. First, tables allow direct analysis using totals and filters. Pivot tables provide a robust reporting and charting tool.
- Microsoft Excel add-ins such as Power Pivot deliver database management tools to Excel and allow users to combine tables from various sources, such as Excel, Access, and other SQL databases.
- Applications such as Tableau Desktop are specifically designed for data analytics and visualizations. They provide easy-to-use analysis tools with extensive charting options.

Key Words

audit data standards (ADS) (*215*) A standard format for data files and fields typically needed to support an external audit in a given financial business process area that was developed by the AICPA.

Big Data (*210*) Datasets that are too large and complex for businesses' existing systems to handle utilizing their traditional capabilities to capture, store, manage, and analyze these datasets.

breach of security (*219*) The unauthorized access to or acquisition of data in electronic form that contain personal information.

DATA (2009) (*217*) Data Accountability and Trust Act of 2009 (DATA) creates a national standard for privacy and data protection.

data analytics (*210*) The science of examining raw data (now often Big Data), removing excess noise from the dataset, and organizing the data with the purpose of drawing conclusions for decision making.

Excel pivot table (*223*) A dynamic summary report generated from a range or table in Excel or an external data file. It allows cross-tabulations and summary reporting of multiple dimensions and levels of detail. In conjunction with slicers, it offers a powerful data analysis tool.

Excel table (*220*) A rectangular range of structured data in one Excel worksheet specifically identified as a table. The table usually has one row of text headings that indicate the contents of each column. Designating a range of data as a table provides access to a set of formatting and analysis tools.

extract, transform, and load (ETL) (*211*) The process of cleaning and scrubbing the data before data analysis can take place.

personally identifying information (*218*) An individual's first name or initial and last name, or address, or phone number, in combination with Social Security number, driver's license number, passport number, military identification number, or other similar number issued on a government document used to verify identity and financial account number and passcodes.

Power Pivot (*228*) Excel add-in that can create an integrated database from various Excel tables and external data sources, such as Access and SQL databases. It supports the creation of calculated fields and the use of pivot tables for the integrated database.

Tableau Desktop (*233*) Software application that supports data analytics and visualizations. It integrates data from multiple data sources. It provides easy-to-use and powerful summary reporting and charting capabilities. It allows users to build dashboards and create stories from their data.

Answers to Progress Checks

1. Analyzing weather patterns and correlating them with corn production is an example of data analytics. We generally know that rain and exposure to sun are key components of corn production, so knowing and measuring rain, sun, temperature, and humidity might all be useful data. Data analytics would figure out how to remove excess noise from the dataset and organize the data in such a way as to draw conclusions and highlight the relationship between weather patterns and characteristics and corn production. Understanding weather patterns might help a farmer choose a variety of corn seed engineered to be resistant to drought or flood or decide how much to plant.
2. Big Data is defined as datasets that are too large and complex for businesses' existing systems to handle utilizing their traditional capabilities to capture, store, manage, and analyze these datasets while data analytics is the science of examining raw data (now often Big Data), removing excess noise from the dataset, and organizing the data with the purpose of drawing conclusions for decision making. Big Data seems to highlight the size of the data—that it is simply so big and unmanageable—but data analytics uses context to figure out what is needed to draw conclusions to be useful in decision making. Specifically, data analytics provides a way to search through large and unstructured data to identify unknown patterns or relationships.
3. The costs of data analytics include the costs to process, store, acquire, reformat, cleanse, and scrub the data to get the information ready for its intended use. Data analytic scientists and the expense of the technological equipment to prepare and analyze the data are also costs.
4. The brand manager at Procter & Gamble might use data analytics to see what is being said about its Olay™ products on social media websites, particularly those that attract an older demographic. This will help them to assess if there is a problem with the perceptions of its skin care products.
5. Data analytics might be used to assess the reasons a firm needed to ask its employees to work overtime. There are many potential questions that might be addressed, such as, Were there problems with the manufacturing process? Was there a malfunction with the machinery on the days where overtime was incurred? Is the order process lumpy, suggesting a short-term, unusually large demand for more products to be produced, or does it suggest something longer term?

6. Data analytics will allow external auditors to spend less time looking for evidence and more time presenting their findings and making judgments.
7. One way is data analytics may also allow an accountant or auditor to assess the probability of a goodwill write-down, warranty claims, or the collectability of bad debts based on what customers, investors, and other stakeholders are saying about the company in blogs and in social media. Such information might help the firm determine both its optimal response to the situation and appropriate adjustment to its financial reporting.
8. Audit data standards allow the external auditor to receive the data they need to perform their audit testing without having to clean, scrub, reformat, or extract the data. This will save them time, effort, and expense.
9. Audit data standards allow the company to provide the required data to the external auditor in a fairly effortless and costless way. It will be especially effortless if the financial reporting system/enterprise system has an option that automatically provides these data with little extra effort on the company's part.
10. According to DATA 2009, a mobile phone number for a customer would be personally identifying information in combination with a Social Security number, driver's license number, or other similar number issued on a government document or financial account number.
11. Be sure your data are formed in a rectangular range with no blank rows or columns. Convert the range to a table by clicking INSERT > Tables > Table. Confirm the area of the range and that the data have a header row. Then select DESIGN > Table Style Options and check Total Row. Navigate to the new last row and use the menus to select sums or other statistics.
12. Start with an Excel table. Select INSERT > Tables > PivotTable. Select the fields to create the pivot table. Select ANALYZE > Filters > Insert Slicer to add the slicer.
13. Select FILE > Options and then select Add-ins. In the Manage drop-down box, select COM Add-ins. Add Power Pivot to Excel. Then, add each table to Power Pivot; set the relationships between tables. Calculate any needed fields. Then, summarize your integrated data with a pivot table.
14. Download the trial of Tableau. Use the same data used for Progress Check13. Open the data sources and create relationships between tables. Use the worksheet to analyze your data and create charts.

Mc Graw Hill Education connect®

Multiple Choice Questions

1. Big Data is often described by the three V's, or: **LO 9-1**
   a. volume, velocity, and variability.
   b. volume, veracity, and variety.
   c. volume, volatility, and variability.
   d. volume, velocity, and variety.
2. According to estimates considered in the chapter, up to what percentage of a data analyst's time is spent cleaning (or scrubbing) the data to be ready for analysis? **LO 9-2**
   a. 90%
   b. 40%
   c. 0%
   d. 20%

3. The acronym ETL, in the process of readying data for use in data analysis, refers to what three words? LO 9-1, LO 9-2
   a. Extrapolate, transform, and learn
   b. Extrapolate, transpose, and load
   c. Extract, transform, and load
   d. Extract, transform, and learn
4. What is the maximum fine imposed by the DATA 2009 law for failure to send notification of a breach of personally identifying information? LO 9-6
   a. $11,000
   b. $1 million
   c. $5 million
   d. No maximum
5. DATA (2009) created a national standard for privacy and data protection. The acronym DATA stands for: LO 9-6
   a. Data Accountability and Trust Act of 2009.
   b. Data Accounting and Trust Act of 2009.
   c. Data Accessibility and Trust Act of 2009.
   d. Data Audit and Trust Act of 2009.
6. Which of these is not part of the security program required by DATA to prevent compromise of critical information? LO 9-6
   a. Develop, document, and maintain a security policy for the collection, use, sale, dissemination, and maintenance of personally identifying information.
   b. Define a protocol to efficiently notify affected parties and regulators in the event of a data breach.
   c. Establish contracts with third parties with access to the information to establish controls that meet the requirements of the act.
   d. Establish a process to identify risks and vulnerabilities of potential breaches and implement administrative and technical controls to mitigate the risk of compromise of the personally identifying information.
7. Which term is used to describe the science of examining raw data, removing excess noise from the dataset, and organizing the data with the purpose of drawing conclusions for decision making? LO 9-1, LO 9-2, LO 9-3, LO 9-4
   a. Big Data
   b. Data analytics
   c. Audit analytics
   d. Extract, transform, and load
8. ADS is a standard format for data files and fields typically needed to support an external audit in a given financial business process area that was developed by the AICPA. The acronym ADS stands for what three words? LO 9-5
   a. Accounting doctoral scholars
   b. Accounting data standards
   c. Audit data standards
   d. Auditor data standards
9. Which of the following, on its own, is not explicitly considered to be personally identifying information? LO 9-6
   a. Date of birth
   b. Biometric data
   c. Personal telephone number
   d. Social Security number

10. Which of the following, on its own, is not explicitly considered to be personally identifying information? **LO 9-6**
    a. Fingerprints
    b. Religion
    c. Mobile telephone number
    d. Personal address
11. Which of the following, on its own, is explicitly considered to be personally identifying information? **LO 9-6**
    a. Race
    b. Business e-mail address
    c. Place of birth
    d. Social Security number
12. Which of the following, on its own, is explicitly considered to be personally identifying information? **LO 9-6**
    a. Credit card number
    b. Business telephone number
    c. Date of birth
    d. Religion
13. Which of the following is not a characteristic of an Excel table? **LO 9-7**
    a. No blank rows
    b. Includes charts
    c. No blank columns
    d. Includes a header row
    e. None of the above
14. Which of the following is true about Excel tables? **LO 9-7**
    a. They are created from rectangular data ranges.
    b. The user can add a totals row.
    c. The header includes filter buttons.
    d. The table is automatically formatted.
    e. All of these are true.
15. Which of the following is a characteristic of a pivot table? **LO 9-8**
    a. It summarizes data in a range, table, or external data source.
    b. It can include multidimensional summaries by designating row and column categories.
    c. Users can format the numbers in the Values field.
    d. Users can choose subtotals and grand totals.
    e. All of these are characteristics of pivot tables.
16. Which of the following is not true about a pivot table? **LO 9-8**
    a. Users can select report row variables.
    b. Users can select report column variables.
    c. Users can select to include grand totals.
    d. Users must sum the values in the pivot table.
    e. Users can format the values in the pivot table.

17. Which of the following best describes Power Pivot? **LO 9-9**
    a. It is an Excel add-in.
    b. It is a database manager.
    c. It allows integrating both Excel tables and tables from external sources.
    d. It supports the creation of sophisticated pivot tables.
    e. All of these describe Power Pivot.
18. How can you tell if you have activated the Power Pivot add-in? **LO 9-9**
    a. Your data have all been converted to tables.
    b. You see a new screen in addition to the standard Excel interface.
    c. You see a new tab titled Power Pivot.
    d. You can insert a slicer.
    e. You can open data from another source.

Discussion Questions

1. How does data analytics relate to Big Data? Why should accountants incorporate data analytics into their work? **LO 9-1, LO 9-4**
2. What is an example of the way data analytics might be used in an airline setting to maximize revenue of selling to business and casual travelers? **LO 9-3**
3. Why is it important to have software vendors (such as SAP, Oracle, etc.) use the audit data standards? **LO 9-5**
4. How could audit data standards make external auditors' work more efficient? **LO 9-5**
5. In field 17 of Figure 9.1, ADS include a record of who approved the journal entry. Why do you think the external auditor might be interested in this field? Why do you think the auditor might also be interested in who modified a journal entry (field 19 of Figure 9.1) and on what date (field 20 of Figure 9.1). **LO 9-3, LO 9-4, LO 9-5**
6. Why should companies have strong policies in place to protect personally identifying information? **LO 9-6**

Problems

connect

1. Identify which of the following, on their own, are personally identifying information (PII) and which are not personally identifying information (non-PII). **LO 9-5, LO 9-6**
    a. Date of birth
    b. Place of birth
    c. Credit card number
    d. Religion
    e. Retina scans
    f. E-mail address (personal)
    g. Race

connect

2. Identify which of the following, on their own, are personally identifying information (PII) and which are not personally identifying information (non-PII). **LO 9-5, LO 9-6**
    a. Financial information
    b. Address of employment
    c. Personal telephone number
    d. Fingerprints
    e. Social Security number
    f. Geographic indicators
    g. Vehicle ID number

connect 3. Data analytics can be disaggregated into two parts: ETL (extract, transform, and load) or analysis. Classify each of the following processes as either ETL or analysis. **LO 9-1, LO 9-2**

a. Removal of extraneous data and noise

b. Looking for trends in the data that might predict new sales opportunities

c. Finding the necessary data from the financial reporting system to give to the external auditor for analysis

d. Performance of a test of internal controls by the external auditor

e. Considering Champaign, Illinois, weather patterns to predict corn production in the immediate area

f. Consolidating large volumes of data from multiple sources and platforms

connect 4. Match these definitions with either of the three V's (volume, velocity, and variety) to describe Big Data. **LO 9-1**

a. Unstructured and unprocessed data, such as comments in social media, e-mails, global positioning system measurements, etc.

b. The massive amount of data involved

c. Data coming in at fast speeds or in real time, such as streaming videos and news feeds

connect 5. Match these terms with their respective definitions: *audit data standards, Big Data, breach of security, DATA (2009), data analytics, ETL,* and *personally identifying information.* **LO 9-1, LO 9-2, LO 9-5, LO 9-6**

a. A standard format for data files and fields typically needed to support an external audit

b. Datasets that are too large and complex for businesses' existing systems to handle using their traditional capabilities to capture, store, manage, and analyze these datasets

c. The science of examining raw data, removing excess noise from the dataset, and organizing data with the purpose of drawing conclusions for decision making

d. The unauthorized access to or acquisition of data in electronic form containing personal information

e. The process of cleaning and scrubbing the data before data analysis can take place

f. Social Security number or driver's license number

6. Explain the penalties accruing to companies that are not in compliance with the Data Accountability and Trust Act of 2009 (DATA), including (a) failure to comply with security program requirements and (b) failure to follow the breach notification rules. Assume a company had a data breach involving failure to notify 100 customers of the loss of their personally identifying information. What are the penalties? What is the penalty for a data breach involving failure to notify 100,000 customers? **LO 9-5, LO 9-6**

For the following three problems, first download the data for the Microsoft PowerPivot tutorial at http://powerpivotsdr.codeplex.com/. The download zip file contains two Access databases, ContosoSales.accdb and ProductCategories.accdb. It also contains two Excel spreadsheets, Geography.xlsx and Stores.xlsx. Extract the files in the zip file to use for the following problems. For each problem, create an Excel worksheet that shows your solution.

7. Open a blank Excel workbook and bring in the FactSales data from the ContosoSales Access database as follows. Select DATA > Get External Data > From Access. Browse to the ContosoSales Access database. When the Select Table box appears, select the FactSales table and click OK. When the Import Data box appears, select PivotTable Report and click OK. **LO 9-7**

a. Create a PivotTable report with the ChannelKey field as the rows and SalesAmount field as the values. Change the number format of the SalesAmount field to currency and rename the column to Total Sales.

b. Insert a bar pivot chart and change the name of the chart to Total Sales by Channel.

c. Insert a slicer to allow selection of one or more ChannelKey. Change the slicer style to Light 2 and change the number of columns in the slicer to 2.

8. Move to a new worksheet. Be sure that you have activated the Power Pivot add-in. Select POWER PIVOT > Manage to open the Power Pivot screen. Move to the Power Pivot for Excel screen. Select HOME > Get External Data > From Database and then select the option to connect to an Access database. Browse to the directory containing the ContosoSales database and select it. When the Table Import Wizard appears, select the DimChannel, DimProduct, and FactSales tables and click FINISH. After the import finishes, click CLOSE to close the Table Import Wizard. Go to Diagram View and make sure that the three tables are linked. Return to Data View and the FactSales table. Add a new calculated column on the right and calculate the month for the datekey field. **LO 9-9**
9. Continue from Problem 8. Select HOME > PivotTable to create a PivotTable report from your integrated Power Pivot tables. **LO 9-8, LO 9-9**
   a. Use the ChannelName from the DimChannel table as the first rows field. Use the calculated column 1 field from the FactSales table as the second rows field. Use the SalesAmount field from the FactSales table as the values field. Change the number format to currency, if necessary; change the name of the calculated column 1 in the PivotTable report to Month; and change the values column name from Sum of SaleAmount to Total Monthly Sales. Change the report layout to tabular form.
   b. Insert slicers for both ChannelName and Month.
   c. Which channel had the highest total sales in January?
   d. Add a column pivot chart. Change the title to Total Monthly Sales. Use the slicers to show the comparison among channels for sales in January.
10. Open Tableau (if you don't have Tableau, you can download a free trial from www.tableau.com).

    After Tableau opens, connect to the Excel data and browse to the location of the Chapter 9 problem data. After importing, there will be two worksheets, Customers and Orders. Drag both of those to the box that says *Drag sheets here*. The two sheets will join and the joined data will appear in the bottom box. You can click on the two icons between the boxes to toggle between showing data and showing file structure.

    Click on Worksheet 1 at the bottom of the page to go to the worksheet associated with the data. Now you are ready to analyze the data. **LO 9-10**
    1. Graph the quantity sold. Drag the Qty Sold measure to the Columns shelf. Notice that the measure is automatically summed.
    2. Change the measure to show the average quantity sold.
    3. Drag the measure from the Columns shelf to the Rows shelf. What changes?
    4. Compare the average quantity sold by state. Drag the State dimension to the Columns shelf. What changes in the graph? Which state has the highest average sales quantity? Which state has the lowest average sales quantity?
    5. Rename sheet 1 to "ave orders by state."
    6. Create a new Dashboard
    7. Add the "ave orders by state" worksheet to the Dashboard.
    8. Save your Tableau file as a Tableau Workbook.
11. Open the Tableau Workbook you created in Problem 10. **LO 9-10**
    1. Click on create a new worksheet.
    2. Create a calculated "amount" field to multiply quantity sold times price (click on the Analysis tab and select Create Calculated field.)
    3. Create a horizontal bar chart to show the sum of sales amounts (the amount field that you calculated) by customer name. (Drag the Amount measure to the Rows shelf. Drag the Name dimension to the Columns shelf.) Which customer made the highest sales? What was that amount? Which customer made the lowest sales? What was that amount?
    4. Rename your worksheet to "sales by customer." Add that to the Dashboard.

5. Return to the "sales by customer" worksheet. Change the color of the horizontal bars to dark green.
6. Add the Customer number to the chart by dragging the Customer# dimension to the Rows shelf and dropping it to the left of the Name dimension on that shelf.
7. Return to the Dashboard. Did the Dashboard update automatically?
8. Save your Tableau file as a Tableau Workbook.

12. Open the Tableau Workbook you created in Problem 10 and updated in Problem 11. **LO 9-10**
    1. Create a vertical bar chart to show total sales (the field calculated in Problem 11) for each store. (Drag the Amount measure to the Rows shelf. Drag the Store# dimension to the Columns shelf.)
    2. Use the "Show Me" palette to change the presentation to a highlight table (click on the option in the first row, right side in the Show Me palette). What changes on the Columns and Rows shelves? Which store has the greatest sales? What is the range of sales? Sort the highlight table in descending order.
    3. Rename your worksheet to "store sales" and add it to the Dashboard.
    4. Save your Tableau file as a Tableau Workbook.
13. Open the Tableau Workbook you saved at the end of Problem 12. **LO 9-10**
    1. Create a new worksheet.
    2. Create a calculated field for the month in which the sale took place and name the new field "month." (Hint: Look for the Month() function in the list of functions available when the dialog box for creating new calculated fields is open.)
    3. Drag the month field from Measures to the Dimensions section in the data panel by dragging it to the Dimensions part of the data pane.
    4. Create a vertical bar chart to show the total sales amount by month. (Drag Amount to the Rows shelf and drag Month to the Columns shelf.) Add the State to the Columns shelf to show sales for each state in each month.
    5. Create a treemap to show sales by state and month. Use the Show Me palette and click on treemap (fourth row, left side). Which state and month had the highest sales? How does the treemap show that?
    6. Filter the month to drop month 4. Use the pull-down menu on the month dimension on the Marks card and select filter.
    7. Rename the worksheet to "sales by state and month." Add it to the Dashboard.
    8. Save your Tableau file as a Tableau Workbook.

Chapter Ten

Reporting Processes and eXtensible Business Reporting Language (XBRL)

A look at this chapter

In this chapter, we explain how accounting information systems facilitate management reporting, including using data warehouses, business intelligence, and dashboards. We then explain the development and emerging use of eXtensible Business Reporting Language (XBRL). We also discuss the potential for XBRL and other emerging technologies to address reporting needs.

A look back

Chapter 9 considered the importance and impact of data analytics on the business world and on the accounting profession. The chapter noted specifically the impact of data analytics on the auditing profession and provides some comprehensive examples of data analytics tools (including the use of data visualization to better understand the data).

A look ahead

Chapter 11 examines issues in ethics and internal controls that are addressed by the Sarbanes-Oxley Act of 2002 (SOX) as well as important control and governance frameworks, including the COSO, COBIT, and ITIL frameworks. In particular, it will examine those areas that are critical to an organization's efficiency and effectiveness in operations, reliability in financial reporting, and compliance with applicable laws and regulations.

© CORBIS RF

TOP Technology leadership at Starbucks supports the use of data warehouses

Starbucks's Jake Ruttenberg doesn't stay awake each night worrying about the data warehouse that delivers 40,000 business dashboards to Starbucks's field leadership team. "Our data warehouse and retail dashboard business intelligence systems are critical to the success of each store and the entire business," says Ruttenberg, Starbucks's IT Manager of Application Development, Business Intelligence Solution Delivery. He notes, "Our managers are asking more difficult questions, and we use the data warehouse to provide the data to answer those questions." With the development of this data warehouse and the support of Starbucks's managers, Jake recently won the Data Warehouse Architect of the Year, by *Oracle Magazine*.

Beyond just the data warehouse, the corporation also clearly recognizes the importance of technology leadership. To support such an agenda, Starbucks recently named Kevin Johnson, the former Microsoft divisional president and Juniper Networks CEO, as its new president and chief operating officer. "Kevin's deep management experience and technology background will help further propel Starbucks's efforts in partner (employee) and customer-facing innovations as we accelerate our global growth agenda," said Howard Schultz, Starbucks's chairman, president, and CEO.

With Jake and Kevin at the helm, and with the assistance of Oracle, Starbucks has built a 10-terabyte data warehouse that supports thousands of users. This data warehouse is used at least on a daily basis by close to 8,000 Starbucks stores to manage inventory, staffing, and much, much more.

Source: David A. Kelly, "Editor's Choice Awards," *Oracle Magazine,* 2009, http://www.oracle.com/technetwork/issue-archive/2009/09-nov/o69awards-100810.html (accessed February 2016); Todd Bishop, http://www.geekwire.com/2015/starbucks-names-former-microsoft-juniper-exec-kevin-johnson-new-president-coo/ (accessed February 2016).

Chapter Outline

Learning Objectives

After reading this chapter, you should be able to:

10-1 Explain how data warehouses are created and used.

10-2 Describe the basic components of business intelligence and how they are utilized in a firm.

10-3 Describe how digital dashboards allow for continuous tracking of key metrics.

10-4 Explain how XBRL works and how it makes business reporting more efficient.

INTRODUCTION

Earlier chapters in this textbook demonstrated how information is gathered and accumulated in a database. We are now interested in the reporting of that information to both internal and external users. We introduce the overall concept of a data warehouse and then specifically explain how data warehouses may be used in business intelligence settings. We also discuss how dashboards are used to manage a company's operations. Finally, we explore the use of XBRL to share financial and nonfinancial information with external users like the Securities and Exchange Commission, the Internal Revenue Service, financial analysts, lenders, and current or potential investors.

LO 10-1
Explain how data warehouses are created and used.

DATA WAREHOUSES AND DATA MARTS

Our discussion thus far in this book has been about operational systems primarily designed and optimized to capture business transactions, such as sales and purchases. In contrast, a data warehouse is essentially a new (often independent) repository designed to be optimized for speed and efficiency in data analysis. More specifically, a **data warehouse** is a collection of information gathered from an assortment of external and operational (i.e., internal) databases to facilitate reporting for decision making and business analysis. Data warehouses often serve as the main repository of the firm's historical data (or, in other words, its corporate memory) and will often serve as an archive of past firm performance.

The best way to illustrate a data warehouse is by using a figure. Figure 10.1 shows operational and external databases that are used as inputs into the data warehouse. The operational databases may all come from within the company's enterprise system or various systems throughout the firm. The external databases may come from a variety of places, including purchased data from the Gartner Group, the Federal Reserve, industry organizations, and so forth.

The actual data warehouse may become too big and overwhelming for specific groups within the firm to use. A **data mart** takes a subset of the information from the data warehouse to serve a specific purpose, such as a marketing data mart, an inventory data mart, or a business intelligence data mart. Whereas a data warehouse is a repository for the overall firm, the data mart is a subset of the data warehouse for a specific purpose or function. In essence, a data warehouse is made up of many data marts.

FIGURE 10.1
Model of Data Warehouse Design

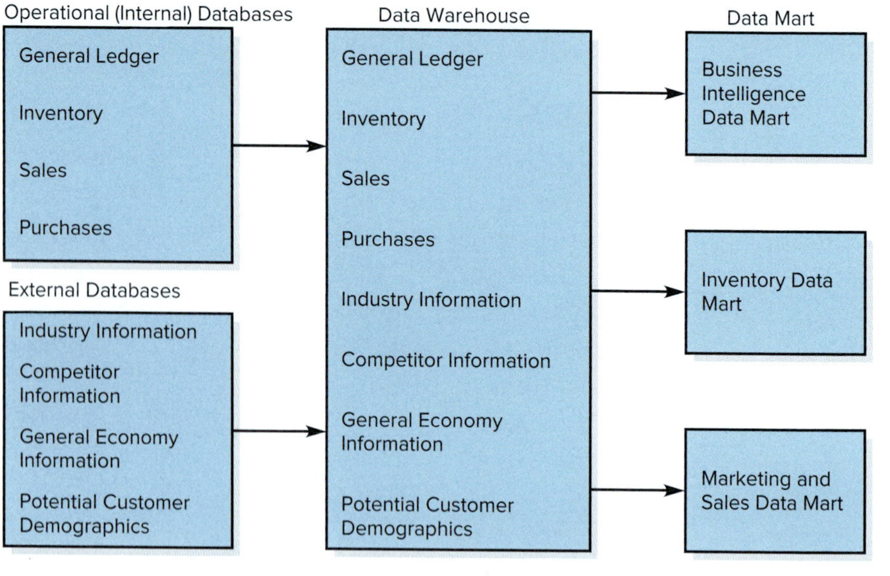

The opening vignette suggests **Starbucks** uses a data warehouse and data marts within its organization. Figure 10.2 provides an example of a potential data warehouse design for Starbucks. The figure highlights four types of data marts (although the potential number of data marts is unlimited) that may be useful to Starbucks: business intelligence, inventory, marketing, and sales and human resources.

The advantages and benefits of using a data warehouse include the following:

- Data warehouses use a common data model for all data in the warehouse, making it easy to quickly compare information all the way from customer invoices, bills of lading, sales journals, purchasing journals, and general ledgers to industry information, competitor information, potential customers, and the like. We discussed some data models in Chapters 3 and 4. Suffice it to say that before the data are loaded into the data warehouse, any data inconsistencies from the input databases are removed so that the data warehouse has homogeneous data that can be readily accessed and analyzed.
- Because the data warehouse is kept separate from the operational database, the information in the warehouse can be stored safely for extended periods of time, and data warehouses can run data queries without affecting the performance (i.e., slowing down) of the company's ongoing operational systems.
- When appropriate, data warehouses work together with operational systems to provide necessary insight, particularly in the case of customer relationship management (CRM) and supply chain management (SCM) systems.
- Data warehouses are often designed to facilitate decision making (such as those often addressed in managerial accounting) and management by exception (such as variance reports, trend reports, variance analysis reports, and reports that show actual performance compared with budgeted information). Often, these types of systems used to support managerial decision making are called **decision support systems (DSSs)**.

FIGURE 10.2
Potential Data Warehouse Design for Starbucks

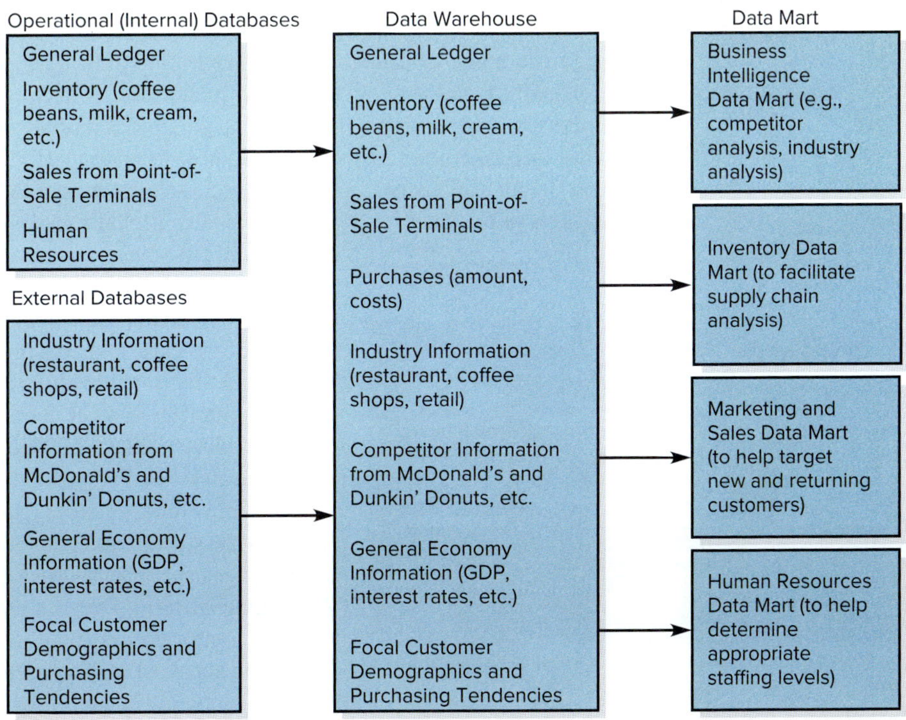

It should also be noted that a key disadvantage of a data warehouse is that it can quickly become obsolete with outdated data unless there is a mechanism to continously update the internal and external databases as time passes.

Progress Check

1. Why would **Apple**'s marketing department only use a subset of the data (using a data mart) instead of the entire data warehouse?
2. Imagine what might be included in a data warehouse for **Best Buy**. How might it be useful?

LO 10-2

Describe the basic components of business intelligence and how they are utilized in a firm.

BUSINESS INTELLIGENCE

Business intelligence is a computer-based technique for accumulating and analyzing data from databases and data warehouses to support managerial decision making. The term *business intelligence* is often used interchangeably with *competitive intelligence.* While competitive intelligence often deals with the examination of external information regarding competitor strategic and tactical actions, the process of business intelligence can be viewed more generically as including these three steps:

1. Gather information (either internal information, external information, or both) from a variety of sources.
2. Analyze (or discern) patterns and trends from that information to gain understanding and meaning.
3. Make decisions based on the information gained.

One way that firms may gather business intelligence is by use of a web crawler, which browses the Internet in a systematic way, collecting information.

There are many different settings in which business intelligence is used. Perhaps the best way to explain business intelligence is to consider potential settings where it might be used.

- Imagine **Tesla** using business intelligence to find indicators of quality issues to pinpoint machinery failures in its assembly plants after collecting and analyzing data on its processes. Sorting through the data may help Tesla predict and prevent failures.
- Imagine **Delta Airlines** trying to decide how to price its flights from New York to Atlanta. It can use business intelligence to track its competitor's prices over different times, days of the week, and so on. It can also use business intelligence to decide the right mix of first-class, business, and economy passengers to maximize revenue. It can also use business intelligence to decide the costs of canceling a flight based on its mix of first-class and economy-class customers.
- Imagine **Morgan Stanley** trying to price an initial public offering of stock for a firm in the Internet retail industry (like **GoDaddy** or **Dropbox**). It can use business intelligence to assess market conditions, assess how other Internet retail firms are performing in the stock market, and assess how initial public offerings have recently performed.
- Imagine **Dunkin' Donuts** using business intelligence to track information about its potential franchisees and the stages of a franchisee contract (see the opening vignette in Chapter 3 for details).

American Airlines relies on business intelligence to price its flights.
© Per Andersen/Alamy

- Imagine **GEICO** or other insurance carriers using business intelligence to forecast claim amounts, medical coverage costs, and important elements that affect medical coverage. Such knowledge can be used to allow the firm to optimize its own insurance coverage and the handling of its medical claims. As the underlying health care requirements change due to recent legislation, such business intelligence will be critical for GEICO's continued success.
- Imagine **ESPN** trying to figure out the demographics of its audience (e.g., age, gender, net worth, interests outside of sports) watching its various sports offerings (e.g., football, basketball, soccer, auto racing, equestrian events). This will facilitate identifying the potential customers buying commercial spots as well as pricing its commercial breaks and finding other sponsorship opportunities.
- Imagine **GoPro** using business intelligence to track pricing information for its various, assorted cameras and video products of its offline and online competitors so that the management can price products appropriately to stay competitive in the market.

Data mining is one technique used to analyze data for business intelligence purposes. Data mining is the process of using sophisticated statistical techniques to extract and analyze data from large databases to discern patterns and trends that were not previously known. Data mining is often used to find patterns in stock prices to assist technical financial stock market analysts, or in commodities or currency trading. Another example of data mining in a retail setting might be analyzing the point-of-sale terminal to find the following trends:

- Items frequently bought in combination (e.g., cereal and milk; wieners, hot dog buns, ketchup, mustard, and relish; ice cream and cones; cayenne pepper and antacid; turkey and stuffing; chips and pop; diapers and baby food).
- Items frequently included in a large $200-plus grocery bill.
- Items frequently purchased by people making relatively small purchases, with "small" perhaps being defined by a dollar amount (i.e., less than $20) or defined by the fact that the customer used the express check-out counter.[1]

The main caveat about data mining is making sure the results are reasonable (or even plausible). While data mining may find a statistical correlation or relationship between two data items, it may or may not have a plausible relationship in the real world. There is a classic example that ice cream sales are correlated with drownings, suggesting that as ice cream sales increase, the number of drownings also increases. That does not mean that ice cream sales cause drownings or that drownings cause more ice cream sales, but rather that warm weather caused both. So it is clear that professional judgment must be used when using data mining techniques.

We must also be careful to communicate clearly (i.e., give or receive information to use appropriate language to describe the relationship) the results of a data mining exercise. For example, if we are describing a correlation, we should use words like "is associated with," "is linked to," or "is related to" to describe the relationship. In contrast, if causation is implied, we could use words like "causes," "impacts," "enhances," or "improves."

Progress Check

3. How would **Starbucks** use business intelligence to monitor **Dunkin' Donuts** or other competitors (like **McDonald's**)? What sources would it monitor?
4. How would the concepts behind business intelligence and data mining be used by the Miami Heat of the **National Basketball Association** to best compete on the court with the Oklahoma City Thunder?

[1] www.cs.ubc.ca/nest/dbsl/mining.html, accessed July 2010.

LO 10-3

Describe how digital dashboards allow for continuous tracking of key metrics.

DIGITAL DASHBOARDS

Your car has a dashboard that is easy to read and contains information that is critical to the driver (e.g., engine status, engine heat, rpms, speedometer, odometer, fuel levels, etc.). The original automobile dashboard designers carefully considered the most important metrics of the automobile's performance and conveniently put them in the best place for the driver to see. Figure 10.3 illustrates an automobile dashboard.

In accounting information systems (AISs), a **digital dashboard** is designed to track a firm's process or its performance indicators or metrics to monitor critical performance. Examples of the metrics that might be continuously tracked include month-to-date orders, days that receivables are outstanding, budget variances, and days without an accident on the assembly line. While the data on the main dashboard may monitor high-level processes, lower-level data can be quickly accessed by clicking through the links. This high-level summary with the lower-level detail allows executives not only to see the summary, but also to drill down deeper as questions arise.

Specialized dashboards may track overall corporate processes and performance or be specialized by function or department. These dashboards may track building projects, customer relationships, sales and

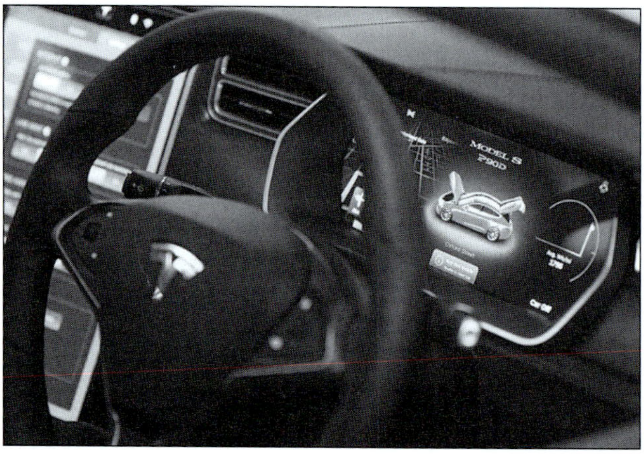

FIGURE 10.3

Automobile Dashboard

Just like automobile dashboards, digital dashboards offer timely, critical information to the decision maker.

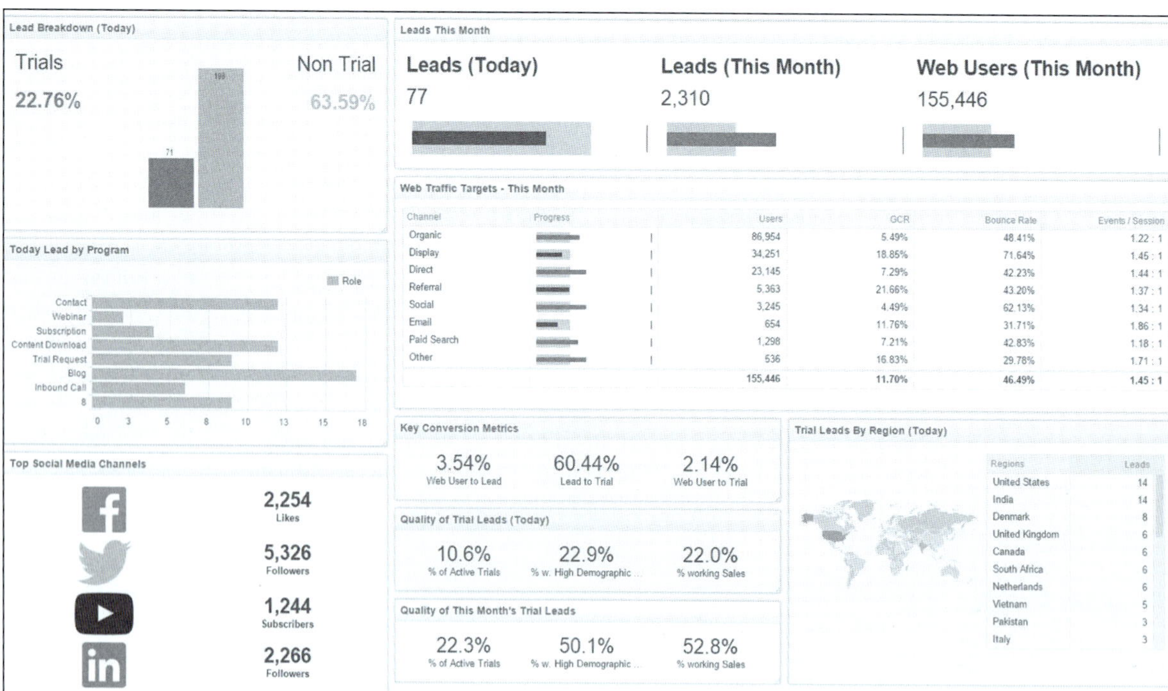

FIGURE 10.4

Example of Digital Marketing Dashboard

Source: Courtesy of Klipfolio.

marketing, security, operations, and the like. Figure 10.4 presents an example of a digital marketing dashboard that provides an example of how marketers are tracking the performance of their online marketing activities. While digital marketing activities may span multiple marketing channels (including social media and more traditional marketing activities like calls, e-mails, and subscriptions), this dashboard is designed to be representative of what a digital marketing manager might use to monitor performance on a continuous basis. The metrics displayed are selected to inform a wide audience, which may span from digital marketing specialists to marketing executives, where the marketing efforts stand.

Progress Check

5. What business processes could be on a digital dashboard for your business school? As retention of students becomes increasingly important for universities and business schools, what metrics could be displayed to monitor and support retention?
6. Why is a dashboard more useful than a standard report shared periodically?

LO 10-4
Explain how XBRL works and how it makes business reporting more efficient.

FINANCIAL REPORTING AND XBRL

XBRL stands for e**X**tensible **B**usiness **R**eporting **L**anguage and is based on the **XML** language (**Extensible Markup Language**), a standard for Internet communication among businesses. XBRL is specifically designed to electronically communicate business information and is used to facilitate business reporting of financial and nonfinancial data.

One of the advantages of XBRL is that it greatly enhances the speed and accuracy of business reporting. **XBRL International** has developed a taxonomy to describe and tag thousands of financial statement items.

XBRL provides major benefits in the preparation, analysis, and communication of business information. Instead of treating financial information as just a block of text that has to be manually reentered into a computer (or digitized) to give it meaning, XBRL gives each financial statement item (both text and numbers) its own unique tag that is computer readable and searchable. Total assets, for example, has its own unique tag telling the database exactly what it is. Accounts receivable has its own tag, and inventory has yet a third tag.

In February 2009, the **U.S. Securities and Exchange Commission (SEC)** passed a new rule titled "Interactive Data to Improve Financial Reporting," which required all large domestic and foreign accelerated filers to begin formatting their financial statements using XBRL. The new rule also requires these same public companies to format their financial statements using XBRL on their corporate websites. XBRL US, a division of XBRL International, was chosen to develop a single taxonomy for SEC financial reporting. Details regarding XBRL and the SEC are available at the SEC's XBRL website: http://xbrl.sec.gov/.

Figure 10.5 presents how financial reporting would look under XBRL. The data begin in the Accounting Information System (AIS). XBRL tags are then assigned to each financial and nonfinancial item either automatically by the enterprise system or manually by a member of the accounting department or its designee. Before the data can be accessed by external parties, assurance must be provided by an external auditor (discussed in more detail later). Once assurance is complete, the database is available for various uses, including reporting on the firm's website, filing to regulators (SEC, IRS, etc.), and providing information to other interested parties (such as financial analysts, loan officers, and investors). Each interested XBRL user can either access standard reports (i.e., 10-K going to the SEC or the corporate tax return going to the IRS) or specialized reports (i.e., only specific data) using what is called an XBRL style sheet (discussed in more detail later). The power of XBRL allows interested parties to either access standardized financial statements and reports or access only the information that is needed most for their own use.

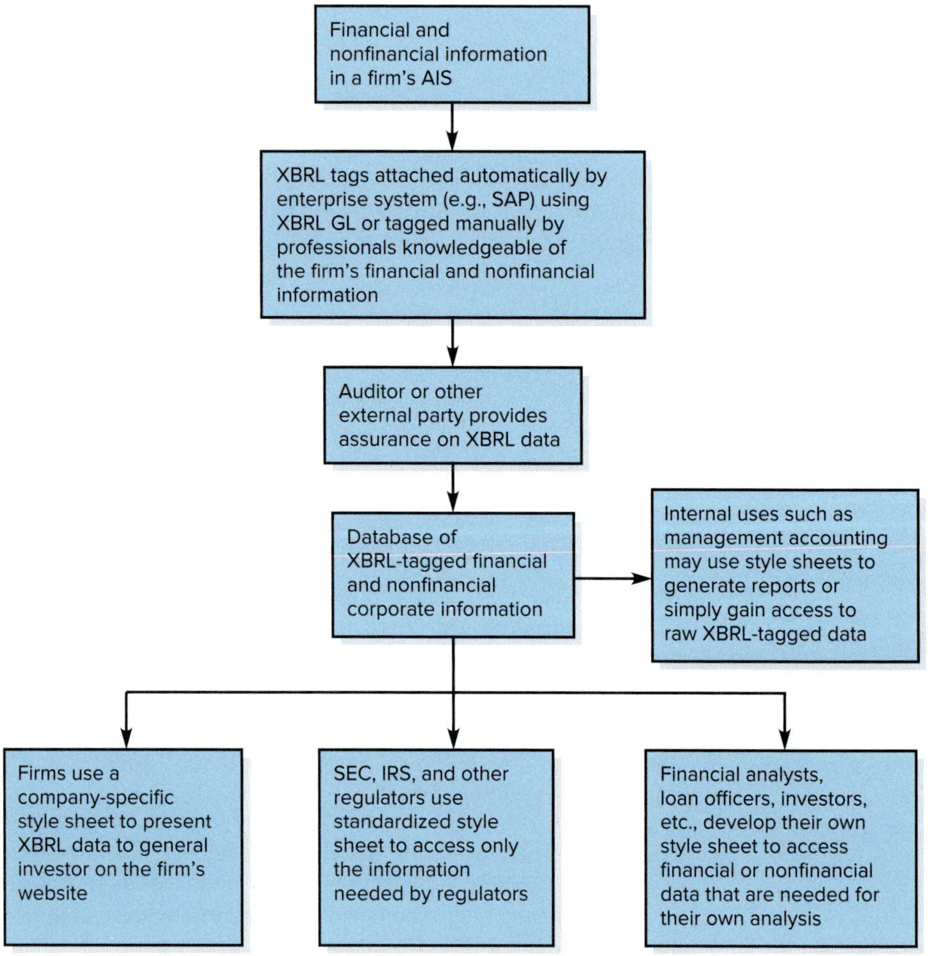

FIGURE 10.5 **Financial and Nonfinancial Reporting Using XBRL: From the Accounting Information System to the End User**

History and Development of XBRL

XBRL has been a few years in the making—from initial concept all the way to SEC adoption. Figure 10.6 provides a brief history of XBRL and highlights the important events in its formation.

How XBRL Works

In this section, we present a description of how the data go from the AIS to ultimately an XBRL report. Figure 10.7 provides a model of how XBRL works.

The **XBRL specification** (currently version 2.1) outlines the technical framework for XBRL. It provides the underlying technical details of what XBRL is and how it works.

XBRL Taxonomy

The **XBRL taxonomy** defines and describes each key data element (e.g., total assets, accounts, payable, net income). Because each national jurisdiction may have different accounting rules and regulations, each country may have its own taxonomy for financial reporting. That is why there are different taxonomies for each country: XBRL-Australia, XBRL-Canada, XBRL-Germany, XBRL IASB, XBRL-Japan, XBRL-Netherlands, and XBRL-UK.

Taxonomies continue to be developed to enable filings to regulators (such as banks), tax authorities (such as the IRS), and other governmental entities. For example, U.S. banks are

FIGURE 10.6
History of XBRL

Source: David Nichtman, "XBRL History," XBRL, https://www.xbrl.org/, accessed May 23, 2016.

April 1998	Charles Hoffman, a CPA from the accounting firm Knight Vale and Gregory in Tacoma, Washington, contemplated how XML could be used as a means to electronically deliver financial information.
January 1999	A prototype of XBRL is presented to the AICPA; the AICPA agrees that XBRL is important to the accounting profession.
July 2000	XBRL releases the first XBRL specification for financial statements for commercial and industrial companies in the United States. The committee announces the formation of an international organization to position for rapid global expansion and adoption.
June 2001	XBRL announces an effort to create XBRL for transactions internal to the company. This is often called XBRL GL, which is essentially XBRL on the general ledger.
October 2001	XBRL recognizes that different countries have different reporting needs and divides up the job of developing specifications to different XBRL jurisdictions, such as XBRL-Australia, XBRL-Canada, XBRL-Germany, XBRL IASB, XBRL-Japan, XBRL-Netherlands, and XBRL-UK.
February 2002	The Australian Prudential Regulatory Agency (APRA), one of the world's largest regulatory agencies, announces that XBRL is being used to overhaul data collection from 11,000 superfunds, insurers, and banks required to report to it on a regular basis.
December 2003	XBRL 2.1 specification is released.
May 2004	XBRL-UK releases taxonomy for UK GAAP.
July 2005	XBRL International releases a new version of its GL taxonomy, which allows the efficient handling of financial and business information contained within an organization.
2008 and early 2009	The SEC mandates that operating firms provide their financial statements to the SEC and on their corporate websites in interactive data format using XBRL.

FIGURE 10.7
How XBRL Works

Source: David Nichtman, "Interactive Data: The Impact on Assurance," Assurance Working Group of XBRL International, XBRL, published November 2006. https://www.xbrl.org/, accessed May 23, 2016.

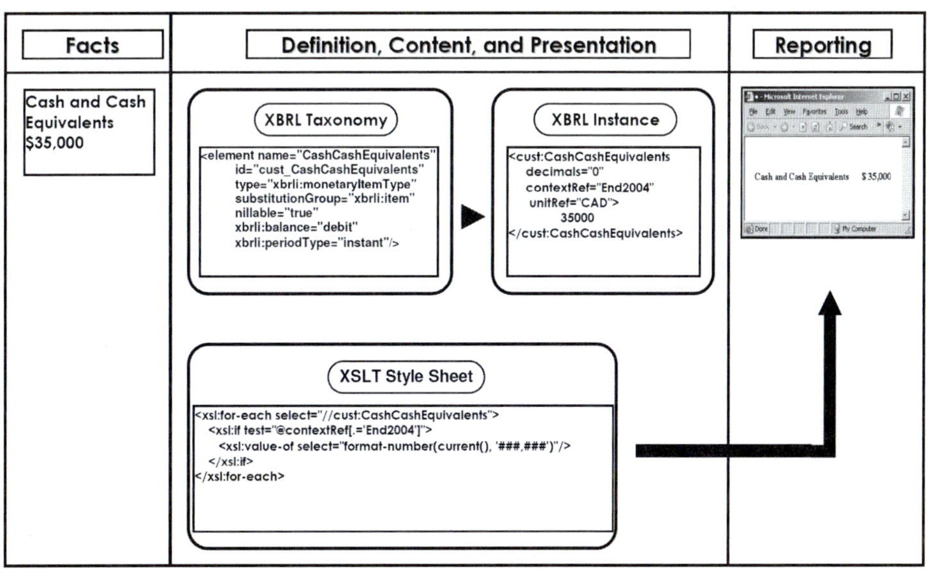

required to submit their quarterly report "Report of Condition and Income" or their Call Report to the Federal Deposit Insurance Corporation (FDIC) using XBRL. The Federal Financial Institutions Examination Council (FFIEC) is responsible for creating XBRL Call Report taxonomy to facilitate filing call reports.

XBRL Instance Documents

The XBRL for U.S. GAAP has approximately 12,000 element labels or tags.[2]

While the XBRL taxonomy describes the data elements, **XBRL instance documents** contain the actual dollar amounts or the details of each of the elements within the firm's XBRL database. Thus, XBRL instance documents are a collection of data in a computer-readable format. It is not until the style sheet is applied that the financial statement information is finally readable by people.

XBRL Style Sheets

XBRL style sheets take the instance documents and add presentation elements to make them readable by people. The data may be presented in a number of formats, including HTML, PDF, Microsoft Word, and Microsoft Excel (among others). The style sheet is made in conformance with a standardized language called Extensible Stylesheet Language (XSL). The official XSL specification for the XSL language is XSLT. This language is not governed by XBRL but is a standard means for taking data from XBRL or XML and presenting computer readable data in a way that is readable to humans. As discussed in Figure 10.4, different users will have different style sheets to access the exact data they are interested in. While the SEC may be interested in a standardized style sheet to retrieve a standardized report, a bank loan officer or financial analyst may be interested in developing his or her own to facilitate analysis.

XBRL Assurance

Before the SEC mandated XBRL submissions, **assurance** on any voluntary XBRL filings generally followed guidance from the Public Company Accounting Oversight Board (PCAOB), which relied on the auditor comparing a paper output of the XBRL-related documents to the information in the official EDGAR (Electronic Data Gathering, Analysis and Retrieval) filing to note any possible differences. Now that the use of XBRL is mandated by the SEC, assuring those XBRL documents is not required. It is expected that investors and other financial statement users will ultimately demand some assurance from an auditor or external party on a firm's use of XBRL.

There is no clear way to predict the future, but we can predict that the assurance afforded to XBRL will be quite different from the common external auditor's report on the auditee's financial statements and more than just matching a paper copy of the financial statements to the output of XBRL reports. However, we do believe that XBRL assurance will include assurance that

1. The most current, standardized XBRL taxonomy is used.
2. The underlying financial and nonfinancial data that are used in XBRL tagging are reliable.
3. The XBRL tagging is accurate and complete.
4. The reports generated using XBRL are complete and received on a timely basis.

XBRL allows highly disaggregated data, so not only is it possible to know the level of sales, but it is possible to know sales revenue in much more detail. For example, it is possible for firms to apply XBRL tagging to sales by state or by country, by product line, by store or by office, and so on. While the extent of disaggregated data that a company will provide is still in question, the possibility allows opportunities for firms to provide this potentially helpful data to external parties. As firms begin to use XBRL to disclose disaggregated data, assurance will be needed on items that have never before been disclosed to investors. It will be especially critical for these items to receive assurance as mentioned under item 2 to ensure that the underlying financial and nonfinancial data used in XBRL tagging are reliable.

[2]"Staff Interpretations and FAQs Related to Interactive Data Disclosure," Securities and Exchange Commission, www.sec.gov/spotlight/xbrl/staff-interps.shtml, accessed July 2009.

XBRL GL

Thus far, we have focused on XBRL for financial reporting. That type of XBRL is meant to facilitate efficient communication between firms and external parties (e.g., shareholders, regulatory bodies like the SEC and IRS, and the like). In contrast, **XBRL GL** (also known as **XBRL Global Ledger Taxonomy**) serves as a means to facilitate efficient communication *within a firm.* XBRL GL allows the representation of anything that is found in a chart of accounts, journal entries, or historical transactions—financial and nonfinancial. The ability to tag using XBRL is generally supported by enterprise systems (ERPs) such as **SAP**, **Oracle**, and **Microsoft**.

According to XBRL International, the advantages of XBRL GL include the following:

- XBRL Global Ledger is *reporting independent.* It collects general ledger and after-the-fact receivables, payables, inventory, and other nonfinancial facts and then permits the representation of that information using traditional summaries and through flexible links to XBRL for reporting.
- XBRL Global Ledger is *system independent.* Any developer can create import and export routines to convert information to XBRL GL format. This means that accounting software developers need only consider one design for their XML import/export file formats. Application service providers can offer to supply XBRL import and output so end users can more easily use their own data. Companies developing operational products, such as point-of-sale systems or job costing, or reporting tools can link with many accounting products without needing specialized links to each one.
- XBRL Global Ledger permits *consolidation.* Popular low-end products and mid-market solutions are not designed to facilitate consolidating data from multiple organizations. XBRL GL can help transfer the general ledger from one system to another, be used to combine the operations of multiple organizations, or bring data into tools that will do the consolidation.
- XBRL Global Ledger provides *flexibility,* overcoming the limitations of other approaches such as electronic data interchange (EDI). It offers an *extensible, flexible, multinational solution* that can exchange the data required by internal finance, accountants, and creditors.[3]

Progress Check

7. Using Figure 10.5 as a guide, how will XBRL GL facilitate the process of tagging the data that are generated by the firm's AIS?
8. What are the four predicted assurance needs for XBRL in the near future?

Summary

- Data warehouses serve as a repository of information that is separate from the operating databases of the firm. Data warehouses include data from a number of operational (internal) and external sources that will be helpful in providing information supportive for decision making across a number of functions in the firm. Data marts represent a slice of data from the data warehouse to meet a specific need.
- Business intelligence uses computer-based techniques to accumulate and analyze data that might be helpful to the firm's strategic initiatives.

[3] www.xbrl.org/GLTaxonomy/, accessed July 20, 2010, used with permission.

- Digital dashboards track critical firm performance in a way that is easily accessible to executives.
- XBRL serves as a means to electronically communicate business information to facilitate business reporting of financial and nonfinancial data to users. XBRL greatly enhances the speed and accuracy of business reporting.

Key Words

assurance (*258*) Independent, professional opinions that reduce the risk of having incorrect information.

business intelligence (*252*) A computer-based technique for accumulating and analyzing data from databases and data warehouses to support managerial decision making.

data mart (*250*) A subset of the information from the data warehouse to serve a specific purpose.

data mining (*253*) A process of using sophisticated statistical techniques to extract and analyze data from large databases to discern patterns and trends that were not previously known.

data warehouse (*250*) A collection of information gathered from an assortment of external and operational (i.e, internal) databases to facilitate reporting for decision making and business analysis.

decision support system (DSS) (*251*) A computer-based information system that facilitates business decision-making activities.

digital dashboard (*254*) A display to track the firm's process or performance indicators or metrics to monitor critical performance.

XBRL (eXtensible Business Reporting Language) (*255*) An open, global standard for exchanging financial reporting information.

XBRL Global Ledger Taxonomy (XBRL GL) (*259*) Serves as a ledger using the XBRL standard for internal purposes.

XBRL instance document (*258*) A document containing XBRL elements.

XBRL specification (*256*) Provides the underlying technical details of what XBRL is and how it works.

XBRL style sheet (*258*) Adds presentation elements to XBRL instance documents to make them readable by people.

XBRL taxonomy (*256*) Defines and describes each key data element (e.g., total assets, accounts payable, net income, etc.).

XML (Extensible Markup Language) (*255*) Open, global standard for exchanging information in a format that is both human- and machine-readable.

Answers to Progress Checks

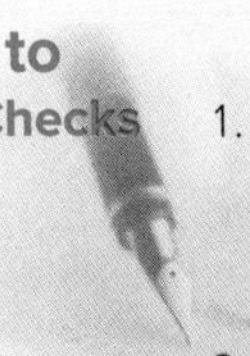

1. Specific functions in a firm, such as marketing, often do not need the whole data warehouse but would prefer a data mart that most closely addresses their needs. **Apple** may be interested in the demographics of the customer segment that purchases iPods and iPhones to best identify those most likely to buy an iPad or other Apple innovation.
2. To answer this question, we'll use Figure 10.2 as a guide. Among other things, **Best Buy** would be interested in general ledger, inventory, sales, and cost information from its internal databases. The company would also be interested in data from the retail industry, specifically from the retail segment that includes consumer electronics, personal computers and entertainment software, and appliances. General economic information and focal customer demographics would all be useful.

3. **Starbucks** could use business intelligence to monitor websites, news articles, court filings, and the like for **Dunkin' Donuts**'s prices, the locations for potential stores, and proposed new products.
4. Business (perhaps better termed as "competitive") intelligence and data mining could be used in the **NBA** to see which defenses work best, who to foul at the end of the game, who would usually take the end-of-the-game shot, who and when to play tight defense at the three-point line, and so on. This would be particularly helpful in a playoff series of five to seven games, where the team plays its competitor in successive games.
5. A business school might use a digital dashboard to track its performance. Many items might be tracked, but if the business school is particularly interested in retention, it might be interested in
   a. Number of students enrolled each semester and number of students returning from previous semesters.
   b. Grades of students dropping out (are they dropping out due to poor performance?).
   c. Student loans of students dropping out (are they experiencing financial trouble, etc.?).
   d. Job placement rates in each major (are students getting jobs when they graduate?).
6. A dashboard is used to monitor, and display, in a user-friendly way, the critical business processes that most affect firm performance. Standard reports may always be used but may not be as accessible as a digital dashboard.
7. XBRL GL will automatically tag the various financial and nonfinancial elements in the enterprise system software. This makes this step of tagging trivial for the firm to perform.
8. The four predicted assurance needs for XBRL include
   a. The most current, standardized XBRL taxonomy is used.
   b. The underlying financial and nonfinancial data that are used in XBRL tagging are reliable.
   c. The XBRL tagging is accurate and complete.
   d. The reports generated using XBRL are complete and received on a timely basis.

Mc Graw Hill Education connect

Multiple Choice Questions

1. A subset of a data warehouse is called a: **LO 10-1**
   a. small data warehouse.
   b. data mart.
   c. data martian.
   d. business intelligence.
2. A data warehouse may include: **LO 10-1**
   a. an XBRL style sheet.
   b. competitor information.
   c. a digital dashboard.
   d. an iPad.

3. **American Airlines** may use business intelligence to: **LO 10-2**
   a. track the cost of snacks on its airplanes.
   b. monitor the cost of its pilots and flight attendants.
   c. track the cost of its airplane fuel.
   d. monitor prices on competitive routes.
   e. all of the above.
4. The computer-based technique to accumulate and analyze data is called: **LO 10-2**
   a. business intelligence.
   b. data warehouse.
   c. digital dashboard.
   d. XBRL.
5. The steps in business intelligence include: **LO 10-2**
   a. analyze data for patterns, gather information, make decision.
   b. create data warehouse, query data warehouse, make decision.
   c. query data warehouse, create data warehouse, make decision.
   d. gather information, analyze data for patterns, make decision.
6. A digital dashboard tracks, in a user-friendly way: **LO 10-3**
   a. automobile speed.
   b. critical business failures.
   c. critical business processes.
   d. critical business markets.
7. XBRL facilitates business reporting of: **LO 10-4**
   a. business processes.
   b. the XML language.
   c. financial and nonfinancial information.
   d. only financial information.
8. The first person to propose using XML as a means to electronically deliver financial information was: **LO 10-4**
   a. Albert Gore.
   b. Charles Hoffman.
   c. Robert Byrd.
   d. Herb Hackett.
9. XBRL GL, or XBRL Global Ledger Taxonomy, is different from XBRL U.S. GAAP because it facilitates: **LO 10-4**
   a. efficient communication between the firm and external parties.
   b. efficient communication within a firm.
   c. efficient communication with the supply chain.
   d. efficient communication with customers.
10. The stated advantages of XBRL GL do not include: **LO 10-4**
   a. reporting independence.
   b. system independence.
   c. scalability.
   d. flexibility.
11. What is the mechanism called that firms may use to track their marketing efforts? **LO 10-3**
   a. XBRL
   b. Business intelligence

c. Data analytics
d. Digital dashboard

12. XBRL assurance might include all but which of the following: **LO 10-4**
    a. The most current, standardized XBRL taxonomy is used.
    b. The XBRL tagging is accurate and complete.
    c. The reports generated using XBRL are complete and received on a timely basis.
    d. The XBRL tagging is useful to investors.
13. The XBRL style sheet is made in conformance with which standardized language? **LO 10-4**
    a. XML
    b. XSL
    c. XBRL GL
    d. XL
14. Which body mandated that operating firms in its jurisdiction submit their financial reports using XBRL? **LO 10-4**
    a. FASB
    b. GASB
    c. SEC
    d. NYSE
15. Which technique or tool is used to analyze data for business intelligence purposes? **LO 10-2**
    a. Data mining
    b. Decision support systems
    c. Data marts
    d. Big Data

Discussion Questions

1. Using Figure 10.2 as a guide, name three internal and three external databases that you think should be included in a data warehouse for **Bank of America**, **Wells Fargo**, or your local bank. Support your answer. **LO 10-1**
2. Using Figure 10.2 as a guide, name three internal and three external databases that you think should be included in a data warehouse for your university. Support your answer. **LO 10-1**
3. Name five items that you think would be included in a digital dashboard for **ESPN** or for **Disney**. Why are these critical business processes for that company? **LO 10-3**
4. Who will rely on XBRL data for decision making? Why is assurance needed on XBRL data? Support your answer. **LO 10-4**
5. Why is there a different XBRL taxonomy for each country, including XBRL-Australia, XBRL-Canada, XBRL-Germany, XBRL-Japan, XBRL-Netherlands, XBRL-US, and XBRL-UK? What would happen if there was only one XBRL taxonomy for all countries? **LO 10-4**
6. How would the XBRL style sheets be different for financial analysts as compared to the Securities and Exchange Commission? How would XBRL style sheets be different for a firm's website as compared to bank loan officers? **LO 10-4**
7. Why is XBRL needed in the financial community? In your opinion, why did the Securities and Exchange Commission mandate its usage? What does it provide that was not available before XBRL? **LO 10-4**
8. Why would XBRL be used for internal uses such as management accounting? (*Hint:* See Figure 10.5.) **LO 10-4**
9. Why do companies need both internal and external databases in a data warehouse? **LO 10-1**
10. How is a digital dashboard different from a financial report? **LO 10-3**

Problems

1. Using Figures 10.1 and 10.2 as guides, name four internal and four external databases that you think should be included in a data warehouse for the marketing function of **Procter & Gamble** or the consumer packaged goods company with whom you are most familiar. Procter & Gamble has products like Gillette razors, Charmin tissue, and Head and Shoulders shampoo. Why are these eight databases you recommend critical to the effective functioning of the marketing department to sell more products? Support your answer. **LO 10-1**
2. Which of the four predicted assurance needs do you believe is most critical to ensuring XBRL accuracy? Support your answer. **LO 10-4**
3. XBRL allows disaggregated data to be presented to interested external parties. Financial analysts often forecast earnings many years ahead and then suggest whether an investor should buy, sell, or hold a stock. Which type of disaggregated data do you think financial analysts would be most interested in receiving when predicting one-year-ahead earnings: detailed sales data, detailed expense data, detailed asset data, and/or detailed liability data? Support your answer. In your opinion, which disaggregated XBRL data would be most useful information in predicting whether an investor should buy, sell, or hold a stock? **LO 10-4**
4. The effectiveness of data mining has been criticized by the *Wall Street Journal*. In one article, the author notes that academic studies have shown that by using data mining, analysts could accurately predict changes in the stock market based on either the population of sheep in Bangladesh, the number of nine-year-olds at a given time, or whether it is smoggy on a given day.[4] While the statistical correlation may be valid, there must be a logical reason that a particular factor will predict stock returns. **LO 10-2**

   Required:

   a. Do you think these findings represent valid relationships or spurious correlations?
   b. What measures do you think might be valid predictors of stock market returns?
5. XBRL touts as its primary advantage that it will increase efficiency for the firm and those interested in its business reports. **LO 10-4**

   Required:

   a. How is XBRL more efficient for the firm that reports its business performance? Does the use of XBRL GL in a firm's accounting software make XBRL more or less efficient than when XBRL GL is not used?
   b. How is XBRL more efficient for those using its business reports for regulator, investing, or other purposes?
   c. Are there any cases when it is less efficient to use XBRL?
6. How would **Coca-Cola** use business intelligence to monitor **Pepsi Cola**'s operations in Russia? What sources of data need to be gathered? How would they be analyzed? **LO 10-2**
7. connect — There are four stated advantages of XBRL GL: reporting independence, system independence, consolidation, and flexibility. Match the advantage with the characteristic of XBRL GL. **LO 10-4**

1. XBRL GL offers an extensible, multinational solution that can exchange the data required by internal finance, accountants, and creditors.	A. Reporting independence
2. Any developer can create import and export routines to convert information from any system to XBRL GL format.	B. System independence
3. Permits the representation of information using traditional summaries and through flexible links.	C. Consolidation
4. XBRL GL can be used to combine the operations of multiple organizations.	D. Flexibility

[4] http://online.wsj.com/article/SB124967937642715417.html, accessed May 2016.

connect 8. Match the description of these XBRL terms with their descriptions. **LO 10-4**

1. A document containing XBRL elements.
2. Adds presentation elements to XBRL instance documents to make them more readable to people.
3. Defines and describes each key data element (e.g., total assets, accounts payable, net income, etc.).
4. Provides the underlying technical details of what XBRL is and how it works.

A. XBRL instance document
B. XBRL specification
C. XBRL style sheet
D. XBRL taxonomy

connect 9. Match the description with these business process terms. **LO 10-1, LO 10-2**

1. A subset of the information from the data warehouse to serve a specific purpose.
2. A computer-based information system that facilitates business decision-making activities.
3. A collection of information gathered from an assortment of external and operational (i.e, internal) databases to facilitate reporting for decision making and business analysis.
4. A computer-based technique for accumulating and analyzing data from databases and data warehouses to support managerial decision making.

A. Business intelligence
B. Data mart
C. Data warehouse
D. Decision support systems (DSSs)

connect 10. The following figure represents a digital cockpit (or dashboard) for **General Electric**. **LO 10-2**

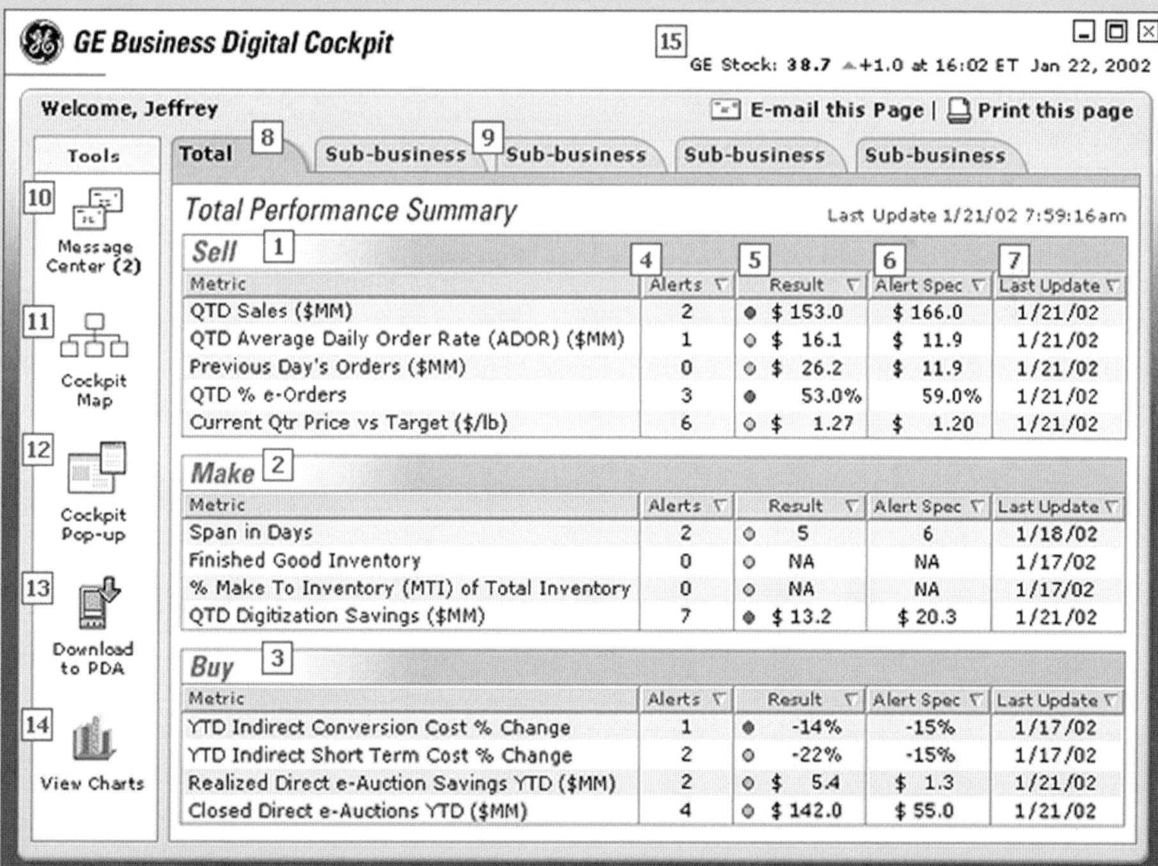

Source: http://www.ge.com/annual01/letter/cockpit/.

The cockpit has 15 items highlighted. Identify which numbered item tracks or shows the following data:

a. The sales of General Electric
b. The detail of the sub-business
c. The previous day's orders
d. The current GE stock price
e. The column reporting the most recent update
f. The "alerts" that need to be investigated further
g. The column reporting the current performance
h. The conversion cost percentage

11. Data mining is the process of using sophisticated statistical techniques to extract and analyze data from large databases to discern patterns and trends that were not previously known. The patterns we find are correlations, but not necessarily causation.

Every time we see a link between the occurrence of one event or action with another, we generally assume that one event or action caused the other. But simply linking one occurrence with another does not always prove that the result has been caused by the other.

For example, such data mining might suggest the following relationship between arcade revenue and computer science doctorates awarded in the United States, with a correlation of 0.985. **LO 10-2**

Total revenue generated by arcades
correlates with
Computer science doctorates awarded in the United States
Correlation: 98.51% (r = 0.985065)

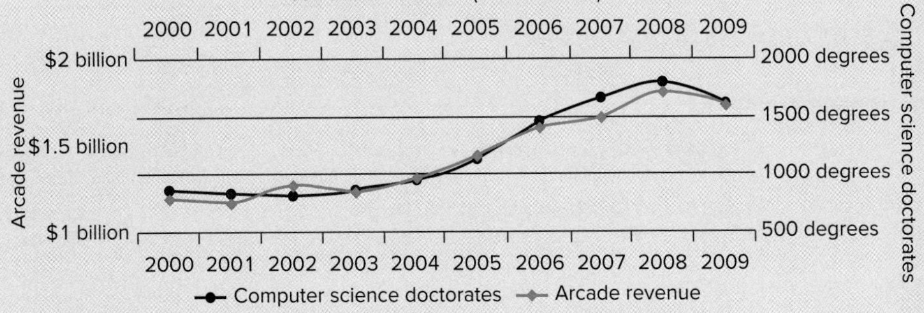

Data sources: U.S. Census Bureau and National Science Foundation.

a. Is this simply a correlation? Or is there a possibility that computer science doctorates affect total revenue generated by arcades or vice versa? Explain your answer.

Number of people who drowned by falling into a pool
correlates with
Films Nicolas Cage appeared in
Correlation: 66.6% (r = 0.666004)

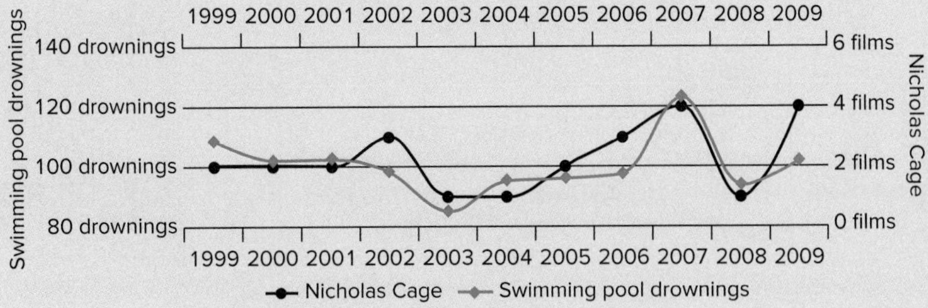

Data sources: U.S. Census Bureau and National Science Foundation.

b. Is this simply a correlation? Or is there a possibility that the number of people who drowned was affected by the films Nicolas Cage appeared in? Explain your answer.

connect 12. Data mining is the process of using sophisticated statistical techniques to extract and analyze data from large databases to discern patterns and trends that were not previously known. The patterns we find are correlations, but we do not necessarily find causation.

Newspaper headlines often link one activity to another and imply causation, rather than a simple correlation or association. Jon Mueller, a professor at North Central College, suggests that when describing a correlation between two variables, there are some acceptable ways to describe this relationship. **LO 10-2**

ACCEPTABLE TERMS for Correlations	AVOID THESE TERMS When Discussing Correlations (but they are acceptable when asserting causation)
Get	Cause
Have	Increase/decrease
Linked	Benefits
More	Impacts
More/less, less	Enhances/undermines
Tied	Effect/affect
Connected/related	Improves/boosts
Tend	If → then type statements (implies one-direction)

Source: http://jfmueller.faculty.noctrl.edu/100/correlation_or_causation.htm.

In light of these suggestions, evaluate each of these headlines as to whether they suggest a causal or noncausal relationship.

1. Facebook users get worse grades in college
2. Link between over-indebtedness and obesity identified
3. Kids' TV habits tied to poorer test scores
4. Recession causes increase in teen dating violence
5. Snooze or lose: Memory retention enhanced by sleep
6. Soda causes obesity, researchers assert
7. Disciplinarian parents have fat kids
8. Social isolation may have a negative effect on intellectual abilities

connect 13. Data mining is the process of using sophisticated statistical techniques to extract and analyze data from large databases to discern patterns and trends that were not previously known. The patterns we find are correlations, but we do not necessarily find causation.

Newspaper headlines often link one activity to another and imply causation, rather than a simple correlation or association. Jon Mueller, a professor at North Central College, suggests when describing a correlation between two variables that there are some acceptable ways to describe this relationship. **LO 10-2**

ACCEPTABLE TERMS for Correlations	AVOID THESE TERMS When Discussing Correlation (but they are acceptable when asserting causation)
Get	Cause
Have	Increase/decrease
Linked	Benefits
More	Impacts
More/less, less	Enhances/undermines
Tied	Effect/affect
Connected/related	Improves/boosts
Tend	If → then type statements (implies one-direction)

In light of these suggestions, evaluate each of these headlines as to whether they suggest a causal or noncausal relationship.

1. Obese girls less likely to attend college, research shows
2. Migraine often associated with psychiatric disorders
3. Your parents are correct, scholars report: Studying pays off
4. Tooth loss in elderly linked to mental impairment
5. Eating fatty fish lowers risk of dementia
6. Political bias affects brain activity, study finds
7. Child anxiety link to ecstasy use

connect 14. Consider each of the following statements and state whether they are true or false. **LO 10-4**

1. XBRL allows tagging to highly disaggregated data
2. XBRL GL allows the representation of anything that is found in a chart of accounts, journal entries, or historical transactions–financial and nonfinancial.
3. XBRL style sheets take the instance documents and add presentation elements to make them readable.
4. XBRL stands for **Extensible Base Reporting Language**.
5. XBRL instance documents contain the actual dollar amounts or the details of each account.
6. XBRL for U.S. GAAP has approximately 2,000 element labels or tags.
7. Assurance of XBRL is required by the Securities and Exchange Commission.
8. XBRL GL serves as a ledger using the XBRL standard for internal purposes.
9. XBRL GL does not allow consolidation of the financials of multiple organizations.
10. There is a specific XBRL style sheet required by financial analysts.

Chapter Eleven

Accounting Information Systems and Internal Controls

A look at this chapter

This chapter provides a general discussion on control issues in accounting information systems. In particular, we examine issues in ethics and internal controls that are addressed by the Sarbanes-Oxley Act of 2002 and important factors in corporate governance. These related areas are critical to an organization's efficiency and effectiveness in operations, reliability in financial reporting, and compliance with applicable laws and regulations. In addition, important control and governance frameworks including COSO, COBIT, and ITIL are covered in this chapter.

A look back

Chapter 10 provided a description of how accounting information systems facilitate management reporting, including using data warehouses, business intelligence, and dashboards. In addition, we also explained the development and emerging use of eXtensible Business Reporting Language (XBRL) in electronic financial reporting.

A look ahead

In Chapter 12, we discuss computer fraud and information security–related issues. The focus includes systems integrity and availability, as well as threats and risks in conducting business.

© Glow Images/Getty Images

You probably often visit **Starbucks** for coffee. Have you ever visited www.starbucks.com to learn more about the firm? You might be surprised to find more than just different types of coffee, a menu, store locations, and so on. You can find a lot of information under the tag called "Responsibility—Ethical, Local, Global." Starbucks believes businesses should be responsible to the communities it serves. The company is committed to "buying and serving the highest-quality, responsibly grown, ethically traded coffee to help create a better future for farmers." The philosophy and ethical values of a firm comprise one of the critical factors that form the firm's control environment. The Committee of Sponsoring Organizations (COSO) indicates that without a good control environment, even the best-designed control systems may fail. The control environment sets the tone of a firm and signifies how the firm values integrity and ethics of its employees.

Chapter Outline

Learning Objectives

After reading this chapter, you should be able to:

11-1 Explain essential control concepts and why a code of ethics and internal controls are important.

11-2 Explain the objectives and components of the COSO internal control framework and the COSO enterprise risk management framework.

11-3 Describe the overall COBIT framework and its implications for IT governance.

11-4 Describe other governance frameworks related to information systems management and security.

INTRODUCTION

Ethics, internal controls, and information security are three closely related areas critical to corporate governance. Safeguarding the assets of a firm has always been the responsibility of its management. Given the swift advancements in computing technology and the pervasive use of IT in all aspects of business operations, managers and accountants have to reexamine how to establish and monitor internal controls. For internal and external auditors, it is important to assess the effectiveness of internal controls to meet the mandate of the Sarbanes-Oxley Act.

LO 11-1
Explain essential control concepts and why a code of ethics and internal controls are important.

ETHICS, THE SARBANES-OXLEY ACT OF 2002, AND CORPORATE GOVERNANCE

The Need for a Code of Ethics

Ethical principles are derived from cultural values, societal traditions, and personal attitudes on issues of right and wrong. Integrity and individual ethics are formed through a person's life experience. Ethics play a critical role when people make choices and decisions. Although individuals have their own values and may behave differently from one another, firms often choose to establish a formal expectation, through a **code of ethics,** on what is considered to be ethical within the group in order to promote ethical behavior. Ethical behavior prompted by a code of ethics can be considered a form of internal control. Given today's diversified and globalized business environment, a firm will have to rely on the ethics of its employees to operate efficiently and effectively. In addition, the importance of a code of ethics should be emphasized because employees with different culture backgrounds are likely to have different values.

In addition, many professional associations have developed codes of ethics to assist professionals in selecting among decisions that are not clearly right or wrong. Some examples include the American Institute of Certified Public Accountants (AICPA), the Information Systems Audit and Control Association (ISACA), the Institute of Internal Auditors (IIA), and the Institute of Management Accountants (IMA). The certification programs of these associations require the knowledge of the codes of ethics in developing professionalism.

WorldCom used shady accounting methods to mask its declining financial condition by falsely professing financial growth and profitability to increase the price of its stock. On March 15, 2005, CEO Bernard Ebbers was convicted of fraud, conspiracy, and filing false documents with regulators. He was sentenced to 25 years in prison.

Corporate Governance as Addressed by Sarbanes-Oxley

The impact of public policy on the accounting profession through the enactment of laws and regulations has been well-documented and can be traced back to the 1930s.[1] Among those policies enforced, the **Sarbanes-Oxley Act of 2002 (SOX)** has probably had the most far-reaching effect on public companies and accounting firms. This bill was a response to business scandals such as Enron, WorldCom, and Tyco International. SOX requires public companies registered with the SEC and their auditors to annually assess and report on the design and effectiveness of internal control over financial reporting.

SOX also established the **Public Company Accounting Oversight Board (PCAOB)** to provide independent oversight of public accounting firms. The PCAOB

[1]See the Securities Act of 1933, Securities Exchange Act of 1934, and Foreign Corrupt Practices Act of 1977.

issues auditing standards and oversees quality controls of public accounting firms. PCAOB Auditing Standard No. 5 (AS No. 5) encourages auditors to use a risk-based, top-down approach to identify the key controls. That is, auditors should start at the financial statement level when analyzing controls, focusing on entity-level controls[2] followed by reviewing significant accounts, disclosures, and management assertions.

SOX is arranged into 11 titles. The first two titles are most relevant to auditors. As far as compliance for public companies, the most important sections within the other titles are considered to be 301, 302, 404, 406, 409, 802, 807, and 906 (see Figure 11.1).

FIGURE 11.1
Titles and Compliance Requirements of Sarbanes-Oxley Act

SOX Titles	Key Sections	Key Compliance Requirements
Title I: Public Company Accounting Oversight Board (PCAOB)	101	Establishment
	103	Auditing, quality control, and independence standards and rules
	104	Inspections of registered public accounting firms
Title II: Auditor Independence	201	Services outside the scope of practice of auditors
	203	Audit partner rotation
	204	Auditor reports to audit committees
	206	Conflicts of interest
Title III: Corporate Responsibility	301	Public company audit committees
	302	Corporate responsibility for financial reports
Title IV: Enhanced Financial Disclosures	404	Management assessment of internal controls
	406	Code of ethics for senior financial officers
	409	Real-time issuer disclosures
Title VIII: Corporate and Criminal Fraud Accountability	802	Criminal penalties for altering documents
	807	Criminal penalties for defrauding shareholders of publicly traded companies
Title IX: White-Collar Crime Penalty Enhancements	906	Corporate responsibility for financial reports

Do you consider SOX helpful to improving corporate governance? Is SOX relevant to a company's social responsibilities? You can find online that some public companies provide a sustainability report on their websites. What is the purpose of the sustainability report?

Corporate governance can be defined as a set of processes and policies in managing an organization with sound ethics to safeguard the interests of its stakeholders. Corporate governance also promotes accountability, fairness, and transparency in the organization's relationship with its stakeholders. At the Global Corporate Governance Forum held by World Bank (2000), Mr. Adrian Cadbury[3] stated: "Corporate governance is concerned with holding the balance between economic and social goals and between individual and communal goals. The corporate governance framework is intended to encourage the efficient use of resources and to require accountability for the stewardship of those resources. The aim is to align as nearly as possible the interests of individuals, corporations and society."

[2] According to the PCAOB Release 2007-005, examples of entity-level controls include internal control environment, risk assessment and management, management override, centralized processing, and monitoring.

[3] Adrian Cadbury was the chairman of Cadbury and Cadbury Schweppes. He was a pioneer in raising the awareness and reforming corporate governance around the world. https://www.washingtonpost.com/business/adrian-cadbury-a-leader-in-corporate-governance-dies-at-86/2015/09/04/e87dd2fe-532e-11e5-8c19-0b6825aa4a3a_story.html, retrieved on May 4, 2016.

Progress Check

1. Why does a firm need a code of ethics? Is it important to corporate governance?
2. The Sarbanes-Oxley Act was enacted in 2002 and established PCAOB. What are the functions of PCAOB?

CONTROL AND GOVERNANCE FRAMEWORKS

Overview of Control Concepts

Internal control involves the processes that an organization implements to safeguard assets, provide accurate and reliable information, promote operational efficiency, enforce prescribed managerial policies, and comply with applicable laws and regulations. Appropriate internal controls support organizations' objectives through accountability and transparency for good corporate governance. According to SOX, the establishment and maintenance of internal controls is a management responsibility.

Firms use internal controls as a means of preventing errors and deterring fraud. The three main functions of internal control are prevention, detection, and correction. **Preventive controls** deter problems before they arise. Preventive controls require compliance with preferred procedures and thus stop undesirable events from happening. For example, a transaction should be authorized to ensure its validity. Hence, a signed source document should be required before recording a transaction. **Detective controls** find problems when they arise. These controls are procedures and techniques designed to identify undesirable events after they have already occurred. For example, bank reconciliations and monthly trial balances are prepared to catch mistakes. **Corrective controls** fix problems that have been identified, such as using backup files to recover corrupted data. Detective controls are often linked to accompanying corrective controls to remediate any issues that are discovered.

In a computerized environment, internal controls can also be categorized as general controls and application controls. **General controls** pertain to enterprisewide issues such as controls over accessing the network, developing and maintaining applications, documenting changes of programs, and so on. **Application controls** are specific to a subsystem or an application to ensure the validity, completeness, and accuracy of the transactions. For example, when entering a sales transaction, use an input control to ensure the customer account number is entered accurately.

Given SOX, the SEC requires management to evaluate internal controls based on a recognized control framework such as the frameworks developed by the **Committee of Sponsoring Organizations (COSO)** of the Treadway Commission.

LO 11-2
Explain the control objectives and components of the COSO internal control framework and the COSO enterprise risk management framework.

Commonly Used Frameworks

COSO is composed of five nonprofit organizations: American Accounting Association (AAA), AICPA, Financial Executives International (FEI), IIA, and IMA. COSO is a voluntary initiative to improve corporate governance and performance through effective internal controls, enterprise risk management, and fraud deterrence. COSO examines the causal factors that lead to fraudulent financial reporting and develops recommendations for public companies, independent auditors, the SEC and other regulators, and educational institutions to improve the quality of financial reporting through internal controls and corporate governance.[4] COSO developed two frameworks to improve the quality of financial reporting through accountability, effective controls, risk management, and corporate governance.

[4]See www.coso.org.

The Committee issued the "Internal Control—Integrated Framework" in 1992 and an updated version in 2013, and the "Enterprise Risk Management—Integrated Framework" in 2004. The COSO internal control framework is one of the most widely accepted authorities on internal control, providing a baseline for evaluating, reporting, and improving internal control. COSO 2013 internal control framework provides the principles for effective internal controls to address changes in the business and operating environments, and to respond to expectations from stakeholders.

The COSO enterprise risk management (ERM) framework expanded the original COSO internal control framework to provide guidance in defining, assessing, managing, and transferring risk in order to maximize firm value. The COSO ERM focuses on the strategic alignment of the firm's mission with its risk appetite. Although most firms in the United States already use the COSO internal control framework in establishing and evaluating their internal control systems, many are still applying the concepts in COSO ERM as the basis for developing risk-based internal control systems. AS No. 5[5] encourages the top-down risk assessment approach in evaluating internal controls. Therefore, the focus of both management and external auditors has become more in line with the COSO ERM framework.

As a future business professional, do you think you need to know so much about control frameworks? Why is this knowledge critical to your success in your future career?

The **control objectives for information and related technology (COBIT)** framework is an internationally accepted set of best IT security and control practices for IT management released by the IT Governance Institute (ITGI). It is a control framework for the governance and management of enterprise IT. COBIT provides management with an understanding of risks associated with IT and bridges the gap among risks, control needs, and technical issues.

The **Information Technology Infrastructure Library (ITIL)** is a set of concepts and practices for IT service management. COBIT defines the overall IT control framework, and ITIL provides the details for IT service management. ITIL is released by the UK Office of Government Commerce (OGC) and is the most widely accepted model for IT service management. ITIL adopts a life-cycle approach to IT services, focusing on practices for service strategy, service design, service transition, service operation, and continual service improvement.

The **International Organization for Standardization (ISO) 27000 series** is designed to address information security issues. The ISO 27000 series—particularly, ISO 27001 and ISO 27002—have become the most recognized and generally accepted sets of information security framework and guidelines.

COSO Internal Control Framework

The updated COSO 2013 internal control framework defines internal control as a process—affected by an entity's board of directors, management, and other personnel—designed to provide reasonable assurance regarding the achievement of objectives in effectiveness and efficiency of operations, reliability of reporting, and compliance with applicable laws and regulations. Accordingly, the COSO framework indicates that[6]

1. Internal control is a process consisting of ongoing tasks and activities. It is a means to an end, not an end in itself.
2. Internal control is affected by people. It is not merely about policy manuals, systems, and forms. Rather, it is about people at every level of a firm who affect internal control.

[5]Auditing Standard No. 5: An Audit of Internal Control over Financial Reporting That Is Integrated with an Audit of Financial Statement, http://pcaobus.org/Standards/Auditing/Pages/Auditing_Standard_5.aspx retrieved on May 4, 2016.

[6]See www.coso.org/resources.htm.

3. Internal control can provide reasonable assurance, not absolute assurance, to an entity's management and board.
4. Internal control is geared toward the achievement of objectives in one or more separate but overlapping categories.
5. Internal control is adaptable to the entity structure.

According to the COSO 2013 framework, an effective internal control system should consist of three categories of objectives and five essential components. The three categories of objectives are

1. *Operations objectives:* effectiveness and efficiency of a firm's operations on financial performance goals and safeguarding assets.
2. *Reporting objectives:* reliability of reporting, including internal and external financial and nonfinancial reporting.
3. *Compliance objectives:* adherence to applicable laws and regulations.

To support a firm in its efforts to achieve internal control objectives, COSO 2013 suggests five components of internal control:

1. *Control environment*—sets the tone of a firm, influences the control consciousness of its employees, and establishes the foundation for the internal control system. Control environment factors include the management's philosophy and operating style, integrity and ethical values of employees, organizational structure, the role of the audit committee, proper board oversight for the development and performance of internal control, and personnel policies and practices.
2. *Risk assessment*—involves a dynamic process for identifying and analyzing a firm's risks from external and internal environments. Risk assessment allows a firm to understand the extent to which potential events might affect corporate objectives. Risks are analyzed after considering the likelihood of occurrence and the potential loss. The analysis serves as a basis for determining how the risks should be managed. This component will be discussed later in the chapter.
3. *Control activities*—occur throughout a firm at all levels and in all functions. A firm must establish control policies, procedures, and practices that ensure the firm's objectives are achieved and risk mitigation strategies are carried out. This component will be discussed later in the chapter.
4. *Information and communication*—supports all other control components by communicating effectively to ensure information flows down, across, and up the firm, as well as interacting with external parties such as customers, suppliers, regulators, and shareholders and informing them about related policy positions. Relevant information should be identified, captured, and communicated in a form and timeframe that enable employees to carry out their duties.
5. *Monitoring*—the design and effectiveness of internal controls should be monitored by management and other parties outside the process on a continuous basis. Findings should be evaluated, and deficiencies must be communicated in a timely manner. Necessary modifications should be made to improve the business process and the internal control system.

The three objectives and five components of the COSO internal control framework are part of the COSO ERM framework. In addition, COSO 2013 codifies 17 relevant principles associated with the five components of internal control (see Figure 11.2). They are essential in assessing the five components. The 17 principles of effective internal controls are listed as follows:

Principles for Control Environment:

1. The organization demonstrates a commitment to integrity and ethical values.
2. The board of directors demonstrates independence from management and exercises oversight of the development and performance of internal control.
3. Management establishes, with board oversight, structures, reporting lines, and appropriate authorities and responsibilities in the pursuit of objectives.
4. The organization demonstrates a commitment to attract, develop, and retain competent individuals in alignment with objectives.
5. The organization holds individuals accountable for their internal control responsibilities in the pursuit of objectives.

Principles for Risk Assessment:

6. The organization specifies objectives with sufficient clarity to enable the identification and assessment of risks relating to objectives.
7. The organization identifies risks to the achievement of its objectives across the entity and analyzes risks as a basis for determining how the risks should be managed.
8. The organization considers the potential for fraud in assessing risks to the achievement of objectives.
9. The organization identifies and assesses changes that could significantly impact the system of internal control.

Principles for Control Activities:

10. The organization selects and develops control activities that contribute to the Mitigation of risks to the achievement of objectives to acceptable levels.
11. The organization selects and develops general control activities over technology to support the achievement of objectives.
12. The organization deploys control activities through policies that establish what is expected and procedures that put policies into place.

Principles for Information and Communication:

13. The organization obtains or generates and uses relevant, quality information to support the functioning of internal control.
14. The organization internally communicates information, including objectives and responsibilities for internal control, necessary to support the functioning of internal control.
15. The organization communicates with external parties regarding matters affecting the functioning of internal control.

Principles for Monitoring Activities:

16. The organization selects, develops, and performs ongoing and/or separate evaluations to ascertain whether the components of internal control are present and functioning.
17. The organization evaluates and communicates internal control deficiencies in a timely manner to those parties responsible for taking corrective action, including senior management and the board of directors, as appropriate.

Progress Check

3. What is the definition of internal control?
4. What are the three main categories of internal control?

Control Environment	Risk Assessment	Control Activities	Information and Communication	Monitoring Activities
1. Demonstrates commitment to integrity and ethical values	6. Specifies suitable objectives	10. Selects and develops control activities	13. Uses relevant information	16. Conducts ongoing and/or separate evaluations
2. Exercises oversight responsibility	7. Identifies and analyzes risk	11. Selects and develops general controls over technology	14. Communicates internally	17. Evaluates and communicates deficiencies
3. Establishes structure, authority, and responsibility	8. Assesses fraud risk	12. Deploys thorough policies and procedures	15. Communicates externally	
4. Demonstrates commitment to competence	9. Identifies and analyzes significant change			
5. Enforces accountability				

FIGURE 11.2
COSO 2013 Control Components and Principles

COSO ERM Framework

All firms encounter uncertainty in daily operations. Uncertainty presents both risk and opportunity, with the potential to reduce or enhance the firm's value. For example, Paul Walsh, CEO of Diageo, indicated that

> [m]anaging risk can be one of the most overlooked areas within a business' structure. It is critical, particularly for global companies such as Diageo, for risk management processes and strategies to be imbedded with its operations. At Diageo, we have an exclusive-level Audit and Risk Committee which is tasked with overseeing and implementing effective risk management and control in the business. Whether it's navigating the global financial crisis or contingency planning for global health epidemics such as avian flu, these are significant issues which can impact your business performance and sustainability.[7]

The COSO enterprise risk management framework (2004) defines **enterprise risk management (ERM)** as "a process, affected by the entity's board of directors, management, and other personnel, applied in strategy setting and across the enterprise, designed to identify potential events that may affect the entity, and manage risk to be within the risk appetite, to provide reasonable assurance regarding the achievement of objectives."[8] Similarly, COSO indicates that

1. ERM identifies potential events that may affect the firm.
2. ERM manages risk to be within the firm's risk appetite.
3. ERM provides reasonable assurance regarding the achievement of the firm's objectives.

[7] M. S. Beasley, Bruce C. Branson, and Bonnie V. Hancock, *Enterprise Risk Oversight—A Global Analysis,* CIMA and AICPA Research Series, September 2010. Retrieved at http://www.aicpa.org/interestareas/businessindustryandgovernment/resources/erm/downloadabledocuments/enterprise%20risk%20v3.pdf, accessed February 2013.

[8] Richard M. Steinberg, Miles E. A. Everson, Frank J. Martens, and Lucy E. Nottingham, *Enterprise Risk Management—Integrated Framework: Executive Summary,* September 2004. Retrieved at http://www.coso.org/documents/coso_erm_executivesummary.pdf, accessed February 2013.

FIGURE 11.3
COSO ERM Model

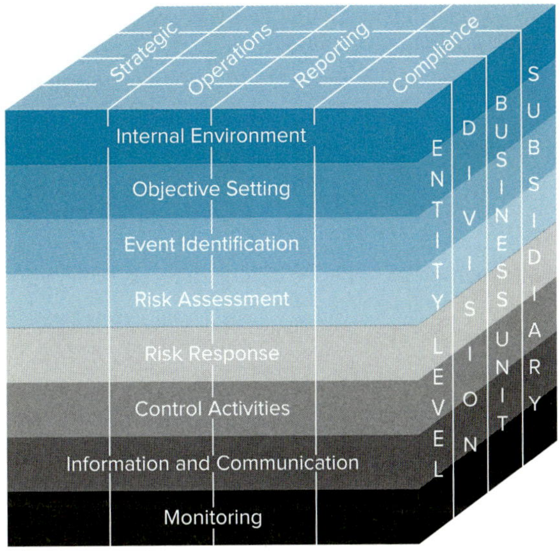

Note that internal control is an integral part of enterprise risk management. The COSO internal control framework is the basis for existing rules, regulations, and laws. It has been incorporated into this ERM framework. In addition to internal controls, COSO ERM expands the COSO internal control framework to provide a broader view on risk management to maximize firm value (see Figure 11.3). The relationship is depicted in a cube. The four objective categories—strategic, operations, reporting, and compliance—are represented by the vertical columns, the eight ERM components by horizontal rows, and the firm's units by the third dimension.

The ERM framework takes a risk-based, rather than a control-based, approach to achieving the firm's objectives in four categories:

1. *Strategic*—high-level goals, aligned with and supporting the firm's mission and vision.
2. *Operations*—effectiveness and efficiency of operations.
3. *Reporting*—reliability of internal and external reporting.
4. *Compliance*—compliance with applicable laws and regulations.

The COSO ERM consists of eight interrelated components. ERM is not strictly a serial process; it is a multidirectional, iterative process in which each component can influence the others. These components are

1. *Internal Environment*—provides the discipline and structure for all other components of enterprise risk management. It encompasses the tone of a firm, influences the risk consciousness of its people, and sets the basis for how risk is viewed and addressed by the firm. Internal environment factors include a firm's risk management philosophy and risk appetite,[9] integrity and ethical values, organizational structure, board of directors and the audit committee, human resource policies and practices, assignment of authority and responsibility, commitment to competence, and development of personnel.
2. *Objective Setting*—based on the firm's mission and vision, management sets specific objectives before identifying potential events[10] affecting their achievement.

[9] A company's risk appetite takes into consideration its risk-taking attitude and how this attitude relates to the expectations of its stakeholders.

[10] COSO defines an event as "an incident or occurrence emanating from internal or external sources that affects implementation of strategy or achievement of objectives. Events may have positive or negative impacts or both." Committee of Sponsoring Organizations of the Treadway Commission, *Enterprise Risk Management—Integrated Framework* (2004), p.16.

Management should have a process in place to set strategic, operations, reporting, and compliance objectives. Objectives are set at the strategic level, establishing a basis for operations, reporting, and compliance, and the chosen objectives shall support and align with the firm's mission and be consistent with its risk appetite.

3. *Event Identification*—internal and external events affecting achievement of a firm's objectives must be identified. After identifying all possible events, management must distinguish between risks and opportunities. Opportunities are channeled back to management's strategy or objective-setting processes. Identified risks should be forwarded to the next stage for assessment and be managed according to the firm's risk appetite.
4. *Risk Assessment*—the same as in the COSO internal control framework. This component will be discussed later in the chapter.
5. *Risk Response*—management selects risk responses and develops a set of actions to align risks with the entity's risk tolerances and risk appetite. The four options to respond to risks are reducing, sharing, avoiding, and accepting risks. This component will be discussed later in the chapter.
6. *Control Activities*—the same as in the COSO internal control framework. This component will be discussed later in the chapter.
7. *Information and Communication*—the same as in the COSO internal control framework.
8. *Monitoring*—the process of evaluating the quality of internal control design and operation and the effectiveness of the ERM model. The ERM components and internal control process should be monitored continuously and modified as necessary. Determining whether a firm's enterprise risk management is effective is a judgment resulting from an analysis of whether the eight components are present and functioning properly. Thus, the components are also criteria for effective enterprise risk management. Monitoring is accomplished through ongoing management activities and conducted by other parties outside the process. ERM deficiencies are reported to top management and the board.

Everyone in a firm is responsible for enterprise risk management. The chief executive officer (CEO) is ultimately responsible and should assume ownership. All others support the firm's risk management philosophy, comply with its risk appetite, and manage risks within their duties. The following comments from Jörg Pässler, group treasurer at Sappi Group Treasury, are about enterprise risk oversight:

> The financial crisis of 2008/09/10 has awakened the need to comprehensively review and manage risk, especially those that seem very remote. If Lehman Bros. can go under, if AIG can go to the brink due to material exposures to a specific market that was deemed "safe," and if government default is viewed as a possibility, then we need to re-assess our risks with a completely different mindset. The comment "that can never happen" will probably never be used in risk assessments again.[11]

Risk Assessment and Risk Response

Risk assessment is the process of identifying and analyzing risks systematically to determine the firm's risk response and control activities. It allows a firm to understand the extent to which potential events might affect corporate objectives. Given AS No. 5,

[11]Beasley, Branson, and Hancock, *Enterprise Risk Oversight—A Global Analysis.*

risk assessment is also a first step in developing an audit plan to meet the mandate of SOX section 404. According to COSO ERM, the risks of an identified event are analyzed on an inherent, control, and residual basis. **Inherent risk** is the risk related to the nature of the business activity itself. It exists already before management takes any actions to address it. For example, an inherent risk of a fast-food corporation is a high number of competitors in the industry. **Control risk** is the threat that errors or irregularities in the underlying transactions will not be prevented, detected, and corrected by the internal control system. For example, an accounts payable clerk is required to get approval if the total dollar amount on any specific purchase order (PO) is more than a predetermined limit (such as $1,000). The possibility that a clerk may create multiple purchase orders for one transaction to avoid the required authorization is a control risk. **Residual risk** is the product of inherent risk and control risk (i.e., Residual risk = Inherent risk × Control risk). In other words, it is the risk that remains after management's response to the risk or after the controls put in place to mitigate the risk. Firms should first assess inherent risk, develop a response or implement a control, and then assess residual risk.

According to COSO ERM, management assesses risks from two perspectives—likelihood and impact—and uses a combination of both qualitative and quantitative risk assessment methodologies. When sufficient and/or credible data for quantitative assessment are not available, management often uses qualitative assessment techniques that depend largely on the knowledge, experience, and judgment of the decision maker. Regarding risk response, COSO ERM indicates four options:[12]

1. Reduce risks by designing effective business processes and implementing internal controls.
2. Share risks by outsourcing business processes, buying insurance, or entering into hedging transactions.
3. Avoid risks by not engaging in the activities that would produce the risk.
4. Accept risk by relying on natural offsets of the risk within a portfolio, or allowing the likelihood and impact of the risk.

In determining risk response, management should evaluate options in relation to the firm's risk appetite, cost versus benefit of potential risk responses, and degree to which a response will reduce impact and/or likelihood. Selections of responses should be based on evaluation of the portfolio of risks and responses.

The process to assess risks is as follows: (1) identify risks to the firm; (2) estimate the likelihood of each risk occurring; (3) estimate the impact (i.e., potential loss in dollars) from each risk; (4) identify controls to mitigate the risk; (5) estimate the costs and benefits of implementing the controls; (6) perform a cost/benefit analysis for each risk and corresponding controls; and (7) based on the results of the cost/benefit analysis, determine whether to reduce the risk by implementing a control, or to accept, share, or avoid the risk. Figure 11.4 illustrates this process.[13]

Cost/benefit analysis is important in determining whether to implement an internal control. The benefits of an internal control should exceed its costs. Costs are easier to measure than benefits. Costs incurred from implementing controls are often for personnel and technology, such as the price of a video camera and the value of additional hours of employee work incurred. They often can be quantified. Conversely, control benefits

[12]Ibid., p. 55.

[13]Adapted from M. B. Romney and P. J. Steinbart, *Accounting Information Systems,* 12th ed. (New York: Prentice Hall, 2012), p. 194.

FIGURE 11.4
Risk Assessment and Response Approach to Selecting Control Activities

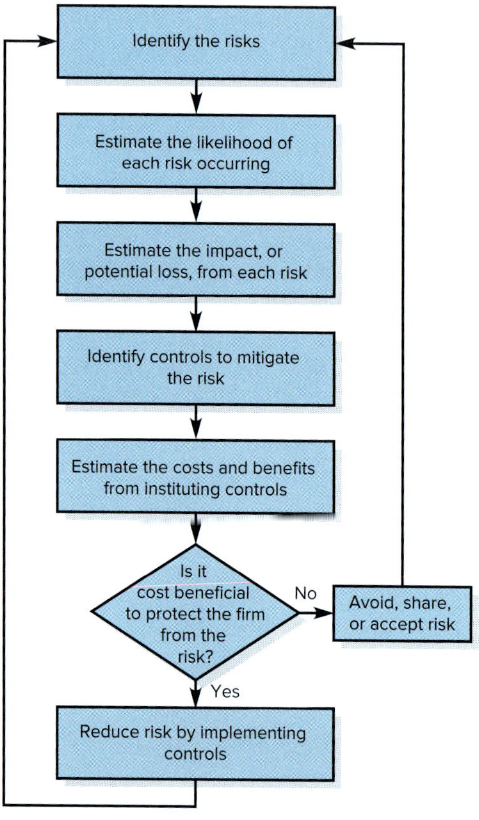

usually involve qualitative factors—such as increased productivity, improved customer satisfaction, better interaction with suppliers, or enhanced employee loyalty—and are difficult to measure. One way to measure the benefits of a control is using the estimated impact of a risk times the decreased likelihood if the control is implemented:

$$\text{Expected benefit of an internal control} = \text{Impact} \times \text{Decreased likelihood}$$

For example, due to input errors in making sales orders, Carlsbad Bottle Company may ship goods to the wrong customers. The company estimates that if this happens, the impact of this type of event will cost about \$15,000 due to lost revenue, rerouting expenses, and so forth. The likelihood of this risk is estimated as 10 percent. If Carlsbad Bottle Company implements a data validation step for input control, the likelihood of this risk could be only 0.5 percent. The cost to implement this control is \$200. Given this information, the expected benefit = \$15,000 × (10% – 0.5%) = \$1,425. The expected benefit of implementing the control (\$1,425) is larger than the cost (\$200), contributing a net benefit of \$1,225 (i.e., the difference between \$1,425 and \$200). Hence, Carlsbad Bottle Company should implement the control.

Progress Check

5. What are the four options of risk response?
6. What is the calculation for the expected benefit of an internal control?

Control Activities

Control activities are the policies and procedures that help ensure that necessary actions are taken to address risks to achieving the firm's objectives. There are two categories of control activities: physical controls and IT controls. IT controls are a subset of a firm's internal controls and are categorized as IT general and application controls.

Physical controls are mainly manual but could involve the physical use of computing technology. These types of control activities include:

- authorization to ensure transactions are valid,
- segregation of duties to prevent fraud and mistakes,[14]
- supervision to compensate imperfect segregation of duties,
- accounting documents and records to maintain audit trails,
- access control to ensure only authorized personnel have access to physical assets and information, and
- independent verification to double-check for errors and misrepresentations.

Business environments have continued to increase in complexity with ever-greater reliance on the information produced by IT systems and processes. **IT controls** involve processes that provide assurance for information and help to mitigate risks associated with the use of technology.[15] Firms need IT controls to protect information assets, remain competitive, and control costs in implementing IT projects.

IT general controls (ITGC) relate to enterprise-level controls over IT:

- IT control environment—sets the tone at the top and forms culture regarding IT service and management.
- Access controls—restrict access to IT facilities, programs, and data. Access controls in IT systems are related to proper authorization and segregation of duties.
- Change management controls—the processes of making sure changes to programs and applications are authorized and documented. Changes should be tested prior to implementation so they do not affect system availability and reliability.
- Project development and acquisition controls—related to the systems development life cycle (SDLC). The controls involve analysis, design, testing, implementation, and evaluation of IT projects. Through management review and approval and user involvement, a firm establishes a formal methodology for developing, acquiring, implementing, and maintaining information systems and related technologies.
- Computer operations controls—involve antivirus protection, backup and recovery procedures, minimizing system downtime, and patch management.

IT application controls are activities specific to a subsystem's or an application's input, processing, and output. Application controls include configured automated input controls, reports or data generated from the system and used in manual controls or accounting procedures, and automated calculations or data processing routines programmed into the application. The application controls are grouped into three categories to ensure information processing integrity: input, processing, and output controls. Most mistakes in an accounting information system occur while entering data. Control efforts are focused on input rather than processing and output activities.

Input controls ensure the authorization, entry, and verification of data entering the system. Authorization of data entry is accomplished by using an access control matrix. This matrix specifies which portion of the system users are allowed to access and what

[14]The general guideline for segregation of duties (SOD) is that transaction authorization, record keeping, and asset custody should be separated from each other.

[15] www.theiia.org.

privilege(s) users have (e.g., view, create, update, and delete). Common data entry controls include the following:

- Field checks ensure the characters in a field are of the proper type.
- Size checks ensure the data fit into the size of a field.
- Range checks test a numerical amount to ensure that it is within a predetermined range.
- Validity checks compare data entering the system with existing data in a reference file to ensure only valid data are entered.
- Completeness checks ensure all required data are entered for each record.
- Reasonableness checks ensure the logical relationship between two data values is correct. For example, an hourly rate of $120 may pass the range check on pay rates (between $8.5 and $150). However, it is not a valid input because the data value of the record for position is "intern"—that is, the pay rate of $120 per hour is not reasonable for an intern.
- Check digit verifications prevent the transpositions of numbers such as entering 5168 for a valid number of 5186. A check digit generated by an algorithm is appended to the original number to create a combination. A number and check digit combination that does not satisfy the algorithm reveals an error.
- Closed-loop verifications retrieve and display related information to ensure accurate data entry. For example, when a receiving clerk enters a part number, the inventory system displays the description of the item so that the receiving clerk can verify that the correct part number had been entered.

Do you know that your understanding on internal controls is a critical success factor being an auditor? SOX requires the external auditor of a public firm to express an opinion on the firm's effectiveness of internal controls.

Processing controls ensure that data and transactions are processed accurately. Important processing controls include the following:

- Prenumbered documents are generated internally to ensure that there is no duplicate or missing record. Prenumbered source documents are used in batch processing[16] to make sure authorized transactions are processed once and once only.
- Sequence checks ensure a batch of data is in sequence for batch processing.
- Batch totals ensure that a batch goes through the processing stages containing the same set of records, with no missing or duplicate record. Three commonly used batch totals are

    1. A record count indicates that the same total records are in the batch.
    2. A control total is the sum of a dollar amount field or a quantity field in the records. Sometimes, the sum of a field containing dollar values is called "financial total."
    3. A hash total is the sum of a numeric field, such as employee number, which normally would not be the subject of arithmetic operations.

- Cross-footing balance tests compare totals provided in multiple methods to ensure accurate processing.
- Concurrent update controls prevent two or more users updating the same record simultaneously.

Output controls provide output to authorized people and ensure the output is used properly. For example, only the required number of copies should be printed. Any additional copies should be disposed of following authorized procedures. Printed output should be delivered promptly to the designated party. Electronic, sensitive material should be encrypted for transmission and data storage.

[16]Batch processing, different from real-time processing, has a delay between the time a transaction occurs and the time it is processed. A batch consists of many records that have been accumulated for processing at the same time.

Progress Check

7. Explain the purposes of physical controls.
8. What are application controls?
9. Give a few examples of input controls.

LO 11-3
Describe the overall COBIT framework and its implications for IT governance.

COBIT Framework

Information technology governance is a subset of corporate governance and includes issues regarding IT management and security. IT governance is the responsibility of management and consists of the leadership, organizational structures, and processes that ensure that the firm's IT sustains and extends its business objectives.[17] To achieve effective IT governance, controls should be implemented within a defined control framework for all IT processes to provide a clear link among IT governance requirements, IT processes, and IT controls. COSO is one of the generally accepted internal control frameworks for enterprises. COBIT (control objectives for information and related technology) is a generally accepted framework for IT governance and management.

The most current version of the COBIT framework is COBIT 5. COBIT 5 expands on COBIT 4.1 by integrating other major frameworks and standards, such as ISACA's Val IT and Risk IT, the Information Technology Infrastructure Library (ITIL), and related standards from the International Organization for Standardization (ISO). COBIT 5 assists firms in creating value from IT by maintaining a balance between realizing benefits and optimizing resource use. COBIT 5 enables IT to be governed and managed in a holistic manner for the firm by taking in the end-to-end IT functional areas of responsibility and considering the IT-related interests of internal and external stakeholders. COBIT 5 defines "governance" as ensuring that firm objectives are achieved by evaluating stakeholder needs; setting direction through decision making; and monitoring performance, compliance, and progress. In most firms, the board of directors is responsible for governance. Per COBIT 5, "management" includes planning (i.e., aligning, planning, and organizing), building (i.e., building, acquiring, and implementing), running (i.e., delivering, servicing, and supporting), and monitoring (i.e., monitoring, evaluating, and assessing) activities in alignment with the direction necessary to achieve the firm's objectives.[18] In most firms, management is the responsibility of the executives under the leadership of the CEO. Figure 11.5 presents the principle of COBIT 5 in separating governance from management.

COBIT provides a supporting tool set that bridges the gap among IT control requirements, technical issues, and business risks. The COBIT framework[19]

- Provides a business focus to align business and IT objectives.
- Defines the scope and ownership of IT process and control.
- Is consistent with accepted IT good practices and standards.
- Provides a common language with a set of terms and definitions that are generally understandable by all stakeholders.
- Meets regulatory requirements by being consistent with generally accepted corporate governance standards (e.g., COSO) and IT controls expected by regulators and auditors.

[17]IT Governance Institute, *COBIT 4.1 Executive Summary* (2007), https://www.isaca.org/Knowledge-Center/cobit/Documents/COBIT4.pdf, retrieved May 5, 2016.

[18]ISACA, *COBIT 5: A Business Framework for the Governance and Management of Enterprise IT,* (Rolling Meadows, IL: ISACA, 2012), p. 31.

[19]*COBIT 4.1 Executive Summary,* p. 8.

FIGURE 11.5
COBIT 5 Governance and Management Key Areas

Source: *COBIT 5,* Figure 30, p. 73.

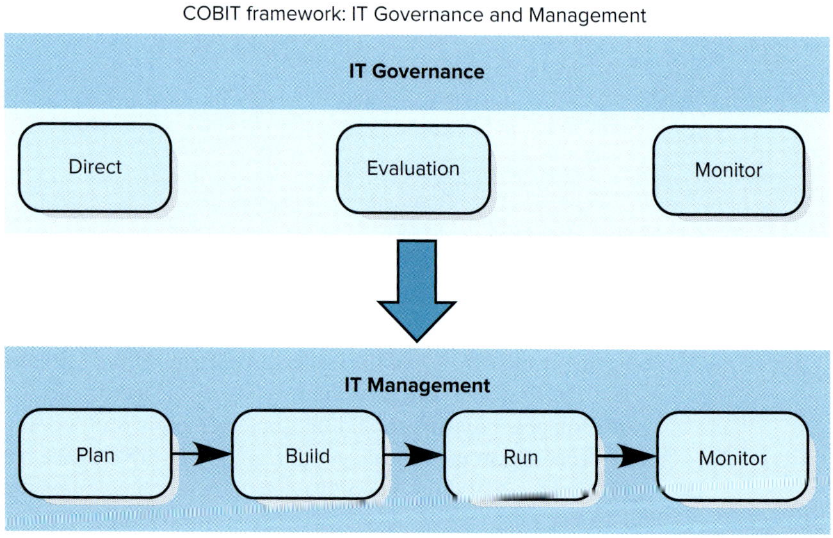

COBIT control objectives provide high-level requirements to be considered for effective control of IT processes. The overall control objectives are to increase business value or reduce risk; to establish and maintain policies, procedures, and organizational structures related to IT; and to provide reasonable assurance that business objectives will be achieved. According to COBIT, the key criteria of business requirements for information are as follows:

- Effectiveness—relevant and timely information.
- Efficiency—information produced economically.
- Confidentiality—protection of sensitive information.
- Integrity—valid, accurate, and complete information.
- Availability—information available when needed.
- Compliance—information produced in compliance with laws and regulations.
- Reliability—reliable information for daily decision making.

COBIT 5 supports IT governance and management by providing a framework to ensure that IT is aligned with the business, IT enables the business and maximizes benefits, IT resources are used responsibly, and IT risks are managed appropriately. In summary, COBIT 5 has five key principles for governance and management of enterprise IT: meeting stakeholder needs, covering the enterprise end-to-end, applying an integrated framework, enabling a holistic approach, and separating governance from management.

Progress Check

10. What are the IT resources and business requirements of information identified in the COBIT framework?

LO 11-4
Describe other governance frameworks related to information systems management and security.

Information Technology Infrastructure Library

The IT Infrastructure Library (ITIL) was developed by the UK government in the mid-1980s and has become a de facto standard in Europe for best practices in IT infrastructure management and service delivery. The ITIL has evolved as a result of firms' increasing dependence on IT. In recent years, there has been growing global recognition and adoption of ITIL.[20]

ITIL's value proposition centers on providing IT service with an understanding of the business objectives and priorities and the role that IT service has in achieving the objectives. Figure 11.6 illustrates the structure of ITIL. ITIL adopts a life-cycle approach to IT services and organizes IT service management into five high-level categories:[21]

1. *Service strategy (SS)*—the strategic planning of IT service management capabilities and the alignment of IT service and business strategies.
2. *Service design (SD)*—the design and development of IT services and service management processes.
3. *Service transition (ST)*—realizing the requirements of strategy and design and maintaining capabilities for the ongoing delivery of a service.
4. *Service operation (SO)*—the effective and efficient delivery and support of services, with a benchmarked approach for event, incident, request fulfillment, problem, and access management.
5. *Continual service improvement (CSI)*—ongoing improvement of the service and the measurement of process performance required for the service.

The ITIL life cycle starts with service strategy. In this phase, IT personnel should identify the customers or users of the IT services.[22] Then, IT personnel and business personnel (i.e., business strategists) should collaborate to develop IT service strategies that are aligned with and support the business strategy. The service design phase ensures that new and changed IT services are designed effectively to meet customer/user expectations in a cost-effective manner. Through the service transition phase of the life cycle, the IT service design is built, tested, and moved into production in order to ensure that the customer/user can achieve the desired value. This phase involves managing changes; controlling the assets and configuration items (e.g., hardware, software, etc.); service validation; testing; and transition planning to ensure that users, support personnel, and the production environment have been prepared for the changed IT assets to function properly. Once transitioned,

FIGURE 11.6
Overview of ITIL Version 3

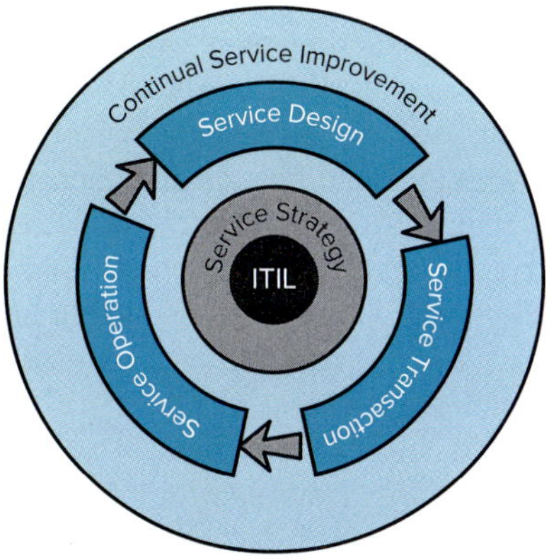

[20]C. Davis and M. Schiller, *IT Auditing Using Controls to Protect Information Assets,* 2nd ed. (New York: McGraw-Hill, 2011), p. 407.

[21]Maggie Kneller, *Executive Briefing: The Benefits of ITIL®* (London: The Stationery Office, 2010), http://addingvalue.se/wp-content/uploads/Executive_Briefing_Benefits_of_ITIL.pdf, retrieved on May 4, 2016.

[22]V. Arraj, *ITIL White Paper: The Basics,* May 2010. Retrieved from http://www.best-management-practice.com/gempdf/itil_the_basics.pdf, accessed February 2013.

the service operation phase delivers and supports the service on an ongoing basis. This process includes managing disruptions to service through rapid restoration of incidents, determining the root cause of problems and detecting trends associated with recurring issues, handling daily routine end user requests, and managing service access. The last phase of the IT service life cycle is continual service improvement. During this phase, a firm should offer a mechanism for IT to measure and improve the service levels, the technology, and the efficiency and effectiveness of IT processes.

FIGURE 11.7
Summary of the Major Standards in the ISO 27000 Series

ISO 27001 This standard replaces BS 7799–2, providing specification for information security management systems (ISMSs).	**ISO 27002** This standard was called ISO 17799, which was formerly known as BS 7799–1.
ISO 27003 A new standard offers guidance for implementing ISMSs.	**ISO 27004** This standard covers ISMS measurement and metrics; includes suggested ISO 27002–aligned controls.
ISO 27005 This standard provides the methodology for information security risk management.	**ISO 27006** This standard provides guidelines for accreditation of ISMS certification.

ISO 27000 Series

The ISO 27000 series of standards are designed to address information security issues. Despite the evolving names and scope, the ISO 27000 series, particularly ISO 27001 and ISO 27002, have become the most recognized and generally accepted sets of information security framework and guidelines. ISO 27001/27002, ISO 17799, and BS 7799 are, essentially, the same core set of standards dealing with various aspects of information security practices and information security management. The ISO 27001 and 27002 standards were published in October 2005, replacing and enhancing BS 7799-1, BS 7799-2, and ISO 17799 standards with harmonization of other generally accepted international standards. Figure 11.7 presents a summary of the major operational standards in the ISO 27000 series.

The main objective of the ISO 27000 series is to provide a model for establishing, implementing, operating, monitoring, maintaining, and improving an information security management system (ISMS). The ISMS standard emphasizes using a "process approach," which is defined as "the application of a system of processes within an organization, together with the identification and interactions of these processes, and their management to produce the desired outcome."[23] It also employs the plan-do-check-act model (PDCA), which is used to structure the process approach. In the "plan" stage, an ISMS is established. Then, the IT personnel maintain and improve the ISMS in the "act" stage. The established ISMS is reviewed and monitored in the "check" stage, followed by the "do" stage to implement and operate the ISMS.

ISO 27001 and 27002 address 11 major areas with regard to information security and outline 133 security controls within those 11 areas:

1. Security policy.
2. Organization of information security.
3. Asset management.
4. Human resources security.

[23]The ISO 27000 Directory, www.27000.org/index.htm.

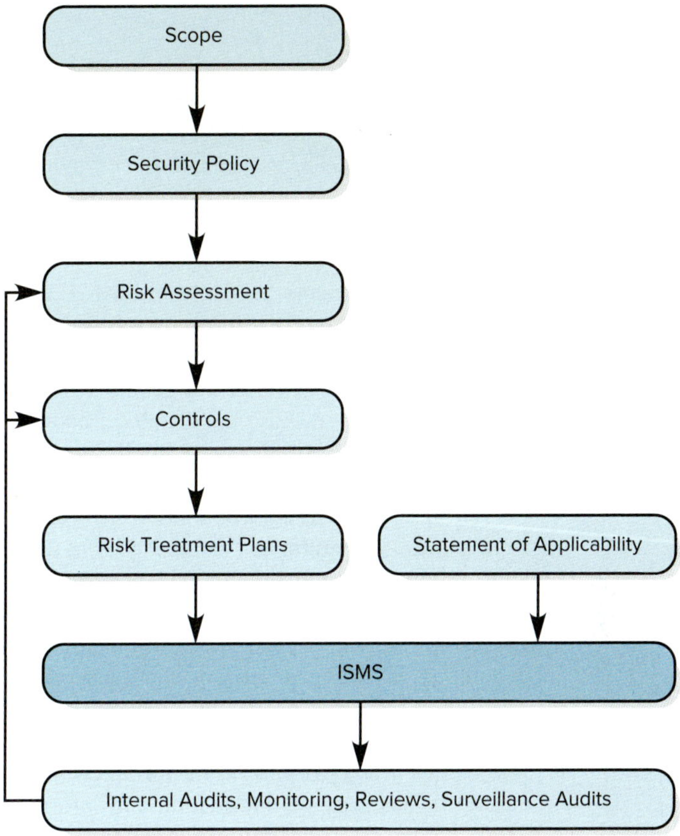

FIGURE 11.8 Steps to Establishing an ISMS Following ISO 27001/27002

Source: http://iso-27000-series.blogspot.com/2008_06_01_archive.html

5. Physical and environmental security.
6. Communications and operations management.
7. Access control.
8. Information systems acquisition, development, and maintenance.
9. Information security incident management.
10. Business continuity management.
11. Compliance.

Figure 11.8 presents the basic steps required to set up an information security management system in accordance with ISO 27001/27002.

COMPARING CONTROL/GOVERNANCE FRAMEWORKS

As we know, COSO 2013 provides a general internal control framework that can be applied to all firms on various systems. COBIT 5 is a comprehensive framework for IT governance and management and provides management and auditors with control objectives, risk and value drivers, best practices regarding information security, and a performance measurement matrix to maximize the benefits from IT. ITIL is a framework focusing on IT infrastructure and IT service management. The ISO 27000 series is a framework for information security management. One of the biggest advantages in adopting COBIT 5 is its general control/security framework for information technology. Because COBIT 5 includes other widely accepted standards, frameworks, and guidance for building effective IT governance and practices, a firm can implement a wide range of desirable IT processes and controls, as well as achieve its business objectives regarding IT security and service management, by using it.

Summary

- Given the mandate of the Sarbanes-Oxley Act of 2002, management is responsible for designing internal controls and evaluating the effectiveness of the controls based on a control framework. COSO is the most commonly accepted internal control framework. COBIT is a generally accepted framework for IT governance and management. Most American firms use COBIT for IT governance and to evaluate IT controls for SOX section 404 compliance.
- There are three general categories of internal controls. Preventive controls deter problems before they arise. Detective controls find out problems when they arise. Corrective controls fix problems that have been identified. In a computerized environment, internal controls can be categorized as general controls and application controls.
- General controls are those applicable to enterprisewide issues. Application controls are specific to a subsystem or an application including input, processing, and output controls.
- COSO publishes two control frameworks: COSO internal control integrated framework and COSO enterprise risk management (ERM) integrated framework. The COSO internal control framework is a widely accepted authority on internal control, providing a foundation for evaluating, reporting, and improving internal control. The COSO ERM framework expanded the COSO internal control framework to provide guidance in defining, assessing, managing, and transferring risk in order to maximize firm value. The COSO ERM focuses on the strategic alignment of the firm's mission with its risk appetite.
- The COBIT framework is a control framework for IT governance and management to ensure the integrity of information and information systems. Two additional governance frameworks related to information technology are the ITIL and the ISO 27000 series. ITIL provides best practices in IT infrastructure management and IT service delivery. The main objective of the ISO 27000 series is to provide a model for establishing, implementing, operating, monitoring, maintaining, and improving an information security system.

Key Words

application controls (*274*) Specific to a subsystem or an application to ensure the validity, completeness, and accuracy of the transactions.

code of ethics (*272*) A formal expectation on what is considered to be ethical within an organization to promote ethical behavior.

Committee of Sponsoring Organizations (COSO) (*274*) Composed of several organizations (AAA, AICPA, FEI, IIA, and IMA); studies the causal factors that lead to fraudulent financial reporting and develops recommendations for public companies, independent auditors, the SEC and other regulators, and educational institutions to improve the quality of financial reporting through internal controls and corporate governance.

control objectives for information and related technology (COBIT) (*275*) An internationally accepted set of best IT security and control practices for IT management released by the IT Governance Institute (ITGI).

control risk (*281*) The threat that errors or irregularities in the underlying transactions will not be prevented, detected, and corrected by the internal control system.

corporate governance (*273*) A set of processes and policies in managing an organization with sound ethics to safeguard the interests of its stakeholders.

corrective controls (*274*) Fix problems that have been identified, such as using backup files to recover corrupted data.

cost/benefit analysis (*281*) Important in determining whether to implement an internal control.

detective controls (*274*) Find problems when they arise.

enterprise risk management (ERM) (*278*) A process, affected by the entity's board of directors, management, and other personnel, applied in strategy setting and across the enterprise, designed to identify potential events that may affect the entity, and manage risk to be within the risk appetite, to provide reasonable assurance regarding the achievement of objectives.

general controls (*274*) Pertain to enterprisewide issues such as controls over accessing the network, developing and maintaining applications, and documenting changes of programs.

Information Technology Infrastructure Library (ITIL) (*275*) A set of concepts and practices for IT service management.

inherent risk (*281*) The risk related to the nature of the business activity itself.

input controls (*283*) Ensure the authorization, entry, and verification of data entering the system.

International Organization for Standardization (ISO) 27000 series (*275*) This series contains a range of individual standards and documents specifically reserved by ISO for information security.

IT application controls (*283*) Activities specific to a subsystem's or an application's input, processing, and output.

IT controls (*283*) Involve processes that provide assurance for information and help to mitigate risks associated with the use of technology.

IT general controls (ITGC) (*283*) Enterprise-level controls over IT.

output controls (*284*) Provide output to authorized people and ensure the output is used properly.

physical controls (*283*) Mainly manual but could involve the physical use of computing technology.

preventive controls (*274*) Deter problems before they arise.

processing controls (*284*) Ensure that data and transactions are processed accurately.

Public Company Accounting Oversight Board (PCAOB) (*272*) Established by SOX to provide independent oversight of public accounting firms.

residual risk (*281*) The product of inherent risk and control risk (i.e., Residual risk = Inherent risk × Control risk).

risk assessment (*280*) The process of identifying and analyzing risks systematically to determine the firm's risk response and control activities.

Sarbanes-Oxley Act of 2002 (SOX) (*272*) A response to business scandals such as Enron, WorldCom, and Tyco International; requires public companies registered with the SEC and their auditors to annually assess and report on the design and effectiveness of internal control over financial reporting.

Appendix

ERP Architecture and Control Issues

Enterprise resource planning (ERP) systems have been steadily growing in popularity since the 1980s. Many firms have come to see integrated systems as an essential competitive edge; the ability to combine all of an enterprise's operations into a single system allows for greater visibility and control over its business concerns.

ERP architecture is generally planned in a way that will meet the needs of the organization from an operational standpoint. The company will need to determine what business processes it needs to put into an ERP system and then determine the proper modules to purchase to begin that process. Most ERP systems will utilize a financial accounting module to record accounting transactions and contain the enterprise's general ledger. Some companies will also need specialized modules (like manufacturing) to track all of the materials and processes needed to produce finished goods.

Modules within an ERP system generally tie together to promote easy integration. For instance, an intercompany sale should easily allow for purchasing and selling legal entities to transact a sale within the system. In a trade sale, costs associated with creating a product in the manufacturing module should easily flow into the cost of sales in the finance module. This easy integration and transferability of data is one of the major advantages granted by an ERP system. However, in some cases, companies still prefer to combine multiple systems to accomplish their business goals. One popular example of this is using a separate customer relationship management system to take customer orders and manage customer-facing interactions. In this case, data must flow from the CRM tool into the ERP system to create an order and then process that order to invoicing and cash collections. This added layer of systems produces more risk because it creates another location—the middleware that manages the flow of data between the systems, where controls must be put in place to protect the confidentiality and integrity of data.

The physical architecture of an ERP system must also be assessed to create a control structure to manage risks. Risk areas include

1. Where will the servers be hosted?
2. Will there be a client/server or a web-based architecture?
3. How will data flow between the servers and the users, and are those lines of communication controlled by the company and secure?
4. Does the company need to utilize encryption or other controls to protect confidential data?
5. How will the company recover from a critical hardware failure or disaster?
6. How will the company maintain services during a primary systems outage?

Businesses must ensure that their systems comply with relevant laws and regulations and contain safeguards to ensure the reliability of their financial reporting. One of the most important controls over an ERP is the assurance of proper change management. Proper change management mandates the creation of at least three separate ERP system instances, referred to as "environments." The lowest environment with the least number of controls is the development environment. This is the only environment where code changes and configurations can be executed. From this environment, changes are migrated to the quality assurance environment for testing. Full testing should be executed in this environment before any changes can be moved to the final environment: production. Change management is designed to prevent disruptions to service or unauthorized code changes that could be used to commit fraud. All steps in the change management process should be monitored and well documented to ensure that all changes are authorized.

ERP systems should be planned with consideration of the control structure of the business for which they are designed. Control activities like segregation of duties and access controls should be utilized in the system security plan to limit the opportunities for fraud in a company's transactions. The company should use the control frameworks that it has adopted to govern its control structure to plan specific control activities. Controls should be considered for all steps of the system's management process:

1. *Plan:* Controls should first be considered in the planning stages of any ERP implementation. Business processes and risks should be assessed and controls should be designed to mitigate the risks that are discovered.
2. *Build:* Controls need to be implemented properly in the build phase of the ERP's life cycle. This includes both initial implementation and any changes that are made through the change management process.

3. *Run:* Once implemented, controls will help to reduce risks to the business while the ERP system is operational. During this time, support needs to be provided to ensure that the control structure continues to function. An example of this activity is that new users must be properly trained and set up within the confines of the control structure.
4. *Monitor:* Once a company has set up an ERP system and integrated the enterprise's control structure, it should continue to monitor the implementation to ensure that the controls are effective. This includes activities such as monitoring for users with segregation of duties conflicts and providing internal audits of risk areas within the enterprise.

An ERP system's architecture and control structure are linked out of necessity. As the architecture of the ERP changes due to the addition of modules, middleware, or additional environments, control risk must be assessed and addressed to ensure the integrity of the system.

Answers to Progress Checks

1. Ethics plays a critical role when people make choices and decisions. To promote ethical behavior, firms often choose to establish a formal expectation of what is considered to be ethical within the group. Ethical behavior prompted by a code of ethics can be considered a form of internal control, so a code of ethics is part of corporate governance.
2. The PCAOB was established by Congress to oversee the audits of public companies in order to protect investors and the public interest by promoting informative, accurate, and independent audit reports. In addition, auditors of U.S. public companies are subject to external and independent oversight by PCAOB. It also issues audit standards.
3. According to a COSO report, an internal control is "a process, affected by an entity's board of directors, management and other personnel. This process is designed to provide reasonable assurance regarding the achievement of objectives in effectiveness and efficiency of operations, reliability of financial reporting, and compliance with applicable laws and regulations."
4. Prevention, detection, and correction.
5. Reduce, share, avoid, and accept risks.
6. Expected benefit of an internal control = Impact (potential loss) × Decreased likelihood (due to control implementation).
7.
   a. Authorization to ensure transactions are valid.
   b. Segregation of duties to prevent fraud and mistakes.
   c. Supervision to compensate for imperfect segregation of duties.
   d. Accounting documents and records to maintain audit trails.
   e. Access control to ensure only authorized personnel have access to assets and information.
   f. Independent verification to double-check for errors and misrepresentations.
8. Application controls are input, processing, and output controls specific to a subsystem or application.
9. Field check, range check, closed-loop verification, reasonableness check, and so on.
10. IT resources are applications, information, infrastructures, and people. The business requirements for information are effectiveness, efficiency, confidentiality, integrity, availability, compliance, and reliability.

connect

Multiple Choice Questions

1. Based on SOX, which of the following sections is about internal controls? **LO 11-1**
   a. 302
   b. 401
   c. 404
   d. 906
2. SOX requires companies to use COSO or COSO ERM as the framework in evaluating internal controls. **LO 11-1**
   a. True
   b. False
3. Controls that are designed to prevent, detect, or correct errors in transactions as they are processed through a specific subsystem are referred to as: **LO 11-1**
   a. general controls.
   b. application controls.
   c. physical controls.
   d. Two of the above are correct.
   e. None of the above are correct.
4. Which of the following is *not* a COSO ERM control objective? **LO 11-2**
   a. Risk assessment
   b. Compliance
   c. Reporting
   d. Operations
   e. Strategic
5. Prenumbering of source documents helps to verify that: **LO 11-2**
   a. multiple types of source documents have a unique identifier.
   b. all transactions have been recorded because the numerical sequence serves as a control.
   c. no inventory has been misplaced.
   d. documents have been used in order.
6. A field check is a(n): **LO 11-2**
   a. preventive control.
   b. detective control.
   c. corrective control.
   d. general control.
   e. output control.
7. Which is not an example of a batch total? **LO 11-2**
   a. Record count
   b. Financial total
   c. Hash total
   d. Exception total
8. Backup is a preventive control. **LO 11-2**
   a. True
   b. False

9. The computer sums the first four digits of a customer number to calculate the value of the fifth digit and then compares that calculation to the number typed during data entry. This is an example of a: **LO 11-2**
   a. field check.
   b. parity check.
   c. check digit verification.
   d. batch total.
10. Which of the following statements is correct? **LO 11-3, LO 11-4**
   a. SOX requires all public companies to use the COSO ERM framework to meet the requirements of section 404.
   b. Regarding IT control and governance, the COBIT framework is most commonly adopted by companies in the United States.
   c. ITIL is the best internal control framework for the high-tech industry.
   d. ISO 27000 series are best practices for IT service management.
11. Based on SOX, which of the following sections is about corporate responsibility for financial reports? **LO 11-1**
   a. 101
   b. 201
   c. 302
   d. 404
12. Based on COSO 2013, which of the following statements is not correct? **LO 11-2**
   a. Employees at any level of an organization play a role in internal control.
   b. Internal controls can provide reasonable assurance only.
   c. Internal control is a process consisting of ongoing tasks and activities.
   d. The responsibility of monitoring the effectiveness of internal controls belongs to the internal audit group.
13. Which of the following is not one of the five essential components in the COSO 2013 framework? **LO 11-2**
   a. Control environment
   b. Control assessment
   c. Control activities
   d. Monitoring activities
14. Access control to ensure only authorized personnel have access to a firm's network is a: **LO 11-2**
   a. general control.
   b. process control.
   c. output control.
   d. input control.
15. The ISO 27000 series are a framework for: **LO 11-4**
   a. IT governance.
   b. IT general controls.
   c. data management.
   d. information security management.

Discussion Questions

1. How has the Sarbanes-Oxley Act affected the audit profession and corporate governance of public firms? **LO 11-1**
2. What are the objectives and components of the COSO ERM framework? **LO 11-2**

3. COSO developed two frameworks: the COSO 2013 internal control framework and the COSO ERM framework. Why did COSO develop the ERM framework? What are the differences between the two frameworks? **LO 11-2**
4. Use a few sentences to describe IT general controls and application controls. Give a few examples of these two types of controls. **LO 11-2**
5. Why would a manager be inclined to use the COBIT framework as a guide for IT governance and management? **LO 11-3**
6. The ISO 27000 series serve different purposes than ITIL. Which one could be more important to accounting professionals and why? **LO 11-4**
7. Segregation of duties is an important internal control. What functions must be separated? If ideal segregation of duties is not economically feasible, what are some compensating controls that would help reduce the risk of fraud or error? **LO 11-2**
8. Use a flowchart to explain the risk assessment process. **LO 11-2**
9. There are three types of controls: preventive, detective, and corrective. List some examples of each type. Explain which type of control auditors would focus on while evaluating a company's effectiveness of controls and why. **LO 11-1**
10. Describe the control activities in the COSO framework. Why are these control activities important for most firms? **LO 11-2**

Problems

1. The global economic crisis of 2008–2010 has stimulated many boards of directors and executives to reevaluate how they assess and manage risks. Use a flowchart to describe the process of risk assessment. **LO 11-2**
2. A newly hired internal auditor discovered that immaterial thefts by employees are pervasive in the company; employees take books from the company's library, tools from the company's laboratories, supplies, products, and so forth. By interviewing some of the employees, the internal auditor discovered that most employees thought their behavior was not detrimental to the company because none of the items had significant value. What should the company do to prevent this type of employee behavior? **LO 11-2**
3. The sales department of a company received several claims from its customers that their payments were not credited to their accounts. Investigation uncovered that the accounts receivable clerk has been stealing some customer payments. What are some of the internal control procedures that could prevent and detect the problem? **LO 11-2**

connect

4. The information system of Carlsbad Bottle Inc. is deemed to be 90 percent reliable. A major threat in the procurement process has been discovered, with an exposure of $300,000. Two control procedures are identified to mitigate the threat. Implementation of control A would cost $18,000 and reduce the risk to 4 percent. Implementation of control B would cost $10,000 and reduce the risk to 6 percent. Implementation of both controls would cost $26,000 and reduce the risk to 2.5 percent. Given the information presented, and considering an economic analysis of costs and benefits only, which control procedure(s) should Carlsbad Bottle choose to implement? **LO 11-2**
5. Which internal control(s) would you recommend to prevent the following situations from occurring? **LO 11-2**
   a. Authorization of a credit memo for a customer's account (on receivables) when the goods were never actually returned.
   b. Theft of funds by the cashier, who cashed several checks and did not record their receipt.
   c. Inventory was stolen by receiving dock personnel. The receiving clerk claimed the inventory was sent to the warehouse, but the warehouse clerk did not record properly.
   d. Writing off a customer's accounts receivable balances as uncollectible in order to conceal the theft of subsequent cash collections.
   e. Billing customers for the quantity ordered when the quantity shipped was actually less due to back-ordering of some items.

connect 6. Which types of input controls would best mitigate the following threats? LO 11-2

a. Posting the amount of a sale to a customer account that does not exist.
b. A customer entering too many characters into the five-digit zip code while making an online purchase, causing the server to crash.
c. An intern's pay rate was entered as $150 per hour, not $15 per hour.
d. Approving a customer order without the customer's address so the order was not shipped on time.
e. Entering the contract number of a critical contract as 13688 instead of 16388, which is a serious mistake for the company.

connect 7. The COSO 2013 internal control framework codifies 17 relevant principles associated with the five components of internal control. Match the following principles with the five components. LO 11-2

COSO Principles	COSO Components
a. Management establishes, with board oversight, structures, reporting lines, and appropriate authorities and responsibilities in the pursuit of objectives.	i. Control environment
b. The organization deploys control activities through policies that establish what is expected and procedures that put policies into place.	ii. Risk assessment
c. The organization considers the potential for fraud in assessing risks to the achievement of objectives.	iii. Control activities
d. The organization holds individuals accountable for their internal control responsibilities in the pursuit of objectives.	iv. Information and communication
e. The organization obtains or generates and uses relevant, quality information to support the functioning of internal control.	v. Monitoring activities
f. The organization evaluates and communicates internal control deficiencies in a timely manner to those parties responsible for taking corrective action, including senior management and the board of directors, as appropriate.	

connect 8. Identify each of the following internal controls as a primarily preventive, detective, or corrective control. LO 11-1

a. Limit access to petty cash funds.
b. Reconcile the petty cash fund before replenishing it.
c. Require two signatures on checks above a specified limit.
d. Enable hidden flags or audit trails on accounting software.
e. Examine credit card statements and corresponding receipts each month, independently, to determine whether charges are appropriate.
f. Keep checks in a locked box or drawer and restrict the number of employees who have access to the key.
g. Back up accounting records daily.

connect 9. Match the following internal controls with the categories of control activities. **LO 11-2**

Internal Controls	Control Activities
a. Separate handling cash (receipt and deposit) functions from record-keeping functions (recording transactions in the accounts receivable subsidiary ledger).	i. Authorization
b. Require purchases, payroll, and cash disbursements to be authorized by a designated person.	ii. Segregation of duties
c. Require accounting department employees to take vacations.	iii. Supervision
d. Separate purchasing functions from payables functions.	iv. Accounting documents and records
e. Ensure that the same person isn't authorized to write and sign a check.	v. Access control
f. When opening mail, endorse or stamp checks "For Deposit Only".	vi. Independent verification
g. Periodically reconcile the incoming check log against deposits.	
h. Require supervisors to approve employees' time sheets before payroll is prepared.	
i. List customer checks on a log before turning them over to the person responsible for depositing receipts.	

connect 10. Match the following control frameworks with their main purposes. **LO 11-3, LO 11-4**

Purposes	Control Frameworks
a. Expand internal controls to provide a broader view on risk management to maximize firm value.	i. COSO 2013
b. Provide management an information technology (IT) governance model that helps in delivering value from IT and understanding and managing the risks associated with IT.	ii. COSO ERM
c. Manage IT infrastructure and service delivery.	iii. COBIT
d. Provide a framework and guidelines for information security.	iv. ITIL
e. Improve quality of financial reporting through internal controls and corporate governance.	v. ISO 27000 series

Chapter **Twelve**

Information Security and Computer Fraud

A look at this chapter

Given today's business environment, computers are at the center of most firms' accounting information systems. Awareness of computer fraud is critical to accountants and auditors. In this chapter, we provide examples of computer fraud and illustrate how AIS can be misused in order to achieve personal gains. We also discuss common vulnerabilities and how to manage and assess such vulnerabilities. These topics are related to information security, which has been a critical technology issue for business professionals in the accounting field.

A look back

In Chapter 11, we discussed internal controls and important factors in corporate governance that are critical to an organization's efficiency and effectiveness in operations, reliability in financial reporting, and compliance with applicable laws and regulations. We also provided detailed information on important control frameworks such as COSO and COBIT.

A look ahead

Given the complicated information systems and the tremendous amount of data to be analyzed and reported, accountants must evaluate the design and monitor the integrity of an accounting information system. In Chapter 13, we examine the risks in accounting information systems and how auditors validate that systems are well designed with embedded internal controls and that the systems process data with integrity.

© Tom Lasseter/MCT via Getty Images

Today, before going to work, you drop by **Starbucks** to grab a cup of coffee. Even early in the morning, Starbucks already has a long line of customers waiting, looking at the menu, and deciding what they want to order. Perhaps they visit Starbucks regularly and have a specific drink they want to order. For example, you already have your drink in mind: iced caramel macchiato, nonfat milk, one extra shot of expresso, light ice, light caramel to start off the day.

While you are waiting, millions of Starbucks customers all over the world are also being served, many with drinks as unique as the one that you just ordered. Throughout the course of an entire day, all the individual Starbucks stores have made countless transactions, which all must be recorded accurately to provide reliable information for decision making to keep Starbucks competitive. The integrity of the systems and the quality of information are critical to companies such as Starbucks in supporting daily operations, as well as providing consolidated data for year-end financial reporting.

Chapter Outline

Learning Objectives

After reading this chapter, you should be able to:

12-1 Describe the risks related to information security and systems integrity.

12-2 Understand the concepts of encryption and authentication.

12-3 Describe computer fraud and misuse of AIS and corresponding risk-mitigation techniques.

12-4 Define vulnerabilities, and explain how to manage and assess vulnerabilities.

12-5 Explain issues in system availability, disaster recovery, and business continuity.

INTRODUCTION

Rapid development in digital technologies has been a driving factor of consumer demand, employee training, and efficient use of firms' resources. As a result of the maturing digital economy, firms across different industries will continue to be reshaped through the application of information technology. In this chapter, we present a discussion of one of the most critical impacts of technology on firms' operations—information security. We first introduce concepts and risks regarding information security and then provide examples of computer fraud and how AIS can be misused in achieving personal gains. We then explain common vulnerabilities and how to manage and assess those vulnerabilities. Frameworks for vulnerability assessment and management, as well as for business continuity management, are also presented in this chapter.

LO 12-1
Describe the risks related to information security and systems integrity.

INFORMATION SECURITY AND SYSTEMS INTEGRITY

The AICPA conducts a survey each year to identify the top 10 technology issues for certified public accountants (CPAs). The purpose of the survey is to indicate the CPAs' unique perspectives on how much each technology will affect financial management and the fulfillment of responsibilities such as safeguarding assets, overseeing business performance, and compliance with laws and regulations. Since 2003, information security management has been ranked as the top technology issue for CPAs. According to AICPA, information security management is "an integrated, systematic approach that coordinates people, policies, standards, processes, and controls used to safeguard critical systems and information from internal and external security threats."[1]

Information security is a critical factor in maintaining system integrity. If users can perform the intended functions of a system without being degraded or impaired by unauthorized manipulation, the system has maintained its integrity. Good information security ensures that systems and their contents remain constant for integrity. In general, the goal of information security management is to protect the confidentiality, integrity, and availability (CIA) of a firm's information.

- Confidentiality—information is not accessible to unauthorized individuals or processes.
- Integrity—information is accurate and complete.
- Availability—information and systems are accessible on demand.

Information Security Risks and Attacks

Given the popularity of the Internet and mobile devices and the complexity of computer technologies, important business information and IT assets are exposed to risks and attacks from internal (such as disgruntled employees) and external parties (such as hackers, foreigners, competitors, etc.). Some of the more common information security risks and attacks include:[2]

- Virus—a self-replicating program that runs and spreads by modifying other programs or files.
- Worm—a self-replicating, self-propagating, self-contained program that uses networking mechanisms to spread itself.

[1] http://infotech.aicpa.org/Resources/Top+Technology+Initiatives/2009+Top+Technology+Initiatives+and+Honorable+Mentions.htm.

[2] Definitions of information security risks and attacks are quoted from National Institute of Standards and Technology (NIST), *Glossary of Key Information Security Terms* (Washington, DC: U.S. Department of Commerce, 2006).

Do you know that mobile devices such as Android phones, tablets, and iPhones/iPads are often the targets for hackers to attack? In addition, mobile apps have emerged as a new attack vector for various security issues.

- Trojan horse—a non-self-replicating program that seems to have a useful purpose in appearance, but in reality has a different, malicious purpose.
- Spam—sending unsolicited bulk information.
- Botnet (bot)—a collection of software robots that overruns computers to act automatically in response to the bot-herder's control inputs through the Internet.
- Denial-of-service (DoS)—the prevention of authorized access to resources (such as servers) or the delaying of time-critical operations.
- Spyware—software that is secretly installed into an information system to gather information on individuals or organizations without their knowledge; a type of malicious code.
- Spoofing—sending a network packet that appears to come from a source other than its actual source.
- Social engineering—manipulating someone to take certain action that may not be in that person's best interest, such as revealing confidential information or granting access to physical assets, networks, or information.

Progress Check

1. What are the general goals of information security?
2. Give an example of social engineering.

LO 12-2
Understand the concepts of encryption and authentication.

Encryption and Authentication

Encryption is a preventive control providing confidentiality and privacy for data transmission and storage. It refers to algorithmic schemes that encode *plaintext* into nonreadable form or *cyphertext.* The receiver of the encrypted text uses a "key" to decrypt the message, returning it to its original plaintext form. The key is the trigger mechanism to the cryptographic algorithm. The main factors of encryption are key length, encryption algorithm, and key management. Longer key length provides for stronger encryption. In general, a key length of 56 bits or less is insufficient for sensitive data; 128-bit and longer key lengths are more than sufficient for secure data transmission. In addition, using a strong encryption algorithm and establishing a strong policy on key management are essential for information security.

In general, cryptographic algorithms are grouped into two categories: symmetric-key and asymmetric-key encryption methods. Figure 12.1 describes the process of using symmetric-key encryption to encrypt and decrypt data/documents in maintaining

FIGURE 12.1
Symmetric-Key Encryption Process

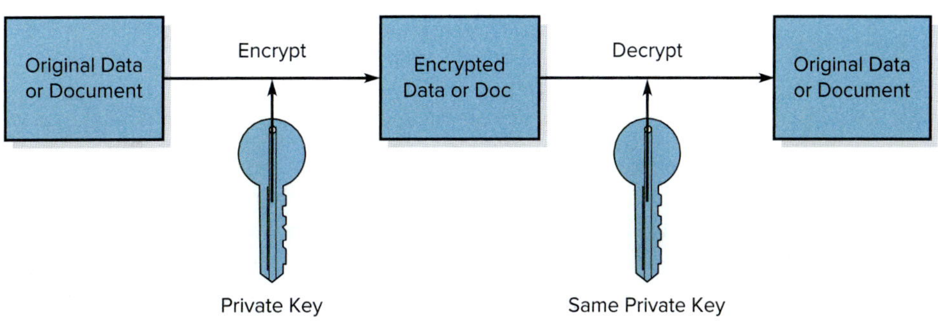

confidentiality. **Symmetric-key encryption** is fast and suitable for encrypting large data sets or messages. However, key distribution and key management are problematic because both the sender and the receiver use the same key to encrypt and decrypt messages. If a firm has many employees and trading partners at different geographical locations, it is very difficult to always distribute keys in a secured way. In addition, managing one key for each pair of users, which results in exponential growth of the number of keys for each additional party, is not cost-effective given the large number of users among the firms.

Conversely, **asymmetric-key encryption** is slow, and is not appropriate for encrypting large data sets. However, because each user has a pair of two keys—the **public key** and the **private key**—asymmetric-key encryption solves problems in key distribution and key management. The two keys are created as one pair and you use one to encrypt and the other to decrypt the data or document. The public keys are widely distributed and available to authorized users. The private key is kept secret and known only to the owner of the key. Hence, to transmit confidential information, the sender uses the receiver's public key to encrypt the message; the receiver uses his or her own private key for decryption upon receiving the message. Refer to Figure 12.2 regarding the process of how to use the asymmetric-key method to transmit data/documents in maintaining confidentiality. Two common names for asymmetric-key encryption are *public-key encryption* and *two-key encryption.*

FIGURE 12.2
Asymmetric-Key Encryption Process

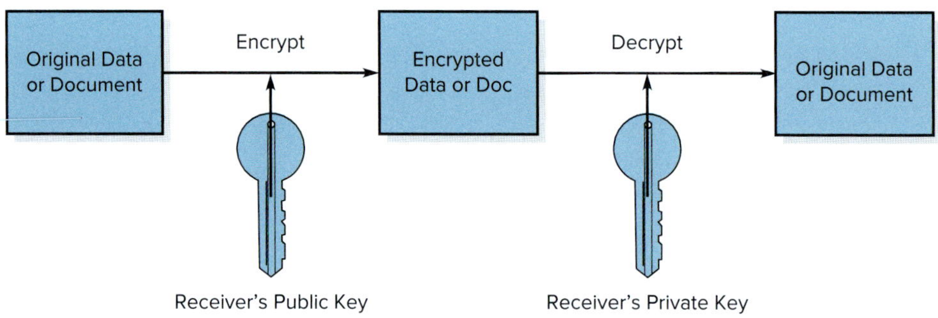

Authentication is a process that establishes the origin of information or determines the identity of a user, process, or device. It is critical in e-business because it can prevent repudiation while conducting transactions online. Using asymmetric-key encryption, authentication can be achieved for electronic transactions. For example, in Figure 12.3, to authenticate the receiver (B), the sender (A) e-mails a challenge message to B. B will use his or her private key to encrypt the challenge message and send it to A. If A is able to use B's public key to decrypt and get the plaintext of the challenge message, A has authenticated B successfully. Please notice that only the pair of one user's two keys is used for encryption and decryption. In this example, B used his or her private key to encrypt the message, and A used B's public key to decrypt the message. Keys from different users cannot be mismatched for encryption and decryption purposes. Please note that this process would need to be repeated in reverse to authenticate both parties involved in the transaction.

To conduct e-business, most firms use a hybrid combination of both methods:

1. Both the sender and receiver use the asymmetric-key encryption method to authenticate each other.
2. Either the sender (or the receiver) generates a symmetric key (called a **session key** because it is valid for a certain timeframe only) to be used by both parties.

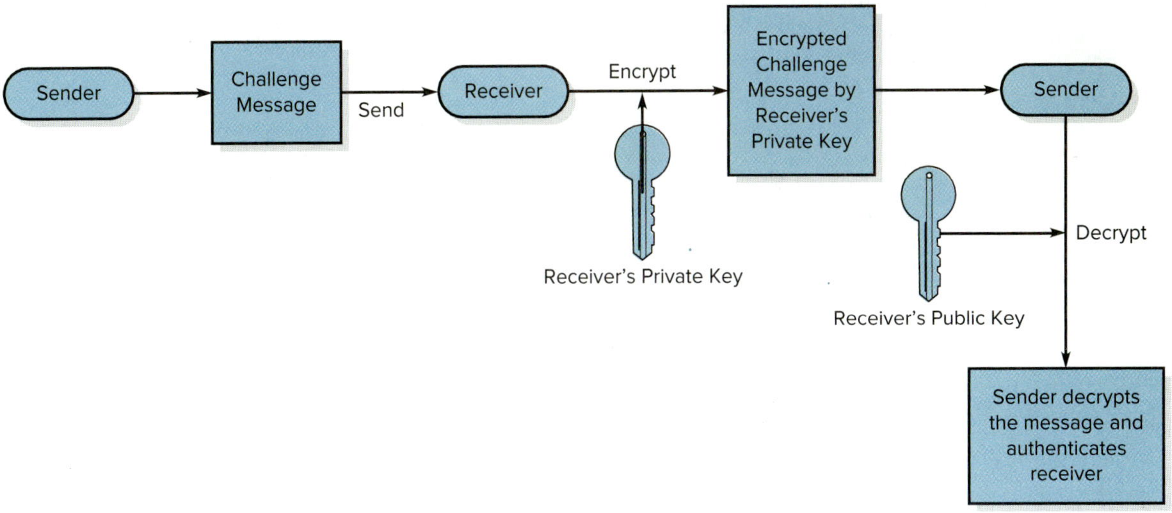

FIGURE 12.3
Authentication Process

3. Asymmetric-key encryption is used to distribute the session key. (For example, the sender uses the receiver's public key to encrypt the session key and sends it to the receiver. The receiver uses his or her own private key to decrypt to get the session key.)
4. After both parties have the session key, the session key is used to transmit confidential data/information. The use of a symmetric key for encryption results in faster data transmission.

A **digital signature** is a **message digest (MD)** of a document (or data file) that is encrypted using the document creator's private key. An MD is a short code (256 bits or 32 characters) that is generated through a process called **hashing,** where the original document passes through an algorithm (a series of steps) to generate the MD. Because popular algorithms such as SHA-256 use every bit in the file to calculate the MD, the change of a single character would result in a completely different hash. Therefore, digital signatures can ensure **data integrity.** In addition, to create a digital signature, the document creator must use his or her own private key to encrypt the MD, so the digital signature also authenticates the document creator. Given the significant attributes of a digital signature (maintaining data integrity and authenticating the document/data creator), it serves a critical role in e-business: No one can record an electronic transaction and then later say that he or she had nothing to do with it. Figure 12.4 depicts the process of using a digital signature to ensure data integrity. The process is described as follows:

1. Both the sender (A) and receiver (B) use an asymmetric-key encryption method to authenticate each other.
2. A makes a copy of the document and uses SHA-256 to hash the copy and get an MD.
3. A encrypts the MD using A's private key to get A's digital signature.
4. A uses B's public key to encrypt the original document and A's digital signature (for confidentiality).
5. A sends the encrypted package to B.
6. B receives the package and decrypts it using B's private key. B now has the document and A's digital signature.

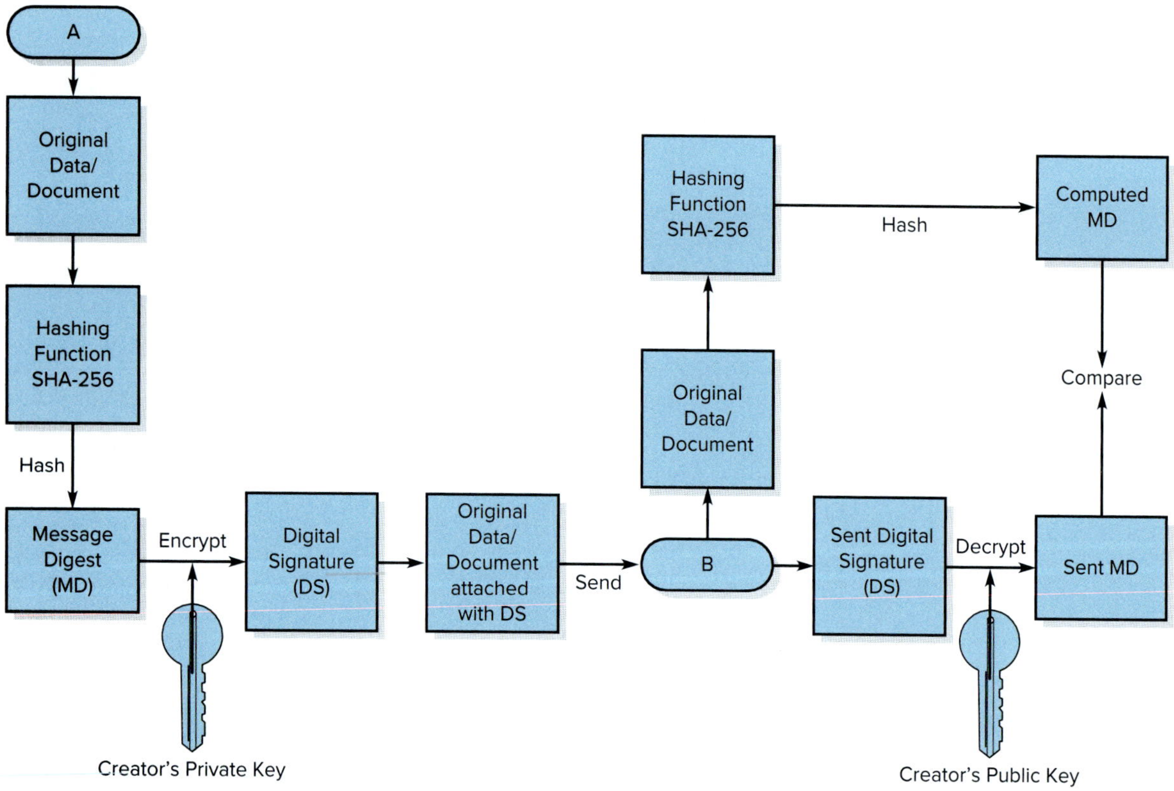

FIGURE 12.4
Digital Signature

7. B decrypts A's digital signature using A's public key to get A's original MD. B also authenticates that A is the document creator (to assure nonrepudiation).
8. B makes a copy of the received document and uses SHA-256 to hash the copy and get a calculated MD.
9. If the original MD is the same as the calculated MD, B ensures data integrity (no changes made to the original document).

To ensure the asymmetric-key encryption method functions well, several key factors must be considered:[3]

1. A **Certificate Authority (CA)** is a trusted entity that issues and revokes digital certificates.
2. A **digital certificate** is a digital document issued and digitally signed by the private key of a Certificate Authority that binds the name of a subscriber to a public key. The certificate indicates that the subscriber identified in the certificate has sole control and access to the private key.
3. A **public-key infrastructure (PKI)** refers to a set of policies, processes, server platforms, software, and workstations used for the purpose of administering certificates and public-/private-key pairs, including the ability to issue, maintain, and revoke public-key certificates.

PKI is an arrangement that issues digital certificates to users and servers, manages the key issuance, and verifies and revokes certificates by means of a CA.

[3]Definitions are quoted from NIST, *Glossary of Key Information Security Terms*.

Because authentication and nonrepudiation are accomplished by using public keys in decryption, the CA plays the most significant role in assuring the effectiveness of asymmetric-key encryption.

Progress Check

3. Can we use the symmetric-key encryption method to authenticate users? Why?
4. What is a digital signature? Why do we need it?

LO 12-3
Describe computer fraud and misuse of AIS and corresponding risk mitigation techniques.

COMPUTER FRAUD AND ABUSE

The International Professional Practices Framework[4] (IPPF) of the Institute of Internal Auditors (IIA) defines fraud as any intended illegal act characterized by deceit, concealment, or violation of trust. "Frauds are perpetrated by parties and organizations to obtain money, property, or services; to avoid payment or loss of services; or to secure personal or business advantage."[5] It is important to understand that intent is a key component defining and differentiating fraud from other acts and behaviors. In addition, the Statement of Auditing Standards (SAS) No. 99, "Consideration of Fraud in a Financial Statement Audit" states that an entity's management has primary responsibility for establishing and monitoring all aspects of the entity's fraud risk-assessment and prevention activities and has both the responsibility and the means to implement measures to reduce the incidence of fraud.

Some of the most valuable items desired by individuals committing computer fraud are the digital assets maintained by the firm. Most firms gather, create, utilize, store, and discard data that have value to others outside the firm. Such data can be in the form of employee or customer personal information such as government-issued identification numbers, bank account numbers, credit card numbers, other personal information, confidential company information, and/or trade secrets. Whether the perpetrator is an individual with authorized access to the data or a hacker, these data can be sold to others or used for personal gain for crimes such as identity theft, unauthorized purchases on stolen credit cards, or stealing or diverting money from a bank account.[6]

Fraud cases bring negative publicity to many companies.
© 2007 Getty Images, Inc.

Insiders, having legitimate access to their firms' data, systems, and networks, pose a significant risk to their firms. Employees experiencing financial problems may tend to use the systems they access at work to commit fraud such as stealing confidential data, proprietary information, or intellectual property from their employers. According to the **fraud triangle** (see Figure 12.5), three conditions exist for a fraud to be perpetrated. First, there is an *incentive* or pressure that provides a reason to commit fraud. Second, there is an *opportunity* for fraud to be perpetrated (e.g., absence of controls, ineffective controls, or the ability of management to override controls.) Third, the individuals committing the fraud possess an attitude that enables them to *rationalize* the fraud. Because research indicates that more than half of the

[4]The IPPF is the conceptual framework that provides authoritative guidance promulgated by IIA.

[5]Global Technology Audit Guides (GTAG), *Fraud Prevention and Detection in an Automated World* (2009).

[6]Ibid.

FIGURE 12.5
The Fraud Triangle

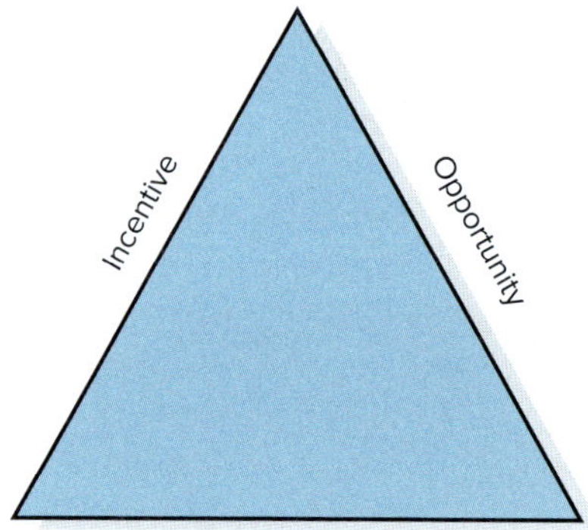

malicious incidents in IT security are caused by insider abuse and misuse, firms should implement a sound system of internal controls to prevent and detect computer frauds perpetrated by insiders. However, the reality seems to be that threats from inside have been overlooked by many firms.[7] We address this gap by introducing computer fraud risks, typical fraud schemes, and strategies/techniques to prevent and detect computer frauds.

Computer Fraud Risk Assessment

According to Global Technology Audit Guides (GTAG) provided by IIA, common computer frauds include the following:

1. The theft, misuse, or misappropriation of assets by altering computer-readable records and files.
2. The theft, misuse, or misappropriation of assets by altering the logic of computer software.
3. The theft or illegal use of computer-readable information.
4. The theft, corruption, illegal copying, or intentional destruction of computer software.
5. The theft, misuse, or misappropriation of computer hardware.

Concerning computer fraud risks, management should first review potential risk exposures. Given an identified possible fraud, exposures are management's estimates of the potential loss from the fraud. Computer fraud risk assessment is a systematic process that assists management and internal auditors in discovering where and how fraud may occur and identifying who may commit the specific fraud. A computer fraud risk assessment is often a component of a firm's enterprise risk management (ERM) program.

Similar to an enterprise risk assessment, a computer fraud risk assessment focuses on fraud schemes and scenarios to determine whether the controls exist and how the controls might be circumvented. According to GTAG, computer fraud risk assessments usually include the following key steps:[8]

1. Identifying relevant IT fraud risk factors.
2. Identifying potential IT fraud schemes and prioritizing them based on likelihood and impact.
3. Mapping existing controls to potential fraud schemes and identifying gaps.
4. Testing operating effectiveness of fraud prevention and detection controls.
5. Assessing the likelihood and business impact of a control failure and/or a fraud incident.

[7] K. C. Brancik, *Insider Computer Fraud: An In-depth Framework for Detecting and Defending against Insider IT Attacks* (Danvers, MA: Auerbach Publications, 2008).

[8] GTAG, *Fraud Prevention and Detection in an Automated World,* p. 2.

Computer Fraud Schemes

It is important to identify potential fraud schemes related to computer systems and include them in the enterprisewide risk assessment plan. The following scenarios are provided to help you understand general computer fraud schemes regarding unauthorized access to systems/data and unauthorized changes to systems programs/data for personal gains.

1. The former controller of the Baierl Acura auto dealership used her position to embezzle more than $10 million from her employer. Between 2004 and 2011, she made over 800 transfers from her employer's bank to her own personal bank accounts. She covered up the thefts by creating fake transactions and listing phantom inventory items to be recorded as assets. She spent the stolen money on luxury items and extravagant purchases for herself, her family, and friends. In 2012, she pleaded guilty and was sentenced to 78 months in prison and three years of probation and ordered to pay nearly $10.35 million in restitution.[9]
2. In November 2013, computer hackers breached Target's IT security and stole customer information, including credit card data and debit card PIN numbers. The hackers used stolen credentials from third-party vendors to gain access and install software to collect customer information from the stores' point-of-sale systems. It was the largest retail hack in U.S. history encompassing 1,797 stores and resulted in 40 million credit card numbers and 70 million addresses, phone numbers, and other pieces of personal information being stolen. Target's IT security software would have stopped the data breach, but the company's security team manually turned off the automated detection function.[10]
3. In September 2014, the same point-of-sale data collecting technology that hacked Target stores also breached Home Depot. The costs associated with these types of cyber attacks were quite expensive and resulted in loss of customer confidence and lost business, lawsuits, regulatory fines, and expenses to cover identity theft and credit monitoring services for customers victimized by the attack. Home Depot estimates that approximately 56 million credit and debit card numbers were exposed. Estimated costs to the company could be as high as $10 billion or $176 per compromised record.[11]
4. In December 2014, a group called Guardians of Peace hacked into Sony Pictures and made off with several terabytes of intellectual property in the form of unreleased movies. In addition to the movies, employee personal information, internal corporate practice information, and account credentials were stolen. The movies and other data were leaked on the Internet within hours of the data theft.[12]
5. In January 2015, the health insurance company Anthem discovered that around 80 million medical and personal data records had been accessed by cyber thieves. The data included names, birthdays, medical IDs, social security numbers, street addresses, e-mail addresses, employment information, and income data. Anthem's public communication about the attack indicated that the attack was so sophisticated that they could not possibly defend against it. However, it turned out that a general laxity exists in regards to cyber security with Anthem.[13]

[9] https://www.fbi.gov/pittsburgh/press-releases/2012/former-baierl-acura-controller-admits-embezzling-10.2-million.

[10] http://www.bloomberg.com/news/articles/2014-03-13/target-missed-warnings-in-epic-hack-of-credit-card-data.

[11] http://krebsonsecurity.com/tag/target-data-breach/

[12] https://www.riskbasedsecurity.com/2014/12/a-breakdown-and-analysis-of-the-december-2014-sony-hack/#mylifeatthecompanypart1.

[13] http://money.cnn.com/2015/02/04/technology/anthem-insurance-hack-data-security/; http://www.latimes.com/business/la-fi-mh-anthem-is-warning-consumers-20150306-column.html.

In addition, the U.S. Secret Service and CERT Coordination Center have also identified computer fraud in the systems development life cycle (SDLC). Figure 12.6 is a summary of such frauds and the corresponding oversights.[14]

One of the main reasons computer fraud is possible is weak access control. The best control over unauthorized access to sensitive information is to require passwords for accessing individual files or subsystems. Logon user IDs should be automatically locked out if the wrong password is entered a predefined number of times. Once locked, a logon user ID should be activated only by appropriate personnel, such as a system administrator. A system itself should enforce password changes on a regular basis (i.e., every 30, 60, or 90 days) and should not permit previous password(s) to be used again for a certain period of time. In addition, the use of two or more types of authentication credentials can achieve a greater level of security. This approach is called a multifactor authentication. For example, requiring a user entering a password and also inserting a smart card in a device is more secure than using either method alone.

Computer Fraud Prevention and Detection

A fraud prevention program starts with a fraud risk assessment across the entire firm, taking into consideration the firm's critical business divisions, processes, and accounts and is performed by management. Management is responsible for fraud risk assessments,

FIGURE 12.6
Fraud Schemes in Systems Development Life Cycle

Phase	Scenario	Oversights
Requirements Definition Phase	195 illegitimate drivers' licenses are created and sold by a police communications officer who accidentally discovers she can create them.	Lack of authentication and role-based access control requirements Lack of segregation of duties
System Design Phase	A special function to expedite handling of cases allows two caseworkers to pocket $32,000 in kickbacks.	Insufficient attention to security details in automated workflow processes
	An employee realizes there is no computerized control in his firm's system, so he entered and profited from $20 million in fake health insurance claims.	Lack of consideration for security vulnerabilities posed by authorized system access
System Implementation Phase	An 18-year-old former web developer uses backdoors he inserted into his code to access his former firm's network, spam its customers, alter its applications, and ultimately put the firm out of business.	Lack of code reviews
System Deployment Phase	A computer technician uses his unrestricted access to customers' systems to plant a virus on their networks that brings the customers' systems to a halt.	Lack of enforcement of documentation practices and backup procedures
	A software engineer did not document or back up his source code intentionally and then deleted the only copy of the source code once the system was in production.	Unrestricted access to all customers' systems
System Maintenance Phase	A foreign currency trader covers up losses of $691 million over a 5-year period by making unauthorized changes to the source code.	Lack of code reviews End-user access to source code
	A logic bomb sits undetected for 6 months before finally performing a mass deletion of data of a telecommunications firm.	Ineffective backup processes

[14] U.S. Secret Service and CERT Coordination Center/SEI, *Insider Threat Study.*

while the audit committee typically has an oversight role in this process.[15] The audit committee often works with the internal audit group to ensure that the fraud prevention and detection program remains an ongoing effort. The audit committee also interacts with the firm's external auditor to ensure that fraud assessment results are properly communicated.

Inappropriate use of IT resources by users exposes an enterprise to fraud risks as well as other information security risks. Making employees aware of their obligations concerning fraud and misconduct begins with practical communication and training. Communicating the firm's policy to employees is one of the most important responsibilities of management. Before new employees receive access to information systems, they should be required to sign an acknowledgment called an acceptable use policy (AUP) or an end-user computing policy. The AUP should explain what the firm considers to be acceptable computer use, with the goal of protecting both the employee and the firm from any illegal act.

A fraud detection program should include an evaluation by internal auditors on the effectiveness of business processes, along with an analysis of transaction-level data to obtain evidence of the effectiveness of internal controls and to identify indicators of fraud risk or actual fraudulent activities.[16] An effective approach is to have a continuous monitoring system with embedded modules to create detailed logs for transaction-level testing.

Progress Check

5. Given your understanding of computer fraud, do you think it happens often? Why or why not?
6. Use the fraud triangle to explain one of the fraud schemes.
7. Search over the Internet to find a recent computer fraud scheme. Given the scenario, identify the oversights of the firm.

LO 12-4
Define vulnerabilities, and explain how to manage and assess them.

VULNERABILITY ASSESSMENT AND MANAGEMENT

The Information Systems Audit and Control Association (ISACA) defines vulnerability as "the characteristics of IT resources that can be exploited by a threat to cause harm."[17] The GTAG considers vulnerabilities as weaknesses or exposures in IT assets or processes that may lead to a business risk, compliance risk, or security risk.[18] Vulnerability management and risk management have the same objective: Reduce the probability of the occurrence of detrimental events. The subtle difference between risk management and vulnerability management is that risk management is often a more complex and strategic process that may take many months or years and is mostly conducted using a top-down, risk-based approach, whereas vulnerability management is often a tactical and short-term effort that may take weeks or a few months and is frequently conducted using an IT asset-based approach. The purpose of an asset-based approach is to categorize and prioritize further investigation efforts on each asset and to identify appropriate control measures based on meaningful criteria, such as a monetary value of assets and significance of the corresponding risks. To use this approach, it is important to properly maintain asset inventory on an ongoing basis.

[15]KPMG, *Fraud Risk Management: Developing a Strategy for Prevention, Detection, and Response* (2006).
[16]GTAG, *Fraud Prevention and Detection in an Automated World.*
[17]ISACA, *Certified Information Systems Auditors Examination Review Manual* (2009).
[18]GTAG, *Managing and Auditing IT Vulnerabilities* (2006).

Types of Vulnerabilities

Because vulnerabilities are the weaknesses or exposures in IT assets or processes, gaining an understanding of existing controls is important to identifying vulnerabilities. In general, vulnerabilities are categorized based on where they commonly exist: within a physical IT environment, within an information system, or within the processes of IT operations. Figures 12.7, 12.8, and 12.9 provide examples of different types of vulnerabilities.

FIGURE 12.7 Examples of Vulnerabilities within a Physical IT Environment

Threats	Vulnerabilities
Physical intrusion	• External parties entering facilities without permission and/or providing access information • Unauthorized hardware changes
Natural disasters	• No regular review of a policy that identifies how IT equipment is protected against environmental threats • Inadequate or outdated measures for environmental threats • Lack of a disaster recovery plan
Excessive heat or humidity	• Humidity alarm not in place • Outdated devices not providing information on temperature and humidity levels
Water seepage in a data center	• Server room located in the basement • Clogged water drain
Electrical disruptions or blackouts	• Insufficient backup power supply • No voltage stabilizer

FIGURE 12.8 Examples of Vulnerabilities within an Information System

Threats	Vulnerabilities
System intrusion (e.g., spyware, malware, etc.)	• Software not patched immediately • Open ports on a main server without router access • Outdated intrusion detection/prevention system
Logical access control failure	• Work performed not aligned with business requirements • Poor choice of password or sharing of passwords • Failure to audit and terminate unused accounts in a timely manner
Interruption of a system	• Improper system configuration and customization • Poor service level agreement (SLA) monitoring of service providers

FIGURE 12.9 Examples of Vulnerabilities within the Processes of IT Operations

Threats	Vulnerabilities
Social engineering	• Employee training not providing information about social engineering attempts
Unintentional disclosure of sensitive information by employee	• Inappropriate data classification rule • Poor user access management allows some users to retrieve sensitive information not pertaining to their roles and responsibilities
Intentional destruction of information	• Approval not required prior to deleting sensitive data • Poor employee morale • Writable disk drive containing data that shall not be deleted, such as transaction logs
Inappropriate end-user computing	• Ineffective training as to the proper use of computer • End-user computing policy not reviewed • Poor firewall rules, allowing users to access illegitimate websites

Progress Check

8. Search the Internet to find additional definitions of vulnerability.
9. Search the Internet to find examples of recent cases for each type of vulnerability presented in Figures 12.7, 12.8, and 12.9.

An Overall Framework for Vulnerability Assessment and Management

There are two prerequisites for vulnerability management. First, a firm should determine the main objectives of its vulnerability management because the firm's resource for managing vulnerabilities is limited. In some cases, a primary purpose of vulnerability management could be to comply with applicable laws, regulations, and standards—in which case, the firm should determine which laws, regulations, and standards it should comply with.

Second, a firm should assign roles and responsibilities for vulnerability management. Management may designate a team (i.e., internal audit group, risk management committee, etc.) to be responsible for developing and implementing the vulnerability management program. When assigning roles and responsibilities (i.e., assigning an owner of each IT asset and/or process, implementing a control self-assessment program, etc.), it is important to note that management's commitment and support, as well as the integration of vulnerability management efforts within all levels of the firm, are critical success factors.

Figures 12.10 and 12.11 provide the overall view and main components of vulnerability management and assessment, as well as brief descriptions of each component.[19]

FIGURE 12.10 Main Components of Vulnerability Management and Assessment

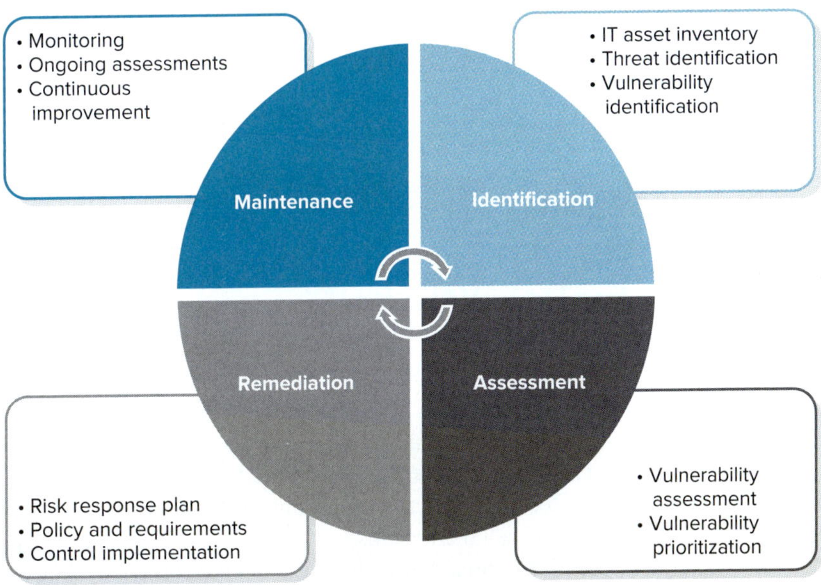

[19]GTAG, *Managing and Auditing IT Vulnerabilities.*

VULNERABILITY ASSESSMENT		**VULNERABILITY MANAGEMENT**	
I. Identification	**II. Risk Assessment**	**III. Remediation**	**IV. Maintenance**
IT Asset Inventory Ensure that all critical IT assets are identified. Ensure IT assets identified are grouped and prioritized. Ensure IT assets are identified and updated periodically.	**Vulnerability Assessment** Identify the approach and criteria to be consistently used for assessing the identified vulnerabilities throughout the organization. Quantify and/or qualify the identified vulnerabilities.	**Risk Response plan** Understand the firm's risk appetite. Conduct a cost/benefit analysis. Select controls and policies to implement.	**Monitoring** Ensure IT assets are maintained in a standardized format to help track logical and physical elements of the IT asset such as model, applications installed, and patches. Ensure change and incident management are integrated with configuration management.
Threat Identification Identify the threats related to each IT asset. If a network scanning or a monitoring tool is used, ensure that the tool reflects updated threats and is used periodically.	**Vulnerability Prioritization** Ensure business impact is included as a measurable priority identifier. Prioritize vulnerabilities based on the significance of risks in an area of focus.	**Policy and Requirements** Policy and procedures for remediation should be consistent across the organization. The following five policies are generally of high importance to vulnerability management: • Change management • Configuration management • Incident management • Patch testing • Contingency plans	**Ongoing Assessment** Conduct monitoring on an ongoing basis to verify whether controls are operating effectively as initially implemented. Automatically scan the systems and devices to detect new vulnerabilities and to meet changes in regulatory requirements.
Vulnerability Identification Identify vulnerabilities associated with each identified threat and IT asset.		**Control Implementation** Analyze whether controls are effective to combat identified vulnerabilities. Any changes of control should be authorized and tested prior to implementation. Changes of control should cause minimal disruptions to business.	**Continuous Improvement** Continuously improve processes to reach best practice, based on prior findings, ongoing assessment, and the benchmark in the industry.

FIGURE 12.11
Brief Descriptions of the Main Components of Vulnerability Management and Assessment

LO 12-5
Explain issues in system availability, disaster recovery, and business continuity.

SYSTEM AVAILABILITY

A key component of IT service delivery and support is making sure the data are available at all times or, at a minimum, in the moment the data are needed. Even a short period of system downtime on an e-commerce application can result in a loss of e-commerce sales and, potentially, a loss of trust in the provider. For example, in 1999, eBay's system for the entire auction site was down for 22 hours. The company not only lost millions in transaction fees from auction sales, but also billions in stock market value as many investors decided to sell their shares.

Firms continue to monitor system availability. Backups are used to alleviate problems of file or database corruptions. An **uninterruptible power supply** is a device using battery power to enable a system to operate long enough to back up critical data and shut down properly during the loss of power. **Fault tolerance** uses redundant units to provide a system with the ability to continue functioning when part of the system fails. Many firms implement a redundant array of independent drives (RAID) so that if one disk drive fails, important data can still be accessed from another disk.

Virtualization and **cloud computing** are often considered good alternatives to back up data and applications. Cloud computing uses redundant servers in multiple locations to host virtual machines. A virtual machine contains system applications and data backups. If the server hosting a virtual machine fails, the virtual machine can be installed to any other redundant server immediately. Using virtualization and cloud computing for system availability could be cost-effective.

Recently, cloud computing has become a popular model for business operations. In general, cloud computing refers to a service model in which a third-party service provider offers computing resources, including hardware and software applications, to cloud users over the Internet, and the service provider charges on a per-user basis. A cloud user company often shares the computing resources with other user companies, and a cloud provider bears the responsibility for managing and maintaining the resources. A survey result showed that 43 percent of 2,014 IT leaders in 50 countries indicated that their companies were projected to have most of their IT efforts running in the cloud by 2015.[20] However, a user company must evaluate a cloud provider's credibility, controls, and security of the systems and networks and its financial viability carefully before using the cloud provider. It is important that a cloud user company obtains and reviews a service organization control (SOC) report from the cloud provider prior to signing an agreement for the service (could be a SOC 1 report). If the business operations are critical to the cloud service user company (such as storing its confidential data and hosting critical applications), the user company should consider requiring an SOC 2 or SOC 3 report. The SOC 1 report focuses on the impact of the cloud provider's controls on the user company's financial statements. On the other hand, SOC 2 and SOC 3 reports provide the evaluations on a broader set of controls relevant to security, availability, processing integrity, confidentiality, or privacy implemented by the service provider.

DISASTER RECOVERY PLANNING AND BUSINESS CONTINUITY MANAGEMENT

Adverse events happen in every daily business environment. For any firm, it is essential to establish and maintain a proper plan to recover from a disaster or any disruptive event and to continue its business operations. In 2011, the severe experience of natural disasters (such as the tsunami in Japan and the tornados in the United States) reinforced the importance of disaster recovery planning and business continuity management.

Disaster recovery planning (DRP) is a process that identifies significant events that may threaten a firm's operations and outlines the procedures to ensure that the firm will resume operations if such events occur. DRP must include a clearly defined and documented plan that covers key personnel; resources, including IT infrastructure and applications; and actions required to be carried out in order to continue or resume the systems for critical business functions within planned levels of disruption. A disaster recovery plan should be reviewed and tested periodically to analyze weaknesses and explore possible ways to improve the plan.

Both DRP and BCM are important to firms because they are about whether the firms can continue their business or not.

While DRP is the process of rebuilding the operations and/or infrastructure after a disaster has occurred, **business continuity management (BCM)** refers to the activities required to keep a firm running during a period of displacement or interruption of

[20] Gartner Inc., *Reimagining IT: The 2011 CIO Agenda*. January 2011. Retrieved at: http://www.gartner.com/id=1524714.

FIGURE 12.12
Components in Business Continuity Management Life Cycle

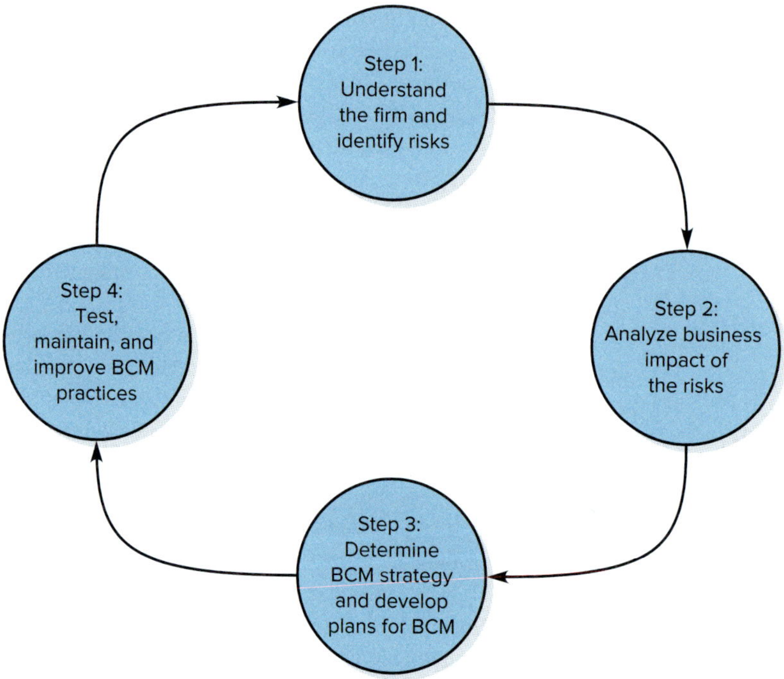

normal operations. DRP and BCM are the most critical corrective controls, and DRP is a key component of BCM.[21] BCM is broader than DRP and is concerned with the entire business processes, rather than particular assets such as IT infrastructure and applications. To achieve business objectives, a firm must continue to perform its critical business processes, as well as IT functions that support the business processes.

British Standard (BS) 25999 is the generally accepted standard for BCM. It establishes the process, principles, and terminology of continuity management for business and its IT functions. BS 25999 is suitable for any firm and is particularly relevant for firms operating in high-risk environments such as health care, finance, and telecommunications, where the ability to continue operations is paramount for the firm itself and for its customers and stakeholders.[22] As shown in Figure 12.12, BCM often includes the following components: (1) understanding the firm and identifying risks; (2) analyzing business impact of the risks; (3) determining BCM strategy and developing plans for the BCM; and (4) testing, maintaining, and improving the firm's BCM practices.

Summary

- Proper use of encryption, authentication, and digital signature technology are important to maintaining information security. Most firms use both symmetric-key and asymmetric-key encryption methods for e-business. Authentication ensures transactions are valid. Encryption maintains confidentiality during data transmission. Digital signatures achieve data integrity and confirm nonrepudiation while conducting e-business.

[21] R. Muthukrishnan, "The Auditor's Role in Reviewing Business Continuity Planning," *Information Systems Control Journal*, 2005.

[22] Business Continuity Institute, www.thebci.org/certificationstandards.htm.

- Disaster recovery planning (DRP) identifies significant events that may threaten a firm's operations, outlining the procedures that ensure the firm's smooth resumption of operations in the case such an event occurs. DRP must include a clearly defined and documented plan that covers key personnel, resources, and actions required to be carried out to resume the systems necessary for critical business functions within a defined, acceptable timeframe. DRP is an essential component of business continuity management (BCM), which refers to the activities required to keep a firm running during a period of interruption of normal operations. BCM is broader than DRP and is concerned with all key business processes, rather than particular assets such as IT infrastructure and applications. To achieve business objectives, a firm must continue to perform its critical business processes, as well as IT functions that support the business processes.

Key Words

asymmetric-key encryption (*304*) To transmit confidential information, the sender uses the receiver's public key to encrypt the message; the receiver uses his or her own private key for decryption upon receiving the message. Also known as public-key encryption or two-key encryption.

authentication (*304*) A process that establishes the origin of information or determines the identity of a user, process, or device.

business continuity management (BCM) (*315*) The activities required to keep a firm running during a period of displacement or interruption of normal operations.

Certificate Authority (CA) (*306*) A trusted entity that issues and revokes digital certificates.

cloud computing (*315*) Using redundant servers in multiple locations to host virtual machines.

data integrity (*305*) Maintaining and assuring the accuracy and consistency of data during transmission and at storage.

digital certificate (*306*) A digital document issued and digitally signed by the private key of a Certificate Authority that binds the name of a subscriber to a public key.

digital signature (*305*) A message digest of a document (or data file) that is encrypted using the document creator's private key.

disaster recovery planning (DRP) (*315*) A process that identifies significant events that may threaten a firm's operations and outlines the procedures to ensure that the firm will resume operations when the events occur.

encryption (*303*) Using algorithmic schemes to encode plaintext into nonreadable form.

fault tolerance (*315*) Redundant units providing a system with the ability to continue functioning when part of the system fails.

fraud triangle (*307*) Three conditions exist for a fraud to be perpetrated: incentive, opportunity, and rationalization.

message digest (MD) (*305*) A short code, such as one 256 bits long, resulting from hashing a plaintext message using an algorithm.

private key (*304*) A string of bits kept secret and known only to the owner of the key.

public key (*304*) A string of bits created with the private key and widely distributed and available to other users.

public-key infrastructure (PKI) (*306*) A set of policies, processes, server platforms, software, and workstations used for the purpose of administering certificates and public-/private-key pairs, including the ability to issue, maintain, and revoke public-key certificates.

session key (*304*) A symmetric key that is valid for a certain timeframe only.

symmetric-key encryption (*304*) Both the sender and the receiver use the same key to encrypt and decrypt messages.

uninterruptible power supply (*314*) A device using battery power to enable a system to operate long enough to back up critical data and shut down properly during the loss of power.

virtualization (*315*) Using various techniques and methods to create a virtual (rather than actual) version of a hardware platform, storage device, or network resources.

Answers to Progress Checks

1. The general goals of information security are to safeguard critical systems and to maintain confidentiality, integrity, and availability of information from internal and external security threats.
2. Social engineering could be an attempt to trick someone into revealing information, such as a password, that can be used to attack systems or networks. For example, a hacker may find a phone number of a salesperson from the company's website. The hacker then pretends that he is one of the IT staff working at the helpdesk and calls the salesperson to ask for the salesperson's password in "fixing" a problem on accessing certain files. If the salesperson gives his or her password to the hacker, the hacker can obtain access to the company's network.
3. We cannot use the symmetric-key encryption method to authenticate users because both the sender and the receiver are using the same key. This method does not provide a unique key for each user when transmitting information among different parties.
4. A digital signature is a message digest encrypted using the sender's private key. We use a digital signature to achieve two purposes. The main purpose is to maintain data integrity. The second purpose is to authenticate the sender. If the receiver can use the sender's public key to decrypt the digital signature, the receiver authenticates the sender. The receiver compares the calculated message digest with the sent-over message digest to confirm data integrity.
5. Computer fraud includes a variety of illegal acts that involve a computer or network. If the internal control of a company is not adequate, the wide use of technologies, computers, and other electronic devices in the business world provide an environment for frequent occurrences of computer fraud.
6. Scenario one: The loose access control of the company's information system provided the employee an opportunity to obtain confidential information after leaving the position. The associate lured the employee to disclose the confidential information for his business by providing financial benefits to the employee. The employee committed the identity theft. She rationalized her behavior—because her position had changed, she was no longer responsible for keeping employees' account information confidential.
7. David Nosal used to work for **Korn/Ferry**, an executive search firm. Shortly after he left the company, he convinced some of his former colleagues who were still working for Korn/Ferry to help him start a competing business. The employees used their login credentials to download source lists, names, and contact information from a confidential database on the company's computer, and then transferred that information to Nosal. (Source: http://www.ca9.uscourts.gov/datastore/opinions/2012/04/10/10-10038.pdf)
8. The Internet Engineering Task Force (IETF) defines vulnerability as a flaw or weakness in a system's design, implementation, or operation and management that could be exploited to violate the system's security policy. The European Network and Information Security Agency (ENISA) defines vulnerability as the existence of a weakness, design, or implementation error that can lead to an unexpected, undesirable event compromising the security of the computer system, network, application, or protocol involved. The Committee on National Security Systems of United States of America defines vulnerability as weakness in an IS, system security procedures, internal controls, or implementation that could be exploited.

9. Examples for each type of vulnerability:
   a. Vulnerabilities in physical IT system
      Threats: Fire
      Vulnerabilities:
      - Nonsensitive automatic fire detection response systems
      - Improper storage of combustible materials
      - Use of malfunctioning heating devices
      - Insufficient training of people about fire prevention and reaction
   b. Vulnerabilities in an information system
      Threats: System intrusion
      Vulnerabilities: No virus scanner on each computer
   c. Vulnerabilities within the process of IT operations
      Threats: Unintentional deletion of information
      Vulnerabilities:
      - Employee mistakes caused by inadequate training about operation
      - Lack of a backup of data and information

Mc Graw Hill Education connect®

Multiple Choice Questions

1. (CISA exam, adapted) Authentication is the process by which the: **LO 12-2**
   a. system verifies that the user is entitled to enter the transaction requested.
   b. system verifies the identity of the user.
   c. user identifies him- or herself to the system.
   d. user indicates to the system that the transaction was processed correctly.
2. (CMA exam, adapted) Data processing activities may be classified in terms of three stages or processes: input, processing, and output. An activity that is not normally associated with the input stage is: **LO 12-2**
   a. batching.
   b. recording.
   c. verifying.
   d. reporting.
3. (CISA exam, adapted) To ensure confidentiality in an asymmetric-key encryption system, knowledge of which of the following keys is required to decrypt the receive message? **LO 12-2**
   I. Private
   II. Public
   a. I
   b. II
   c. Both I and II
   d. Neither I nor II

4. To authenticate the message sender in an asymmetric-key encryption system, which of the following keys is required to decrypt the received message? **LO 12-2**
   a. Sender's private key
   b. Sender's public key
   c. Receiver's private key
   d. Receiver's public key
5. To ensure the data sent over the Internet are protected, which of the following keys is required to encrypt the data (before transmission) using an asymmetric-key encryption method? **LO 12-2**
   a. Sender's private key
   b. Sender's public key
   c. Receiver's private key
   d. Receiver's public key
6. Which of the following groups/laws was the earliest to encourage auditors to incorporate fraud examination into audit programs? **LO 12-3**
   a. COSO
   b. COBIT
   c. PCAOB
   d. SAS No. 99
   e. Sarbanes-Oxley Act
7. Incentive to commit fraud usually will include all of the following, except: **LO 12-3**
   a. inadequate segregation of duties.
   b. financial pressure.
   c. personal habits and lifestyle.
   d. feelings of resentment.
   e. alcohol, drug, or gambling addiction.
8. (CPA exam, adapted) An information technology director collected the names and locations of key vendors, current hardware configuration, names of team members, and an alternative processing location. What is the director most likely preparing? **LO 12-5**
   a. Internal control policy
   b. System hardware policy
   c. System security policy
   d. Disaster recovery plan
   e. Supply chain management policy
9. A message digest is the result of hashing. Which of the following statements about the hashing process is true? **LO 12-2**
   a. It is reversible.
   b. Comparing the hashing results can ensure confidentiality.
   c. Hashing is the best approach to make sure that two files are identical.
   d. None of the above is true.
10. Which one of the following vulnerabilities would create the most serious risk to a firm? **LO 12-4**
   a. Using open source software (downloaded for free) on the firm's network
   b. Employees recording passwords in Excel files
   c. Employees writing instant messages with friends during office hours
   d. Unauthorized access to the firm's network

11. Which of the following statements is correct? **LO 12-1, LO 12-2, LO 12-5**
    a. A spam will send a network packet that appears to come from a source other than its actual source.
    b. Multifactor authentication is less secure than requiring a user always entering a password to access a network.
    c. Fault tolerance uses redundant units to provide a system with the ability to continue functioning when part of the system fails.
    d. SOC 1 reports provide the evaluations on a broader set of controls implemented by the service provider.
12. Which of the following can be considered as a good alternative to back up data and applications? **LO 12-5**
    a. Continuous monitoring
    b. Disaster recovery planning
    c. Business continuity management
    d. Cloud computing
13. A digital certificate: **LO 12-2**
    a. is used to certify public-key and private-key pairs.
    b. is a trusted entity to certify and revoke Certificate Authorities (CA).
    c. indicates that the subscriber identified has sole control and access to the private key.
    d. ensures that the symmetric-key encryption method functions well.
14. The symmetric-key encryption method: **LO 12-2**
    a. is slow.
    b. is not appropriate for encrypting large data sets.
    c. solves problems in key distribution and key management.
    d. uses the same key for both senders and receivers for encryption and decryption.
15. The fraud triangle indicates which of the following condition(s) exist for a fraud to be perpetrated? **LO 12-3**
    a. rationalization.
    b. pressure.
    c. legal environment.
    d. Only a and b are correct.
    e. a, b, and c are correct.

Discussion Questions

1. Phishing is an example of social engineering where the attacker attempts to trick people into giving them personal information. Give two examples of phishing. **LO 12-1**
2. If social engineering is a common reason that confidential information was revealed, what needs to be done to prevent this from occurring? **LO 12-1**
3. What is the goal of each of the general security objectives (e.g., confidentiality, integrity, availability, access control)? Why should a company care about these? **LO 12-1**
4. There are restrictions on how U.S. companies store and share customer data. For healthcare providers, HIPAA is designed to protect patient data. A handful of states require companies processing customer payments to comply with PCI-DSS. Search the Internet for information about these regulations, and discuss the major requirements of each. **LO 12-3**
5. Consider the following scenarios and identify the incentive, opportunity, and rationalization that exist which would enable a person to commit fraud: **LO 12-3**
    a. A manager increases the value of inventory in the computer system so she can show higher cost of goods sold. As a result, she embezzles the additional income.
    b. A college student pirates a newly released movie over the Internet.
    c. An employee creates a new vendor account for his spouse and submits invoices for services that were never performed.

6. What are the differences between authentication and authorization? LO 12-2
7. Explain how to use the asymmetric-key encryption method to maintain confidentiality in transmitting a business document electronically. LO 12-2
8. What are the differences between asymmetric- and symmetric-key encryption, and when is each used? LO 12-2
9. How can data integrity be ensured when conducting e-business? Why is it critical to e-business? LO 12-2
10. The previous chapter identifies COBIT and ISO 27000 as information security frameworks. How do they relate to GTAG's Vulnerability Assessment? What similarities and differences are there between these three? LO 12-4
11. Disaster recover planning (DRP) and business continuity management (BCM) help businesses manage security risks. What similarities and differences exist between these two approaches? LO 12-5

Problems

1. Compare and contrast symmetric-key and asymmetric-key encryption methods in conducting e-business. Why do companies prefer one method over the other? If a company chooses to use both methods, what might be the reasons? How can the company truly use both methods for e-business? LO 12-2
2. Many internal auditors and IT professionals believe wireless networks and mobile devices pose high risks in a firm's network system. Collect information to examine whether this concern is valid. If so, identify the risks and the general controls to help reduce these risks. LO 12-1
3. Under PKI, Certification Authority (CA) plays a critical role in the success of maintaining information security. Search over the Internet to find a few public firms that are CAs. Compare these firms, and provide suggestions on how to choose a CA as part of information security management. LO 12-2

connect

4. Match the descriptions with each encryption method. LO 12-2

Descriptions	Encryption Method
a. Good for large data sets	i. Symmetric-key encryption
b. Slow in processing	ii. Asymmetric-key encryption
c. Convenient for key distribution and key management	
d. Each user has a public key and a private key	
e. Good for authentication	

connect

5. Match correct statement(s) with each term regarding system availability. LO 12-5

Internal Controls	System Availability Terms
a. Activities required to keep a firm running during a period of displacement or interruption of normal operations	i. Uninterruptible power supply
b. A process that identifies significant events that may threaten a firms operations and outline the procedures to ensure that the firm will resume operations if such events occur	ii. Fault tolerance
c. A service model in which a third-party service provider offers computing resources, including hardware and software applications, to cloud users over the Internet, and the service provider charges on a per-user basis	iii. Cloud computing
d. A clearly defined and documented plan that covers key personnel, resources including IT infrastructure and applications, and actions required to be carried out in order to continue or resume the systems for critical business functions	iv. Disaster recovery planning
e. Using redundant units to provide a system with the ability to continue functioning when part of the system fails	v. Business continuity management
f. A device using battery power to enable a system to operate long enough to back up critical data and shut down properly during the loss of power	

connect 6. Identify the main components of vulnerability management and assessment. **LO 12-4**

Component	Category
a. Prioritize vulnerabilities	i. Vulnerability management
b. Design a risk response plan	ii. Vulnerability assessment
c. Monitor vulnerabilities	
d. Establish policy and requirements	
e. Identify vulnerabilities	

7. There are five types of fraud schemes in systems development cycles (refer to Figure 12.6). Identify an example of each type. **LO 12-3**

8. Internal auditors are often tasked with testing vulnerabilities. How would you suggest testing for system intrusion, logical access control, natural disasters, and intentional destruction of information? **LO 12-4**

9. Browse the Internet to identify some recent cases related to system availability. What are the risks and issues in system availability of these cases? Indicate possible controls to mitigate the risks. **LO 12-5**

10. Consider each of the following fraud cases. Identify the incentive, opportunity, and rationalization present in each case. **LO 12-3**

    a. An employee of a telecommunications firm's payroll department moved to a new position within the department in which she no longer has privileged access to payroll accounts. However, when changing positions, her access rights to the payroll accounts were left unchanged. An associate told her that he was starting a financial service business and needed some contact information. Using the privileged access rights that she had retained, the employee provided her associate with confidential information of many employees, including 401(k) account numbers, credit card account numbers, and social security numbers, which he then used to commit more than 100 cases of identity theft. The insider's actions caused more than $1 million worth of damages to the firm and its employees.[23]

    b. A database analyst of a major check authorization and credit card processing company went beyond his authorized computer access rights. The employee obtained his firm's consumer information of 8.4 million individuals. The stolen information included names and addresses, bank account information, and credit and debit card information. He sold the data to telemarketers over a five-year period.[24]

    c. An IT consultant working under contract for an offshore oil platform company was denied an offer for a permanent job with the same company. He then accessed the firm's computer systems without approval and caused damage by impairing the integrity and availability of data.[25]

    d. A manager responsible for payment authorization hired an offshore programmer to insert a couple of independent contractors to the vendor table of his company's database. He then authorized payments to the independent contractors on fictitious services for personal gain. He spent the stolen money on luxury items and extravagant purchases for himself, his family, and friends.

[23]U.S. Secret Service and CERT Coordination Center/SEI. 2 Insider Threat Study: Illicit Cyber Activity in the Information Technology and Telecommunications Sector (2008).

[24]U.S. Department of Justice Website, Computer Crime and Intellectual Property Section, http://usdoj.gov/criminal/cybercrime.

[25]U.S. Department of Justice Website, Computer Crime and Intellectual Property Section, http://usdoj.gov/criminal/cybercrime.

Chapter Thirteen

Monitoring and Auditing AIS

A look at this chapter

In today's business environment, almost all firms rely on computerized systems in daily operations, in particular, to perform accounting functions. The swift advances in technologies have changed business models and the approaches to collecting data and communicating business information. Given the complicated information systems and the tremendous amount of data to be analyzed and reported, it is challenging for managers, accountants, and auditors to validate that the systems are well designed with embedded internal controls and that they process data with integrity. Accountants' role in the business world is to provide quality information for decision making. Hence, they must understand and be involved in monitoring and auditing accounting information systems.

A look back

In Chapter 12, we provided examples of computer fraud and illustrated how AIS can be misused in order to achieve personal gains. We also discussed common vulnerabilities and how to manage and assess such vulnerabilities.

A look ahead

As managers of IT systems and business partners, accountants are often involved in formulating and implementing company strategies. Chapter 14 explains how the Balanced Scorecard might be used to formulate, implement, and monitor strategic performance on information technology and information systems.

© Tim Boyle/Getty Images

If you visit the website of **Starbucks Corporation**, at the bottom of the page, under "Investor Relations," you can access its annual reports in the Financial Information section. There, you can find two audit reports, both titled "Report of Independent Registered Public Accounting Firm," on pages 88 and 90 of Starbucks' 2015 annual reports. The first audit report is the auditor's opinion on whether the financial statements of Starbucks Corporation fairly represent the company's financial conditions; the second audit report examines the internal control over financial reporting of Starbucks Corporation. The external auditors from **Deloitte & Touche LLP** conducted audits on the information systems, internal controls, and financial information of Starbucks before they rendered these audit opinions. External auditors need to understand a firm's information systems and examine the reliability of the systems before they audit the financial information that is produced by those systems.

Chapter Outline

Learning Objectives

After reading this chapter, you should be able to:

13-1 Understand the risks involved with computer hardware and software.

13-2 Understand and apply computer-assisted audit techniques.

13-3 Explain continuous auditing in AIS.

INTRODUCTION

In Chapters 11 and 12, we provided a general discussion of control, security, and fraud issues in accounting information systems with regard to managing threats and risks in conducting business. In Chapters 5, 6 and 7, we indicated specific internal controls for each major business process—such as sales, cash collections, purchases, cash disbursement, and conversion/manufacturing. This chapter discusses important concepts of monitoring and auditing controls and verifying the accuracy and completeness of the information produced by the systems. We introduce fundamental concepts of critical computer hardware and software, including the operating system, the database, local area networks and wide area networks, and wireless networks. More importantly, we discuss computer-assisted audit techniques (CAATs) and continuous auditing in AIS.

LO 13-1
Understand the risks involved with computer hardware and software.

COMPUTER HARDWARE AND SOFTWARE

Chapter 12 discussed information technology–related frauds and vulnerabilities. To enhance the understanding of those concepts, in this section we discuss important computer hardware and software: the operating system (OS), database systems, local area networks (LANs) and wide area networks (WANs), wireless networks, and remote access.

The Operating System

The **operating system (OS)** is the most important system software because it performs the tasks that enable a computer to operate. The operating system is comprised of system utilities and programs that[1]

- Ensure the integrity of the system.
- Control the flow of multiprogramming and tasks of scheduling in the computer.
- Allocate computer resources to users and applications.
- Manage the interfaces with the computer.

To consistently and reliably perform these tasks listed, the operating system must achieve five fundamental control objectives:[2]

- *The operating system must protect itself from users.* User applications/software must not be able to gain control of or damage the operating system.
- *The operating system must protect users from each other.* One user must not be able to access, destroy, or corrupt the data or programs of another user.
- *The operating system must protect users from themselves.* A user's applications/software may consist of several modules stored in separate memory locations, each with its own data. One module must not be allowed to destroy or corrupt another module.
- *The operating system must be protected from itself.* The operating system is also made up of individual modules. No module should be allowed to destroy or corrupt another module.
- *The operating system must be protected from its environment.* In the event of a power failure or other disaster, the operating system should be able to achieve a controlled termination of activities from which it can later recover.

Operating system security should be included as part of IT governance in establishing proper policies and procedures for IT controls which determine who can access the operating system, which resources (e.g., files, programs, printers, or servers) they can use, and

[1]Information Systems Audit and Control Association (ISACA), *CISA Exam Review Manual* (2011), p. 260.

[2]F. M. Stepczyk, "Requirements for Secure Operating Systems," *Data Security and Data Processing* 5 (1974).

what actions they can take.[3] With an ever-expanding user community sharing greater levels of computer resources, operating-system security becomes one of the most important IT control issues.

It should be noted that many firms are now turning toward virtualization of their computer resources. In this architecture, hardware resources are split among multiple separate operating systems that exist only as separate environments on the server. In this situation, additional care must be taken to govern and secure the IT environments used.

Database Systems

In today's competitive business environment, data are often the core assets of many companies. In our electronic world, all or most accounting records are stored in a database. A **database** is a shared collection of logically related data that meet the information needs of a firm. Understanding a **database system** is crucial to accounting professionals. Since they have superior knowledge of risks, controls, and business processes, accountants increasingly participate in designing internal control systems and improving the business and IT processes in a database environment.

A **data warehouse** is a centralized collection of firmwide data that are stored for a relatively long period of time. The data in a data warehouse are pulled periodically from each of the operational databases (ranging from a couple of times a day to once a year), and the data are maintained in the data warehouse for 5 to 10 years. Firms use **operational databases** for daily operations. An operational database often includes data for the current fiscal year only. The data in an operational database are updated when transactions are processed. Such updates do not happen in a data warehouse, so the data in a data warehouse are nonvolatile. Periodically, new data are uploaded to the data warehouse from the operational databases for analysis. The purpose of a data warehouse is to provide a rich data set for management to identify patterns and to examine trends of business events.

Data mining is the process of searching for patterns in the data within a data warehouse and analyzing these patterns for decision making. Data mining is often used to identify patterns in predicting customers' buying behavior for making better selling and production decisions. The tools used in data mining are called online analytical processing (OLAP). Typical approaches in OLAP include drill-down, consolidation, time series analysis, exception reports, and what-if simulations.

Data governance, a discipline that has emerged in recent years, has an evolving definition. It is the convergence of data quality, data management, data policies, business process management, regulation compliance, and risk management surrounding the handling of data in a firm.

Connection with Practice

JPMorgan Chase's IT Failure: An Apology and Some Informed Speculation

Customers whacked by JPMorgan Chase's information system debacle—the bank's online banking site was down for three days—finally got an apology, but it's still a little fuzzy about what exactly went wrong. JPMorgan Chase's online site crashed Monday night and stayed offline through Wednesday. On Thursday, the bank said:

> We are sorry for the difficulties that recently affected Chase.com, and we apologize for not communicating better with you during this issue. Giving you 24-hour access to your banking is of the utmost

(continued)

[3] J. A. Hall, *Information Technology Auditing and Assurance,* 3rd ed. (Cincinnati, OH: South-Western College, 2010), p. 69.

importance to us. This was not the level of service we know you expect, and we will work hard to serve you better in the future and to communicate with you better if a situation like this should arise again.

Online Bill Payments scheduled for September 13, 14, or 15 were processed by Wednesday night, September 15. It is not necessary to reschedule these payments. If you scheduled a payment during those dates, but do not see it reflected in your payment activity by September 16, please contact us. We will refund any late fees that you may have incurred as a result of our delay in processing your payment.

Thank you for your patience and for the opportunity to work harder to serve you in the future.

Online banking.

© Radius Images/CORBIS

The big question here is what exactly went wrong. *Computerworld* notes that JPMorgan Chase blamed a third-party database company's software. That third party is Oracle. Curt Monash, principle of Monash Research, offered some informed speculation in a blog post. Citing tips from readers of his DBMS 2 blog, Monash said:

- A corruption in the Oracle database led to the outage.
- The Oracle database stored user profiles.
- Portals, ACH transactions, loan applications, and trading portfolio access for private clients (i.e., the wealthy types) were affected.

The overall conclusion from Monash is that JPMorgan Chase wasn't to blame. More details are likely to emerge. Let's hope JPMorgan Chase does a thorough post mortem. These days banks are their online sites.

Source: Larry Dignan, "JPMorgan Chase's IT Failure: An Apology and Some Informed Speculation," ZDNet, September 17, 2010. https://www.zdnet.com. Copyright © 2010 by Larry Dignan. All rights reserved. Used with permission

LANs and WANs

A **local area network (LAN)** is a group of computers, printers, and other devices connected to the same network and covers a limited geographic range such as a home, small office, or a campus building. LAN devices include **hubs** and **switches.** A packet, which is a formatted, small unit of data, is part of the message or data set that is transmitted over the networks.

A hub contains multiple ports. When a data packet from a computer arrives at one port of a hub, it is copied to *all* other ports so that all other equipment connected to the LAN can receive the arrived packet (like a broadcast). A switch is an intelligent device that provides a path for each pair of connections on the switch by storing address information in its switching tables. From a security perspective, switches provide a significant improvement over hubs because each device connected via the network only sees traffic that has been directed to it via its designated **MAC (media access control) address** and cannot

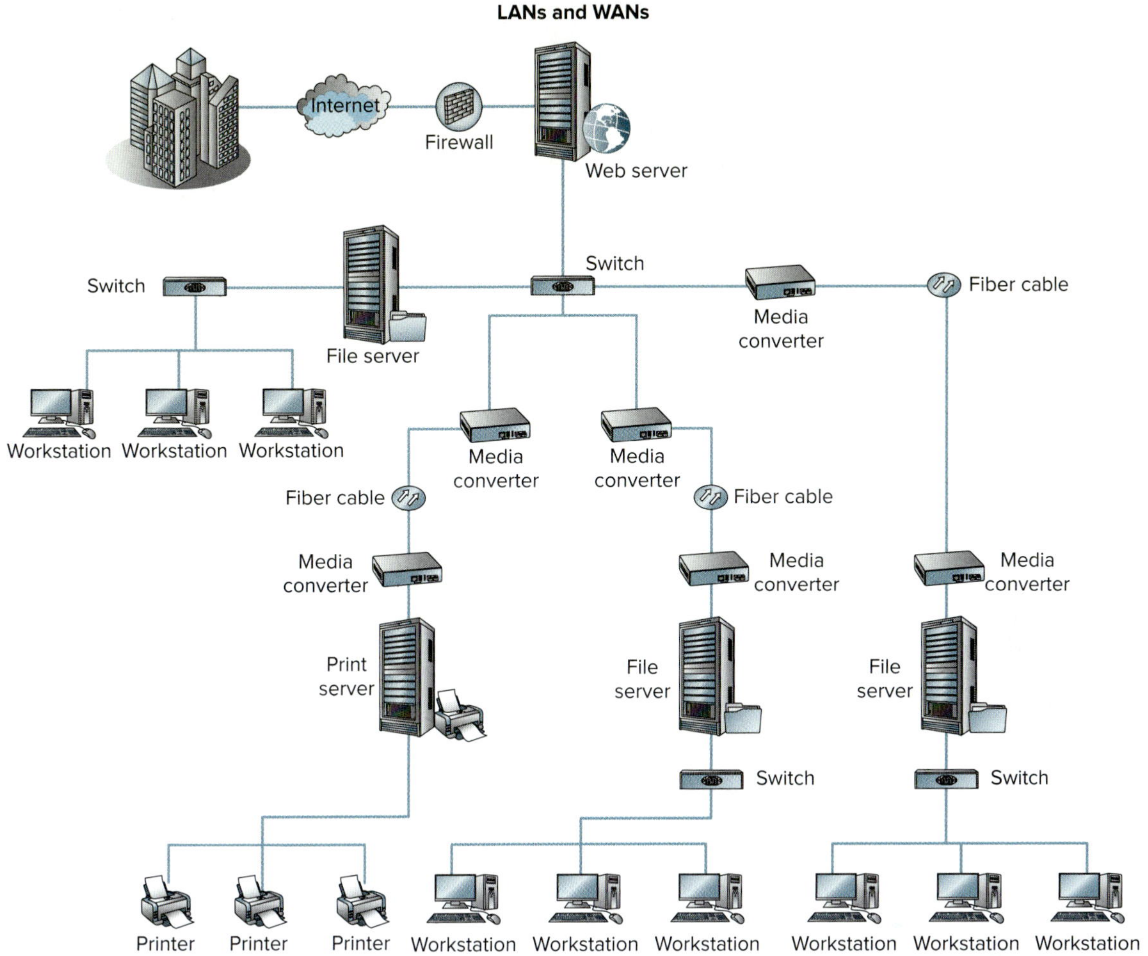

FIGURE 13.1
A Local Area Network Sample

Source: SanketShukla Blog (http://sanketshukla.blogspot.com/2009/11/local-area-network-lan.html)

eavesdrop on network traffic intended for other recipients. Figure 13.1 illustrates a sample local area network.

Wide area networks (WANs) link different sites together; transmit information across geographically dispersed LANs; and cover a broad geographic area such as a city, region, nation, or an international link. The three main purposes of WANs are (1) to provide remote access to employees or customers, (2) to link two or more sites within the firm, and (3) to provide corporate access to the Internet.[4] In general, WANs are slower than LAN communication in transmitting data but are often implemented over connectivity that offers guaranteed data rates. Enterprises are often willing to pay for these connections because of the guaranteed quality of service (QoS) and security offered by the point-to-point dedicated connection. WAN devices include **routers** and **firewalls.** Figure 13.2 illustrates a sample wide area network.

A router connects different LANs. Routers are software-based intelligent devices that choose the most efficient communication path through a network to the required

[4]R. Panko and J. Panko, *Business Data Networks and Telecommunications,* 8th ed. (Upper Saddle River, NJ: Prentice Hall, 2011).

FIGURE 13.2
A Wide Area Network Sample
Source: *OTC company (http://www.otc.pl/en/tm_med.html)*

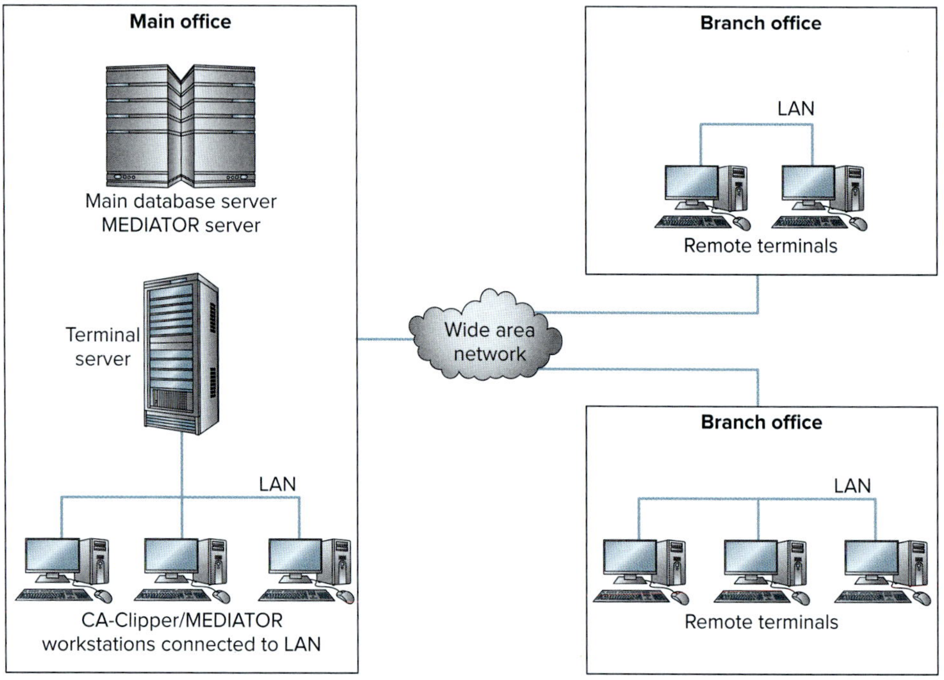

destination. A router examines the Internet Protocol (IP) address of senders and recipients and makes decisions to direct the packet to its recipient's IP address through the most efficient communication path. Routers can also divide and interconnect network segments or link two more physically separate network segments, similar to a switch.

In a computer network, a firewall can be defined as a security system comprised of hardware and software that is built using routers, servers, and a variety of software.[5] Whenever a data packet arrives, the firewall examines each incoming and outgoing data packet to determine whether a data packet should be allowed to continue in the transmission process. Also, a firewall allows individuals on the corporate network to send/receive a data packet from the Internet.

In today's business environment, VPN is an important technology. Many firms need to provide secure access for employees who are traveling and for those who work from home.

A **virtual private network (VPN)** securely connects a firm's WANs by sending/receiving encrypted packets via virtual connections over the public Internet to distant offices, salespeople, and business partners. Rather than using expensive dedicated leased lines, VPNs take advantage of the public Internet infrastructure with encryption and authentication technology to create a virtual private network that provides users with secure, **remote access** to their firm's network using the Internet. VPNs are a cheaper alternative to leased lines, yet they carry the disadvantage of not having guaranteed QoS. VPNs allow for companies to utilize a widely dispersed workforce without losing the productivity provided by a LAN.

Progress Check

1. Identify one LAN and one WAN that you have been using.

[5] Ibid.

Wireless Networks

Wireless technologies, which use radio-frequency transmissions and electromagnetic signals as the means for transmitting data, enable devices to communicate without physical connections. According to the Institute of Electrical and Electronics Engineers (IEEE) 802.11 standard, a **wireless network** is comprised of two fundamental architectural components: access points and stations. An **access point** logically connects stations to a firm's network. Access points can also logically connect wireless stations with each other in an ad hoc wireless network.[6] A **station** is a wireless endpoint device equipped with a wireless network interface card (NIC). Common benefits of using wireless technology include[7]

- Mobility—convenient online access without a physical network using cables for connections.
- Rapid deployment—time saved on implementing networks because of reduction in using physical cables/media.
- Flexibility and scalability—freely setting up or removing wireless networks at different locations.

General security objectives for both wired LANs and wireless LANs include

- Confidentiality—ensure that communication cannot be read by unauthorized parties.
- Integrity—detect any intentional or unintentional changes to the data during transmission.
- Availability—ensure that devices and individuals can access a network and its resources whenever needed.
- Access control—restrict the rights of devices or individuals to access a network or resources within a network.

Most threats with regard to wireless LANs involve an attacker with access to the radio link between a station and an access point or between two stations. The most common security threats for wireless LANs include[8]

- Eavesdropping—the attacker passively monitors wireless networks for data, including authentication credentials.
- Man-in-the-middle—the attacker actively intercepts communications between wireless clients and access points to obtain authentication credentials and data.
- Masquerading—the attacker impersonates an authorized user and gains certain unauthorized privileges to the wireless network.
- Message modification—the attacker alters a legitimate message sent via wireless networks by deleting, adding to, changing, or reordering it.
- Message replay—the attacker passively monitors transmissions via wireless networks and retransmits messages, acting as if the attacker was a legitimate user.
- Misappropriation—the attacker steals or makes unauthorized use of a service.
- Traffic analysis—the attacker passively monitors transmissions via wireless networks to identify communication patterns and participants.
- Rogue access points—the attacker sets up an unsecured wireless network near the enterprise with an identical name and intercepts any messages sent by unsuspecting users who log onto it.

[6]National Institute of Standards and Technology (NIST), "Establishing Wireless Robust Security Networks: A Guide to IEEE 802.11i," SP 800-97 (2007), p. 22.

[7]Cyber Security Malaysia, *Wireless Local Area Network (WLAN) Security Guideline* (2010), p. 12.

[8]NIST, "Establishing Wireless Robust Security Networks: A Guide to IEEE 802.11i," pp. 27–28.

Security controls for wireless networks can be categorized into three groups: management, operational, and technical controls.[9] Management controls are security controls that focus on management of risk and information system security. Management controls include, but are not limited to, assigning roles and responsibilities, creating policies and procedures, and conducting risk assessment on a regular basis. Examples include determining which parties are authorized and responsible for installing and configuring access points and other wireless network equipment; types of information that may or may not be sent over wireless networks; and how transmissions over wireless networks should be protected, including requirements for the use of encryption and for cryptographic key management.[10]

Operational controls in wireless networks typically include protecting a firm's premises and facilities; preventing and detecting physical security breaches; and providing security training to employees, contractors, or third-party users. For example, a firm should define and document the security roles and responsibilities of employees, contractors, and third-party users based on the firm's policies, procedures, and security requirements. It is also important to produce terms and conditions of employment that state the responsibilities of the employees, contractors, and third-party users for the firm's wireless network. They should agree to and sign the terms and conditions of their employment contract prior to beginning work. In addition, conducting appropriate awareness training on wireless networks and providing regular updates on organizational policies and procedures to employees, contractors, and third-party users can strengthen a firm's security control.

Technical controls are security controls that are primarily implemented and executed through mechanisms contained in computing-related equipment, including access-point management and encryption setup. A firm should immediately change the default configuration of all access points that have been deployed, including service set identifier (SSID), administrator credentials, radio signal strength, remote web-based configuration (e.g., administrator's username and password), and Internet protocol service configuration.[11] Regarding data transmission security, all access points should be configured with encryption to maintain confidentiality and data integrity. Using the wired equivalent privacy (WEP) algorithm is not recommended because it is not secure enough. It is better to use the wi-fi protected access (WPA) or the WPA2 algorithm as the cryptography technique to provide more effective authentication and for encryption.

Progress Check

2. Do you own a laptop, a cell phone, or an iPad? Can you identify a few security issues while using these devices over a wireless network?

LO 13-2
Understand and apply computer-assisted audit techniques.

COMPUTER-ASSISTED AUDIT TECHNIQUES

For most large and medium-sized enterprises, there are few business processes that are not driven by computers.[12] Almost all the data needed while conducting an audit are digital. Given today's business environment, it is very difficult to audit effectively and efficiently without using technology, such as **computer-assisted audit techniques (CAATs).**

[9] Federal Information Processing Standards (FIPS), "Minimum Security Requirements for Federal Information and Information Systems," Publication 200 (2006).

[10] NIST, "Guide to Securing Legacy IEEE 802.11 Wireless Networks," SP 800-48 Rev 1 (2008), p. 29.

[11] Cyber Security Malaysia, *Wireless Local Area Network (WLAN) Security Guideline,* p. 12.

[12] S. A. Sayana, "Using CAATs to Support IS Audit," *Information Systems Control Journal* 1 (2003).

CAATs are essential tools for auditors to conduct an audit in accordance with heightened auditing standards. Generally accepted auditing standards (GAAS) are broad guidelines regarding an auditor's professional responsibilities in three areas: general standards, standards of fieldwork, and standards of reporting. GAAS require auditors to gather sufficient and appropriate evidence in the course of audit fieldworks. The Information Systems Audit and Control Association (ISACA) issues Information Systems Auditing Standards (ISASs) that provide guidelines for conducting an IS/IT audit. Recently, ISASs were renamed as IT Standards, Guidelines, Tools, and Techniques for Audit and Assurance and Control Professionals. In "Performance of Audit Work" (S6), ISACA indicates that "during the course of the audit, the IS auditor should obtain sufficient, reliable, and relevant evidence to achieve the audit objectives. The audit findings and conclusions are to be supported by appropriate analysis and interpretation of this evidence."[13] In addition, according to the Institute of Internal Auditors' (IIA) professional practice standard section 1220.A2, internal auditors *must* consider the use of computer-assisted, technology-based audit tools and other data analysis techniques when conducting internal audits.[14]

The term "computer-assisted audit techniques" refers to any automated audit techniques that can be used by an auditor to perform audits in achieving audit objectives. In particular, CAATs enable auditors to gather and analyze audit evidence to test the adequacy and reliability of financial information and internal controls in a computerized environment. Some common areas in which auditors can use CAATs include the following:

- Test of details of transactions and balances.
- Analytical review procedures.
- Compliance tests of IT general and application controls.
- Operating system (OS) and network vulnerability assessments.
- Application security testing and source code security scans.
- Penetration testing.

Auditors may use two CAAT approaches in auditing systems: **auditing around the computer** (or **black-box approach**) and **auditing through the computer** (or **white-box approach**). Using the black-box approach, auditors test the reliability of computer-generated information by first calculating expected results from the transactions entered into the system. Then, the auditors compare these calculations to the processing or output results. If they prove to be accurate and valid, it is assumed that the system of controls is effective and that the system is operating properly. That is, auditors do not need to gain detailed knowledge of the systems' internal logic. The advantage of this approach is that the systems will not be interrupted for auditing purposes. The black-box approach could be adequate when automated systems applications are relatively simple.

The white-box approach requires auditors to understand the internal logic of the system/application being tested. Using this approach, auditors need to create test cases to verify specific logic and controls in a system. The auditing through the computer approach embraces a variety of approaches: the test data technique, parallel simulation, integrated test facility (ITF), and embedded audit module.[15]

The **test data technique** uses a set of input data to validate system integrity. When creating the test data, auditors need to prepare both valid and invalid data to examine critical logics and controls of the system. **Parallel simulation** attempts to simulate the firm's

[13] ISACA, *IT Standards, Guidelines, Tools, and Techniques for Audit and Assurance and Control Professionals* (2010), www.isaca.org.

[14] Institute of Internal Auditors (IIA), *International Standards for the Professional Practice of Internal Auditing (Standards)* (2010), www.theiia.org.

[15] Hall, *Information Technology Auditing and Assurance.*

key features or processes. Under this approach, the auditors write a computer program to reprocess the firm's actual data for a past period to generate simulated results. The simulated results are compared with the actual results to determine the validity of the system. The **integrated test facility (ITF)** approach is an automated technique that enables test data to be continually evaluated during the normal operation of a system. The auditor creates fictitious situations and performs a wide variety of tests over the system. This approach requires more computer expertise and is time-consuming and expensive. The **embedded audit module (EAM)** is a programmed audit module that is added to the system under review. Hence, the auditors can monitor and collect data over online transactions. The collected data are analyzed by auditors in evaluating control risks and effectiveness. The application of this approach requires auditors to have good knowledge and skills in computer programming.

In addition to the aforementioned techniques in auditing controls in a system, one widely used tool in auditing a system is **generalized audit software (GAS).** GAS is frequently used to perform substantive tests and is used for testing of controls through transactional data analysis.[16] GAS refers to standard software that has the capability to directly read and access data from various database platforms. GAS provides auditors with an independent means to gain access to data for analysis and the ability to use high-level, problem-solving software to invoke functions to be performed on data files.[17] Features include mathematical computations, stratification, statistical analysis, sequence checking, duplicate checking, and re-computation. Two of the most popular software packages are Audit Command Language (ACL) and Interactive Data Extraction and Analysis (IDEA). GAS is ideal for investigating large data files to identify records needing further audit scrutiny.

LO 13-3
Explain continuous auditing in AIS.

CONTINUOUS AUDITING

A **continuous audit** occurs when audit-related activities are performed on a continuous basis. With continuous auditing, theoretically, an audit report/opinion can be issued *simultaneously* with, or shortly after, the occurrence of the events under review.[18] Testing in continuous audits often consists of continuous controls monitoring and continuous data assurance.[19] Using automated audit procedures, the audit activities related to continuous auditing range from continuous control assessment to continuous risk assessment and include internal control assurance, financial attestation, fraud examination, audit scope and objective identification, audit records follow-ups, and annual audit plans preparation. For management, related continuous monitoring activities are control and performance monitoring, use of the Balanced Scorecard for total quality management, and enterprise risk management. Because continuous auditing is highly dependent on automated audit procedures, technology plays a key role in analyzing trends and patterns of transactions, identifying exceptions and anomalies, and testing controls.[20] Figure 13.3 illustrates the concepts and hierarchy of continuous auditing.

There are many benefits of conducting continuous audits. Most firms can reduce errors and frauds, increase operational effectiveness, better comply with laws and regulations, and increase management confidence in control effectiveness and financial information.

[16]M. V. Cerullo, "Impact of SAS No. 94 on Computer Audit Techniques," *Information Systems Control Journal* 1 (2003).

[17]ACL and IDEA are the most widely used GAS applications for data analysis.

[18]Global Technology Audit Guides (GTAG), *Continuous Auditing: Implications for Assurance, Monitoring, and Risk Assessment* (2005), p. 7.

[19]M. G. Alles, A. Kogan, and M. A. Vasarhelyi, "Putting Continuous Auditing Theory into Practice: Lessons from Two Pilot Implementations," *Journal of Information Systems* 22, no. 2 (2008), pp. 195–214.

[20]GTAG, *Continuous Auditing.*

Approach	Focus	Analysis Techniques	Related Audit Activities	Related Management Activities
Continuous controls assessment	Control-based (ensure financial controls are working)	Real-time/detailed transaction testing on financial data	Control assurance Financial data attest Fraud/waste/abuse examination Audit scope and objectives Follow-up on audit recommendations Annual audit plan	Control monitoring Performance monitoring Balanced Scorecard Total quality management (TQM) Enterprise risk management (ERM)
Continuous risk assessment	Risk-based (identify and assess risks on financial and operational controls)	Trend/comparison analysis on financial and operational data		

FIGURE 13.3
Concepts in Continuous Auditing

Source: D. Coderre, "Concepts in Continuous Auditing," Continuous Auditing, Pub/2005. https://www.iia.nl/.

In addition, continuous auditing allows internal and external auditors to monitor transaction data in a timely manner; better understand critical control points, rules, and exceptions; perform control and risk assessments in real time or near real time; notify management of control deficiencies in a timely manner; and reduce efforts of routine testing while focusing on more valuable investigation activities. However, if costs outweigh benefits, continuous auditing should not be implemented.

A 2006 study by Kuhn and Sutton analyzes the particular fraudulent activities that WorldCom's management used to deceive investors and assesses whether the "continuous auditing alarms" would have caught the fraudulent activities. This study provides guidance to auditors who are establishing continuous auditing initiatives to leverage the lessons learned from the WorldCom debacle and ensure that their continuous auditing routines are able to identify the type of financial fraud that occurred at WorldCom.[21]

Figure 13.4 summarizes the Kuhn and Sutton study and indicates the fraud schemes and the corresponding proposed alarms under continuous audits that would have flagged the activity for further review.

Although the concept of continuous auditing was introduced more than 20 years ago, it was not widely implemented by firms before the proliferation of information technologies in recent years. Today's advanced data analytics, ERP systems, and web-based programming languages such as Extensible Markup Language (XML) and Extensible Business Reporting Language (XBRL) make the implementation of continuous auditing more feasible and less costly than before.

Common IT techniques needed to implement continuous auditing include database management systems, transaction logging and query tools, data warehouses, and data mining or CAATs. Using these techniques, some key functions of continuous audits can be performed, such as accessing and normalizing data from across the enterprise, extracting large transactional volumes without having a negative impact on operational system performance, and testing data and reporting results in a timely manner.

[21] J. R. Kuhn and S. G. Sutton, "Learning from WorldCom: Implications for Fraud Detection through Continuous Assurance," *Journal of Emerging Technologies in Accounting* 3, no. 1 (2006), pp. 61–80.

FIGURE 13.4
Continuous Auditing Alarms and the WorldCom Fraud Schemes

WorldCom Fraud Scheme	Proposed Continuous Auditing Alarm
Operating expenses were illegitimately reclassified as capital expenditures, which improved the "expenditure-to-revenue" (E/R) ratio by reducing the amount of expenses recorded in current fiscal year.	Create an alarm that simultaneously identifies (1) reductions in operating expenses that exceed the industry average and (2) increases in capital expenditures that exceed the industry average.
Book values of acquired entities were illegitimately reclassified as goodwill on the books, which improved the E/R ratio by increasing the effective amortization period of the amounts in question.	Create an alarm that identifies increases in plant, property, equipment, and goodwill that differ significantly from historical averages.
"Taking a bath" by excessively writing down the assets included in the corporate acquisitions gave "the false impression that expenses were declining over time in relation to revenue (i.e., reducing the E/R ratio and increasing net income from operations)."	Benchmark key ratios (e.g., E/R) against industry averages, and generate an alarm when there is a significant discrepancy between the two.
Allowance for doubtful accounts was underestimated (along with the corresponding expense entry bad debts expense) to falsely improve the E/R ratio.	Generate an alarm if the allowance for doubtful accounts differs significantly from the last month's ratio (i.e., to Accounts Receivable).

The most significant nontechnical barriers[22] and technical challenges[23] encountered in implementing continuous auditing include

- Perceived negative impact of continuous auditing on the firm, such as the cost of initial investments, changes in internal audit group's head count, and the quality of audits.
- Priority of implementation in determined key areas, such as which controls should be monitored on a continual basis and which audit activities could be automated.
- Readiness of the internal audit group to develop and adopt continuous auditing.
- Unrealistic expectations of the benefits of continuous auditing.
- Access to all relevant data in a timely manner.
- Accumulating and quantifying the risks and the exposures that have been identified.
- Defining the appropriate analytic that will effectively identify exceptions to controls.
- Developing a suitable scoring/weighting mechanism to prioritize exceptions.
- Balancing the costs and efforts of reviewing large volumes of exceptions against the exposures of the exceptions themselves.

Although there is no universal, well-accepted approach to implementing continuous auditing, there is a general template that a steering team or the internal audit function can use.[24] When a firm considers whether or not to implement continuous auditing, it should first evaluate the overall benefit and cost of having continuous auditing as part of the firm's overall governance, risk, and compliance (GRC) effort. After careful evaluations to rationalize the decision, the firm should develop a strategy in identifying and prioritizing potential areas for continuous audits. Once the strategy is developed, the firm should plan and design how to implement continuous auditing, such as determining the scope of the audit objectives, designing the continuous auditing processes, allocating resources, and creating a reasonable timeline for implementation. Once the resources are approved and in place, the firm can implement continuous auditing followed by periodic performance monitoring on the implementation.

[22] Deloitte & Touche, *Continuous Monitoring and Continuous Auditing: From Idea to Implementation* (2010), p. 10.

[23] ACL, *Building and Implementing a Continuous Controls Monitoring and Auditing Framework* (2005), p. 3.

[24] Deloitte & Touche, *Continuous Monitoring and Continuous Auditing,* p. 10.

Summary

- Essential concepts of critical computer hardware and software are introduced in this chapter, including the operating system, the database, local area networks, wide area networks, and wireless networks.
- There are two approaches to auditing an information system: auditing around the computer (the black-box approach) and auditing through the computer (the white-box approach).
- Most auditors would like to use computer-assisted audit techniques (CAATs) in auditing a system, such as the test data technique, parallel simulation, and the embedded audit module. CAATs are often used in continuous auditing. Performing audit-related activities on a continuous basis may narrow the gap between daily operations and the required improvements resulting from an audit.

Key Words

access point (*331*) Logically connects stations to a firm's network.

audit around the computer (or black-box approach) (*333*) Auditors test the reliability of computer-generated information by first calculating expected results from the transactions entered into the system. Then, the auditors compare these calculations to the processing or output results.

audit through the computer (or white-box approach) (*333*) Requires auditors to understand the internal logic of the system/application being tested.

computer-assisted audit techniques (CAATs) (*332*) Essential tools for auditors to conduct an audit in accordance with heightened auditing standards.

continuous audit (*334*) Performing audit-related activities on a continuous basis.

data governance (*327*) The convergence of data quality, data management, data policies, business process management, and risk management surrounding the handling of data in a firm.

data mining (*327*) A process of using sophisticated statistical techniques to extract and analyze data from large databases to discern patterns and trends that were not previously known.

data warehouse (*327*) A collection of information gathered from an assortment of external and operational (i.e, internal) databases to facilitate reporting for decision making and business analysis.

database (*327*) A shared collection of logically related data for various uses.

database system (*327*) A term typically used to encapsulate the constructs of a data model, database management system (DBMS), and database.

embedded audit module (*334*) A programmed audit module that is added to the system under review.

firewall (*329*) A security system comprised of hardware and software that is built using routers, servers, and a variety of software.

generalized audit software (GAS) (*334*) Frequently used to perform substantive tests and used for testing of controls through transactional data analysis.

hub (*328*) Contains multiple ports.

integrated test facility (ITF) (*334*) An automated technique that enables test data to be continually evaluated during the normal operation of a system.

local area network (LAN) (*328*) A group of computers, printers, and other devices connected to the same network that covers a limited geographic range such as a home, small office, or a campus building.

MAC (media access control) address (*328*) A designated address that is connected to each device via the network and only sees traffic.

operating system (OS) (*326*) Performs the tasks that enable a computer to operate; comprised of system utilities and programs.

operational database (327) Often includes data for the current fiscal year only.

parallel simulation (333) Attempts to simulate the firm's key features or processes.

remote access (330) Connection to a data-processing system from a remote location e.g., through a virtual private network.

router (329) Software-based intelligent device that chooses the most efficient communication path through a network to the required destination.

station (331) A wireless endpoint device equipped with a wireless network interface card.

switch (328) An intelligent device that provides a path for each pair of connections on the switch by storing address information in its switching tables.

test data technique (333) Uses a set of input data to validate system integrity.

virtual private network (VPN) (330) Securely connects a firm's WANs by sending/receiving encrypted packets via virtual connections over the public Internet to distant offices, salespeople, and business partners.

wide area network (WAN) (329) Links different sites together; transmits information across geographically dispersed LANs; and covers a broad geographic area such as a city, region, nation, or an international link.

wireless network (331) Comprised of two fundamental architectural components: access points and stations.

Answers to Progress Checks

1. Two or more computers in a small office connected to the same printer form a local area network. The Internet is the most popular and largest wide area network.
2. Mobile devices are subject to man-in-the-middle attacks when using unsecured wi-fi networks. Also, if an iPad user gets applications from any apps store, he or she is at risk of getting malicious applications from the store.

connect

Multiple Choice Questions

1. A local area network (LAN) is best described as a(n): LO 13-1
   a. computer system that connects computers of all sizes, workstations, terminals, and other devices within a limited proximity.
   b. system that allows computer users to meet and share ideas and information.
   c. electronic library containing millions of items of data that can be reviewed, retrieved, and analyzed.
   d. method to offer specialized software, hardware, and data-handling techniques that improve effectiveness and reduce costs.
2. Which of the following network components is set up to serve as a security measure that prevents unauthorized traffic between different segments of the network? LO 13-1
   a. Switch
   b. Router
   c. Firewall
   d. Virtual local area networks (VLANs)

3. Unauthorized alteration of records in a database system would impair which of the following components of the CIA (related to security)? **LO 13-1**
   a. Confidentiality
   b. Integrity
   c. Availability
   d. Authorization
4. Which of the following is not a task performed by an operating system? **LO 13-1**
   a. Translate high-level languages to machine-level language
   b. Manage job scheduling and multiprogramming
   c. Support applications and facilitate their access to specified resources
   d. Provide controlled access to data and process data
5. Managers at a consumer products company purchased personal computer software from only recognized vendors and prohibited employees from installing nonauthorized software on their personal computers by enforcing a new end-user computing policy. To minimize the likelihood of computer viruses infecting any of its systems, the company should also: **LO 13-1**
   a. restore infected systems with authorized versions.
   b. recompile infected programs from source code backups.
   c. institute program change control procedures.
   d. test all new software on a stand-alone personal computer.
6. Unauthorized alteration of records in a database system can be prevented by employing: **LO 13-1**
   a. key verification.
   b. computer matching.
   c. regular review of audit trails.
   d. database access controls.
7. An organization is planning to replace its wired networks with wireless networks. Which of the following approaches provides the most secure wireless network? **LO 13-1**
   a. Implement wired equivalent privacy (WEP) protocol
   b. Allow access to only authorized media access control (MAC) addresses
   c. Disable the network interface card (NIC)
   d. Implement wi-fi protected access (WPA2)
8. The vice president of human resources has requested an audit to identify payroll overpayments for the previous year. Which would be the best audit technique to use in this situation? **LO 13-3**
   a. Test data
   b. Generalized audit software
   c. Integrated test facility
   d. Embedded audit module
9. Which of following statements about CAATs is not correct? **LO 13-2**
   a. Parallel simulation attempts to simulate or reproduce the firm's actual processing results.
   b. The test data technique uses a set of hypothetical transactions to examine the programmed checks and program logic in programs.
   c. The integrated test facility is a programmed module or segment that is inserted into an application program to monitor and collect data based on daily transactions.
   d. The embedded audit module may require the auditor to have a good working knowledge of computer programming and a solid understanding of IT risks that may exist in a system.

10. Which of the following audit techniques should an IS auditor use to detect duplicate invoice records within an invoice master file? **LO 13-3**
    a. Test data
    b. Generalized audit software
    c. Integrated test facility
    d. Embedded audit module
11. A group of computers, printers, and other devices connected to the same network and covering a limited geographic range is called a: **LO 13-1**
    a. LAN.
    b. VAN.
    c. VPN.
    d. WAN.
12. The most common security threats for wireless LANs include: **LO 13-1**
    a. man-in-the-middle.
    b. system malfunction.
    c. social engineering.
    d. virus.
13. The test data technique uses: **LO 13-3**
    a. a programmed audit module that is added to the system under review.
    b. a computer program to reprocess the firm's actual data for a past period to generate simulated results.
    c. a set of input data to validate system integrity.
    d. an automated technique that enables test data to be continually evaluated during the normal operation of a system.
14. Which of the following is not one of the main purposes for a WAN? **LO 13-1**
    a. Provide remote access to employees and/or customers
    b. Link two or more geographically dispersed sites within a company
    c. Provide corporate access to the Internet
    d. Securely connect a network to distant offices in a building by sending encrypted packets
15. An operational database: **LO 13-1**
    a. contains data that are volatile.
    b. covers the data of current and previous fiscal years.
    c. is updated before transactions are processed.
    d. contains data that are uploaded from a data warehouse.

Discussion Questions

1. What are the main reasons for using a VPN? **LO 13-1**
2. Consider the computer attacks in the previous chapters. How would a VPN protect a user from one or more of them? **LO 13-1**
3. We often use regression analyses in data mining. Are accountants required to understand data mining? Why? **LO 13-1**
4. What is the main purpose of using firewalls? **LO 13-1**
5. Firewalls rely on a list of allowed and blocked services and locations. What would happen if a company's firewall rules were too weak? If the firewall rules were too strict? **LO 13-1**
6. Are there differences among hubs, switches, and routers? **LO 13-1**
7. Identify a few critical security issues in using a wireless network. **LO 13-1**

8. Using a brute-force attack, hackers can crack the password to a WEP access point in about 5 minutes and WPA2 in about 2 days. What does this tell you about the security of wireless networks? **LO 13-1**
9. Auditors are constantly developing new CAAT analyses to help them in the assurance process. Use a search engine to identify some of the techniques that are being used currently. **LO 13-2**
10. When would an auditor prefer to conduct a black-box audit? A white-box audit? **LO 13-2**
11. Continuous auditing allows auditors to validate data and monitor transactions in near real-time. What advantages does this provide to auditors? What are some potential problems with continuous auditing? **LO 13-3**
12. Auditing an accounting information system requires knowledge and skills in both accounting and computers. However, most auditors may not have sufficient expertise in the technical side of computing and information systems. Given today's business environment, how much computer- and information systems-related knowledge and skills must an auditor have to be effective in performing auditing? **LO 13-2, LO 13-3**

Problems

connect

1. Match the descriptions with each type of network. **LO 13-1**

Descriptions	Network
a. This computer network covers a broad area (e.g., includes any network whose communications link cross metropolitan, regional, or national boundaries over a long distance).	i. LAN
b. The Internet is a good example of this type of network.	ii. WAN
c. This type of network often uses Layer 2 devices like switches and Layer 1 devices like hubs.	iii. VPN
d. The purpose of this type of network is mainly for remote access.	iv. Wireless LAN
e. This type of network comprises of two fundamental architectural components: stations and access points.	
f. This type of network has a large geographical range generally spreading across boundaries and often needs leased telecommunication lines.	

connect

2. Match the continuous auditing alarms to flag the fraud schemes. **LO 13-3**

Fraud Scheme	Continuous Auditing Alarms
a. Operating expenses were illegitimately reclassified as capital expenditures, which improved the "expenditure-to-revenue" (E/R) ratio by reducing the amount of expenses recorded in the current fiscal year.	i. Generate an alarm if the allowance for doubtful accounts differs significantly from the last month's ratio (i.e., to Accounts Receivable).
b. Book values of acquired entities were illegitimately reclassified as goodwill on the books, which improved the E/R ratio by increasing the effective amortization period of the amounts in question.	ii. Benchmark key ratios (e.g., E/R) against industry averages and generate an alarm when there is a significant discrepancy between the two.
c. Excessively wrote down the assets included in the corporate acquisitions, which gave "the false impression that expenses were declining over time in relation to revenue (i.e., reducing the E/R ratio and increasing net income from operations)."	iii. Create an alarm that identifies increases in plant, property, equipment, and goodwill that differ significantly from historical averages.
d. Allowance for doubtful accounts was underestimated (along with the corresponding expense entry bad debts expense) to falsely improve the E/R ratio.	iv. Create an alarm that simultaneously identifies (1) reductions in operating expenses that exceed the industry average and (2) increases in capital expenditures that exceed the industry average.

3. (CIA adapted) As an internal auditor, you have been assigned to evaluate the controls and operation of a computer payroll system. To test the computer systems and programs, you submit independently created test transactions with regular data in a normal production run. Identify advantages and disadvantages of this technique. **LO 13-3**
4. Describe how an auditor would use each of the following audit techniques: ITF, parallel simulation, EAM, GAS. **LO 13-2**
5. Identify the key feature and components of a continuous audit. **LO 13-3**
6. (CMA adapted) As chief executive auditor, Mallory Williams heads the internal audit group of a manufacturing company in southern Texas. She would like to purchase a CAAT tool to assist her group in conducting internal audit functions. She has asked you to prepare a report on the following tools: ACL, IDEA, Microsoft Visio, Oversight, and Tableau. In your report, identify key features and how an auditor would incorporate the tool into the audit, and recommend one or two of the tools for purchase. **LO 13-2, LO 13-3**

Chapter Fourteen

The Balanced Scorecard and Business Value of Information Technology

A look at this chapter

As managers and designers of IT systems as well as business partners, accountants are often involved in helping formulate and implement company strategy. The Balanced Scorecard is a well-known strategic performance management system that many companies use to formulate, implement, and monitor strategic performance. In this chapter, we explain concepts embodied in the Balanced Scorecard and describe how information technology supports a company's strategic objectives from a Balanced Scorecard viewpoint.

A look back

Chapter 13 explained the accountants' role in the business when monitoring and auditing accounting information systems.

A look ahead

Chapter 15 presents a process for assessing the business value of IT initiatives. As users, managers, designers, and evaluators of the firm's IT systems, accountants are important members of the team that will develop the business case for AIS initiatives. Additionally, as users, managers, and evaluators, they can also be asked to review business cases for IT initiatives in general.

According to an August 2009 article in *The Wall Street Journal*, **Starbucks** is adopting "lean Japanese techniques" in a quest for greater efficiency in its 11,000 U.S. stores. Scott Heydon, Vice President of Lean Thinking at Starbucks, has been known to challenge store managers to assemble and disassemble Mr. Potato Head toys in less than 45 seconds. This challenge is intended to get them to think about wasted steps in their processes.

An Oregon City, Oregon, Starbucks store was among the first to adopt lean techniques. The store manager first took more than 2 minutes to put Mr. Potato Head together and then take him apart. After reducing extra steps, she reduced the time to about 15 seconds. Then, she examined the steps that her partners took to fill drive-through window orders, including moving and reaching for different ingredients. After streamlining the process, the store reduced the time to fill an average drive-through order to 25 seconds, one of the fastest times in the company.

© Muskopf Photography, LLC/Alamy

Starbucks' management believes that reducing waste will give its store partners more time to interact with customers and allow them to improve service. This is important for a couple of reasons. First, the recent economic downturn has reduced customer traffic and forced Starbucks to close almost 900 stores. Second, personnel costs amount to 24 percent of Starbucks' revenue, one of its largest operating expenses. While reducing waste is important, it won't deliver real value unless Starbucks' partners can improve customer service and increase customer traffic. This chapter describes how a company's investment in people and technology can affect the business process performance and how business process performance affects the company's customer value proposition and, subsequently, its financial performance.

Chapter Outline

Learning Objectives

After reading this chapter, you should be able to:

14-1 Describe the Balanced Scorecard framework.

14-2 Explain the purpose of strategy maps.

14-3 Describe different types of IT and why IT initiatives can be difficult to evaluate.

14-4 Define the Balanced Scorecard management process.

14-5 Describe how an AIS system contributes to a Balanced Scorecard management process.

14-6 Describe the IT Governance Val IT Framework

14-7 Explain how organizations implement the Val IT framework

LO 14-1
Describe the Balanced Scorecard framework.

BALANCED SCORECARD FRAMEWORK

According to a recent survey by the Financial Executives Institute,[1] more than 40 percent of responding financial officers reported that their company's investments in IT are providing little or no return on investment. When existing IT systems and new IT initiatives fail to deliver expected returns, companies have a management problem—not an IT problem. According to a recent article in *IndustryWeek* magazine, "A formal, structured approach that links IT investment to business performance can help companies avoid many of these problems by providing a focus to the investment that is often missing."[2] This chapter offers frameworks that describe the potential value of IT relative to a company's strategic objectives. The next chapter describes methods for evaluating return on investment for individual, or portfolios of, IT investments.

Investments in information technology, such as AIS, take on value only in the context of the company's strategy. Executives should analyze each proposed investment as part of a portfolio of potential investments that help to implement a strategy.[3]

The Balanced Scorecard provides a tool that can describe the contribution of IT to the company's strategy. The Balanced Scorecard is a performance measurement framework that allows managers to measure the firm's performance from multiple perspectives that follow from the firm's mission, strategy, and objectives. According to the Balanced Scorecard Institute (www.balancedscorecard.org),

> The balanced scorecard is a strategic planning and management system that is used extensively in business and industry, government, and nonprofit organizations worldwide to align business activities to the vision and strategy of the organization, improve internal and external communications, and monitor organization performance against strategic goals.

The **Balanced Scorecard framework** describes performance from four different perspectives based on the firm's strategy to achieve shareholder value. Objectives for each perspective describe the strategy in a series of cause-and-effect relationships (see Figure 14.1).

FIGURE 14.1
Relationships between Balanced Scorecard Perspectives

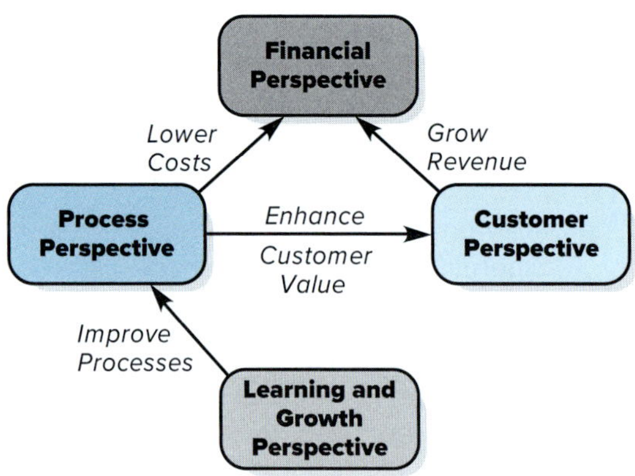

[1]Computer Sciences Corporation and Financial Executives Research Foundation, *Technology Issues for Financial Executives,* Financial Executive Institute (2008).

[2]D. Schrock, J. Cole, and J. Shaffer, "Getting IT Right: How to Plan, Manage and Deliver on Technology's Promise," *IndustryWeek,* December 16, 2010, www.IndustryWeek.com.

[3]See, for example, Deloitte, *Value Matters: Getting Back to What's Really Important in Planning, Budgeting, and Forecasting,* Deloitte Consulting, LLP (2010).

Connection with Practice

Bain and Company, a prominent consulting company, conducts an annual survey of almost 1,500 international executives. The survey asks about the use of the 25 most popular management tools and techniques. For 2015, 39 percent of North American and 44 percent of European respondents were using some form of the Balanced Scorecard for strategic management.

Learning and Growth Perspective

The **learning and growth perspective** describes the firm's objectives for improvements in tangible and intangible infrastructure. The firm addresses its goals for investments in human capital, information capital, and organizational capital to make sure that the firm is strategically ready to continuously improve its process performance. Managers use metrics to focus investments, such as employee training or new systems development, to achieve the firm's learning and growth objectives and also link those changes to process objectives.

Customer management process in action.
© Plush Studios/DH Kong/Getty Images

Process Perspective

The **process perspective** describes the firm's objectives for its business processes so that the firm operates efficiently while delivering products and services that meet its customers' requirements. In their book, *Strategy Maps,*[4] Kaplan and Norton describe four types of business processes:

1. Operations management processes, such as supply, production, distribution, and risk management.
2. Customer management processes, such as those involved with the selection, acquisition, and retention of customers and growth of the firm's market.
3. Innovation processes, such as identifying opportunities, research and development, product design and development, and product launch.
4. Regulatory and social processes, such as financial reporting, accounting, and those that manage environmental, safety and health, employment, and community issues.

Firms invest in learning and growth to improve business process performance, which in turn affects customer and financial performance objectives. Process performance can be

[4]R. S. Kaplan and D. Norton, *Strategy Maps: Converting Intangible Assets into Tangible Outcomes.* (Boston: Harvard Business School Press, 2004).

measured generally in terms of cost, time, quality, and throughput. Process cost directly affects financial productivity measures, as shown in Figure 14.2. Time measures, such as cycle time and on-time delivery, directly affect customer service. Process quality affects product quality and customer service and thus drives customer satisfaction and retention. Throughput describes the quantity of products and services that the process can deliver. Financial perspective productivity measures, such as return on assets or return on sales, relate costs to throughput. In general, companies seek to lower process costs, lower cycle times, improve process quality, and increase process throughput to deliver their value proposition to their customers and achieve financial objectives.

Customer Perspective

Within the **customer perspective,** customer satisfaction is considered a leading indicator of firm performance. By operating its business processes, the firm creates a **value proposition** that differentiates it from its competition. The value proposition includes attributes of the firm's products, such as price, quality, and selection, as well as attributes of its relationship with its customers, such as the level of service and efforts to build long-term relationships, and its brand image (see Figure 14.2). When the firm's value proposition meets or exceeds customers' requirements, customer satisfaction results in customer retention and new customer acquisition, which drives sales growth.

Financial Perspective

The final measure is the **financial perspective.** Accounting-based performance measures are considered lagging indicators of firm performance. They confirm the success of the firm's investments in learning and growth, process performance, and ability to deliver value to customers. Balanced Scorecard financial objectives usually relate to firm productivity and long-term growth, both of which drive shareholder value.

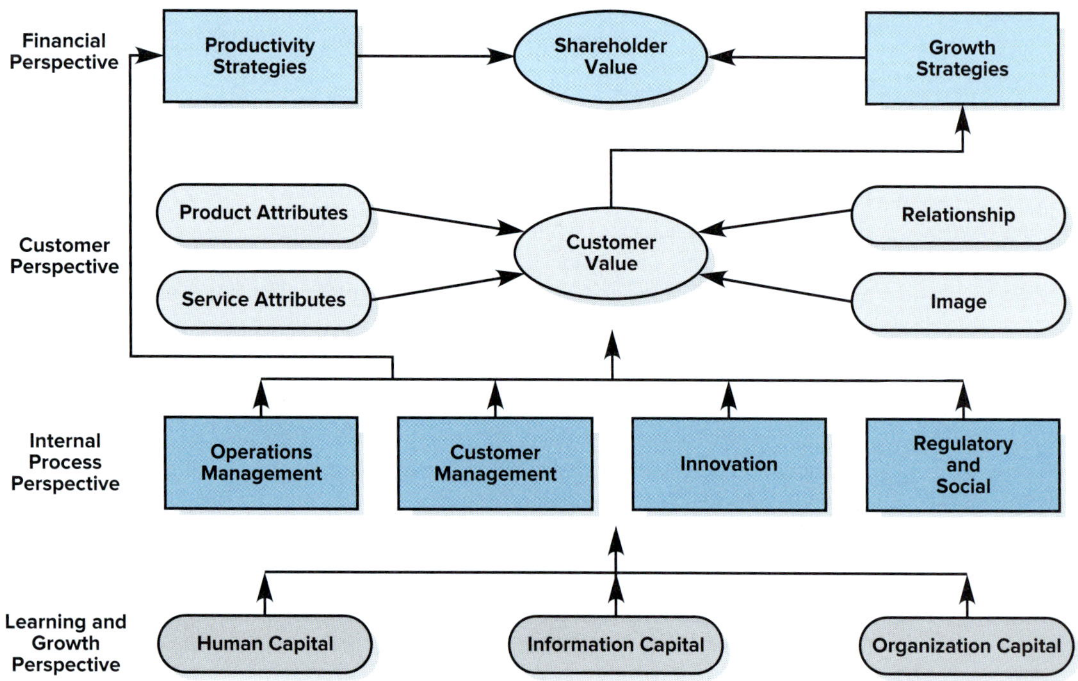

FIGURE 14.2
Generic Strategy Map

LO 14-2
Explain the purpose of strategy maps.

One important feature of strategy maps is the identification of expected cause-and-effect links among perspectives.

FRAMEWORK INTEGRATING STRATEGY, OPERATIONS, AND IT INVESTMENT

The Balanced Scorecard provides a useful integrating framework to examine a company's strategy/operations management system as well as the potential contributions of IT to company success. A Balanced Scorecard strategy map illustrates the various components of a company's strategy across the four perspectives described in the preceding section.

A **strategy map** is a one-page representation of the firm's strategic priorities and the cause-and-effect linkages among those strategic priorities.[5] It illustrates the firm's strategic objectives (also called critical success factors, as shown in Table 14.1) for each perspective as well as the cause-and-effect links among perspectives. A strategy map allows firms to assess and prioritize gaps between their current and desired performance levels.

LO 14-3
Describe different types of IT and why IT initiatives can be difficult to evaluate.

ROLE OF AIS/IT IN A BALANCED SCORECARD FRAMEWORK

A Balanced Scorecard framework allows companies to assess the value of IT investments in terms of contribution to strategic objectives, regardless of whether they employ a Balanced Scorecard performance management system. A Balanced Scorecard framework recognizes the difference between investments in tangible information technology and the capabilities provided by that technology. **Information capital** is an intangible asset that reflects the readiness of the company's technology to support strategic internal processes. In other words, information capital includes:

- Computing hardware, such as individual computers.
- Infrastructure, such as communications networks.
- Applications, such as accounting and decision support software.
- Employees' abilities to use the technology effectively.

To understand the value of IT in a Balanced Scorecard framework and the importance of portfolios of IT investments rather than individual investments, it is helpful to consider different ways to characterize the nature of IT. The following classifications (see Table 14.2)

Perspective	*Performance Objectives*	*Critical Success Factors*	*Key Performance Indicators*
Financial	How does the firm's performance drive shareholder value?	Demonstrate productivity and growth necessary to create shareholder value.	Return on assets/equity/sales, earnings per share growth rate, sales growth rate, market value added
Customer	How does the firm deliver value to its customers to create long-term growth?	Create customer value necessary to drive revenue growth.	Market share, new customer acquisition rate, repeat purchase rate, customer satisfaction
Process	How do the firm's processes deliver value to customers while operating efficiently?	Conduct business processes to create customer value and achieve profitable growth.	Process cost, quality, timeliness, and outputs
Learning and growth	How do investments in employee, organizational, and information systems capabilities support continuous improvement of the firm's business processes and customer relationships?	Invest in human capital, organizational capital, and information capital to improve processes and deliver strategic objectives.	Assessments of employee knowledge, skills, and values; employee change readiness and strategic awareness surveys; readiness ratings of software applications; levels of spending

TABLE 14.1
Balanced Scorecard Perspectives, Objectives, Sample Critical Success Factors, and Key Performance Indicators

[5]Ibid.

TABLE 14.2
Three Categories of Information Technologies

IT Category	*Description*	*Characteristics*
Function IT	Assists execution with discrete tasks.	Does not require complements, but impact can increase with users' skill.
Network IT	Facilitates interactions.	Does not require complements, but impact increases with users' skill and extent of teamwork.
Enterprise IT	Specifies the nature of business processes and requires interactions.	Requires complements and impact often depends on users' skills, teamwork, changes to the way work is performed, and changes in the way decisions are made.

characterize the nature of information technologies and can indicate which initiatives could be harder to implement and evaluate.[6]

1. **Function IT (FIT)**—those that perform a single function, such as enhancing worker productivity for stand-alone tasks. Examples of FIT include word-processing and spreadsheet applications and computer-aided design applications. Function information technologies can improve the productivity of skilled workers, but they can be used without affecting the remainder of the organization.
2. **Network IT (NIT)**—those that allow people to communicate with one another. Examples of NIT include e-mail, instant messaging, network technologies, and blog applications. Network information technologies allow collaboration, foster teamwork, and improve information exchange within the organization, but they do little to change the way that work is performed or decisions are made.
3. **Enterprise IT (EIT)**—those that restructure interactions within the organization as well as with external partners. Examples of EIT include customer relationship management (CRM) and supply chain management (SCM) applications. Enterprise information technologies often change the way business processes are performed as well as the way decisions are made.

Compared to function and network IT, enterprise IT provides more capabilities but requires more complementary resources to achieve its potential benefits. Enterprise IT can provide the following organizational capabilities.

- *Transaction automation*—the EIT can automate transaction processing, replacing personnel while ensuring that each transaction is performed in a uniform and controlled manner. This allows—and forces—standardized work flow and applications of business rules.
- *Process management automation*—the EIT can automate administrative processes, incorporating business rules and decision heuristics and reducing the need for administrative specialists.
- *Process integration*—the EIT can integrate processes previously managed separately, reducing the need for separate systems and separate administration.
- *Customer service*—the EIT can provide general and customized service to both internal and external clients, thereby reducing the need for customer service agents.
- *Performance monitoring and decision support*—the EIT can record various process performance indicators and more timely summarize information on **key performance indicators** for management use.

After enterprise IT is implemented, its performance becomes embedded in one or more organizational processes, making it difficult for firms to evaluate the benefit of the IT investment separately from the performance of the process. However, the performance of business processes usually depends on a variety of factors. For example, when an EIT

[6] A. McAfee, "Mastering the Three Worlds of Information Technology," *Harvard Business Review*, November 2006, pp. 141–149.

improves decision support, the impact on business value depends on the decisions, and it can take 3 to 5 years for managers to learn how to use better and timelier information.

IT systems provide relative few business benefits on their own. The value of IT can depend on the existence of complementary organizational capabilities, such as skilled workers, teamwork, the way that work is performed, and the authority to make decisions. Furthermore, the level of these complementary resources can change over time after an IT system is implemented.

Progress Check

1. Describe how you think IT creates value for **Starbucks**, whose CIO is now also general manager of digital ventures. Based on what you know about the company, what category of IT best describes Starbucks's digital ventures?
2. From your own experience, describe examples of function IT and network IT.

LO 14-4
Define the Balanced Scorecard management process.

USING A BALANCED SCORECARD MANAGEMENT PROCESS

While the relationships among Balanced Scorecard perspectives shown in the generic strategy map (Figure 14.2) shows how information capital contributes to critical business processes, which in turn contribute to customer acquisition and retention and result in financial performance, the strategy map does not describe how companies go about implementing their strategy. According to the creators of the Balanced Scorecard, companies can plan, implement, and monitor performance using the following **Balanced Scorecard management process.**[7] The steps in the process can be thought of as continuous, with the last step feeding back to the first step, as shown in Figure 14.3.

1. *Formulate*—the company examines its competitive environment and identifies ways in which it can best compete consistent with its mission, vision, and values.
2. *Translate*—the company establishes specific objectives, measures, targets, and initiatives and develops capital, initiative, and other long-term budgets to guide resource allocation and action according to its strategy.

FIGURE 14.3
Balanced Scorecard Management Process

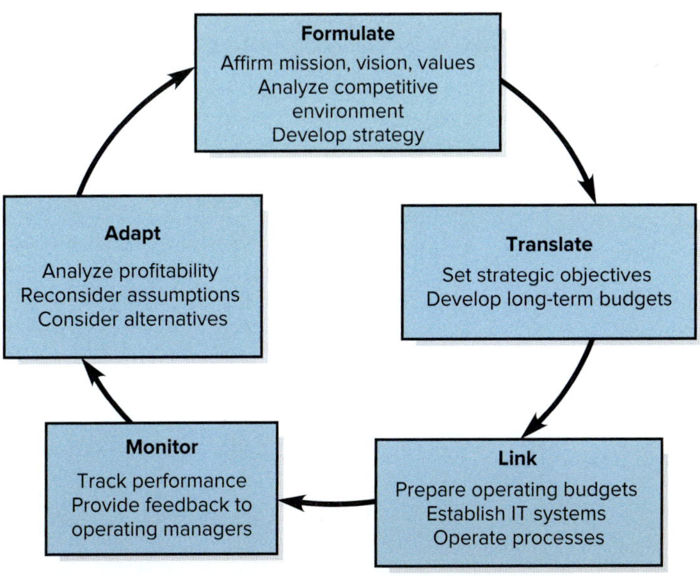

[7] R. S. Kaplan and D. Norton, *The Execution Premium* (Boston: Harvard Business Press, 2008).

3. *Link to operations*—the company prepares operating budgets, prioritizes business process improvements, and develops key performance indicators. At this point it establishes necessary IT systems to support strategic business processes as well as management reporting and review capabilities.
4. *Monitor*—the company monitors performance to ensure processes are meeting objectives and provides feedback to operating managers for continuous improvement.
5. *Adapt*—the company evaluates the effectiveness of its strategy, conducts profitability analytics, tests the cause-and-effect assumptions of the strategy, and identifies potential alternatives.

LO 14-5
Describe how an AIS system contributes to a Balanced Scorecard management process.

ROLE OF AIS/IT IN THE BALANCED SCORECARD MANAGEMENT PROCESS

IT also has an important role in implementing and managing a Balanced Scorecard management process or similar planning, forecasting, and budgeting processes. Beginning with strategy formulation, companies rely on a variety of information technology systems and capabilities to support their strategy execution and management process. Table 14.3 provides some examples. Business intelligence and financial reporting systems provide data to support strategy development, and business analytics systems provide forecasts and analysis to support senior executives' decisions. Those broad strategic decisions are translated into objectives that guide the capital budgeting process, supported by a variety of systems. Strategic objectives then link to operations. Specific budgets are set, and the company conducts operations, supported by appropriate enterprise IT, such as ERP systems. The enterprise IT performance monitoring and decision support capabilities then assess operational performance against the strategic objectives. Operational managers adjust operations based on feedback. Finally, senior executives use information from business intelligence and financial reporting systems to reevaluate the strategy and consider alternatives.

Think about how the models that you prepared in Chapters 5, 6, and 7 would support the information requirements outlined here.

The use of structured strategic management processes, such as the Balanced Scorecard, ties the effective use of supporting technologies, as described in Table 14.3, to successful performance. Standardized, integrated, and networked technology enhances decision making and performance management. While the capabilities of function IT systems, such as

TABLE 14.3
AIS/IT Contributions to the Balanced Scorecard Management Process

Process Step	Information Technology Capabilities
1. Formulate	Enterprise IT (business intelligence systems, financial reporting systems)
	Function IT (business analytics, executive dashboards)
	Network IT (communication and collaboration)
2. Translate	Function IT (Balanced Scorecard systems, business analytics)
	Enterprise IT (budgeting systems, performance monitoring and decision support)
	Network IT (communication and collaboration)
3. Link to operations	Enterprise IT (budgeting systems, transaction processing, process management, customer service, process integration)
4. Monitor	Integrated Enterprise IT (performance monitoring and decision support)
	Function IT (operational dashboards with key performance indicators)
	Network IT (communication and collaboration)
5. Adapt	Enterprise IT (business intelligence systems)
	Function IT (business analytics, executive dashboards)
	Network IT (communication and collaboration)

business analytics and executive dashboard applications, are important, companies need to gather data from multiple sources, linking dashboards to an integrated view of operating processes. A complete picture of the company's value chain enhances data analysis and accelerates decision making and planning.

LO 14-6
Describe the IT Governance Val IT Framework.

IT GOVERNANCE INSTITUTE VAL IT FRAMEWORK

Recently, the IT Governance Institute also developed a structured framework for IT investment and management. The **Val IT** framework is intended to help managers create business value from IT investments. It aligns with and complements the COBIT control framework described in Chapter 11. Val IT is aimed at the management of IT benefits over an investment's life cycle net of any costs and adjusted for risk. It is similar to the Balanced Scorecard since it requires organizations to define value in terms of the organization's strategic objectives.

Val IT requires managers and executives to focus on four major questions,[8] as shown in Figure 14.4.

1. Are we doing the right things? To answer this question, managers must examine whether investments are consistent with their business principles and contributing to the achievement of strategic objectives.
2. Are we doing them the right way? This requires managers to consider whether the investment is consistent with their current IT architecture and other IT initiatives.
3. Are we doing them well? This question focuses on processes. Managers must evaluate whether the organization has the right technical and business resources to support the investment.
4. Are we getting the benefits? Managers must understand what the investment will deliver and establish clear metrics to help assess whether the investment delivers those benefits.

Val IT distinguishes among (1) projects, activities to deliver a defined capability; (2) programs, structured groups of interdependent projects; and (3) portfolios, groups of

FIGURE 14.4
Fundamental Val IT Questions

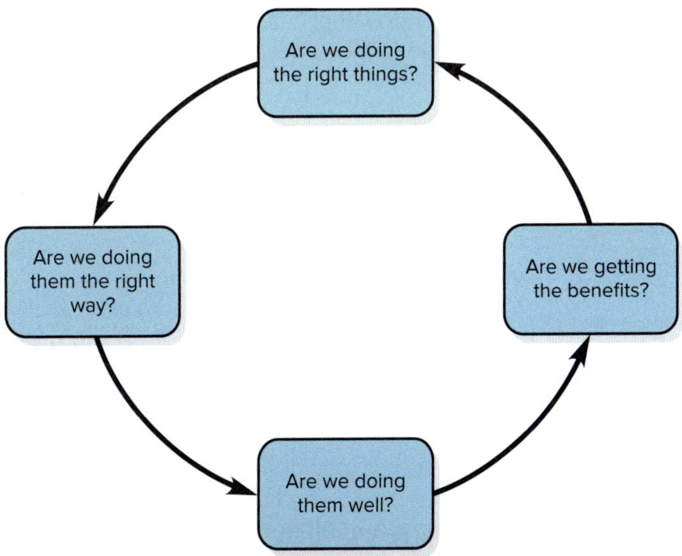

[8]For further information on Val IT, see *Enterprise Value: Governance of IT Investments. The Val IT Framework 2.0*, published by the IT Governance Institute.

programs, projects, services, and other IT resources. The Val IT framework establishes three domains with corresponding governance, portfolio management, and investment management processes.

- Value governance establishes the governance part of the framework, which includes defining the various portfolios as well as mechanisms for monitoring the effectiveness of all Val IT processes.
- Portfolio management establishes strategic priorities, determines required characteristics of the investment portfolios, and monitors the performance of the overall portfolio. It also sets program priorities within funding constraints, based on strategic alignment, net benefits, and risks.
- Investment management proposes potential programs and the projects that make up those programs, executes authorized programs, reports investment and program performance, and retires programs when the desired business value is delivered or it is clear that the business value cannot be delivered.

Thus, the three domains interact to provide oversight and management of individual projects, combinations of projects within programs, and programs within the overall portfolio.

When properly implemented, Val IT focuses on delivering business value while COBIT focuses on managing risk. Both are essential elements of IT governance.

LO 14-7
Explain how organizations implement the Val IT framework.

IMPLEMENTING VAL IT GOVERNANCE

The steps to implement and use Val IT are similar to the steps of the Balanced Scorecard management process outlined earlier in this chapter. Organizations often fail to realize value from their IT investments. Experts agree that the most common problem is the lack of a structured approach; however, the second most common problem is lack of knowledge of how to begin. Four Val IT implementation steps are designed to assist organizations in developing a structured approach to managing IT investments.

1. *Recognize problems with prior IT investments.* In this step, organizations should assess the state of their IT governance. They should consider whether the roles and responsibilities of the IT function and other business functions are clearly defined. They should also assess whether IT and business functions collaborate fully to deliver value from IT investments.
2. *Define characteristics of the ideal future state.* These include awareness and communication of roles and responsibilities. Managers are responsible and accountable for their roles in delivering business value. Investments are aligned with business strategies. Investment performance is continuously monitored against goals. Management processes are effective, and standard tools are available across the enterprise to evaluate investments and respond to problems.
3. *Assess the organizations' readiness to undertake IT business value management.* This self-assessment examines whether the organization is aware of and recognizes the need for Val IT management principles. This assessment provides insight into current levels of understanding of value management principles and the commitment to practices that implement those principles. It also provides information about gaps between current and desired attitudes and practices.
4. *Take action.* Build awareness of value management principles. Redefine processes, roles, and responsibilities. Identify and create an inventory of IT investments both planned and ongoing. Review the business cases for individual investments. Evaluate and prioritize investments to form new programs and an overall portfolio.

Summary

- The Balanced Scorecard provides a framework that allows managers to measure firm performance from multiple perspectives using both financial and nonfinancial measures.
- The four Balanced Scorecard perspectives are as follows:
    - Learning and growth.
    - Business processes.
    - Customer.
    - Financial.
- Strategy maps illustrate the components of a company's strategy across the four Balanced Scorecard perspectives.
- Investments in AIS/IT create information capital.
- Three classes that describe the nature of information technologies are as follows:
    - Function IT supports individual employees.
    - Network IT allows collaboration among employees.
    - Enterprise IT structures interactions within the organization and with external partners.
- The Balanced Scorecard management process involves the following:
    - Formulating ways to improve competitiveness.
    - Translating objectives into specific targets and initiatives to attain those targets.
    - Linking objectives and initiatives to operations.
    - Monitoring performance.
    - Adapting to continuously improve performance.
- The Val IT framework helps managers create business value from IT investments.
    - It examines IT investments in terms of contribution to strategic objectives.
    - Investments should be consistent with current IT architecture and other IT initiatives.
    - Organizations should develop resources necessary to support the investments.
    - Investments should deliver benefits according to established metrics.
- Val IT creates an investment management hierarchy.
    - Projects are structured into programs, and overall portfolios include programs and projects as well as supporting resources.
    - Value governance involves implementing and maintaining the Val IT framework.
    - Portfolio management sets priorities for investments and monitors performance.
    - Investment management executes authorized IT investment programs.
- Organizations implement Val IT in four major steps.
    - Recognize issues with prior performance.
    - Define characteristics of desired future state.
    - Assess readiness to undertake change.
    - Institute the necessary change.

Key Words

Balanced Scorecard framework *(346)* Provides an integrating framework that describes organizational performance relative to its strategic objectives across four perspectives: learning and growth, process, customer, and financial. Objectives for each perspective describe the strategy in a series of cause-and-effect relationships.

Balanced Scorecard management process *(351)* The process by which companies plan, implement, and monitor performance. It consists of five steps: formulate the strategy, translate the strategy, link the strategy to operations, monitor performance, and adapt.

customer perspective (*348*) The Balanced Scorecard perspective that describes the organization's customer-related objectives and corresponding customer measures; it views organization performance from the customers' perspective.

enterprise IT (EIT) (*350*) A type of information technology that restructures interactions within an organization and with external partners, such as customer relationship management systems.

financial perspective (*348*) The Balanced Scorecard perspective that describes the organization's financial objectives and corresponding financial measures of performance; it views organizational performance from the shareholders' perspective.

function IT (FIT) (*350*) A type of information technology that performs/supports a single function, such as spreadsheet applications.

information capital (*349*) An intangible asset that reflects the readiness of the company's technology to support strategic internal processes. It includes computing hardware, infrastructure, applications, and employees' abilities to use technology effectively.

key performance indicator (*350*) Those measures that the organization feels best indicate the performance of a particular activity.

learning and growth perspective (*347*) The Balanced Scorecard perspective that describes the organization's objectives and corresponding measures related to improvements in tangible and intangible infrastructure, such as human, information, and organizational capital.

network IT (NIT) (*350*) A type of information technology that allows people to communicate with one another, such as e-mail and instant messaging.

process perspective (*347*) The Balanced Scorecard perspective that describes the organization's internal, process-related, objectives and corresponding measures; it views organizational performance from an internal perspective.

strategy map (*349*) A one-page representation of the firm's strategic priorities and the cause-and-effect linkages among those strategic priorities.

Val IT (*353*) An IT investment framework developed by the IT Governance Institute.

value proposition (*348*) Represents the product and service characteristics, such as price, quality, selection, and brand image, that the firm attempts to deliver to customers to meet or exceed its customers' expectations and thereby result in customer retention and new customer acquisition; summarizes the costs and benefits of a preferred alternative IT investment, describing (1) the relevant time frames in which the costs will be incurred and benefits realized, (2) the corresponding discount rates to apply to future cash flows, and (3) the sensitivity of the results to assumptions.

Answers to Progress Checks

1. At the least, IT creates value by supporting operations management processes, including supply chain management. It also creates value in the regulatory and social process by supporting internal and external financial reporting and compliance with myriad local laws, regulations, and tax requirements. **Starbucks**'s digital ventures are most likely an example of network IT because they will support content delivery.
2. The answers can vary, but function IT includes individual tax preparation software and other personal applications. Network IT includes e-mail, local wireless networks, and perhaps social media.

connect

Multiple Choice Questions

1. Which of the following is not a Balanced Scorecard perspective? **LO 14-1**
   a. Learning and growth
   b. Customer
   c. Business process
   d. Financial
   e. All of the above are Balanced Scorecard perspectives.
2. Which of the following is not a type of business process in the Balanced Scorecard framework? **LO 14-1**
   a. Operations management
   b. Customer management
   c. Innovation
   d. Regulatory and social
   e. All of the above are types of business processes.
3. Which of the following describes the purpose of a strategy map? **LO 14-2**
   a. A graphical description of expected cause-and-effect linkages among Balanced Scorecard perspectives
   b. A list of the company's mission, vision, and values
   c. A representation of the company's strategic priorities
   d. Both a and b
   e. Both a and c
4. Which of the following does not describe a step in the Balanced Scorecard management process? **LO 14-4**
   a. Formulate the strategy
   b. Translate the strategy into strategic objectives
   c. Link objectives to operations
   d. Monitor performance and provide feedback
   e. All of the above describe steps in the Balanced Scorecard management process.
5. Which of the following do not describe characteristics of enterprise IT? **LO 14-3**
   a. Enhance individual worker productivity
   b. Automate transaction processing
   c. Integrate processes
   d. Provide general customer service
   e. Monitor performance and support decision making
6. Which of the following would be an example of network IT? **LO 14-3**
   a. Spreadsheets
   b. E-mail
   c. ERP systems
   d. CRM systems
   e. None of the above

7. Which of the following is an example of function IT? **LO 14-3**
   a. Spreadsheets
   b. E-mail
   c. ERP systems
   d. CRM systems
   e. None of the above
8. Which of the following is not a role of IT in the Balanced Scorecard management process? **LO 14-5**
   a. Strategy development support
   b. Long-term budget forecasting
   c. Transaction processing
   d. Reporting
   e. All are roles of IT in the Balanced Scorecard management process.
9. What is one reason that a Balanced Scorecard might be considered "balanced"? **LO 14-1**
   a. It includes four perspectives.
   b. It includes both leading and lagging performance indicators.
   c. It includes a large base.
   d. It is widely used by organizations around the world.
   e. All of these are reasons that it is balanced.
10. Which of the following is the ultimate objective for the financial perspective in for-profit organizations? **LO 14-1, LO 14-2**
    a. Brand image
    b. Productivity
    c. Growth
    d. Shareholder value
    e. None of these is the ultimate objective
11. Which of the following is part of an organization's value proposition? **LO 14-1**
    a. Product price
    b. Product quality
    c. Product availability
    d. Brand image
    e. All of these are part of the value proposition.
12. Which of the following is a typical key performance indicator for the financial perspective? **LO 14-1**
    a. Process cost
    b. Satisfaction
    c. New customer acquisition rate
    d. Return on equity
    e. Change readiness
13. Which of the following is a typical key performance indicator for the customer perspective? **LO 14-1**
    a. Process cost
    b. Satisfaction
    c. Process quality
    d. Return on equity
    e. Change readiness

14. Which of the following is a typical key performance indicator for the process perspective? **LO 14-1**
    a. Return on equity
    b. Employee skills
    c. Market share
    d. Process cycle time
    e. Sales growth
15. Which of the following is a typical key performance indicator for the learning and growth perspective? **LO 14-1**
    a. Return on equity
    b. Market share
    c. Process cost
    d. Sales growth
    e. Employee skills
16. Information capital can include which of the following? **LO 14-1**
    a. Employee ability to use technology
    b. Communications networks
    c. Accounting systems
    d. Computing hardware
    e. All of these are information capital.
17. Which of the following is the best description of Val IT? **LO 14-6**
    a. A Balanced Scorecard system
    b. A customer relationship management system
    c. An enterprise resource planning system
    d. A structured IT investment management system
    e. None of these describe Val IT.
18. Which one of the following is not one of the four major questions that Val IT focuses on? **LO 14-6**
    a. Doing the right thing
    b. Doing things differently
    c. Doing things well
    d. Doing things the right way
    e. Getting the benefits
19. In the Val IT framework, a program is which of the following? **LO 14-6**
    a. An IT governance practice
    b. An individual IT investment
    c. The description of a portfolio
    d. A collection of interdependent projects
    e. All of these are programs.
20. In the Val IT framework, portfolio management includes which of the following? **LO 14-6**
    a. Establishing strategic priorities
    b. Determining required characteristics of the portfolio
    c. Monitoring performance of the portfolio
    d. Setting program priorities under funding constraints
    e. All of these are portfolio management.

21. In the Val IT framework, investment management includes which of the following? **LO 14-6**
   a. Governs the Val IT framework
   b. Establishes strategic priorities
   c. Monitors portfolio performance
   d. Executes projects within authorized programs
   e. None of these are investment management.
22. Val IT is designed to work in concert with COBIT. Which of the following is true with respect to the roles of these two frameworks? **LO 14-6**
   a. Val IT focuses on delivering business value; COBIT focuses on managing risk.
   b. Val IT focuses on IT; COBIT does not.
   c. Val IT focuses on portfolio management; COBIT focuses on project management.
   d. Val IT focuses on financial performance; COBIT focuses on process performance.
   e. None of these is true about the two frameworks.
23. Which of the following is the first step in implementing Val IT? **LO 14-7**
   a. Forming programs of IT investments
   b. Making specific IT investments
   c. Recognizing problems with prior IT investments
   d. Assessing the readiness to change
   e. None of these is the first step.
24. Which of the following is the second step in implementing Val IT? **LO 14-7**
   a. Defining the ideal future state for IT investments
   b. Making specific IT investments
   c. Recognizing problems with prior IT investments
   d. Assessing the readiness to change
   e. None of these is the second step.
25. Which of the following is the third step in implementing Val IT? **LO 14-7**
   a. Defining the ideal future state for IT investments
   b. Making specific IT investments
   c. Recognizing problems with prior IT investments
   d. Assessing the readiness to change
   e. None of these is the third step.
26. Which of the following is the fourth step in implementing Val IT? **LO 14-7**
   a. Defining the ideal future state for IT investments
   b. Taking action to redefine processes, roles, and responsibilities
   c. Recognizing problems with prior IT investments
   d. Assessing the readiness to change
   e. None of these is the fourth step.

Discussion Questions

1. Consider a company that competes on price, such as **Walmart**, in comparison to a company that competes on other factors, such as **Starbucks**. Describe how their Balanced Scorecard objectives and the corresponding measures would differ across the four perspectives. **LO 14-2**
2. One criticism of the Balanced Scorecard is that it can lead to information overload by measuring too many performance indicators. Do you agree with this criticism? Why or why not? **LO 14-1, LO 14-2**

3. If a company does not want to implement a formal Balanced Scorecard performance management system, is it still beneficial for the company to develop a strategy map? Why or why not? **LO 14-1, LO 14-2**
4. Some companies create a Balanced Scorecard by taking some current objectives and key performance indicators (KPI) and assigning them to the four Balanced Scorecard perspectives. Describe the advantages and disadvantages of that approach. **LO 14-1, LO 14-2**
5. Does the Balanced Scorecard framework provide a performance measurement system or a performance management system? Why? **LO 14-1, LO 14-2**
6. A biotech company is considering developing an IT system that will track the progress of its drug compounds through the **Food and Drug Administration (FDA)** approval process. Describe, as specifically as possible, how that IT initiative might affect performance across all four Balanced Scorecard perspectives. **LO 14-1, LO 14-2**
7. A company is developing key process indicators (KPI) for the information capital aspect of its learning and growth. It is considering measuring the amount spent on information technology hardware and software as its measure. What advice would you give it about that choice? **LO 14-1, LO 14-2**
8. Outline a Balanced Scorecard for your business school. How would using your Balanced Scorecard system affect the management of the school? **LO 14-1, LO 14-2**
9. Describe likely differences in a Balanced Scorecard between a for-profit company and a not-for-profit (or governmental) organization. Which perspectives are each organization more likely to focus on? **LO 14-1, LO 14-2**
10. The CEO of a midsized company is considering purchasing an ERP system but may not have fully considered the other changes that the company needs to make to maximize the value of the system. Using a Balanced Scorecard framework, create a strategy map that describes how the ERP system could benefit company performance with the right set of complementary changes. **LO 14-1, LO 14-2, LO 14-3**

Problems

1. Select a prominent public company, such as **Apple**, **Google**, or **Microsoft**. Obtain recent annual reports and news articles about the company. Using that information, develop a strategy map that describes the company's performance. Start by defining its value proposition, and then identifying key business processes that deliver that value proposition. **LO 14-1, LO 14-2**
2. Use the company that you selected for Problem 1. Identify examples of its learning and growth efforts and explain how those might affect its business process performance. **LO 14-1, LO 14-2**
3. Select a prominent company that experienced problems during the 2008–2010 economic downturn, such as **Bank of America**, **Goldman Sachs**, or **AIG**. Use annual reports and news articles from that time to develop a strategy map that describes the elements that caused the company's financial problems. **LO 14-1, LO 14-2**

connect

4. Using the following objectives, create a strategy map that places them at the proper perspective and links them together. For each objective, develop two possible measures. **LO 14-1, LO 14-2**
   a. Manage the product portfolio for superior innovation.
   b. Acquire new customers.
   c. Improve fixed asset utilization.
   d. Lower cost of serving customers.
   e. Grow revenue.
   f. Create a climate of knowledge sharing.
   g. Implement an IT infrastructure necessary to support growth.
   h. Improve return on assets.
   i. Increase market share.
   j. Achieve just-in-time supplier capability.

connect 5. A company has elected to pursue the initiatives listed in part a. For each initiative, describe which Balanced Scorecard perspectives the initiative will address and, specifically, which of the performance measures in part b it will affect. **LO 14-1, LO 14-2**

a. Initiatives

Purchase new, more efficient, production equipment.
Train employees.
Renovate older retail stores.
Implement a business intelligence/business analytics system.
Create a new advertising campaign.

b. Performance measures

Sales growth percentage.
Percent of repeat customers.
Employee turnover.
Percent of defective products.
Number of new customers.
Number of product warranty claims.
Employee satisfaction.

Chapter **Fifteen**

Evaluating AIS Investments

A look at this chapter

In this chapter, we describe the process by which firms economically justify IT initiatives. Accounting information systems and information technology initiatives in general often involve substantial costs. As users, managers, designers, and evaluators of the firm's IT systems, accountants are important members of the team that will develop the business case for AIS initiatives. Additionally, as users, managers, and evaluators, they can also be asked to review business cases for IT initiatives in general.

A look back

Chapter 14 described the Balanced Scorecard framework and explained how information technology delivers value by supporting a company's strategic objectives. It also outlined a Balanced Scorecard management process whereby companies plan, implement, monitor, and adjust strategic objectives and showed AIS/IT roles in that context.

A look ahead

Chapter 16 highlights the use of project management in AIS projects. It also describes constraints to successful AIS project implementations and tools that are used to overcome them. Additionally, it discusses a model that indicates whether a new system will actually be useful to the intended AIS users.

© *Tom Pennington/Getty Images*

Starbucks recently named Gerri Martin-Flickinger as its chief technology officer to lead the global IT function and play a key role in shaping the technology agenda across the Starbucks business.

In the press release announcing her hire, Kevin Johnson, Starbucks's president and chief operating officer, noted, "Gerri is a technologist at heart and has a 30-year track record of leveraging technology-based solutions to *drive business value*. As we continue to shape our global technology agenda at Starbucks, we needed leadership talent with deep experience in cloud, big data analytics, mobile and security to take us to the next level. As we searched for that leader, Gerri stood out as someone who has years of experience in Silicon Valley and brings deep management and technical expertise to help us navigate the future."

You can be sure that Gerri will carefully evaluate all AIS investments to ensure that they drive business value. There may well be some great new technologies for Starbucks to try, but if they do not create value, you can guess that Gerri will not approve the investment.

Source: Starbucks press release, October 6, 2015 (emphasis added).

Chapter Outline

Large IT Projects Require Economic Justification

The Business Case for IT Initiatives

Assessing Business Requirements for IT Initiatives

Estimating Benefits

Estimating Costs

Acquisition Costs

Operating Costs

Assessing Risks

Developing the Value Proposition

Test the Sensitivity of Estimates to Changes in Assumptions

Prepare the Value Proposition

Learning Objectives

After reading this chapter, you should be able to:

15-1 Articulate similarities and differences between major IT initiatives and other capital investments.

15-2 Explain the major steps in the economic justification of an IT initiative.

15-3 Explain potential benefits of IT initiatives and how to evaluate them.

15-4 Assess potential costs of IT initiatives and how to evaluate them.

15-5 Describe potential risks of IT initiatives and corresponding risk-mitigation techniques.

15-6 Apply capital budgeting techniques to assess the value proposition for an IT initiative.

LO 15-1
Articulate similarities and differences between major IT initiatives and other capital investments.

LARGE IT PROJECTS REQUIRE ECONOMIC JUSTIFICATION

Information technology (IT) projects involve substantial costs and offer important **benefits** to organizations. According to the IT research firm IDC, business-funded technology spending in the United States will be more than $330 billion in 2017.[1] It is estimated that approximately 70 percent of that spending will be in the form of capital expenditures. Additionally, most investments that are aimed at sustaining, growing, or transforming the business include a central IT component. When managed well, these investments offer organizations significant opportunities to create value. However, **Gartner Inc.**, a prominent consulting firm, estimates that 20 percent of all IT spending is wasted.[2]

Most organizations have developed specific techniques for evaluating IT projects for several reasons:

1. IT projects often require large amounts of capital, and for most firms, capital resources are limited.
2. Selecting one investment often means forgoing other potentially value-increasing investments.
3. IT projects often involve changes in business processes that will affect substantial portions of the organization.

Capital budgeting techniques provide a systematic approach to evaluating investments in capital assets. Yet, many organizations find it difficult to evaluate IT projects using traditional capital budgeting techniques. To understand why IT projects can be difficult to evaluate, managers need to consider the different characteristics of IT.

LO 15-2
Explain the major steps in the economic justification of an IT initiative.

THE BUSINESS CASE FOR IT INITIATIVES

"A goal without a plan is just a wish."
—Antoine de Saint Exupéry, French writer and aviator

Good governance requires that all significant investments be justified. Therefore, information technology planning requires thorough consideration of alternative approaches and justification of the value of the selected alternative. According to the International Federation of Accountants, a global organization committed to the development of the accounting profession, organizations should create a **business case** for an IT investment. That business case should answer the following questions:[3]

1. Why are we doing this project?
2. How does it address key business issues?
3. How much will it cost, and how long will it take?
4. What are the return on investment and the payback period?
5. What are the risks of doing the project?
6. What are the risks of not doing the project?
7. What are the alternatives?
8. How will success be measured?

As users, managers, designers, and evaluators of the firm's IT systems, accountants are important members of the team that will develop business cases for AIS initiatives. Additionally, as users, managers, and evaluators, they can also be asked to review business cases for IT initiatives in general.

[1] IDC, "United States Technology Buyer Forecast by Vertical: 2012 to 2017," accessed February 2016, www.eweek.com/small-business/business-technology-spending-to-top-330-billion-by-2017.html.

[2] The Gartner Group, *The Elusive Business Value of IT* (2002).

[3] International Federation of Accountants, *Managing Information Technology; Planning for Business Impact,* Information Technology Committee Guideline 2 (December 1999).

Developing an economic justification.
© Dmitriy Shironosov/Alamy

So, how do firms create a business case to justify their IT initiatives? Figure 15.1 describes this **economic justification process.**[4]

1. The project team assesses the business requirements for the IT initiative.
2. The team identifies potential solutions that will address those business problems.
3. For each alternative solution, the team evaluates potential benefits, costs, and risks.
4. All of the information gathered is combined to form the estimated value propositions for the alternatives and the team formalizes their business case recommendations.

The following sections describe each step in this process.

FIGURE 15.1
Economic Justification Process

Note: The gateway symbol with the plus sign indicates that the process takes all three paths.

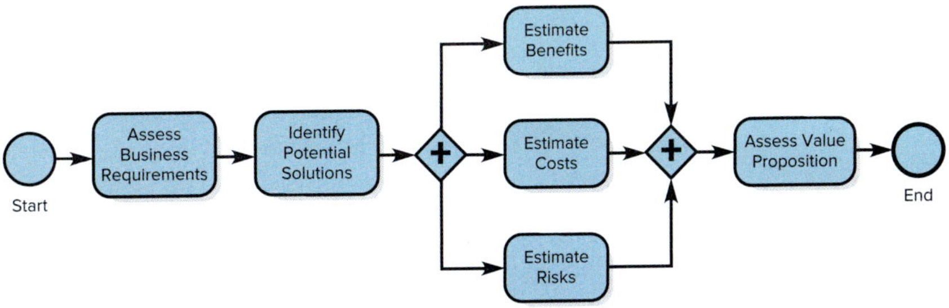

Assessing Business Requirements for IT Initiatives

In a company, IT exists to support the business goals and business strategies. To support those goals and strategies, IT must carefully align with the business requirements. IT initiatives should reduce one or more gaps between the firm's current and desired performance levels as indicated by the firm's strategy map. Therefore, the project team must explicitly link the proposed technology with the overall business performance improvements for one or

[4]See Microsoft Corporation's *Rapid Economic Justification, Enterprise Edition* (2007), for additional information.

FIGURE 15.2
Benefit Dependency

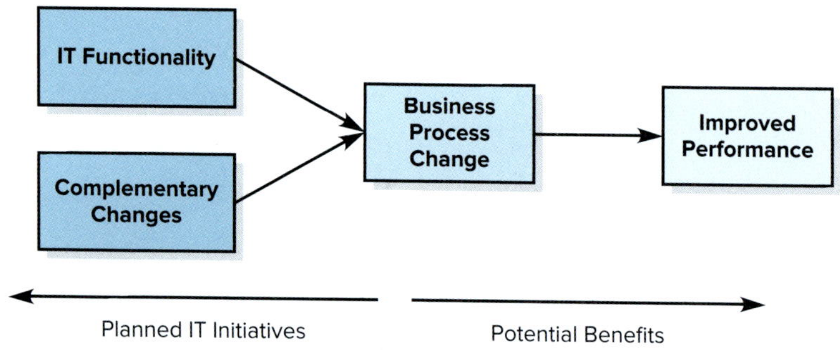

more selected critical success factors. IT alone is usually not sufficient to achieve important changes, so the project team must also consider other enabling changes that, in conjunction with the technology, will accomplish substantial business change, as shown in Figure 15.2.

Examples of complementary changes include providing training, redefining job descriptions, reconfiguring tasks, or offering incentives. For each critical success factor to be addressed by the IT initiative, the project team identifies (1) the specific business processes that affect that critical success factor, (2) problems with those business processes, (3) opportunities to address those problems, and (4) the specific technology that would enable changes.

Progress Check

1. Think back to the discussion of the Balanced Scorecard framework in Chapter 14. Like other firms, **Starbucks**'s value proposition includes attributes of its products, such as price, quality, and selection; attributes of its relationship with its customers, such as the level of service and efforts to build long-term relationships; and its brand image. Which of those attributes are most important to Starbucks customers' satisfaction?
2. What elements of the value proposition are **Starbucks**'s digital ventures likely designed to improve? Why?

LO 15-3
Explain potential benefits of IT initiatives and how to evaluate them.

ESTIMATING BENEFITS

Once the opportunities for improvement are identified and alternative solutions are proposed, the project team next assesses the potential benefits of each alternative. A benefit is a positive consequence—such as a reduction in the performance gaps for a critical success factor—of an IT investment. Benefits should be measurable in financial terms:

Ultimately, benefits must be measured in terms of the financial impact of the project.

1. Revenue enhancement—creating all-new sales opportunities, such as using e-commerce capabilities to expand the firm's market.
2. Revenue protection—protecting existing revenue streams. For example, a data encryption system protects the loss of customer data and encourages customers to share data.
3. Cost savings—opportunities to modify business processes to reduce low value-added or manually intensive activities, to improve capabilities to manage assets to increase efficiencies, or to reduce errors. For example, improving inventory management information allows reduced inventory investments.
4. Cost avoidance—opportunities to modify business processes to avoid cost increases in the future, such as installing current software that will accommodate changes to international financial reporting standards when required.

Note that the benefits should be measured in comparison to the revenues and costs that will occur if the IT initiative is not implemented. These revenues and costs can be different than current levels of revenues and costs. Often, the project team must estimate the amount and timing of future benefits for a number of reasonable alternative situations without complete information. There are several possible approaches that can be used to quantify expected benefits:

- Simulation—using simulation software to test the impact of a change in a key performance indicator on the firm's financial statements under a variety of assumptions to establish the likely benefit.
- Expert opinion—consulting with experts to establish the likely benefit or the probability of achieving a particular level of benefit.
- Real option theory—using sophisticated financial techniques that compare the probability of achieving benefits with an investment against the benefits of not making that investment.
- External benchmarks—using the actual experience of other firms that made similar investments in similar contexts to estimate the likely benefit.

These approaches start with an assessment of the effectiveness of current performance based on the current outputs and inputs for the process or processes under consideration, as shown in Figure 15.3. Then, they consider the potential impact of the change and forecast the long-term benefit.

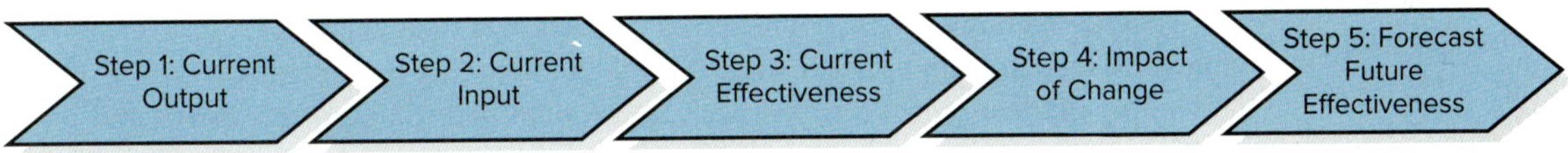

FIGURE 15.3
Forecasting Effects of Change

LO 15-4
Assess potential costs of IT initiatives and how to evaluate them.

ESTIMATING COSTS

Relevant costs include the incremental expense of developing, implementing, and operating the proposed IT initiative over its life cycle. The total **acquisition cost** includes all direct and indirect costs required to acquire and deploy the technology. The total **operation cost** includes all direct and indirect costs of operating, maintaining, and administering the technology over its expected life. Technology consulting firms, such as **Gartner Inc.** and **International Data Corporation**, publish widely used total cost of ownership figures for various technologies, and Gartner has developed an extensive chart of accounts to classify IT initiative costs.[5]

Acquisition Costs

Direct Costs

The direct acquisition costs include all costs necessary to acquire and implement the IT initiative:

Hardware
Software
Networking and communications
Development
Project management
Consulting
Training

[5]Gartner Inc., *Distributed Computing Chart of Accounts* (2003), available at www.gartner.com/4_decision_tools/modeling_tools/costcat.pdf.

Indirect Costs

The indirect acquisition costs include costs not directly related to the acquisition and implementation, such as business disruption and employee downtime.

Operating Costs

Direct Costs

The direct operating costs include all costs necessary to operate, maintain, and administer the technology:

Hardware replacements
Software upgrades
Maintenance contracts
Help desk support
Ongoing training
Administration
Decommissioning the old system

Indirect Costs

The indirect operating costs include costs of user downtime and lost productivity, such as time spent on self-training, peer support, and end user data management.

The project team must also estimate the amount and timing of the direct and indirect costs of acquisition and operation of IT initiatives without complete information. The various approaches to quantifying benefits, outlined earlier, also apply to estimating costs. Additionally, there are several commercial software products designed to help firms estimate total cost of ownership.

Progress Check

3. Do you own a laptop, a cell phone, an iPod, or an iPad? What is your total cost of ownership for each of those? Is it more expensive than just the initial purchase? Do you have any indirect costs of owning those products?

LO 15-5
Describe potential risks of IT initiatives and corresponding risk-mitigation techniques.

ASSESSING RISKS

Each alternative IT initiative carries risks of failing to achieve the prospective benefits and exceeding the estimated costs. To help identify risks, it is usually helpful to consider the following categories of risks. One classification scheme is as follows:[6]

- **Alignment risk**—the solution is not aligned with the strategy of the firm.
- **Solution risk**—the solution will not generate projected benefits.
- **Financial risk**—the solution will not deliver expected financial performance.
- **Project risk**—the project will not be completed on time or within budget.
- **Change risk**—the firm or part of the firm will not be able to change.
- **Technological risk**—the technology will not deliver expected benefits.

After identifying relevant risks, the project team should assess the financial impact on the firm if the risk scenario occurs, the probability that the risk scenario will occur, and

[6]Risk categories taken from Microsoft Corporation, *Rapid Economic Justification, Enterprise Edition* (2007).

Systems implementation problems kept Hershey's from accepting Halloween orders.

costs of mitigating the risk. Some of the risk assessment can be done during the quantification of costs and benefits, and the estimated costs and benefits can be adjusted for risk. Risk-mitigation techniques include considering portfolios of IT initiatives, rather than single initiatives, and considering outsourcing where contracts can protect against certain risks. Table 15.1 describes examples of risk-mitigation techniques for each risk category.

Progress Check

4. A few years ago, **Hershey's Corp.**, a leading manufacturer of chocolates, confectionaries, and beverages, implemented SAP's R/3 enterprise resource planning software using a big bang approach, where all the software was implemented at once. Because of problems with the implementation during a busy period, Hershey's could not take orders or deliver products for Halloween. By the time the problems were corrected, they had cost Hershey's more than $100 million. What risks were involved? Was this the fault of the software? Do you think Hershey's planning allowed for this contingency when it justified the IT initiative?

TABLE 15.1
Examples of Risk-Mitigation Techniques

IT Initiative Risks	Risk-Mitigation Examples
Alignment risk	Use the Balanced Scorecard framework (Chapter 14) to assess the link to strategy.
Solution risk	Use sensitivity analysis to consider likely alternative benefit levels.
Financial risk	Interview other users of similar IT; follow a structured Balanced Scorecard management process (Chapter 14).
Project risk	Ensure active top management support for the project.
Change risk	Conduct training, and create employee incentives for successful use of the new IT.
Technological risk	Require hardware and software vendors to demonstrate that their systems can meet requirements.

LO 15-6
Apply capital budgeting techniques to assess the value proposition for an IT initiative.

The business case establishes the value proposition for the preferred alternative or alternatives.

DEVELOPING THE VALUE PROPOSITION

The last step in the IT economic justification process is to combine the information developed in the previous steps to describe the **value proposition** for the preferred alternative. This value proposition is unrelated to the term used in Chapter 14. The firm's senior executives need to understand the financial implications of the IT initiative so they can decide whether to allocate resources to it. The project team will employ capital budgeting techniques using the expected cash flows for each alternative:

1. Determine the relevant time frame for costs and benefits.
2. Select appropriate discount rates to apply.
3. Prepare capital budgeting financial metrics.
4. Assess the sensitivity of results to the assumptions.

The relevant time frame for most IT initiatives is 3 years or less because technology changes rapidly. The appropriate discount rates usually run from 5 to 15 percent, depending on the firm's cost of capital and the riskiness of the particular project. Financial metrics commonly used include the following and are summarized in Table 15.2:

- **Payback period** and **breakeven analysis**—both compare the costs with benefits of an IT project. The breakeven point is where the total value of benefits equals that of total costs. The payback is the number of periods needed to recover the project's initial investment.

Payback period = Initial investment/Increased cash flow per period

Assume an IT project is expected to cost $20,000 up front, and it will provide net benefits that average $16,000 per year for the next 3 years.

Payback period = $20,000/$16,000 = 1.25 years

- **Net present value (NPV)**—sum of the present value of all cash inflows minus the sum of the present value of all cash outflows. Each cash outflow/inflow is discounted to its present value.

$$\text{Present value} = CF_t/(1+r)^t$$

where:
CF = cash flow for period t
r = discount rate (typically the firm's weighted average cost of capital)

Again, assume an IT project that is expected to cost $20,000 up front and return $16,000 per year for 3 years. Assume a discount rate of 10 percent. Then, the NPV is calculated as follows.

Year 0	Present value = −$20,000/(1.10⁰)	−$20,000
Year 1	Present value = $16,000/(1.10¹)	14,545
Year 2	Present value = $16,000/(1.10²)	13,223
Year 3	Present value = $16,000/(1.10³)	12,021
NPV	Sum of present values	$19,790

- **Internal rate of return (IRR)**—the discount rate that makes the project's net present value equal to zero. There is no solvable formula for internal rate of return. Instead, financial calculators and spreadsheet software, such as Microsoft Excel, use an iterative technique for calculating IRR. Starting with a guess, they cycle through the

Financial Metric	Strength	Weakness
Payback period	Easy to calculate and understand. Widely used.	Ignores the time value of money as well as both costs and benefits occurring after the payback period.
Accounting rate of return	Relates estimates to standard accounting ratios using accrual accounting. Shows impact on operating income.	Ignores the time value of money. Assumes cash flows in all periods are similar.
Net present value	Considers the time value of money. Incorporates cash flows over the life of the IT initiative. Compares the dollar value of the benefits from an IT initiative to the initial investment.	Larger projects tend to have larger net present values. Does not show rate of return on investment. Sensitive to discount rate applied.
Internal rate of return	Considers the time value of money. Incorporates cash flows over the life of the IT initiative. Computes the unique rate of return for the initiative. Not sensitive to a selected discount rate.	Fails to consider the size of the project. Sensitive to timing of the cash flows.

TABLE 15.2
Financial Metric Strengths and Weaknesses

calculations until the result is accurate. The IRR and NPV functions are related in that if you use the IRR as the discount rate (r) in calculating NPV, your NPV is zero.[7]

- **Accounting rate of return (ARR)**—the average annual income from the IT initiative divided by the initial investment cost.

ARR = (Average annual income from IT initiative)/(Total IT initiative investment cost)

Again, using the same assumed initial outlay and subsequent net cash flows described earlier, the accounting rate of return would be calculated as follows.

ARR = \$16,000/\$20,000 = 80%

Table 15.3 shows an example of the financial metrics applied to an IT initiative with an implementation cost of \$20,000 and positive net cash flow for the subsequent 3 years.

TABLE 15.3
Example Comparing Payback, NPV, and IRR

Discount Rate	10%					
Project 1	**Year 0**	**Year 1**	**Year 2**	**Year 3**	**Total**	**Average**
Benefits		\$20,000	\$20,000	\$30,000	\$70,000	\$23,333
Costs	\$20,000	\$7,500	\$7,500	\$7,500	\$42,500	\$10,625
Cash flow	−\$20,000	\$12,500	\$12,500	\$22,500	\$27,500	\$15,833
Payback	1.26					
NPV	\$16,908					
IRR	52%					
Project 2	**Year 0**	**Year 1**	**Year 2**	**Year 3**	**Total**	**Average**
Benefits		\$30,000	\$20,000	\$20,000	\$70,000	\$23,333
Costs	\$20,000	\$7,500	\$7,500	\$7,500	\$42,500	\$10,625
Cash flow	−\$20,000	\$22,500	\$12,500	\$12,500	\$27,500	\$15,833
Payback	1.26					
NPV	\$18,342					
IRR	71%					

Note that total cash flow is equal, but NPV and IRR are not, due to time value of money.

[7]Note that Excel assumes that the cash flows occur at the end of the year, so the initial outlay would be assumed to be for year 1. Try this by entering the data and using the Excel NPV and IRR functions.

The two projects have equal payback periods, but project 1 has a higher net present value (NPV), and project 2 has a higher internal rate of return (IRR). This illustrates how risks resulting in increased costs and reduced benefits can affect the value of the IT initiative, especially when considering the time value of money.

Test the Sensitivity of Estimates to Changes in Assumptions

Before prioritizing the alternative IT initiatives based on the financial metrics, the project team should test the impact of changes in assumptions on the various financial metrics. These tests can be performed using spreadsheet or simulation software. The assumptions can also be reviewed by subject matter experts. Because each financial metric has both strengths and weaknesses, IT initiatives should be evaluated using several metrics (see Figure 15.4).

FIGURE 15.4
Project Value

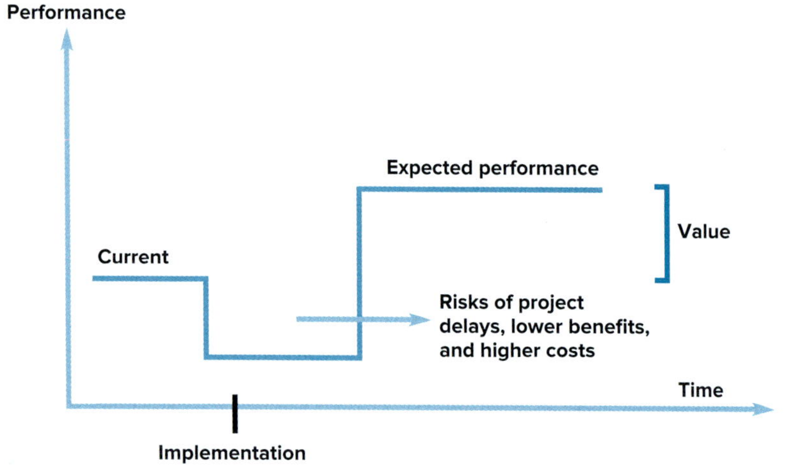

Prepare the Value Proposition

The final step is to assemble the analysis for each alternative IT initiative and recommend the preferred alternatives. The value proposition must address the business case questions listed earlier in the section "The Business Case for IT Initiatives" especially focusing on these five areas:

1. The change and technology proposed.
2. The anticipated benefits (related to the firm's critical success factors).
3. The group(s) within the firm that will benefit.
4. The timing of the benefits.
5. The likelihood of achieving those benefits as planned.

Summary

- Large projects require economic justification comparing the costs against the benefits.
- One step in the economic justification process is the preparation of the business case that identifies the purpose of the project, costs, expected return on investment, risks of doing the project, risks of not doing the project, alternatives considered, and how success will be measured.

- The economic justification process occurs in a series of steps:
    - Assess business requirements.
    - Identify potential solutions.
    - Estimates costs, benefits, and risks.
    - Assess the overall value proposition for each potential solution.
- IT initiatives must also include complementary changes in business processes to improve performance.
- Estimated benefits involve revenue enhancement, revenue protection, cost savings, and cost avoidance.
- Estimated costs involve direct and indirect acquisition and operating costs over the life cycle of the project.
- Relevant risks can be categorized as alignment, solution, financial, project, change, and technological risks.
- The business case should identify ways to mitigate relevant risks.
- The value proposition depends on capital budgeting financial metrics that consider the time value of money and the anticipated timing of the costs and benefits.

Key Words

accounting rate of return (ARR) (*373*) The average annual income from the IT initiative divided by the initial investment cost.

acquisition costs (*369*) All direct and indirect costs necessary to acquire and implement the IT initiative.

alignment risk (*370*) The risk that an IT initiative is not aligned with the strategy of the organization.

benefits (*366*) The positive consequences to the organization of an IT investment.

breakeven analysis (*372*) Determines the breakeven point, where the total value of benefits equals that of total costs.

business case (*366*) Economic justification for an IT investment or other major project.

change risk (*370*) The risk that the organization will be unable to make the changes necessary to implement the IT initiative successfully.

economic justification process (*367*) The process by which an organization creates a business case for an IT investment or other major project.

financial risk (*370*) The risk that the IT investment will not deliver expected financial benefits.

internal rate of return (IRR) (*372*) The discount rate (return) that makes a project's net present value equal to zero.

net present value (NPV) (*372*) The sum of the present value of all cash inflows minus the sum of the present value of all cash outflows related to an IT investment or other capital investment.

operation cost (*369*) The recurring cost necessary to operate, maintain, and administer an IT initiative.

payback period (*372*) The amount of time necessary to recoup a project's initial investment.

project risk (*370*) The risk that the project will not be completed on time or within budget.

relevant costs (*369*) Those costs that will change as a result of an IT initiative or other major project.

solution risk (*370*) The risk that the proposed solution will not generate expected benefits.

technological risk (*370*) The risk that the technology will not perform as expected to deliver the planned benefits.

value proposition (*372*) Summarizes the costs and benefits of a preferred alternative IT investment, describing (1) the relevant time frames over which the costs will be incurred and benefits realized, (2) the corresponding discount rates to apply to future cash flows, and (3) the sensitivity of the results to assumptions.

Answers to Progress Checks

1. **Starbucks** competes on quality, image, and relationship. All three are important to the company's customer satisfaction, but one could argue that image gets the customer into the store and quality and relationship keep the customer coming back.
2. Digital ventures seemed to be aimed at (a) improving the customer relationship and (b) expanding their selection so new and returning customers buy more per visit.
3. Each of these personal devices costs far more than the original investment in hardware. You have to buy applications (software), Internet access, and perhaps insurance. Each time you purchase one of these, you incur indirect costs of self-training, potential loss of personal information, and any loss of productivity connected with using the new device.
4. The **Hershey** ERP project likely carried all the risks listed in Table 15.1. The fault was not likely related to the software alone. It was more likely related to implementation and training issues. It is highly unlikely that Hershey considered this possibility in its planning, or the company would have had contingency plans to mitigate the problems.

connect

Multiple Choice Questions

1. Which of the following is a question that companies should answer when preparing the business case for an IT investment? **LO 15-2**
   a. How much will it cost?
   b. What are the risks?
   c. What are the alternatives?
   d. How will success be measured?
   e. All of the above
2. What is the first step in the economic justification process? **LO 15-2**
   a. Identify potential solutions.
   b. Assess the value proposition.
   c. Assess business requirements.
   d. Estimate costs.
   e. All of the above
3. Which of the following is a not an example of a complementary change necessary to allow an IT initiative to achieve its goals? **LO 15-2**
   a. Outsource the IT initiative.
   b. Retrain employees.
   c. Redefine job descriptions.
   d. Provide incentives for employees to make the change successfully.
   e. None of the above
4. Which of the following is not an example of benefits of an IT investment? **LO 15-3**
   a. Increased revenues from access to new markets
   b. Decreased costs from automating manual tasks
   c. Facilitating employee work-from-home arrangements
   d. Allowing compliance with new federal regulations
   e. Reducing the number of inventory count errors
   f. All of the above

5. Which of the following can be used to quantify benefits on an IT investment? **LO 15-3**
   a. Gathering expert opinions
   b. Benchmarking against competitor performance
   c. Comparing against the probability of future benefits if investment is forgone
   d. Conducting simulations
   e. All of the above
6. Which of the following are examples of direct costs of acquiring and implementing an IT investment? **LO 15-4**
   a. Cost of hiring consultants to assess system requirements
   b. Personnel costs of the project team
   c. Training costs of employees who will use the system
   d. Cost of new computer hardware necessary to run the system
   e. All of the above are direct costs of acquiring and implementing an IT investment.
7. Which of the following are not examples of operating costs for an IT investment? **LO 15-4**
   a. Costs of routine hardware replacements over time
   b. Cost of contract for help desk support
   c. Costs of disposal of electronics at end of life
   d. Costs of software license renewals
   e. All of the above are examples of operating costs.
8. Which of the following is not a category of IT initiative risk? **LO 15-5**
   a. Alignment
   b. Technological
   c. Financial misstatement
   d. Solution
   e. All of the above are examples of IT initiative risk.
9. If an IT project costs $150,000 and returns net cash flows of $100,000 per year, what is the payback period? **LO 15-6**
   a. 1 year
   b. 1.5 years
   c. 2 years
   d. 2.5 years
   e. None of the above
10. If an IT project costs $150,000 and returns net cash flows of $100,000 per year, what is the accounting rate of return? **LO 15-6**
    a. 33 percent
    b. 50 percent
    c. 67 percent
    d. 75 percent
    e. None of the above
11. What is the order of events for the economic justification process? **LO 15-2**
    a. Identify potential solutions → Assess business requirements → Estimate costs → Assess value
    b. Assess business requirements → Estimate costs → Identify potential solutions → Assess value
    c. Identify potential solutions → Estimate benefits → Assess business requirements → Assess value
    d. Assess business requirements → Identify potential solutions → Estimate costs → Assess value
    e. None of the above

12. Which of the following would be considered direct acquisition costs when estimating costs associated with an IT initiative? **LO 15-4**
    a. Networking and communications
    b. Business disruption
    c. Employee downtime
    d. Help desk support
    e. None of the above
13. Which of the following would be considered indirect acquisition costs when estimating costs associated with an IT initiative? **LO 15-4**
    a. Networking and communications
    b. Business disruption
    c. Ongoing training
    d. Software upgrades
    e. None of the above
14. What type of IT initiative risk is it if top management does not have active support for the project? **LO 15-5**
    a. Alignment risk
    b. Solution risk
    c. Financial risk
    d. Project risk
    e. Technological risk
15. What type of IT initiative risk is it if hardware/software vendors do not meet system requirements? **LO 15-5**
    a. Alignment risk
    b. Solution risk
    c. Financial risk
    d. Project risk
    e. Technological risk

Discussion Questions

1. An important first step in the economic justification process is to assess business requirements. How would the Balanced Scorecard framework presented in Chapter 14 help companies assess their business requirements for IT? **LO 15-2**
2. Chapter 14 described three types of IT: function, network, and enterprise IT. Consider the diagram shown in Figure 15.2. Which type of IT is likely to have the greatest impact on business performance? Which type of IT would require the most complementary changes? Why? **LO 15-2**
3. The benefits of an IT initiative should be measured in comparison to the revenues and costs that will occur if the IT initiative is not implemented. What issues would a project team face when making this comparison? How does it affect the team's assessment of risks? **LO 15-3**
4. Use Microsoft Excel to assess the NPV of an IT initiative. The initiative will require an initial investment of $250,000 and is expected to return $150,000 per year for the next 3 years. Assume a discount rate of 10 percent. What is the NPV? How does the NPV change if the discount rate is 15 percent? Describe how changes in the discount rate assumption can affect the NPV. **LO 15-6**
5. Use Microsoft Excel to assess the internal rate of return for an IT initiative. Suppose the initial investment is $70,000. The returns on investment in dollars for the following 5 years are (a) $12,000, (b) $15,000, (c) $18,000, (d) $21,000, and (e) $26,000. Use the IRR function to

compute the internal rate of return after 2, 3, and 5 years. Next, assume that the loan for the initial $70,000 is at 8 percent and you are earning 15 percent on the annual returns. Use the MIRR function to calculate the internal rate of return. Is the annual rate of return higher when using the MIRR function than the IRR function? Under what circumstances would it be lower? **LO 15-6**

6. Consider two projects. Project 1 costs $272,000 and returns $60,000 per year for 8 years. Project 2 costs $380,000 and returns $70,000 per year. Project 2 is determined to be less risky, so your company only requires an 8 percent minimum annual return compared to 10 percent for project 1. What is the NPV of each project? What is the absolute maximum that the company should consider investing in each project? **LO 15-6**
7. Your company has just completed a major IT initiative and is reviewing the outcome. It notes that the project took 3 months longer than expected. As part of the project, the company wanted to use some automatic bar code readers, but the rate of correct bar code reads was below the expected rate. Although managers were worried about employee acceptance of the new system, it appears that the employees have embraced it and, as a result, are making it work better than expected. Refer to Table 15.1 and identify how these results address the risk categories listed in the table. **LO 15-6**
8. Congratulations. You've won the state lottery. You have a choice of three options: (a) $12 million 5 years from now, (b) $2.25 million at the end of each year for 5 years, or (c) $10 million 3 years from now. Assuming you can invest at 8 percent, which option would you prefer? **LO 15-6**
9. Moore's law suggests that computing power for the same cost doubles every two-and-a-half years. A combination of Moore's law and the commoditization of computer components has made it possible to buy a $500 computer today that is more powerful and portable than a similar offering that cost $2,000 just a few years ago. How does this affect planning for major IT projects? **LO 15-6**

Problems

1. SlowRider Inc. had a rudimentary business intelligence (BI) system. Analysts at SlowRider Inc. pulled data from three different ERP systems, loaded the data into Excel spreadsheets, and e-mailed those spreadsheets to the senior managers each month. However, some managers complained that they didn't understand how to get the information they needed, others complained that the data were not accurate, and still others ignored the spreadsheets. SlowRider established a project team to look at acquiring a state-of-the-art business intelligence system. After several interviews with all the managers, the project team was ready to develop the business case.

   The project team estimated benefits of the new BI system as follows:

   - 5 percent increase in sales through better-focused sales campaigns, which should increase gross margins by $200,000 in year 1 and $300,000 in years 2 and 3.
   - 10 percent increase in inventory turnover through better purchasing, which should reduce inventory carrying costs by $100,000 in year 1 and $150,000 in years 2 and 3.

   The project team estimated costs over an expected 3-year life as follows:

Cost Element	Year 0	Year 1	Year 2	Year 3
Acquisition cost (new software and implementation)	$400,000			
Operating cost (annual licenses, upgrades, support)		$50,000	$50,000	$50,000
Training	$10,000	$5,000	$5,000	$5,000
Lost productivity during implementation	$20,000			
Total	$430,000	$55,000	$55,000	$55,000

After interviewing managers at other firms that have already implemented similar BI systems, the project team then estimated that the initiative would have the following risks. **LO 15-6**

Risk Description	Probability	Mitigation Steps
Managers will not use the system, resulting in:		Top management support; incentives to use the system
Revenue growth of 3%	25%	
Inventory turnover increase of 5%	25%	

a. Disregarding the risk, calculate the following for the BI investment:
   1. The payback period
   2. The NPV (assume 10 percent discount rate)
   3. The IRR
   4. The accounting rate of return

b. Recalculate the payback period, NPV, IRR, and ARR considering the risk.

c. Prepare a value proposition for the BI investment. Should SlowRider pursue the investment? What other issues should they consider?

2. The Beach Dude Inc. (BD) sells surf gear and clothing to retail stores around the country. It outsources the production of most of its items, so its warehouse is very busy receiving incoming shipments and preparing deliveries to customers. After a thorough review of its warehouse processes, the company determined that it could save substantial employee time and improve its on-time delivery rates if it adopted a warehouse management system using RFID chips and readers. RFID (radio-frequency identification) is a technology that uses radio waves to automatically identify people or objects. RFID tags are applied to packages, and then RFID readers can be used to track the location and movement of the inventory.

   BD estimates that the RFID system—including fixed and mobile scanners, software, servers, installation, and integration with its existing AIS—will cost $400,000. The system has an expected useful life of 5 years and is expected to have a negligible value at that time. Training for the warehouse, IT, and accounting employees is expected to cost an additional $25,000. Additionally, the company's estimate for the cost of RFID tags is $30,000 per year based on the current $0.15 cost per tag. However, it believes there is a 50 percent probability that the cost per tag will decrease to $0.10 per tag in 2 years. BD estimates that it will save $150,000 per year in reduced employee overtime, fewer priority shipments, reduced inventory losses, and improved inventory turnover. Assume that BD has a cost of capital of 6 percent. **LO 15-6**

   a. Calculate the following for BD's investment, assuming there is no reduction in the cost of RFID tags:
      1. The payback period
      2. The NPV
      3. The IRR
      4. The accounting rate of return

   b. Recalculate those values, assuming that the cost of RFID tags does decrease in 2 years as expected.

   c. Identify some potential risks and possible omissions in BD's planning. Provide examples of situations that would lead to the risks that you identify.

3. Refer to the **Starbucks** vignette at the beginning of this chapter. Starbucks has aggressively pursued digital ventures to improve the customer experience and increase the amount of customer transactions per visit. Among other things, Starbucks mines the data from customer loyalty cards to examine buying patterns to predict what customers will buy in the future. It is looking for an increased "wallet-share." **LO 15-3; LO 15-6**

   a. Describe why it is difficult to evaluate Starbucks' digital ventures' investments using traditional capital budgeting techniques.

   b. What are some other ways that Starbucks could evaluate the benefit of its digital ventures?

4. Sunset Graphics is considering two mutually exclusive projects. Both require an initial investment of $100,000. Assume a marginal interest rate of 10 percent and no residual value for either investment. The cash flows for the two projects are expected to be the following: **LO 15-6**

Year	Project 1	Project 2
1	$30,000	$0
2	$30,000	$20,000
3	$30,000	$20,000
4	$30,000	$50,000
5	$30,000	$75,000

a. Compute the NPV, payback, and IRR for both projects. Which is more desirable?

b. Assume straight-line depreciation is used for both projects; compute the accounting rate of return. What do you think of the ARR criterion?

c. Assume a change in interest rate to 15 percent. Does that change your views on which project the company should adopt?

d. Assume a change in interest rate to 6 percent. Does that change your views on which project the company should adopt?

e. For investments in technology, which cash inflow projection is most likely?

5. Sunset Graphics is considering moving to a cloud-based accounting system because its current system only runs on outdated computers. The cloud-based system is very similar to the current system, so there would be no additional training required. The cloud-based system will cost $1,500 per month for the next 36 months. The company will write off its old equipment and record a corresponding loss of $2,000. It will buy five new computers to access the cloud at a total cost of $2,200.

Its alternative is to purchase a new local accounting system. If it pursues this alternative, the company will also spend $2,200 on five new computers and write off the old hardware and software. The new software will cost $40,000. Sunset Graphics uses a discount rate of 10 percent. **LO 15-6**

a. Which alternative is the better solution? Why? What factors would influence your decision?

b. Assume the local accounting system is expected to last 5 years but will require a major upgrade costing $15,000 at the end of year 3. Also assume that the cost of the cloud-based system will fall to $1,200 per month for months 37–60. Neither alternative will have any residual value. Compare the two alternatives again.

connect

6. Each alternative IT initiative carries risk of failing to achieve the respective benefits and exceeding the estimated costs. Match the description of risk with each risk term. **LO 15-5**

1. The solution will not generate projected benefits.
2. The solution is not aligned with the strategy of the firm.
3. The project will not be completed on time or within budget.
4. The solution will not deliver expected financial performance.

A. Project risk
B. Solution risk
C. Alignment risk
D. Financial risk

connect 7. After identifying relevant risks, the project team often employs risk-minimization techniques to lessen the probability or impact of the risk. Match the description/example of the risk mitigation technique with the type of risk being mitigated. **LO 15-5**

1. Ensure active top management support for the project.
2. Use sensitivity analyst to consider likely alternative benefit levels.
3. Ask **Microsoft** to demonstrate that its software can meet the system requirements.
4. Give employees adequate incentive to use the new IT.

A. Change risk
B. Project risk
C. Technological risk
D. Solution risk

connect 8. Match the description of these financial metrics to their terms. **LO 15-6**

1. The average annual income from the IT initiative divided by the initial investment cost
2. The sum of the present value of all cash inflows less the sum of the present value of all cash outflows
3. The discount rate (return) that makes a project's net present value equal to zero
4. The amount of time necessary to recoup a project's initial investment

A. Accounting rate of return
B. Internal rate of return
C. Net present value
D. Payback period

connect 9. Project benefits may come from a variety of sources. Match the examples of these project benefits to their terms. **LO 15-3**

1. The new system will be able to identify additional products that customers might be interested in.
2. Installing an accounting system that supports international financial standards will lower the cost when international financial standards are required.
3. A supply chain system will help us source cheaper sources of raw materials to build our projects.
4. Adding tracking information to shipments was important to not lose sales to competitors.

A. Revenue enhancement
B. Revenue protection
C. Cost savings
D. Cost avoidance

connect 10. Which of these project costs would be considered to be acquisition costs and which would be considered to be operating costs? **LO 15-4**

1. Hardware replacement
2. Help desk support
3. Software upgrade
4. Development
5. Initial training
6. Ongoing training
7. Maintenance contracts
8. Project management

connect 11. There are several approaches to quantifying expected project benefits. Which of the following uses simulation, external benchmarks, real option theory, or expert opinion to help with the quantification? LO 15-3

1. Software that allows you to consider the impact under a variety of assumptions
2. Compare and contrast the results with projects of competitors or similar firms
3. Sophisticated financial analysis comparing the probability of achieving expected benefits
4. Consulting with a seasoned consultant to establish a likely benefit

connect 12. A firm is considering two projects. Both have an initial investment of $1,000,000 and pay off over the next five years in this fashion. The cost of capital is 6%. LO 15-6

	Option 1	Option 2
Year 0	−1,000,000	−1,000,000
Year 1	1,000,000	250,000
Year 2	0	250,000
Year 3	0	250,000
Year 4	0	250,000
Year 5	100,000	250,000

a. Which of these has a faster payback period?
b. Which of these options has a higher net present value?
c. Which of these options has a higher internal rate of return (IRR)?

connect 13. A firm is considering two projects. Both have an initial investment of $1,000,000 and pay off over the next five years in this fashion. The cost of capital is 8%. LO 15-6

	Option 1	Option 2
Year 0	−1,000,000	−1,000,000
Year 1	1,000,000	500,000
Year 2	100,000	500,000
Year 3	200,000	400,000
Year 4	300,000	300,000
Year 5	400,000	200,000

a. Which of these has a faster payback period?
b. Which of these options has a higher net present value?
c. Which of these options has a higher internal rate of return (IRR)?

Chapter Sixteen

The Systems Development Life Cycle and Project Management: Addressing the Challenges of Building AIS Systems

A look at this chapter

This chapter highlights the systems development life cycle and project management. We make the case that management needs to understand how AIS systems are developed and describe the roles of the project manager and project sponsor. We also highlight the constraints to successful AIS project implementations and the tools that are used to overcome them. Finally, we discuss a model to determine whether a new system will actually be useful to the intended AIS users.

A look back

Because accounting information systems and information technology initiatives in general often involve substantial costs, Chapter 15 discussed ways firms economically justify IT initiatives and ensure that those initiatives align with objectives of the overall business.

© Danny Johnston/AP Photo

Starbucks certainly seems to control one corner of the retail market. But **Walmart** has to be viewed as retail's 10-ton gorilla. Walmart initially relied entirely on home-grown internal systems, and its technology has helped it lead the market in many respects, including supply chain management, Retail Link, RFID tags, and electronic commerce. Recently, however, Walmart chose **SAP** to help it with its accounting information system and embarked on one of the world's largest software installations. With almost $500 billion in global sales annually and more than 2,200,000 employees, the project management of a new accounting information system for Walmart has to be carefully planned and meticulously completed. Choosing the right people to serve as project manager, project sponsor, and project team members is just the beginning of ensuring a successful AIS implementation.

Chapter Outline

Learning Objectives

After reading this chapter, you should be able to:

16-1 Describe each phase in the systems development life cycle.

16-2 Explain the core principles of information systems planning.

16-3 Define *project management,* and describe the positions of those who lead the project.

16-4 Explain why IT projects are challenged and the tools that are used to overcome these challenges.

16-5 Explain why users do or do not want to use a new information system designed for them.

LO 16-1
Describe each phase in the systems development life cycle.

INTRODUCTION

We have learned about many of the processes and components of an accounting information system (AIS) thus far in this book. Another key component in understanding the accounting information system is to know how these AIS systems are envisioned, designed, and ultimately brought into operation. In an organization, accountants play a key user role in telling systems developers what information is needed in an accounting information system and often play an important role in implementing projects. Managing and carrying out the systems development life cycle to achieve an intended outcome is called **project management** and is the topic of this chapter.

DESCRIPTION OF THE SYSTEMS DEVELOPMENT LIFE CYCLE

To best understand the design, use, management, and evaluation of an accounting information system, it is important to understand the systems development life cycle. The **systems development life cycle (SDLC)** is the process of creating or modifying information systems to meet the needs of its users. The SDLC is generally viewed as the foundation for all systems development that people use to develop such systems. The SDLC has five phases: planning, analysis, design, implementation, and maintenance.

1. The **planning phase** of the SDLC begins with a business need for a new or better information system. This phase involves summarizing the business needs with a high-level view of the intended project. A feasibility study is often used to evaluate economic, operational, and technical practicability. This includes making a business case for the system. It is also used as a basis to get buy-in and funding from upper management.
    - *Example:* Let's suppose that the **Starbucks** marketing department wants to analyze what type of pastries sell best with its various hot and cold drinks. In order to do so, it will need to change the software on its POS (point-of-sale) terminals and develop an easy system for the marketing department to run what-if analyses with its data. A feasibility analysis suggests that it is operationally and technically practical to make this change, and if this information is captured, the chief marketing officer of Starbucks will be much more successful when she presents her case for potential marketing promotions featuring the sale of both drinks and pastries. The marketing officer expects the payoff in profits for such systems to be greater than the approximately $63,000 needed to plan, design, and implement this system.
2. The **analysis phase** of the SDLC involves a complete, detailed analysis of the systems needs of the end user. The analysis phase further refines the goals of the project into carefully specified functions and operations of the intended system. This step may involve looking at the entire system in different pieces and drawing various flowcharts and diagrams to better analyze the situation and project goals.
    - *Example:* **Starbucks**'s systems analysis team meets with all of the desired users of the enhanced system (including the chief marketing officer). The users want to make sure that considerable flexibility is built into the system in order to address both current and potential data analysis needs it may have in the future.
3. The **design phase** of the SDLC involves describing in detail the desired features of the system that it uncovered in the analysis phase. These features may be described using screen layouts, process and event diagrams (such as we learned earlier in this book), and other documentation. A **systems analyst** is responsible for both determining the information needs of the business and designing a system to meet those needs.
    - *Example:* The **Starbucks** systems designers take the requested business requirements from the analysis stage and begin to design how the new what-if Starbucks analysis system would look on a screen and the business rules and process diagrams needed to make such a change in the system.

4. The **implementation phase** of the SDLC involves development, testing, and implementation of the new proposed system. Development is the process of transforming the plan from the design phase into an actual, functioning system. The testing of the system involves testing for errors, bugs, and interoperability with other parts of the system. It also serves to verify that all of the business requirements from the analysis phase are met. Implementation involves placing the system into production such that users can actually use the system that has been designed for them.
    - *Example:* The **Starbucks** systems developers write the computer code and test it. Once testing is complete and the business requirements are met, the users are trained and given incentives to use the new system, and the new software is put into actual use. At this point, the users can begin to perform what-if analyses using the new software.
5. The **maintenance phase** of the SDLC is the final phase and includes making changes, corrections, additions, and upgrades (generally smaller in scope) to ensure the system continues to meet the business requirements that have been set out for it. The maintenance phase continues indefinitely because the system must continue to evolve as the underlying business evolves.
    - *Example:* The **Starbucks** system undergoes continuous and regular maintenance to ensure that it meets the underlying business requirements. Specifically, as new products are introduced and new information is needed, the system continues to be modified and upgraded. The bigger the needed changes, the more likely that the SDLC will start all over again to address the expected changes.

During the maintenance phase, new, substantive changes are often needed to meet the changing, evolving needs of the firm. The systems development life cycle starts again and the planning phase begins anew in a recursive manner to assess whether a new or upgraded system needs to be developed. This recursive nature is a reason why it is called a life cycle. The recursive nature of the systems development life cycle is illustrated in Figure 16.1.

FIGURE 16.1
The Recursive Nature of the Systems Development Life Cycle

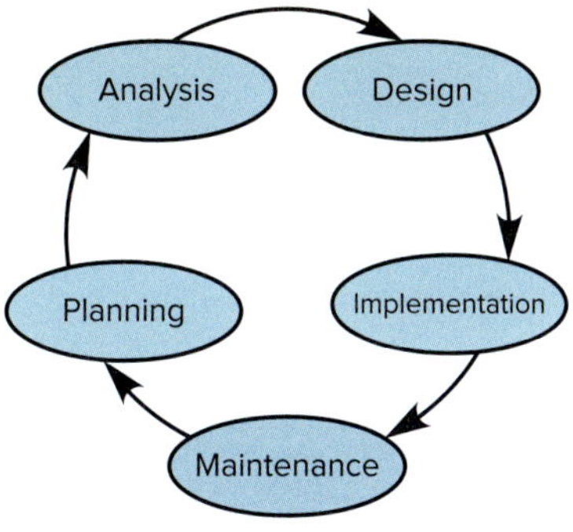

Connection with Practice

The Information Systems Audit and Control Association (ISACA) and the IT Governance Institute (ITGI) developed Control Objectives for Information and Related Technology (COBIT) to serve as a set of best practices for information technology (IT) management. COBIT provides managers, auditors, and IT users with a set of generally accepted measurements, processes, indicators, and best practices to assist them in maximizing the benefits derived through the use of information technology. COBIT's guidance corresponds to the SDLC, namely, plan and organize, acquire and implement, deliver and support, and monitor and evaluate.

LO 16-2
Explain the core principles of information systems planning.

EFFECTIVE INFORMATION TECHNOLOGY PLANNING

As the title of this chapter suggests, we want to emphasize the importance of effective IT planning. During the first phase of the SDLC, the planning phase, an information technology plan should be developed to support the overall firm strategy. The plan should provide a roadmap of the information technology required to support the business direction of a firm. This should include an outline of the required resources and the expected benefits that will be realized when the IT plan is implemented. While each information technology plan is unique to the needs and circumstances of a firm, the International Federation of Accountants suggests that these 10 core principles be followed to ensure effective information technology planning:[1]

- Alignment—the planning phase should support and complement the business strategy of a firm.
- Relevant scope—the overall scope of the planning phase should be established to facilitate formulation of effective ways to address the business needs.
- Relevant timeframe—the appropriate planning horizon should be formulated that provides both short- and medium-term deliverables as well as long-term alignment with the business strategy.
- Benefits realization—costs of implementation should be commensurate with the tangible and intangible benefits that are expected to be realized. The expected benefits should be bigger than the costs.
- Achievability—the planning phase should recognize the capability and capacity of the firm to deliver solutions within the stated planning timeframe.
- Measurable performance—the planning phase should provide a means to measure and monitor project performance and serve as a means of communicating success to both stakeholders inside and outside the firm.
- Reassessment—the plan should be periodically reassessed to ensure it is relevant to the evolving business strategy of the firm.
- Awareness—the resulting plan that comes out of the planning phase should be communicated widely.
- Accountability—identification of those responsible for implementing the plan should be explicitly clear.
- Commitment—management commitment to the plan's implementation should be clear and evident.

Each of these core principles is important to effective information technology planning.

Progress Check

1. Why is the systems development life cycle recursive? Will systems development ever be completed?
2. Why is measurable performance important to consider in the planning phase of the systems development life cycle?

The Sarbanes-Oxley Act of 2002 (SOX) highlights the importance of accounting information system controls by requiring management and auditors to report on the effectiveness of internal controls over the company's accounting information system.

Consider these two excerpts taken from two companies announcing misstatements. In both cases, the firms revealed a material weakness that allowed a material misstatement in the financial reports.

[1]International Federation of Accountants, *Managing Information Technology Planning for Business Impact* (January 1999).

Consider this 10-K filing from **Landauer Inc.** (2014):

> We did not design and maintain processes and procedures that restrict access to key financial systems and records to appropriate users and evaluate whether appropriate segregation of duties is maintained. Specifically, certain personnel had access to financial application, programs and data beyond that needed to perform their individual job responsibilities without independent monitoring.

Landauer Inc. provides technical and analytical services, outsourced medical physics services, and radiology-related medical products worldwide. This misstatement in the accounting information system suggests that the software was not designed to restrict access to the accounting systems or to provide adequate segregation of duties. Had the software been designed correctly, it would not have caused a misstatement.

This one is from **WaferGen Bio-Systems Inc.**'s 8-K filing:

> In addition, due to a spreadsheet error, the Company's previously filed financial statements recorded basic and diluted net loss per share in the nine months ended September 30, 2013, based on a weighted average of 709,639 shares outstanding during the period, when the correct number of shares was 1,226,570.

WaferGen Bio-Systems presents a case of ineffective controls around the use of spreadsheets. As accountants understand the design of accounting information systems, they are better equipped to address potential weaknesses in the accounting information system.

Connection with Practice

Segregation of Duties

In nearly all accounting textbooks, the importance of segregation of duties (SOD) is discussed. The general rule is that accounting controls, whether they be manual or computerized, should be set up to separate (1) custody of assets, (2) authorization of transactions, and (3) record-keeping responsibilities.

As in the 2014 case of **Landauer** disclosed earlier, it notes that the company "did not design and maintain processes and procedures that restrict access to key financial systems and records to appropriate users and evaluate whether appropriate segregation of duties is maintained."

Segregation of duties is not just a concept you read in a textbook. It continues to be a real issue at companies today.

In both examples, the design of the information system was ineffective and was the source of a potential material weakness in the accounting information system. This highlights the real need for accountants to understand the design and development of accounting information systems, which is the topic of this chapter.

LO 16-3
Define *project management,* and describe the positions of those who lead the project.

PROJECTS, PROJECT MANAGEMENT, AND PROJECT SPONSORS

Projects are a series of tasks that are generally performed in a defined sequence to produce a predefined output. The history of project management has its roots in engineering and construction projects. In an information technology setting, a project might include the creation of a new, unique IT product or service such as replacing old computers, moving data to a different cloud computing environment, installing a new financial reporting database, or merging financial reporting databases. For example, can you imagine merging an accounting information system from two different systems into one? We'll highlight this IT project management setting throughout the rest of this chapter.

Can you imagine merging the databases of customers, flights, accounting information, and frequent flyer miles for the recent combined merge of American Airlines and US Airways? Now that's a big project!

As defined earlier in the chapter, project management is the planning, organizing, supervising, and directing of an IT project. A **project manager** is the lead member of the project team and is responsible for the project. The project manager's mission is to coordinate the entire project development process to successfully complete the project. A project manager must also be able to analyze the project charter, a document that details the objectives and requirements of the project.

The third important concept surrounding a project is the presence of a project (or executive) sponsor. The **project sponsor** will often be a senior executive in the company who takes responsibility for the success of the project. The project sponsor is generally a different person than the project manager but often serves as the project champion. In addition, this person takes on critical roles in the project, including the following:

- Supporting the project manager in managing the project.
- Advocating for the project to the company management and also to those outside the company (e.g., vendors, suppliers, shareholders, etc.).
- Obtaining necessary resources for successful completion.
- Monitoring overall scope for the project to ensure successful completion and work to prevent scope creep (as discussed later).
- Accepting responsibility for issues and problems that arise that the project manager cannot handle alone.

The modern project management concept began with the Manhattan Project, which the U.S. military led to develop the atomic bomb.
© Bettman/Getty Images

All IT projects move through these five phases of the project management life cycle: initiating, planning, executing, monitoring and controlling, and closing. These phases contain the needed processes to move the project from the initial idea to project implementation and subsequent maintenance.

Progress Check

3. Why is the project sponsor so important?
4. Why should accountants be interested in project management?

LO 16-4
Explain why IT projects are challenged and the tools that are used to overcome these challenges.

CHALLENGES OF IT PROJECT MANAGEMENT

Before we get too far into discussing the details of the challenges of IT project management, it should be noted that IT projects are frequently canceled, late, or over budget or don't deliver the intended consequences. To illustrate the problem, here are some statistics on the outcomes of recent IT projects. Every few years, the Standish Group performs a survey to evaluate the outcomes of IT projects. Figure 16.2 provides a summary of its 2013 report.

FIGURE 16.2
Information Technology Project Outcomes

Source: Standish Group, 2013 and 2009.

	2012	2009	2006	2004	2002	2000	1998	1996	1994
Successful	39%	32%	35%	29%	34%	28%	26%	27%	16%
Challenged	43%	44%	19%	53%	15%	23%	28%	40%	31%
Failed	18%	24%	46%	18%	51%	49%	46%	33%	53%

The report shows that software projects now have a 39 percent success rate, compared with 32 percent from the previous study in 2009 and 16 percent in 1994. On the other hand, 43 percent of projects were challenged (i.e., late, over budget, and/or with less than the required features and functions) while 18 percent failed (i.e., canceled prior to completion or delivered and never used). While there seems to be improvement since 1994's low successful outcome percentage, there are still 61 percent (43 percent challenged + 18 percent failed) of the projects that either outright failed or were challenged in 2012. This low success rate can be attributed to poor project management and helps illustrate why project management is so critical in firms today. In the next section, we consider the specific obstacles, or constraining factors, that project managers face and the tools to overcome those challenges.

CONSTRAINING FACTORS OF IT PROJECTS

There are many reasons information technology projects fail to meet expectations. First, there are project management concerns that exist for all projects—such as deadlines, budget constraints, and limited resources (i.e., people) to focus efforts on completing the project successfully. Second, information technology projects face unique challenges because technology continues to change and oftentimes has glitches. These changes and glitches may come from hardware, operating systems, or databases. Third, there might also be security risks or interoperability issues between computer systems.

A project manager is generally told that a project must be completed by a certain date or for a certain cost or both. All information technology and other projects are constrained by three factors: cost, scope, and time constraints. This is often called the Dempster's triangle or the **triple constraints.** For a project to be successful, these three constraints must be held in balance. Once any of the constraints becomes out of balance, the project is likely headed for an unsuccessful outcome. Figure 16.3 provides an illustration of the triple constraint. Notice that in the center of these three constraints is quality. While the

FIGURE 16.3
The Triple Constraints of Project Management (Dempster's Triangle)

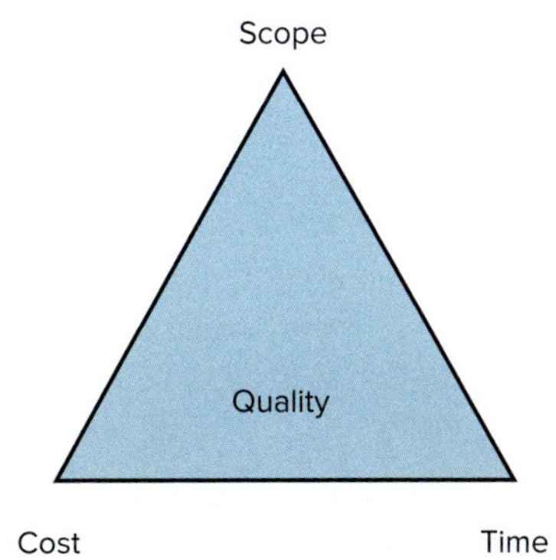

triple constraints do need to be carefully addressed, some level of quality must be met to be useful to the firm. As a project manager, you are often told that a project must be completed by a certain date or for a certain amount of money (cost) or both. At the same time, the deliverable (or result) of your project must also meet some minimum specifications (quality) to meet the firm's intended purposes.

Scope

The size or scope of the project is often defined in the initial stages of the project. However, in most projects, the scope begins to expand when additional features are added to the original specifications to add desired functionality. **Scope creep** is the broadening of a project's scope that occurs after the project has started. The change in scope often comes about from small, relatively insignificant change requests that the project team accepts to keep the project sponsor satisfied (e.g., information system available in Spanish or an e-commerce program able to transact with euros as well as U.S. dollars). Eventually, the number of change requests may become numerous enough to become significant, or some of the individual requests may be big enough to require much more work than originally expected.

The larger the scope expands beyond its initial specifications, the more the project will drift away from its original purpose, timeline, and budget. To help control scope creep, the project sponsor must be involved in the process to ensure that scope changes are absolutely needed and to assess if the benefits of the enhanced scope outweigh the costs. If the project scope is expanded, there must be additional time and funding to complete it.

Cost

A major challenge for IT projects is keeping the project within the planned budget. Often, the initial budget at the start of a project may not reflect all of the costs to bring the project to completion. As the IT project manager becomes aware of the costs to date and the expected costs to complete the project, she must share this information with the project sponsor and other company leadership. She then suggests a reconfiguration of resources or tasks that do not significantly change the scope of the project. This can be a challenge if additional costs are needed to successfully complete the project but additional needed funds are not available.

Time

Due to the rapid evolution of business and technology, most information technology projects are constrained by time. The results of these information systems often serve as a basis for a competitive advantage within the firm. Sometimes, systems implemented quickly can have a first-mover advantage. For this reason, the project manager is often given a deadline by which the project needs to be completed and delivered. Likewise, if software or hardware vendors don't deliver their solutions on time, the project will not be completed on time. To help address these time constraints, there are several project management tools available, including the PERT and Gantt charts, which are discussed later.

The 15-15 Rule

Sometimes it is important to know when an IT project will not reach a successful conclusion. At that point, it may make sense to stop investing in the IT project. As some would say, you need to know when to "quit throwing good money after bad" or in a poker game, "to know when to fold." One indicator that the project might have serious difficulty in achieving a successful outcome is called the **15-15 rule,** which states that if a project is more than 15 percent over budget or 15 percent off the desired schedule, it will likely never recoup the time or cost necessary to be considered successful. Of course, to know if the project is 15 percent over budget or 15 percent off the desired schedule requires careful monitoring by the project manager (and possibly the project sponsor).

Progress Check

5. What are the triple constraints of project management? How can scope creep cause distortions in cost and time?
6. When should the project manager and project sponsor approve scope changes? When should they deny scope changes?

PROJECT MANAGEMENT TOOLS

The previous section mentioned that one of the triple constraints of projects is time. There are two project management tools to help with this time constraint by scheduling, organizing, and coordinating the tasks within a project. The most popular tools in use today are the PERT and Gantt charts.

PERT is actually an acronym for **Program Evaluation Review Technique.** PERT was originally developed in the 1950s by the U.S. Navy to manage the building of the Polaris submarine missile.

The first step in a PERT chart is to identify all tasks needed to complete a project. This breakdown of all of the project tasks is often called the **work breakdown structure (WBS).** These tasks generally define all events and deliverables. After the tasks have been identified, the next step is to establish the sequencing of those events. The sequencing suggests which tasks need to precede the other tasks and which are dependent on the other tasks. A key part of making sure the PERT and the Gantt chart work is being able to define all of the tasks—including all internal, external, and interim tasks. This identification of all tasks is sometimes called the **100% rule.** The 100% rule, therefore, requires thorough and complete project planning.

The best way to explain a PERT chart is to see one and explain how it works. Consider the PERT chart in Figure 16.4. A PERT chart is a graphical representation of a project that consists of numbered *nodes* (either circles or rectangles) representing milestones in the project linked together by labeled directional lines representing tasks that need to be completed in the project. The numbers on the various directional lines indicate how much time has been allotted to the task. The sequencing of the tasks is denoted by the direction of the arrows on the lines. Some of the tasks must be completed in a certain sequence, like the set of tasks between numbered nodes 1, 6, 7, and 9 in Figure 16.4. These are called *dependent tasks* because they require that the previous task be completed before they can begin the next task. The tasks between nodes 10 and 11 cannot begin until all the preceding tasks (incoming directional lines) for node 10 are completed, including tasks 5, 8, and 9.

Because these all must be done in order, the longest string of time allotted to dependent tasks must be determined. We call this the critical path. The **critical path** is the longest path for a project and represents the minimum amount of time needed for the completion of the project when sufficient resources are allocated. The critical path helps the project manager figure out how resources should be allocated in order to complete the project within the shortest amount of time. In Figure 16.4, that path is 1, 2, 3, 4, 5, 10, 11, 12.

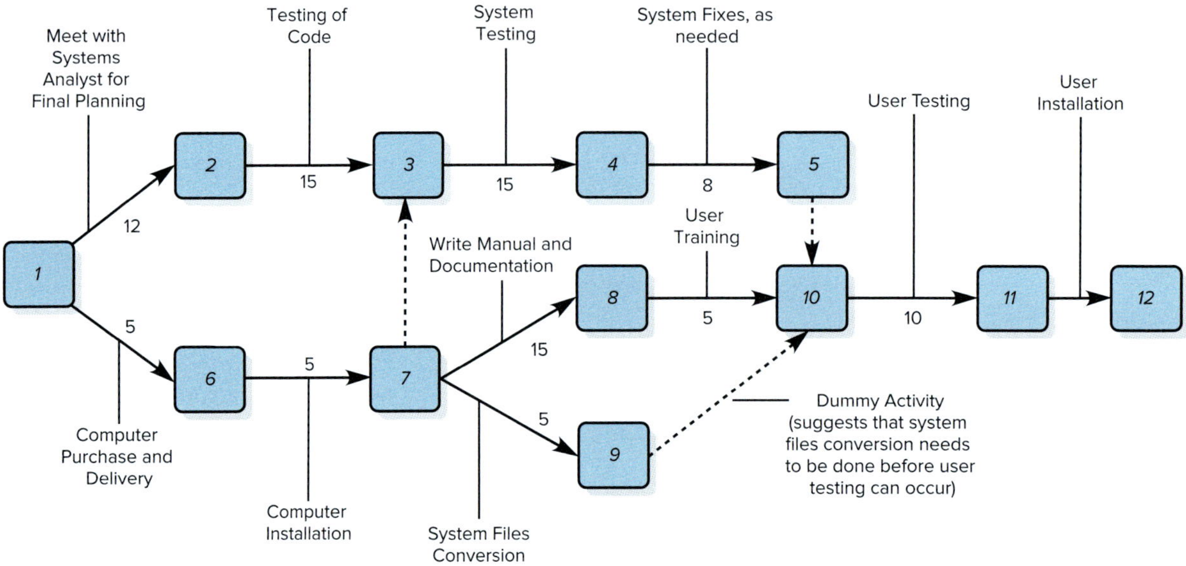

FIGURE 16.4
Example of a PERT Chart

Some tasks are not dependent on the completion of one to start the other, such as the tasks between nodes 7 and 8, and nodes 7 and 9. Tasks 5 and 8 are called *parallel,* or *concurrent tasks* because they can be done at the same time. Tasks that must be completed in a specific sequence but don't require additional resources or a specific completion time are considered to have *task dependency.* These are called *dummy tasks* and are represented by dashed lines with arrows. For example, the dashed lines between nodes 9 and 10 suggest that the software testing and related fixes must be completed before user testing can take place.

Henry Gantt, an American mechanical engineer, is generally credited with inventing the Gantt chart.

Another similar, but complementary project management tool is the use of the Gantt chart. A **Gantt chart** is a graphical representation of the project schedule by mapping the tasks to a project calendar. Gantt charts are especially useful when monitoring a project's progress.

A Gantt chart illustrates the start and finish dates of the various tasks of the project. Some Gantt charts also show the dependency between the tasks. Figure 16.5 shows an illustration of both a PERT chart and a related Gantt chart and how they might work together. Each letter represents a task to be performed. The PERT chart shows the critical path; the Gantt chart also shows the term "margin" and ". . ." to signify the slack time before the next critical path task needs to be completed. As the project progresses through time, the Gantt chart is used to show the current status.

One noted advantage of the PERT chart over the Gantt chart is that it clearly illustrates the dependence of one task on another. At the same time, one disadvantage of the PERT chart is that it can be much more difficult to interpret, especially on complex projects.

Progress Check

7. Why is the 100% rule critical for identifying the work to be done? How is it different from the 15-15 rule?
8. What is a parallel or concurrent task? Are these tasks required to be done at the same time? If you have to choose, which parallel or concurrent task should be done first?

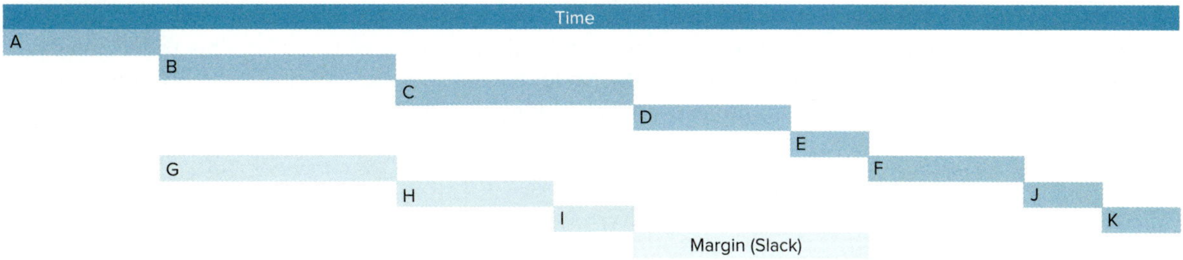

Gantt Chart

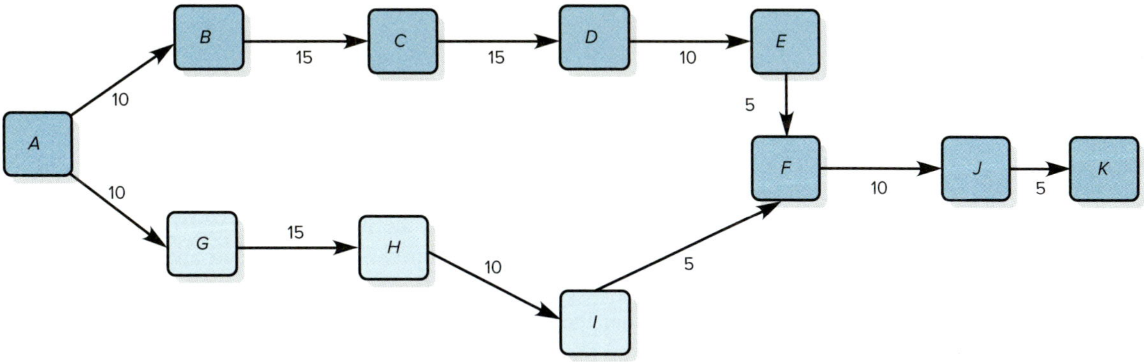

PERT Chart

FIGURE 16.5
Example of Gantt Chart and Its Relationship to the PERT Chart

LO 16-5
Explain why users do or do not want to use a new information system designed for them.

WILL THE SYSTEM BE USED, AND WILL IT BE USEFUL?

Outside of the triple constraints is the challenge of whether the system will actually be used by the intended users once it is completed. In other words, even though the system is on time, on budget, and built to the firm's specifications, users may not use the system. There are some systems that are scrapped because the users simply don't want to use them.

Let's assume the systems department sends you an e-mail and tells you they are ready to install a new accounting system's module for accounts payable on your computer. While the old system will still be available for a short time, your boss and the systems department would like you to start to use the new system and get used to it. They will even pay you to go to training at a nice hotel and for a nice lunch. But because change is hard for everyone, you wonder "if the new system will work as good as the old," "if you'll ever figure out how to use it," or "if this is the system that will ultimately replace your job."

In a study by Fred Davis,[2] a model was proposed that predicts whether a system will be adopted or whether the system will be scratched. The model, titled the **technology acceptance model (TAM),** suggests that users will adopt a new or modified system to the extent they believe the system will help them perform their job better. TAM would call this **perceived usefulness.** At the same time, TAM defines the extent to which a person believes that the use of a particular system would be free of effort. We call this concept

[2] F. Davis, "Perceived Usefulness, Perceived Ease of Use, and User Acceptance of Information Technology," *MIS Quarterly* 13, no. 3 (1989), pp. 319–40.

perceived ease of use. So if the user believes that the system is easy to learn and use (i.e., perceived ease of use) and will help the user to perform his or her job better (i.e., perceived usefulness), the model predicts the user will make the effort to learn the new system and ultimately adopt it. Figure 16.6 offers an illustration of the technology acceptance model.

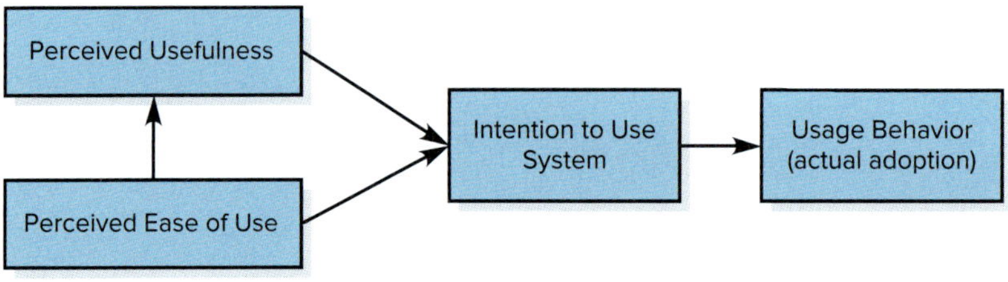

FIGURE 16.6
The Technology Acceptance Model

Source: F. Davis, "Perceived Usefulness, Perceived Ease of Use, and User Acceptance of Information Technology," *MIS Quarterly* 13, no. 3 (1989), pp. 319–40.

Addressing Perceived Usefulness

Project managers, project champions, systems analysts, and developers alike all take responsibility for building a system that will be useful to the users. One way to make the perception that the new system will be useful to users a reality is by extensive communication between the systems builders and the user base and meeting their needs. As the project progresses, feedback on what features will be included and which will not be included will keep all users involved in the process. To achieve the milestone and ensure on-time delivery, project managers usually create a *specification,* which includes a feature list from the feedback of the potential users. The features can be further categorized into "must-have" features, "nice-to-have" features, and "future improvements" to determine their priorities. Based on the features and priorities, system developers implement the most important must-have features within the specified timeframe and continue on to the nice-to-have features. Future improvements are usually more sophisticated and time-consuming to implement but cannot be addressed in the allowable timeframe, so they are often considered in the second (or maintenance) phase.

In Figure 16.6, we also note the directional arrow going from perceived ease of use to perceived usefulness. This recognizes the possibility that if the system is perceived to be easy to use, it will also be perceived to be more useful. Likewise, if a new system is fraught with errors and issues and has not been completely tested, it will not be perceived to be useful or easy to use.

In an accounting information system, system features to address new regulatory requirements (e.g., new FASB standards, new SEC disclosures, Sarbanes-Oxley laws, etc.) would be considered "must-have" features. In contrast, an accounting information system that allows the user to track the cost of shipping from China to the United States for each product may be considered a "nice-to-have" feature. However, if management requires this information to adequately manage the business and make critical decisions, it may rise to "must-have" feature status. In either case, we learn that as the new AIS system meets the needs of the users, they will perceive it to be more useful and be more likely to adopt it.

Addressing Perceived Ease of Use

There are many things that can be done to help new users prepare to actually use the system. Systems analysts and developers can mock up the computer screen to show the look and feel of the system well before the new system is written. Project managers can also ensure that users undergo extensive training before the system goes into operation so they feel comfortable with it.

At times, instead of rolling out the computer system for the whole staff at the same time, it may make sense to pilot test the new system with some peer leaders who can ultimately help steer adoption for the rest of the users to the new system. For example, in August 2010, **Walmart** piloted its new **SAP** accounting information system at its Asda subsidiary in the United Kingdom before the worldwide rollout. They found that the UK implementation was so successful that the company proceeded in rolling it out globally. This certainly helps make an AIS implementation at other Walmart locations less stressful. All of these strategies can help users feel confident they can learn and use the new system.

Systems analysts, systems developers, and project managers should all be aware of how a new system is perceived by those who will ultimately be using it. They should consistently communicate with this user group to make sure the system will be useful and easy to use.

Connection with Practice

Perceived Usefulness or Failure?

The **London Ambulance Service** (LAS) developed a brand-new software system of routing ambulances throughout the London area. The system was put into operation on the morning of October 26, 1992. After just a few hours' use, however, problems began to appear in the routing system. The system was unable to track ambulance location or status. Not knowing the relative location of the ambulances, the system then began to send multiple ambulances to some locations, but none to others. The problem was further exacerbated when customers kept calling back when their requested ambulances did not arrive. As additional calls, both new and call-backs, were entered into the system, it became further clogged, and the problems increased. The next day, the LAS switched back to the original, manual system to make sure to keep up with demand.

Because of the huge population served only by the LAS network, many people were affected by the failure of this computer system. Forty-six avoidable deaths could be attributed to the failure of the computer system had the requested ambulance arrived on time. One ambulance crew arrived so late that they found that the patient had not only died, but his body had already been taken to the mortician. In a different case, a heart attack patient waited more than 6 hours for an ambulance before finally having her son take her to the emergency room. Almost 4 hours later, the LAS called to see if the ambulance was still needed. Finally, another woman kept calling the ambulance service every 30 minutes for 3 hours before an ambulance finally came. By then, it was too late—her husband had already died.

A useful system? No, this was a failure.

Sources: A. Finkelstein and J. Dowell, "A Comedy of Errors: The London Ambulance Service Case Study," *IWSSD*, 8th International Workshop on Software Specification and Design (1996), p. 2; and D. Dalcher, "Disaster in London: The LAS Case Study," *ECBS*, IEEE Conference and Workshop on Engineering of Computer-Based Systems (1999), p. 41.

Progress Check

9. What can be done to address perceptions of usefulness of a new accounting information system?
10. What can be done to address perceptions of ease of use of a new accounting information system?

Summary

- Users and auditors of an accounting information system need to understand the basics of AIS project management to understand how accounting information systems are developed.
- The systems development life cycle is the foundation for all systems development, models, and methodologies that people use to develop such systems. The SDLC has five phases: planning, analysis, design, implementation, and maintenance.

- Effective information systems planning is of critical importance to the firm because it is the stage that the firm uses to evaluate needed changes to the system. Ten core principles of effective information systems planning were highlighted.
- Project managers and project sponsors each plays a key role in managing system development.
- Many AIS and IT projects fail to meet expectations. If we can understand the reason these projects fail, we can better design the project management process to address these reasons.
- Scope, time, and cost represent the triple constraints of project management. If any of these constraints get out of control, the project will likely face overwhelming challenges. The project manager and project sponsor use various project management tools to monitor and control the scope, time, and costs.
- AIS developers, project managers, and project sponsors should all be aware of how a new system is perceived by those who will ultimately be using the new system. They should consistently communicate with the end-user group to make sure the system will be (or at least perceived to be) useful and easy to use.

Key Words

15-15 rule (*392*) A rule suggesting that if a project is more than 15 percent over budget or 15 percent off the planned schedule, it will likely never recoup the time or cost necessary to be considered successful. At this point, a decision needs to be made on if or how to proceed.

100% rule (*393*) A rule requiring 100 percent planning of all tasks, including all of the internal, external, and interim tasks.

analysis phase (*386*) The phase of the SDLC that involves a complete, detailed analysis of the systems needs of the end user as well as a proposed solution.

critical path (*393*) The longest path for a project and represents the minimum amount of time needed for the completion of the project when sufficient resources are allocated.

design phase (*386*) The phase of the SDLC that involves describing in detail the desired features of the system that were uncovered in the analysis phase.

Gantt chart (*394*) A graphical representation of the project schedule that maps the tasks to a project calendar.

implementation phase (*387*) The phase of the SDLC that involves development, testing, and implementation of the new proposed system.

maintenance phase (*387*) The final phase of the SDLC that includes making changes, corrections, additions, and upgrades (generally smaller in scope) to ensure the system continues to meet the business requirements that have been set out for it.

perceived ease of use (*396*) The extent to which a person perceives that the use of a particular system will be relatively free from effort.

perceived usefulness (*395*) The extent to which users believe the system will help them perform their job better.

planning phase (*386*) The phase of the SDLC that summarizes the business needs with a high-level view of the intended project.

Program Evaluation Review Technique (PERT) (*393*) A project management tool used to help identify all tasks needed to complete a project. It is also helpful in determining task dependencies.

project (*389*) A series of tasks that are generally performed in a defined sequence to produce a predefined output.

project management (*386*) The process of carrying out the systems development life cycle to achieve an intended outcome.

project manager (*390*) The lead member of the project team who is responsible for the project.

project sponsor (*390*) Generally a senior executive in the company who takes responsibility for the success of the project.

scope creep (*392*) The change in a project's scope after the project work has started.

systems analyst (*386*) Person responsible for both determining the information needs of the business and designing a system to meet those needs.

systems development life cycle (SDLC) (*386*) The process of creating or modifying information systems to meet the needs of its users. It serves as the foundation for all processes people use to develop such systems.

technology acceptance model (TAM) (*395*) A model that predicts when users will adopt a new system to the extent they believe the system will help them perform their job better.

triple constraints (*391*) Three factors that constrain information technology and other projects: cost, scope, and time. Also known as Dempster's triangle.

work breakdown structure (WBS) (*393*) The process of identifying all tasks needed to complete a project.

Answers to Progress Checks

1. The recursive nature of the SDLC reflects that the firm continues to evolve, always needing new and different information. While a particular system may be completed and put into use, because the business is always changing, a firm's systems development should never be considered complete.
2. It is important to set expectations clearly and measure whether a system has met those expectations (or not). This is particularly important to consider in the earliest planning phases.
3. For a project to be successfully implemented, there must be executive support. A project sponsor ensures that the project has initial and continuing executive support to ensure the necessary and appropriate resources are available. One of the most important responsibilities for the project sponsor is to monitor the overall scope of the project and make sure there is enough support for any scope changes that might occur.
4. Accountants use and audit the information that comes out of an accounting information system. But how was the system designed? Can they trust the numbers that come out of the system? Accountants must understand the design and development of an accounting information system to be able to trust the information coming out of that system.
5. Scope, cost, and time are the triple constraints of project management. If the scope becomes different and/or larger, the cost and time to complete can quickly become overwhelming and become a source of failure.
6. Generally, scope changes are made to satisfy potential users and executives. They may make the system more useable and have desired features. The project manager and project sponsor must assess and balance the costs and benefits of scope changes. If a change has too little impact, costs too much, or can easily be done in a future upgrade to the system, the project manager and project sponsor should deny the scope change.
7. In order to plan the project, the work breakdown structure must be complete, or 100 percent planned. This will help in sequencing the tasks, figuring out which tasks are dependent on other tasks, and allowing for planning of the complete project. In contrast, the 15-15 rule states that if a project is more than 15 percent over budget or 15 percent off the desired schedule, it will likely never recoup the time or cost necessary to be considered successful.

8. A parallel, or concurrent, task is a task that can be done or completed at the same time as another task. All other things equal, the parallel task that is on the critical path should be completed first because subsequent tasks depend on that task being completed.
9. To address perceptions of usefulness by the ultimate user, extensive communication between the systems builders and the user base needs to occur. As the new system assesses and addresses user needs, users will feel more comfortable that the new system will be useful. Accountants who will use the system should be included in the discussion of what the new system needs to have and how the new system will address them.
10. To address perceptions of ease of use by the ultimate user, project managers should ensure that users have extensive training and that those who feel most comfortable with the new system use it first in a pilot test.

Mc Graw Hill Education connect

Multiple Choice Questions

1. Which phase of the systems development life cycle would include a feasibility analysis? **LO 16-1**
   a. Analysis phase
   b. Planning phase
   c. Design phase
   d. Implementation phase
2. The IFAC suggested 10 core principles of effective information technology planning. Which of the following is not one of those 10 core principles? **LO 16-1**
   a. Achievability
   b. Reassessment
   c. Accountability
   d. Justifiable cost
3. Projects are considered challenged if they: **LO 16-4**
   a. are late, are over budget, or do not have the required features and functions.
   b. are canceled prior to completion.
   c. are delivered but never used.
   d. are completed early.
4. The triple constraints of project management do not include the constraint of: **LO 16-4**
   a. technical issues.
   b. time.
   c. cost.
   d. scope.
5. The PERT and Gantt charts primarily address the triple constraint of: **LO 16-4**
   a. technical issues.
   b. time.
   c. cost.
   d. scope.

6. The 100% rule suggests that before a PERT chart is done, a project manager must: **LO 16-4**
   a. make sure 100 percent of the project is funded.
   b. make sure the project team is devoted solely, or 100 percent, to the project.
   c. make sure 100 percent of the project tasks are defined.
   d. make sure that each person on the project team got 100 percent on his or her project management final exam.
7. The critical path in a PERT chart represents: **LO 16-4**
   a. the sequencing of tasks.
   b. the most important tasks of the whole project.
   c. the longest path of tasks needed for project completion.
   d. the tasks that must be completed without errors.
8. The technology acceptance model does not address: **LO 16-5**
   a. perceived usefulness.
   b. perceived systems quality.
   c. perceived ease of use.
   d. intention to use.
9. The Sarbanes-Oxley Act's section 404 reports require management and auditors to report on: **LO 16-2**
   a. the financial condition of the firm.
   b. the quality of the project management planning.
   c. the academic background and experience of the company's accounting leadership.
   d. the effectiveness of the internal controls of the company's accounting information system.
10. In this chapter, *projects* are defined as: **LO 16-3**
    a. a series of tasks performed in a defined sequence.
    b. turning raw talent into an NFL-quality quarterback.
    c. turning blueprints from an architect into a completed building.
    d. merging two databases into one.
11. The technology acceptance model addresses: **LO 16-5**
    a. intention to adopt mobile technology.
    b. perceived ease of use.
    c. perceived usage.
    d. perceived ability to address technical difficulties.
    e. none of the above.
12. Which phase of the systems development life cycle would include describing in detail the desired features of the system? **LO 16-1**
    a. Analysis phase
    b. Planning phase
    c. Maintenance phase
    d. Design phase
    e. Implementation phase
13. Which phase of the systems development life cycle summarizes the business needs with a high-level view of the intended project? **LO 16-1**
    a. Analysis phase
    b. Planning phase
    c. Maintenance phase
    d. Design phase
    e. Implementation phase

14. Which member of the project team will take responsibility for the success of the project? **LO 16-3**
    a. IT lead
    b. Project manager
    c. Project sponsor
    d. CEO
    e. None of the above
15. Which term defines the broadening of a project that occurs after the project begins? **LO 16-4**
    a. Project planning
    b. Scope creep
    c. Cost overrun
    d. 15-15 rule
    e. None of the above

Discussion Questions

1. Rank the 10 core principles of effective information technology planning in order of importance in your opinion. Provide support for your top 5 important principles. **LO 16-2**
2. Imagine the role of the project sponsor when a leader of the accounting bookkeepers comes to complain that the new information system could possibly result in the loss of five bookkeeper jobs. The bookkeepers argue that they will get the union involved if needed to protect their jobs. What should the project sponsor do? **LO 16-3**
3. Explain the 100% rule. Assume you are telling your roommate about this rule, and use an example that is relevant to him or her. **LO 16-4**
4. Your grandmother regularly listens to oldies music on a collection of cassette tapes using a Sony Walkman (vintage 1989). She appreciates the ability to take her music with her when she goes on walks. You are convinced that a newer music player, such as an iPod touch, would bring her into the current era, even though cassettes are making a comeback among the hip crowd.
    a. What features of the music player would you point out to her to help ease her concerns of "perceived usefulness" and "perceived ease of use"? and
    b. Use the technology acceptance model discussed in the chapter to determine whether she will actually use a new music player if she received it as a birthday present. **LO 16-5**
5. What are the differences between the situation in Question 4 and that of users of a brand-new accounting information system? **LO 16-5**
6. Compare and contrast a PERT chart and a Gantt chart. How do they complement each other? **LO 16-4**
7. Using the 15-15 rule as a guide, when would a project manager and/or project sponsor proceed with completion of a project even if it is both 15 percent over budget and 15 percent off the initial schedule? **LO 16-4**

Problems

1. As part of effective IT planning in the systems development life cycle, a return on investment (ROI) calculation may be performed as part of the economic feasibility analysis. Often, many of the benefits from a new information system may be intangible benefits (e.g., system is easier to use or system enhances customer service, etc.) that are hard to quantify in an income statement. How would you suggest this be included in the economic feasibility analysis? **LO 16-2**
2. In the chapter, we discussed an example of **Starbucks** using the systems development life cycle to develop the capability to analyze what type of pastries sell best with its various hot

and cold drinks. Now, let's suppose that **NASDAQ** requires all of the firms trading on the exchange to report their financial statements not only using GAAP but also International Financial Reporting Standards (IFRS). Because Starbucks's current system cannot handle the IFRS requirements, the financial reporting system must be modified. Using Starbucks as an example, explain what types of activities would occur in each of the five phases of the systems development life cycle in preparation for reporting financial results according to IFRS. **LO 16-1**

3. Accountants generally do not have all of the necessary systems analyst and systems development skills needed to develop accounting information systems. Why should you be interested in project management of an accounting information system? **LO 16-3**

4. For your personal consulting business, you decide to set up an accounting information system to help with taxes as well as to help monitor your revenues and expenses. You've heard that **QuickBooks** is easy to set up, so you buy it, install it on your computer, enter in recent transactions, and begin to use it. **LO 16-1, LO 16-2**

   Required:

   1. Explain one or two ways you could be a user of this accounting information system. (*Hint:* Use the discussion in the text considering the role of accountants in accounting information systems.)
   2. Explain one or two ways you could be a manager of this accounting information system. (*One possibility:* What practices do you employ to make sure your system is safe?)
   3. After a few months, you decide to expand your QuickBooks with additional modules (payroll, inventory, etc.). Access the QuickBooks website (http://quickbooks.intuit.com) and consider one or two ways in which you could be a designer of your accounting information system.

5. Brainstorm a list of reasons why 61 percent (including 43 percent challenged plus 18 percent failed) of the information technology projects either failed or were challenged in 2012. Consider specifics of each of the elements of the triple constraints model and any other common delays, including the challenges of working with programmers, software and hardware suppliers and vendors, and the like. What is the best way to overcome these issues and decrease the number of projects failed or challenged? **LO 16-4**

6. As mentioned in the opening vignette, **Walmart** is implementing its SAP system throughout its worldwide operations. If Walmart has the choice, should it implement this system in China before, at the same time, or after the implementation in the United States? Use the technology acceptance model (in particular, perceived ease of use) to explain your answer. **LO 16-5**

7. The following PERT chart (Figure 16.7 on page 404) represents the tasks to be done to implement a system. Can you think of other steps that should be included? Is there adequate time for training given the technology acceptance model's recommendation to focus on perceived usefulness and perceived ease of use? What is the critical path for this project? **LO 16-4**

8. Consider the triple constraints diagram in Figure 16.3. Why is quality included in that figure even if it is not one of the triple constraints? Why is quality a concern (or not a concern, based on your point of view) for the project manager and project sponsor? **LO 16-4**

connect

9. We discussed 10 core effective information technology planning principles. Match the description of each with its respective principle. **LO 16-2**

1. The planning phase should support and complement the business strategy of the firm.	A. Alignment
2. Costs of implementation should be commensurate with the tangible and intangible benefits expected to be realized.	B. Relevant scope
3. An appropriate planning horizon should be developed.	C. Relevant timeframe
4. The overall scope of the planning phase should be established to facilitate formulation of effective ways to address the business needs.	D. Benefits realization

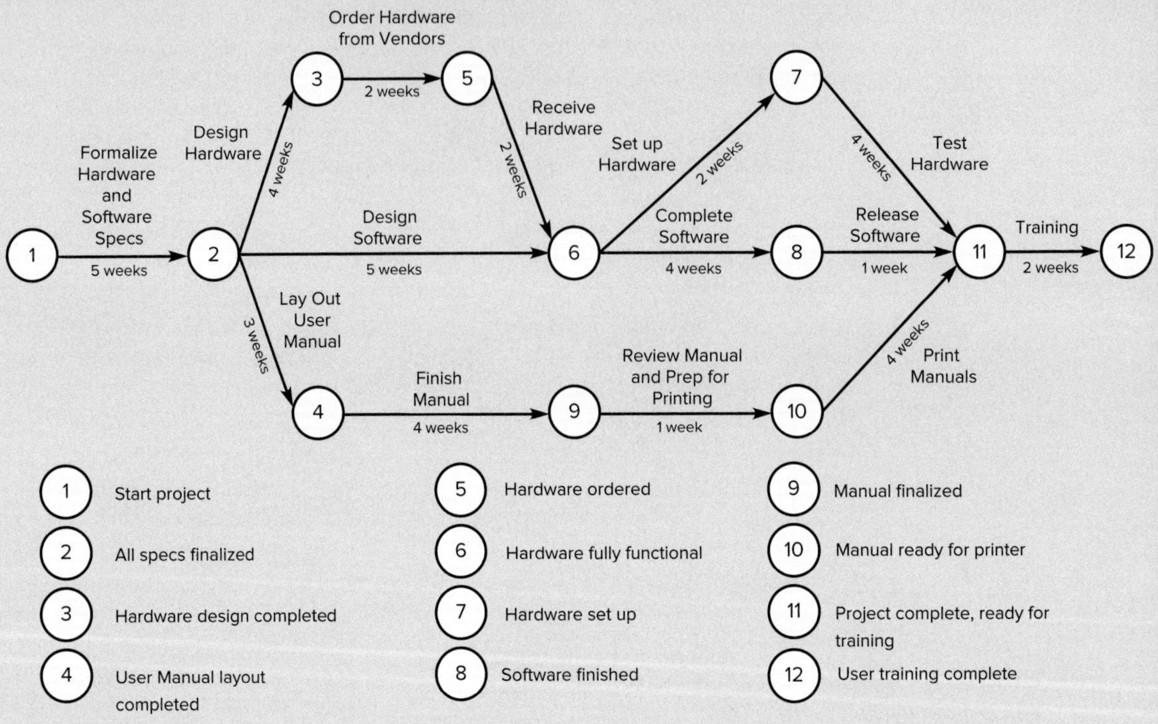

FIGURE 16.7
PERT Chart for Problem 7

connect 10. We discussed 10 core effective information technology planning principles. Match the description of each with its respective principle. **LO 16-2**

1. The resulting plan that comes out of the planning phase should be communicated widely.
2. The planning phase should recognize the capability and capacity of the firm to deliver solutions within the stated planning timeframe.
3. The plan should be periodically reassessed to ensure it is relevant to the evolving business strategy of the firm.
4. The planning phase should provide a means to measure and monitor project performance and a means of communicating success to stakeholders both inside and outside the firm.

A. Achievability
B. Awareness
C. Reassessment
D. Measurable performance

connect 11. The textbook emphasized the challenges of IT project management. In 2012, what were the outcomes of IT projects (as reported in the text)? **LO 16-4**

1. Successful
2. Challenged (late, over budget, and/or with less than the required features and functions)
3. Failed (canceled prior to completion or delivered and never used)

A. 18%
B. 39%
C. 43%

connect 12. There are five phases in the systems development life cycle (SDLC). Match the description of each phase to the correct phase. **LO 16-1**

1. The phase of the SDLC that involves a complete, detailed analysis of the systems needs of the end user as well as a proposed solution.
2. The phase of the SDLC that involves development, testing, and implementation of the new proposed system.
3. The phase of the SDLC that involves describing in detail the desired features of the system that were uncovered in the analysis phase.
4. The final phase of the SDLC that includes making changes, corrections, additions, and upgrades (generally smaller in scope) to ensure the system continues to meet the business requirements that have been set out for it.
5. The phase of the SDLC that summarizes the business needs with a high-level view of the intended project.

A. Analysis phase
B. Design phase
C. Implementation phase
D. Maintenance phase
E. Planning phase

connect 13. Decide whether each of these statements regarding the technology acceptance model are true or false. **LO 16-5**

1. The technology acceptance model predicts whether systems will be adopted or scratched.
2. Perceived usefulness is the extent to which users believe the system will help them perform their job faster.
3. Perceived ease of use is the extent to which a person perceives that the use of a particular system will be relatively free from effort.
4. To help users adopt a new system, systems analysts and developers may mock up the computer screen to show the look and feel of the system well before the new system is written.
5. To help users adopt a new system, systems analysts and developers may stop discussing with users features of the new system after the planning phase to make sure the users get exactly what they say they need.

connect 14. For each of the following, please define these as either work breakdown structure, triple constraint, 100% rule, or 15-15 rule. **LO 16-4**

1. The process of identifying all tasks needed to complete a project.
2. Three factors that constrain information technology and other projects: cost, scope, and time.
3. A rule requiring 100 percent planning of all tasks, including all of the internal, external, and interim tasks.
4. A rule suggesting that if a project is more than 15 percent over budget or 15 percent off the planned schedule, it will likely never recoup the time or cost necessary to be considered successful. At this point, a decision needs to be made on if or how to proceed.

Glossary of Models

This glossary presents various structure and activity models to show modeling options. It is not intended to be all inclusive, but rather to provide examples of how to model common situations. For the structure models, the basic assumption is that resources, agents, and type images are added to the database before they are linked to other classes, so the minimum multiplicity is zero. Otherwise, the models show the most common multiplicities.

The glossary presents examples of structure models in the following section and then presents some generic activity models in the last section. The models are presented in the following order: sales and cash receipts process, purchases and cash disbursements process, and the conversion process, and for the structure models, it includes miscellaneous and integrated models.

Structure Models Using the REA Framework

1. Sales—Generic Model

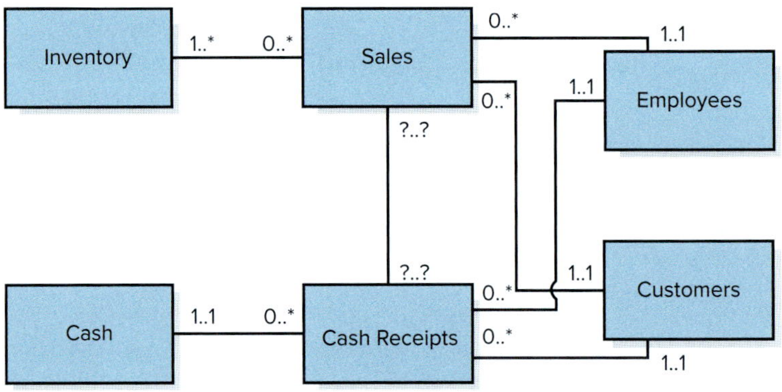

The generic model represents typical economic resources, events, and agents involved in the sales process. This model assumes that inventory items are not tracked individually (like high-value items such as automobiles and houses), but rather by UPC code such that all products with the same UPC code are considered to be the same item.

2. Sales—With Invoice Tracking

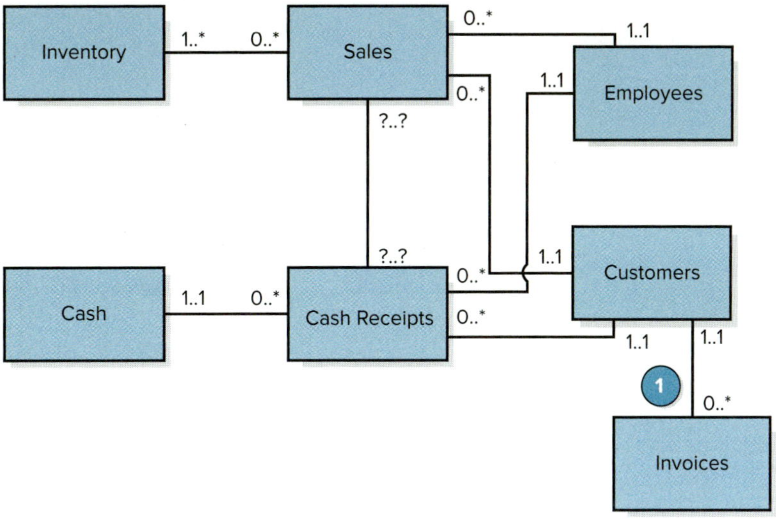

This model extends the generic model to track the invoices issued to each customer as shown in the association (1) between Customers (Agent) and Invoices (Type Image).

3. Sales—Where Employees Are Assigned to Service Particular Customers

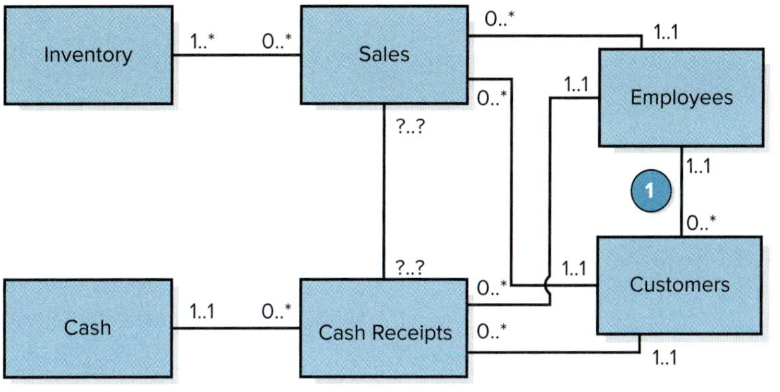

This model extends the generic model to represent assignment of employees to customers. The association (1) links customers to the assigned employee, such as when sales take place on commission. Similarly, employees can be assigned to inventory when specific employees manage specific inventory items.

4. Sales with Summary

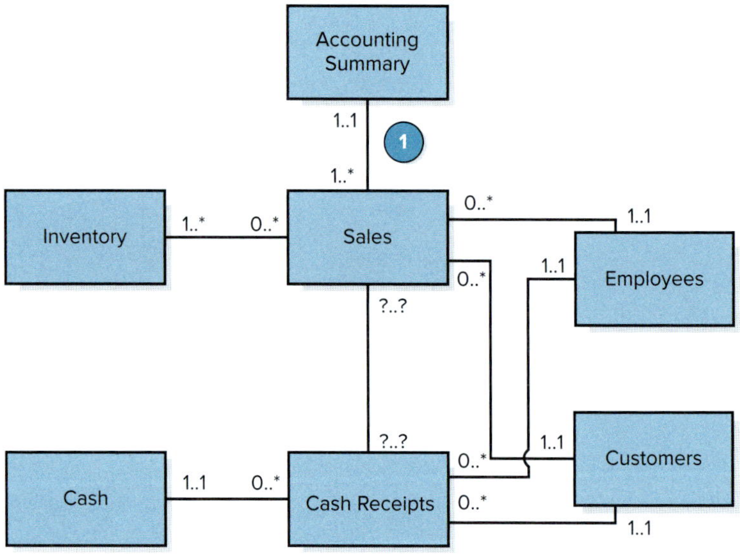

This model presents a simplified example of the summarization of economic activity by fiscal period in order to prepare financial reports. In this case, sales are summarized by fiscal period as shown in the association (1) between Accounting Summary and Sales.

5. Purchases—Generic Model

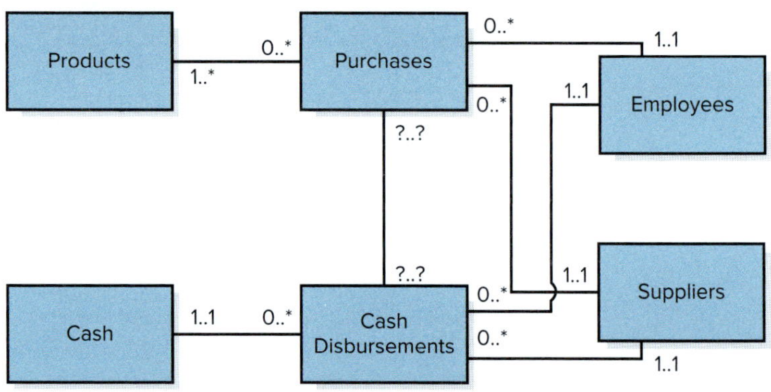

The generic model represents typical economic resources, events, and agents involved in the purchases process. Like the generic sales model, this model assumes that inventory items are not tracked individually, but rather by UPC code or similar identifier.

6. Purchases—With Commitment Event

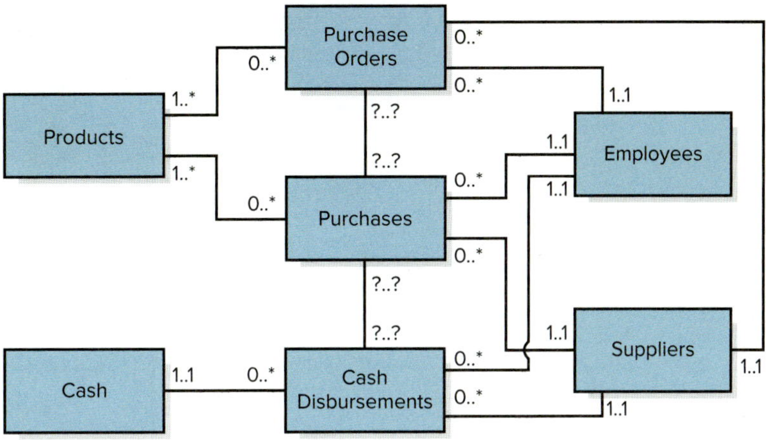

This model adds the commitment event, Purchase Orders, to the generic model. A commitment precedes the economic event. It records anticipated purchases but does not directly affect the financial statements. Note that this model requires tracking both the items ordered and the items received, which is a level of complication that many organizations avoid. Thus, they use a structure that combines the Purchase Orders and Purchases event as shown in the next model.

7. Purchases—With Combined Purchase Orders and Purchases

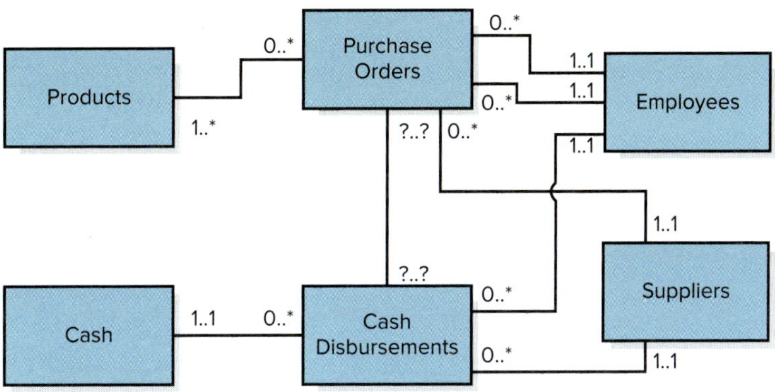

This model shows the combined Purchase Orders and Purchases event (still titled Purchase Orders). The Purchase Order class would track both the date of the order and the date of the receipt of products (the purchase date). The organization is now concerned with only one association between Purchase Orders/Purchases and the Products classes. However, there are now two associations between the Employees and Purchase Orders class, representing the requirement to track the two roles (purchasing agent and receiving agent) separately for internal control.

8. Purchases—With Type Images to Manage the Purchases Process

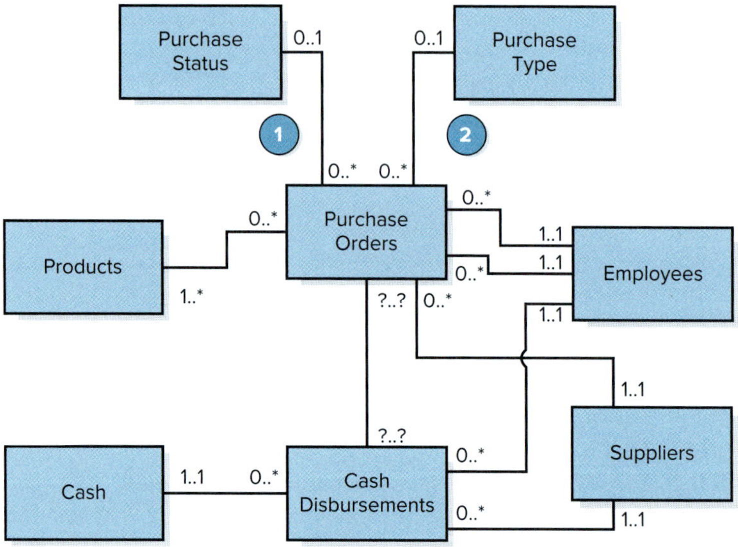

This model shows potential use of two type images to manage the purchase process. The Purchase Status type (1) would summarize information based on the point in the purchase process at the end of a fiscal period—for example, amounts on order, amounts received, amounts paid. The Purchase Type (2) would summarize information according to the type of purchase—for example, routine organizational supplies and services, inventory replenishment, and asset acquisition.

9. Purchases—With Type Images Linked for Summary Information

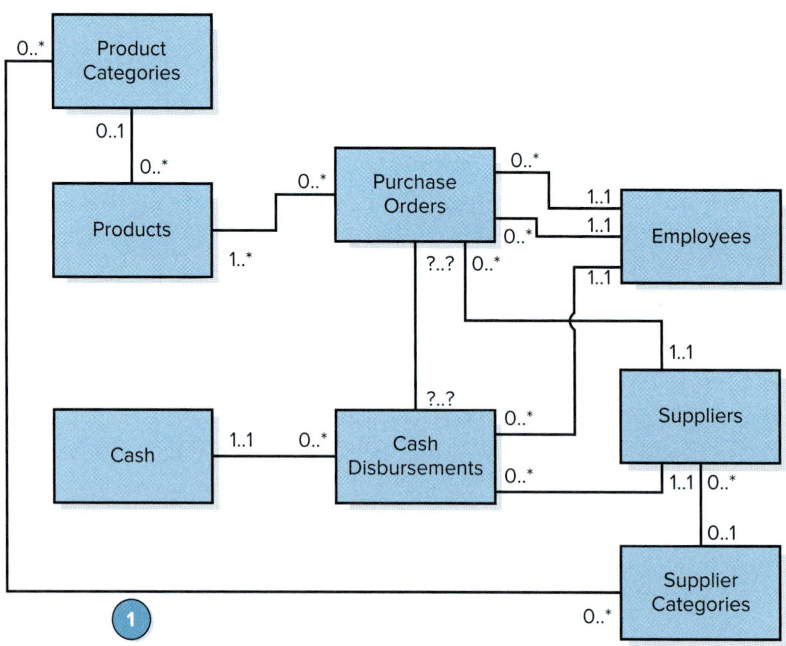

This model provides an example of the use of type images to summarize information. In this case, the organization could use the category classes to obtain summary information about supplier characteristics and activity, about product characteristics and activity, and about the common activity for each product and supplier category combination (1). For example, annual sales for each supplier category and product category combination would be recorded in the linking table between those two type images.

10. Conversion—Basic Model

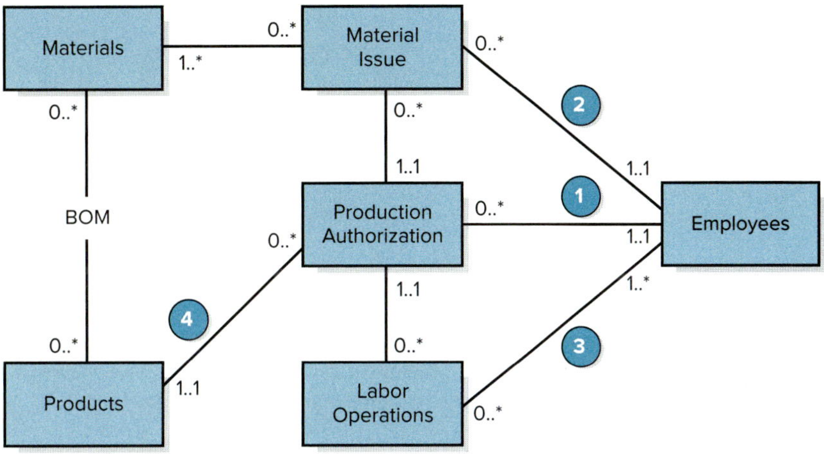

This basic conversion process model shows the structure related to (1) a supervisor authorizing production, (2) raw material issued into work-in-process, (3) labor applied to work-in-process, and (4) finished goods (products) increased when production completes.

11. Conversion—Production in a Series of Steps

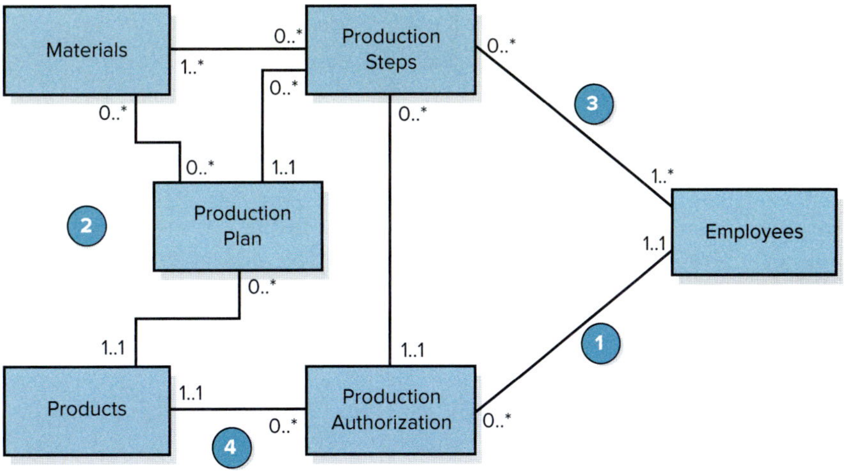

This revised conversion model shows production in a series of steps according to a production plan (a type image). The model shows (1) the supervisor authorizing production, (2) the production plan determining the raw material and labor needed to produce a specific product, (3) how employees work and materials are issued into work-in-process, and (4) how finished goods (products) increase when production completes. This model can be expanded to include accounting for equipment (a resource) use in the production steps.

12. Miscellaneous—Recursive Relationships

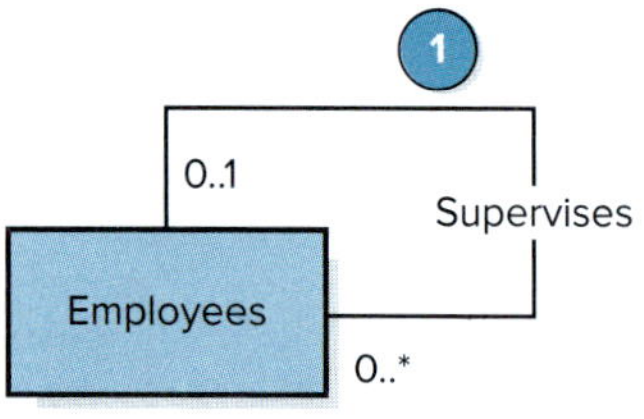

This is an example of a class related to itself. In this case, the association describes the supervisory relationship between an employee and several other employees. Similar common uses include products related to other substitute products and organizational departments that are parts of other organizational departments.

13. Miscellaneous—Associations Indicating Roles

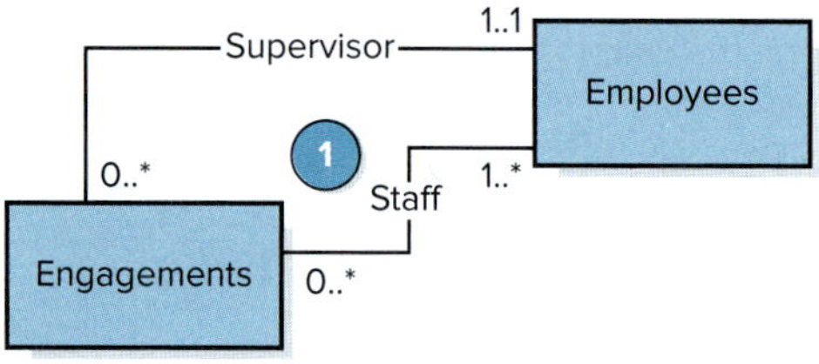

This is an example where two associations link the same two classes to indicate different agent roles in the event. In this case, each engagement (e.g., audit or consulting engagement) has one supervisor as well as several staff members. Placing the name of the role on the association can help clarify the purpose of the associations.

14. Integrated Models—Sales and Purchases

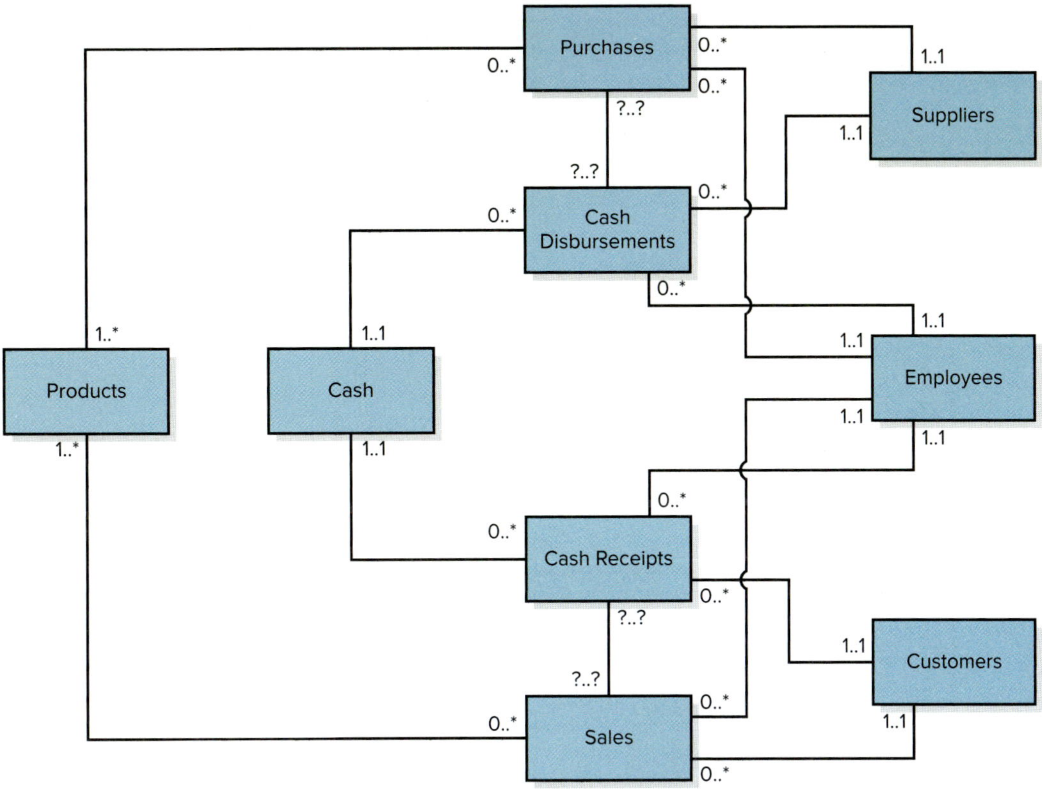

This is a basic example of a model integrating the sales (and cash receipts) and purchases (and cash disbursements) processes. Note that the two duality events (Purchases and Cash Disbursements or Sales and Cash Receipts) as well as the external agents (Customers and Suppliers) are unique to one process. However, the internal agent (Employees) and resources (Products and Cash) are shared across processes.

15. Integrated Models—Sales, Conversion, and Purchases

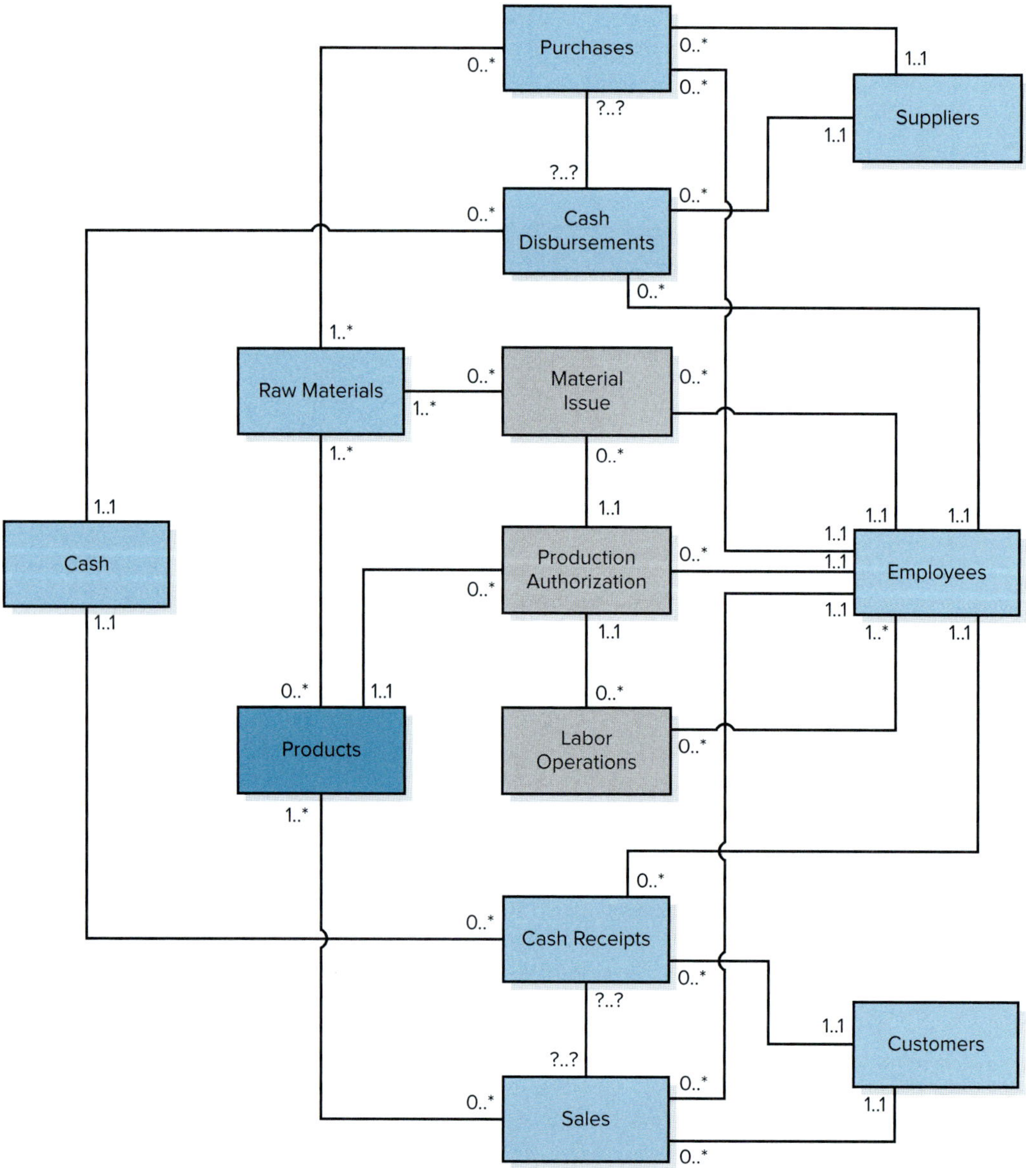

This is an example of a model integrating the sales (and cash receipts), conversion, and purchases (and cash disbursements) processes. In this case, the organization purchases raw materials that are converted into products (finished goods) that are then sold to customers. Again, the duality events (Purchases and Cash Disbursements, Sales and Cash Receipts, Production Authorization and Material Issue and Labor Operations) as well as the external agents (Customers and Suppliers) are unique to one process. However, the internal agent (Employees) and resources (Raw Materials, Products, and Cash) are shared across processes.

Activity Models Using BPMN

16. Sales—Basic Model

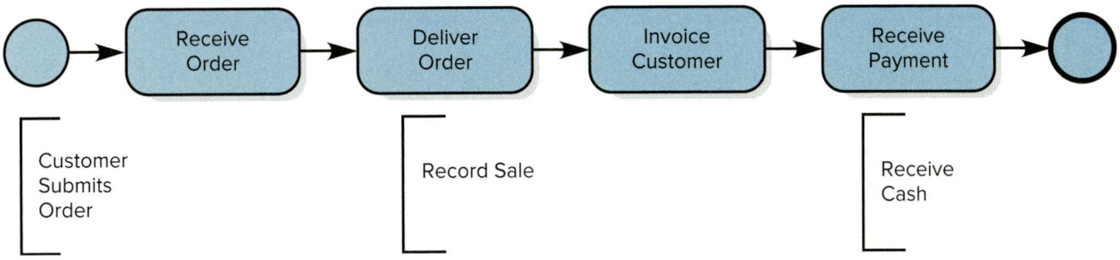

This model shows typical activity flow for a business that takes orders. Note that the steps in the model generally correspond to events in an REA diagram: commitment (receive order), sale (deliver order), and cash receipt (receive payment).

17. Sales—Basic Model with Pools and Swimlanes

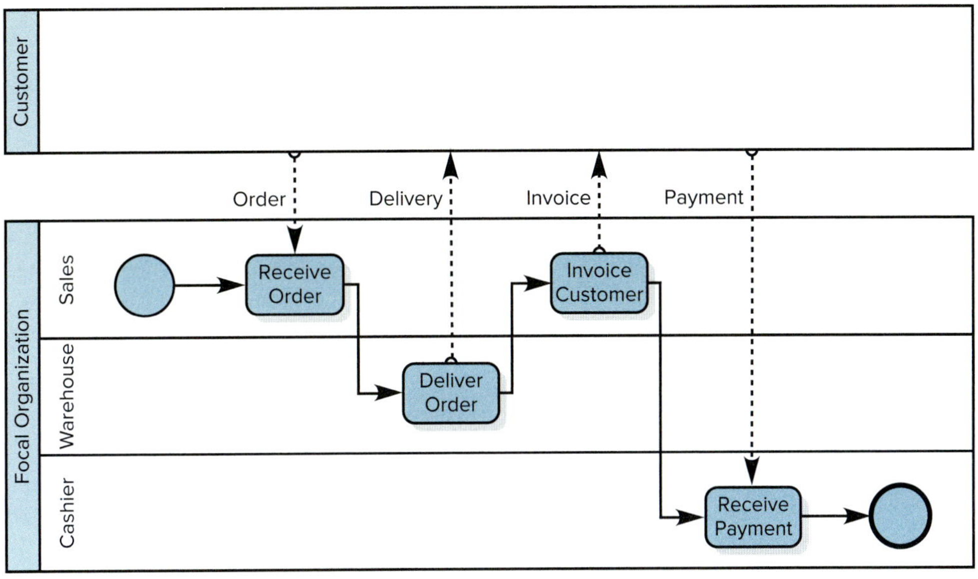

This is the basic model with pools and swimlanes to show responsibility for the various tasks. Note that there are no visible activities in the Customer pool because we are normally not interested in the specific steps they take. Instead, the focus moves to the interactions between pools, shown as message flows (dashed lines). It is good practice to put labels on the message flows to clarify the nature of the interactions. Within the pool of interest, the sequence flows connect the start and end events without any break.

18. Purchases—Basic Model

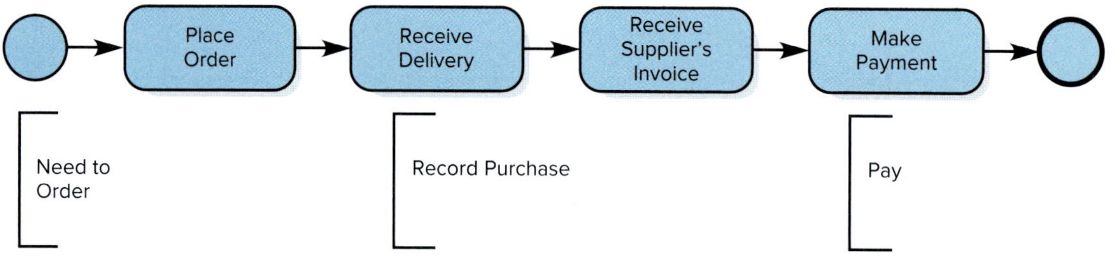

This model shows typical activity flow related to issuing purchase orders. Note that the steps in the model generally correspond to events in an REA diagram: commitment (place order), purchase (receive order), and cash disbursement (make payment).

19. Purchases—Basic Model with Gateway

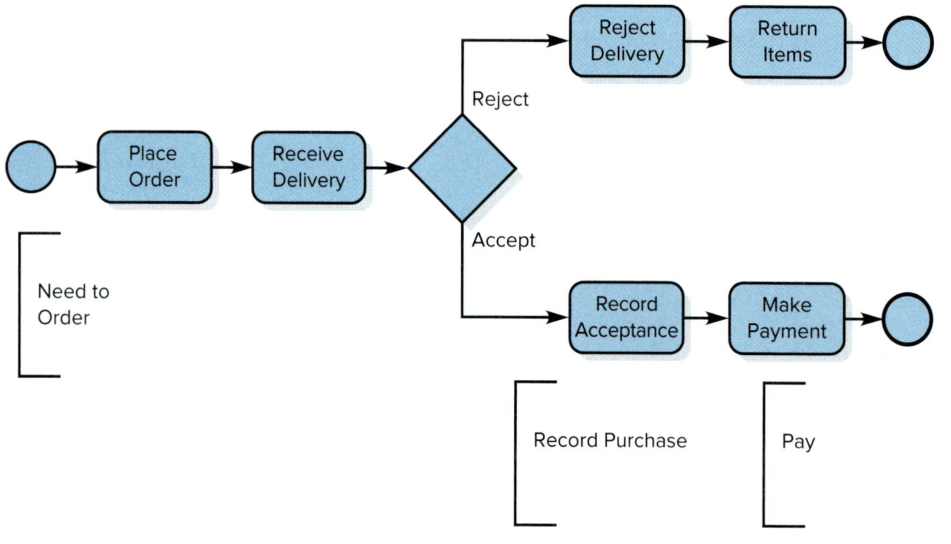

This model is similar to the basic model, except it includes the gateway to show the different flow options after the receipt of the delivery: (1) accept and make payment and (2) reject and return the items to the supplier.

20. Purchases—Basic Model with Error Event

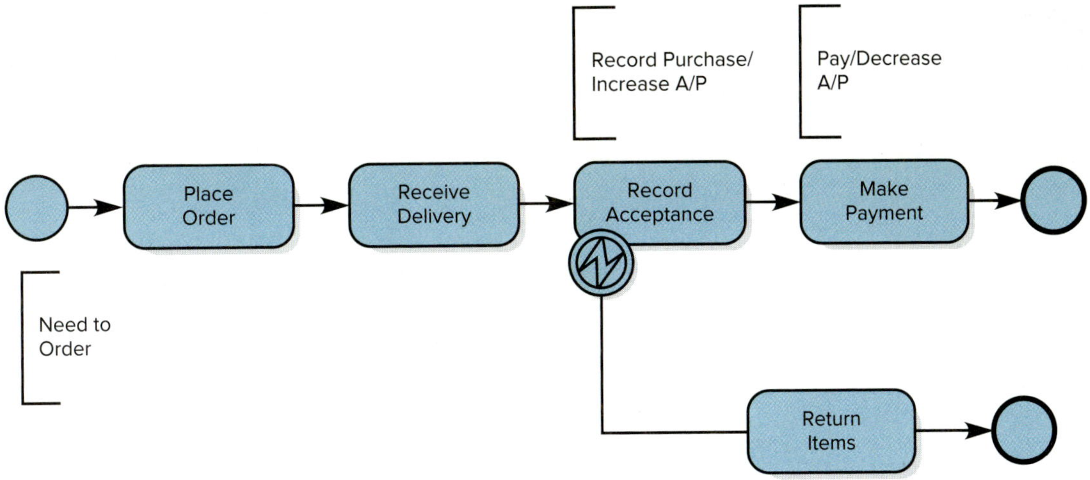

In this model, the intermediate error event shows flow when the items are rejected.

21. Purchases—With Pools and Lanes

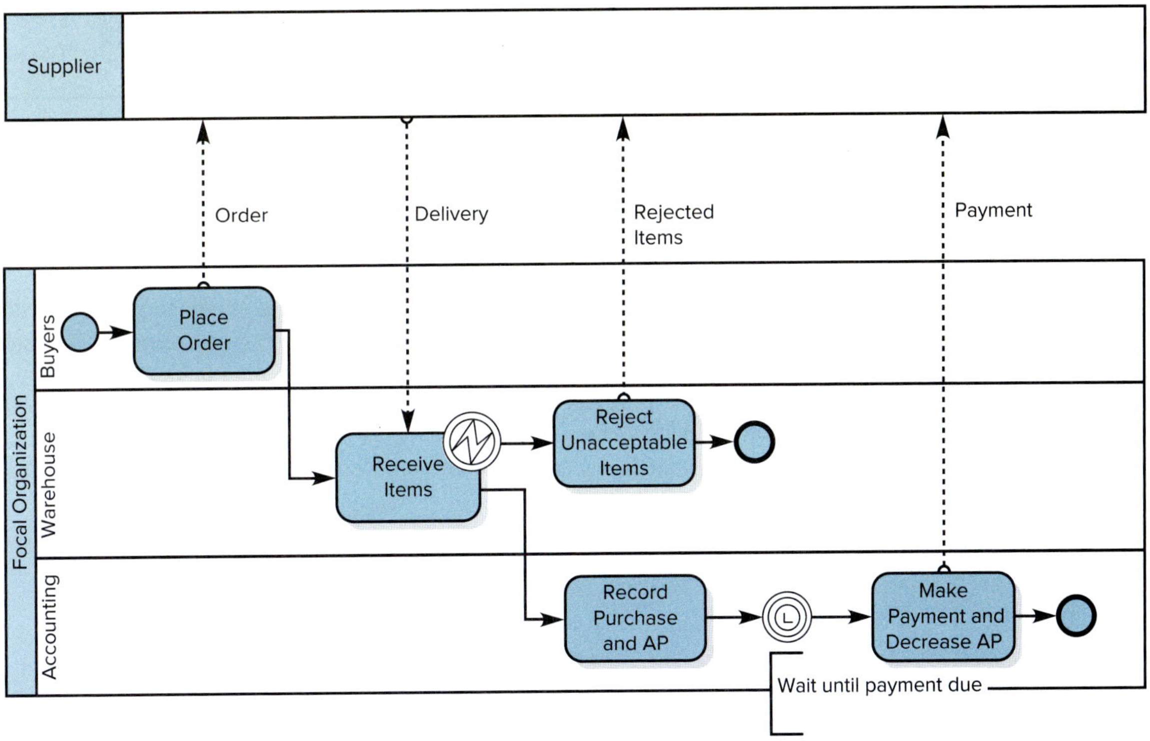

This model uses pools to show the process participants and lanes to show responsibility in the focal organization. It again employs an intermediate error event to show rejected items. It includes an intermediate timer event to show the delay until the payment to the supplier is due.

22. Purchases—With Pools and Lanes and Data Objects

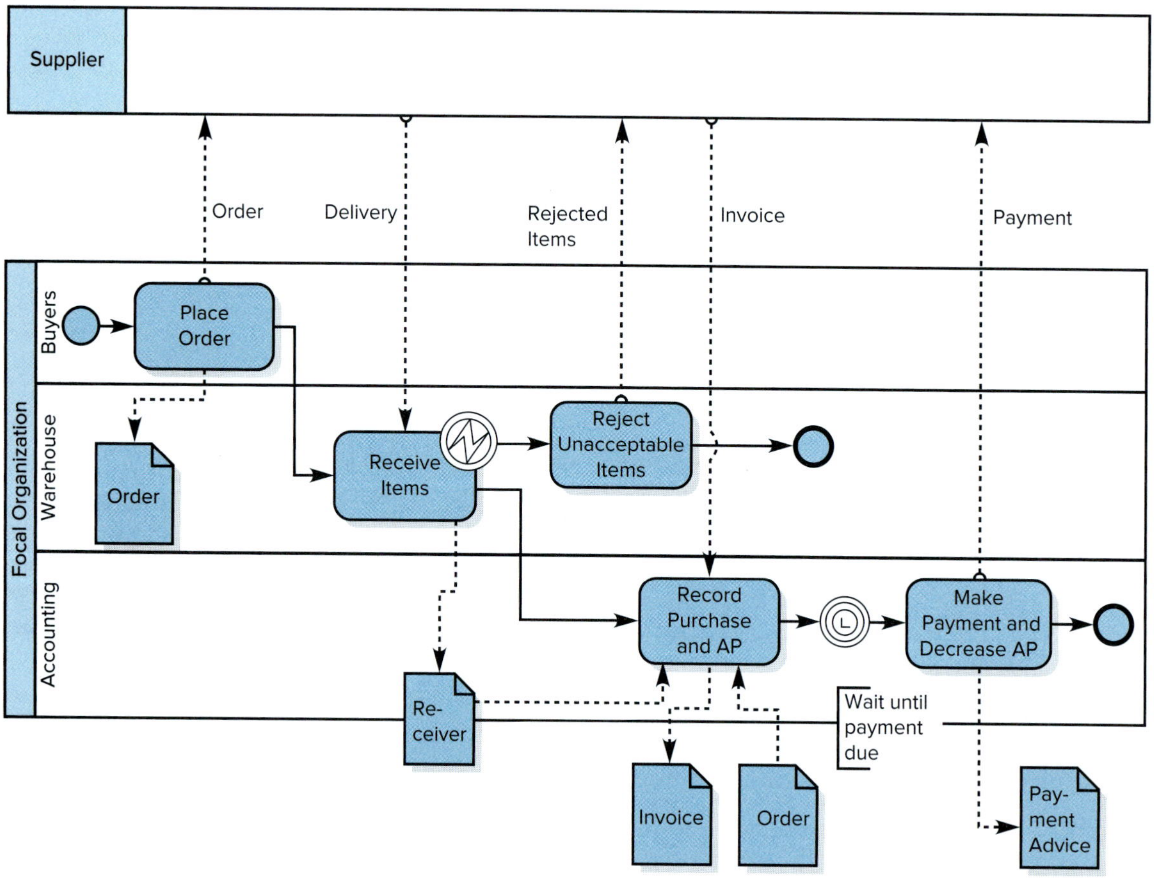

This model builds on the previous model. It also uses pools to show the process participants and lanes to show responsibility in the focal organization. It again employs an intermediate error event to show rejected items, and it includes an intermediate timer event to show the delay until the payment to the supplier is due. It adds data objects to show the documents/information being created or used at the various steps in the process. It assumes a standard three-way match—matching invoices, receipts, and orders—before payments are authorized.

23. Conversion—Basic Model with Repeated Activities or a Looping, Collapsed Subprocess

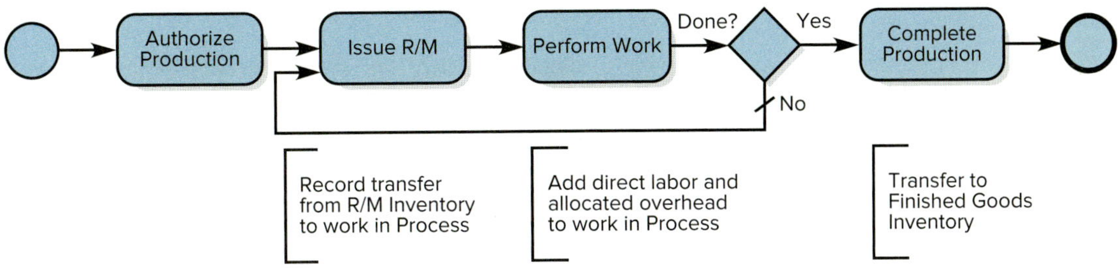

These models provide alternate descriptions of the basic conversion process. The model on top is closely related to the REA model that shows (1) the authorization, (2) raw material issue into work-in-process, (3) labor (and equipment) applied to work-in-process, and (4) completion of production and transfer to finished goods. The gateway routes the flow back until all production to carry out the authorization is complete. The model on the bottom places Work-in-Process activities in a collapsed subprocess. The looping arrow shows that the process loops until complete.

24. Conversion—Basic Model with Repeated Activities and Batches

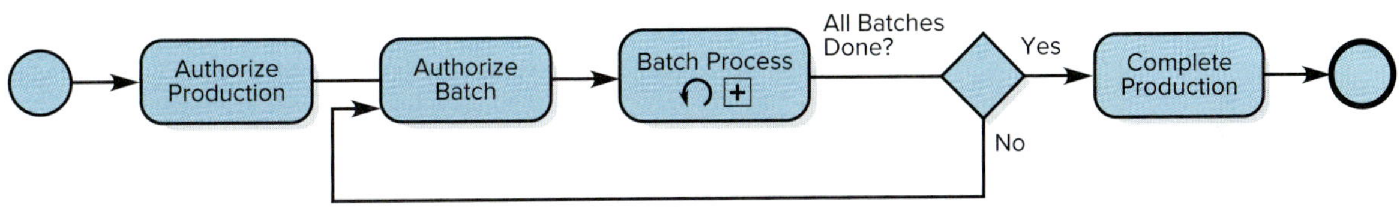

Batch Process Subprocess

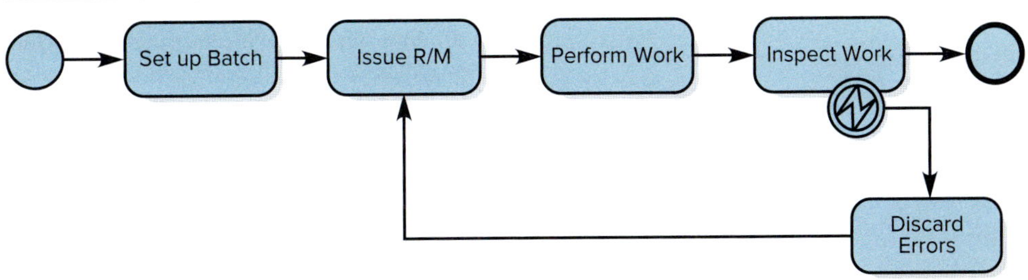

This model expands on the previous model to include batches. In this case, the flow starts with production authorization, to batch authorization, to the batch process, which then repeats until all batches are done. The contents of the collapsed Batch Process subprocess are shown separately. The subprocess also includes an intermediate error event that halts the normal process flow when items fail inspection.

Glossary

15-15 rule *(392)* A rule suggesting that if a project is more than 15 percent over budget or 15 percent off the planned schedule, it will likely never recoup the time or cost necessary to be considered successful. At this point, a decision needs to be made on if or how to proceed.

100% rule *(393)* A rule requiring 100 percent planning of all tasks, including all of the internal, external, and interim tasks.

A

access controls *(125)* Limit who can use and change records in the system; for example, passwords control who can use an application.

access point *(331)* Logically connects stations to a firm's network.

accounting information system (AIS) *(4)* A system that records, processes, and reports on transactions to provide financial and nonfinancial information to make decisions and have appropriate levels of internal controls for those transactions.

accounting rate of return (ARR) *(373)* The average annual income from the IT initiative divided by the initial investment cost.

accounts payable *(152)* Amounts owed to suppliers for goods and services received. In a data modeling context, accounts payable are calculated based on receipts (purchases) from each supplier less the corresponding payments (cash disbursements) to those suppliers.

accounts receivable *(120)* Monies owed by customers for prior sales of goods or services. In a data modeling context, accounts receivable are calculated as each customer's sales less corresponding cash receipts.

acquisition costs *(369)* All direct and indirect costs necessary to acquire and implement the IT initiative.

activities *(37)* In business process modeling, activities represent specific steps in a business process.

activity models *(36)* Models that describe the sequence of workflow in a business process or processes.

agents *(126, 157, 183)* The people or organizations who participate in business events, such as customers and salespeople.

aggregation relationship *(65)* A special-purpose UML notation representing the relationship between two classes that are often considered together, such as when a sports league is made up of a collection of teams.

alignment risk *(370)* The risk that an IT initiative is not aligned with the strategy of the organization.

analysis phase *(386)* The phase of the SDLC involves a complete, detailed analysis of the systems needs of the end user as well as a proposed solution.

annotations *(37)* Model elements that allow the modeler to add additional descriptive information to the model. Annotations are modeled with text inside a bracket connected to other model symbols with a dashed line.

application controls *(125, 274)* Ensure data integrity and an audit trail; for example, new invoices are assigned sequential numbers; specific to a subsystem or an application to ensure the validity, completeness, and accuracy of the transactions.

association *(63)* UML symbol that depicts the relationship between two classes; it is modeled as a solid line that connects two classes in a model.

assurance *(258)* Independent, professional opinions that reduce the risk of having incorrect information.

asymmetric-key encryption *(304)* To transmit confidential information, the sender uses the receiver's public key to encrypt the message; the receiver uses his or her own private key for decryption upon receiving the message. Also known as public-key encryption or two-key encryption.

attributes *(64, 73, 85)* Data elements that describe instances in a class, very much like fields in a database table; characteristics, properties, or adjectives that describe each class.

audit around the computer (or black-box approach) *(333)* Auditors test the reliability of computer-generated information by first calculating expected results from the transactions entered into the system. Then, the auditors compare these calculations to the processing or output results.

audit data standards *(215)* A standard format for data files and fields typically needed to support an external audit in a given financial business process area that was developed by the AICPA.

audit through the computer (or white-box approach) *(333)* Requires auditors to understand the internal logic of the system/application being tested.

authentication *(304)* A process that establishes the origin of information or determines the identity of a user, process, or device.

automate *(19)* The use of technology to replace human labor in automating business processes.

B

Balanced Scorecard framework *(346)* Provides an integrating framework that describes organizational performance relative to its strategic objectives across four perspectives: learning and growth, process, customer, and financial. Objectives for each perspective describe the strategy in a series of cause-and-effect relationships.

Balanced Scorecard management process *(351)* The process by which companies plan, implement, and monitor performance. It consists of five steps: formulate the strategy, translate the strategy, link the strategy to operations, monitor performance, and adapt.

benefits *(366)* The positive consequences to the organization of an IT investment.

Big Data *(210)* Datasets that are too large and complex for businesses' existing systems to handle utilizing their traditional capabilities to capture, store, manage, and analyze these datasets.

breach of security *(219)* The unauthorized access to or acquisition of data in electronic form that contain personal information.

breakeven analysis *(372)* Determines the breakeven point, where the total value of benefits equals that of total costs.

business analysis *(33)* The process of defining business process requirements and evaluating potential improvements. Business analysis involves ascertaining, documenting, and communicating information about current and future business processes using business process modeling and related tools.

business case *(366)* Economic justification for an IT investment or other major project.

business continuity management (BCM) *(315)* The activities required to keep a firm running during a period of displacement or interruption of normal operations.

business intelligence *(252)* A computer-based technique for accumulating and analyzing data from databases and data warehouses to support managerial decision making.

business model *(33)* A simple, abstract representation of one or more business processes. A business model is typically a graphical depiction of the essential business process information.

business process *(33)* A defined sequence of business activities that use resources to transform specific inputs into specific outputs to achieve a business goal.

business process modeling notation (BPMN) *(36)* A standard for the description of activity models.

business rule *(70)* Succinct statements of constraints on business processes; they provide the logic that guides the behavior of the business in specific situations.

business value *(11)* Items, events, and interactions that determine the financial health and well-being of the firm.

C

cardinalities *(74)* *See* multiplicities.

cash *(120, 157)* The organization's monies in bank or related accounts. The instances of the class are individual accounts. This is considered a resource.

cash disbursements *(152)* Record payments of cash to external agents (e.g., suppliers) and the corresponding reduction in cash accounts. This is considered an event.

cash receipts *(127)* Record receipts of cash from external agents (e.g., customers) and the corresponding deposit of those receipts into cash accounts. This is considered an event.

Certificate Authority (CA) *(306)* A trusted entity that issues and revokes digital certificates.

Certified Information Systems Auditor (CISA) *(10)* The CISA designation identifies those professionals possessing IT audit, control, and security skills. Generally, CISAs will perform IT audits to evaluate the accounting information system's internal control design and effectiveness.

Certified Information Technology Professional (CITP) *(10)* The CITP designation identifies accountants (CPAs) with a broad range of technology knowledge and experience.

Certified Internal Auditor (CIA) *(10)* The CIA designation is the certification for internal auditors and is the standard to demonstrate competency and professionalism in the internal auditing field.

change risk *(370)* The risk that the organization will be unable to make the changes necessary to implement the IT initiative successfully.

choreography *(122, 153)* The interaction (message flows) between two participants (modeled as pools) in a process modeled using BPMN.

class *(62)* Any separately identifiable collection of things (objects) about which the organization wants to collect and store information. Classes can represent organization resources (e.g., trucks, machines, buildings, cash, investments), persons (e.g., customers, employees), events (e.g., sales, purchases, cash disbursements, cash receipts), and conceptual structures (e.g., accounts, product categories, budgets). Classes are typically implemented as tables in a relational database, where individual instances of the class are represented as rows in the table.

class diagrams (62) Structure models prepared using UML notation.

cloud computing *(104, 315)* Internet-based computing, where shared resources, software, and information are provided to firms on demand; using redundant servers in multiple locations to host virtual machines.

code of ethics *(272)* What is considered to be ethical within an organization to promote ethical behavior.

collaboration *(122, 153)* A BPMN model showing two participant pools and the interactions between them within a process.

Committee of Sponsoring Organizations (COSO) *(274)* Composed of several organizations (AAA, AICPA, FEI, IIA, and IMA); studies the causal factors that lead to fraudulent financial reporting and develops recommendations for public companies, independent auditors, the SEC and other regulators, and educational institutions to improve the quality of financial reporting through internal controls and corporate governance.

composition relationship *(65)* A special-purpose UML notation representing the relationship between two classes that are often considered together, similar to aggregation relationships, except in composition relationships, one class cannot exist without the other, such as a book and the chapters that compose the book.

computer-assisted audit techniques (CAATs) *(332)* Essential tools for auditors to conduct an audit in accordance with heightened auditing standards.

constraints *(64)* Optional or mandatory guidance about how a process should perform in certain situations.

continuous audit *(334)* Performing audit-related activities on a continuous basis.

control objectives for information and related technology (COBIT) *(275)* An internationally accepted set of best IT security and control practices for IT management released by the IT Governance Institute (ITGI).

control risk *(281)* The threat that errors or irregularities in the underlying transactions will not be prevented, detected, and corrected by the internal control system.

corporate governance *(273)* A set of processes and policies in managing an organization with sound ethics to safeguard the interests of its stakeholders.

corrective controls *(274)* Fix problems that have been identified, such as using backup files to recover corrupted data.

cost/benefit analysis *(281)* Important in determining whether to implement an internal control.

critical path *(393)* The longest path for a project and represents the minimum amount of time needed for the completion of the project when sufficient resources are allocated.

customer *(121)* The external agent in the sales and collection process.

customer perspective *(348)* The Balanced Scorecard perspective that describes the organization's customer-related objectives and corresponding customer measures; it views organization performance from the customers' perspective.

customer relationship management (CRM) software *(16)* Software used to manage and nurture a firm's interactions with its current and potential clients. CRM software often includes the use of database marketing tools to learn more about the customers and to develop strong firm-to-customer relationships.

D

data *(6)* Raw facts or statistics that, absent a context, may have little meaning.

DATA (2009) *(217)* Data Accountability and Trust Act of 2009 (DATA) creates a national standard for privacy and data protection.

data analytics *(210)* The science of examining raw data (now often Big Data), removing excess noise from the dataset, and organizing the data with the purpose of drawing conclusions for decision making.

data dictionary *(85)* Describes the data fields in each database record such as field description, field length, field type (e.g., alphanumeric, numeric), etc.

data flow diagram (DFD) *(52)* Another type of activity model that graphically shows the flow of data through a system and also incorporates elements of structure models.

data governance *(327)* The convergence of data quality, data management, data policies, business process management, and risk management surrounding the handling of data in a firm.

data integrity *(305)* Maintaining and assuring the accuracy and consistency of data during transmission and at storage.

data mart *(250)* A subset of the information from the data warehouse to serve a specific purpose.

data mining *(253, 327)* A process of using sophisticated statistical techniques to extract and analyze data from large databases to discern patterns and trends that were not previously known.

data models *(62)* A graphic representation of the conceptual contents of databases; data models support communication about database contents between users and designers of the database.

data warehouse *(250, 327)* A collection of information gathered from an assortment of external and operational (i.e, internal) databases to facilitate reporting for decision making and business analysis.

database *(84, 327)* A shared collection of logically related data for various uses.

database administrator *(85)* The person responsible for the design, implementation, repair, and security of a firm's database.

database management system (DBMS) *(84)* A computer program that creates, modifies, and queries the database. Specifically, the DBMS is designed to manage a database's storage and retrieval of information.

database system *(327)* A term typically used to encapsulate the constructs of a data model, database management system (DBMS), and database.

decision support system (DSS) *(251)* A computer-based information system that facilitates business decision-making activities.

design phase *(386)* The phase of the SDLC that involves describing in detail the desired features of the system that were uncovered in the analysis phase.

detective controls *(274)* Find problems when they arise.

digital certificate *(306)* A digital document issued and digitally signed by the private key of a Certificate Authority that binds the name of a subscriber to a public key.

digital dashboard *(254)* A display to track the firm's process or performance indicators or metrics to monitor critical performance.

digital signature *(305)* A message digest of a document (or data file) that is encrypted using the document creator's private key.

disaster recovery planning (DRP) *(315)* A process that identifies significant events that may threaten a firm's operations and outlines the procedures to ensure that the firm will resume operations when the events occur.

discretionary information *(7)* Information that is generated according to one's own judgment.

documentation *(33)* An information transmission and communication tool that explains how business processes and business systems work.

E

economic justification process *(367)* The process by which an organization creates a business case for an IT investment or other major project.

embedded audit module (EAM) *(334)* A programmed audit module that is added to the system under review.

encryption *(303)* Using algorithmic schemes to encode plaintext into nonreadable form.

enterprise IT (EIT) *(350)* A type of information technology that restructures interactions within an organization and with external partners, such as customer relationship management systems.

enterprise risk management (ERM) *(278)* A process, affected by the entity's board of directors, management, and other personnel, applied in strategy setting and across the enterprise, designed to identify potential events that may affect the entity, and manage risk to be within the risk appetite, to provide reasonable assurance regarding the achievement of objectives.

enterprise system (ES) *(13, 102)* A centralized database that collects data from throughout the firm. Commercialized information system that integrates and automates business processes across a firm's value chain located within and across organizations.

entities *(73)* The people, things, and events in the domain of interest; in UML notation, entities are modeled as classes.

entity integrity rule *(87)* The primary key of a table must have data values (cannot be null).

error event *(123)* An intermediate event in a BPMN model showing processing for exceptions to the normal process flow.

events *(36, 126, 157, 184)* Important occurrences that affect the flow of activities in a business process. BPMN includes symbols to define start, intermediate, and end events.

Excel pivot table *(223)* A pivot table is a dynamic summary report generated from a range or table in Excel or an external data file. It allows cross-tabulations and summary reporting of multiple dimensions and levels of detail. In conjunction with Slicers, it offers a powerful data analysis tool.

Excel table *(220)* A rectangular range of structured data in one Excel worksheet specifically identified as a table. The table usually has one row of text headings that indicate the contents of each column. Designating a range of data as a table provides access to a set of formatting and analysis tools.

extract, transform, and load (ETL) *(211)* The process of cleaning and scrubbing the data before data analysis can take place.

F

fault tolerance *(315)* Redundant units providing a system with the ability to continue functioning when part of the system fails.

financial perspective *(348)* The Balanced Scorecard perspective that describes the organization's financial objectives and corresponding financial measures of performance; it views organizational performance from the shareholders' perspective.

financial risk *(370)* The risk that the IT investment will not deliver expected financial benefits.

finished goods inventory *(179)* For a manufacturing company, the inventory (REA resource) that has completed the manufacturing process and is held for sale to customers.

firewall *(329)* A security system comprised of hardware and software that is built using routers, servers, and a variety of software.

firm infrastructure *(12)* Activities needed to support the firm, including the CEO and the finance, accounting, and legal departments.

flowcharts *(47)* Visualizations of a process activity; they are activity models much like models using BPMN.

foreign key (FK) *(65, 86)* Attribute that allows database tables to be linked together; foreign keys are the primary keys of other tables placed in the current table to support the link between the two tables.

form *(87)* Forms are utilized by users to enter data into tables and view existing records.

fraud triangle *(307)* Three conditions exist for a fraud to be perpetrated: incentive, opportunity, and rationalization.

function IT (FIT) *(350)* A type of information technology that performs/supports a single function, such as spreadsheet applications.

G

Gantt chart *(394)* A graphical representation of the project schedule that maps the tasks to a project calendar.

gateways *(37, 154, 180)* Show process branching and merging as the result of decisions. Basic gateways are depicted as diamonds. Usually, gateways appear as pairs on the diagram. The first gateway shows the branching, and the second gateway shows merging of the process branches.

general controls *(274)* Pertain to enterprisewide issues such as controls over accessing the network, developing and maintaining applications, and documenting changes of programs.

generalization relationship *(65)* A special-purpose UML symbol that supports grouping of things that share common characteristics; it reduces redundancy because the shared characteristics need only be modeled once.

generalized audit software (GAS) *(334)* Frequently used to perform substantive tests and used for testing of controls through transactional data analysis.

H

hierarchical data model *(84)* Organizes data into a tree-like structure that allows repeating information using defined parent/child relationships.

hub *(328)* Contains multiple ports.

human resource management *(12)* Activities include recruiting, hiring, training, and compensating employees.

I

implementation phase *(387)* The phase of the SDLC that involves development, testing, and implementation of the new proposed system.

inbound logistics *(11)* Activities associated with receiving and storing raw materials and other partially completed materials and distributing those materials to manufacturing when and where they are needed.

informate-down *(19)* The use of computer technology to provide information about business activities to employees across the firm.

informate-up *(19)* The use of computer technology to provide information about business activities to senior management.

information *(6)* Data organized in a meaningful way to the user.

information capital *(349)* An intangible asset that reflects the readiness of the company's technology to support strategic internal processes. It includes computing hardware, infrastructure, applications, and employees' abilities to use technology effectively.

information overload *(6)* The difficulty a person faces in understanding a problem and making a decision as a consequence of too much information.

Information Technology Infrastructure Library (ITIL) *(275)* A set of concepts and practices for IT service management.

information value chain *(7)* The overall transformation from a business need and business event to the collection of data and information to an ultimate decision.

inherent risk *(281)* The risk related to the nature of the business activity itself.

input controls *(283)* Ensure the authorization, entry, and verification of data entering the system.

integrated test facility (ITF) *(334)* An automated technique that enables test data to be continually evaluated during the normal operation of a system.

intermediate error event *(180)* Occurs between start and end events and affects the flow of the process. Intermediate error events represent interruptions to the normal flow of the process and start the exception flow.

intermediate event *(155)* Occurs between start and end events and affects the flow of the process.

intermediate timer event *(155)* Intermediate events that indicate a delay in the normal process flow until a fixed amount of time has elapsed.

internal rate of return (IRR) *(372)* The discount rate (return) that makes a project's net present value equal to zero.

International Organization for Standardization (ISO) 27000 series *(275)* This series contains a range of individual standards and documents specifically reserved by ISO for information security.

IT application controls *(283)* Activities specific to a subsystem's or an application's input, processing, and output.

IT controls *(283)* Involve processes that provide assurance for information and help to mitigate risks associated with the use of technology.

IT general controls (ITGC) *(283)* Enterprise-level controls over IT.

K

key performance indicator *(350)* Those measures that the organization feels best indicate the performance of a particular activity.

L

labor operations event *(184)* In the conversion process, an event that represents the recording of labor (and any associated overhead) costs applied to work-in-process.

learning and growth perspective *(347)* The Balanced Scorecard perspective that describes the organization's objectives and corresponding measures related to improvements in tangible and intangible infrastructure, such as human, information, and organizational capital.

local area network (LAN) *(328)* A group of computers, printers, and other devices connected to the same network that covers a limited geographic range such as a home, small office, or a campus building.

M

MAC (media access control) address *(328)* A designated address that is connected to each device via the network and only sees traffic.

macro *(88)* Macros are defined by Access users to automate processes such as opening a specific form.

maintenance phase *(387)* The final phase of the SDLC that includes making changes, corrections, additions, and upgrades (generally smaller in scope) to ensure the system continues to meet the business requirements that have been set out for it.

mandatory information *(7)* Information that is required to be generated or provided by law or regulation.

many-to-many relationship *(126, 158, 185)* Exists when instances of one class (e.g., sales) are related to many instances of another class (e.g., inventory) and vice versa. These relationships are implemented in Access and relational databases by adding a linking table to convert the many-to-many relationship into two one-to-many relationships.

marketing and sales activities *(11)* Activities that identify the needs and wants of their customers to help attract them to the firm's products and buy them.

message digest (MD) *(305)* A short code, such as one 256 bits long, resulting from hashing a plaintext message using an algorithm.

message flows *(39)* BPMN represents exchanges between two participants (pools) in the same process as message flows, which are modeled as dashed arrows.

module *(88)* Some Microsoft applications come with modules built in that will be automatically added onto Access.

multiplicities *(63)* UML symbols that describe the minimum and maximum number of times an instance of one class can be associated with instances of another class for a specific association between those two classes; they indicate whether the two classes are part of one-to-one, one-to-many, or many-to-many relationships.

N

net present value (NPV) *(372)* The sum of the present value of all cash inflows minus the sum of the present value of all cash outflows related to an IT investment or other capital investment.

network data model *(84)* A flexible model representing objects and their relationships; allows each record to have multiple parent and child records or M:N mapping, also known as many-to-many relationships.

network IT (NIT) *(350)* A type of information technology that allows people to communicate with one another, such as e-mail and instant messaging.

O

one-to-many relationship *(126)* Exists when instances of one class are related to multiple instances of another class. For example, a customer can participate in many sales, but each sale involves only one customer.

one-to-one relationship *(158)* Exists when instances of one class (e.g., sales) are related to only one instance of another class (e.g., cash receipts) and each instance of the other class is related to only one instance of the original class.

operating system (OS) *(326)* Performs the tasks that enable a computer to operate; comprised of system utilities and programs.

operation cost *(369)* The recurring cost necessary to operate, maintain, and administer an IT initiative.

operational database *(327)* Often includes data for the current fiscal year only.

operations *(11)* Activities that transform inputs into finished goods and services.

orchestration *(122, 153)* In BPMN, the sequence of activities within one pool.

outbound logistics *(11)* Activities that warehouse and distribute the finished goods to the customers.

output controls *(284)* Provide output to authorized people and ensure the output is used properly.

P

pages *(88)* Access pages allow data to be entered into the database in real time from outside of the database system.

parallel simulation *(333)* Attempts to simulate the firm's key features or processes.

payback period *(372)* The amount of time necessary to recoup a project's initial investment.

perceived ease of use *(396)* The extent to which a person perceives that the use of a particular system will be relatively free from effort.

perceived usefulness *(395)* The extent to which users believe the system will help them perform their job better.

personal identifying information *(218)* An individual's first name or initial and last name, or address, or phone number, in combination with Social Security number, driver's license number, passport number, military identification number, or other similar number issued on a government document used to verify identity and financial account number and passcodes.

physical controls *(283)* Mainly manual but could involve the physical use of computing technology.

planning phase *(386)* The phase of the SDLC that summarizes the business needs with a high-level view of the intended project.

pools *(38)* BPMN symbols used to identify participants, actors, or persons that perform activities and interact with other participants in a process.

Power Pivot (228) Excel add-in that can create an integrated database from various Excel tables and external data sources, such as Access and SQL databases. It supports the creation of calculated fields and the use of pivot tables for the integrated database.

preventive controls *(274)* Deter problems before they arise.

primary key (PK) *(64, 85)* An attribute or a combination of attributes that uniquely identifies an instance of a class in a data model or a specific row in a table.

private key *(304)* A string of bits kept secret and known only to the owner of the key.

process maps *(48)* Simplified flowcharts that use a basic set of symbols to represent a business process activity.

process perspective *(347)* The Balanced Scorecard perspective that describes the organization's internal, process-related, objectives and corresponding measures; it views organizational performance from an internal perspective.

processing controls *(284)* Ensure that data and transactions are processed accurately.

procurement *(12)* Activities that involve purchasing inputs such as raw materials, supplies, and equipment.

product *(120, 157)* Class representing the organization's goods held for sale, that is, the organization's inventory. This is considered a resource.

production authorization event *(184)* In a UML class model of the conversion process, an event that records the authorization to produce one or more finished goods inventory items.

Program Evaluation Review Technique (PERT) *(393)* A project management tool used to help identify all tasks needed to complete a project. It is also helpful in determining task dependencies.

project *(389)* A series of tasks that are generally performed in a defined sequence to produce a predefined output.

project management *(386)* The process of carrying out the systems development life cycle to achieve an intended outcome.

project manager *(390)* The lead member of the project team who is responsible for the project.

project risk *(370)* The risk that the project will not be completed on time or within budget.

project sponsor *(390)* Generally a senior executive in the company who takes responsibility for the success of the project.

Public Company Accounting Oversight Board (PCAOB) *(272)* Established by SOX to provide independent oversight of public accounting firms.

public key *(304)* A string of bits created with the private key and widely distributed and available to other users.

public-key infrastructure (PKI) *(306)* A set of policies, processes, server platforms, software, and workstations used for the purpose of administering certificates and public-/private-key pairs, including the ability to issue, maintain, and revoke public-key certificates.

purchase discount *(152)* An offer from the supplier to reduce the cost of a purchase if payment is made according to specified terms, usually within a specified time.

purchase order *(152)* A commitment event that precedes the economic purchase event. It records formal offers to suppliers to pay them if the supplier complies with the terms of the purchase order.

purchases *(152)* Records the receipt of goods or services from a supplier and the corresponding obligation to pay the supplier. These are considered events.

Q

query *(87)* Query in Access is a tool used to retrieve and display data derived from records stored within the database.

quote *(121)* Description of the products and/or services to be provided to a customer if ordered.

R

raw material issue event *(184)* In a UML class diagram of the conversion process, an event that records the transfer of raw materials into work-in-process.

raw materials inventory *(179)* For a manufacturing company, the inventory (REA resource) acquired for use (conversion) in the manufacturing process.

REA *(126, 157, 183)* Resource-event-agent framework for modeling business processes, originally developed by William McCarthy.

receipt *(157)* Same as the purchases event.

referential integrity rule *(87)* The data value for a foreign key must either be null or match one of the data values that already exist in the corresponding table.

relational data model *(84)* Stores information in the form of related two-dimensional tables.

relationship *(73)* The business purpose for the association between two classes or two database tables; *see* association.

relevance *(5)* Information that is capable of making a difference in a decision.

relevant costs *(369)* Those costs that will change as a result of an IT initiative or other major project.

reliability *(5)* Information that is free from bias and error.

remote access *(330)* Connection to a data-processing system from a remote location, e.g., through a virtual private network.

report *(88)* Reports in Access are used to integrate data from one or more queries and tables to provide useful information to decision makers.

residual risk *(281)* The product of inherent risk and control risk (i.e., Residual risk = Inherent risk × Control risk).

resources *(126, 157, 184)* Those things that have economic value to a firm, such as cash and products.

risk assessment *(280)* The process of identifying and analyzing risks systematically to determine the firm's risk response and control activities.

router *(329)* Software-based intelligent device that chooses the most efficient communication path through a network to the required destination.

S

sales *(120)* Events documenting the transfer of goods or services to customer and the corresponding recognition of revenue for the organization.

sales order *(121)* Event documenting commitments by customers to purchase products. The sales order event precedes the economic event (sale).

Sarbanes-Oxley Act of 2002 (SOX) *(9, 272)* A federal law in the United States that set new and enhanced standards for all U.S. public companies, management, and public accounting firms; a response to business scandals such as Enron, WorldCom, and Tyco International. It requires public companies registered with the SEC and their auditors to annually assess and report on the design and effectiveness of internal control over financial reporting.

scope creep *(392)* The change in a project's scope after the project work has started.

sequence flows *(37)* BPMN symbols that show the normal sequence of activities in a business process. Sequence flows are modeled as solid arrows, with the arrowhead showing the direction of process flow.

service activities *(11)* Activities that provide the support of customers after the products and services are sold to them (e.g., warranty repairs, parts, instruction manuals, etc.).

session key *(304)* A symmetric key that is valid for a certain timeframe only.

solution risk *(370)* The risk that the proposed solution will not generate expected benefits.

station *(331)* A wireless endpoint device equipped with a wireless network interface card.

strategy map *(349)* A one-page representation of the firm's strategic priorities and the cause-and-effect linkages among those strategic priorities.

structure model *(62)* A conceptual depiction of a database, such as a UML class model or an entity-relationship model.

Structured Query Language (SQL) *(96)* A computer language designed to retrieve data from a relational database.

subprocess *(122, 154)* Represents a series of process steps that are hidden from view in BPMN. The use of subprocesses in modeling helps reduce complexity.

suppliers *(152)* In the UML diagram of the purchases and payments process, the external agents from whom goods and services are purchased and to whom payments are made.

supply chain *(14)* The flow of materials, information, payments, and services from raw materials suppliers, through factories and warehouses, all the way to the final customers of the firm's products.

supply chain management (SCM) software *(15)* Software that connects the focal firm with its suppliers. It generally addresses segments of the supply chain, including manufacturing, inventory control, and transportation.

swimlanes (or lanes) *(38)* BPMN symbols that provide subdivisions of pools to show, for example, functional responsibilities within an organization.

switch *(328)* An intelligent device that provides a path for each pair of connections on the switch by storing address information in its switching tables.

symmetric-key encryption *(304)* Both the sender and the receiver use the same key to encrypt and decrypt messages.

systems analyst *(9, 386)* Person responsible for both determining the information needs of the business and designing a system to meet those needs.

systems development life cycle (SDLC) *(386)* The process of creating or modifying information systems to meet the needs of its users. It serves as the foundation for all processes people use to develop such systems.

T

Tableau Desktop *(233)* Software application that supports data analytics and visualizations. It integrates data from multiple data sources. It provides easy-to-use and powerful summary reporting and charting capabilities. It allows users to build dashboards and create stories from their data.

technological risk *(370)* The risk that the technology will not perform as expected to deliver the planned benefits.

technology *(12)* Supports value-creating activities in the value chain. These technologies also include research and development to develop new products or determine ways to produce products at a cheaper price.

technology acceptance model (TAM) *(395)* A model that predicts when users will adopt a new system to the extent they believe the system will help them perform their job better.

test data technique *(333)* Uses a set of input data to validate system integrity.

timer events *(155)* Indication of a delay in the flow of a process to a specific date, an elapsed time (for example, 30 days), or a relative repetitive date, such as every Friday.

transform *(19)* The use of computer technology to fundamentally redefine business processes and relationships.

triple constraints *(391)* Three factors that constrain information technology and other projects: cost, scope, and time. Also known as Dempster's triangle.

type image *(128, 159, 184)* Class that represents management information (such as categorizations, policies, and guidelines) to help manage a business process. Type image often allows process information to be summarized by category.

U

uninterruptible power supply *(314)* A device using battery power to enable a system to operate long enough to back up critical data and shut down properly during the loss of power.

V

Val IT *(353)* An IT investment framework developed by the IT Governance Institute.

value chain *(11)* A chain of critical business processes at a company that creates value.

value proposition *(348, 372)* Represents the product and service characteristics, such as price, quality, selection, and brand image, that the firm attempts to deliver to customers to meet or exceed its customers' expectations and thereby result in customer retention and new customer acquisition; summarizes the costs and benefits of a preferred alternative IT investment, describing (1) the relevant time frames in which the costs will be incurred and benefits realized, (2) the corresponding discount rates to apply to future cash flows, and (3) the sensitivity of the results to assumptions.

virtual private network (VPN) *(330)* Securely connects a firm's WANs by sending/receiving encrypted packets via virtual connections over the public Internet to distant offices, salespeople, and business partners.

virtualization *(315)* Using various techniques and methods to create a virtual (rather than actual) version of a hardware platform, storage device, or network resources.

W

wide area network (WAN) *(329)* Links different sites together; transmits information across geographically dispersed LANs; and covers a broad geographic area such as a city, region, nation, or an international link.

wireless network *(331)* Comprised of two fundamental architectural components: access points and stations.

work breakdown structure (WBS) *(393)* The process of identifying all tasks needed to complete a project.

work-in-process inventory *(184)* For a manufacturing company, the value of raw materials, direct labor, and manufacturing overhead in production but not yet finished.

X

XBRL (eXtensible Business Reporting Language) *(255)* An open, global standard for exchanging financial reporting information.

XBRL Global Ledger Taxonomy (XBRL GL) *(259)* Serves as a ledger using the XBRL standard for internal purposes.

XBRL instance document *(258)* A document containing XBRL elements.

XBRL specification *(256)* Provides the underlying technical details of what XBRL is and how it works.

XBRL style sheet *(258)* Adds presentation elements to XBRL instance documents to make them readable by people.

XBRL taxonomy *(256)* Defines and describes each key data element (e.g., total assets, accounts payable, net income, etc.).

XML (Extensible Markup Language) *(255)* Open, global standard for exchanging information in a format that is both human- and machine-readable.

Index

Bold page numbers indicate definitions or key discussions of terms; page numbers followed by *n* indicate footnotes or source notes.

T